FORM AND POWER IN MEDIEVAL AND EARLY MODERN LITERATURE

FORM AND POWER IN MEDIEVAL AND EARLY MODERN LITERATURE

A BOOK FOR JAMES SIMPSON

Edited by
Daniel Donoghue, Sebastian Sobecki, and Nicholas Watson

D. S. BREWER

© Contributors 2024

All Rights Reserved. Except as permitted under current legislation
no part of this work may be photocopied, stored in a retrieval system,
published, performed in public, adapted, broadcast,
transmitted, recorded or reproduced in any form or by any means,
without the prior permission of the copyright owner

First published 2024
D. S. Brewer, Cambridge

ISBN 978 1 84384 711 3

D. S. Brewer is an imprint of Boydell & Brewer Ltd
PO Box 9, Woodbridge, Suffolk IP12 3DF, UK
and of Boydell & Brewer Inc.
668 Mt Hope Avenue, Rochester, NY 14620–2731, USA
website: www.boydellandbrewer.com

A CIP catalogue record for this book is available
from the British Library

The publisher has no responsibility for the continued existence or accuracy of
URLs for external or third-party internet websites referred to in this book, and
does not guarantee that any content on such websites is, or will remain, accurate
or appropriate

This publication is printed on acid-free paper

CONTENTS

List of Illustrations	ix
Contributors and Editors	xi
Acknowledgments	xiii
List of Abbreviations	xv

Simpson: An Interim Report   1
Daniel Donoghue, Sebastian Sobecki, and Nicholas Watson

PART I: THE HERMENEUTICS OF RECOGNITION

1. The Shock of the Old: Recognition in the Humanities;
The 2022 Morton W. Bloomfield Memorial Lecture   13
James Simpson

2. "Stuffed with Divine Words": Undigested Texts in Early
Medieval England   35
Erica Weaver

3. The "Physician's Tale" and Chaucer's Art of Prosopopoeia   49
Julie Orlemanski

4. "Troilus can afford to fall in love … with whomsoever he will":
Free Will and Recognition in *Troilus and Criseyde*   67
Laura Ashe

CONTENTS

PART II: GENRE AND FIGURE

5. Rarely Obscure and Not a Genre: Medieval Allegorical Narrative   87
Nicolette Zeeman

6. "Thynke nat the contrary": Field Notes in the Ecology of
Medieval Romance   107
Nicholas Perkins

7. Filling in the Lines: Text, Image, and Late Medieval Literary Forms   121
Jessica Brantley

8. Catching at Words: The Literal, the Metaphorical, and the Obvious   147
Chris Barrett

PART III: CULTURE AND INSTITUTIONS

9. Petition, Justice, and Peace in *Piers Plowman*   167
Yun Ni

10. In Place of the Past: *Saint Erkenwald*'s Versions of Conversion   183
Aparna Chaudhuri

11. Proverb and Satirical Time: The Digby Poems and Their
Fifteenth Century   201
Spencer Strub

12. Common Style and the Bourgeois Ethos in John Lydgate's *Dietary*   223
Taylor Cowdery

PART IV: REFORMATIONS

13. Rewriting *Robert the Devil*: Thomas Lodge and Medieval Romance   241
Cathy Shrank

14. Iconoclasm and the Epigraphic Image   259
Jessica Berenbeim

CONTENTS   vii

15. **The Letter Kills but the Spirit Gives Life (2 Corinthians 3:6):**
      Or, What Happened to Enemy Love?   275
      David Aers

16. **James Simpson's Freedoms: An Appreciation**   293
      Jason Crawford

      James Simpson's Publications from 1984 to 2024   301

      Bibliography   311

      A Note on the Bloomfield Conferences   345

      General Index   347

      Tabula Gratulatoria   357

ILLUSTRATIONS

Brantley, "Filling in the Lines: Text, Image, and Late Medieval Literary Forms"

Fig. 1.   Line-fillers: simple penwork flourishes. Psalter with Canticles, fourth quarter of the twelfth century to first quarter of the thirteenth century, England. London, British Library MS Harley 5102, f. 2r.   124

Fig. 2.   Line-fillers: geometrically patterned ornament. Psalter ("Rutland Psalter"), c. 1260, England. London, British Library MS Additional 62925, f. 13v.   125

Fig. 3.   Line-fillers: figural paintings. Book of Hours, c. 1300, England. Baltimore, Walters Art Museum MS W.102, f. 2r.   126

Fig. 4.   Line-fillers: dragons. Book of Hours, c. 1300, Liège. Baltimore, Walters Art Museum MS W.37, f. 128r.   128

Fig. 5.   Elephant and castle. Book of Hours, c. 1300, England. Baltimore, Walters Art Museum MS W.102, f. 28r.   129

Fig. 6.   Adam. Book of Hours, c. 1300, England. Baltimore, Walters Art Museum MS W.102, f. 28v.   131

Fig. 7.   Holy Face and game of chess. Book of Hours, c. 1300, England. Baltimore, Walters Art Museum MS W.102, f. 29r.   132

Fig. 8.   Index with line-fillers. Gaston Phoebus, *Livre de la Chasse*, first quarter of the fifteenth century, Paris. New York, The Morgan Library & Museum MS M.1044, f. 2r.   134

Fig. 9.   Table of contents with line-fillers. Nicole Oresme's translation of Aristotle's *Ethics*, mid-fifteenth century, Rouen. Rouen, Bibliothèque municipale de Rouen MS I 2, f. 410r.   135

Fig. 10.   Table of contents with line-fillers. Custumal, early fourteenth century. Ipswich, Suffolk Record Office, Ipswich C/4/1/1, f. 9a.   136

Fig. 11.   Layout of Psalm-verses. Psalter ("Vespasian Psalter"), second quarter of the eighth century to mid-ninth century, England. London, British Library Cotton MS Vespasian A I, f. 31r.   138

x   ILLUSTRATIONS

Fig. 12.   Vernacular verse with line-fillers. Book of Hours ("Entwisle
            Hours"), c. 1440, England. London, British Library MS Sloane
            2321, f. 14r.   141

Fig. 13.   Poetic fragments with line-fillers. Collection of fragments,
            fourteenth–sixteenth century, England. Oxford, Bodleian MS
            Rawlinson D. 913.   142

Fig. 14.   "Ho that sith him one the rode." Miscellany, ?fourteenth
            century, England. London, British Library MS Harley 7322, f. 7.   142

Fig. 15.   John Lydgate, "The reignes of the kyngis of Englande," mid-
            fifteenth century to the second quarter of the sixteenth century,
            England. London, British Library MS Royal 18 D 2, f. 181r.   145

Barrett, "Catching at Words: The Literal, the Metaphorical, and the Obvious"

Fig. 1.   Facing pages in Michael Drayton, *Ideas Mirrour* (London:
            James Roberts, for Nicholas Linge, 1594), B3v to B4r. From
            the collection of the Folger Shakespeare Library.   151

Fig. 2.   a.   Detail from John Gerard, *The Herball or Generall Historie
            of Plantes* … (London: John Norton, 1597); QK41 .G3 1597
            OVER, page 53. Special Collections, Louisiana State University
            Libraries, Baton Rouge, LA.   157

            b.   Detail from Gerard's *Herball*. QK41 .G3 1597 OVER, page
            54. Special Collections, Louisiana State University Libraries,
            Baton Rouge, LA.   157

Fig. 3.   Detail from facing pages of Gerard's *Herball*. QK41 .G3 1597
            OVER, pages 112–13. Special Collections, Louisiana State
            University Libraries, Baton Rouge, LA.   158

Fig. 4.   From the Second Folio: *Mr. William Shakespeares comedies,
            histories, and tragedies: published according to the true originall
            copies* (London: Thomas Cotes, for Robert Allot, 1632);
            PR2751 .A2 1632 VAULT, page 261 (Y5r). Special Collections,
            Louisiana State University Libraries, Baton Rouge, LA.   162

Berenbeim, "Iconoclasm and the Epigraphic Image"

Fig. 1.   Binham Priory screen, detail of surviving bay fragment.   258

Fig. 2.   Binham Priory site, view from south-east.   262

Fig. 3.   Binham Priory screen, full surviving bay.   263

Fig. 4.   Binham Priory screen, full surviving bay.   264

Fig. 5.   Binham Priory screen, full surviving bay.   265

ILLUSTRATIONS

xi

Fig. 6.   Binham Priory screen, full surviving bay.   266

Fig. 7.   Binham Priory screen, detail of full surviving bay in figure 4.   267

Fig. 8.   Thornham church screen, north bays.   273

Full credit details are provided in the captions to the images in the text. The editors, contributors and publisher are grateful to all the institutions and persons for permission to reproduce the materials in which they hold copyright. Every effort has been made to trace the copyright holders; apologies are offered for any omission, and the publisher will be pleased to add any necessary acknowledgement in subsequent editions.

Contributors and Editors

David Aers	Duke University
Laura Ashe	University of Oxford
Jessica Berenbeim	University of Cambridge
Chris Barrett	Louisiana State University
Jessica Brantley	Yale University
Aparna Chaudhuri	Ashoka University
Taylor Cowdery	University of North Carolina
Jason Crawford	Union University
Daniel Donoghue	Harvard University
Yun Ni	Peking University
Julie Orlemanski	University of Chicago
Nicholas Perkins	University of Oxford
Cathy Shrank	University of Sheffield
James Simpson	Harvard University
Sebastian Sobecki	University of Toronto
Spencer Strub	Princeton University
Nicholas Watson	Harvard University
Erica Weaver	University of California, Los Angeles
Nicolette Zeeman	University of Cambridge

Peter Sacks, *Summoning 22*, 2007–09. Mixed media on canvas.

ACKNOWLEDGMENTS

Funding for this book was provided by the Morton W. Bloomfield Fund at Harvard University. The editors would like to thank our contributors for their hard work, patience, and punctuality. Special thanks are due our colleague Anna Wilson, the fourth organizer of the conference at which first versions of its essays were read, "Illuminated and Unsettled: Literary Forms and Cultural Power, Medieval to Early Modern" (Harvard University, 26–28 September 2022), who did much to shape this book's intellectual direction. Thanks also to Ellie Powell, who prepared the bibliography, and to Diana Myers, who prepared the index. Sebastian Sobecki is grateful for the Morton W. Bloomfield Fellowship that allowed him to work on this volume in Cambridge, Mass., with his fellow editors.

Among the many who participated in "Illuminated and Unsettled" or helped with its complicated logistics, we especially thank Peter X. Accardo, Kailey Bennett, Sol Kim Bentley, Sean Gilsdorf, Michelle DeGroot, Steven Rozenski, and Misha Teramura. We also thank Rob Brown and Bailey Sincox, who curated an exhibition at the Houghton Library to coincide with the conference. An essay by Sincox reporting on this exhibition has subsequently been published online in the *Harvard Library Bulletin*: see https://harvardlibrarybulletin.org/illuminated-unsettled-exhibition.

Finally, we thank James's longtime friend and department colleague at Harvard, Peter Sacks, for allowing us to reproduce *Summoning 22*. The painting, which featured on the poster advertising "Illuminated and Unsettled," suggests the interior of a chapel, in the past or perhaps the *cellula mentis*, whitewashed but also richly textured and colored. Outlines of the trees from which the building might have been made are picked out in lace on the back wall. An open book, its lines of text undulating, lies diagonally on the floor, near where a medieval bishop, consecrating the space, would trace the great letters of the divine name, Alpha and Omega, on the floor with his staff. A representation of the unexpected vibrancy of the human past, still available to memory and reconstruction across time, *Summoning 22* captures a number of James's deepest interests and investments: in the controversial power of images and the imagination; in the interweavings of nature and culture; in the dark violences but also the continuities of history; and in the urgency of keeping the human past available to the present, not only as a sounding-board but as a reservoir.

Abbreviations

CCCM	Corpus Christianorum Continuatio Mediaevalis
CCSL	Corpus Christianorum Series Latina
CSEL	Corpus Scriptorum Ecclesiasticorum Latinorum
DIMEV	*Digital Index of Middle English Verse*
DOML	Dumbarton Oaks Medieval Library
EETS	Early English Text Society
es	Extra Series
os	Original Series
ss	Supplementary Series
ESTC	Electronic Short Title Catalogue
MED	*Middle English Dictionary*
OED	*Oxford English Dictionary*
PL	Patrologia Latina. Migne, Jacques-Paul, gen. ed. *Patrologia Cursus Completus, Series Latina*. 221 vols. Paris: Imprimerie Catholique, 1844–65
TEAMS	Teaching Association for Medieval Studies

SIMPSON: AN INTERIM REPORT

Daniel Donoghue, Sebastian Sobecki, and Nicholas Watson

> What unites all his work is an attention to the way in which literary texts both illuminate and unsettle discursive patterns in disciplines that might seem more powerful (e.g. theology, economics, psychology, politics).
>
> Simpson on Simpson, 1998[1]

This book honors the scholarship and, no less, the teaching of James Simpson, one of the most influential figures in medieval and early modern literary studies over the past half century, and perhaps the single figure who has come to represent the center of the field of late Middle English studies in the form it has taken over most of the past twenty-five years in particular. More specifically, it honors Simpson's signal commitment to the distinctive category of the literary. Over the past four decades, his energetic work has illuminated new intersections between literary and more dominant public discourses, while unsettling received hierarchies of power and disrupting intellectual systems centered on periodization, literalism, and liberalism, especially in relation to what he has taught us to call the Trans-Reformation period. At the heart of these interventions is always the transformative and thus central role of literature as agent and instigator, instrument and subject. Simpson's scholarship tests the boundaries of literary history, exposing tacit cultural structures and passive myths of cultural alterity. His contributions have profoundly shaped scholarship on late medieval literature, from nudging the canon to embrace John Gower, Thomas Hoccleve, and John Lydgate to influencing how an entire generation of students and scholars approaches William Langland's *Piers Plowman*. Meanwhile, the revisionist bent of

---

[1] Taken from James Simpson's archived web profile at the Faculty of English, University of Cambridge, 13 February 1998. Available online: https://web.archive. org/web/19980213180334/http://www.english.cam.ac.uk/members.htm (accessed 29 April 2023).

2   DANIEL DONOGHUE, SEBASTIAN SOBECKI, AND NICHOLAS WATSON

Simpson's cultural narratives continues to dislocate the periodizing wedge that has long been driven between the medieval and the proto-modern. In turn, Simpson's hermeneutics of periodization and his polemical probing of the origin myths of modernity (e.g. humanism, liberalism, literalism, iconoclasm, and Protestant triumphalism) have opened up fruitful paths for thinking about literary and intellectual history over the *longue durée*.

The book grew out of a conference held at Harvard University in the fall of 2022 to mark the occasion of Simpson's retirement from the Donald P. and Katherine B. Loker Professorship of English, which he held for almost twenty years, six of them as Department Chair. Like the conference, the book is a celebration of the whole of his career, including both the quarter century he spent in the United Kingdom after his arrival from Melbourne, at Oxford, then London, then Cambridge, and the indefinite period that has opened out for him recently as he continues his scholarly journey unencumbered by the institutional duties he long carried out so effectively. Two of the three editors of this volume have been his colleagues at Harvard, and more than half its chapters are by scholars who studied with him there. The third editor and another four chapter writers, in addition to his long-term collaborator David Aers and his former colleague Nicolette Zeeman, were his students at the "other Cambridge" (as Cambridge University is fondly known at Harvard). This is where, in retirement, he and his wife Luisella now make their home for half the year. Appropriately so: as the ties he has continued to maintain with medieval literary studies in Australia also show, Simpson's career has been famous not only for his eagerness to strike out in new conceptual as well as geographical directions but also for his determination to leave nothing, whether ideas, friends or places, behind. His has been, and will surely remain, a recursive kind of journey, characterized by gathering as much as movement, recognition as much as discovery, as his own contribution to this book, given at the conference as the 2022 Morton W. Bloomfield Lecture, so beautifully suggests. Simpson's is also an uncompleted journey, a journey without limits, however passionately aligned around a set of themes, interests and affections. Thus the title of this introduction: all we can offer in celebration of this superbly wide-ranging, ambitious and large-hearted career is an interim report.

To move to the form of that journey, it thus seems proper, indeed inevitable, that in James's beginning – to call him now by his *kynde name* – was *Piers Plowman*, that exploratory, recursive and forever uncompleted journey through late-medieval English society and the conflicting institutions, beliefs, ideologies, injustices, hypocrisies, hopes, fears and feelings that subtended it. For much of the long period James spent in Oxford, London and Cambridge, he was known for his brilliant work on William Langland's intricate poem, as he developed an account of its several versions that focuses on its intensive exploration both of the forms of knowledge (authority-based, reason-based, experimental, affective) and their embodiment in

SIMPSON: AN INTERIM REPORT

late-medieval English society. Typically, he also devoted careful attention to how best to bring the fruits of this work to the widest number of readers. His first monograph, *Piers Plowman: An Introduction to the B-Text*, somehow manages to be a scholarly tour-de-force and a textbook rolled into one, rendering intelligible the most complex of Middle English poems to thousands of grateful readers, from students to fully paid-up Langlandians. The book has gone through several printings and two distinct editions, and to this day remains a lucid and immensely significant contribution to scholarship on this central canonical poem.[2]

Thus the first phase of James's career, which also included a co-edited festschrift for his Melbourne *Doktorvater*, George Russell, and the first dozen of what has been a continuous stream of essays, notably a brilliant and much-cited one on "The Constraints of Satire in *Mum and the Sothsegger* and *Piers Plowman*," published, like his first book, in 1990. After that year, even as he continued to publish on *Piers Plowman* – Langland has been one of James's great constants – he then embarked on a decade-long trek toward early modernity, building towards and away from his superb second book, *Sciences and the Self in Medieval Poetry: Alan of Lille's "Anticlaudianus" and John Gower's "Confessio amantis"*, published in 1995. *Sciences and the Self* signals his increasingly explicit attachment to the relationship between literary, intellectual and institutional history, while also focusing on what was becoming his abiding interest in the history and character of humanism. This is humanism with a lowercase "h," the holistic view of human relevance in the greater scheme of things that the book traces back to the twelfth century, rather than seeing it "born" in the fifteenth, and that in James's subsequent work features as an important early stage in the continuing history of what he calls liberalism.

It was while working on Gowerian humanism that James also began to direct the field's attention towards that unlikely pair of fifteenth-century titans – Thomas Hoccleve and John Lydgate – with remarkable effects. Before James began writing on Hoccleve in 1991, the study of his poetry was confined to a handful of scholars, most prominently John Burrow.[3] Fast forward to 2024, when only work on Chaucer and Langland surpasses in volume publications on Hoccleve. James's impact on the study of Lydgate was even more transformative. Before the two great articles James published on *The Siege of Thebes* and *Troy Book* in 1997 and 1998 respectively, Lydgate, too, had been languishing in obscurity, the butt of jokes about tedium and prolixity whose unquestioning repetition had become an impediment to

---

[2] For the essays and books by Simpson mentioned below, see the list of his publications at the end of this volume.

[3] See, e.g., Burrow's "Autobiographical Poetry in the Middle Ages: The Case of Thomas Hoccleve," *Proceedings of the British Academy* 68 (1982), 389–412.

4   DANIEL DONOGHUE, SEBASTIAN SOBECKI, AND NICHOLAS WATSON

research into fifteenth-century English literature as whole.[4] Then James showed us why England's favorite and central fifteenth-century poet was deserving of our attention, paving the way for the great revival in fifteenth-century English literary studies that has been one of the most notable field developments of the previous twenty-five years. By demonstrating what is to be gained by seeking to understand their poetry on their own cultural, aesthetic and intellectual terms, James's work on Hoccleve and Lydgate showed just how much there was still to be said about them, turning what had seemed slim pickings into a bumper crop.

After what in retrospect can be seen as a transitional decade, James went on to make the epoch-challenging argument around which much of his twenty-first century work to date has circled, initially building on the twin pillars of the history of humanism and its antagonists and fifteenth-century poetry as read on its own terms. The outlines of this argument were announced in his Oxford English Literary History of the later Middle Ages, published in 2002 as *Reform and Cultural Revolution, 1350–1547*, an ambitious and extraordinarily influential book that launched what we can view as the second and at present longest phase of his work. *Reform and Cultural Revolution* joyously reverses a venerable account of the fifteenth century as a pre-Renaissance "dark ages," a time of dullness, stasis or decadence – to invoke Johan Huizinga's wistful swan song, *The Waning of the Middle Ages* – by showing the ways in which the Henrician Reformation of the 1530s represented a closing down of possibilities, not an opening out. Using the history of institutions as a meeting-point between intellectual, literary and religious history, the book argues that the diversity and openness of Middle English literature, grounded in the "multiple jurisdictions" that coexisted across the late medieval period, was systematically destroyed under the early Tudor monarchs, which from the 1520s on set out to cut English thought and culture off from its immediate past in the name of unity and conformity. This is necessarily a polemical

---

[4]   See, e.g., Derek Pearsall, *John Lydgate* (Charlottesville, VA: University of Virginia Press, 1970), a blend of learned appreciation freely interspersed with derogatory judgments typical of twentieth-century studies of this poet, including Pearsall's own crucial later work on him. David Lawton's "Dullness and the Fifteenth Century," *ELH* 54 (1987), 761–99 is an important exception. Arguments here have been surprisingly fierce. For Pearsall's last word on this topic, which squarely takes aim at the new body of work pioneered by Simpson, see "Medieval Literature and Historical Enquiry," *Modern Language Review* 99 (2004), xxxi–xlii, and "The Apotheosis of John Lydgate," *Journal of Medieval and Early Modern Studies* 35 (2005), 25–38. Simpson responded in "John Lydgate," in *The Cambridge Companion to Medieval Literature*, ed. Larry Scanlon (Cambridge: Cambridge University Press, 2009), pp. 205–16. Pearsall later softened his position, but the lines of disagreement here were generational, and paralleled the dismay with which *The Cambridge History of Medieval English Literature* (Cambridge: Cambridge University Press, 1999), edited by David Wallace, was met in certain quarters for what was seen as the failure of its contributors to acknowledge the primacy of an aesthetic understanding of the literary.

argument, organized along dialectical lines in order to disentangle ruptures from continuities and lay the focus not where historians have placed them but where the intellectual trajectories of our subject demand them. It is also an argument that set the late-medieval cat fiercely among the early modern pigeons, using terms recognizable to the New Historicism that then dominated sixteenth-century literary studies but refuting its assumptions, both about the absolutely distinct character of the "early modern" era and the desirability of dissolving the history of literature and literary forms into cultural history more broadly.

Crowned with the British Academy's Sir Israel Gollancz Prize, *Reform and Cultural Revolution* prompted dedicated journal issues, extensive responses and a harvest of monograph tributes. In this work, James gives us the long fifteenth century in widescreen format, flanked by its later fourteenth-century antecedents and its early Tudor ripples. The reward was instantaneous: only by viewing the literature of the later Middle Ages through the lens of its cultural investments can we appreciate the central contribution of this period to literary and, thus, western history. A careful listener and gifted close-reader, James still made it his cause to weed out the remnants of an anachronistic aestheticism in determining which authors count, which do not. *Reform and Cultural Revolution* also takes not a chisel but a hammer (as James might put it) to entrenched notions of periodization, pulverizing the barriers between the medieval and the early modern that had imposed tunnel vision on generations of literary scholars. In the process, it also created for its author a major new role as an interlocutor (and sometimes gadfly) in the broad field of early modern and modern literary and religious studies.

James's next three books cemented this role. *Burning to Read: English Fundamentalism and its Reformation Opponents* (2007), marked a return to the targeted case study, only this time a series of dialogues took center stage, the bitter exchanges between Thomas More and William Tyndale. James uses these exchanges to show how humanism (More) and evangelicalism (Tyndale) were not mutually supporting projects, alike dedicated to pushing away from a discarded medieval past, but had profoundly contradictory understandings of the character of truth and human history, and the connections between them. *Under the Hammer: Iconoclasm in the Anglo-American Tradition* (2011), based on the series of Clarendon Lectures he gave at Oxford in 2009, then extrapolated the arguments of both its two predecessors into a correspondingly broad account of the history of liberalism itself, told from a particular vantage-point. Diverse cultural voices, enabled by the permissive institutional structures of late medieval England, blossomed in the literary experiments of the fifteenth century. What followed was a dramatic narrowing of institutional and cultural possibilities. Authoritarianism had replaced curiosity. James first noticed this trend in Tudor England, but in *Under the Hammer* he extends his observations to the study of Protestant iconoclasm. By now,

6   DANIEL DONOGHUE, SEBASTIAN SOBECKI, AND NICHOLAS WATSON

the transhistorical arc in his writing, and the revisionist historiography it enables, were clear: late-medieval permissiveness was a form of freedom, yielding to illiberal narratives of Protestant triumphalism. James's fourth and perhaps culminating intervention was published in 2019 as *Permanent Revolution: The Reformation and the Illiberal Roots of Liberalism*. This work dismantles Protestant origin myths of liberty at the end of the early modern period, not now dealing directly with the late Middle Ages at all, but presupposing James's understanding of the era in ways that seek to illuminate and unsettle standard accounts of sixteenth- and seventeenth-century literary and religious history in equal measure.

With its revisiting and updating of *Reform and Cultural Revolution*, *Permanent Revolution* would be easy to mistake as a career culmination, looking not only back over a twenty-five-year intellectual project but forward towards a richly deserved retirement. Nothing could be further from the truth. To look carefully at James's other publications since around 2015 in the light of his newest work is to see that he has spent the past few years preparing for a third phase of his career, one that is now well launched. This phase is less invested in *grand récit*, showcasing instead a different kind of Simpsonian scholarship that has nevertheless been a strand in his work from the beginning. James is, and has always been, a fine textual scholar who continues to open up important works and archives. In the later 1980s, he catalogued the manuscripts in Parisian libraries that contain Middle English prose. In the early 2000s, he effectively reinvented the medieval portion of the *Norton Anthology of English Literature*. More recently, he has translated Caxton's *Reynard the Fox* while continuing to edit John Hardyng's *Chronicle*, with Sarah Peverley. Only a few years ago, together with Christopher Cannon, he stunned us all by announcing an authoritative text of Chaucer's works, just published in a two-volume, 1500-page edition by Oxford University Press. Meanwhile, his energies for producing articles have scarcely diminished, some of them occasional pieces, most of them "interventions," almost all of them organized around defining and defending the literary in one sort or another. The vigor and clarity with which James shapes the field continue unabated. Hot on the heels of the Cannon-Simpson *Chaucer*, are a long-awaited book project on romance, which traces the form all the way to Homer, and several targeted essays. And clearly there will be yet more, much more, to come.

What, now, of James as a teacher? In his forty-year career, he has left his mark on the study of medieval literature not just in his native Australia, but especially in the UK and the US. Before coming to Harvard in 2004, James had already shaped a generation of medievalists in the UK, initially at Westfield College, and then at Cambridge University, where, at the time of his departure, he had succeeded Jill Mann to the endowed chair in Medieval and Renaissance English, a post initially created for C. S. Lewis. During his years in that post, he energized the medieval graduate seminar by transforming it into an occasion where, instead of admiring faculty as they sparred with visiting speakers, students were urged to formulate questions of their own and join the discussion, in a style long familiar in North America. This innovation then made his transition to Harvard and its medieval colloquium, which had long been organized along these lines, a good deal smoother.

A guiding passion behind James's research and teaching has been the belief in the primacy and centrality of the argument in scholarship: the lived practice of *Streitkultur*, where starkly differing views are respectfully and productively exchanged. Empirically grounded, his mind has always been led by a love of first principles, by political convictions he calls "liberal" that appeal to collective or even universal values. "I put it to you," with a smile and a tilt of the head, is a typically Simpsonian opening in reply to a presentation – collegial and challenging in equal measure – followed by a well-structured question that adds clarity to the speaker's ideas. James has brought this same style to his classroom, office hours, and conversations, championing and exemplifying a pedagogy centered around dialectic, debate, categorization, and the drive for simple, lucid, punchy argumentation. The contributors to this volume, like many others, encountered James beyond his research: as a colleague, teacher, friend, mentor, or in several combinations of the four. Many of us can attest to his remarkable gifts as a demanding yet encouraging teacher – supportive, kind, and caring for his students and colleagues alike – as someone who not only expects your finest work but empowers you to achieve it, in ways we hope this book has been successful in capturing.

~

In what follows, sixteen essays, divided into four clusters and an Appreciation, range across the extensive terrain of James's intellectual preoccupations, many of them taking his ideas in new directions or adapting his methodology to new topics. James's own essay, "The Shock of the Old: Recognition in the Humanities," anchors the first cluster, *The Hermeneutics of Recognition*, by offering the three essays that follow both as an inspiration and a point of departure. Working outwards from an argument about how humanities disciplines understand knowledge, the essay extends James's recent preoccupation with the Platonic theme of cognition as re-cognition to an Old English riddle, whose solution, the Bible, "astonishes by virtue of depending on other life forms to reproduce the Word of God," but affirms a model of knowledge as recovery that remains relevant to this day. Focusing now on what remains resistant to recognition, Erica Weaver continues James's project of unravelling enigmatic texts in Old English by turning to the familiar yet unsettling motif of reading as digestion. Concluding with an analysis of two evocative severed heads in texts from the *Beowulf* manuscript, which "trouble the lines between human and animal reading, eating, and understanding," Weaver offers a more jagged, yet still fundamentally optimistic account of medieval hermeneutics as her seventh- to tenth-century sources understood it.

8   DANIEL DONOGHUE, SEBASTIAN SOBECKI, AND NICHOLAS WATSON

Moving to the late fourteenth century in "'The Physician's Tale' and Chaucer's Art of Prosopopoeia," Julie Orlemanski expands on the way Chaucer deploys the trope of prosopopoeia in fashioning a face or mask for Virginia, giving her a voice, or at any rate a brief space to speak, where other versions of her story do not. Orlemanski illustrates an instance of what James calls "recognition of textual face," but one where the "face" in question – that of a daughter whose death at her father's hands precipitates political, social and aesthetic questions the tale can raise but cannot answer – is presented as so heavily mediated as to remain undecipherable. Finally, Laura Ashe's essay, "'Troilus can afford to fall in love … with whomsoever he will': Free Will and Recognition in *Troilus and Criseyde*," takes as its starting-point James's remark quoted in the title, only again to trouble it, so far as premodern culture at large is concerned. For Ashe, Troilus's freedom of the will forms part of the poem's innovative fashioning of what she calls the radical and "mutually self-constituting bonds of recognition, between non-substitutable individuals" as a foundation for creating "a theory of human love" that Chaucer can only imagine, experimentally and via tragedy.

Genre and Figure, the second cluster of essays, springs from James's formalist sensitivity to different categories of writing and, in particular, to several substantial works that draw on the figurative modes, such as *Piers Plowman* or the *Confessio Amantis*. Nicolette Zeeman opens this cluster with "Only Rarely Obscure and Not a Genre: Medieval Allegorical Narrative." Asking whether "allegorical narratives or allegories do indeed constitute a recognizable and cohesive medieval textual genre," rather than a localized trope, the essay traces the complex history of the poetic fictions we now consider allegorical in relation to accounts of *allegoria* in medieval rhetorical theory. In the process Zeeman offers yet another instance where definitions crystallized only in the early modern period fail to capture, even as they can be used to dismiss, the fluid workings of a major medieval literary form. Nicholas Perkins's "'Thynke nat the contrary': Field Notes in the Ecology of Medieval Romance" then offers his own revisionist account of a major medieval literary form, focusing on what he calls "haunted romances," especially *Sir Degaré* and Sir Thomas Malory's *Tale of Balyn*. Developing James's insight that "Romance compacts a kind of ecological, pre-ethical thought about the civilized order" or social structure, Perkins examines what unhappy endings reveal about structural coherence in what most scholars, including James, view as an inherently comic genre.

Turning from genre to figure and from broad literary forms to the more specific forms generated by the makers of later medieval books, Jessica Brantley's "Filling in the Lines: Text, Image, and Late Medieval Literary Forms" focuses attention on decorative line-fillers, a manuscript feature that arose at a specific moment, the late twelfth and early thirteenth centuries, but seems to have aroused little or any direct comment and still resists interpretation, for example as decoration or punctuation. Even at their plainest – and some of Brantley's examples are far from plain – line-fillers transform pages of text into images by giving definition to the rectangular block of text on a manuscript folio, unsettling what our own, post-Reformation reading protocols teach us to insist is a clear distinction between the two. Finally, moving to the sixteenth and early seventeenth centuries to focus on a different, little-noticed codicological detail, Chris Barrett turns to another feature of early book culture, in "Catching at Words: The Literal, the Metaphorical, and the Obvious." Beginning with the observation that nothing could be more obvious than the catchword, which functions less as part of the text than a convenience for book-binders, Barrett links "obviousness with interpretive suggestiveness" and an against-the-grain invitation for the reader to make an illuminating detour.

The third cluster of essays, *Culture and Institutions*, pays tribute to James's long-standing commitment to understanding the role of literature in intellectual and institutional history. This cluster begins with Yun Ni's "Petition, Justice, and Peace in *Piers Plowman*," which takes up a specific instance of James's observation that the poem "develops its meanings out of the dynamics of different institutional discourses." In an argument that also speaks to Zeeman's account of medieval allegory, Ni exposes Peace as a deliberately problematic personification, rife with ethical and social as well as epistemological contradiction, dramatized in the scene of Peace's legal petition before the King at the end of Langland's first vision. Aparna Chaudhuri's essay, "In Place of the Past: *Saint Erkenwald*'s Versions of Conversion," shows how the poem raises questions about Christianity's claim of territory, especially in light of London's built environment in the fourteenth century, which had witnessed a series of conversions and inhabitants and architecture over the centuries. *Saint Erkenwald* dramatizes how the assimilation of the past to the needs of the present can itself create historical ruptures.

Spencer Strub's "Proverb and Satirical Time: The Digby Poems and Their Fifteenth Century" takes up the relation between context and form in the twenty-four lyrics contained in Digby 102. Although the poems have been faulted for lacking specificity and abounding in truisms, they nevertheless speak to an urban audience in exhorting virtues that move across the blurry boundary between the citizen and the realm. Continuing the association between the specific context of London and institutional discourses, Taylor Cowdery examines Lydgate as a public poet in "Common Style and the Bourgeois Ethos in John Lydgate's *Dietary*." Recuperating the poem from critical neglect, Cowdery shows how the *Dietary* authorizes the values of its urban readership by validating its tastes and viewpoints.

James has made the specific and broader meanings of the word *Reformations* a focal interest in his work, and the three essays in the final cluster explore the various senses of this word. In "Rewriting *Robert the Devil*: Thomas Lodge and Medieval Romance" Cathy Shrank shows how Lodge's "Life of Robert I of Normandy" interrogates and stress-tests the

10 DANIEL DONOGHUE, SEBASTIAN SOBECKI, AND NICHOLAS WATSON

ideological foundations of his own humanist education as it "probes the double-edged nature of verbal proficiency."

Inspired by James's incisive critiques of iconoclasm, Jessica Berenbeim re-examines the Binham rood screen in "Iconoclasm and the Epigraphic Image," in which words overlay an earlier, medieval image. She shows how "this inscription, its evangelical medium on a persisting orthodox surface, expresses iconoclasm's insistent but unstable articulation of a periodic break." Finally, in "The Letter Kills but the Spirit Gives Life (2 Corinthians 3:6): Or, What Happened to Enemy Love?" David Aers draws from the legacies of Origen, Augustine, Calvin, and Milton to expose "the relation between the distinctive hermeneutics of the Reformation, and the practices of persecutory violence (and vehement legitimizations of such violence) germane to the period," as opposed to the more expansive reconciliations of letter and spirit allowed by the figural hermeneutics of the Middle Ages.

Finally, in an Appreciation, Jason Crawford recounts his personal encounters with "James Simpson's Freedoms," first as the stunning assertion that opens *Reform and Cultural Revolution*, and later as "James's pedagogy of freedoms, his affirmation of the plural selves and stories that emerge in the work of intellectual exchange." We are all engaged, as he reminds us, in a still-unfinished history of freedoms.

Taken together, the seventeen contributions gathered here respond to a wide range of James's intellectual interests and approaches, connecting creatively with his enduring interventions in medieval and early modern culture. We hope that this collection, our *Book for James Simpson*, will not only celebrate an exceptionally distinguished career but also exemplify just how stimulating and inspirational James's work continues to be.

PART I

THE HERMENEUTICS OF RECOGNITION

1 THE SHOCK OF THE OLD: RECOGNITION IN THE HUMANITIES; THE 2022 MORTON W. BLOOMFIELD MEMORIAL LECTURE

James Simpson

So here's how it went. I'm walking into Harvard Yard on a summer's day, as a rather plump, entirely bald male is walking towards me. I do not recognize him. I cannot, however, help noticing that the person coming towards me exhibits, in very low level and understated form, signs of having recognized me. There is, I intuit, something in his eye movement that expresses greeting. This is always a troubling social predicament. One is caught in a dilemma we have all experienced: either one will be thought rude, if one does not respond to the manifested signs of recognition; or, if one does respond, one runs the risk of being thought slow-witted, on discovering, to one's acute embarrassment, that one had misread those tiny, ambiguous signs of possible recognition – the minuscule eye movements of a complete stranger had not meant "hello" after all.

"After all" is in fact an exaggeration in such circumstances, since encounters of this kind happen in real time, as two creatures approach each other, both walking at brisk pace, from a distance of only two or three yards. With only a couple of seconds available, one's judgment goes into overdrive, but mine wasn't coming up with a decision in time. The apparent stranger, however, released me from this mini-agony.

The dénouement: as we are about to pass beyond each other, the apparent stranger breaks out into a broad smile. Suddenly there is no ambiguity: within a millisecond I stop observing and start recognizing: this is my friend John, who has been absent from campus for many months undergoing chemotherapy.

JAMES SIMPSON

John had been trim, with plenty of hair, when last I saw him, just before he went in for treatment. "John!" I exclaimed as we warmly shook hands and enjoyed our mutual relief, not to say joy. John was perhaps happy to be back in the land of the living, but I was much more than happy: that sudden flash of my friend's smile transformed everything in an instant – it transformed one quick moment of embarrassment into blissful cognitive certainty; and it transformed months of uncertainty about the fate of my friend into the joy that here he was, fully alive and present. Not least, it transformed observation into recognition.

Let me introduce the main themes of this short essay by isolating the cognitive features of the recognitional drama embedded in this small narrative.

I focus on these features in part because recognition has a rather weak place in the epistemological armory of the research university. When university presidents defend the humanities, that is, they do so in the same way they defend the sciences: as *discovery* of *original* knowledge. That may be true of the sciences, but in this essay I aim to persuade you that there is a distinctive form of thinking and pedagogy in the humanities. Thinking in the humanities is more a matter of *re*covery than of *dis*covery. Moments of revelation in the humanities are more inventions in the older sense (finding the already known) than scientific inventions in the newer sense (discovering the never previously known). To know in the humanities is "to recover what has been lost / And found and lost again and again."[1] Knowledge in the humanities is more, that is, a matter of recovering and refreshing the old than of discovering the wholly new. Cognition, to put the case in its crispest form, is re-cognition.

The suggestion that scholars in the humanities recover the old and the known runs counter, as I say, to the ways university presidents talk about research university knowledge production in these fields. The same suggestion also runs athwart the way in which teachers in university humanities departments, and especially in literature departments, speak about how and what students learn.

The deepest posture of Anglo-American literary pedagogy is grounded, rightly, on the conviction that literature liberates. We prize what is new and original, what destabilizes the solidities of official culture, and what points to liberation from the strictures of the norm. My essay is not at all designed to undo these Enlightenment-derived convictions about liberation from the past. I want, however, to persuade you that the reading practice and the pedagogy of the humanist are differently grounded, on opposed premises. Our reading practice, that is, in fact depends on deeply instilled norms, and begins by assuming that every work in a certain genre is, somehow, the "same" work, a work that we "knew" before we began reading the "new" work. Literary knowledge, that is, is dependent on recognition. We know because, in part, we knew. Literary cognition is fundamentally a matter of re-cognition. If true, such a claim has implications for the way we generate syllabi and curricula.

---

[1] T. S. Eliot, "East Coker," in *Collected Poems 1909–1962* (London: Faber and Faber, 1963), Section 5, p. 203.

THE SHOCK OF THE OLD: RECOGNITION IN THE HUMANITIES 15

In this essay, therefore, I focus less on represented moments of recognition in literary texts. Such moments are, to be sure, both the focal points and the narrative motor of many great works,[2] and of course I make reference to some extraordinary examples here. But my aim is to persuade you that a recognitional drama, with the associated pleasures and pedagogic affordances of repetition, is being played out in every literary reading experience. Beyond such individual reading experiences, cultural history produces recognitional self-knowledge.

The iterative quality of such knowledge is underlined in a variety of European languages, ancient and modern, each of which prefixes the lexical element designating cognition with a particle signaling iteration: *re-cognitio*, *re-connaisance*, *ri-conoscenza*, *Wieder-erkennung*, *ana-gnorisis*, for example. Re-cognition involves seeking again, a re-petition (< Latin *re-petere*, to seek again). In this essay I burrow into the logic and implications of that search for, and illuminating, pleasurable experience of, re-sought knowledge.

～

I begin by highlighting the distinctive cognitive features of recognition. Aristotle (382–24 BCE) famously defined what he called *anagnorisis* (literally "re-cognition") with regard to the complex plot of ancient drama.[3] Here I take up the connection between recognition and drama to argue that the cognitive act of recognition is itself a mini-drama, with its own timing, emotional tension and release, *dramatis personae*, and its own happy ending of nostalgic, non-tragic plot resolution. Recognition is dramatic, in both senses. As such, like drama itself, the event of recognition is performative: the truth it discloses is inseparable from the experience of perceiving that truth.

The drama of recognition includes the following features: first, momentary timing; second, powerful emotional experience; third, the centrality of the viewer; and four, the fact that the knowledge was already known. I take each of these in turn.

---

[2]   As brilliantly discussed in Terence Cave, *Recognitions: A Study in Poetics* (Oxford: Oxford University Press, 1988), and Piero Boitani, *Riconoscere è un dio: scene e temi del riconoscimento nella letteratura* (Milan: Einaudi, 2014). See also the collection of essays *Recognition and Modes of Knowledge: Anagnorisis from Antiquity to Contemporary Theory*, ed. Teresa G. Russo (Edmonton: University of Alberta Press, 2013). For the parallelisms between facial and textual recognition, see James Simpson, "Cognition is Recognition: Literary Knowledge and Textual 'Face,'" *New Literary History* 44 (2013), 25–44; and "Textual Face: Cognition as Recognition," in *Contemporary Chaucer across the Centuries, a Festschrift for Stephanie Trigg*, ed. Helen M. Hickey, Anne McHendry and Melissa Raine (Manchester: Manchester University Press, 2018), pp. 218–33.

[3]   For Aristotle on anagnorisis, see especially Aristotle, *Poetics*, in *Aristotle, Poetics. Longinus, On the Sublime. Demetrius, On Style*, tr. W. Hamilton Fyfe, ed. Stephen Halliwell (Cambridge, Mass.: Harvard University Press, 1995), 1452a.23–1452b.7, pp. 65–66.

THE MOMENTARY TIMING OF RECOGNITION

Recognitional knowledge happens in a moment. It is an example of what has been called a "disclosure model" of knowing – a model, that is, where the knowledge derives from the whole experience of apprehension, and arrives in a single moment of apprehension.[4] Thus in my introductory story, understanding happened in two temporal stages, cognition and recognition: I began by looking at a person for a certain period of time (cognition); that "looking at" suddenly gave way to "seeing as" (i.e. recognition). The moment of recognition was indeed a moment, and it was transformative.

My introductory story embeds a key aspect of the timing of a recognitional event, that of *resistance*. The recognition moment occurred in a temporal flash, but the arrival of the flash had been retarded. In fact, the flash may have struck all the more forcefully precisely *because* it had been delayed. "Looking at" was a prelude of resistance to "seeing as"; I naturally and unconsciously remained in that prelude, but then passed through it suddenly.

Maybe all "seeing as" (i.e. perception that involves understanding) involves such a flash, but we become aware of the flash effect only when there's a retardation resisting its access. In real life, Covid masks that hid the smile prompted many retarded, amusing recognitions, just as summer sunglasses do. Recognitions in literature and the visual arts often involve retardation: literary recognition scenes often involve poor light quality (I think of Odysseus turned away from the fire in order that Eurycleia not see his face in full light,[5] or Mary Magdalene not recognizing the resurrected Christ in the early morning obscurity ["while it was still dark"], looking from inside the tomb to beyond its mouth).[6] Sometimes in literature it's the facial change caused by trauma of one kind or another. Thus the baked face, the "cotto aspetto," of Dante's former teacher Ser Brunetto, now suffering in hell, brakes the speed of, and thereby magnifies the force of, recognition by Ser Brunetto's former pupil Dante.[7] Retardation or not, however, the recognitional event itself is brief.

THE EMOTIONAL FORCE OF RECOGNITION

The brief event is also emotionally memorable: recognitional knowledge involves a certain *emotional rush*. With my resuscitated friend, for example, the emotional effect was intense and unforgettable. This story produced an

---

[4] For the concept of the "disclosure model," see David Aers, *Piers Plowman and Christian Allegory* (London: St. Martin's Press, 1975), p. 13, and further reference.

[5] Homer, *The Odyssey*, tr. A. T. Murray, rev. George E. Dimock, 2 vols. (Cambridge, Mass: Harvard University Press, 1995), 2:19.388–91. Further references to Homer, *The Odyssey*, will be made in the text by book and line number.

[6] John 20:11–16.

[7] Dante Alighieri, *La Divina Commedia*, ed. Natalino Sapegno, 2nd ed., 3 vols. (Florence: Nuova Italia, 1971), *Inferno*, 1:15.22–30.

THE SHOCK OF THE OLD: RECOGNITION IN THE HUMANITIES   17

experience that is much more frequent in art: the intense, indistinguishable mix of joy and total understanding, the coincidence of which seems, for a moment at least, to set the world to rights. One thinks again of Eurycleia recognizing Odysseus: Eurycleia recognizes the scar "at once" ("αὐτίκα" (19.392)). Things and liquids threaten suddenly to spill out of control: the cradled leg falls, the basin tips, the water spills, confused emotions of joy and grief compete in Eurycleia, and tears overspill her eyelids: "Surely you are Odysseus, dear child, and I did not know you, until I had handled all the body of my master" (19.474–75). To observe is to leave the emotions barely touched, if at all; to recognize is to activate the emotions to high pitch. Of course the recognitional emotion is not necessarily joyful: one can also think of moments of literary recognition that produce horror (Oedipus is the obvious example), but these too are, if we are lucky, more frequent in art than life.

In sum, mind and heart, reason and emotion, move in exactly the same direction, and fire at the same moment when we move from "looking at" to "seeing as." Aristotle defines recognition in cognitive terms in *The Poetics*: "Recognition," he says, "… is a change from ignorance to knowledge …." Aristotle here emphasizes cognitive change, but my citation is incomplete: by the time the sentence in which this claim is made has ended, it's clear that Aristotle also includes high emotion as an essential part of the recognition package: "Recognition is a change from ignorance to knowledge, leading to friendship or to enmity, and involving matters which bear on prosperity or adversity."[8] Close relationships associated with understanding of friendship or enmity generate high emotion.

THE CENTRALITY OF THE VIEWER

The scientific model of knowledge production, dominant in the research university, sets us as curious, disengaged observers of the world. As scientific observers, we design our observation deck so as to take us off it. We minimize our input, in order to avoid skewing our results, and to avoid the circularity of prejudice. When we recognize, by contrast, we are inextricably in the picture, even on stage, bringing the pre-judgments of our past experience into the event.

Recognizing is an event; in part, it's an event we activate, even if we become passive recipients of the cognitive gift of surprise triggered by the event. That we activate recognition is evident in our search for the green-spined book thinking that it has a blue spine; we see the green-spined book we are in fact looking for any number of times before we recognize it, since our incorrect programming has us passing over it as we search for a blue spine. In my initial story, the cognitive trigger of unusual eye movements prompted me

---

[8]   Aristotle, *Poetics*, tr. Fyfe, ed. Halliwell, 1452a.30–31, p. 65.

JAMES SIMPSON

consciously to look at the person before me differently, to see him really again. Recognition is partially active preception, partially passive perception.[9]

Beyond the age of three or so we move from cognition to object recognition thousands of times per day, without being conscious of so doing, both because we are so accustomed to the experience, and because our perception is not retarded by ambiguity or wonder. By age three, say, we are accustomed, and remain forever thereafter accustomed, to seeing the big white cube in the kitchen, opposite the oven, as a fridge. With each perceptual recognition, we have nonetheless come home, however rapidly and uneventfully. Our basic perceptual habits are, that is, modeled on the *nostos* (homecoming) plot: we hunt for home with every perceptual act, with whatever sense. Nostalgia is a Greek-derivation meaning "home-pain" (νόστος + αλγία).[10] Nostalgia, we might say, drives the native operations of the psyche: we don't like feeling cognitively unwell, and want swiftly to move home, almost every time. *Almost* every time: works of art, and very occasionally and memorably lived experience, involve kinds of ambiguity that slow us down; they retard the movement from "looking at" to "seeing as"; they keep us homesick for a bit, and they prompt us to become conscious of, and to see afresh, what we routinely do, when there is no perceptual ambiguity. We hunt for cognitive home; we are conscious, volitional players within this cognitive event.

Saint Augustine (354–432 CE) articulates the volitional prompt and mechanism of recognition beautifully in Book 10 of the *Confessions* (c. 397), where he provides a searching account of the psychic operations of memory. We cannot quite remember fully what we are looking for, but we hunt with a remembered fragment, until the whole crops up, when "we say 'this is it!'" We cannot make that claim unless we recognize the lost object (*"nisi agnosceremus"*).[11] We hunt not by recalling the whole to mind, since the whole

---

9   The amusing experiment in which viewers, directed to look for something non gorilla-related miss the anomalous figure in gorilla costume, also proves the point. See http://www.theinvisiblegorilla.com/gorilla_experiment.html.

10 Though the *OED* points out that the word is of relatively recent origin: "< post-classical Latin nostalgia (J. Hofer Dissertatio Medica de Nostalgia, oder Heimwehe (1688)) < ancient Greek νόστος return home (see NOSTOS *n.*) + -αλγία ALGIA *comb. form*, after German Heimweh HEIMWEH *n.*"

11 "If the memory is coming up with one thing in place of another, we reject it, until the thing we are looking for crops up. And when it does crop up, we say, 'this is it!' We would not say that unless we recognized it, and we would not recognize it unless we remembered it. But we had definitely forgotten it" ["et ibi si aliud pro alio forte offeratur, respuimus donec illud occurrat quod quaerimus. Et cum occurrit, dicimus, 'hoc est'; quod non diceremus nisi agnosceremus, nec agnosceremus nisi meminissemus. Certe ergo obliti fueramus …"]. Augustine, *Confessions*, tr. Carolyn J. B. Hammond, 2 vols. (Cambridge, Mass.: Harvard University Press, 2014), 10.19, pp. 116–17. Further references to Augustine's *Confessions* will be made in the body of the text, by book, paragraph and page number.

THE SHOCK OF THE OLD: RECOGNITION IN THE HUMANITIES   19

is precisely what we have forgotten. On the contrary, we recall only a fragment (e.g. the initial letter of the name we cannot remember), which, limping ("*claudicans*"), goes obediently in search of the whole memory to which it wishes to be restored:

> [What we were seeking] had not vanished completely: the fraction that remained present went in search of the rest of the whole because the memory was aware that what it was ruminating upon was not exactly the same as usual, and so, as if its normal shape was mutilated, it went limping, *insistent* that the missing element be restored [my emphasis].[12]

Augustine describes the limping fragment as the sole agent ("the fraction that remained present went in search of the rest of the whole"), but he might have mentioned that it's our will that orders the fragment to search in the first place. That the fragment is indeed an agent is revealed by the fact that the searched-for item will often pop up unexpectedly from the memory, a while after we have consciously, volitionally given up the search. But the fragment would not have performed its work without our commanding it to start in the first place.

Augustine's account of a personified, limping fragment going in search of the whole to which it wishes to be restored is also transferrable to the experience of many art forms. The work of art, that is, deliberately retards the process of recollection by imposing some form of mental "limp," as it were. Works of art deliberately activate the limping fragment seeking the missing whole. It's altogether fitting that the clue for Eurycleia to recognize Odysseus should be the scar of the leg wound.[13] Oedipus, too, comes to the very boundary of appalling self-recognition by understanding the event that gave him his name, meaning "swollen-foot."[14]

In sum, recognitional knowledge is unashamedly relational; we contribute to the knowledge acquired; the dutiful, agential limping recognizer is inherently part of the story. This is obviously true for the mutual recognitions of real life, but it applies equally to recognitions across time: we recognize ourselves in history by actively seeking historical mirrors. We no longer neutrally observe the alterity of the past, standing outside it, but see ourselves afresh by mutual recognition of both the past and ourselves within history's restored continuum.

---

[12] "… an non totum exciderat, sed ex parte quae tenebatur pars alia quaerebatur, quia sentiebat se memoria non simul volvere quod simul solebat, et quasi detruncata consuetudine claudicans reddi quod deerat flagitabat." Augustine, *Confessions*, tr. Hammond, 10.19, p. 117 (translation altered).

[13] I thank Homi Bhabha for this point.

[14] Sophocles, *Oedipus Tyrannos*, ed. and tr. Hugh Lloyd-Jones (Cambridge, Mass.: Harvard University Press, 1994), lines 1031–37, pp. 431–33. Illuminating name etymology will of course have high profile in genres that wish to excavate immanent knowledge.

WHAT BECAME KNOWN WAS IN SOME SENSE ALREADY KNOWN

With scientific method we seek new knowledge, something that has never previously been thought. My example, by contrast, recycles old knowledge. That knowledge was explicitly known to me, and refreshed by the particular experience. The knowledge was, one way or another, immanent: the story I told rehearses the recovery of buried knowledge; it performs a conceptual archaeology; its knowledge effect and affect are indissociably connected to an already-known face.

The need already to have known what one claims to know is perhaps the most implausible, illogical aspect of recognitional, or what we can also call immanent, knowing. A moment's pause over stories precisely of the kind to which I point persuades us, however, that such a claim has at least an emotional plausibility. After all, our most intense and memorable experiences often derive from emotional recognitions of old faces. The emotional effect of recognitional knowledge is powerful because somehow familiar, *not* because it is wholly new and original. Thus Augustine points to the especial pleasure we take in rediscovery of the known and lost: "So what is at work in the soul when it takes more pleasure in whatever it finds or recovers and then loves than it would if it had always possessed them?"[15] The persuasion that recognition is wisdom survives even in ages of disenchantment. Thus what Samuel Beckett says of the old questions and answers in *Fin de partie* (*Endgame*) (1957) is no less true of old recognized faces: "Ah, the *old* questions, the *old* answers, *there's nothing like them!*" [my emphases].[16]

There's "nothing like them," nothing like these old questions and faces (except, apparently, themselves of course): the old faces, the recovered faces, have the power to move us to a distinctive cognitive novelty. Precisely as they move to reform us, they become new and unlike anything else – there is, indeed, "nothing like them."

~

The main aspect of my recognition story is, however, the final one treated immediately above: recognition itself. In this section I offer a very brief intellectual history of this cognitive phenomenon.

In my story, I saw and understood something I'd seen before. In the history of epistemology, this is the default position of European thought from at least Plato (428/27–348/47 BCE) until John Locke (1632–1704). Within that reasonably long chronology, two powerful, related traditions of intellectual history – Platonic and

---

15 "Quid ergo agitur in anima, cum amplius delectatur inventis aut redditis rebus quas diligit quam si eas semper habuisset?" Augustine, *Confessions*, tr. Hammond, 8.7, p. 367.
16 Samuel Beckett, *Endgame*, in Samuel Beckett, *The Complete Dramatic Works* (London: Faber and Faber, 1986), pp. 92–134 (at p. 110).

THE SHOCK OF THE OLD: RECOGNITION IN THE HUMANITIES   21

Christian – posit and account for a recognitional response to the natural and divine world. Those traditions argue that we are both prompted and *enabled* to understand the natural and the supernatural precisely because we are made of the same stuff, by the same maker, on the same generative models, as those worlds. Primal, generative ideas are innate to humans. Those primal forms invest both humans and the cosmos with a desire to achieve their own ideal form. The human desire to achieve a perfected, even divinized form is, therefore, characterized by *backward* movement, an effort to remember whence we came. Cognitive perfection is achieved by making it back home, by recognition.

In Platonic thought, the powerful desire for, and the rich affordances of, the backward gaze derive from the soul's own history. In the *Meno*, Socrates summarizes the logic of recollection (*anamnesis*) thus:

> Seeing then that the soul is immortal and has been born many times, and has beheld all things both in this world and in the nether realms, she has acquired knowledge of all and everything; so that it is no wonder that she should be able to recollect all that she knew before about virtue and other things. For as all nature is akin, and the soul has learned all things, there is no reason why we should not, by remembering but one single thing – an act which men call learning – discover everything else, if we have courage and faint not in the search; since, it would seem, research and learning are wholly recollection (ἀνάμνησις, anamnesis).[17]

The soul's history, then, generates an epistemology: knowledge is most richly archived in the past, given the soul's prior existences. All true knowledge is, for Plato, recovered only after *la recherche du temps perdu*.

Plato's recognitional epistemology is doubly grounded: on innate ideas derived from prior existences; and on a cosmological persuasion that the elements of the cosmos, including human souls and bodies, are thickly inter-related both materially and through the principles of their creation. Given that "all nature is akin," by learning one thing, we can "discover everything else."

Anamnesis was taken up by Christian neo-Platonists such as St. Augustine. The Christian, neo-Platonic epistemological *nostos* plot works by a Platonic logic, but with differences: Christian theology denies any prior existence to the soul;[18] and, given the Incarnation, awards a different and more significant place to corporeality.[19] Christian neo-Platonists nonetheless posit that the Word was with God from the beginning, and that our progress

---

[17] Plato, *Meno*, ed. and tr. W. Lamb (Cambridge, Mass.: Harvard University Press, 1924), 81c, p. 303.

[18] For Augustine's explicit repudiation of the Platonic formulation of anamnesis, see Augustine, *The Trinity*, tr. Stephen McKenna (Washington: Catholic University of America Press, 1963), 12.15, pp. 366–68.

[19] For an introduction to Augustine's epistemology, see Marcia L. Colish, *The Mirror of Language: A Study in the Medieval Theory of Knowledge*, rev. ed. (Lincoln, Nebr.: University of Nebraska Press, 1983), pp. 7–54.

22   JAMES SIMPSON

towards knowledge is a progress of getting back to beginnings, though now Christological beginnings. For Augustine, the fact that we are part of God's creation activates an intense cognitive and affective desire to seek out, and to recognize, the incarnate source of that creation; until we recognize that source, we find no peace.[20] The Christian, in this scenario, replays the *nostos* plot (Augustine is here addressing God): "let us not fear that we have nowhere to return, just because we once broke away. Even while we were away, our house has not fallen into decay, since it is your eternity."[21]

Augustine brilliantly reformulates Plato's psychological view with regard to memory in Book 10 of the *Confessions*.[22] Augustine says he can account for the vast, cavernous memory banks of sensory perception but simply cannot understand how abstract knowledge entered his psyche, or where it lies. He articulates the classic Platonic epistemological position with regard to eternal Ideas thus:

> Where from, and how, did these things enter into my memory? I do not know how. For when I learned them, I did not rely on someone else's mind, but *recognized* them in my own, and agreed that they were true (*non credidi alieno cordi, sed in meo recognovi et vera esse approbavi et commendavi*), and entrusted them to my memory as if I were tucking them away ready to be retrieved when I wanted them. So they were in my mind even before I had learned them, but they were not yet in my memory (*ergo erant et antequam ea didicissem, sed in memoria non erant*). Where, then, and how did I *recognize* them when they were spoken of, and so remark, "It is so, it is true," unless it was because they were already in my memory, but buried so distant and deep – in the most hidden hollows, as it were (*cum dicerentur, agnovi et dixi, "ita est, verum est," nisi quia iam erant in memoria, sed tam remota et retrusa quasi in cavis abditioribus*) – that unless someone's reference to them had dragged them out, I might perhaps not have been able to think them at all [my emphases].[23]

---

20 The ending of Dante's *Divine Comedy* (*Divina Commedia*, ed. Sapegno, *Paradiso*, 3:33.133–45) at which Dante's journey must end with the vision of Christ at the summit of paradise, works wholly within this Christian, Neo-Platonic tradition. See also Augustine, *The Trinity*, tr. McKenna, 15.8, pp. 469–70 for the significance of recognizing the image of God through self-knowledge.

21 "… Et non timemus ne non sit quo redeamus, quia nos inde ruimus. Nobis autem absentibus, non ruit domus nostra, aeternitatis tua." Augustine, *Confessions*, tr. Hammond, 4.15.31, p. 183.

22 For a survey of scholarship on memory studies in Augustine, see Kevin G. Grove, *Augustine on Memory* (Oxford: Oxford University Press, 2021), pp. 2–21.

23 "unde et qua haec intraverunt in memoriam meam? Nescio quomodo. Nam cum ea didici, non credidi alieno cordi, sed in meo recognovi et vera esse approbavi et commendavi ei, tamquam reponens unde proferrem cum vellem. Ibi ergo erant et antequam ea didicissem, sed in memoria non erant. Ubi ergo aut quare, cum dicerentur, agnovi et dixi, 'ita est, verum est,' nisi quia iam erant in memoria, sed tam remota et retrusa quasi in cavis abditioribus ut, nisi admonente

THE SHOCK OF THE OLD: RECOGNITION IN THE HUMANITIES   23

The epistemology and the cosmological-anthropological persuasions are variously transmitted to the medieval and early modern periods, in, for example, the fourth-century Calcidian commentary on the *Timaeus*, and in Boethius's *Consolation of Philosophy* (523–24). That larger Platonic theory, which "part d'une cosmologie pour aboutir à une anthropologie,"[24] is fully present in Plato's *Timaeus*. This is the one Platonic dialogue known, at least in significant part, throughout the Middle Ages, via the commentary (321 CE) upon it by Calcidius.[25] In the rich and influential post-Classical response to the *Timaeus*, the human was understood to be the microcosm of the macrocosm (i.e. the cosmos as a whole). The human form replicates in small the structure of the larger universe, and is made of the same materials. This tradition was optimistic because it held out the possibility of perfection, even divinization of sorts, to humans capable of knowing themselves.[26] For humans to know themselves (their highest calling), that is, they must know the cosmos; micro-cosmic humans are both prompted and enabled to know the cosmos by virtue of being part of, made of the same materials as, and arranged in the same structure as, the macrocosm. Microcosmic humans were hard-wired to want to understand themselves, and *to succeed* in fulfilling that desire, through their material and intellectual commonality with the macrocosm. Knowledge of self was, in this tradition, a graded sequence of recognitions, seeing oneself in the universe.

Boethius's *Consolation* also transmits both the Platonic epistemology of anamnesis and the Timaean micro-macrocosmic understanding. Further, the *Consolation* expresses the aesthetic beauty and narrative dynamism of that worldview. Thus at the work's central point (Book 3, meter 9 [*O qui perpetua*]), Philosophy draws on the *Timaeus* to address the generative principle of the cosmos, who shapes the beautiful natural world on the model of the divine Idea. In Book 4, meter 1 (*Sunt etenim pennae volucres mihi*), Philosophy outlines the upwardly-mobile yet finally circular dynamism of the heavenly itinerary to which the enlightened soul naturally aspires.

---

aliquo eruerentur, ea fortasse cogitare non possem?" Augustine, *Confessions*, tr. Hammond, 10.17, pp. 97–99.

[24] Philippe Delhaye, *Le Microcosmos de Godefroy de St.-Victor: étude théologique* (Lille: Facultés catholiques, 1951), p. 148. Cited by Winthrop Wetherbee, in *Platonism and Poetry in the Twelfth Century* (Princeton, N.J.: Princeton University Press, 1972), p. 34.

[25] Plato, *"Timaeus", a Calcidio translatus commentarioque instructus*, ed. Jan H. Waszink (Leiden and London: Brill and Warburg Institute, 1975).

[26] For the larger history and varieties of the tradition of self-knowledge, see Pierre Courcelle, *Connais toi-même de Socrate à saint Bernard*, 2 vols. (Paris: Etudes Augustiniennes, 1974). For the optimism of the Timaean tradition for self-knowledge, see André Jean Festugière, *La revelation de Hermes Trismegiste*, 4 vols. (Paris: Les Belles Lettres, 1944–54), vol. 2, *Le dieu cosmique* (1949).

24   JAMES SIMPSON

The profound inter-relatedness of the fields of cosmology, psychology and aesthetics are all underwritten by recognition and recollection.[27] Thus in Book 3, meter 11 (*Quisquis profunda mente vestigat verum*), Philosophy underlines that the seeker after truth must "on himself turn back (*revolvat*) the light of his inward vision, / Bending and forcing his far-reaching movements / Into a circle ... For why, being asked a question, do you rightly judge / Out of yourself, unless the kindling lived / Deep down in your heart? If Plato's muse rings true, / What each man learns, forgetful he recalls (*recordat*)."[28] Words prefaced by the iterative particle "re" describe the entire epistemological process, from *revolvat* to *recordatur*, just as the circular shape of learning (*in orbem*) models the aesthetic form such learning will inevitably take.

The optimistic, elitist, humanist, micro-macrocosmic *Timaean* tradition flourished with extraordinary brilliance from the twelfth to the seventeenth century, especially in literary traditions.[29] It ceased to command philosophical respect in 1689 with John Locke's publication of *An Essay Concerning Human Understanding*. Put simply, Locke strenuously denies the existence of innate ideas, and posits that the mind at birth is like a sheet of white paper, "void of all characters, without any ideas" on whose surface the observed world writes onto memory.[30] Understanding the perceptual world no longer involves recognition.

~

Cognition, to repeat my theme, is recognition. This is true in the experience of both life and art, but much more common in art. Works of art very often produce the illuminating thrill of recognition, and they do so by reverse engineering, and by deliberately slowing down, the quotidian, cognitive

---

27 See Elaine Scarry, "The Well-Rounded Sphere: Cognition and Metaphysical Structure in Boethius's *Consolation of Philosophy*," in *Resisting Representation* (Oxford: Oxford University Press, 1994), pp. 143–80.

28 "In se revolvat intimi lucem visus / Longosque in orbem cogat inflectens motus ... Nam cur rogati sponte recta censetis, / Ni mersus alto viveret fomes corde? / Quod si Platonis musa personat verum, / Quod quisque discit immemor recordatur." Boethius, *Consolatio Philosophiae*, ed. and tr. S. J. Tester (Cambridge, Mass.: Harvard University Press, 2014), 3.m11, lines 3–11, pp. 296–97.

29 See James Simpson, "Humanism," in *Dictionary of the Middle Ages*, gen. ed. William Chester Jordan (New York: Charles Scribner's Sons, 2004), Supplement 1, pp. 279–82. For the twelfth-century reception, see Wetherbee, *Platonism and Poetry*, and Peter Dronke, *Fabula: Explorations into the Uses of Myth in Medieval Platonism* (Leiden: Brill, 1974). For later medieval reception, in the context of twelfth-century texts, see Kathryn L. Lynch, *The High Medieval Dream Vision* (Stanford: Stanford University Press, 1988), and James Simpson, *Sciences and the Self in Medieval Poetry: Alan of Lille's* Anticlaudianus *and John Gower's* Confessio amantis (Cambridge: Cambridge University Press, 1995), chapters 4–6.

30 John Locke, *An Essay Concerning Human Understanding*, ed. Alexander Campbell Fraser (Oxford: Clarendon Press, 1894), Book 2, chapter 1, p. 121. The theme of Book 1 of this text is that there are no innate principles in the mind.

THE SHOCK OF THE OLD: RECOGNITION IN THE HUMANITIES   25

processes of recognition. When we dramatically recognize a person or artefact, our experience is extraordinary and memorable. The moment we stop "looking at" and start "seeing as" produces a charge of high, simultaneous degrees of cognitive illumination and emotional intensity. We certainly experience such moments in real life, when we recognize the lost parent, spouse, lover, child, student, teacher, or friend, for example. But great (and often not so great) art specializes in recognition: it frequently represents and provokes recognitional moments of high cognitive illumination and great emotional intensity. That may be one reason why we love great art (and, sometimes, popular art): we love watching others recognize; we love recognizing; and we love communal recognition. In sum, we love coming home, not by any means least when "home," as in the reaches of much great art, turns out to be a home that we'd never thought of as such. As we have seen, recognition has its own drama, in which we all play the part of Odysseus's nurse Eurycleia, the second human to recognize Odysseus come home; if we are lucky, we can also play the part of Odysseus himself, being recognized in Ithaca.

I have, I hope, reinvested this epistemological model with some credibility in the presence of its competitor, scientific method. The humanist might, however, quickly join the scientist in repudiating certain crucial aspects of the recognition model. Recognition is a past-friendly cognitive model. Appeals to the past are, in the humanities, often dismissed as either reactionary and/or nostalgic, both of which charges need only be stated to be complete and effective. So far from seeking to recognize the past, the freedom seeker will argue that we must inoculate ourselves against past-virus. We do so by alienating ourselves from it. We cultivate what the revolutionary playwright Bertolt Brecht in the 1930s dubbed the "Alienation Effect" (*Verfremdungseffekt*),[31] or, more aggressively, we subject the past to "critique," an interpretative regime that interrogates the object of its enquiry with unrelenting suspicion.[32] Recognition, or so critique would have it, is precisely what we must guard *against*. Treat the past as hostile, as toxic

---

[31] For a succinct but inadequate history of the term, first formulated conceptually by Viktor Shklovsky in 1917, and adopted by Brecht in 1936, see "Defamiliarization," in *The Princeton Encyclopedia of Poetry and Poetics*, ed. Roland Greene, Stephen Cushman, Clare Cavanagh, Jahan Ramazani, Paul Rouzer, 2 vols. (Princeton, N.J.: Princeton University Press, 2012), 1:343–44, and further references. The Wikipedia entry is in fact much superior: https://en.wikipedia.org/wiki/Distancing_effect. The history of defamiliarization's value in reading is of course a long one; see, for example, Augustine, *De doctrina Christiana*, translated by D. W. Robertson as *On Christian Doctrine* (New York: Liberal Arts Press, 1958), Book 2.6, where the provisional obscurity of figural expressions is defended as producing pleasure in resolution.

[32] For a penetrating set of reflections on the practice of critique in literary criticism, see Rita Felski, *The Limits of Critique* (Chicago: University of Chicago Press, 2015). For use of the word "interrogation," with its connotations of the practices of the police state, in the liberal academy, see James Simpson, "Interrogation Over. A Review Essay of Rita Felski, *The Limits of Critique*," PMLA 132 (2017), 377–83.

26 JAMES SIMPSON

stranger, or else fall victim to the malady of the past, a malady whose first, surest and most baleful symptom will be nostalgia. When we spake naively as children, we sought recognitions, but when we grew up and put away childish things, then we began to interrogate texts with the instruments of critique. Recognition? It's kids' stuff.

Let me turn, then, to kids' stuff, which turns out to be full of illuminating and liberating surprises.

I turn to the children's genre of the riddle. I do so partly because linguistic recognition is fascinating in itself, but also in order to answer the skeptics, both the scientist and the critical humanist, who wish to restrict recognition to the nursery. By understanding how children learn from, and play with, the recognition plot, we also learn about how adults engage with art.

Children's games revive the process of recognition, because it's fun. "What's black and white and [rəd] all over?" Trapping the assembled grown-ups with this puzzler was of course a source of childish delight at family parties, even if, in retrospect, the adults were no doubt only pretending not to know the answer. The source of the riddle's delight, for the children, was that the answer was staring the adults in the face all the while, even if they seemed unable to see it.

Part of the fun for children was watching the adults' failed intellectual struggle, but a better part was enjoying the moment of resolution: everyone smiling in relief at having a satisfactory answer, and also smiling in shared, resigned sympathy for the crooked cognitive timber of humanity. We are, after all, so easily given not to seeing what stares us in the face, because we are searching for the wrong recognition. The pleasure of springing the solution was precisely that the answer was, as in all good riddles, buried within the question, but just visible. None of us discovered anything new, but pleasurably recovered something old (i.e. not the trivial fact that we read (or used to read) newspapers, but the fact that we enjoy recognitions).

The rehearsal of fundamental linguistic recognition routines is fun not only for children. Adults also enjoy going through the motions of recognition. We learn nothing whatsoever about newspapers in the children's riddle. When ambitious literary artists deploy riddles, however, they do so in order to produce illuminating re-visions of the world.

From early medieval England, for example, we have a collection of riddles, in a late tenth-century collection of Old English poetry, the so-called Exeter Book.[33] These riddles are evidently derived from a longer, learned and Latin tradition of riddling poetry, known formally as *aenigmata*.[34] The vernacular

---

[33] *The Exeter Book*, ed. George Philip Krapp and Elliot van Kirk Dobbie (New York: Columbia University Press, 1936).

[34] For a survey, see Andy Orchard, ed. and tr., *The Old English and Anglo-Latin Riddle Tradition* (Cambridge, Mass.: Harvard University Press, 2021). For a survey of scholarship on the Exeter Book riddles, see Andy Orchard, *A Commentary on the Old English and Anglo-Latin Riddle Tradition* (Washington:

THE SHOCK OF THE OLD: RECOGNITION IN THE HUMANITIES   27

riddles often begin with a variation on the infinitely repeated question parents pose to infants as they acquire language. Whereas the parents are forever saying "What is it?" to their long-suffering infants, many of the poems begin more mysteriously, by potentially animating the world: "What am I?" ("*Saga hwæt ic hatte*" ["Say what I am called"]).

Many examples of Old English poetry (i.e. vernacular poetry written between the seventh and the eleventh century in England) are voiced in the first-person singular. Some of these first-person-singular poems are elegiac, where the speaker's refusal to disclose his or her full identity and story is the result of, and serves further to underline, the speaker's intense pain. In the case of the riddles, however, the effect of refusing to disclose identity is in the first instance cognitive uncertainty. That uncertainty produces intellectual wonder and only then emotional release.

Take for example the beginning of this riddle (#24),[35] whose opening lines, in retrospect, do not offer enough to work out the definitive solution (not to me, at any rate):

> A certain foe snatched away my life,
> deprived me of earthly powers, then soaked me,
> dipped me in water, drew me out again,
> set me in sunlight, where I soon lost
> those hairs I had.
>   Then a hard knife's edge
> shaved me, impurities thoroughly removed;
> fingers folded me; and a bird's delight
> spread on me serviceable drops, often made tracks
> across a brown rim, swallowed wood dye,
> in some solution, stepped back upon me,
> and traveled, leaving a dark track.

> Mec feonda sum   feore besnyþede
> woruld-strenga binom   wætte siþþan
> dyfde on wætre   dyde eft þonan
> sette on sunnan   þær ic swiþe beleas
> herum þam þe ic hæfde.
>   Heard mec siþþan
> snað seaxses ecge   sindrum begrunden
> fingras feoldan ond mec fugles wyn
> geondsprengde sped-dropum   spyrede geneahhe

Dumbarton Oaks, 2021), pp. 321–27, and Andy Orchard, "Enigma Variations: The Anglo-Saxon Riddle Tradition," in *Latin Learning and English Lore: Studies in Anglo-Saxon Literature for Michael Lapidge*, ed. Katherine O'Brien O'Keeffe and Andy Orchard, 2 vols. (Toronto: University of Toronto Press, 2005), 1:284–304.

[35] The numbering of Exeter Book Riddles is revised in Orchard's *The Old English and Anglo-Latin Riddle Tradition*. Older scholarship labels this riddle as #26.

ofer brunne brerd   beam-telge swealg
streames dæle   stop eft on mec
siþade sweartlast.[36]

The first line might prompt sympathy for the victim of a killer, but sympathy is quickly displaced by the cognitive dissonance of a puzzle: who is speaking? Who, or what, is the "I"? That question is unavoidable, because the voice of the poem denies its claim: the claim is that the speaker was killed in the past, while the voice of the poem is still speaking, in the present.

A word within the riddle gives us the clue to our own interpretative task: the "joy of the bird" (whatever that might be) often "spyrede" over the brown surface of the speaker. The Old English word *spyrian* (simple past tense *spyrede*) is the ancestor of Modern German *Spur* or "track." In other Old English texts, *spyrian* translates Latin *investigare*, meaning to "trace footsteps" (Latin *vestigia*).[37] So we as readers must become trackers, or in*vestiga*tors, along interpretative paths, on high alert for each trace of where the speaker has trodden before us. If we are to find our way home along the paths of this riddle, we must educe more about the speaker than the speaker seems ready to disclose.

We are invited to track the speaker's path with the clues of fundamental binaries by which we tend to organize perception: in this case, passive/active; and human/animal. The speaker is totally passive: "it" (the safest pronoun for the moment) is never active, but only subject to a bewilderingly wide range of other agents (i.e. the enemy who killed and drenched it; the hostile knife; the folding fingers; the "joy of the bird," which (the joy, not the bird) walks across, or even steps on, "it"). We are invited to look for human versus animal co-ordinates to gain traction. The fingers are almost certainly human, just as the knife is certainly wielded by a human. "The joy of the bird," by contrast, seems to be animal, producing things that animals produce (droppings, the Old English word "*dropa*," a drop of liquid), or consuming other biological products (tree dye), or treading over other things, in this case the speaker. These clues do not add up to a track, and set us off in many different directions. All we can say for sure is that the speaker, whether dead or alive, is a biological entity (it can be deprived of life; it has hairs (plural)); it is subject to an apparently bizarre range of technological and biological treatments, inflicted by both humans and, apparently, animals.

---

[36] *The Old English and Anglo-Latin Riddle Tradition*, ed. and tr. Orchard, pp. 332–35. Further references to this edition will be made by line number in the body of the text. I have changed Orchard's translation thus: where I translate "Then a hard knife's edge / shaved me, impurities thoroughly removed," Orchard's translation reads "Then a hard knife's edge / its roughness rubbed off, cut me up." For a defense of the translation I adopt, see Elena Afros, "*Sindrum begrunden* in Exeter Book Riddle 26: the Enigmatic Dative Case," *Notes and Queries* n.s. 51 (2004), 7–9.

[37] Dictionary of Old English, Web Corpus, s.v. "spyrede," https://tapor-library-utoronto-ca.ezp-prod1.hul.harvard.edu/doecorpus/ (accessed 23 January 2023).

THE SHOCK OF THE OLD: RECOGNITION IN THE HUMANITIES 29

At this point we could look to the rest of the riddle, where things become a little clearer. But riddles ask that we press each clue maximally before we pass on to others. So before we move on, we should examine our available clues more closely. The one clue that turns out to be most explicit is the circumlocution "joy of the bird" ("fugles wyn"). I happen to know the riddle's solution, and acknowledge that I might be jumping the gun by using this as my *Spur*. But birds have only one joy that is capable of making drops and of swallowing. If we reach for the solution "feather," then we suddenly have a set of recognitions.

With "feather" in hand, as it were, we no longer look at, but see happily as. The drops are useful because the feather is a quill, writing profitable words; the feather swallows tree dye in the way the quill replenishes itself with ink. Working out from writing, we might now change from looking *at* the "I" speaker, to seeing it *as* the vellum skin that has been prepared by killing a sheep or calf; *as* the vellum that is being soaked; and *as* the skin product being excised of all impurities with a knife, in order to produce a perfect writing surface. The droppings and the dark tracks were decoys. They are not, once we have our bearing, typically animal behaviors but rather the mysterious, productive, meaning-making marks of tracing letters on vellum. The letters are repeatedly tracing on the ample expanse of the parchment ("spyrede geneahhe / ofer brunne brerd") because they are copying from an exemplar. Just as we track across the riddle, the pen tracks back and forth across the manuscript page: both reader and quill are tracking, retracing, investigating.

With "quill," the riddle suddenly has what we might call a textual face. The solution is "The Bible." What's left of the riddle springs readily into clarity: "Now those decorations, and that red dye ... / Spread wide the fame / of the protector of noble nations" (lines 15–17). By the time we arrive at the final prompt ("*frige hwæt ic hatte*" ["ask what I am called"] [line 26]) the answer has been recovered. But the opacity of the riddle's opening sequence has taken us into the very interpretative practices (i.e. allegory, or saying one thing and meaning another) that the divine book itself demands.

The solution even accounts for the apparent contradiction in the opening lines: the book, like the God it proclaims, is, if you will, capable of resurrection: it had been killed but is now speaking; it has been transformed from a "what" to an animated "who." The child-like genre of the riddle discloses the theological phenomenon, just as St. Paul chooses the word *aenigma* (i.e. riddle) for all earthly knowing.[38] He chooses the genre of the riddle that more than any other promises to disclose immanent truth, the truth that is already in there: *nunc vidimus per speculum in aenigmate* (now we see through a mirror, as in a riddle).

---

[38] For the theological resonances of the dead letters speaking, see Mary Hayes, "The Talking Dead: Resounding Voices in Old English Riddles," *Exemplaria* 20 (2008), 123–42 (at pp. 127–33 for the riddle under discussion here).

Our tracking into this riddle conforms in every way to our model of recognitional knowledge: we are asked to approach an artefact as if it were a question, whose answer is visible within the artefact if only we "see as"; we look for what we know, and what we know is there already (the premise of every riddle); our prior knowledge of the solution is precisely what makes recovery of the solution so illuminating.

Is the model of finding prompted by this riddle epistemologically weak (the scientific experimentalist's objection)? Can its path home be described as conservative, even reactionary (the humanist's objection)?

Answers to both questions are made by pointing to the way we rediscover the world we thought we knew by finding the riddle's track. The riddle generates its mystery by not telling us who is speaking. That simple deprivation of a readily intelligible grammatical subject, around which a reader habitually and rapidly organizes understanding, here transforms everything around that subject. Suddenly the standard technical procedures for preparing parchment are defamiliarized, and thereby invested with wonder and surprise. The violence of sheep killing behind every piece of parchment; the technological treatments to which the parchment is subject; the other biological necessities of writing (i.e. bird's feathers); the resurrection of the dead parchment into a new creature speaking divine truths: all are defamiliarized and given high, wonder-producing, thought-provoking profile by the missing subject. The missing subject slows our routine cognitive processes down, and, as they slow down, the everyday world becomes surprising and marvelous.

The object itself ("The Bible") is completely transformed in unexpected ways. Here the Bible is not extraordinary by virtue of containing the Word of God; instead, it astonishes by virtue of depending on other life forms to reproduce the Word of God. Divine Word and parchment transform each other; life forms are miraculously transformed, so as to produce, in part because of the violence they must endure, meaning-making words in very durable form. We learn about the immaterial Word of God through the very material, and even violent, processes of its production, not the other way around. We also learn though humble vernacular words, not glorious, stable Latin.

To be allegorical is to say one thing and to mean another. The Biblical text, in a Christian reading, is made dynamic by allegory, whereby the events of the Hebrew Scriptures narrate an event from the pre-Christian past so as to point forward to a future Christian fulfilment. The aenigma functions in a parallel way, by creating an allegory of sorts; it does so by applying brakes to the speed with which we approach meaning through recognition. It does so, in fact, *only* by doing that: the poem's illuminating meaning derives wholly from its retarded cognitive mechanics.

THE SHOCK OF THE OLD: RECOGNITION IN THE HUMANITIES   31

The riddles as a corpus often explicitly describe the mundane as a wonder.[39] Aristotle posits that wonder and knowledge stand in inverse proportion to each other: we first respond to the world with wonder, which prompts us to move to knowledge; so the more knowledge we gain, the less wonder we experience.[40] These poems set knowledge and wonder into a richer epistemological relation: knowledge of the everyday is itself wondrous when you look at it from a certain angle. We recognize what we knew all along, but we see them afresh. Outworn metaphors spring into rich conceptual life; that which is regarded as purely conceptual is returned to its richly material condition; the everyday event becomes a wonder. Things and creatures disclose their mysterious, layered, life in the world.

We aim to get home with riddles, and we know, from the genre, that home is in there somewhere. We track our way home by seeking more information than the words seem to disclose, looking for signs of where the riddle voice has passed before us. We learn at an extraordinary rate, and with surprising intensity, through this disclosure model. But we learn unexpected things – less the answer to the riddle, but more the world transformed as we hunt for that answer.

Thus we might attempt to persuade the neutral observer scientist to start taking recognition serious as a way of knowing. Our skeptical humanist may be unpersuaded: should such a tracking home be described as conservative, even reactionary?

Insofar as the aim is to get home, and insofar as the neutral sense of "conservative" is "preserving," then yes, the project of riddles is conservative. But that is not for a moment to say that the knowledge so gained is reactionary, merely recapitulating and reconfirming what has already been achieved in the past, merely setting up the past as a bulwark against the present and the future. On the contrary, the past is refreshed and renewed, having been recovered in new circumstances; we know it, as it were, for the first time. The past refreshes and renews the present, and points future-ward.[41]

---

[39] For the Old English riddles' explicit interest in provoking wonder, see Patricia Dailey, "Riddles, Wonder and Responsiveness, in Anglo-Saxon Literature," in *The Cambridge History of Early Medieval English Literature*, ed. Claire A. Lees (Cambridge: Cambridge University Press, 2013), pp. 451–72, especially at pp. 468–70. See also Orchard, "Enigma Variations," pp. 289–91.

[40] See Aristotle, *Metaphysics*, in *The Complete Works of Aristotle*, ed. and tr. Jonathan Barnes, 2 vols. (Princeton, N.J.: Princeton University Press, 1984), 2:1552–728 (at 1982b, p. 1554). For the wide later medieval reception of this idea, see Patrick Boyde, *Dante Philomythes and Philosopher* (Cambridge: Cambridge University Press, 1981), pp. 50 and 310, n. 20.

[41] For a persuasive argument that riddles permit expression of social thought that would be otherwise unsayable, see Jennifer Neville, "The Unexpected Treasure of the 'Implement Trope': Hierarchical Relationships in the Old English Riddles," *RES* 62 (2011), 505–19.

The newest of those new truth circumstances is the experience of almost having lost our way to truth. That is to say, the riddle not only rehearses coming home, but also first rehearses getting lost. Riddles, like romance plots, are full of near misses, misses that remind us of just how close catastrophe is, and how easy it would have been to lose that which was finally found again. In this case the poet surely sends us off on false tracks deliberately: the "droppings" of the bird's joy on the surface of the speaker must evoke the entropy of a soiled surface, animal defecation on the humanly crafted, folded object. The poet does that by way of adding to our relief at discovering not a soiled artifact, but the retraced Word of God on the beautifully traced skin surface. That Word resuscitates the biological world, just as the riddle resuscitates our own understanding.

The recognition depends, that is, on something already pre-existent, and for this riddle our task is to recover it, to arrive at it, as our home. But – and this is the big "but" characteristic of greater recognitions – the pre-existent object must be in some way defaced, distressed, and ambiguous as we look at it.

The Old English word for riddle is *raedels* (> "riddle"). The root of this word is Old English *raedan*, a word of wide semantic range from "interpret" to "read" to "instruct."[42] This riddle is, like all the Old English riddles, and in keeping with the root of the word, in good part about the processes of reading. But in this riddle the reading process is also communal. Cracking this riddle trains one to read the scriptural text, successful reading of which is a communal experience. The final sequence of the riddle, which will make sense only as long as the individual reader has recognized the riddle's textual face, focuses both on the spiritual strength *and* the communality of the reading experience. Life will feel wholly renewed socially through recognitional reading: "*habbaþ freonda þy ma / swæsra ond gesibbra soþra ond godra*" ("they will have the more friends / more loved ones and kinsmen, more loyal and close," lines 21–23).

Conservative and reactionary? It's a "conservative" reading practice, to be sure, looking as it does to see what was already there. But it is not "conservative" in the sense of *merely* preserving what was there: this is a reformist conservatism, which transforms the social world through more intense bonds, in wider social groups, of fellow readers. It is emphatically not reactionary, turning aggressively and costively back to a prior, protective form. As Erica Weaver has so succinctly said, the riddles prompt a reading practice that is "neither suspicious nor purely formalist but a probing, meditative kind of reading that blends paranoid and reparative, symptomatic and surface approaches."[43]

---

[42] *OED*, respectively, senses I.1, 2; II; and IV.18. Cf. ancient Greek ἀναγιγνώσκω (to know again), *A Lexicon Abridged from Liddell and Scott's Greek-English Lexicon*, ed. H. G. Liddell, R. Scott, and J. M. Whiton (New York: American Book Company, 1906), s.v. 3 "to read."

[43] Erica Weaver, "Premodern and Postcritical: Medieval Enigmata and the Hermeneutic Style," *New Literary History* 50 (2019), 43–64 (at p. 46).

THE SHOCK OF THE OLD: RECOGNITION IN THE HUMANITIES 33

I respond, then, to the humanist's charge that the knowledge gained through recognition is necessarily "conservative": such knowledge is indeed gained only by excavating the past, but such knowledge is fresh and liberating in the new circumstances of its reinvention.

This non-reactionary, recognitional experience is not at all exclusive to the experience of art. It is, however, universal to the experience of great art. Literary understanding of that art is most fully itself when it is an act of recovery.

～

The grand traditions of anamnesis – Platonic and Christian neo-Platonic – are theologically grounded. What becomes of recognition when readers are no longer persuaded of those theological traditions? One answer to that question might be to point to the programming of our DNA, which does connect us to vast natural worlds recognition of which is gripping, deeply pleasurable and innate. That is beyond my ken, so I point to a second answer, which does not at all rely on innate ideas, so much as on culturally absorbed protocols of perception.

Recognition survives as the routine perceptual mechanism of seeing meaning even when it's wholly learned. Faced with the potential chaos of perceptual experience, or at least the separate imaginative worlds (i.e. genres) of the literary field, we need constantly to "see as." We gain our perceptual and cognitive footholds on literary texts through learned protocols. We learn the protocols through patterns of experience gained both prior to and during our reading of a given work.

With that posture in focus, we suddenly notice that the fundamental analytical tools at our disposal for the analysis of literary texts are features of repetition and retardation. This is no less true of large-scale categories such as genre, than it is of the following: medium-scale features of narrative (e.g. recapitulation, *in medias res* narrative order); and much smaller features of style. Many separate figures of speech in a text point us backward: the very etymology of "verse" turns us backwards, just as the schemes of rhyme, alliteration, anaphora and chiasmus, are, for example, all figures of repetition, turning us back even as we move forward. Each operates like the refrain of a lyric. Each offers forms of recapitulation. Each invites cognition through recognition.[44]

As we read, we are always looking for the familiar face or feature, or topos (i.e. commonplace) from the past. To read any work well, we need to understand how such works operate, what kinds of meaning they habitually offer and what kinds of meaning they habitually do *not* offer. We need, it might be said, to recognize their "face." Our texts, that is, train us how to read

---

[44] More fully argued in Simpson, "Cognition is Recognition," p. 34.

and recognize them. What in an earlier critical idiom we might have called intertextual allusion, we might now also call cognitive cues.

This has pedagogic implications: our students need training in the formal features that prompt our capacity to recognize. Learned recognition also has curricular consequences: our literary history is but an evolutionary eye blink (4,000 or so years). There is no such thing as a truly long literary history, since all are, relatively, short in evolutionary time. As we devise curricula, we should extend their chronological range so as to maximize the recuperative illuminations of recognition.

2

"STUFFED WITH DIVINE WORDS": UNDIGESTED TEXTS IN EARLY MEDIEVAL ENGLAND

Erica Weaver

"[T]he students of monuments and records … ought to amass no more than they can digest"

Samuel Johnson[1]

From the fifteenth century, when the verb "digest" first entered the English language, the act could refer both to the scholarly work of mulling over food for thought and the bodily one of breaking down organic matter in the stomach.[2] One could hope to digest both "hye witt" and "baskettes of breedes."[3] I say *hope* because, of course, digestion sometimes fails. While there is a longstanding understanding of reading as a kind of consuming, there is an equally long tradition of readers who fail to take in their reading matter or who

---

[1] Samuel Johnson, "No. 71" (November 20, 1750), in *The Rambler* (London: P. Dodsley, R. Owen, and Other Booksellers, 1794), II: 95. On the necessity of eating no more than one may digest, see also Vercelli VII, ed. D. G. Scragg, *The Vercelli Homilies and Related Texts*, EETS, os 300 (Oxford: Oxford University Press, 1992), pp. 133–38.

[2] *OED*, s.v. "digest, v.," https://www.oed.com (accessed 2 November 2022).

[3] These quotations are included for "digest, v." senses 3 and 4a in the *OED*. The first derives from Blind Harry or Henry the Minstrel's *The Actis and Deidis of The Illustere and Vailðeand Campioun Schir William Wallace, Knicht of Ellerslie*, Book 8, line 1430, ed. James Moir (Edinburgh: William Blackwood and Sons, 1889), p. 226. Later known as *The Wallace*, this poem survives in a single 1488 manuscript (Edinburgh, National Library of Scotland, Adv. MS 19.2.2 [ii]) but became the most popular printed book in Scotland after the Bible and inspired the 1995 movie *Braveheart*. The second quotation is drawn from William Bonde's *Pilgrimage of Perfection*, ESTC S108952 (London: Wynkyn de Worde, 1531), fol. clxxxxii.

36   ERICA WEAVER

only absorb it incompletely. In more ways than one, then, reading was a matter of taste. As the opening to the Old English poem now known as *Solomon and Saturn I* hints, however, when we read something carefully, we do not merely taste it; we digest, even as some texts prove frustratingly inedible.[4]

Many early medieval English riddles center on precisely that range of readerly (in)digestibility. While all riddles are designed to provide food for thought and consequently invite close and careful reading, some resist any easy digestion. Several even foreground this kind of unproductive reading directly by presenting tantalizing scenes of empty consumption, from Aldhelm's *Enigma* 89, in which a bookchest is "stuffed with divine words" ("divinis complentur … verbis") but fails to profit from the books that fill it, to Exeter Book Riddle 45, whose moth similarly "was not a whit the wiser" ("ne wæs / wihte þy gleawra") although he "ate words" ("word fræt").[5] Centering on these two figures, this essay explores the motif of reading as failed digestion, in contrast to the ruminative reading practice advocated by thinkers like Bede. Together, these acts of consumption invite us to reconsider two of the most puzzling digestive remnants in early medieval literature: the Donestre's victims, whose heads they weep over after consuming the rest of their bodies, and the beheaded figure of Æschere, the king's counselor in *Beowulf*.

READER'S DIGEST:
RUMINATION AND EARLY MEDIEVAL RIDDLES

These voracious readers, who consume without deriving any nutritive advantage, remind us that rumination, that art of chewing up, relishing, and fully taking in texts, was at the heart – or, better, the gut – of early medieval reading.[6] In his description of the workflow of the first known English poet,

---

4   Saturn boasts that he has "tasted" (line 2, *onbyrged*) the books of all the islands but is unable to experience the Lord's Prayer. *The Old English Dialogues of Solomon and Saturn*, ed. Daniel Anlezark (Cambridge: D. S. Brewer, 2009). As Jonathan Wilcox observes, there are several Biblical precedents for eating books in order to acquire divine knowledge (most notably Apocalypse 10:9–10, Jeremiah 15:16, and Ezechiel 3:1–3), "but in Saturn's case such a diet is ineffectual," so that he resembles the bookworm of Riddle 45, in "Eating Books: The Consumption of Learning in the Old English Poetic *Solomon and Saturn*," *ANQ* 4 (1991), 115–18 (at 117).
5   Aldhelm, *Enigma* 89 ("*Arca libraria*"), ed. Rudolf Ehwald, *Aldhelmi Opera*, Monumenta Germaniae Historica Auct. Antiq. 15 (Berlin: Weidmann, 1919), p. 138; and Riddle 45, ed. Andy Orchard, *The Old English and Anglo-Latin Riddle Tradition*, DOML 69 (Cambridge, Mass.: Harvard University Press, 2021), p. 364. Unless otherwise noted, all translations are my own.
6   For the classic account of monastic *ruminatio*, see Jean LeClercq, *The Love of Learning and the Desire for God: A Study of Monastic Culture* (New York: Fordham University Press, 1982), p. 73 and following. On the role of rumination in Old English poetic composition, see also Ruth Wehlau, "Rumination and Re-Creation: Poetic Instruction in *The Order of the World*," *Florilegium* 13 (1994), 65–77; and Francis Leneghan, "Making the Psalter Sing: The Old English Metrical

UNDIGESTED TEXTS IN EARLY MEDIEVAL ENGLAND 37

the cowherd Cædmon, Bede famously compares the poet's work – listening to scripture and replying with poetry – to an animal chewing cud.[7] In the words of editor and scholar Charles Plummer, "This metaphor ... is a very favourite one with Bede," and it appears several times across his corpus.[8] Although Plummer assumed that it was a scriptural reference to the ruminants in Leviticus and Deuteronomy, J. M. Pizarro has revealed that this association of poetic and intestinal rumination instead derives from Rufinus of Aquileia's addition to his translation of Eusebius, where he describes his former teacher, Didymus the Blind of Alexandria, similarly taking in and digesting what he had heard.[9] As Antonina Harbus observes, "[i]n view of Cædmon's duties as a cattle-herd, the image of the clean beast adds an ironic completeness to the story," but the ruminative ideal was widespread.[10] As a monastic practice, *ruminatio* asked readers not only to read but to digest as they chewed on devotional texts in search of spiritual nourishment.

For this reason, it is perhaps unsurprising that the first attested instance of "soul food" in English appears in the work of the prolific homilist Ælfric of Eynsham.[11] While bodily feasting could be gluttonous, the eager ingestion of soul food – in the form of spoken or written language – could mark one's progression in the faith, as in the graduation from milk to solid food in 1 Corinthians 3:2. When Ælfric maintains that "Hlaf is ðæs lichaman bigleofa, and lar is ðære sawle foda" (bread is the food of the body, and learning is the food of the soul), he thus invites his listeners to participate in a kind of textual transubstantiation, in which body and bread find a spiritual counterpoint in the nourishment of instruction.[12] Found in the tenth-century Exeter Book (Exeter, Cathedral Library MS 3501), Exeter Riddle 45 conflates these two very different kinds of consumption, as a bookworm devours words but fails

---

Psalms, Rhythm, and *Ruminatio*," in *The Psalms and Medieval English Literature: From Conversion to the Reformation*, ed. Tamara Atkin and Francis Leneghan (Cambridge: D. S. Brewer, 2017), pp. 173–97, esp. pp. 193–97.

[7] In Bede's terms, Cædmon proceeds "quasi mundum animal ruminando," in *Ecclesiastical History of the English People*, 4.24, ed. Bertram Colgrave and R. A. B. Mynors (Oxford: Clarendon Press, 1969), p. 418.

[8] Charles Plummer, *Venerabilis Baedae Opera Historica* (Oxford: Oxford University Press, 1896), vol. 2: 250. For further discussion, see Philip J. West, "Rumination in Bede's Account of Cædmon," *Monastic Studies* 12 (1976), 217–26.

[9] J. M. Pizarro, "Poetry as Rumination: The Model for Bede's Caedmon," *Neophilologus* 89 (2005), 469–72 (at 470). As Pizarro notes, G. A. Lester has also traced Greek, Icelandic, and Arabic analogues that were likely unknown to Bede in "The Caedmon Story and its Analogues," *Neophilologus* 58 (1974), 225–37.

[10] Antonina Harbus, *The Life of the Mind in Old English Poetry* (Amsterdam: Rodopi, 2002), p. 19.

[11] *OED*, s.v. "soul food, n.," sense 1, https://www.oed.com (accessed 6 February 2023).

[12] Ælfric of Eynsham, "Dominica VIII Post Pentecosten," ed. Malcolm Godden, *Ælfric's Catholic Homilies: The Second Series, Text*, EETS, ss 5 (Oxford: Oxford University Press, 1979), p. 233, lines 110–11.

38   ERICA WEAVER

to treat them as a spiritual, rather than bodily, matter. The entire poem dwells
on this metaphor:

> Moððe word fræt.   Me þæt þuhte
> wrætlicu wyrd,   þa ic þæt wundor gefrægn,
> þæt se wyrm forswealg   wera gied sumes,
> þeof in þystro,   þrymfæstne cwide
> ond þæs strangan staþol.   Stælgiest ne wæs
> wihte þy gleawra,   þe he þam wordum swealg.[13]

> A moth gnawed up words. To me that seemed
> a wondrous circumstance, when I heard of that wonder,
> that that worm should swallow down some man's song,
> a thief in the dark, the splendid speech,
> and its strong support. The stealing guest was not
> a whit the wiser, even though he swallowed those words.

Much like the genre of the riddle itself, which seems simple but is revealed to
be richly rewarding on closer analysis, this riddle invites a series of deceptively
straightforward questions: What, precisely, is the moth eating? Are these
words written or spoken?[14] And, as always with riddles, how do we solve the
conundrum? If the solution is "moth," or bookworm, then we have the answer
from the very first word, but if we go a step further, the riddle invites us to
think about the fragility of textual circulation and survival, or of the arrogance
of thinking that we have fully digested what we have read.

On closer analysis, it becomes a much richer meditation on the nature
of reading and rumination. Indeed, Exeter Riddle 45 has itself digested and
repurposed another text: the *Tinea* (moth) riddle by the fourth- or fifth-
century North African poet Symphosius, who is credited with pioneering the
riddle form:

> Littera me pauit, nec quid sit littera noui.
> In libris uixi, nec sum studiosior inde.
> Exedi Musas, nec adhuc tamen ipsa profeci.[15]

> Letters fed me, but I'm not aware what letters are.
> I lived in books, although I'm no more studious from that.
> I've eaten up the Muses, yet so far I haven't made anything of myself.

---

[13] Riddle 45, ed. Orchard, *The Old English and Anglo-Latin Riddle Tradition*, p. 364.
[14] As Geoffrey Russom observes, the moth seemingly consumes both the written
words of the book and the oral song (*gied*) of the poet, in "Exeter Riddle 47: A Moth
Laid Waste to Fame," *Philological Quarterly* 56 (1977), 129–36.
[15] Symphosius, *enigma* 16, ed. Fr. Glorie, *Variae collectiones aenignmatvm Merovingicae
aetatis (pars altera)*, CCSL 133a (Turnhout, Belgium: Brepols, 1968), p. 637.

UNDIGESTED TEXTS IN EARLY MEDIEVAL ENGLAND

The Old English bookworm riddle is double the length of Symphosius's, however, and reworks several aspects. Symphosius's bookworm speaks to us directly, recounting his life between the pages, whereas Riddle 45 narrates the wonder from the perspective of a distinct first-person speaker, who heard or asked (*gefrægn*) about the marvel. Rather than invoking the Muses, the Old English *þrymfæstne cwide* also has associations with divine speech, leading John D. Niles to posit that "some man's song" (*wera gied sumes*) refers to the Psalms of David.[16]

Moreover, as Fred C. Robinson has highlighted, Riddle 45 is made up of "successions of interconnected puns," including the gap between *swealg* as swallowing and as understanding as well as the ruminative association between *cwide* (speech) and *cwidu* (cud or what is chewed).[17] As in *Solomon and Saturn I*, the poem is thus invested in the particular reading practice suited to prayer: the careful chewing and digestion of words. Mercedes Salvador-Bello solves it as "a monk or a student … unsuccessfully 'ruminating' the contents of excellent learned books."[18] In chewing the words, the moth does exactly what a good monastic reader should do, except that it sets to work literally rather than figuratively. Its mindless consumption emphasizes the need for consideration and intentionality by contrast, lest spiritual food become bodily matter.

While the opening word might at first seem to give away the answer, defeating the purpose of the riddle, it ultimately cautions against uncritical reading or mindless munching. If we stop at "moððe," then we are no better than the moth itself, whose engagement with the text remains entirely at the surface level. As Martin Foys puts it, "[e]ither the riddle is doing it wrong, or we are doing the riddle wrong."[19] From this perspective, the moth is not the answer but a metaphor for the true solution: the careless reader, who takes in texts but does not digest them. This negotiation of answers that first seem straightforward but gain in complexity illustrate how many of the Latin riddle collections of early medieval England work as well. They give us an answer, perhaps embedded in an acrostic or written in the margins, and then they ask us to consider it more deeply, to read in all of the senses of the Old English

---

[16] John D. Niles, *Old English Enigmatic Poems and the Play of the Texts* (Turnhout, Belgium: Brepols, 2006), pp. 120–21 and 142, solves it as "maða ond sealm-boc" (maggot and psalm book).

[17] Fred C. Robinson, "Artful Ambiguities in the Old English 'Book-Moth' Riddle," in *Anglo-Saxon Poetry: Essays in Appreciation, for John. C. McGalliard*, ed. Lewis E. Nicholson and Dolores Warwick Frese (Notre Dame, Ind.: University of Notre Dame Press, 1975), pp. 355–62 at p. 356.

[18] Mercedes Salvador-Bello, *Isidorean Perceptions of Order: The Exeter Book Riddles and Medieval Latin Enigmata* (Morgantown, W.Va.: West Virginia University Press, 2015), p. 147.

[19] Martin Foys, "The Undoing of Exeter Book Riddle 47: 'Bookmoth,'" in *Transitional States: Cultural Change, Tradition and Memory in Medieval England*, ed. Graham D. Caie and Michael D. C. Drout (Tempe, Ariz.: Arizona Center for Medieval and Renaissance Studies, 2018), pp. 101–30 at p. 105.

40 ERICA WEAVER

rædan, from processing the text to riddling to giving counsel, or teaching.[20] Implicit in reading or recognition, then, is pedagogy.

From this perspective, our moth munching his way through pages without understanding might lead us to another bookish riddle with a similarly cautionary revelation:

> Nunc mea divinis complentur viscera verbis
> Totaque sacratos gestant praecordia biblos;
> At tamen ex isdem nequeo cognoscere quicquam:
> Infelix fato fraudabor munere tali,
> Dum tollunt dirae librorum lumina Parcae.[21]

> Now my entrails are stuffed with divine words,
> and all my insides bear sacred books;
> but even so, out of them, I can't recognize a thing.
> Unlucky, I am cheated of such a reward by destiny,
> while the awful Fates
> run off with the books' illuminations.

This riddle, by Aldhelm of Malmesbury (d. 709), is the earliest surviving reference to a library or bookchest (*arca libraria*) from pre-Conquest England. It is a useful reminder that even the most basic accouterments of reading can now unsettle our expectations; indeed, that we may not even recognize an early medieval library, which often consisted of a chest of books more than a dedicated room.[22] It is also a beautiful, brief meditation on the difficulties of reading and recognition: how, like moths, we can stuff ourselves with words or pack a chest full of sacred books and nonetheless falter in our recognitions.

Like the uncomprehending bookchest of Exeter Riddle 47 (sometimes also solved as "oven") or the similarly witless bookchest of Eusebius's enigma 33, Aldhelm's *arca libraria* may physically hold knowledge, but it lacks any corresponding mental storehouse or internal engagement. This deadening lack of sensation or perception is all the more striking when read together with the following riddle in Aldhelm's collection, enigma 90 (*puerpera geminas enixa* or woman bearing twins). Whereas the bookchest bears books but does not profit by them, with *gestant* even suggesting a kind of bookish pregnancy, the mother's

---

[20] On Old English *rædan* and its Indo-European cognates, see Nicholas Howe, "The Cultural Construction of Reading in Anglo-Saxon England," in *The Ethnography of Reading*, ed. Jonathan Boyarin (Berkeley, Calif.: University of California Press, 1993), pp. 58–79.

[21] Aldhelm, *Enigma* 89 ("Arca libraria"), ed. Ehwald, *Aldhelmi Opera*, p. 138.

[22] Michael Lapidge has surmised that "when an Anglo-Saxon scholar wished to consult a book," he didn't so much sequester himself in a wood-paneled room as "he got down on his hands and knees and rummaged around in the chest until he came upon the book he required." Michael Lapidge, *The Anglo-Saxon Library* (Oxford: Oxford University Press, 2005), p. 62.

UNDIGESTED TEXTS IN EARLY MEDIEVAL ENGLAND 41

womb holds the unborn infants, or those not yet capable of speaking.[23] Across the pair of riddles, who or what speaks or knows moves from the inside out and the outside in in a chiastic structure, as the books full of divine words are replaced by the speechless twins, and the uncomprehending bookchest gives way to a living pregnant woman. Indeed, unlike the bookchest's shelves, her insides magnify her powers of observation, and she introduces herself by noting, "Sunt mihi sex oculi, totidem simul auribus hausi" (I have six eyes; with just as many ears I drink in simultaneously).[24] As in the bookworm riddle, embodiment – literal or figurative – becomes central to the nature of observation and understanding, or recognition, on display. Indeed, we are tasked with recognizing how inner and outer do not necessarily form unified wholes.

At the same time, the books that populate early medieval riddles are vulnerable not only to improper digestion but also to outright destruction and fragmentation. Across the Exeter riddles, which number roughly a hundred split into two discrete groupings, Dieter Bitterli has identified several "scribal riddles," which deal with the making and unmaking of books, from the preparation of parchment to pen and ink to the moth, who devours them all.[25] And just as the bookworm is a thief, whose persistent swallowing grows increasingly worrisome as he eats up more and more words, so, too, do Aldhelm's terrible Fates run off with the books' illuminations, denying the bookchest any chance of reading or seeing the books it holds both because of its unlucky status as an illiterate object and, presumably, because of the depredations of time and use causing ink to fade, folios to loosen, and bindings to break apart. While the bookchest at first seems harmless, even protective, then, its holdings are still vulnerable to loss. The books are not merely unread or uncomprehended, but actively destroyed in the process – even if only by the passage of time and destiny, *wrætlicu wyrd* and *Parcae*. We might even imagine a kind of double consumption, in which the bookworm of Riddle 45 chews a path through the books that stuff the entrails of Aldhelm's illiterate *arca libraria*.

Although the moth seems to fulfill the terms of monastic rumination, by working steadfastly in silence, his rumination destroys the book at hand.[26] He eats his way through the pages, consuming the words altogether as he swallows. As in the children's classic *The Very Hungry Caterpillar*, which follows an initially "tiny" protagonist through a week of meals that transform him into "a big, fat caterpillar," wormholes get larger and more numerous as

---

[23] On pregnancy imagery in Aldhelm's *Enigmata*, see Salvador-Bello, *Isidorean Perceptions of Order*, pp. 213–16.

[24] Aldhelm, *Enigma 90*, line 1, ed. Ehwald, *Aldhelmi Opera*, p. 139.

[25] Dieter Bitterli, *Say What I Am Called: The Old English Riddles of the Exeter Book & the Anglo-Latin Riddle Tradition* (Toronto: University of Toronto Press, 2009), p. 135.

[26] For further discussion, see John Scattergood, "Eating the Book: *Riddle 47* and Memory," in *Text and Gloss: Studies in Insular Learning and Literature Presented to Joseph Donovan Pheifer*, ed. Helen Conrad O'Brian, Anne Marie D'Arcy, and John Scattergood (Dublin: Four Courts Press, 1999), pp. 119–27.

an insect consumes more and more of a book.[27] And however destructive worms were to parchment and vellum, they found cloth and paper even more appetizing. As Foys makes clear, for early medieval English books, these bugs thus posed a threat not only to the words of the texts inside but also to the covers and bindings meant to protect them.[28] By eating "þrymfæstne cwide / ond þæs strangan staþol" (the splendid speech, / and its strong support), the worm undoes the book altogether, so that the riddle draws attention to the fragility of the material object and consequently the precariousness of textual circulation and the written record. Such a risk is visible within the pages of the Exeter Book itself, now badly burned, but also, incidentally marked by a hole on fol. 112r–v, six lines before the bookworm riddle begins.[29] The putative strength of the support is always relative, for even the strongest medium risks environmental damage if not eventual obsolescence or wholesale destruction.

PICKY EATING: ITERATIVE READING

In the essay that anchors this volume, "The Shock of the Old: Recognition in the Humanities," James Simpson draws a clear distinction between looking and seeing, or we might say tasting and digesting, highlighting the role of delay as a crucial juncture between the two. Yet, he argues that literature's purview is that juncture, as great works dwell in blur, shadow, ambiguity, and doubt – Odysseus turned from his nurse, or perhaps Orpheus from Eurydice, his moment of sight ultimately one of both recognition and irretrievable loss. Riddles highlight this movement between ambiguity and certainty. Like the modern mystery or detective novel, the form is often dismissed as childish or low-brow, perhaps because we as critics do not want to recognize ourselves in children's games and pulps. But as James Simpson notes, solving the Exeter riddle about a holy book requires the same modes of reading as the Bible itself. It is, in miniature, an object lesson in how to read the book it describes. So, while the riddles may seem to be but "a quaint coda to a sober field,"[30] closer inspection reveals that they are at the heart of what we do as readers, then and now.

The known riddlers of early medieval England comprise some of the greatest men of learning, such as Aldhelm and Boniface, and their riddles are

---

[27] Eric Carle, *The Very Hungry Caterpillar* (New York: World Publishing Company, 1969), n. pag.

[28] Martin Foys notes that true bookworms generally favor papyrus, paper, and other plant matter to parchment and vellum, but there were many hole-borers in early medieval England, if not bookworms *per se* in "Undoing of Exeter Book Riddle 47," 121.

[29] On fol. 112v, the hole is in the margin just above Riddle 44, and Riddle 45 begins at the bottom of the page. Drawing attention to this hole, Jordan Zweck argues that, as it transforms Symphosius's Latin riddle, the Old English poem "becomes an echo of the signal noise of the wormhole in the manuscript: entropic, but creative; not a lacuna, but a way of responding to one," in "Silence in the Exeter Book Riddles," *Exemplaria* 28 (2016), 319–36 (at 330).

[30] Orchard, *The Old English and Anglo-Latin Riddle Tradition*, p. vii.

UNDIGESTED TEXTS IN EARLY MEDIEVAL ENGLAND   43

tours de force of erudition even as they engage with ordinary objects and with faltering, or destructive reading practices.[31] Although the Old English riddles operate differently in some ways from their Latin precedents, it is worth noting that two of them are translations of *enigmata* by Aldhelm and several rework earlier riddles by Symphosius. They make similar demands of us as readers, and many still prove elusive. Indeed, if the basic conceit of the riddle is that we already know the answer, if we can only get back to it, then what do we do with some of the other Exeter Book riddles whose subjects – like the one-eyed garlic seller of Exeter Riddle 86 – now prove decidedly unrecognizable? In this instance, the solution hinges on a recognition of its similarity to another one-eyed garlic seller in Symphosius's enigma 95. To read one riddle, we must recognize another. Such recognition reveals that each achieves its identity in a closed textual community.

For this reason, ambiguity – or delayed recognition – does not only mediate between likenesses, languages, and texts. It is also a modulator of pace. The riddles invite lingering, sitting with opening lines before hastening onward to the poem's end, trying to make the clues add up, or even to see in one poem the details of another. This is all the more striking in those riddles where the normal solving process is reversed, when we are given the answer at the outset and then asked to examine it at greater length, as with the bookworm riddle. As Jordan Zweck observes, if Exeter 45 gives us the answer in its very first word, "then it does not really make us *re*read" the moth; rather, "it creates the experience of rereading on one's first encounter with the riddle … the worm is a bad reader and creates only silence. But considered from a different angle, it produces a signal noise meant to (mis)lead the audience, who are encouraged from the opening lines to read outside, across, and back and forth."[32] From this perspective, the bookworm moves through the text just like the quill that "tracks back and forth across the manuscript page" in James's account of Riddle 24 ("The Bible").[33] Instead of writing, however, the bookworm unwrites or even rewrites, creating new pathways between texts and pages.

Whether by snatching away the life of the animal whose skin becomes parchment or by munching through the pages, these riddles offer careful consideration of a reading process both destructive and generative. In short, they present something that initially seems unambiguous, like writing or reading, and then steadily unsettle assumptions and foundations, poems

---

[31] Patrick W. Conner has demonstrated that when Sidemann and monks from Glastonbury were sent to Exeter in 968 to introduce the reformed Benedictine order, the move inaugurated a flurry of bookish activity, which resulted in the production of manuscripts of Amalarius, Bede, Boethius, Cassian, and other curriculum authors, who provide a backdrop to the production and dedication of the Exeter Book under Bishop Leofric. See Conner, *Anglo-Saxon Exeter: A Tenth-Century Cultural History* (Woodbridge, UK: Boydell, 1993), p. 30.

[32] Zweck, "Silence in the Exeter Book Riddles," 331.

[33] James Simpson, "The Shock of the Old: Recognition in the Humanities," above, p. 29.

44 ERICA WEAVER

and parchment. They call any snap judgement or too-hasty recognition into question. After all, the winged moth that opens Riddle 45 misleads us, too. It is simultaneously a metonym for the true solution and a misdirection, for we need to picture not a mature moth so much as its larval state. It is *se wyrm* that eats the book.

While Riddle 45 foregrounds this iterative reading practice from the beginning, many other riddles make use of a closing challenge to invite similar re-engagement. At the end of Exeter Riddle 24, for instance, the speaker implores, "frige hwæt ic hatte" (ask what I am called).[34] Throughout the collection, we find similar prompts – "say what I am called" or "tell what I mean" – but this command to the reader to ask seems particularly interesting, for to recognize is not merely to read or to interpret, but to ask. Although recognition, or digestion, might seem passive, it is better understood as the triumphant result of careful inquiry. As James notes of Riddle 24, "we as readers must become trackers, or in*vestiga*tors, along interpretative paths, on high alert for each trace of where the speaker has trodden before us. If we are to find our way home along the paths of this riddle, we must educe more about the speaker than the speaker seems ready to disclose."[35] Even the narrator of the bookworm riddle learns about the wonder through asking. Such an investigation requires us to abandon certainty in order to find it again, some other way.

In the process, certainty becomes uncertain, unfamiliar familiar and then joyful. Observation gives way to recognition, and we are released from the awkwardness, or even agony, of not knowing. This is what the riddles ask us and their subjects to undergo; in order to elicit proper rumination and digestion, they first obscure and even threaten, for "[r]iddles, like romance plots, are full of near misses, misses that remind us of just how close catastrophe is, and how easy it would have been to lose that which was finally found again."[36] To be sure, this mode of temporary obscurity pertains across many texts and genres, but Old English riddles are perfect models for this mode of reading, in part because one of the really remarkable things about them is the way in which they self-consciously invite us all, even the most seasoned professors of literature, to become beginning readers again: students unsure of whether our questions are apt, whether we are mis- or over-reading, whether we can be quite sure of how to pronounce or parse a word, or of what to do with a runic letterform. As Foys notes of the larval bookworm wending

---

[34] Riddle 24, line 26b, ed. Orchard, *The Old English and Anglo-Latin Riddle Tradition*, p. 334.

[35] Simpson, "The Shock of the Old," p. 28.

[36] Simpson, "The Shock of the Old," p. 32. Like the lovers in James's favorite movie, the 1993 Nora Ephron classic *Sleepless in Seattle* (TriStar Pictures, 1993), it is often only at the very last minute that everything comes together. And as it happens, this movie, too, is another kind of bookworm, replaying and rewriting another eleventh-hour recognition atop the Empire State Building, from Leo McCarey's 1957 film *An Affair to Remember* (20th Century Fox, 1957).

UNDIGESTED TEXTS IN EARLY MEDIEVAL ENGLAND

its way through the text, "the immature creature that devours a learned man's sayings with no intellectual gain can also evoke a more specific figure, that of the monastic schoolboy who cannot or will not learn the wisdom set before him."[37] As monastic customaries make clear, however, monks are always, somehow, schoolboys. The *Rule of Benedict* invokes this directly, beginning, "Heed, oh son, the precepts of a master" or, we might say, "the lessons of a teacher" ("Obsculta, o fili, praecepta magistri").[38] So, too, the earliest solvers might have read a series of riddles about books, as they held another, the Exeter Book, in their hands, inescapably reminded of its shared origins in hair and flesh and bone. Some of the Old English riddles even ask us, like them, to rearrange the letters on the page in order to spell out their answers. Indeed, six hinge on embedded runes.[39] To reach a solution, we must become participants in writing as well as reading them, mentally re-enacting their inscription on the page or re-voicing them for oral circulation. And in doing so, we are taught how to recognize, or identify, ourselves and others through a paradoxical relationship to unreliable narrators, missing subjects, withheld wholes, and fragments.

LEFTOVERS

For the voracious readers of the riddles discussed above, reading has not altogether failed, since the reading happens, or at least the superficial motions do; it is just not properly digested, or it effaces the text. In each case, we are left with crucial leftovers, remnants that call into question the broader enterprise. What begins as a moth quickly becomes a *þeof in þystro* (thief in the dark) and a *stælgiest* (stealing guest). As I draw this essay to a close, these questions of theft, undigested remains, and readability lead me to juxtapose Riddle 45 with the figures from the *Beowulf* manuscript mentioned above: Æschere and the Donestre, both intimately tied to language and its loss, reading and eating. Although they are very different figures, drawn from very different texts, an act of recognition – of "looking," as James invites us to do, "for the familiar face or feature, or topos (i.e. commonplace)" – draws them together and lets them speak.[40] When Grendel's mother comes to avenge her son's death as another *þeof in þystro*, she reclaims his severed arm along with Hrothgar's *hæleþa leofost* (line 1296b, most loved hero), subsequently named as Æschere, in an exchange (*gewrixle*, line 1304b) that, in understated fashion, "was not good" (*ne wæs …*

---

37 Foys, "Undoing," 122.

38 Benedict of Nursia, *Regula*, 1.1, ed. Rudolph Hanslik, in *Benedicti Regula*, CSEL 75 (Vienna: Hoelder-Pichler-Tempsky, 1960), p. 1.

39 For discussion, see Exeter Book Riddles 17 ("Ship"), 22 ("Jay"), 34 ("Ship"), 40 ("Cock and Hen"), 62 ("Ship"), and 73 ("Piss") in Craig Williamson, *The Old English Riddles of the "Exeter Book"* (Chapel Hill, N.C.: The University of North Carolina Press, 1977).

40 Simpson, "The Shock of the Old," p. 33.

til, line 1304b).[41] In mourning him, Hrothgar laments that he has lost "min runwita ond min rædbora" (line 1325, my rune-counselor and my advisor), leading James Paz to deem Æschere "Hrothgar's reader."[42] Without him, the community is mired in interpretive difficulties, following Grendel's mother's inky tracks (*lastas*, line 1402b) only to come up short "syðþan Æscheres / on þam holmclife hafelan metton" (lines 1420b–21, when they met Æschere's head on the mere's edge). With Æschere beheaded, Hrothgar struggles to read the runes inscribed on the sword hilt Beowulf brings back from the scene.

Though once a sentient *rædbora*, or a bearer of both reading and counsel, Æschere himself becomes like the bookchests of Latin and Old English riddles – filled with knowledge but unable to profit by it. Where Eusebius's bookcase even imagines a mute mouth taking in and dispensing books, Æschere's has been closed, and his ability to read extinguished. Examining the inscrutable sword hilt, inscribed with runes that the community cannot or does not fully read, Paz concludes, "We might imagine that if he still lived, Æschere would be able to read the runes on our behalf. But that is only a fantasy. As such, the hilt must remain a mysterious thing, and the story it tells must remain alien to us."[43] It is a riddle without a solution, and it invites only partial recognition. By consuming all but the head, Grendel's mother underscores Æschere's silencing, for this head, unlike the fantastical dismembered heads that continue to speak in Ælfric's *Life of St. Edmund* or in stories of Orpheus, is mute.

So, too, are we confronted with a similarly curious set of circumstances in *The Wonders of the East*, a copy of which accompanies *Beowulf* in London, British Library, Cotton Vitellius A.xv. Here, we are confronted with the misleading recognition and strange beheadings of the Donestre, who

> cunnon eall mennisce gereord. Þonne hy fremdes cynnes mannan geseoð, þonne nemnað hy hyne ond his magas cuþra manna naman, ond mid leaslicum wordum hy hine beswicað ond hine gefoð, ond æfter þan hy hine fretað ealne buton þon heafde ond þonne sittað ond wepað ofer þam heafde

> … know all human languages. When they see a person of a foreign race, they name him and his kinsmen with the names of acquaintances, and with devious words they delude him, and they get hold of him, and after that they eat him, all but the head, and then sit and weep over the head[44]

---

41 Here and elsewhere, I cite *Beowulf* from R. D. Fulk, Robert E. Bjork, and John D. Niles, eds., *Klaeber's Beowulf*, 4th ed. (Toronto: University of Toronto Press, 2008), without vowel lengths and other diacritics.

42 James Paz, "Æschere's Head, Grendel's Mother, and the Sword That Isn't a Sword: Unreadable Things in *Beowulf*," *Exemplaria* 25 (2013), 231–51 (at 232).

43 Paz, "Æschere's Head, Grendel's Mother, and the Sword That Isn't a Sword," 247.

44 *The Wonders of the East*, ed. and tr. R. D. Fulk, *The Beowulf Manuscript*, DOML 3 (Cambridge, Mass.: Harvard University Press, 2010), pp. 24 and 25.

UNDIGESTED TEXTS IN EARLY MEDIEVAL ENGLAND 47

Mobilizing a seeming recognition and even intimacy – shared language and relations – in order to convert the familiar and the known into the alien and strange, the Donestre "embody a monstrosity both corporeal and linguistic," as Jeffrey Jerome Cohen observes, taking the traveler in not only through conversation but also through "[t]he material incorporation of one body into the flesh of another."[45] Unlike the bookworm or the bookcase, the Donestre know how to read their victims, but the consumption is nonetheless still partial and unfulfilling, leading only to tears.

Whereas the riddles ask us to rethink reading and rumination, or whether we can say that we have read or known a text, the Donestre call attention to a different breakdown of speech and knowledge. They call out not to engage but to destroy. So, too, do Beowulf and Grendel's mother exchange an arm for a head, for a head – first Grendel's broken grip, then Æschere's decapitated head, and finally Grendel's own, enormous head. Each side pays and repays the other, and even Hrothgar concedes that her reprisal is a recognizable action under the law: as he acknowledges, "heo þa faehðe wræc" (line 1333b, she avenged that feud). Although she operates within the law, she also subverts it, leaving Æschere's severed head as its own obvious sign. *Runwita* and *rædbora* have been removed from the equation, and what is left is painfully readable. Rather than the moth riddle that looks beyond the moth to consider myriad relationships to oral and written literature, good and bad readers, Grendel's mother replaces a careful reader with an obvious sign of his ineffectuality.

Similarly, in order to map an imagined "elsewhere," as Nicholas Howe notes of the Donestre's consumption, "the foreign must be assimilated in an almost physical way so that it can be made part of the traveler's body, and yet that act of incorporation can never be complete – the head remains – and becomes the object of regret to the traveler … some residue remains that cannot be normalized or naturalized into a complete narrative."[46] Even their tears, like the drops of James's quill, demand further consideration, for this may not be weeping that we can altogether recognize. Do the Donestre weep because they have inadvertently consumed their new acquaintances or because they cannot consume them entirely, head and all? Are they tears of grief or of frustration, a recognition of a lost friend or a lost meal, something that should not or merely could not be digested? Whereas Exeter Riddle 45 takes in Symphosius's earlier Latin riddle, digests it, and puts forth new poetry, the Donestre's consumption is most notable for what it fails to take in: the forlorn heads, which elicit so much weeping, much as Æschere's does. Pitted against the usual expectations for reading and rumination, these figures become ciphers for a breakdown in communication. At the same time, even so, these strange all-too-readable

---

[45] Jeffrey Jerome Cohen, *Of Giants: Sex, Monsters, and the Middle Ages* (Minneapolis, Minn.: University of Minnesota Press, 1999), p. 2.

[46] Nicholas Howe, *Writing the Map of Anglo-Saxon England: Essays in Cultural Geography* (New Haven, Conn.: Yale University Press, 2008), pp. 172–73.

and recognizable leftovers can still, somehow, speak. Like the riddles, they ask us to recognize and reassemble them, to make meaning out of systems of communication that have come undone.

It is significant, then, that so much Old English poetry is concerned with the breakdown or the impossibility of recognition – the inability of a lone wanderer or seafarer to identify themselves without recourse to a larger community, or how a mysterious voyager can identify himself to a coast guard or to a crowd. We have scenes of failed recognition, populated by birds whose cries resemble human laughter, or hecklers, who recognize as an accusation: "Are you *that* Beowulf?"[47] Yet, in this system of words and deeds, to be unrecognizable is to pose a threat. Here, we might think again of Grendel and his mother – "in the likeness of a man and woman" – dangerous because unperceivable.[48] So, recognition – or full digestion in the mind and memory – is not just joyful but essential, even life-saving.

Re-reading Riddle 45 with Bruce Holsinger's call to consider the animal nature of medieval manuscripts (or, we might add, with James's resurrected animal-turned-Bible), Foys draws attention to "how a worm's unthinking destruction encodes a cultural resistance of a different sort – a resistance to a human unthinking and unfounded sense of superiority."[49] If this riddle is, in part, about an animal kind of consumption (a chewing of the cud that is more ruminant than *ruminatio*), then the bookworm, Grendel's mother, and the Donestre all similarly trouble the lines between human and animal reading, eating, and understanding. With their strange remnants and damaged text-bearers, they invite a reading practice that balances parts against wholes (and holes), letting readers choose when to fill gaps in the record and when to let them stay.

In their engagement with language and with time, they all remind us that what remains to us is necessarily partial and fragmentary. Like Hrothgar examining the inscribed sword, we may only receive paraphrase or outline instead of full stories of ancient strife. Language falters across time and distance, as wonders are asked and heard about at a remove, whether in Riddle 45 or in *The Wonders of the East*. And yet, even if we falter, like moths or schoolboys, we can learn to read, and reread, and hope, like the solvers of riddles, that we will come to recognize – and to digest.

---

[47] "Eart þu se Beowulf" (line 506a) initiates Unferth's questioning about Beowulf's swimming match with Breca.

[48] Hrothgar recounts how two figures were seen: one "idese onlicnæs" (of the likeness of a woman) and the other "on weres wæstmum" (in the form of a man) (lines 1351a and 1352a).

[49] Foys, "Undoing," 126. Bruce Holsinger, "Of Pigs and Parchment: Medieval Studies and the Coming of the Animal," *PMLA* 124 (2009), 616–23.

3 THE "PHYSICIAN'S TALE" AND CHAUCER'S ART OF PROSOPOPOEIA

Julie Orlemanski

Geoffrey Chaucer's "Physician's Tale" is a story centrally concerned with the making and unmaking of literary persons. It focuses on the facture and destruction of one figure in particular, that of the maiden Virginia, whose creation is recounted in the opening lines and whose death at her father's hands constitutes the narrative climax. At issue, I suggest, is not only the meaning of her short life but the validity of the rhetorical and narrative techniques that have animated her within the framework of Chaucer's account. The present essay argues that the "Physician's Tale" is fruitfully read as a Chaucerian investigation into prosopopoeia, or the trope of fashioning a mask or face, the *poiesis* of a *prosopon*. To borrow a phrase from James Simpson, Virginia's "textual face" is at the center of Chaucer's retelling.[1] Most readers agree that the "Physician's Tale" is not a work that sustains hermeneutic optimism, not in the identification of its genre or moral nor in the parsing of its heroine's fate. Yet it is precisely because the tale is dissonant and self-divided that it makes an apt site for reexamining certain aspects of Chaucer's art.

What do I mean by *prosopopoeia*? In its broad sense, the figure differs from allegorical personification, or the trope of "lending voice and body to abstract ideas," as Katharine Breen has recently glossed it.[2] The broader phenomenon (of which allegorical personification would be a particular case) appears in works of classical and medieval rhetorical theory under labels like prosopopoeia, *ethopoeia, conformatio, adlocutio, effictio, sermocinatio, ficta*

---

[1] James Simpson, "Cognition is Recognition: Literary Knowledge and Textual 'Face,'" *New Literary History* 44 (2013), 25–44.

[2] Katharine Breen, *Machines of the Mind: Personification in Medieval Literature* (Chicago: University of Chicago Press, 2021), p. 3.

50   JULIE ORLEMANSKI

oratio, fictio personarum, and *personarum ficta inductio.* Definitions of these figures emphasize the mercurial interplay of voice, embodiment, presence, and liveliness. The account of *conformatio* in the *Rhetorica ad Herennium* is representative, where the figure is explained as "that by which an absent person is represented as though present, or a mute or formless thing is rendered articulate, attributed a definite form and language, or a certain behavior, in conformity with its character."[3] The definition sets several aspects of personhood in circulation together and would seem to include literary techniques that range from quoting speech to animating formless things, or, in the examples offered by the *Ad Herennium* author, from giving a city a voice to ventriloquizing the dead.[4] Needless to say, this is a wide, even diffuse, set of possibilities. In his *Institutio Oratoria,* Quintilian seems to give up on the task of distinguishing among the trope's possibilities, choosing instead to gather the associated practices under the label of *fictiones personarum* or *prosōpopoiiai*:

> We are even allowed in this form of speech to bring down the gods from heaven or raise the dead; cities and nations even acquire a voice. Some confine the term Prosopopoeia to cases where we invent both the person and the words (*et corpora et verba fingimus*); they prefer imaginary conversations between historical characters to be called Dialogues, which some Latin writers have translated *sermocinatio*. I follow the now established usage in calling them both by the same name, for we cannot of course imagine a speech except as the speech of a person.[5]

Like Quintilian, I use *prosopopoeia* as an umbrella term for the set of techniques that center on the propensity to imagine speech by imagining persons. Like the *Ad Herennium* author, I understand the figure to entail changeable combinations of voice, bodily form, action, animation, and phenomenality – combinations that are particular and characterizing ("in conformity with its character") but also counterfactual, insofar as prosopopoeia bestows form on the formless, language on the mute, or presence on those who are absent.

It is in this capacious sense that prosopopoeia is especially relevant to Chaucer's corpus, where it helps to demarcate an important "problem space," or a literary and conceptual terrain to which Chaucer's texts again and again

---

3   *Conformatio est cum aliqua quae non adest persona confingitur quasi adsit, aut cum res muta aut informis fit eloquens, et forma ei et oratio adtribuitur ad dignitatem adcommodata aut actio quaedam.* Pseudo-Cicero, *Rhetorica ad Herennium*, 4.53, tr. Harry Caplan (Cambridge, Mass.: Harvard University Press, 1954), pp. 398–99. Translation modified.

4   Pseudo-Cicero, *Rhetorica ad Herennium*, 4.53, tr. Caplan, pp. 398–401.

5   Quintilian, *The Orator's Education* 9.2, ed. and tr. Donald A. Russell (Cambridge, Mass.: Harvard University Press, 2002), pp. 50–51. For discussion of this passage from Quintilian and the broader rhetorical tradition of theorizing prosopopoeia, see James J. Paxson, *The Poetics of Personification* (Cambridge: Cambridge University Press, 1994), pp. 11–22.

THE "PHYSICIAN'S TALE" AND CHAUCER'S ART OF PROSOPOPOEIA   51

recur. In the larger project from which my reading here grows, I argue that episodes of literary animation across Chaucer's oeuvre show us literary personhood pulled taut between two poles – between the contrivance of literary persons, on the one hand, and their vivacity, on the other; or, to put it another way, between their status as fabulations, imagined by author, speaker, or dreamer, and the reality of these persons' independent presence – their existence "in themselves," not just "for us." Episodes of literary animation in Chaucer's poems leave readers puzzling over whether prosopopoeia confers (as it were) a mask, which the poet dons, or whether it summons another's face, someone else and other. What is distinctive about Chaucer's art of prosopopoeia is his works' commitment to staging the entangled hermeneutic and ethical stakes of literary persons' undecidable natures, their flickering between artifice and intersubjective encounter.

In one of his several essays on prosopopoeia, Paul de Man remarks, "[v]oice assumes mouth, eye and finally face, a chain that is manifest in the etymology of the trope's name, *prosopon poien*, to confer a mask or a face (*prosopon*) …. Our topic deals with the giving and taking away of faces, with face and deface, figure, figuration and disfiguration."[6] Mask and face, face and deface: these terms constitute a shorthand deriving from the trope's own etymology, useful for talking about the tensions that structure prosopopoeia in Chaucer. Recourse to the metaphorics of the face also helps us to think anew about literary recognition as James Simpson has movingly described it.[7] As Simpson's several overlapping accounts insist, the quotidian experience of flicking one's gaze across someone's visage, and all at once knowing who it is, is a nearly indispensable model for recognition as such. Yet "The Physician's Tale" strains the humane optimism that runs through Simpson's reflections, by foregrounding the misrecognition with which recognition is mingled, or how face may harden into mask.

Any new account of the "Physician's Tale" sets forth from two coordinates well-established in literary scholarship on the text. The first is that the sympathetic attention focused on the Roman maiden in Chaucer's version is unprecedented in earlier tellings, which concentrate instead on the narrative's male antagonists, a predatory judge and an upstanding Roman patriarch.[8] In the *Romance of the Rose*, Chaucer's immediate source, the theme is the corruption of justice: Appius plots; Virginius kills his daughter rather than

---

[6]   Paul de Man, "Autobiography as De-facement," *MLN* 94 (1979), 919–30, at 926.
[7]   See Simpson, "Cognition Is Recognition"; "Textual Face: Cognition as Recognition," in *Contemporary Chaucer across the Centuries, a Festschrift for Stephanie Trigg*, ed. Helen M. Hickey, Anne McHendry and Melissa Raine (Manchester: Manchester University Press, 2018), pp. 218–33; and "The Shock of the Old: Recognition in the Humanities," pp. 13–34, in the present volume.
[8]   In Livy's original account in *Ab urbe condita* and Pierre Bersuire's French translation, a young man betrothed to Virginia also features prominently. There is no persuasive evidence that Chaucer worked with textual sources other than the *Romance of the Rose*, but the popularity of Livy's history, in visual as well as textual culture, means he could well have been acquainted with other versions.

JULIE ORLEMANSKI

let her fall into his clutches; and the Roman people rise up and overthrow the corrupt magistrate. While the key events of Jean de Meun's rendition all appear in the "Physician's Tale," the story's center of gravity has shifted. Description of Virginia's beauty and virtue dominate the first quarter of the tale, and the scene of her death has been amplified, such that she speaks, both to lament and consent to her fate. Chaucer's version is unique in endowing Virginia with a voice, a change connected to various deep-rooted tendencies in his corpus – his Ovidianism, his investment in the moral dignity of feminine suffering, and his concern, in the *House of Fame* and elsewhere, for how contingencies of discursive transmission (who speaks and who does not, whose name is recorded and whose is not) redound on the constitution of literary persons. By all appearances, the tale is designed to give Virginia a voice, an act of prosopopoeia not in the sense of a rhetorical ornament, confined to the figurative register, but as a project of narrative reimagining.

Yet the ultimate significance of the tale's alterations to its source material remains uncertain. This brings me to the second point of literary-critical consensus, namely, that the "Physician's Tale" is mis-made, badly put together, and that readers must struggle to understand its vacillating focus, contradictory generic cues, and wayward moralization. These inconsistencies threaten what Simpson calls "literary knowledge and textual 'face,'" – inhibiting not only the recognition of genre and meaning but the apprehension of who its doomed heroine is. Without dissenting from such a negative evaluation, I would place these inconsistencies under the sign of a genuinely experimental mode of writing, an experiment driven by the conviction that Virginia is at the heart of the story. The tale explores what is at stake in lending her a voice. In many scholars' readings, the interpretive and ethical dissatisfactions of the tale have been blamed on the Physician, the infelicity of whose tale-telling has been understood to characterize and satirize him. Yet as Helen Cooper observes, there is no evidence that the story was written with the Physician firmly in mind:

> Even if it was composed specifically for the *Canterbury Tales* and not earlier, many tales seem to have been written before their ascription to particular tellers. The only lines that link the tale to the Physician come after it is finished, so there is no prologue, such as Chaucer supplies for the Pardoner, to cue an ironic interpretation.[9]

More broadly, calls to rethink the role of "the narrator" in Chaucer studies offer compelling reasons not to explain the tale's design by way of the Physician's moral or intellectual shortcomings.[10] Still, as I explore below, the tale's language invites

---

[9] Helen Cooper, *Oxford Guides to Chaucer: The Canterbury Tales*, 2nd ed. (Oxford: Oxford University Press, 1996), pp. 253–54.

[10] For critique of modern interpreters' assumptions regarding Chaucerian narrators, see David Lawton, *Chaucer's Narrators* (Cambridge: D. S. Brewer, 1985); C. David Benson, *Chaucer's Drama of Style: Poetic Variety and Contrast in the Canterbury Tales* (Chapel Hill, N.C.: University of North Carolina Press, 1986), pp. 3–25;

THE "PHYSICIAN'S TALE" AND CHAUCER'S ART OF PROSOPOPOEIA 53

close attention to the unstable boundary between the act of telling and what is recounted, and between narration and the speech of characters. This boundary is where prosopopoeia takes place, where one voice leaps forth into other voices and other personae, a boundary to which Chaucer's writings again and again recur.

As I argue below, from the moment of Virginia's allegorical creation in the opening lines, readers are made aware of the interplay between literary animation and rhetorical artifice, maiden and made thing. Ironically, or perhaps fittingly, it is in the scene of her death that Virginia comes most vividly to life, assuming a voice to reflect on her own condition, just before her head is struck off and her face recast as object. The "Physician's Tale" is distinctive in literary and historiographic tradition for lending Virginia speech, even if (as I explore below) her person continuously collapses back into those who would speak on her behalf. "Our recognition of textual face," writes Simpson, "implies, and realizes, a transformative affective claim we make on that known face."[11] He offers this statement in relation to literary endeavors of recovery and return. Recovery and return are aspirations that pulse through the "Physician's Tale" as well, but the story does not escape the disfiguring effects of its affective claims on the past, as the face-to-face encounter passes over to the assumption of another's person as a mask.

To begin: Virginia enters the "Physician's Tale" in a flourish of prosopopoeial invention. Just at the point when she is introduced, an unexpected feminine voice breaks out in the text. The Roman "knyght" Virginius, we are told, has a daughter who stands far above everyone else in beauty,

> For Nature hath with sovereyn diligence
> Yformed hire in so greet excellence,
> As though she wolde seyn, "Lo, I, Nature,
> Thus kan I forme and peynte a creature,
> Whan that me list; who kan me countrefete?
> Pigmalion noght, though he ay forge and bete,
> Or grave, or peynte, for I dar wel seyn
> Apelles, Zanzis, sholde werche in veyn
> Outher to grave, or peynte, or forge, or bete,
> If they presumed me to countrefete."[12]

---

and A. C. Spearing, *Textual Subjectivity: The Encoding of Subjectivity in Medieval Narratives and Lyrics* (Oxford: Oxford University Press, 2005), pp. 101–36, and *Medieval Autographies: The "I" of the Text* (Notre Dame: University of Notre Dame Press, 2012), pp. 65–97. Robert Meyer-Lee offers a different, also bracing, treatment of the issue in *Literary Value and Social Identity in the "Canterbury Tales"* (Cambridge: Cambridge University Press, 2019). Spearing treats narration of the "Physician's Tale" directly in "What is a Narrator? Narrator Theory and Medieval Narratives," *Digital Philology* 4 (2015), 59–105, at 80–87, and "Narration in Two Versions of 'Virginius and Virginia,'" *The Chaucer Review* 54 (2019), 1–34.

11 Simpson, "Cognition Is Recognition," 43.

12 "Physician's Tale," in *The Riverside Chaucer*, 3rd ed., gen. ed. Larry Benson (Boston: Houghton Mifflin, 1987), lines 9–18; henceforth cited parenthetically by line number.

54   JULIE ORLEMANSKI

Nature's speech continues for ten more lines and concludes with the narrator's remark, "Thus semeth me that Nature wolde seye" (29). *Natura artifex*, or "Nature the artisan," belongs to a well-established allegorical tradition, familiar to Chaucer and his readers from its development by writers like Alan of Lille and Jean de Meun.[13] Her utterance thus summons around it a self-consciously poetic mode, one known for playing with the paradoxes of representing nature with art and employing fiction to communicate philosophical truths. The interpolated speech, which is original to Chaucer's version, immediately opens the tale to speculative and metafictional considerations.

Nature's voice is certainly unexpected. After all, the tale's opening couplet has identified the story as Roman historiography: "Ther was, as telleth Titus Livius, / A knyght that called was Virginius." The attribution, which is present in the *Romance of the Rose* as well, is "the only instance in the *Canterbury Tales* that a specific historian is cited as the source for a tale," Angus Fletcher observes.[14] The polysyllabic, Latinate rhyme on the two men's names emphasizes the masculine final syllable and the reciprocity between historian and paterfamilias. (It is only in this final syllable that Virginia's name will be distinguished from her father's.) If the audience knows anything about Livy – as they likely do, given the high profile of his Roman history in late-medieval culture – then the opening couplet invites readers into a narrative that would seem to be Latinate, vericonditional, non-Christian, and patriarchal.[15] Worth noting is the fact that a similar moment occurs later in the tale, when the genre is identified again as history and that definition is marked with another rhyme on Roman men's names. After the corrupt judge recruits a co-conspirator to take part in his plan to gain sexual possession of Virginia, we are told:

> Hoom gooth the cherl, that highte Claudius.
> This false juge, that highte Apius,
> (So was his name, for this is no fable,
> But knowen for historial thyng notable ...) (153–56)

The recording of men's proper names – Claudius and Appius, Virginius and Titus Livius – signals that the text is "historial" and "no fable."[16] Contrastingly, when Nature pipes up, poetry disrupts history, and the simple historical

---

[13] For an excellent general discussion, see Barbara Newman, *God and the Goddesses: Vision, Poetry, and Belief in the Middle Ages* (Philadelphia: University of Pennsylvania Press, 2003), pp. 51–137.

[14] Angus Fletcher, "The Sentencing of Virginia in the *Physician's Tale*," *The Chaucer Review* 34 (2000), 300–08, at 300.

[15] Jessica Berenbeim remarks of Livy's popularity in the Middle Ages, "Livy's history was ultimately read everywhere in Europe, in its transmitted, translated, revised, re-translated, redacted, and derivative forms" ("The Past of the Past: Historical Distance and the Medieval Image," *New Medieval Literatures* 21 (2021), 191–220, at 193).

[16] On the relatively unusual word "historial," see Diane Speed, "Language and Perspective in the *Physician's Tale*," in *Words and Wordsmiths: A Volume for H. L. Rogers*, ed. Geraldine Barnes et al. (Sydney: University of Sydney, 1989), pp. 119–36, at pp. 128–29.

THE "PHYSICIAN'S TALE" AND CHAUCER'S ART OF PROSOPOPOEIA 55

givenness of persons is thrown into question. This is one manifestation of Chaucer's Ovidianism: the author mischievously assumes a feminine voice – here, Nature's – to challenge the patriarchal fixity of literary tradition. Just as Nature dismisses her puny male rivals, and usurps Virginius's role, the narrator borrows her bravado for his departure from Livy. Insofar as the subsequent plot of the "Physician's Tale" revolves around who has the authority to determine Virginia's origins – whether it lies in civil law, which declares her a stolen servant of Claudius, or with Virginius, who asserts his paternal authority by killing her – it is notable that Nature introduces yet another narrative of Virginia's beginnings, one that is playfully femininized and self-consciously poetic.

Chaucer has gone out of his way to emphasize artistic facture in the passage, an emphasis that has reflexive and metafictional significance. The repetitions are hard to ignore: Nature can "forme and peynte" (12) better than Pygmalion can "forge and bete, / Or grave, or peynte" (14–15) and better than Apelles or Zanzes are able to "grave, or peynte, or forge, or bete" (17). The end-rhyme of "bete" and "countrefete" repeats (lines 13–14, 17–18). The heavy-handed emphasis on aesthetic craftsmanship continues beyond Nature's bragging, as the narrator describes Nature fashioning Virginia: "For right as she kan *peynte* a lilie whit, / And reed a rose, right with swich *peynture* / She *peynted* hath this noble creature" (32–34). The final lines of Nature's discourse – "So do I alle myne othere creatures / What colour that they han or what figures," (27–28) – have metapoetic connotations. "Color" and "figure" are part of Chaucer's vocabulary for rhetorical art – as when, elsewhere in the *Canterbury Tales*, Harry Bailey refers to the Clerk's high style as "Youre termes, youre colours, and youre figures."[17] The passage thus riffs on the familiar paragonal model of ekphrasis, by which the media of word and image comment on one another and their shared capacities for representation, fabrication, and ingenuity.[18]

Painting, forming, forging, engraving, copying: in her claim to surpass fabled artisans, Nature also places herself in their company and, by extension, analogizes Virginia to a made thing, the product of artistic – and, poetic – skill. Nature's triple reference to Apelles, Zeuxis, and Pygmalion is a clue that in crafting her speech Chaucer almost certainly drew on another passage from the *Romance of the Rose*, one in which the *Rose*'s dreamer-narrator confesses at length that his abilities are not equal to the task of describing Nature.[19] Although Chaucer transposes the dreamer's modesty topos to Nature's boast, the self-reflexivity of the two passages is similar, as the limits of human art become a rhetorical occasion for the vernacular poet. Not

---

17   "Clerk's Prologue," in *Riverside Chaucer*, line 16.
18   On paragonal ekphrasis, see Gabriele Rippl, "Ekphrasis," in *Oxford Research Encyclopedia of Literature*, 25 June 2019 (accessed 1 February 2023).
19   See lines 16146–55 of Guillaume de Lorris and Jean de Meun, *Le Roman de la Rose*, 3 vols., ed. Félix Lecoy (Paris: Librairie Honoré Champion, 1965–70).

quite an allusion (since its precise source would probably not have been recognizable), the intertext is nonetheless evidence of Chaucer's wide-ranging engagement with the *Rose* as he worked on the "Physician's Tale."[20] The French poem's analytical handling of personae, its reification and fragmentation of the feminine beloved, and its bold claims for the powers of art might all be relevant to Chaucer's rewriting of Virginia.

I have already quoted the lines where Chaucer makes explicit that Nature's voice has the status of trope or fiction: it is "*as though* she wolde seyn" what follows, and "Thus *semeth me* that Nature wolde seye" (11, 29). The poet-narrator thus responds to Livy's account with the seeming it inspires, and it is he who rather whimsically invents her utterance. As Elizabeth Allen observes, this admission "points toward the narrator's mediating role" and associates his efforts "with imaginative poetry more than history."[21] Nature is a personification who personifies, supposedly making persons even as the narrator's rhetoric fashions her. In philosophically conventional readings of *Natura artifex*, she is already a paradoxical figure: her artisanal labors are meant to mark the superiority of natural reproduction over human craft – even as the former is necessarily imagined in terms of the latter.[22] In the "Physician's Tale," in turn, that conventional figure is appropriated to embody the narrator's rhetorical power over his sources, of poetic seeming over historical record. The result is a kind of metaphysical pastiche, presented as having more to do with poetic whim than with cosmological hierarchies governing the world of the tale.[23] Indeed, Nature's abrupt appearance and disappearance foreshadow the confused mixture of pagan, Hebrew, and Christian cosmologies that crowd together at the story's conclusion and muddy any sense of metaphysical order or coherence.

What connections can we draw between the animations of Nature and Virginia, two feminine figures newly attributed speech in Chaucer's telling of the story and both closely bound up with his literary craft? It is important that Nature is explicitly a mask, a mouthpiece, for the poet-narrator, who

---

[20] On the tale's relation to the *Rose*, see Philip Knox, *The Romance of the Rose and the Making of Fourteenth-Century English Literature* (Oxford: Oxford University Press, 2021), pp. 146–50.

[21] Elizabeth Allen, *False Fables and Exemplary Truth: Poetics and Reception of Medieval Mode* (New York: Palgrave Macmillan, 2005), p. 86.

[22] For a lucid overview of the philosophical and literary paradoxes of *Natura artifex*, see Jonathan Morton, *The* Roman de la Rose *in Its Philosophical Context: Art, Nature, and Ethics* (Oxford: Oxford University Press, 2018), pp. 36–61.

[23] In this, my reading departs somewhat from Anne Middleton ("The *Physician's Tale* and Love's Martyrs: Ensamples Mo than Ten as a Method in the *Canterbury Tales*," *The Chaucer Review* 8 (1973), 9–32, at 22) and Kellie Robertson (*Nature Speaks: Medieval Literature and Aristotelian Philosophy* (Philadelphia: University of Pennsylvania Press, 2017), pp. 257–74), who associate Chaucer's Nature with, respectively, "a natural law above civil justice" (p. 22) and "a necessary hierarchy of orders that all stand in analogous relation to one another: divine, natural, human, familial" (p. 271).

THE "PHYSICIAN'S TALE" AND CHAUCER'S ART OF PROSOPOPOEIA   57

responds to Livy's record with the seeming it inspires in him. She introduces confusion about whether Virginia enters the story under the sign of history or poetry. The metapoetic significance of Nature's words lies in the double fact that they are *about* the fabrication of the tale's central figure, Virginia, and that they *enact* the process by which subjective language and persona constitute one another, as Nature assumes imaginative presence. Finally, as we will see, Virginia to some degree resembles Pygmalion's statue, whose limbs grew warm beneath the sculptor's hands. Her origins in poetic artifice will not confine her to lifelessness, and the pathos of the tale's conclusion proves her reality on our pulses. Of course, in Virginia's case, it is not her ability to love that demonstrates her liveliness, as in the *Metamorphoses*, but rather her capacity to be killed and mourned. Lest readers miss or mistrust this quality, Chaucer has Harry Bailey lament her fate vociferously after the tale's conclusion: "Algate this sely mayde is slayn, allas! / Allas, to deere boughte she beautee!'" (292–93).

The latter part of the present essay concentrates on the scene of Virginia's conjoined speaking and dying, or in de Man's terms, "the giving and taking away of faces." On the way to that, however, two intervening passages warrant mention. First is the narrator's excursus on the responsibility of governesses and parents for the moral education of those in their charge, which has been generatively discussed by Lianna Farber and Holly A. Crocker, among others.[24] The admonishment is notable for its apparent irrelevance to Virginia, who, after all, "So kepte hirself hir neded no maistresse" (106). The solicitous, opinionated tenor of the narrator's address, which (superficially at least) is untethered to anything taking place in the plot, effects what I see as an intensification of the free play, or even waywardness, of the narrator's voice, unconstrained by the "matere" he recounts (104). If we think of narrative discourse as an economy of voices, "in which the poet both speaks in his own voice and introduces characters who speak," then in this part of the story, the tale-teller's own voice dominates.[25] In fact, the narration draws attention to its own activity at many points, constructing an "I" in relation to an audience's plural "you" – for instance, with performative signposting ("As ye shul heere it after openly," "as ye shul heere," and "as ye bifore / Han herd" [152, 177, 229–30]) and imperatives ("Ne taketh of my wordes no displesaunce" [74] and "taketh kep of that that I shal seyn" [90]). The digression on childcare

---

[24] See Lianna Farber, "The Creation of Consent in the *Physician's Tale*," *The Chaucer Review* 39 (2004), 151–64 and Holly A. Crocker, *Chaucer's Visions of Manhood* (New York: Palgrave Macmillan, 2007), pp. 51–76.

[25] This duality is characteristic of the "'common' or 'mixed' genre" of poetry, which stands in between "dramatic" poetry (exclusively in direct speech) and "expository" poetry (entirely in the poet's voice), according to a taxonomy dating back to Plato. I quote from Bede's *De schematibus et tropis*, translated in Rita Copeland and Ineke Sluiter, eds., *Medieval Grammar and Rhetoric: Language Arts and Literary Theory, AD 300–1475* (Oxford: Oxford University Press, 2009), p. 266.

only exaggerates these effects, by specifying the imagined audience ("ye maistresses, in youre olde lyf" and "Ye fadres and ye moodres eek also" [72, 93]). As A. C. Spearing has observed, "we are kept continuously aware of the telling of that story, or rather its retelling," and this retelling "persistently appeals outside itself to possible human responses."[26] This is evidence for what voice *is* in the tale, or how a speaking "I" constitutes itself. Later in the tale, this opinionated, subjective voice will give way to the direct speech of Virginia and Virginius.

The second intervening passage of interest recounts what happens in Appius's courtroom. In all versions of the narrative, the court is the venue for what is presented as an act of outrageous dispersonification, which lies in the silencing and incapacitation of Virginius. In Jean de Meun's version and Chaucer's as well, Virginius is physically present but not allowed to answer the charges made against his paternity: "Virginius was quite ready to reply and confound his adversaries, but, as the case went, Appius spoke before he did and made the hasty judgment."[27] Appius manipulates formal procedures to control speech and agency within the legal domain. The law, of course, is a crucible for the formation of persons. Like literary narrative, it institutes its own order of beings by distributing recognition and agency, personhood and animacy, in a manner that may be at odds with seemingly straightforward, natural relations.[28] Virginius violently punctures law's self-referring system by destroying the body that Appius seeks: as Jean de Meun tells it, he "instantly cut off the head of his beautiful daughter Virginia and then presented it to the judge before all, in open court."[29] This bloody act, a second dispersonification, apparently breaks the legal spell, rendering the sphere of law vulnerable to political reclamation.

Appius's courtroom is particularly notable for the part it must have played in Chaucer's reworking of the narrative. As he examined the events recounted in the *Rose* for occasions where Virginia could come to the fore and reckon with her fate, the courtroom, original scene of her death, would have been the most obvious possibility. In the not unlikely event that Chaucer had seen or read other representations of Virginia's death, these all would have

---

[26] Spearing, "Narration in Two Versions of 'Virginius and Virginia,'" 18, 19.

[27] *Et con li plez ainsint alast, / ainz que Virginius palast, / qui touz estoit prez de respondre / por ses aversaires confondre, / juja par hastive sentance / Appius que sanz atendance / fust la pucele au serf rendue.* Roman de la Rose, ed. Lecoy, lines 5587–93; translation cited from *The Romance of the Rose*, tr. Charles Dahlberg, 3rd ed. (Princeton, N.J.: Princeton University Press, 1995), p. 114.

[28] For a recent and generative overview of legal personhood in the literature of late-medieval England, see Andreea Boboc, "Theorizing Legal Personhood in Late Medieval England," in *Theorizing Legal Personhood in Late Medieval England*, ed. Andreea Boboc (Leiden: Brill, 2015), pp. 1–28.

[29] *Roman de la Rose*, ed. Lecoy, lines 5606–09; translation, Dahlberg, *Romance of the Rose*, p. 114.

THE "PHYSICIAN'S TALE" AND CHAUCER'S ART OF PROSOPOPOEIA   59

depicted the maiden's final moments in public view.[30] Yet Chaucer evidently found the courtroom and forum unpromising locations for Virginia's speech, choosing instead to install her at home, a space of private domesticity to which Virginius retreats. This change bears on one of the liveliest and most unpredetermined variables in Chaucer's narrative craft: the degree and kind of malleability he sensed in his narrative materials. What counted as the "objective constraints" of the "story facts," and what, by contrast, could be altered or invented, to borrow A. C. Spearing's distinction?[31] Spearing, in his account of the "Physician's Tale," places the story of Virginia's death firmly in the genre of history: "For Chaucer that event was not a fiction, it was 'knowen for historial thyng notable' ...; it really happened, and the challenge was to find a way of making sense of it."[32] However, I have already suggested how Chaucer contests the masculine, Latinate regime of history, presided over by Titus Livius and Virginius, Claudius and Appius, by means of the prosopopoeial license of the vernacular poet, who assumes a feminine voice, first as Nature, then as Virginia. This puts the "Physician's Tale" in what Allen calls "a narrative no-man's-land" that is "neither fabulous nor historically coherent."[33] Such uncertain terrain is precisely where Chaucer carries out his labor of "formation," or his reworking of received narrative.[34]

Chaucer's earliest blueprint for intervening in traditional literary materials was undoubtedly Ovid's *Heroides*, a collection of plaintive first-person letters that positioned their inscription within well-known narratives: after Aeneas has abandoned her but before her suicide, Dido writes; after Paris has abducted Helen but before the Trojan War, Oenone writes; and so forth. As Simpson has shown, Chaucer's commitment to this Ovidian model opened opportunities for the "recognition of the pain of marginal, rejected, belated, experiential, and often feminine voices" and "an understanding of the ways in which those experiential narratives can destabilize, through subtle changes of perspective, the apparent solidities of the masculine, imperialist, epic tradition."[35] As his writing career went on, Chaucer continued to follow the Ovidian imperative to refashion received narratives through feminine perspectives. This is what

---

[30]   In Livy's original, Virginius kills his daughter near the temple of Venus Cloacina, and his action immediately incites a public outcry; see *Ab Urbe Condita* 3.48.
[31]   Spearing, "Narration in Two Versions of 'Virginius and Virginia,'" 2.
[32]   Spearing, "What Is a Narrator?," 86.
[33]   Allen, *False Fables and Exemplary Tales*, p. 89.
[34]   On the idea of "formation," see Kara Gaston, *Reading Chaucer in Time: Literary Formation in England and Italy* (Oxford: Oxford University Press, 2020), especially pp. 15–47.
[35]   James Simpson, "Chaucer as a European Writer," in *The Yale Companion to Chaucer*, ed. Seth Lerer (New Haven, Conn.: Yale University Press, 2006), pp. 55–86, at p. 64. Also see Jill Mann, "Chaucer and the 'Woman Question,'" in *This Noble Craft: Proceedings of the Xth Research Symposium of the Dutch and Belgian University Teachers of Old and Middle English and Historical Linguistics*, ed. Erik Kooper (Amsterdam: Rodopi, 1991), pp. 173–88.

he does, at least in part, in the "Physician's Tale." But insofar as these suffering women in his later works are not just the victims of erotic betrayal, they require other, different genres to frame the significance of their words, beyond Ovidian elegiacs. What, then, should Virginia say?

Chaucer seeks to work out an answer by adding the new episode of Virginius's return home, to a setting that is quite the opposite of the courtroom's claustrophobic formalism and conspiratorial displacement of intentions. Virginius

> gooth hym hoom, and sette him in his halle,
> And leet anon his deere doghter calle,
> And with a face deed as asshen colde
> Upon hir humble face he gan biholde,
> With fadres pitee stikynge thurgh his herte,
> Al wolde he from his purpos nat converte.
> "Doghter," quod he, "Virginia, by thy name …." (207–13)

Father and daughter look at each other, face to face, and the narration delivers an expressive cascade of feelings, bodily signs, and words. As Farber observes, the terms of the description mean that the reality of "Virginius's love and emotion cannot be in question."[36] This is also the only time in the tale that Virginia is named, albeit with a significance that is ambiguous. Her proper name associates her with the abstract virtue of "virginitee" (44), which she will embody in death, and it onomastically expresses her dependence on her father.[37] It is as this dubiously individualized persona that she is named and called upon to respond.

The tale here opens a space for Virginia's voice. Her father labors to explain to her the reasons for her impending death, a task broached in no other version of the tale:

> "O doghter, which that art my laste wo,
> And in my lyf my laste joye also,
> O gemme of chastitee, in pacience
> Take thou thy deeth, for this is my sentence.
> For love and nat for hate, thou most be deed;
> My pitous hand moot smyten of thyn heed." (221–25)

We might notice how urgently, even frantically, Virginius relays between first and second person. As John Hirsch notes, Virginius "uses the pronouns

---

[36] Farber, "The Creation of Consent in the *Physician's Tale*," p. 158.
[37] On Virginia's naming, see Elizabeth Scala, *Desire in the Canterbury Tales* (Columbus, Ohio: The Ohio State University Press, 2015), p. 179, and Speed, "Language and Perspective in the *Physician's Tale*," p. 129.

THE "PHYSICIAN'S TALE" AND CHAUCER'S ART OF PROSOPOPOEIA   61

thou, the, and thyn nine times, and the pronouns *I* and *my* eight."[38] In some instances, these pronouns are employed oxymoronically, so as to confuse the relations between self and other, passivity and action. Most starkly Virginius calls the maiden "deere doghter, endere of *my* lyf" (218). While it is "thou" who "most suffer," "allas, that *I* was bore!" (215). Despite her imminent death, he implies that his own end is near: "doghter, which that art my laste wo, / And in my lyf my laste joye also" (221–22). The modal verbs insist that his violence is constrained and forced: "my pitous hand *moot* smyten of thyn heed." As Hirsch observes, "It is as though Virginius is being forced to aim the blow against himself."[39] In Allen's words, "he renders her an instrument of his own social self-assertion and affective torment."[40]

Readers have often argued for the blameworthy irony of Virginius's words. He seems unable to acknowledge that someone besides himself is about to die. But we might also read in his address a torqued literary energy, a poetic confusion or ambivalence, gathered around the halting and perhaps only incomplete emergence of Virginia as a fully other person. After all, Virginia has been, in all previous versions, "a non-person – the particular *object* of the dialectic, but not a controlling factor in it," as Anne Middleton describes her.[41] Useful here is the observation of the twentieth-century linguist Émile Benveniste that linguistic personhood "belongs only to *I/you* and is lacking in *he*," or, more pithily, that the third-person is a "non-person."[42] Benveniste's point is that within the play of discourse, personhood inheres only in the poles of the communicative situation, *I* and *you*. Or, if we consider language as a kind of ontological system (as literary narratives encourage us to do), there is something special about the first- and second-person: they bestow linguistic animacy, while the third-person does not. According to this logic, the personhood of the tale thus far has been concentrated in the narrator and his posited audience (as I discussed above). Virginius's feverish play upon "I" and "thou" displaces what have been the fixed poles of linguistic personhood in the tale, redefining the time and place of discourse. As he apostrophically calls his daughter toward speech, he does so in a way that emphasizes the subjective dependencies, the oxymoronic confusion of self and other, that condition her voice.

The inchoate state of Virginia's personhood has both an intra-diegetic dimension and a metapoetic significance. Internal to the narrative world, and according to the patriarchal order of Rome, she belongs to her father

---

[38] John C. Hirsh, "Modern Times: The Discourse of the *Physician's Tale*," *Chaucer Review* 27 (1993), 387–95, at 388.

[39] Hirsh, "Modern Times," 388.

[40] Allen, *False Fables and Exemplary Tales*, p. 91.

[41] Middleton, "*Physician's Tale* and Love's Martyrs," 13.

[42] Émile Benveniste, "The Nature of Pronouns," in *Problems in General Linguistics*, tr. Mary Elizabeth Meek (Coral Gables, Fla.: University of Miami Press, 1971), pp. 217–22, at p. 217 and p. 221.

– or alternately, under Appius's ruling, to Claudius's household. She is an adolescent, a female, a daughter, a "thrall." Under the law and within Virginius's impassioned address, she is a partial subject, confused with and to some degree submerged in masculine claimants. The other, more poetological dimension of her incompletion reflects the conditions of her literary animation. Her voice, unattested in the historical record, emerges with only partial autonomy from the tale-teller's. Like Nature's words, Virginia's speech is what it *seems to him* she would say. This seeming is not something that Chaucer remarks on directly, as he does in the case of Nature ("Thus semeth me that Nature wolde seye" [29]). Instead, we can define its contours by comparing the "Physician's Tale" to other versions of the story, thereby perceiving Chaucer's work of prosopopoeial reinvention. Virginia's figurality, or her quality of merely *seeming* to be present and speak, is apprehensible in the evanescence of her person; her persona, I will suggest, disaggregates into a series of enigmatic utterances.

Readers who criticize the Physician as an unreliable narrator often emphasize the close relation between Virginius and the tale's teller during this scene. While I remain skeptical of a sharp distinction between narrator and authorial consciousness – especially one that would treat the former as a self-consistent object of critique for the latter – this focalization through Virginius remains important. Virginius participates in a drama of recognition and misrecognition that is the poet-narrator's as well. Father addresses daughter in terms that put himself clumsily into her plight, in terms that lose their dialogic character even as they insist on it: "deere doghter, endere of my lyf," "which that art my laste wo, / And in my lyf my laste joye also" (218, 221–22). Likewise, as the scene moves toward Virginia's prosopopoeial animation – "'O mercy, deere fadre!' quod this mayde" (231) – the tale-teller must shift perspectives, from gazing pityingly "Upon hir humble face," as Virginius does, to conceiving how *she* would see her plight – an act of sympathetic imagination that is not quite persuasively achieved (as I argue below). Yet if Virginius serves as an avatar for the poet-narrator, that relationship casts both as figures of pained constraint. In a powerful essay, Jill Mann identifies Virginius as an example of what she calls the motif of the "enthralled lord," or one of a number of characters in Chaucer who "at first look like figures of authority but turn out to be figures of subordination."[43] Mann argues for the moral seriousness of Chaucer's "enthralled lords," whom she connects to the role of parents throughout the *Canterbury Tales* and "the mystery of the relation between power and love."[44] The "enthralled lord" is metafictionally suggestive, mirroring the

---

[43] Jill Mann, "Parents and Children in the *Canterbury Tales*," in *Literature in Fourteenth-Century England*, ed. Piero Boitani and Anna Torti (Tübingen: Narr, 1983), pp. 165–83, at p. 171.

[44] Mann, "Parents and Children in the *Canterbury Tales*," p. 165.

THE "PHYSICIAN'S TALE" AND CHAUCER'S ART OF PROSOPOPOEIA   63

poet-narrator who is bound to the "story facts" but who nonetheless seeks to extend conditions of affection and pity, recognition and voice.

But what does this voice have to say? Who is the self expressed? The crucial quality of Virginia's remarks is their peculiar externality, or the fact that they seem to come from elsewhere, from a genre and time not her own. This is clearest in her very last utterance, when she says to her father, "'Blissed be God that I shal dye a mayde; / Yif me my deeth, er that I have a shame. / Dooth with youre child youre wyl, a Goddes name'" (248–50). As many readers have noticed, these words abruptly inscribe Virginia into the genre of hagiography, but they do so apart from the framework of Christian salvation. As Catherine Sanok writes, Virginia "only impersonates a Christian saint."[45] Hirsch remarks that its hagiographic aspects "do not partake of the philosophical or theological context which would establish their authority."[46] Derek Pearsall comments, "Virginia has all the attributes of a Christian virgin-martyr except a good reason, in Christian faith, for dying."[47] Lee Patterson describes the tale as "a fraudulent or 'counterfeit' hagiography ... unable to transcend its own fallen historicity."[48] The awkward incongruity of Virginia's virgin-martyr tones would likely have been apparent to Chaucer and his readers. While there is relatively little emphasis on paganism in the tale, Livy's Rome was known to be a non-Christian one, and Virginia's visit earlier in the narrative to a "temple" (119) – a word that Chaucer largely reserves for places of pagan worship – confirms her culturally and historically delimited religious practice.

I thus agree with A. C. Spearing's contention that the "Physician's Tale" partakes of the "pathos of paganism" that Chaucer explored throughout his career; it should be counted as one of his "several thought-experiments in the exploration of pagan worlds, worlds in which human beings live without the comfort and constraint of the Christian revelation."[49] But the "Physician's Tale" is also messier than other such experiments. It lacks the tidy boundaries of works like the "Knight's Tale" and *Troilus and Criseyde*, where polytheistic characters run up against the carefully limned edges of their metaphysics. The "Physician's Tale" does not maintain those limits. Instead, Virginia's voice proves to be historically porous, duplex, contaminate. The misfit of what she says indicates the composite nature of her voice, divided between her subjectivity and her "seeming" to the story's teller, or between her existence *for us* and *in herself*.

---

45 Catherine Sanok, "The Geography of Genre in the *Physician's Tale* and *Pearl*," *New Medieval Literatures* 5 (2002), 177–201, at 184.
46 Hirsh, "Modern Times," p. 390.
47 Derek Pearsall, *The Life of Geoffrey Chaucer: A Critical Biography* (Oxford: Blackwell, 1992), p. 265.
48 Lee Patterson, *Chaucer and the Subject of History* (Madison, Wis.: University of Wisconsin Press, 1991), p. 162.
49 Spearing, "Narration in Two Versions of 'Virginius and Virginia,'" 32, and "What is a Narrator?," 87.

64   JULIE ORLEMANSKI

Virginia's recourse to the licensing example of Jephthah's daughter, to bolster her request for time to lament, constitutes an even more complex example of her voice's anachronistic drift:

> "Thanne yif me leyser, fader myn," quod she,
> "My deeth for to compleyne a litel space;
> For, pardee, Jepte yaf his doghter grace
> For to compleyne, er he hir slow, allas!
> And, God it woot, no thyng was hir trespas
> But for she ran hir fader first to see,
> To welcome hym with greet solempnitee." (239–244)

Several scholars have written thoughtfully on the exegetical history of the passage from Judges 11 to which Virginia refers, pointing out both the aptness and the ironies of its invocation.[50] I agree with Samantha Katz Seal that these lines represent a peculiar "fantasy of historical supersession," according to which "pagan and Jewish pasts blur together, or rather, the Jewish past is … deliberately superimposed onto a pagan one."[51] But the significance of that superimposition is difficult to unpack. I would argue that it necessarily implicates another, later historical moment, indeed the one within which the act of superimposition is accomplished. It is within Chaucer's own Christian future that classical antiquity and Judaism belong together, as part of a structurally fungible "before." Certainly, Chaucer does not have the same sense of historicist propriety that marks our post-Enlightenment world, but he is elsewhere profoundly sensitive to the limits of a non-Christian, classical thought-world. Virginia can function typologically here only in the most inconsequential sense – not as part of a sacred history of prophetic resemblance but of similarities recognized *post hoc*, of mere narrative homologies. Like the motif of a saint embracing death, which fits superficially but not soteriologically, Virginia's invocation of Jephthah's daughter is based in schematic resemblances between the two situations: a sole daughter, a father bound by his perceived obligations, and the daughter's direct speech, both accepting her death and bewailing it. Virginia's words call upon a likeness that she can glimpse only obliquely, in the mirror of modernity, which catches both Hebrew and Roman maiden in its gaze and then projects its perspective through her eyes.

---

[50] E.g., Richard L. Hoffman, "Jephthah's Daughter and Chaucer's Virginia," *Chaucer Review* 2 (1967), 20–31; Daniel T. Kline, "Jephthah's Daughter and Chaucer's Virginia: The Critique of Sacrifice in the Physician's Tale," *Journal of English and Germanic Philology* 107 (2008), 77–103; Samantha Katz Seal, "Reading Like a Jew: Chaucer's *Physician's Tale* and the Letter of the Law," *Chaucer Review* 52 (2017), 298–317; and David Wallace, "'She Lives!': Jephthah's Daughter and Chaucer's Virginia, Jews and Gentiles, Bad Narrative, and Ending Happily," *Chaucer Review* 58 (2023), 403–15.

[51] Seal, "Reading Like a Jew," 306, 307.

THE "PHYSICIAN'S TALE" AND CHAUCER'S ART OF PROSOPOPOEIA   65

Yet it is also the case that the "Physician's Tale" insists on the moral seriousness of Virginia's speech. Like the reanimated figure of Ceyx in the *Book of the Duchess*, whose utterance partakes not only of the poet-god Morpheus but also the king's own drowned flesh, Virginia's person is pulled up from the depths of the historical record. Her powerful, if partial, alterity is legible in the recursiveness of what she has to say. She asks for "leyser" to lament her death and "a litel space" for complaint. It would seem, superficially at least, that Virginia's request goes unanswered in the tale, and that it is swiftly superseded by her hagiographic consent to her fate. Yet we might also notice that the scene itself functions as an answer to her request. It overwrites the briskness of Jean de Meun's version, where Virginius *tantost*, "instantly, immediately" strikes off his daughter's head.[52] Here, by contrast, time is slowed down, dilated for complaint and lament. Strikingly, though, the content of that complaint is a petition for more of the "leisure" and "space" that its utterance already occupies. We might think of this as the hunger of Virginia's voice in the "Physician's Tale." The theme she speaks on at greatest length is the desire for more voice. The swoon that follows this request marks the spot where such an interval might be – here a non-space, an aporia of absolute privacy, of the self sealed up in the self, which interrupts her composite words. It was presumably in such a non-space, an interval with no extension, where Chaucer recognized in previous versions a "space" for Virginia's voice.

The grotesque literalization of dispersonification soon follows. While Virginia's figural creation set the tale on its way, here we witness the transition from the linguistic personhood of "you" and "I," to "she" ("And with that word aswone doun she fil," (253)), and finally to "it" ("Hir fader ... hir heed of smoot, and by the top it hente" (254–55)). Textual face evaporates, and Virginius wields her head as an instrument of affective shock, which sends the narrative careening to its chaotic close.

In James Simpson's resonant meditations on literary recognition, he explains that literary interpretation entails "deep-seated, ingrained, and circular protocols that give us access to truths immanent within the separate realms of literary experience."[53] On this account, "As we read, we are always looking for the familiar face or feature, or topos (that is, commonplace) from the past."[54] Face and commonplace, in Simpson's treatment, are metaphors for one another; both are fundamental grounds for recognition. Yet the "Physician's Tale" also points out the disfiguring force of such recognitions. Prosopopoeia, lending Virginia voice and face, is essential to her sympathetic Ovidian recovery, but what she speaks in response to the tale's apostrophic solicitation are commonplaces alien to her, though familiar to her readers.

---

[52] *Roman de la Rose*, ed. Lecoy, line 5607.
[53] Simpson, "Cognition is Recognition," 25. See also Simpson, "Textual Face" and "The Shock of the Old."
[54] Simpson, "Cognition is Recognition," 30.

Despite the connotative force of her words, she remains marooned from the resources of Christian salvation. Anticipating a potential critique of his claims, on the basis of the utter singularity and otherness of individuals, Simpson warns that "the recognized textual face is not in any way the experience of a radical, Levinasian alterity."[55] What is notable about the "Physician's Tale," as well as other instances of Chaucerian prosopopoeia, is that they agree with this principle, that the face of the text, and the faces that texts lend a mode of appearing, are not radically Other in a Levinasian sense. In fact, they partake of the readers and writers, dreamers and tale-tellers, to whom they appear. Yet Chaucer's works return again and again to exploring in narrative and figural terms the fissuring and disfiguring effects of this hybridity, which nonetheless do not prevent the utterance of an "I" not heard before, and heard in no other way. He works consistently between face and mask, in the uneasy prosopopoeial arena of the first-person.

So, what kind of thing is literary person in the "Physician's Tale"? Virginia is a composite phenomenon, dependent on and derivative of not only her father Virginius but also the narrating voice, whose time interfuses hers without the capacity to redeem her. Simultaneously, she is not treated as mere narrative prop and adjunct, and the introduction of her voice seems to mark the irreducibility of her ethical claim upon us. Like Ceyx, whose sodden body is dragged up from the sea floor in Chaucer's peculiar retelling of Ovid, Virginia weighs heavily on the "Physician's Tale," pulling us into her recursive hunger for more voice. Chaucer recognizes that (to return to Simpson's phrase) the "transformative affective claim that we make on that known face" alters it, figuring and disfiguring it at once, summoning it as face and mask, person and made thing. The hermeneutic failures of the "Physician's Tale" stage the mixed ontology of the prosopopoeial figure and help to map the unstable grounds for lending a voice.

---

[55] Simpson, "Cognition is Recognition," 43.

4 "TROILUS CAN AFFORD TO FALL IN LOVE ... WITH WHOMSOEVER HE WILL"[1]: FREE WILL AND RECOGNITION IN *TROILUS AND CRISEYDE*

Laura Ashe

In his important discussion of Chaucer's Criseyde in *Reform and Cultural Revolution*, James Simpson offers the aside that provides my title quotation. "However painful it finally turns out to be," he observes, Troilus possesses a freedom profoundly different from the circumstances that constrain Criseyde. Contrasting Troilus's immediate vision of love with her painful decision-making, he establishes the former's comparative social freedom as a foil to his real focus: the intense psychological narrative of Criseyde's "shrewd appraisal of the conditions in which she finds herself."[2] I will return to James's account of Criseyde shortly; but despite its brevity, I want to engage with this comment on Troilus's limited and painful freedom, and with James's work elsewhere on the concept of recognition, to propose this observation as a rather unexpected departure point: toward a theory of human love, and a changed understanding of tragedy. By a "theory of human love," I mean the model of a freely willed, mutually self-constituting bond between individual, non-substitutable human beings; and when I say "toward," I mean to suggest that lacking such a culturally sanctioned model, Chaucer responded to human reality with a radical

---

[1] James Simpson, *The Oxford English Literary History, Vol. 2: 1350–1547. Reform and Cultural Revolution* (Oxford: Oxford University Press, 2002), p. 147.

[2] Simpson, *Reform and Cultural Revolution*, p. 147.

68   LAURA ASHE

experiment. That experiment, rooted in the freedom of the will and the ethical necessity of recognition, performed an act of transformation upon his sources: and so he also, I will argue, created a new form of tragedy.

There were of course many culturally sanctioned theories of love in the Middle Ages. Perfect divine love was idealized for humanity as universal *caritas* for God and neighbour; Aristotle's highest form of love between persons, *philia*, a relation between "men who are good, and alike in virtue," had with Aquinas been Christianized as the necessary inclination of the soul toward the good, a participant in the greater love that leads to God.[3] Responding to Cicero's classic treatise on friendship, Aelred of Rievaulx's *On Spiritual Friendship* defined love as "quidam animae rationalis affectus" ("a particular affection of the rational soul"),[4] which in its highest form ("spiritual" as opposed to "carnal" and "worldly") "inter bonos vitae, morum studiorumque similitudo conglutinat" ("is cemented between the good by similitude of life, morals and pursuits"). This *vera amicitia*, true love, is "ad Dei dilectionem et cognitionem gradus" ("a stage toward the love and knowledge of God"), rather than a distraction from the divine:

> Itaque amicus, in spiritu Christi adhaerens amico, efficitur cum eo cor unum et anima una, et sic per amoris gradus ad Christi conscendens amicitiam, unus cum eo spiritus efficitur in osculo uno. (2.151)

---

[3] Thomas Aquinas, *Summa Theologica*, ed. and tr. the Fathers of the English Dominican Province, 3 vols. (New York: Benziger Brothers, 1947–48), I–I q. 20 a. 2, on divine love which "provocat," "calls forth," human love of the good; *STh* II–II q. 26 a. 3 on the perfection of *caritas*; *STh* II–II q. 27 a. 8 on love of God and one's neighbour. On Aristotelian friendship, *Commentary on the Nicomachean Ethics*, ed. and tr. C. I. Litzinger, O.P., 2 vols. (Chicago: Henry Regnery Company, 1964), Book VIII (1538–1756), esp. 1574–84, 1605, 1650. See, e.g., James McEvoy, "*Philia* and *amicitia*: the Philosophy of Friendship from Plato to Aquinas," *Sewanee Mediaeval Colloquium Occasional Papers* 2 (1985), 1–23; Lars Hermanson, *Friendship, Love, and Brotherhood in Medieval Northern Europe, c. 1000–1200*, tr. Alan Crozier (Leiden: Brill, 2019). For an account of the difficulties of reconciling Aristotelian and Christian conceptions of love, and the argument that Chaucer seeks to depict the love between Troilus and Criseyde as a species of *philia*, see Jessica Rosenfeld, *Ethics and Enjoyment in Late Medieval Poetry: Love after Aristotle* (Cambridge: Cambridge University Press, 2010), esp. pp. 106, 135–59. On the difficulty (and necessity) of reconciling God's love with human individuality see Marcel Sarot, "The Value of Infused Love: Nygren, Brümmer and Aquinas on *Agape and Caritas*," *Jaarboek Thomas Instituut te Utrecht* 33 (2013), 111–23; Vincent Brümmer, *The Model of Love: A Study in Philosophical Theology* (Cambridge: Cambridge University Press, 1993), pp. 206–18.

[4] *De spirituali amicitia, in Aelredi Rievallensis Opera omnia: I. Opera ascetica*, ed. A. Hoste and C. H. Talbot (CCCM I. Turnhout, Belgium: Brepols, 1971), Book 1.109.

FREE WILL AND RECOGNITION IN *TROILUS AND CRISEYDE*   69

And so, friend bonded with friend in the spirit of Christ, he is made one heart and one soul with him, and so through the stages of love climbing to friendship with Christ, he is made one spirit with him in one kiss.[5]

As this passage itself shows, such expressions of spiritualized love were wholly compatible with erotic (and homoerotic) imagery and expression.[6]

Courtly romance, meanwhile, offered love as an adaptable metaphor, an ethical justification for the protagonist's pursuit of worldly ambition and success: the chivalric hero, struck by love of the most beautiful lady, suffers and strives as he embarks on the quest to prove his worth and win her love, and his victory brings wealth, status, and power.[7] Finally, the love-lyric proposed an Ovidian model of solitary love-longing, a lone voice required to navigate between absurdity and despair, whose real purpose is often the exploration of quite different relationships – such as that between ruler and courtier – or the instantiation of the desiring subject itself, independent of the object of desire.[8] All these characterize love as a mixture of compulsive reaction and reason, the response of the corporeal senses and the rational soul to what they perceive as the good.[9] There were, too, prescriptive models of married love – albeit usually regarded as much inferior to that possible between virtuous male equals – but these were exactly that, theories of the ways in which love can be conducted

---

[5]   On the hierarchy of human and divine love, and Dante's achievement in transforming the former to the latter, see Jerome Mazzaro, "From *Fin Amour* to Friendship: Dante's Transformation," in *The Olde Daunce: Love, Friendship, Sex, and Marriage in the Medieval World*, ed. Robert R. Edwards and Stephen Spector (Albany, N.Y.: State University of New York Press, 1991), pp. 121–37; Elena Lombardi, *The Wings of the Doves: Love and Desire in Dante and Medieval Culture* (Montreal: McGill-Queen's University Press, 2012).

[6]   Heloise's letters to Abelard represent a virtuosic extremity of this combination, in their "extraordinary interweaving of the discourses of *amicitia* … *amor* … and religious devotion": see Martin Irvine, "Heloise and the gendering of the literate subject," in *Criticism and Dissent in the Middle Ages*, ed. Rita Copeland (Cambridge: Cambridge University Press, 1996), pp. 87–114, at p. 101.

[7]   For this argument see Laura Ashe, *The Oxford English Literary History, Vol. 1: 1000–1350. Conquest and Transformation* (Oxford: Oxford University Press, 2017), pp. 241–68.

[8]   See Sarah Kay's succinct overview "Desire and subjectivity," in *The Troubadours: An Introduction*, ed. Simon Gaunt and Sarah Kay (Cambridge: Cambridge University Press, 1999), pp. 212–27.

[9]   On the complex relations between competing (literary and cultural) models of love emergent in the period see, e.g., C. Stephen Jaeger, *Ennobling Love: In Search of a Lost Sensibility* (Philadelphia: University of Pennsylvania Press, 1999); Peter L. Allen, *The Art of Love: Amatory Fiction from Ovid to the Romance of the Rose* (Philadelphia: University of Pennsylvania Press, 1992); R. Howard Bloch, *Medieval Misogyny and the Invention of Western Romantic Love* (Chicago: University of Chicago Press, 1991).

70 LAURA ASHE

between unequal partners, and models for the experience and conduct of the roles of wife and husband.[10]

Missing from all these capacious and overlapping paradigms is a model of love that can explain why any individual might love this person, and not another: and why that act of choosing matters. To speak of the beloved's virtue or goodness or beauty is to elide any question of individuality or non-substitutability: as the hero of Marie de France's *Guigemar* sadly observes, encountering a beautiful lady and not recognizing her as his beloved, "Femmes se resemblent asez" ("Women all look the same");[11] the philosophy of *philia* and Aelred's *spiritualis amicitia*, correspondingly, rooted love in the friends' essential likeness, their equality of virtue. More importantly, this meritocratic view of love as a response to the beloved's value implicitly subordinates human love to divine love: for if love is rational in its pursuit of the good, who is better than Christ?[12] As such, any model of human, individual love must address an essential question: why this one, and not another? We do not need – and we cannot have – an answer that actually explains why we love; Montaigne, who elsewhere dismissed "love" as a sexual desire for satisfaction in a particular object, famously said of his greatest friendship that he could only offer the reason "Because it was he, because it was I."[13] This clarifies that what we must have, in the absence of a universal explanation for particular love, is an epistemological framework within which the categories of this self and that other are rendered capable of signifying at all; and for this we need two things. The first is a theory of individuality – the idea that people are importantly, substantially different from one another, and not merely accidentally or categorically or quantitatively so – and hence the understanding that individuals are non-substitutable. The second is a theory of recognition: the idea that it is possible – or at the least a genuinely moral aspiration – to recognize another, in all their unique individuality, their paradoxically unknowable otherness.

---

[10] See Michael M. Sheehan, "*Maritalis Affectio* Revisited," and Erik Kooper, "Loving the Unequal Equal: Medieval Theologians and Marital Affection," in *The Olde Daunce*, ed. Edwards and Spector, pp. 32–43, 44–56.

[11] Marie de France, *Guigemar*, in *Lais*, ed. A. Ewert (Oxford: Blackwell, 1965), line 779.

[12] This ontological reality is most famously set out in Part 7 of the *Ancrene Wisse*: see *Ancrene Wisse: A Corrected Edition of the Text in Cambridge, Corpus Christi College, MS 402, with Variants from Other Manuscripts*, ed. Bella Millett, with E. J. Dobson and Richard Dance, 2 vols. EETS, os 325, 326 (Oxford: Oxford University Press, 2005), I.145–54.

[13] "Par ce que c'estoit luy; par ce que c'estoit moy": "De l'Amitié," in *Les Essais de Michel de Montaigne*, ed. Pierre Villey with Verdun L. Saulnier, 3rd ed. (Paris: Presses universitaires de France, 1978), I.25 (188). On love: III.5 (877): "je trouve après tout que l'amour n'est autre chose que la soif de cette jouyssance en un subject desiré."

FREE WILL AND RECOGNITION IN *TROILUS AND CRISEYDE*   71

Difficulties immediately arise. The European Middle Ages developed sophisticated theories of selfhood, but selfhood is not the same as individuality. The assertion of individuality was the original sin of Lucifer, the angel who made himself his own end, who "appetiit finalem beatitudinem per suam virtutem habere" ("sought to have final beatitude of his own power").[14] As a hermeneutic for lived experience, the idea of individuality simply had a very weak place in available cultural models, largely subordinated to social roles and to shared ideals of worldly or spiritual ambition. Each soul is of infinite moral responsibility and of infinite value to God, and in this sense all souls are alike; they are distinguished by God's judgment, not by ours. "Then shall I know, even as I am known":[15] but that *I* stands for everyone.[16]

Unsurprisingly, similar and deeper difficulties arise in searching for the concept of recognition of the other. This idea, Hegel's *Anerkennung*, acknowledgement-recognition, is usually regarded as the product of modernity. Distinct from – though obviously not unrelated to – Aristotelian recognition, *anagnorisis*, by which the subject encounters new knowledge about the world and the self, recognition of the other is an intensely controversial philosophical concept, perhaps even a fundamentally incoherent one.[17] James has worked a great deal on the broader concept of recognition (as his contribution to the present volume shows); in his analysis the process of recognition emerges as our only available hermeneutic, the essential prior structure within which and by which we can approach the (any) text:

> [B]efore, that is, we can understand the meaning of any communicative act, we need to understand what kinds of meaning are likely to be available in that kind of communicative act. We need to know about the communicative act *before* we decode it, precisely in order that we can see the text's "face," or recognize it. This kind of cognition implies,

[14] Aquinas, *Summa Theologica*, I–I q. 63 a. 3.

[15] "tunc autem cognoscam sicut et cognitus sum": 1 Cor. 13:12.

[16] There is a large hinterland of scholarship on the "discovery of the individual" in the twelfth century, though much of that discussion concerned ideas of subjectivity and selfhood, rather than (non-substitutable) individuality: major contributions include Peter Dronke, *Poetic Individuality in the Middle Ages: New Departures in Poetry, 1000–1150* (Oxford: Clarendon Press, 1970); Colin Morris, *The Discovery of the Individual: 1050–1200* (London: S.P.C.K., 1972); Robert W. Hanning, *The Individual in Twelfth-Century Romance* (New Haven, Conn.: Yale University Press, 1977); Caroline Walker Bynum, "Did the Twelfth Century Discover the Individual?," in *Jesus as Mother: Studies in the Spirituality of the High Middle Ages* (Berkeley, Calif.: University of California Press, 1982), pp. 82–109 (revised from *Journal of Ecclesiastical History* 31 (1980), 1–17); John F. Benton, "Consciousness of Self and Perceptions of Individuality," in *Renaissance and Renewal in the Twelfth Century*, ed. Robert L. Benson and Giles Constable, with Carol D. Lanham (Cambridge, Mass.: Harvard University Press, 1982), pp. 263–95.

[17] I treat this topic at length in a monograph on Chaucer and (mostly modern) philosophy, forthcoming with Oxford University Press.

paradoxically, recognition. … Absent our effort to perceive unstated meaning, and to suppose intended meaning, all verbal signs, literary or not, remain forever cut off, floating helplessly as *disiuncta membra* in a world of perpetual unreadability.[18]

As an approach to the text, this is a doctrine of readerly engagement and participation, a shared creation of cultural meaning. But it carries with it a dark ethical risk, hinted at in James's "literary or not": for the problem with this hermeneutic closing down of possibility, as Judith Butler observes, is that the same limitations apply to our encounter with the human face, as well as the textual "face": for what is another person to us but a series of signs?

> The other only appears to me, only functions as an other for me, if there is a frame within which I can see and apprehend the other in her separateness and exteriority … I am caught up not only in the sphere of normativity but in the problematic of power … norms work not only to direct my conduct but to condition the possible emergence of an encounter between myself and the other.[19]

The only way we can "recognize" another is by placing drastic – false – limitations on their capacity for meaning; but if we dispense with those limitations we cannot see them at all.

However: if, as many philosophers have claimed, we can never truly recognize another, I suggest that does little to remove what amounts to an ethical imperative: that we must nonetheless make the attempt. The first ethical question is, how should I treat another person; the first answer is, by recognizing them to be a person, with the same capacity for significance, for infinitely various meaning-making, as I grant to myself. The problem is that this is impossible – put very simply, we cannot ever know what the other person *means*, in the fullest sense of that word. But we have to try: and this is an act of will, a radical act of human freedom. By not leaving it to God, by continually attempting the impossible, we acknowledge the ethical bonds and responsibilities that lie between human individuals; and with that we enable the possibility of creating mutually self-constituting bonds of recognition, between non-substitutable individuals – this one and no other – a theory of human love.

I suggest that in *Troilus and Criseyde*, the changes Chaucer makes in the process of adapting Boccaccio's *Il Filostrato* show him to be engaged in just such an experiment. This is pursued in different ways through the two protagonists, commensurate with their different positioning in the narrative: lover and beloved, faithful and faithless, male and female; with some vital

---

[18] James Simpson, "Cognition is Recognition: Literary Knowledge and Textual 'Face,'" *New Literary History* 44 (2013), 25–44, at 30–31.

[19] Judith Butler, *Giving an Account of Oneself* (New York: Fordham University Press, 2005), p. 25.

FREE WILL AND RECOGNITION IN *TROILUS AND CRISEYDE* 73

oscillations, active and passive. James has described Chaucer's unprecedented mimesis of subjectivity in the figure of Criseyde:

> [Criseyde's] emotional life is represented as a matter of circumstance, decision, and, therefore, of process ... an astonishing poetic achievement of sustained intimacy, the first of its kind in English poetry. The very persuasiveness of that representation of psychological "process," however, is the premise of Criseyde being unrepresentable in Book 5. For in Book 5 her repetition of almost the same process, under an equally pressing male advance, produces a discontinuity of self that threatens to compromise sympathy, and certainly disables the resources of narrative.[20]

I will return to this final claim of "discontinuity," for I wish to offer a different interpretation of the closing stages of the narrative; for now, however, it suffices to note that the impressive psychological conviction James identifies is vital both to our sense of Criseyde's mimetic personhood – her availability *as face* for us to recognize – and, I suggest, to our understanding of the characters' free will. In contrast with his source, Chaucer does not present Criseyde to our recognition as a textual type, the beautiful faithless woman. Rather he creates the textual mimesis of an at times unrepresentably complex subjectivity, a creature of freedom and constraint, of self-knowledge and self-deception, part revealed and part hidden. Essential to our recognition of Criseyde as a (mimetic) subjectivity is the perception of her freedom of will: a sense of agency, and of moral responsibility, that is generated in the text despite the narratorial voice's frequent, anguished recourse to the rhetoric of fortune and destiny. Just as Troilus's misunderstanding of the implications of divine omniscience is ironized by its direct dependence on Boethius's famous resolution of the problem,[21] so the narrator's frequent apostrophes to "Fortune" are continually destabilized by the narrative's much more mundane representation of causality.

On the night the lovers finally consummate their relationship, brought together by Pandarus's manipulations both verbal and bodily, Criseyde is said to have been on the point of leaving Pandarus's house:

> But O Fortune, executrice of wierdes,
> O influences of thise hevenes hye!
> Soth is, that under God ye ben oure hierdes,
> Though to us bestes ben the causez wrie.
> This mene I now: for she gan homward hye,
> But execut was al bisyde hire leve
> The goddes wil, for which she moste bleve. (III.617–23)

---

[20] Simpson, *Reform and Cultural Revolution*, pp. 147–48.

[21] The relevant passage is Geoffrey Chaucer, *Troilus and Criseyde*, ed. Stephen A. Barney, in *The Riverside Chaucer*, gen. ed. Larry D. Benson, 3rd ed. (Boston: Houghton Mifflin, 1987), IV.953–1078.

74 LAURA ASHE

This apostrophe appears to be the grandest statement of Fortune's power over human affairs: fortune steers us against our will to its fated conclusions, people herded like sheep, their destiny hidden from them. But the object of these narratorial histrionics is pure bathos: the fact that it starts raining heavily. And indeed, when Pandarus had first asked Criseyde to dinner, she objected that "'It reyneth; lo, how sholde I gon?'" (III.562): nothing, actually, has changed, and we are invited to wonder whether that includes Criseyde's mind. Similarly, our judgement of the effect of Pandarus's dishonesty is troubled by the narrator's disclaiming ignorance: when Pandarus unconvincingly swears that Troilus is away from besieged Troy, scepticism is archly entertained:

> Nought list myn auctour fully to declare
> What that she thoughte whan he seyde so
> That Troilus was out of towne yfare,
> As if he seyde therof soth or no;
> But that, withowten await, with hym to go
> She graunted hym, sith he hire that bisoughte,
> And, as his nece, obeyed as hire oughte. (III.575–81)

The silence of the "auctor" here is a device to alert us to our absolute uncertainty: this whole section departs from *Il Filostrato*, and depicts a character whose intentions are occluded not only from the narrator and from us, but very likely from herself. Criseyde has sex with Troilus that night for multiple reasons, including familial piety and familial pressure, empathy, excitement, desire, love, and the idea of love, her growing knowledge of Troilus's character, the concatenation of circumstance that reassures her of secrecy, the susceptibility of human beings to aesthetic patterns, and the fact that it rained a lot.[22] When in bed she responds to Troilus's uncharacteristic forcefulness by declaring that "'Ne hadde I er now, my swete herte deere, / Ben yolde, ywis, I were now nought here!'" (III.1210–11), she both confirms her consent and yet abstracts it from the narrative present, locating it in some unknowable – and narratively nonexistent – earlier moment. At numerous points of crisis Chaucer shows us the (oxymoronic but real) elective inevitability we are capable of creating in our own lives, and imposing upon our future selves. Some weeks earlier Criseyde had reflected on the question of whether to act or not, of whether to accept the offered role of protagonist in a love-plot. Her natural desire simply to *be* such a protagonist generated a series of irresistible arguments in favour; irresistible because they are not justifications of particular action, but of action rather than passivity, of being rather than non-being:

---

[22] On the generation of contingency within the text, see Peter Buchanan, "Reading bodies, books, and beyond: experience and contingency in *Troilus and Criseyde*," *Textual Practice* 36 (2022), 1892–912; and for a powerful recent revisioning of the "consummation" scene see Clare Davidson, "Reading in Bed with *Troilus and Criseyde*," *Chaucer Review* 55 (2020), 147–70.

FREE WILL AND RECOGNITION IN *TROILUS AND CRISEYDE*   75

> "But swich is love, and ek myn aventure." (II.742)
> "What shal I doon? To what fyn lyve I thus?" (II.757)

> And after that, hire thought gan forto clere,
> And seide, "He which that nothing undertaketh,
> Nothyng n'acheveth, be hym looth or deere." (II.806–08)

Similarly, critics have long observed that even though Troilus is struck down by the god of love, he nevertheless chooses to consent:[23] "Thus took he purpos loves craft to suwe ... For with good hope he gan fully assente / Criseyde forto love and nought repente." (I.379; 391–92). This is stronger than Boccaccio's lover's "inclination" to love, manifest not in a promise of willed permanence but in one of exclusive attention to Criseyde:

> Perchè disposto a seguir tale amore ...
> ... lieto si diede a cantare
> Bene sperando, e tutto si dispose
> Di voler sola Criseida amare,
> Nulla apprezzando ogni altra che veduta
> Glie ne venisse, o fosse mai piaciuta.[24]

> Therefore inclined to pursue this love ... joyfully he began to sing, high in hope and all disposed to want to love Criseida alone, giving no value to any other he might see, or who had ever pleased him.

What Chaucer's passages capture so clearly is the human capacity to generate a feeling of inevitability out of contingency: our desire to set things going, simply to enter into narrative existence, in all the patterns made available to us by our particular cultural moment – and also our self-deceiving insistence on conscious, rational decision-making. It is not that we do not decide – it is crucial to my argument that we do; but that we decide very quickly, and in ways that we hide from ourselves, and that we rehearse as a painful weighing of alternatives and surveying of dangers long after the decision has been made. Once Criseyde has thought to herself "But swich is love, and ek myn aventure," she has chosen the kind of pseudo-fatalism that is no such thing: that is, in

---

[23] See Elizabeth D. Kirk, "'Paradis Stood Formed in Hire Yën': Courtly Love and Chaucer's Re-Vision of Dante," in *Acts of Interpretation: The Text in its Contexts, 700–1600: Essays on Medieval and Renaissance Literature in honor of E. Talbot Donaldson*, ed. Mary J. Carruthers and Elizabeth D. Kirk (Norman, Okla.: Pilgrim Books, 1982), pp. 257–77 (at p. 263); and with much less certainty about this "assente," J. Allan Mitchell, "Romancing Ethics in Boethius, Chaucer, and Levinas: Fortune, Moral Luck, and Erotic Adventure," *Comparative Literature* 57 (2005), 101–16, at 107.

[24] Giovanni Boccaccio, *Il Filostrato: The Filostrato of Giovanni Boccaccio*, ed. and tr. Nathaniel Edward Griffin and Arthur Beckwith Myrick (Philadelphia: University of Pennsylvania Press, 1929), 1.36–37 (here and elsewhere, translation sometimes amended for style).

76 LAURA ASHE

fact, a determination to act. And of course this is also because there is no such thing, in life, as not acting. We are inescapably moral agents: we live in a plurality of beings, and all our acts and our failures or refusals to act form and constitute our ethical relation to others. That is free will.

However, the most important point to grasp about free will is that it is nothing at all like freedom. We all have free will; the problem is, so does everyone else; and then there is chance and consequence and deception and self-deception to be thrown in. Everywhere in *Troilus* – not least in the events that lead to Criseyde's removal to the Greek camp – Chaucer emphasizes the infinite plurality of human decision-making, and the concatenation of intended and unintended events, that renders the unrepresentable complexity of causality really no different from mere chance. We can call this inscrutability "fortune" if we wish, but however it is understood, it does nothing to attenuate the moral responsibility we carry as agents with free will.

A traditional reading of this crux suggests that beneath the narrator's rhetorical complaints, Chaucer simply reminds us that "Fortune" is not *really* a malevolent force, but rather a useful metaphor for the essential instability of earthly life. In the face of that painful instability, the immanent tragedy of our mortality, he offers at the end of his great poem the Boethian answer, which is to turn away from what is unstable to embrace what is eternal. However, I suggest that in *Troilus and Criseyde* Chaucer offers a radical critique of the Boethian view, even as he also finally endorses it. He shows that the whole idea of Fortune as something to be transcended by giving up on worldly things is both true, and a complete misunderstanding of contingency and of humanity: because in light of the human world in all its plurality, the Boethian response is profoundly inhumane.

This philosophy posits a sole protagonist amid the things of the world: he is raised on Fortune's wheel and then dashed to the ground, deprived of the objects of worldly desire – love, wealth, status, power; the only answer to this confusion is to recognize the inevitability of loss, and to rise above "This world that passeth soone as floures faire" (V.1841). But we cannot just "rise above" the things of the world, because the things of this world include, most importantly, other people. And here we reach an uncomfortable truth about our dominant hermeneutic models, which is their inherent loneliness, their inability to account for other minds. Writing about the experience of reading, James has offered a poignant model of textual recognition as repeated longing, encounter, and loss, virtuosically explored in the series of brief meetings and irrevocable partings that structure Dante's great work:

> ... the frequent topos of the otherworldly recognition in which the embrace of the recognized loved one is in vain ... suppl[ies] us with an even sharper model for our own literary experience: we are immeasurably enlivened by reaching towards the recognized loved one, even as we are painfully deluded by her or his absence.

FREE WILL AND RECOGNITION IN *TROILUS AND CRISEYDE*   77

> Dante's *Commedia* is the great example of a text whose entire narrative of self-knowledge ... is driven by a complex interaction of recognitions and painful leave takings ... as Dante himself is propelled forward.[25]

Dante's progress to paradise, to divine love, is the one that we take alone – just as our experience as readers posits us as subjectivity, and texts as fleetingly recognized, half-understood, vanishing faces. The problem with this – the moral scandal that it adumbrates for us – is that other *people* appear to us in much the same way. But in *Troilus and Criseyde*, Chaucer attempts to show us what it would be to recognize another *as* other, as infinite as the self. This is where I turn from Criseyde's experience to Troilus's, as the forlorn lover becomes, ironically or otherwise in his loss, Chaucer's protagonist in an experimental theory of human love. It matters here that Troilus's loss of Criseyde is brought about not by his subjection to fortune, but by his attempt to accommodate Criseyde as another moral agent, to make a joint decision with another person driven by their own motivations and fears. In *Il Filostrato*, as the request is made for Criseida's removal, Boccaccio's "timido" Troilo is trapped in indecision, the impulse to resist stymied by fear:

> Amore il facea pronto ad ogni cosa
> Doversi oppor, ma d'altra parte era
> Ragion che'l contrastava, e che dubbiosa
> Faceva molto quell'impresa altiera,
> Non forse che di cio fosse crucciosa
> Criseida per vergogna; e in tal maniera,
> Volendo e non volendo or questo or quello,
> Intra due stava il timido donzello. (*Fil.* 4.16)

> Love made him ready to oppose everything as a matter of duty, but Reason stood against it on the other side, casting grave doubt on that high undertaking in case Criseida might be enraged for the shame of it; and so the timid youth stood trapped between two alternatives, willing and unwilling and not knowing this from that.

Here "Amore" instructs him to act without reference to Criseida's feelings, while "Ragion" urges him to consider her possible reaction as a further external obstacle to his happiness. In subtle but clear departure from his source, Chaucer both adapts this moment and makes significant additions to it, by which Troilus determines to act only on Criseyde's agreement, with her full understanding, consent and assent:

> Love hym made al prest to don hire byde,
> And rather dyen than she sholde go;
> But Resoun seyde hym, on that other syde,

---

[25] Simpson, "Cognition is Recognition," 41.

"Withouten assent of hire ne do nat so ..."
For which he gan deliberen, for the beste ...
He wolde lat hem graunte what hem leste,
And telle his lady first what that they mente;
And whan that she hadde seyd hym hire entente,
Therafter wolde he werken also blyve,
Theigh al the world ayeyn it wolde stryve. (IV.162–75)

"Reason" does not caution Troilus against her unpredictable reactions, but rather counsels him to find out what she thinks; "hire entente" is all. This difference is maintained throughout: in the final decision not to act, Boccaccio's Troilo persuades himself to believe something he wants to be true, when love itself – again without reference to Criseida's wishes, and now in opposition to her own words – tells him it isn't right:

E quasi verisimil gli sembrava
Dover ciò che diceva certamente
Esser così, ma perchè molto amava,
Pur fede vi prestava lentamente;
Ma alia fin, come che vago fosse,
Seco cercando, a crederlo si mosse. (*Fil.* 4.137)

And it seemed to him fairly likely that what she said with such conviction ought to be true, but because he loved a great deal, he gave faith to it only slowly. But in the end, like one anxious for something, searching for reasons to do so, he brought himself to believe.

By contrast Troilus – who actually loves Criseyde – shares her thought (the "selve wit"); his love for Criseyde leads him not to mistrust her word, but simply to feel pain and fear at the thought of letting her go; and in the end, despite these fears, he wilfully moves his heart to trust her, acceding to her interpretation of their situation:

And verrayliche him semed that he hadde
The selve wit; but yet to late hir go
His herte mysforyaf hym evere mo;
But fynaly, he gan his herte wreste
To trusten hire, and took it for the beste. (IV.1426–28)

This respect for Criseyde as another person, another moral agent, culminates in Chaucer's handling of the final proof of Criseyde's infidelity. Boccaccio's Troilo is given a shocking and terrible discovery, the recognition, Aristotelian anagnorisis, that his lady is untrue and that therefore he has lost himself; there is nothing for him now but grief and rage, and the wish for vengeance.

"Del tutto veggio che m'hai discacciato
Del petto tuo, ed io contra mia voglia

FREE WILL AND RECOGNITION IN *TROILUS AND CRISEYDE*   79

Nel mio ancora tengo effigiato
Il tuo bel viso con noiosa doglia:
O lasso me, che'n malora fui nato,
Questo pensier m'uccide e mi dispoglia
D'ogni speranza di futura gioia …
Ma spero pur la divina giustizia
Rispetto avrà al mio dolore amaro,
E similmente alia tua gran nequizia.
O sommo Giove …
Che fanno le tue folgori ferventi,
Risposan elle? …
Togliete via colei nelli cui seni
Bugie e inganni e tradimenti sono,
Ne più la fate degna di perdono." (*Fil.* 8.15–18)

"I see you have entirely driven me out of your breast, and against my
will, I still hold in mine the image of your fair face, with grievous
anguish! Oh alas for me, born in an evil hour! This thought kills me,
robs me of all hope of future joys … But I hope divine justice attends
to my love's agonies, and likewise to your great iniquity … Oh great
Jove, where are your burning thunderbolts – are they at rest? Get rid
of her, whose heart hides lies and treacheries and betrayals, and never
judge her worthy of pardon."

Chaucer first alters, and then excises, the excesses of Troilo's vituperation against
his lady. Where Troilo cannot forget Criseida's "bel viso," Troilus, in Chaucer's
famous and devastating coinage, cannot "unloven" Criseyde; where Troilo
thinks of the ending of his happiness, Troilus asserts the continuation of his love:

"Thorugh which I se that clene out of youre mynde
Ye han me cast – and I ne kan nor may,
For al this world, withinne myn herte fynde
To unloven yow a quarter of a day!
In corsed tyme I born was, weilaway,
That yow, that doon me al this wo endure,
Yet love I best of any creature!" (V.1686–701)

What matters above all is that Troilus continues to love Criseyde; he does not
wish her harm; he pities her the loss of her good name; he barely accuses her of
wrongdoing, and shows none of Troilo's vengeful bitterness. Boccaccio's lesson
from the whole sorry business is to advise greater care in choosing which
lady to love; he – ironically like Chaucer's Criseyde in the Greek camp – is a
protagonist with eyes on *this* horizon, taking chances amid constraints, trying
to choose wisely among the things of this world for the sake of earthly thriving.
The Boethian response to these events, and to the poem *Il Filostrato* itself – and
a response which Chaucer offers in his poem's coda – is to rise above all this, to

understand that worldly joys are fleeting, and turn instead to eternal happiness: but, to reiterate, that is not what Troilus does. And it matters what he does, because he *is* carried up to the eighth sphere: as a pagan, Chaucer grants him the closest thing to a heavenly ascent available.

The point is that Troilus's awful recognition of the situation is not only an example of anagnorisis – the world is not as he thought it was – and it is not the same as Troilo's anagnorisis. Troilus's recognition here is also, vitally, an act of acknowledgement-recognition: he sees that Criseyde is a wholly other, independent person, whose intentions and desires he can only read by signs, but whose intentions and desires are thereby not one whit less important than his own. She is absolutely free to abandon him, notwithstanding that she will be blamed for it. And in continuing to love the woman who has abandoned him, who does not love him, whom he will never see again, he exercises the most extreme free will, and hence the greatest self-determination.

I believe it is this radical freedom that constitutes the ground for a theory of human love. This was a theory that required a particular philosophical departure. Aquinas, following Aristotle, had established the orthodoxy that free will is a capacity of rationality: the intellect recognizes what is good, and the will desires it. If an object is presented to the intellect as the best possible – he of course is speaking of God – then the will *must* give its assent.

> Sunt enim quaedam particularia bona, quae non habent necessariam connexionem ad beatitudinem, quia sine his potest aliquis esse beatus, et huiusmodi voluntas non de necessitate inhaeret. Sunt autem quaedam habentia necessariam connexionem ad beatitudinem, quibus scilicet homo Deo inhaeret, in quo solo vera beatitudo consistit. Sed tamen antequam per certitudinem divinae visionis necessitas huiusmodi connexionis demonstretur, voluntas non ex necessitate Deo inhaeret, nec his quae Dei sunt. Sed voluntas videntis Deum per essentiam, de necessitate inhaeret Deo, sicut nunc ex necessitate volumus esse beati. (*STh*, I.82.2)

> There are certain individual goods which have not a necessary connection with happiness, because without them a man can be happy: and to such the will does not adhere of necessity. But there are some things which have a necessary connection with happiness, by means of which things man adheres to God, in Whom alone true happiness consists. Nevertheless, until through the certitude of the Divine Vision the necessity of such connection be shown, the will does not adhere to God of necessity, nor to those things which are of God. But the will of the man who sees God in His essence of necessity adheres to God, just as now we desire of necessity to be happy.

This understanding of the rational will, inasmuch as it bears upon the concept of love, provides for the turn away from "feynede loves" and "wrecched worldes appetites" (V.1848, 1851); at its best, human love can only be a shadow of, or a pathway to, divine love; at its worst, it prevents the soul from reaching

FREE WILL AND RECOGNITION IN *TROILUS AND CRISEYDE*   81

salvation. For Aquinas, however, rationality is supreme, and supremely directed toward the good: no one can desire to be unhappy, or perceive the nature of God and not be compelled to love him. William of Ockham took a different view of human freedom. For him, the will is absolutely free to desire and to reject anything at all:

> Voluntas respectu cuiuscumque obiecti libere et contingenter agit.

> The will acts freely and contingently in relation to any object.

> Conclusio est quod videns divinam essentiam et carens fruitione beatifica *potest nolle* illam fruitionem.

> The conclusion is that someone who sees the divine being while lacking a beatific love is *able not to want* that love.[26]

This means that no act of cognition compels any kind of volition: a man could discover that his beloved had betrayed him, and that he had every reason to reject her – that, indeed, loving her would bring protracted suffering and no reward – and nonetheless continue to love her as an act of will. This is what Troilus does. And it matters, I suggest, because this is what enables a theory of human love. For Aquinas, the proper working of intellect and will lead inexorably to the love of God. But by stating that love cannot be compelled, that it must be freely given, and that it can be given to any object, Ockham provides for a theory of human love that renders supreme the individual's choice of another individual: not as a rational appreciation of their qualities (for how could that end other than with the love of God?) but as a radical act of freedom, dignifying human individuality.

This is where we can return to James's observation of Criseyde's "unrepresentability" in Book V. I absolutely agree that Criseyde becomes illegible to the narrative; but I disagree that this is because of a "discontinuity of self." I think Criseyde at this stage is the mimesis of something greater, illuminated by James's point about the limitations of textual recognition. The woman in Book V is inscrutable to us, is beyond our capacity to understand, because in the poem's established terms she *cannot be recognized*: either as the faithful Criseyde who loved Troilus, or as Boccaccio's faithless *domna* (even though she herself says this is how she will be represented and understood, since she too is a reader); but the poem can offer no other framework by which to see her. She is, in this "unrepresentability," something else: the mimesis of a whole person, a subjectivity that cannot be so contained by any limited framework we might readily recognize. If we find her change of heart shocking, inexplicable,

---

[26] William of Ockham, *Ordinatio* I.1.2, I.1.6: *Opera Theologica: Vol. I: Scriptum in Librum Primum Sententiarum Ordinatio (Prol. et Dist. I)*, ed. Gedeon Gál et al. (St. Bonaventure, N.Y.: The Franciscan Institute, 1967), I. 399, 505: my translation and emphasis.

a "discontinuity of self," then we betray our own unwillingness to allow to another the infinite capacity for agency and self-determination that we grant to ourselves. In metaliterary terms, she has become the protagonist of a different, unwritten narrative: the heroine of a story we are not in, and that we will never read. But in terms of lived experience, we are being shown something profound about the sheer difficulty of this inescapable and unfulfillable moral duty to recognize the other. We lose access to Criseyde – lose our ability to read her, both figuratively and literally – in a brilliant mimesis of what it actually feels like when someone falls out of love with you. More: with that parallel, we can see that the act of recognition *is* an act of love. The lived experience of the loss of love is a severe challenge to our capacity to see other people as people, rather than as things that happen to us; but that experience is itself metonymic of a greater truth. What Chaucer has done with Criseyde is to produce an effect of textual unrepresentability that is a near-perfect mimesis of our real experience of the inaccessibility of other people. So when Troilus refuses to do anything other than to see Criseyde as his ontological equal, as her own protagonist, with independent significance and reality that exists regardless of his own experience, he has achieved a radical recognition of the other.

Chaucer's apotheosis of Troilus serves, then, to acknowledge the essential truth that lies uneasily alongside the truth of divine reality: we cannot just ignore the things of this world, for in our mortality we are ethical agents bound into willed and necessary obligations with others. The most important things in this world are not things; they are people; but they are still in and of this world: mortal, in some absolute sense inaccessible, and always to be lost. That is why the divine coda to the poem is simultaneously always already and eternally true. Nevertheless, to abandon this world is to deny a great part of our ethical reality: and so Troilus laughs.

This is Chaucer's experiment. Nevertheless, if, as I have argued, Troilus's freely-willed, loving recognition of Criseyde amounts to a theory of human love, Chaucer did not invent its bare parameters, and he had inspiration beyond Boccaccio. Troilus had determined to love Criseyde "and nought repent": in fact he follows the model of the betrayed knight in Guillaume de Machaut's *Le Jugement dou roy de Behaingne*:

> *Ne departir*
> *N'en vueil mon cuer*, pour doubte dou partir,
> Qui trop demeure en vie, et, sans mentir,
> Je ne saroie amer a repentir.
> Et si seroie
> Faus amoureus se je me'en departoie,
> Car sans nul "si" li donnai l'amour moie.[27]

---

[27] Guillaume de Machaut, *Le Jugement dou roy de Behaingne*, in *Guillaume de Machaut: The Complete Poetry and Music, Volume 1: The Debate Series*, ed. R. Barton Palmer

FREE WILL AND RECOGNITION IN *TROILUS AND CRISEYDE*   83

> *I do not wish to take back my heart* for fear of desertion, I who remain too long alive, and – it's no lie – I do not know how to repent of loving. And I would be a faithless lover if I left her, because with no "but" I gave her my love.

And in the *Remede de Fortune*, Machaut had the lady Esperance counsel the despairing lover never to abandon his unrequited love:

> Qu'amy vray ne sont pas en compte
> Des biens Fortune, qui bien compte,
> Mais entre les biens de vertu. …
> Et loiauté ja ne despite,
> Se ça jus n'en as la merite,
> Qu'elle ne puet estre perdue
> Qu'à cent doubles ne soit rendue.
> Se ci ne l'est, c'est chose voire,
> Se l'iert elle en sige de gloire.[28]

> A true lover is not counted among the goods of Fortune, if we account properly, but among the goods of virtue … And do not despise loyalty, even if you get no reward from it, for it will not be lost but redoubled a hundredfold, if not here, then truly, in heaven's seat of glory.

This is a genuinely outrageous gambit – it might be regarded as a fundamentally unserious, wilful manipulation of Boethius;[29] and it goes directly against the conventional view – also expressed in Machaut's poetry – that worldly love is inherently sinful. In the *Jugement*, the suffering knight is repeatedly counselled to give up on his faithless lover. Machaut's *dits* sit in a courtly world where such assertions and counter-assertions pass by in the flux of *fin'amor* rhetoric; but Chaucer, in showing Troilus's unwavering love of the unreachable Criseyde, and rewarding him with a glimpse of heaven, is experimenting with taking it seriously, and making it true.

Finally, then, this humane seriousness – this willingness to regard the absurdity of human suffering without rendering the sufferer absurd – allows for a striking development in the concept and understanding of tragedy.

---

and Yolanda Plumley, with Dominic Leo and Uri Smilansky (Kalamazoo, Mich.: Medieval Institute Publications, 2016), lines 1141–46 (emphasis mine).

[28] Guillaume de Machaut, *Remede de Fortune*, in *Guillaume de Machaut: The Complete Poetry and Music, Volume 2: The Boethian Poems*, ed. R. Barton Palmer, with Dominic Leo and Uri Smilansky (Kalamazoo, Mich.: Medieval Institute Publications, 2019), lines 2801–12.

[29] On the highly selective adaptation of Boethian philosophy in the *Remede* see Sarah Kay, "Touching Singularity: Consolation, Philosophy, and Poetry in the *Dit*," in *The Erotics of Consolation: Desire and Distance in the Late Middle Ages*, ed. Catherine E. Léglu and Stephen J. Milner (New York: Palgrave Macmillan, 2008), pp. 21–38; James I. Wimsatt, "Reason, Machaut, and the Franklin," in *The Olde Daunce*, ed. Edwards and Spector, pp. 201–10, gives a more positive reading.

Chaucer had inherited a narrative we might think of as a classical tragedy – a predestined outcome, pitiless gods striking down the protagonist, a terrible moment of anagnorisis. It's long been said that he rewrites his tale as a medieval Christian tragedy – a fully heartfelt yet ultimately exemplary story of the instability of worldly fortune, ending with the turn to the divine comedy that lies beyond. I would argue that he has rewritten it as something more radical. This is a tragedy that did not have to happen, made by people's actions in a world of unknowably complex causality. But it possesses the seriousness, and the shape, of tragedy because in all its contingency it is also inevitable. We are free and moral agents capable of significant choices only because we inhabit a populated world in which we are all mortal. Because other people exist, our ethical identity rests on our capacity to recognize their reality; and because we are mortal and bounded creatures, all our acts of recognition will end in loss. *Troilus and Criseyde* is a tragedy simultaneously inevitable and contingent, just as mortality and loss is our inescapable condition, but our choices within that finitude are wholly our own.

A theory of human love requires radical freedom of will – the capacity to choose in defiance of rationality. It requires recognizing and acknowledging the alterity of others, as an ethical reality that imposes a particular, not a general, moral responsibility upon the self; and it demands that we honour the bonds made between individuals, the bonds which are themselves constitutive of individuality (*because it was he, because it was I*). It endows mortal love with a dignity that stands it up against eternity in a true, unresolvable contradiction; but it does nothing to resolve – indeed locates us absolutely within – the desperate-hopeful tragedy of our mortality. Troilus responds to loss with recognition and with love; it doesn't save him, but it does save *him*, his full existence as a moral agent regardless of what is inflicted upon him. And that is the stuff of great tragedy.

PART II

GENRE AND FIGURE

5

Rarely Obscure and Not a Genre: Medieval Allegorical Narrative[1]

Nicolette Zeeman

The first time I met James Simpson – tireless scholar, bold critic and shifter of paradigms, generous collaborator and friend – we had a wonderfully exciting conversation about *Piers Plowman*. I hope that this essay will speak to his transforming work on that allegorical poem, but also to his interest in allegorical hermeneutics and his suspicion of its Reformation opponents.

In the essay I will be taking a hard look at what we mean by medieval "allegorical narrative." This phrase usefully foregrounds the elements of imaginative figuration and narrative diegesis to be found in these texts. However, many readers have used the term "allegory" synonymously with it, and in long-standing literary-critical practice the two usages seem to be substantially interchangeable. As we will further see, the word "allegory" is also locked into the history of the theorization of the mode. For these reasons, I will keep the two terms in play.

I will be asking three questions. First, why is allegorical narrative/allegory still so often associated with a negatively-loaded notion of obscurity? This obscurity is usually assumed to be a form of purposive esotericism, intended to keep certain kinds of reader out. Of course it is true that there are some medieval texts and commentators that subscribe to a hermetic or "gatekeeping" view of allegorical composition and hermeneutics;[2] but

---

[1] My warmest thanks to Rita Copeland, Mary Franklin-Brown, Simon Goldhill, Sarah Kay, Michael Silk, Sebastian Sobecki, David Wallace, and Nicholas Watson for advice, shared texts, critique and some crucial corrections.

[2] See Peter T. Struck, "Allegory and Ascent in Neoplatonism," in *The Cambridge Companion to Allegory*, ed. Rita Copeland and Peter T. Struck (Cambridge:

should we read all medieval narrative allegory in light of it? I will suggest not. This first question is almost certainly linked to a second one: is it helpful to describe narrative allegory as structured around a binary polarity that opposes, on the one hand, the languages of diegesis, figuration, indirection or obscurity, and, on the other hand, the languages of elucidation and explication? It is true that a polarity of this sort, along with a recognition of the pervasive presence of glossatory practices in medieval culture more generally, has in recent decades proved a productive hermeneutic in discussions of these texts.[3] Nevertheless, it may be that the critical emphases encouraged by this polarity have had the effect of distorting our sense of the texts they have been used to analyze; in this essay I will be putting this polarized view of narrative allegory under the spotlight. Finally, these theories may have helped to reinforce the idea that the texts we have called allegorical narratives or allegories do indeed constitute a recognizable and cohesive medieval textual genre. I will be asking if this is actually the case.

If we think of the medieval texts that are usually described by modern readers as narrative allegories, it is not clear that their dominant structure opposes figuration and obscurity to commentary and elucidation. I have in mind such varied texts as the *Consolatio Philosophiae*, the *Cosmographia*, *De planctu Naturae*, the *Roman de la rose*, *Perlesvaus*, the *Commedia*, the *Mirouer des simples ames*, the *Pèlerinage de vie humaine*, the *Remede de Fortune*, *Piers Plowman* and the *House of Fame*. Rather, I suggest that what links these texts is their foregrounding of features such as multi-discursivity, several kinds of narrative, figural variety, conceptual interplay or dialogism. These texts are characterized by the intersection and overlap, but also opposition, not of two but of several different types of discourse or voice, some present, some implied. They can contain a wide variety of narrative, figurative and imaginative structures; they use their different formal dimensions to make innovative connections and self-commentaries, all the while also being marked by gaps, lacunae and the manifestations of incompletion. These texts are prismatic – that is, linguistically and conceptually contrastive and conversational. If it is helpful to describe them as "allegorical," I believe that the term should be understood in this capacious sense.[4]

If we do understand narrative allegory in this inclusive sense, then the category relates not only to medieval or early modern texts, but also to

---

Cambridge University Press, 2010), pp. 65–68; also Copeland and Struck's Introduction to the volume, p. 3.

[3] See pp. 89–90 below.

[4] For a fuller explanation of this view with references, see my *Arts of Disruption: Allegory and* Piers Plowman (Oxford: Oxford University Press, 2020), pp. 2, 5–16. For a recent allegory bibliography, see Vladimir Brljak, "Introduction: Allegory Past and Present," in *Allegory Studies: Contemporary Perspectives*, ed. Vladimir Brljak (New York: Routledge, 2021), pp. 1–40, at pp. 2–3.

works from other periods. Narrative allegory is a metamorphic and various phenomenon, as alive in modernity as it was in the Middle Ages. It includes works as diverse as *Gulliver's Travels*, "O rose, thou art sick," *Bleak House*, *Moby Dick*, *Before the Law*, *The Crying of Lot 49* and "Sunday Morning." Indeed, given that the characteristics I have mentioned can be found in many kinds of writing (again, either overtly present or implied), we might fairly ask if this is an identifiable category at all. I would argue that it is, although I agree with those who think that allegorical narrative/allegory is best thought of not as a genre but as a mode of textuality that can appear in different generic forms.[5] There are equivalent modes in the visual arts. Understood in this sense, narrative allegory – a prismatic form of textuality – is any kind of diegetic and figurative text that makes an issue out of the polysemousness and intersectionality of language, along with the conceptual conjunctions, links, contrasts, polarities and clashes that they enable.

Nevertheless, a substantial, but post-medieval, tradition of readers has claimed that there is also a more specific genre of writing which can be called allegorical narrative or allegory. This proposed genre is associated with a narrower group of late antique, medieval and early modern literary and philosophical texts, a group that nevertheless usually includes those cited above. Although this genre is recognized to have an (increasingly depleted) legacy in later centuries, its heyday has been said to be the later Middle Ages – famously, for Jacob Burckhardt and Johan Huizinga, this period was defined by the existence of this type of writing and the thought it was considered to presuppose.[6] Descriptions or definitions of the proposed genre are various. One tradition identifies it with the figure of personification;[7] another describes it in terms of its use of "extended metaphor";[8] another has located it at the confluence of the languages of figuration and the

---

[5] See Gordon Teskey, *Allegory and Violence* (Ithaca, N.Y.: Cornell University Press, 1996), p. 10, and references.

[6] See Vladimir Brljak, "The Age of Allegory," *Studies in Philology* 114 (2017), 697–719; "Introduction: Allegory Past and Present," p. 6; also Katharine Breen, *Machines of the Mind: Personification in Medieval Literature* (Chicago: University of Chicago Press, 2021), pp. 16–19.

[7] On this view and its first expression in the early modern period, see Michael Silk, "Invoking the Other: Allegory in Theory, from Demetrius to de Man," in *Allegory Studies*, ed. Brljak, pp. 41–65, at pp. 46–52; also C. S. Lewis, *The Allegory of Love: A Study in Medieval Tradition* (Oxford: Clarendon Press, 1936), pp. 44–111; Jill Mann, "Langland and Allegory," Morton W. Bloomfield Lectures on Medieval Literature 2 (Kalamazoo, Mich.: Medieval Institute Publications, 1992); Jon Whitman, *Allegory. The Dynamics of an Ancient and Medieval Technique* (Cambridge, Mass.: Harvard University Press, 1987). For a philosophical reading of personification, see Breen, *Machines of the Mind*.

[8] See Rosemond Tuve, *Allegorical Imagery: Some Mediaeval Books and Their Posterity* (Princeton, N.J.: Princeton University Press, 1966), pp. 3–55; also Teskey, *Allegory and Violence*, p. 56; Copeland and Struck, "Introduction," *The Cambridge Companion to Allegory*, pp. 1–11, at p. 2, n. 1.

90 NICOLETTE ZEEMAN

gloss. Although these descriptions overlap and influence each other,[9] it is the third that will primarily interest me here.

The modern critics who describe this late antique and medieval genre of narrative allegory in terms of this binary opposition locate it at the intersection of "myth" and elucidation, the indirect and the explicit, the concealed and the revealed. It has been subtly described as a balancing act; an interplay between "compositional and interpretative strains";[10] or as a frictional encounter between discourses that (even when they have a powerfully literal dimension) are narratival, troped, oblique or somehow opaque, and other discourses that attempt to exert interpretative control through explicatory, analytical or preceptive commentary.[11] Michael Murrin puts it flatly: "the poet expresses a truth ... through the medium of tropological figures[;] the learned auditor, knowing how to interpret this kind of language, sees through the veil."[12] Silk puts it more carefully: "we need to put special weight on allegory's claim to *hidden* significance."[13] Gordon Teskey has provocatively described the work of interpretation in narrative allegory as the imposition of coherence on narrative incoherence ("allegory ... in essence" is "violence emerging from noise"), but his underlying assumption remains clear: "in an allegory interpretation is an intended and to some extent managed effect."[14]

But is figural obscurity necessarily an essential component of *De planctu Naturae*, the *Roman de la rose*, or *Piers Plowman*? Is the primary structure here really a binary opposition between the figured or opaque and the elucidatory? These texts are not notably covert or obscure. "Despite the fact that most writing about allegory assumes its figurative or hidden meaning is what matters," says Masha Raskolnikov, it "is not ... consistently concerned

---

9 It seems possible, for example, that the binary view of narrative allegory has encouraged reductively binary versions of the other two (now seen as personification and abstraction, metaphor and referent, even "shell and kernel").

10 Whitman, *Allegory*, p. 9, and passim for many eloquent analyses. For Angus Fletcher allegory is characterized by "a peculiar doubleness of intention[:] while it can ... get along without interpretation, it becomes much richer and more interesting if given interpretation"; see *Allegory: The Theory of a Symbolic Mode* (repr. Princeton, N.J.: Princeton University Press, 2012), p. 7; also pp. 2–10.

11 Teskey, *Allegory and Violence*, pp. 3, 5, 19.

12 Michael Murrin, *The Veil of Allegory: Some Notes towards a Theory of Allegorical Rhetoric in the English Renaissance* (Chicago: University of Chicago Press, 1969), p. 70. Compare Suzanne Conklin Akbari, *Seeing through the Veil: Optical Theory and Medieval Allegory* (Toronto: University of Toronto Press, 2004), pp. 9, 11.

13 Silk, "Invoking the Other," p. 64.

14 Teskey, *Allegory and Violence*, p. 74, and Gordon Teskey, "Langland's Golden Bough," *Yearbook of Langland Studies* 25 (2011), 189–96. Compare Jason Crawford, who describes allegory in terms of a dialectical relation between "history" and the "immaterial order of the idea," or "narrative" and "static meaning," in *Allegory and Enchantment: An Early Modern Poetics* (Oxford: Oxford University Press, 2017), pp. 10–18.

with obscure meanings."[15] Indeed, these texts are often vividly immediate and graphically overt. This does not mean that they are never challenging, puzzling or difficult – they often are. But if they are, this is perhaps not because they are structurally or generically required to be so, but because they are doing challenging, puzzling, and difficult conceptual work. And, in this respect, they are no different from any other hard-working literary text. And what about the language of the gloss? It is true that these texts sometimes use the language of commentary to clarify, nuance, or critique their narratives, ecphrases and figuration: the contrast between the figured or opaque and the elucidatory certainly appears here. But it is also true that these texts sometimes use narratives, ecphrases and figuration to clarify, nuance, or critique the language of commentary; and of course their diegetic and troped forms sometimes talk to and comment on each other without any reference to a gloss at all. The dialogue between figured form and overt interpretation, in other words, is only one of many discursive interactions going on here.

Behind all these questions is a larger one: would medieval writers and readers have recognized the group of texts that modern readers call medieval narrative allegory as a distinct genre? If not, in what sense can modern readers group them as one? In a companion piece, I will be revisiting the relationship between medieval narrative and the figure of personification/*prosopopoeia*; it may be that that "prosopopoeiac narrative" does indeed represent a textual genealogy of sorts, though it may not be helpful to call this allegory. Below, I will in passing discuss whether medieval thinkers would have classed a group of texts in terms of their use of "extended metaphor." Here, my project is to ask whether medieval thinkers would have identified a group of texts in terms of a binary that opposes diegesis, figuration, indirection, and obscurity to the language of explication; and whether – and if so, how – they would have associated this with the terminology of *allegoria*/allegory.

~

The binarizing view of narrative allegory has a long and tenacious history. Among medieval and early modern scholars, the view has been connected to the attempt to read narrative allegory through two bodies of classical and medieval theory, both associated with the Latin term *allegoria* and its vernacular equivalents. One is rhetorical and the other hermeneutic. Scholars argue that at some point these two bodies of theory merged, jointly producing a polarity that opposes the diegetic, the figured, and the obscure to the glossatory. They have also claimed that, in parallel, there was a merger

---

[15] Masha Raskolnikov, *Body against Soul: Gender and Sowlehele in Middle English Allegory* (Columbus, Ohio: Ohio State University Press, 2009), p. 5. See also Richard Goulet and Gilbert Dahan, "Présentation," in their edited *Allégorie des poètes, allégorie des philosophes: Etudes sur la poétique et l'herméneutique de l'allégorie de l'Antiquité à la Réforme* (Paris: Vrin, 2005), pp. 5–8, at p. 7.

92 NICOLETTE ZEEMAN

of the two usages of the term *allegoria*, the one rhetorical and the other hermeneutic. This combined notion of *allegoria* underlies many modern readers' binary understanding of what they call medieval allegorical narrative/ allegory. Scholars are undoubtedly right that these two bodies of theory are hugely influential and that there was real interference and overlap between them over the classical and medieval periods. Nevertheless, I will be asking if a full "merger" of the two theories, and, even more important, of the two usages of *allegoria*, took place. For if not, we are making a mistake in using the term *allegoria* (narrowly understood) and its vernacular equivalents to describe a genre that supposedly includes texts as diverse as *De planctu Naturae*, the *Roman de la rose*, the *Commedia*, and *Piers Plowman*.

In the next pages I will look at the classical and medieval conceptualization and terminology of *allegoria*, first considering the two separate traditions and then reviewing the evidence for a merger.

Rhetorical *allegoria*, also sometimes called *permutatio* or *inversio*, is the trope that entails saying something other than is meant; this can be by means of metaphor or, provoking much later critical discussion, irony.[16] I will focus on the metaphorical dimension of the trope, though this is not to deny the role played by irony in allegorical narrative, especially when it is more capaciously defined. The rhetorical description of this trope that was most widely known in the Middle Ages occurs in the anonymous *Ad Herennium*, attributed in the Middle Ages to Cicero, where it is defined as an ornament denoting "aliud verbis aliud sententia" ("one thing by the letter of the words, but another in meaning") and named *permutatio*.[17] Not so well known in the Middle Ages was Cicero's *Orator*, which uses the term *allegoria* and notes that the trope is made up of a series of metaphors;[18] also not well known was Book 8 of Quintilian's *Institutio oratoria*, which says that *allegoria* or *inversio* "presents one thing by its words and either a different or sometimes even a contrary thing by its sense" ("aut aliud verbis, aliud sensu ostendit, aut etiam interim contrarium").[19] Very well disseminated in the Middle Ages, however, was the fourth-century grammarian Donatus, for whom in *allegoria* "something else

---

[16] The Greek term *allēgoria* is already used in this sense: see Whitman, *Allegory*, pp. 263–64; Rita Copeland, "Allegory and Rhetoric," in *The Oxford Handbook to Allegory*, ed. David Parry (Oxford: Oxford University Press, forthcoming); also below. I am much indebted to Copeland's cogent and insightful essay.

[17] Pseudo-Cicero, *Rhetorica ad Herennium*, tr. Harry Caplan (Cambridge, Mass.: Harvard University Press, 1954), 4.34.46.

[18] Cicero, *Orator*, in *Brutus. Orator*, tr. H. M. Hubbell (Cambridge, Mass.: Harvard University Press, 1962), pp. 295–509 (27.94); also *De oratore*, in *De oratore Book III, De Fato, Paradoxa Stoicorum, De partitione oratoria*, tr. H. Rackham (Cambridge, Mass.: Harvard University Press, 1942), pp. 3–185 (3.41.166).

[19] Quintilian, *Institutio oratoria*, in *The Orator's Education*, ed. and tr. Donald A. Russell, 5 vols. (Cambridge, Mass.: Harvard University Press, 2001), 8.6.44.

MEDIEVAL ALLEGORICAL NARRATIVE

is signified than is said."[20] Rhetorical theorists often note that the trope runs the risk of obscurity (*aenigma*), though it does not necessarily involve it. As Rita Copeland has made clear, in all these early rhetorical and grammatical contexts, *allegoria* is a trope, not a type of text or a complete text.[21]

However, this is not how some passages from these texts have been read by modern critics, in particular Cicero's statement that *allegoria* results from "a series of several metaphors" ("continuae plures tran[s]lationes"),[22] and Quintilian's observation that metaphorical *allegoria* "generally consists of a succession of metaphors" ("fit … plerumque continuatis translationibus").[23] Jon Whitman, for example, claims that early on *allegoria* had come to denote "the *compositional* technique of creating an allegorical text." Later he cites Cicero and Quintilian on *allegoria* as a series of metaphors, and comments that "the sense of a sustained rhetorical composition retains a firm hold on rhetorical theory after Quintilian."[24] However, when we look at the theorists' examples of metaphorical *allegoria*, it is not clear that this is the case. The *Ad Herennium*, for example, gives: "For when dogs act the part of wolves, to what guardian, pray, are we going to entrust our herds of cattle?" Cicero has: "Neither will I endure that I make shipwreck, / Like the Achaean fleet in days gone by, / A second time upon the self-same rock."[25] Quintilian does illustrate the trope with the metaphor that shapes a complete Horatian ode ("in which he represents the state as a ship, the civil wars as waves and storms, and peace and concord as the harbour"), but his other examples are mostly short sections of longer texts.[26] Donatus exemplifies the trope from *Georgics* 2.542: "'and now it is time to unharness the steaming necks of the horses,' that is, 'to finish up the poem.'"[27] These theorists are discussing a trope, not a genre of textuality or a complete text, and medieval readers seem to have known this. In the *Poetria nova*, for example, Geoffrey of Vinsauf discusses transferred or metaphorical uses of words and notes that these can be multiplied, turning them into a

---

[20] *Donati ars grammatica*, in *Grammatici latini*, ed. Heinrich Keil, 7 vols. (Leipzig: Teubner, 1857–80), 4.353–402 (3.6); tr. in *Medieval Grammar and Rhetoric: Language Arts and Literary Theory, AD 300–1475*, ed. Rita Copeland and Ineke Sluiter (Oxford: Oxford University Press, 2009), p. 96.

[21] Copeland, "Allegory and Rhetoric."

[22] Cicero, *Orator*, 27.94; also *De oratore*, 3.41.166. The description of the trope as "extended metaphor" is available in Aristotle, *Poetics*, ed. Stephen Halliwell, tr. W. Hamilton Fyfe, in *Aristotle, Poetics. Longinus, On the Sublime. Demetrius, On Style* (Cambridge, Mass.: Harvard University Press, 1995), pp. 28–142 (at 22, 1458a); *Demetrius, On Style*, ed. Doreen C. Innes, based on the translation of W. Rhys Roberts, ibid., pp. 309–525 (at 99–102); see also *Ad Herennium*, 4.34.46: "a number of metaphors originating in a similarity in the mode of expression are set together."

[23] Quintilian, *Institutio oratoria*, 8.6.44.

[24] Whitman, *Allegory*, pp. 264–65.

[25] *Ad Herennium*, 4.34.46; Cicero, *De oratore*, 3.41.166.

[26] *Institutio oratoria*, 8.6.44–45, referring to Horace Ode 1.14; also 8.6.45–59.

[27] *Donati ars grammatica*, 3.6; tr. *Medieval Grammar*, ed. Copeland and Sluiter, p. 96.

"scema verbi" ("figure of words").[28] The passages from Cicero and Quintilian cited above may have been read differently after the Middle Ages, when they may have been increasingly understood as allusions to a mode of writing or even a genre that had now begun to be called allegory – and to be described in terms of continued metaphor (see below). But there is no evidence that this is how rhetorical *allegoria* was understood in the Middle Ages.

The second classical and medieval use of the term *allegoria* is hermeneutic and connected to practices of *allegoresis*, whereby texts are read with a view to identifying other, sometimes, but not necessarily, non-overt levels of sense. This *allegoria* (Greek ἀλληγορία, *allēgoria*) constitutes a much thornier topic. It denotes primarily the meanings to be extracted from a text, whether they are only indirectly or implicitly expressed, whether they are thought to be somehow signaled or hidden, and whether they are thought to be intended by the author or not.[29] The term comes, by association, to be linked to the "allegorical" technique of extracting these meanings, and also to allegorical senses intentionally placed in a text, which means that it does have an implicitly rhetorical dimension. On the one hand, this *allegoria* allows for the possibility of textual opacity, "veiling" and even hermeticism; on the other hand, in many contexts the allegorical meanings revealed by commentary are not necessarily especially difficult or recherché, and might even be quite traditional or commonplace. Although there certainly is a medieval tradition of claiming that some texts are composed with an allegorical sense in order to keep out a denigrated class of readers, the hermeneutic notion of *allegoria* does not necessarily assume that the allegorical sense is obscure. For most of the Middle Ages hermeneutic *allegoria* is primarily associated with the reading and interpretation of Christian scriptural and religious writings, where it is used both as a general term and as a sub-category of interpretation that elucidates particular types of scriptural meaning within a multi-leveled wider practice.[30] Nevertheless, a second version of interpretative *allegoria* is also found in the medieval reading of antique literature and myth, in particular the verse tradition of classical *poetria*, an association that may have been encouraged by the links between classical *poetria* and myth, that is, non-Christian versions of theurgy and the supernatural. Later in the Middle Ages, hermeneutic *allegoria* is also used to read medieval Latin and vernacular

---

28 Geoffrey of Vinsauf, *Poetria nova*, in E. Faral, *Les Arts poétiques du XIIe et XIIIe siècle* (Paris: Champion, 1924), pp. 194–262 (line 937); *Poetria nova*, tr. M. F. Nims, rev. ed. (Toronto: Pontifical Institute of Mediaeval Studies, 2010), pp. 49–50. Also Matthew of Vendôme, *The Art of Versification*, tr. Aubrey E. Galyon (Ames, Iowa: Iowa State Press, 1980), 3.43.

29 These notions of *allegoria*, also associated with the Greek term *hyponoia*, predate the rhetorical notion of *allegoria*: see Copeland and Struck, "Introduction," pp. 2–4; Copeland, "Allegory and Rhetoric."

30 See Gilbert Dahan, *L'Exégèse chrétienne de la Bible en Occident médiévale, XIIe–XIVe siècle* (Paris: du Cerf, 1999); *Medieval Literary Theory and Criticism c. 1100–c. 1375. The Commentary Tradition*, ed. A. J. Minnis and A. B. Scott, with the assistance of David Wallace (Oxford: Clarendon Press, 1988), pp. 65–112, 383.

MEDIEVAL ALLEGORICAL NARRATIVE

mythographical and philosophizing texts – texts often, but not exclusively, written in imitation of classical or Latin *poetria*.[31]

This hermeneutic version of *allegoria* also brings with it a whole set of views about the characteristics and formal qualities of the texts that supposedly require this "extractive" or elucidatory reading. Over the course of the Middle Ages, scriptural hermeneutics brings its own distinctive focus on the pluri-dimensionality of the Bible. In grammatical and rhetorical contexts more generally, the figured, oblique, inexplicit and even obscure textual structures that are thought often to invite commentary or *allegoresis* are analyzed in increasingly sophisticated forms, and described as *figurae* ("figures"), *fabulae* ("fables," "[fictional] narratives"), textual *integumenta* ("coverings"), and *involucra* ("wrappings," "veilings"). This vocabulary, along with the archival and glossatory hermeneutic practices that underlie it, is frequently found in medieval descriptions of philosophical and literary texts, and it is undeniable that these hermeneutic practices (along with their inevitable polarity of "myth and interpretation") play an important role in the composition of these texts. But we should not assume that these terms and practices map onto a supposed genre of allegorical narrative/allegory, or that they authorize us to identify such a genre: for in fact they have a powerful impact on medieval rhetorical and compositional invention more generally, imbuing it with a radical sense of the creative potential of the diegetic, figural, or conversational "gloss" in the literary reworking of prior texts. Medieval literature is in many ways a masterclass in the creative and subversive work that can be done with commentary; but it also reveals that there are no limits to the forms that this commentary can take. If much medieval literature revels in the interplay of the narrative and the *glose*, it also revels in undermining the distinction between the two.[32]

Despite the huge impact of the practices associated with allegorical hermeneutics on medieval imaginative and fictive writing more generally, the term *allegoria* is still used in these contexts to describe writing primarily in terms of its possession of an allegorical sense – whether this is with a view to reading and interpretation, or with a view to composition, for others to read and interpret. *Allegoria* thus continues to describe a particular feature of texts: it is not used to describe imaginative and fictive writing more generally, or a subgroup of it, or a whole text.

Because of this, modern readers have argued that at some point these two usages merged: only when these two usages were linked in some kind of parallel relationship did they provide what looked like a plausible version of the polarity that had become so important to definitions of the supposed

---

[31] For earlier examples, see *Medieval Literary Theory*, ed. Minnis and Scott, pp. 113–64.

[32] Rita Copeland, *Rhetoric, Hermeneutics, and Translation in the Middle Ages: Academic Traditions and Vernacular Texts* (Cambridge: Cambridge University Press, 1991); Douglas Kelly, *The Art of Medieval French Romance* (Madison, Wis.: University of Wisconsin Press, 1992), pp. 15–67.

96   NICOLETTE ZEEMAN

genre of allegorical narrative. On the one side was the narratival, figured, inexplicit or obscure material of rhetorical "other speaking" and the text subject to allegorical interpretation; on the other side, whether actually present or implied and assumed, was a supposedly elucidatory discourse that unpacked narrative diegesis, rhetorical figures, and the covert text. For this process to be complete, of course, these two usages of *allegoria* not only had to fall into alignment with each other but also to shift so that they now denoted a style of writing, a genre of textuality or even a complete text – as the equivalent English term does in Thomas Wright's 1846 reference to "the spirited and extremely popular political allegory of the *Vision of Piers Ploughman*."[33]

But what evidence do we have that this happened in the Middle Ages? There is undoubtedly all kinds of evidence for conceptual interplay and overlap; but to what degree does this affect the term *allegoria*? Copeland and Struck are clear that the problem is the survival of two distinct usages of the term: a Latin tradition "muddied by the common terminology inherited from antiquity" in which a single term denoted two different things; Copeland speaks of "various attempts to resolve [the] conceptual difference" but also cites Isidore of Seville who includes both definitions in different places (though he only names the rhetorical one, calqued into Latin as *alieniloquium*, "other speaking").[34] This remains a vast and contested area of study. In what follows I cannot provide conclusive evidence but will review some classic texts that have been cited in support of a merger; I want simply to point to the continued instability of, and frictions between, the various usages of the terminology of *allegoria*.

Glen Most, Brljak, and Silk document forms of conceptual elision of the two theories associated with *allēgoria* in Greek antiquity, citing Aristotle, Demetrius, and the grammarian Heraclitus.[35] They cite Aristotle's discussion in the *Poetics* of the use of clear and obscure language, though he does not here use the terminology of *allēgoria*, nor does he refer to explication or commentary. Demetrius uses the term in a rhetorical sense: "allegory is also impressive, particularly in threats, for example that of Dionysius, 'their cicadas will sing from the ground'"; although he notes the different interpretations to which the figure is open, he does not here use the term *allēgoria* to describe them. In charting Homer's many usages of *allēgoria*, on the other hand, Heraclitus focuses on the

---

[33] See *OED*, s.v. "allegory, n.," sense 2.
[34] Copeland and Struck, "Introduction," p. 4; Copeland, "Allegory and Rhetoric"; Copeland argues that "outside the precincts of Scripture or profound philosophical commentary, there was no need to balk at the doubleness of the term." See Isidore of Seville, *Etymologiarum sive originum libri XX*, ed. W. M. Lindsay (Oxford: Clarendon Press, 1957), 1.37.22, 26; 6.1.10. Brljak, in contrast, alludes to the "conceptual flexibility" of the term ("Introduction: Allegory Past and Present," pp. 4–5).
[35] Glen W. Most, "Hellenistic Allegory and Early Imperial Rhetoric," in *Cambridge Companion to Allegory*, pp. 26–38; Brljak, "Introduction: Allegory Past and Present," p. 4 and n. iv; Silk, "Invoking the Other," p. 44. Also Jean Pépin, "Allegoria," *Enciclopedia Dantesca*, ed. Umberto Bosco (Rome: Istituto della Enciclopedia Italiana, 1970), pp. 151–65, at p. 151.

MEDIEVAL ALLEGORICAL NARRATIVE 97

hermeneutical, but acknowledges its rhetorical dimension, as he notes both allegorical sense and Homer's role in creating it: "In each book I will use subtle learning to expound the allegorical statements about the gods" ("ἐν ἑκάστῃ ῥαψῳδίᾳ διὰ λεπτῆς ἐπιστήμης ἐπιδεικνύντι τὰ περὶ θεῶν ἠλληγορημένα"); "Homer has not used allegory covertly here, or in a way demanding a certain subtle interpretation [λεπτῆς τινος εἰκασίας]."[36] These are rich examples and must indicate conceptual cross fertilization; but do they illustrate the conflation of the two usages of the terminology of *allēgoria*? That seems less clear.

Whitman makes the case for the elision of the two usages taking place in the twelfth century and being illustrated by Bernardus Silvestris's philosophical personification narrative, the *Cosmographia*: "as these two traditions increasingly influence each other, their strategies gradually interact and finally transform the original dilemmas." As Whitman writes, what he initially calls two "allegorical traditions" turns into "allegory," a single noun, defined by the over-arching characteristic of "obliquity."[37] This is a period in which exciting new forms of "integumentalist" philosophical literature are emerging, forms that may well include both rhetorical and hermeneutic *allegoria*. But would the authors or readers of these texts have described the texts themselves as *allegoriae*? Bernardus does not use this term to describe the *Cosmographia*. Nor does it appear in the commentary on the first six books of the *Aeneid* attributed to Bernardus, where the author instead explains that Virgil teaches with an *integumentum*, "a type of vivid representation that wraps a perception of the truth under a fictive narrative, whence it is called a 'wrapping'" ("genus demonstrationis sub fabulosa narratione veritatis involvens intellectum, unde etiam dicitur involucrum").[38] Alain of Lille similarly does not use *allegoria* to speak of his philosophical *De planctu Naturae*, although in the prologue to his philosophical *Anticlaudianus*, he comments that the more elementary literal and moral senses are for the young, while the "keener subtlety of the allegory" sharpens the intellect of the advanced reader ("acutior allegoriae subtilitas proficientem acuet intellectum").[39] Here he is using *allegoria* in a strictly hermeneutic sense, to denote one the senses that can be extracted

---

[36] Aristotle, *Poetics*, 22 (1458a–b); *Demetrius, On Style*, 99–102; Heraclitus, *Homeric Problems*, ed. and tr. Donald A. Russell and David Konstan (Leiden: Brill, 2005), 6.2, 29.4; see also 5.3–6.2; 24.1–7; 29.4–7; 37.4–6, 70.

[37] Whitman, *Allegory*, pp. 8–10, 266–67 (see also pp. 3–5, 205, 221–23). See also Teskey, *Allegory and Violence*, p. 122: "There were in antiquity two distinct notions of allegory that would be fused in the Middle Ages and have seldom been kept apart since."

[38] *The First Commentary on the First Six Books of the* Aeneid *of Vergil commonly attributed to Bernardus Silvestris*, ed. Julian Ward Jones and Elizabeth Frances Jones (Lincoln, Nebr.: University of Nebraska Press, 1977), Prologue, p. 3.

[39] Alan of Lille, *Anticlaudianus*, Prologus (prose) 4, in *Literary Works*, ed. and tr. Winthrop Wetherbee (Cambridge, Mass.: Harvard University Press, 2013); in *De planctu* Alan does use the terms *integumentum* and "integumentale involucrum," but to refer to local figures (8.24, 32).

98   NICOLETTE ZEEMAN

from the text. Evidence such as this does not seem to suggest that the two usages of *allegoria* are merging and evolving to denote an identifiable genre of text. On the contrary, a text such as the *Compendium rhetorice* (*Compendium of Rhetoric*), written by a Cistercian in Paris in 1332, suggests that writers in the later Middle Ages are still happy to accept that *allegoria* is a figure "quo aliud in verbi[s] et aliud in sentencia demonstratur" ("by which one thing is represented in words and another in meaning"), while also accepting that the main use of the same term is in reading the scriptures, where it denotes the hermeneutic "allegorical sense."[40]

It has been suggested that the elision of the two usages of *allegoria* in fact takes place among the classicizing poets, writers, and theorists working in Italy and France in the later thirteenth and first half of the fourteenth centuries: Dante Alighieri, Petrarch, Giovanni Boccaccio, and the commentators Giovanni del Virgilio and Pierre Bersuire. Much has been made of these Italian writers' arguments for the deep connections between the schools-derived categories of *poetria*, *philosophia* and *theologia*, and their application of these categories to works of vernacular writing, including those of living writers.[41] These arguments involve the development of earlier schools theories about the allegorical interpretation of *poetria* into ambitious ideas about the moral and philosophical meanings (*allegoriae*) to be extracted from Latin and vernacular literature, whether verse or prose, whether written by others or by themselves. The possibility that these theories might relate to the supposed genre of allegorical narrative looks as if it might be supported by the fact that several of these writers compose texts that modern readers have identified with the genre.

Nevertheless, sweeping claims about the innovations of these poets and theorists may have had the effect of blurring our sense of their use of the term *allegoria* – and our understanding of the history of our supposed genre. These Italian writers certainly describe "poetry" using both hermeneutic and rhetorical notions of *allegoria*. Early on in the *Convivio* Dante offers to explain "la vera sentenza" ("the true meaning"), which is "nascosa sotto figura d'allegoria" ("hidden beneath the figure of allegory"). Dante's rather loose use of the term *figura* here indicates that he is using the term *allegoria* in a rhetorical and tropological sense (he may also understand the meaning to be elicited from it by readerly interpretation as a form of hermeneutic *allegoria*, but he does not say so). However, elsewhere in the same text he also repeatedly uses the terminology of *allegoria* in a hermeneutic sense, as when he distinguishes the "esposizione ... litterale" ("literal exposition") from the "[esposizione] allegorica," or when he explains first the literal sense and then "la sua allegoria, cioè la nascosa veritade" ("its allegory, that is, the

---

40 See James J. Murphy, *Rhetoric in the Middle Ages: A History of Rhetorical Theory from St. Augustine to the Renaissance* (Berkeley, Calif.: University of California Press, 1974), p. 238, citing Bibliothèque Nationale MS Lat. 16252, fol. 24v.

41 See Pépin, "Allegoria;" *Medieval Literary Theory*, ed. Minnis and Scott, chapters 9 and 10.

hidden truth").[42] Dante seems to have no problem in using these two distinct versions of *allegoria* side by side. Both here and in the *Epistle to Can Grande* (in the early parts attributed to the poet by most readers)[43] Dante also speaks of the "allegorical sense" of the theologians and the poets. Indeed, the *Epistle* only uses the terminology of *allegoria* in a hermeneutic sense, sometimes speaking of the "literal sense, [and] the second, allegorical one," sometimes of looking "ad literam" ("to the letter") and "ad allegoriam" ("to the allegory").[44] Jean Pépin and Albert Ascoli argue that it is Dante's originality to have elided ("deliberately blurr[ed]") hermeneutic and rhetorical *allegoria* – the text as object of interpretation and as form of expression; they may be right, but Dante does not use the vocabulary of *allegoria* to say this.[45] Copeland puts it clearly: "Dante may speak of the 'allegory' of his poem, but that is not the same as naming the poem itself 'allegory' as a kind of literary 'style' … medieval poets do not seem to extend the name of the trope to encompass a certain poetic method."[46]

In one of his letters on *Familiar Matters* Petrarch describes Christ's parables in rhetorical terms, as "speech differing from the usual senses … *alieniloquium*, which, using a more common word, we call *allegoria*"; "it is," he goes on, "from a type of this speech that all poetry is woven" ("ex huiusce sermonis genere poetica omnis intexta est"). Petrarch's underlying assumptions about the figural and fictional nature of this rhetorical and poetic *allegoria* are clarified by logical opposition when he opposes it to the "bare truth" ("nuda veritas") and to "historical" speech.[47] Nevertheless, while there is no doubt real conceptual interference here, and Petrarch's allusion to "the senses" of the text may reflect the presence of ideas about hermeneutic *allegoria*, he does not here use the term to describe it. Boccaccio in his *Trattatello* in praise of Dante treads a similar line. He claims that "poets conceal the plain truth beneath many things which seem to be in opposition to it" ("li poeti sotto cose molto ad essa contrarie apparenti nascosero [la verità piana]"). Like Petrarch, he explains how the figured modes of the scriptures and poetry are the same, and notes that "this manner of speaking we call, to use a more common word, 'allegory'" ("il quale parlare noi con più usato

---

42 Dante, *Convivio: A Dual-Language Edition*, ed. and tr. Andrew Frisardi (Cambridge: Cambridge University Press, 2018), 1.2.17; 2.1.2; 2.1.8; 2.1.15.

43 *Medieval Literary Theory*, ed. Minnis and Scott, pp. 440–45.

44 *Convivio*, 2.1.4–5; *Epistle to Can Grande*, in *Dantis Alagherii Epistolae. The Letters of Dante*, ed. Paget Toynbee, 2nd ed. (Oxford: Clarendon Press, 1966), Epistola 10.7; my translation.

45 Pépin, "Allegoria," pp. 163–64; Albert R. Ascoli, "Dante and Allegory," in *Cambridge Companion to Allegory*, pp. 128–35, citation at p. 134.

46 Copeland, "Allegory and Rhetoric."

47 Francesco Petrarca, *Le Familiari*, ed. Vittorio Rossi, 4 vols. (Florence: G. C. Sansoni, 1933–41), 10.4.2; 10.4.22; 10.4.31 (my translation). For Aristotelian logical teaching on how to specify terms through their opposites, see Zeeman, *Arts of Disruption*, pp. 121–36.

100   NICOLETTE ZEEMAN

vocabolo chiamiamo 'allegoria'").[48] Once again, the remit of the rhetorical
terminology of *allegoria* may here be expanding to allude to something more
like a type of writing characterized by saying one thing and meaning another,
rather than just a local trope; nevertheless, it is not clear that we are seeing
any conflation of the rhetorical and hermeneutic senses of the word. In books
14 and 15 of his *Genealogia deorum gentilium* Boccaccio does not use the
rhetorical trope *allegoria* to speak of poetry, though he is clearly thinking in
loosely compositional terms. He speaks of poetry's "integumenta fictionum"
("coverings of fictions") and remarks that "whatever is placed as under a veil
and ... exquisitely expressed is pure poetry" ("mera poesis est, quicquid sub
velamento componitur et expositur exquisite"). Later, citing Virgil, Boccaccio
comments, "this is poetry from which the sap of philosophy runs pure,"
asking if anyone can believe "that he wrote such lines without some meaning
hidden beneath the superficial veil of myth" ("absque abscondito sub fabuloso
velamine intellectu scripsisse");[49] but he does not, as we might have expected,
use *allegoria* in a hermeneutic sense. Across his different writings, then, we
do not see Boccaccio conflating the rhetorical and hermeneutic usages of
allegoria; and neither for him nor for Petrarch does the term *allegoria* denote
a textual genre or a complete text.[50]

The early commentators on Dante's *Commedia* also read it allegorically.
Guido da Pisa uses a version of the figure of the "shell and kernel" to describe
hermeneutic *allegoria* when he speaks of the *Commedia* as "written within
and without, as it contains both literal and allegorical senses" ("scripta dicitur
intus et foris, quia continet non solum licteram, sed etiam allegoriam").[51]
Boccaccio's *Esposizioni* of the *Commedia* also systematically analyzes each

---

48   Boccaccio, *Trattatello in laude di Dante*, ed. Pier Giorgio Padoan, in *Tutte le opere*,
     gen. ed. Vittore Branca, vol. 3 (Florence: Arnoldo Mondadori, 1974), pp. 423–911;
     prima redazione 152; 154; translated in *Medieval Literary Theory*, ed. Minnis and
     Scott, pp. 497–98.
49   Boccaccio, *Die Proemia, Lib. XIV und Lib. XV, sowie die Conclusio der Genealogia
     deorum im Wortlaut des Originals des Laurenziana*, in *Boccaccio-Funde*, ed. Oskar
     Hecker (Braunschweig: George Westermann, 1902), pp. 159–299; XIV, cap. 7, cap.
     10; tr. in *Boccaccio on Poetry: Being the Preface and the Fourteenth and Fifteenth
     Books of Boccaccio's* Genealogia Deorum Gentilium, tr. Charles G. Osgood (repr.
     Indianapolis, Ind.: Bobbs-Merrill, 1956), pp. 42, 52–53.
50   Book 14 of *Genealogia* also contains a thoughtful discussion of obscurity, where
     Boccaccio says that, while poetry is sometimes obscure and requires hard
     interpretative work, it is not always so; his nuanced discussion counters Murrin's
     claim that for the Italians "poetry *essentially* requires obscurity"; see *Genealogia
     deorum* XIV, cap. 12; tr. Osgood, pp. 58–62; Michael Murrin, "Renaissance Allegory
     from Petrarch to Spenser," in *Cambridge Companion to Allegory*, pp. 162–76, at p.
     163.
51   See Guido da Pisa, *Expositiones et glose super Comediam Dantis, or Commentary on
     Dante's Inferno*, ed. Vincenzo Cioffari (Albany, N.Y.: State University of New York
     Press, 1974), prologue, p. 2; tr. in *Medieval Literary Theory*, ed. Minnis and Scott, p.
     470; on Guido, see pp. 445–49; on this figure, see Pépin, "Allegoria," pp. 156–57.

MEDIEVAL ALLEGORICAL NARRATIVE

canto first with an "esposizione litterale" and then an "esposizione allegorica."[52] Dante's son, Pietro Alighieri, defines the allegorical sense of the *Commedia* in terms of its fictionality, figuration and requirement for explication: this includes Dante's fictional descent into hell, narrated *mistice* ("figuratively"). Dante, he tells us, deals "with a real and an allegorical" hell ("de essentiali et allegorico").[53] Pietro also illustrates conceptual interplay, however, as he formulates his description of the poem in rhetorical and intentional terms, as "enclosed and hidden in its covering" ("in suo integumento clausum et absconsum"); as expressed "in figures and diverse rhetorical colours" ("sub figuris et coloribus diversimodis"); and, using the terminology of *allegoria*, "with a certain allegorical fiction, by analogy and type" ("cum allegorico quodam figmento, sub analogia et typo").[54] In another passage Pietro invokes rhetorical *allegoria*, now perhaps coming close to aligning rhetorical and hermeneutic versions of *allegoria*:

> Scribit ipse auctor aliqua ac multa sub allegorico intellectu; dicitur enim "allegoria" quasi "alieniloquium, ut cum lictera unum sonat et aliud intellegi debet," ut ecce dum sic Apostolus dicit ... "Scriptum est enim quomodo Habraam duos filios habuit, unum de ancilla, et unum de libera ... que sunt ita per allegoriam dicta. Hec enim sunt duo Testamenta, Vetus scilicet et Novum."

> The author writes things, indeed much, in the allegorical sense. "Allegory" is to be understood as an "other speaking, as when the letter says one thing and ought to be understood [as saying] another," as when the Apostle [Paul] ... says: "For it is written how Abraham had two sons, one by a bondwoman and one by a free woman ... these things are said through allegory. For these are the two Testaments, the Old and the New."[55]

And yet, even here I suggest we still see Pietro sliding between the two versions of *allegoria* (first hermeneutic, then rhetorical and then perhaps back to the hermeneutic?), rather than actually merging them.

Even amongst these later medieval Italians with their ambitious claims about the fundamentally figured and "allegorical" nature of poetry, the terminology of *allegoria* still swings between rhetorical and hermeneutic meanings. Posing the

---

[52] Boccaccio, *Esposizioni sopra la Comedia di Dante*, in *Tutte le opere di Giovanni Boccaccio*, gen. ed. Vittore Branca, vol. 6 (Florence: Arnoldo Mondadori, 1965); on Boccaccio, see *Medieval Literary Theory*, ed. Minnis and Scott, pp. 387–92, 453–58.

[53] Pietro Alighieri, *Comentum super poema Comedie Dantis: A Critical Edition of the Third and Final Draft of Pietro Alighieri's "Commentary" on Dante's "The Divine Comedy"*, ed. Massimiliano Chiamenti (Tempe, Ariz.: Arizona Center for Medieval and Renaissance Studies, 2002), Inferni prohemium, 24, 33. On Pietro, see *Medieval Literary Theory*, ed. Minnis and Scott, pp. 449–53; extract of the commentary translated at pp. 476–91.

[54] Pietro Alighieri, *Comentum*, Inferni prohemium, 1; 17; 12.

[55] See Gal. 4.22–24. Pietro Alighieri, *Comentum*, Inferni prohemium, 21–22.

102 NICOLETTE ZEEMAN

question of whether medieval *allegoria* is a rhetorical figure or a hermeneutic technique, Richard Goulet and Gilbert Dahan comment: "les auteurs du Moyen Age passent sans cesse de l'une à l'autre, le plus souvent en toute connaissance de cause" ("the authors of the Middle Ages pass ceaselessly from one to the other, mostly quite knowingly").[56] Most important, even if it is the case that among these Italian writers compositional *allegoria* sometimes looks more like a type of writing than a figure, and even if it does sometimes overlap in increasingly unstable but also frictional ways with hermeneutic *allegoria*, it does not denote a whole text or the supposed genre of narrative allegory.

This is still true in sixteenth-century England, when the identification of "poetry" and "allegory" is well established;[57] in this period rhetorical theorists also increasingly stress the "dark" or obscure nature of poetic figuration.[58] Nevertheless, Thomas Wilson's *Arte of Rhetorique* (1560) still defines *allegorie* as a trope: "none other thing, but a Metaphore used throughout a whole sentence, or Oration"; proverbs too are "commenly ... nothyng elles but Allegories and darcke devised sentences."[59] For Puttenham's *Art of English Poesy* (1589), *allegoria* is the "courtly" trope, linked to political hypocrisy, "False Semblant or Dissimulation," as well as speaking "under covert and dark terms."[60] Spenser's description of the *Faerie Queene* as "a continued Allegory, or a darke conceit" is very much of its moment.[61] What does he mean by "continued Allegory"? The phrase echoes the "series of metaphors" ("continuae translationes") that make the trope of *allegoria* in Quintilian, now recovered in its entirety; both Spenser's qualifying adjective "continued" and comments elsewhere that the poem is "clowdily enwrapped in Allegoricall deuises"[62] suggest that for him what he calls *Allegories* are still tropes. Spenser's "continued Allegory" looks different, in other words, depending on whether you read it from the perspective of Quintilian or Coleridge. In the early modern period, then, the rhetorical trope of *allegoria* still "lives somewhere uncomfortably between metaphor and the various species of *alieniloquium*,

---

56 Goulet and Dahan, "Présentation," p. 7.
57 Murrin, *Veil of Allegory*, pp. 66–74.
58 See Silk, "Invoking the Other," pp. 54–55; also Brljak, "Age of Allegory." On poetry's "cloudy fygures" and the "clok[ing of] sentence under mysty fygures," see Stephen Hawes, *The Pastime of Pleasure*, ed. William Edward Mead, EETS, os 173 (London: Oxford University Press, 1928), lines 701–1407, at lines 720, 932.
59 Thomas Wilson, *Arte of Rhetorique*, ed. Thomas J. Derrick (New York: Garland: 1982), p. 352.
60 George Puttenham, *The Art of English Poesy: A Critical Edition*, ed. Frank Whigham and Wayne A. Rebhorne (Ithaca, N.Y.: Cornell University Press, 2007), pp. 270–71. See also the references in Crawford, *Enchantment*, p. 18, n. 41.
61 Edmund Spenser, "A Letter of the Authors," in *The Faerie Queene*, ed. A. C. Hamilton, assisted by R. J. Manning (London: Longman, 1977), pp. 737–38.
62 "Letter of the Authors," in *Faerie Queene*, p. 737; see Andrew Zurcher, *Edmund Spenser's The Faerie Queene: A Reading Guide* (Edinburgh: Edinburgh University Press, 2011), pp. 182–86.

MEDIEVAL ALLEGORICAL NARRATIVE

saying one thing and meaning another."[63] There is no evidence that for Spenser, any more than for his contemporaries, it denotes a whole text or a genre.

∼

Brljak has proposed a solution to the question of what medieval "allegory" is, according to which the later medieval Italian poets and theorists simply make explicit a long-standing medieval assumption that all *poetria* (not just what we have come to call narrative allegory) is *allegoria*, a figured and imaginative form of textuality that "covers" a body of philosophical doctrine. Brljak's proposal has the useful effect of sidestepping the problem of the genre of narrative allegory by claiming that in the Middle Ages all literature is "allegorical" (though with the ambiguous proviso that not "every single work" was necessarily regarded as such).[64] But I have some doubts about this solution. First, it backdates and generalizes claims only made in a forceful way in later thirteenth- and fourteenth-century Italy and France. Second, it assumes that all medieval imaginative writing was read from the perspective of a schools-driven, grammatical, rhetorical and philosophical culture, homogenized as a version of *poetria*. Third, this argument depends on the "merged" notion of *allegoria*, with its binary opposition of the figured or obscure and the gloss, that I have been questioning in this essay.

However, along with a number of other readers, Brljak has made a different but absolutely crucial point:

> premodern authors did not write – did not see themselves as writing – allegories. They wrote poems and stories of various generic affiliations, which may or may not, comprehensively or episodically, use or contain allegories.[65]

Marco Nievergelt reminds us that "during the medieval period the term *allegoria* was *never* used to categorize a particular literary text, genre, or mode"; Copeland insists that "we do not see the term 'allegory' (*allegorie, allegoria*) [used to describe] the poetic fictions that we would now call 'allegorical.'"[66] We have not taken this fact seriously enough. For if the terminology of *allegoria* was multiple and divided to the end of the Middle Ages, and denoted neither a type of text nor a whole text, it is clear why medieval imaginative writers did not use it to describe their compositions, never mind a particular sub-genre of them.

In fact, the terms used to describe the texts that we have called allegories – whether in titles, rubrics or descriptions internal to the texts, whether authorial or scribal – are hugely various. They include: *consolatio, planctus/compleynte,*

---

[63] Copeland, "Allegory and Rhetoric." By this period, the full text of Quintilian's *Institutio* had been recovered.

[64] Brljak, "Introduction: Allegory Past and Present," pp. 8–10.

[65] Brljak, "Introduction: Allegory Past and Present," pp. 8–9.

[66] Marco Nievergelt, "Allegory," *The Encyclopedia of Medieval Literature in Britain*, ed. Siân Echard and Robert Rouse (Chichester, UK: Wiley Blackwell, 2017), pp. 50–59, at p. 51; Copeland, "Allegory and Rhetoric"; see also Goulet and Dahan, "Présentation," p. 7; Silk, "Invoking the Other," pp. 46–49.

romans/romaunce, visio/songe/dreme, dit/dite, mirouer/mirrour, livre/book/ quair, chartre/charter (the "charters of Christ"), *breviari* (*Breviari d'amor*), *testament* (*Testament of Love*) or *dialogus* (*Piers Plowman*). Some of these terms correspond with textual categories used in Latin writing and clerical or learned contexts, and some do not. Particularly revealing are vernacular terms such as *romans* or *dit* that etymologically and originally seem to mean no more than "(vernacular) speaking," but come to denote forms of narrative or song.[67] The development of these terms into semi-generic but fluid categories has much to tell us about how vernacular writing did not just avoid the textual categories of the schools, but actually refused the schools' classificatory systematics.[68] The manner in which most of these terms differentiate texts from each other is arguably in its own way precise and yet also open. Sometimes they describe texts in terms of the form of speech or writing (complaint, saying, dialogue), sometimes in terms of notional sources (vision, dream, mirror), sometimes in terms of material textuality (book, charter, letter, *cosmographia*). Indeed, many of these texts' titles evade the question of genre altogether by referring instead to diegetic or iconographic "contents": *De nuptiis Philologiae et Mercurii*, the *Queste del sanc graal*, the *Pèlerinage de vie humaine*, *Piers Plowman*, the *Parliament of Fowls*, *Confessio amantis*. The variety of these descriptive terms is so great as to indicate that writers and readers do not identify what we have called medieval allegorical narrative/allegory as a distinct genre; rather, it suggests a pervasive sense of overlap with other types of writing, whether imaginative or otherwise. And none of these terms gives special weight either to obscurity, or to the binary opposition of the figured or obscure with the elucidatory.

[67] On *romans*, see Laurence Harf-Lancner, "Chrétien's Literary Background," in *A Companion to Chrétien de Troyes*, ed. Norris J. Lacy and Joan Tasker Grimbert (Cambridge: D. S. Brewer, 2005), pp. 26–42, at pp. 27–28; Emmanuèle Baumgartner, "Le livre et le roman (XII–XIIIe siècles)," in *Livre et littérature: dynamisme d'un archétype* (Nanterre: Université de Paris X-Nanterre, 1986), pp. 7–19. For *dits*, see "dité, n.," 2 (and "dire, v.," 2) in *Anglo-Norman Dictionary*, https://www.anglo-norman.net/entry/ (accessed 21 March 2023); "dit, n.," B (and "dire, v.," II.A) in *Dictionnaire de moyen français* (1330–1500), http://zeus.atilf.fr/dmf/ (accessed 21 March 2023); Michel Zink, *Medieval French Literature: An Introduction*, tr. Jeff Rider (Binghamton, N.Y.: Medieval and Renaissance Texts and Studies, 1995), pp. 81–83; Sarah Kay, *Parrots and Nightingales: Troubadour Poetry and the Development of European Poetry* (Philadelphia: University of Pennsylvania Press, 2013), p. 34, who intriguingly further notes the term *chans* used to describe the Occitan language in Terramagnino da Pisa's Occitan grammar.

[68] On vernacular literature's "active resistance to classificatory schemas," see Alfred Hiatt, "Genre without System," in *Oxford Twenty-first Century Approaches to Literature. Middle English*, ed. Paul Strohm (Oxford: Oxford University Press, 2007), pp. 277–94, at p. 280; also Simon Gaunt, *Gender and Genre in Medieval French Literature* (Cambridge: Cambridge University Press, 2009), pp. 4–10; Julie Orlemanski, "Genre," in *A Handbook of Middle English Studies*, ed. Marion Turner (Chichester, UK: Wiley-Blackwell, 2013), pp. 207–21.

MEDIEVAL ALLEGORICAL NARRATIVE

This brings us back to my opening comments, where I proposed that if we are going to describe any medieval texts as allegorical narratives or allegories, we should use these terms in a capacious, not a narrowly generic, sense. The inclusive – and prismatic – version of allegory is cross-generic, multi-perspectival and dialogic; if we think of allegory as a mode and not a genre, then Brljak is right that allegory is both "deeply embedded in premodern poetic thought" and cannot be separated from the many genres in which it participates."[69] This more capacious version of allegory is reflected in *De planctu naturae*, where Alain of Lille allows grammar and invective to criss-cross with moral and philosophical discourse; in the first part of the *Roman de la rose*, where Guillaume de Lorris splices song with courtly narrative and advice text; and in *Piers Plowman*, where Langland transforms pastoralia by intercutting it with the discourses of dialogue, hypocrisy and poetic paradox.

But this changed understanding of the notions of allegorical narrative and allegory means that we cannot continue using these terms for exactly the same group of texts as before. After all, many of the works associated with the supposed genre of allegory turn out to be (at the very least) rather unexciting examples of allegory as I have redefined it; but, equally well, other texts that, although they have not been associated with the supposed genre, might now be usefully and provocatively thought of in terms of a more inclusive notion of allegory. One example might be the narratively contrastive techniques of Arthurian romance, especially in the interlaced forms of prose romance. Another example might be multi-discursive lyrics such as "Blow, northerne wind" or the "Corpus Christi Carol," with their internal contrasts and startling refrains. Another might be Chaucer's *Canterbury Tales*. These have not usually been read as allegorical in the narrow sense of being organized round systematic "other speaking" or the presence of substantial hidden meaning; nevertheless, the *Tales* are built around contrasting and opposing perspectives, and use myriad genres and discursive forms to comment on, critique and illuminate each other. If allegory is writing that espouses the striking conjunctions and conceptual conflicts that result from self-consciously exploring, complicating and breaking generic boundaries, then the *Canterbury Tales* are surely this. To make this claim is not to revert by another route to the proposal that all medieval literature is somehow allegorical; it is to recognize that, if we redefine allegory as something fundamentally dynamic and prismatic, then we find that it turns up in unexpected places.

The argument of this essay entails discarding our post-medieval generic understanding of the terminology of *allegoria*/allegory. It has led us to believe that there was once a medieval genre called allegory defined in terms of an allegorical polarity of the figured or obscure and its explication. Many medieval imaginative texts use the trope of *allegoria*, often elaborately and at length; and many medieval imaginative texts also suggest or explain their own

[69] Brljak, "Introduction: Allegory Past and Present," p. 9.

allegorical senses, or demand allegorical interpretation from the reader. These features no doubt enhance these texts' rich tropology and figuration. But if the writers of the Middle Ages did not acknowledge a textual genre called *allegoria* or allegory (any more than writers and readers have identified one in modernity), then probably one did not exist.

POSTSCRIPT

Why has this idea of the supposed genre of allegorical narrative/allegory – along with the associated emphasis on the polarity of the figured or obscure and the gloss – seemed so persuasive for so long? It seems likely that part of the answer might lie in the theories linking poetry, allegory and (later) "darke conceit" that took an increasingly bold form in later medieval Italy and became widespread in the early modern period. But the real answer is even more substantially post-medieval. It is in the neoclassical and romantic periods that the term allegory comes to denote a specific type or genre of writing associated with personification, extended metaphor or a preoccupation with obscurity and clarity. It is also notoriously in this period that a particular negative set of views about this thing called allegory really set in.[70] On the one hand, neoclassical and romantic critics attacked allegorical narrative and its animate abstractions for their supposedly fantastical elements and obscurity; but on the other hand, they also issued critical instructions that redefined allegory in more confined, "clearer" terms, mainly as a streamlined version of personification narrative, only then to attack it for being simplistic and mechanistic. Although we are in theory aware of this history, we still live with its latent legacy. For the crude version of this legacy is a caricatural version of the polarity of the obscure and the explicatory, the suspicion that allegorical narrative is fantastical, hermetic, archaic and elitist, and yet also somehow reductively and banally "readable."

But there is a subtler version of this legacy that, although it seems more positive, is equally problematic. This version involves the retrospective co-option of the classical and early to high-medieval terminology of *allegoria*, its rhetorical and hermeneutic usages retrospectively conflated to confirm a shared polarization of the obscure and the explicatory, and then used to theorize texts that only after the Middle Ages came to be called allegories. It is a co-option that has misled us badly.

---

[70] The history of this process has often been told: Teskey, *Allegory and Violence*, pp. 98–121; Crawford, *Enchantment*, pp. 27–44; Brljak, "Age of Allegory"; "Introduction: Allegory Past and Present," p. 13; Silk, "Invoking the Other," pp. 49, 57–60; Breen, *Machines*, pp. 15–16; Copeland, "Allegory and Rhetoric."

6

"Thynke nat the contrary": Field Notes in the Ecology of Medieval Romance

Nicholas Perkins

It is an honor to contribute to this volume celebrating James Simpson, whose teaching, publications and friendship have been central to what being a scholar means to me. Among the many qualities of his work, I have found some to be particularly influential. First, clear-eyed argument, identifying key questions to ask in a way that invites us to investigate alongside him.[1] Second, his willingness to take many kinds of writing seriously, despite the consensus view about their merits.[2] Third, analyzing how a range of discourses (both in the sense of discursive fields in texts, but also critical discourses) help to not only communicate ideas but to form them.[3] And finally (for this essay, at least), the

---

[1] For example, James Simpson, "Desire and the Scriptural Text: Will as Reader in *Piers Plowman*," in *Criticism and Dissent in the Middle Ages*, ed. Rita Copeland (Cambridge: Cambridge University Press, 1996), pp. 215–43.

[2] For example, writing and teaching about Thomas Hoccleve and John Lydgate, when their reputations were still relatively low. See James Simpson, "Madness and Texts: Hoccleve's *Series*," in *Chaucer and Fifteenth-Century Poetry*, ed. Julia Boffey and Janet Cowan (London: King's College, 1991), pp. 15–29; "Nobody's Man: Thomas Hoccleve's *Regement of Princes*," in *London and Europe in the Later Middle Ages*, ed. Julia Boffey and Pamela King (London: Centre for Medieval and Renaissance Studies, Queen Mary and Westfield College, 1995), pp. 149–80; and *The Oxford English Literary History, Vol. 2: 1350–1547. Reform and Cultural Revolution* (Oxford: Oxford University Press, 2002), ch. 2.

[3] For example, "Spirituality and Economics in Passus 1–7 of the B Text," *Yearbook of Langland Studies* 1 (1987), 83–103; and more broadly in *Piers Plowman: An*

108   NICHOLAS PERKINS

ability not only to find larger patterns among texts and ideas but also to test those patterns against acute readings of individual examples.[4] In James's work, then, we see both wood and trees – sometimes both the topography or ecology of whole regions and also the markings on individual leaves, with plausible connections made between those scales of analysis. Further, he draws on previous creative and critical books to develop a productive field for debate about a wide range of texts, ideas and institutions. Here I shall discuss one of those areas of debate: that of romance's thinking and its genre.

James is better known for his work in other areas (amply reflected in this volume), but he has written about romance several times, making powerful arguments about the structure of romances, their generic affiliation, and the way that they yield ethical value. This position is most clearly presented in "Derek Brewer's Romance," but also developed in several other pieces.[5] While giving support to some of James's insights – how his work helps to illuminate romances – I shall also ask how his work unsettles, or provokes debate, and how we might develop or modify some of those insights. In particular, how do we approach the relationship between overall structural coherence and local variation or counter-current; and how do unhappy endings pressurize our understanding of romance, which is, in James's argument, an inherently comic genre?

In "Derek Brewer's Romance," James notes how Brewer pushed against well-established orthodoxies (both New Critical and poststructuralist) about romance reading and value. Brewer argued that structure, not style, is the most important level of analysis to understand romances; that character development is not important to this genre; and that realism is not prized in romance, and so should not be used as a criterion to assess its success, or its value. All these have had a major impact on how we read romances. James then extends one of Brewer's arguments by defining romance as generically comic:

> These stories end happily. The logic of their episodic structure is driven by the logic of the ending: the structure carefully defines what events, in what order, are necessary to achieve that happy ending. The narrative evokes the irreparable disintegrations of tragedy (notably incest) only to evade them, often by near misses.[6]

   Introduction, rev. ed. (Exeter: Exeter University Press, 2007).
4 For example, *Under the Hammer: Iconoclasm in the Anglo-American Tradition* (Oxford: Oxford University Press, 2010); *Burning to Read: English Fundamentalism and its Reformation Opponents* (Cambridge, Mass.: Harvard University Press, 2007).
5 James Simpson, "Derek Brewer's Romance," in *Traditions and Innovations in the Study of Medieval English Literature: The Influence of Derek Brewer*, ed. Charlotte Brewer and Barry Windeatt (Cambridge: D. S. Brewer, 2013), pp. 154–72. See also *Reform and Cultural Revolution*, ch. 6; "Unthinking Thought: Romance's Wisdom," in *Thinking Medieval Romance*, ed. Nicola McDonald and Katherine C. Little (Oxford: Oxford University Press, 2018), pp. 36–52; and "Violence, Narrative and Proper Name: *Sir Degaré*, 'The Tale of Sir Gareth of Orkney', and the *Folie Tristan d'Oxford*," in The *Spirit of Medieval English Popular Romance*, ed. Jane Gilbert and Ad Putter (London: Routledge, 2000), pp. 122–41.
6 "Derek Brewer's Romance," p. 169.

FIELD NOTES IN THE ECOLOGY OF MEDIEVAL ROMANCE   109

James particularly has in mind Brewer's structural and broadly Freudian readings of romance as part of "the family drama" in his book *Symbolic Stories*. There, Brewer notes that "[m]ost medieval romance is deliberately orientated towards 'comedy', in the sense of achieving a happy ending."[7] However, James critiques scholarship's apparent failure to clarify and focus its generic definitions:

> If there are indeed no significant generic distinctions to be made within the vast textual terrain often classed as romance then there is no call to proceed, since there is nowhere to go …. On the other hand, it may be that we can perceive clear generic differences between works habitually classed as romance. If that were true, then we are in a strikingly retrograde position, after more than 200 years of scholarship, of lost opportunity.[8]

This passage's bold, even polemic, tone reinforces a flank of debate elsewhere in his work, which is to identify critical space for historical, ethical, and/or tragic texts that reflect on human (in)capacities to handle power, to manage political relationships, or to order their public and private desires.[9] This need for clarity is a long-held position of James's. In preparing for the talk on which this essay is based, I found my undergraduate notes from a 1992 seminar about romance, taught by James. Alongside comments on Chrétien de Troyes's *Yvain*, I had scribbled: "define romance? Simpson: not difficult."[10] This sense of focus has enabled some revelatory work on texts that had often been classed as unsatisfactory romances, but defining genre is nevertheless a problematic task, especially with the "inherently slippery" romance. Many scholars have instead explored how these narratives are themselves composite, or engage with other genres and discourses; or how they undermine our expectations, incorporating reversal and generic play into the larger networks of romance narrative.[11]

---

[7] Derek Brewer, *Symbolic Stories: Traditional Narratives of the Family Drama in English Literature* (London: Longman, 1980), p. 111. Compare Northrop Frye's influential characterization of romance as having a "perennially childlike quality … marked by its extraordinarily persistent nostalgia" in his *Anatomy of Criticism: Four Essays* (Princeton, N.J.: Princeton University Press, 1957), p. 186.

[8] "Derek Brewer's Romance," p. 163.

[9] See *Reform and Cultural Revolution*, pp. 106–20 (on the Alliterative *Morte Darthur* and *The Wars of Alexander*); and "'Dysemol daies and fatal houres': Lydgate's *Destruction of Thebes* and Chaucer's *Knight's Tale*," in *The Long Fifteenth Century: Essays for Douglas Gray*, ed. Helen Cooper and Sally Mapstone (Oxford: Oxford University Press, 1997), pp. 15–33.

[10] I now think that the complex resolution to *Yvain* is itself a test of what a romance's "happy" ending might contain or obscure. See for example Tony Hunt, *Chrétien de Troyes:* Yvain (London: Grant and Cutler, 1986), esp. ch. 2; and Fredric L. Cheyette and Howell Chickering, "Love, Anger, and Peace: Social Practice and Poetic Play in the Ending of *Yvain*," *Speculum* 80 (2005), 75–117.

[11] Quoting Corinne Saunders, "Introduction," in *A Companion to Romance: From Classical to Contemporary*, ed. Corinne Saunders (Oxford: Blackwell, 2004), pp. 1–9 (at p. 1). For the flexible use of narrative "memes," see Helen Cooper's *The English Romance in Time: Transforming Motifs from Geoffrey of Monmouth to the Death*

NICHOLAS PERKINS

In "Unthinking Thought" James returns to his understanding of romance as generically comic, and based on an underlying narrative structure of integration–disintegration–reintegration. This pattern is inviting but very broad, and any individual text has a habit of straying from even the largest categories that we shepherd them towards. James's reflection on romance's recuperative narrative structure uses the metaphor of ecology:

> These narratives are less about ethics than about the ecology of family structure that must pertain before we can even begin to think about ethics. Romance compacts a kind of ecological, pre-ethical thought about the civilized order. By "ecological thought," I mean structuralist rather than genealogical thought. Ecological thought locates meaning in the synchronic interrelations of systems, rather than the derivation in time of individual elements within a system. In Middle English romances, as in all comic narratives of this kind, that ecological "thought" must confront relations between the civilized and the wild in any social structure. Such thinking demands that we understand individual episodes in a larger, interdependent, synchronic system.[12]

This passage challenges us to consider what sort of thought is happening, and where, in the romance text, and whose thought we prioritize. Its appeal to narrative structure again echoes Brewer, while the ecological language stresses organizing and balancing relationships within the text.[13] This is a powerful mode of reading, but I want to lead it in a direction that extends or challenges James's claims about romance generically, since interrelation, complex time, and a more messy form of reckoning are also at work between texts and amongst genres. The ecological metaphor can help us not only to read individual romances as bounded structures defined by their endings but also as participants in larger systems and networks.[14] In addition, romances frequently – while directing a

---

of Shakespeare (Oxford: Oxford University Press, 2004). For romances in relation to their manuscript co-texts, see for example *Codex Ashmole 61: A Compilation of Popular Middle English Verse*, ed. George Shuffleton, TEAMS: Middle English Texts (Kalamazoo, Mich.: Medieval Institute Publications, 2008) and scholarship referenced there; Arthur Bahr, *Fragments and Assemblages: Forming Compilations of Medieval London* (Chicago: University of Chicago Press, 2013), esp. ch. 2, on the Auchinleck Manuscript; Nicholas Perkins, *The Gift of Narrative in Medieval England* (Manchester: Manchester University Press, 2021), ch. 2, discussing Auchinleck romances in relation to larger patterns of exchange in the manuscript. Another, overlapping, approach is via readership, as for example in Michael Johnston, *Romance and the Gentry in Late Medieval England* (Oxford: Oxford University Press, 2014).

12 "Unthinking Thought," p. 48.

13 Brewer says of Malory's Lancelot: "In terms of the total pattern of the whole tragedy, and in his relation to Arthur and Guinevere, Lancelot at the latent level never grows up. He is always the brilliant youth" (*Symbolic Stories*, p. 111).

14 James's use of "ecology" is based etymologically on the *oikos*, or household, but more recent biological understandings of ecology have also been used to study cultural relations; see, for example, Mark Q. Sutton and E. N. Anderson, *Introduction to Cultural Ecology*, 3rd ed. (Lanham, Md.: Altamira Press, 2014). See also D. Vance Smith, *Arts of*

FIELD NOTES IN THE ECOLOGY OF MEDIEVAL ROMANCE 111

line of narrative towards a (usually) comic conclusion – seed further narrative in the face of that apparent closure. The very ingredients of romance's endings, especially inheritance, marriage and children, are the material for further storytelling, and not always for comfortable reintegration.[15]

How can ecological thought help to open relationships between languages, discourses and genres? My example is *Degaré*, a fourteenth-century romance which survives in four pre-1500 manuscripts, several early print editions, and in the Percy Folio, suggesting its long-lasting appeal.[16] In his own discussion of *Degaré* in "Unthinking Thought," James moves swiftly to the structural principles holding the text together, quickly accepting – even reinforcing – the view that it has little literary merit, in the sense of linguistic richness or subtlety.[17] Likewise, the extraordinary reversals of its plot; the inclusion of a fairy knight who rapes a princess (Degaré's mother) but is at the end absorbed into the family structure; the motifs of incest: in James's reading these elements, though strikingly problematic for us as readers, must eventually settle themselves into order, to complete its story about family and identity. Romance "unthinking" is partly a way of coping with questions that might become too difficult if faced directly:

> I present romance non-thought as an especially subtle form of cybernetic (in the etymological sense of "self-governing") reformism. This especially subtle form of thought requires a holiday from explicit, rational thought, from thinking out loud, and from thinking too explicitly about shame. Instead, such "thought" operates by disabling thought; it requires "unthinking."[18]

Possession: The Middle English Household Imaginary (Minneapolis, Minn.: University of Minnesota Press, 2003), which takes *economic* ideas and their balancing structures at the household level as a context for enlightening readings, including of romances.

[15] See for example Cooper, *English Romance in Time*, pp. 361–408. A recent study, Grace A. Timperley, "The Idea of Disinheritance in Middle English Romances" (unpublished Ph.D. dissertation, Manchester University, 2020), suggests how (dis)inheritance complicates romance beginnings and endings; and see Walter Wadiak, *Savage Economy: The Returns of Middle English Romance* (Notre Dame, Ind.: University of Notre Dame Press, 2016) for powerful readings of romances enforcing "happy" outcomes through violence or its looming potential.

[16] The pre-1500 manuscripts are Edinburgh, National Library of Scotland MS Advocates 19.2.1 (the Auchinleck MS, c. 1330s); London, British Library MS Egerton 2862 (late fourteenth century); Cambridge, University Library MS Ff.2.38 (c. 1425x1450); Oxford, Bodleian Library MS Rawlinson poet. 34 (late fifteenth century). Along with the Percy Folio [London, British Library, Additional MS 27879 (c. 1650)], some folios in Oxford, Bodleian Library MS Douce 261 contain part of the poem, copied by Edward Bannister from an early print in 1564. There were at least four print editions in the sixteenth century. See Nicolas Jacobs, *The Later Versions of* Sir Degarre: *A Study in Textual Degeneration* (Oxford: Society for the Study of Medieval Languages and Literature, 1995); texts and editions are listed in *Degaré's* entry in the *Database of Middle English Romance* (University of York), https://www.middleenglishromance.org.uk.

[17] "Unthinking Thought," pp. 39–40.

[18] Ibid., p. 37.

NICHOLAS PERKINS

One question that arises here is about the nature of reformism, when a text includes acts of abuse, including sexual violence, but then attempts to rebalance or absorb them into its narrative structure. How can and should that violence be reckoned with?[19] Another question is "Whose thought?" – that is, which parts of an audience "unthink" these moments, are they all involved in the same reading/listening enterprise, and can we differentiate them?[20] I shall consider two moments in *Degaré* to suggest how it allows both for explicit reflection on shame, and a more variegated repertoire of perspective and language than most readings allow. These moments are "both/and": they can contribute to the overall narrative drive of the text (integration–disintegration–reintegration), but also provide counter-currents – trials of ethics and emotion – that open the text to other responses, and which are part of a wider ecology of narrative or textuality. Though at times partial or clumsy, they give opportunities for insight, reflection or dissent. They both tell and think.

Early in the story, the king and his household set out to visit the tomb of his dead wife on her "mynnyng" (memorial) day.[21] The king's daughter becomes doubly separated, first from her father's entourage and then, in a dream-like state, from her female companions. She wanders off and encounters a fairy knight. He claims to have long admired her, and is described as handsome and elegant, but he then rapes her. Later, one of her maids notices her weeping:

> On a dai, as hi wepende set,   159
> On of hire maidenes hit underyet.
> "Madame," she seide, "par charité,
> Whi wepe ye now, telleth hit me."
> "A! gentil maiden, kinde icoren,
> Help me, other ich am forloren!

---

[19] See for example Amy N. Vines, "Invisible Women: Rape as a Chivalric Necessity in Medieval Romance," in *Sexual Culture in the Literature of Medieval Britain*, ed. Amanda Hopkins et al. (Cambridge: Cambridge University Press, 2014), pp. 161–80; Corinne Saunders, *Rape and Ravishment in the Literature of Medieval England* (Cambridge: Brewer, 2001).

[20] One approach might be to focus on women as readers. See for example Jennifer R. Goodman, "'That Wommen Holde in Ful Greet Reverence': Mothers and Daughters Reading Chivalric Romances," in *Women, the Book, and the Worldly*, ed. Lesley Smith and Jane H. M. Taylor (Cambridge: Brewer, 1995), pp. 25–30; Nicola McDonald, "Chaucer's *Legend of Good Women*, Ladies at Court, and the Female Reader," *The Chaucer Review* 35 (2000), 22–42; Corinne Saunders, "Affective Reading: Chaucer, Women, and Romance," *The Chaucer Review* 51 (2016), 11–30; and more broadly *Women and Literature in Britain, 1150–1500*, ed. Carol M. Meale, 2nd ed. (Cambridge: Cambridge University Press, 1996). Recent research by Alana Bennett uses evidence of reading from manuscripts, theories of performance and experiments in reading aloud from facsimile manuscripts to explore different possible audience responses. See "'Romanz reding on the bok': 'Reauralising' Romances from Later Medieval English Household Manuscripts" (unpublished Ph.D. dissertation, University of York, 2022).

[21] *The Middle English Breton Lays*, ed. Anne Laskaya and Eve Salisbury, TEAMS: Middle English Texts (Kalamazoo, Mich.: Medieval Institute Publications, 1995), line 39. Subsequent quotations referenced in the text.

FIELD NOTES IN THE ECOLOGY OF MEDIEVAL ROMANCE 113

Ich have ever yete ben meke and milde: 165
Lo, now ich am with quike schilde!
Yif ani man hit underyete,
Men wolde sai bi sti and street
That mi fader the King hit wan
And I ne was never aqueint with man!   170
And yif he hit himselve wite,
Swich sorewe schal to him smite
That never blithe schal he be,
For al his joie is in me,"
And tolde here al togeder ther   175
Hou hit was bigete and wher.
"Madame," quad the maide, "ne care thou nowt:
Stille awai hit sschal be browt.
No man schal wite in Godes riche
Whar hit bicometh, but thou and iche."   180

This episode is inadequate to fully account for the knight's crime and the suffering of the princess. Nevertheless, it does not take a total "holiday" from explicit thought, nor represent it as governed by a singly authorized perspective. The king's daughter speaks privately, away from men, about her rape and the shame that it could bring her. The maid notices ("underyet" (160)) the princess's distress, but if others find out ("underyete" (167)) that she is pregnant, she would be ruined. The words "man," "men" (167, 168) can be translated "anyone," "people," but they also point to the fact that male expectations of female sexual purity will potentially ruin her. This exchange, then, focuses on women's support, and women's ways of knowing: the two make a pact to deceive the princess's powerful father and save her child. The princess's initial speech (163–66) echoes those found in female-voiced lyrics and carols lamenting extra-marital pregnancies.[22] There is even potential humor (hard to stomach in the context of a rape story) in the parallels here with narratives about Mary's conception of Jesus: "And I ne was never aqueint with man!" (170) bears comparison with the York Play known as "Joseph's Troubles about Mary," where Mary insists "Forsuth, I am a mayden clene" to the doubtful Joseph.[23]

---

[22] See the texts discussed in Neil Cartlidge, "'Alas, i go with chylde': Representations of Extra-Marital Pregnancy in the Middle English Lyric," *English Studies* 79 (1998), 395–414. As Cartlidge suggests, the tone and perspective of these lyrics are often complex, and not always one of misogynistic moralizing. For conversations about this tradition, my thanks to Alice Raw, who explores it in "Gender, Sexual Discourse, and Women's Pleasure in Later Medieval England, c. 1300–c. 1550" (unpublished D.Phil. dissertation, Oxford University, 2023). For another kind of interplay between romance and lyric forms, focusing on *King Horn*, see Christopher Cannon, "Lyric Romance," in *What Kind of a Thing is a Middle English Lyric?*, ed. Christina Maria Cervone and Nicholas Watson (Philadelphia: University of Pennsylvania Press, 2022), pp. 88–105.

[23] *The York Corpus Christi Plays*, ed. Clifford Davidson, TEAMS: Middle English Texts (Kalamazoo, Mich.: Medieval Institute Publications, 2011), Play 13, line 208. In the

114   NICHOLAS PERKINS

This passage directly raises the question of incest: many will think that the king will be the child's father, the princess says. Although incest has not taken place, she acknowledges that "al his joie is in me." The familiar dynamic of the widowed king being at least over-protective of his daughter helps drive this story, connecting the princess to other women who are maligned because of pregnancy, the accusation of improper sex, or the threat of incest, as in the Constance legend, or the eponymous protagonist of *Emaré*, or Cristabel in *Eglamour of Artois*.[24] The princess's "Men wolde sai bi sti and street" (168) predicts that further storytelling, in the form of gossip, lyric or romance, might develop about her situation. This moment echoes Criseyde's prediction that "rolled shal I ben on many a tonge," but here the princess both acknowledges the powerful drive of misogynistic retelling, and at the same time challenges it by refuting the gossip before it has started.[25] *Degaré* has been a byword for poor style and lack of depth, but the language of this passage is at interplay with numerous other narratives, discourses, and genres. Its style is not irrelevant or simply an embarrassment to be overcome; it is integral to the story's plot, and provokes acts of thinking in the text and about the text. Those discursive, intertextual links are part of larger networks: their ecology is broader based than we might initially think, and reaches out both within and beyond romance.

A later passage further complicates *Degaré*'s thinking. In the interim, the baby Degaré has been left with a hermit, whose sister has brought him up. Once his education is completed by the hermit, Degaré sets off with a pair of gloves left to him by his mother, which will fit only her. After various adventures, he hears that the King of Litel Bretaygn will give his daughter in marriage only to someone who can defeat him in a tournament. Degaré takes on the challenge and defeats the king, who is (unbeknownst to Degaré) his own grandfather:

> The King was sor asschamed forthi;   580
> The lordinges comen with might and mein
> And broughte the King on horse agein,
> An seide with o criing, iwis,
> "Child Degarre hath wonne the pris!"
> Than was the damaisele sori,   585

Auchinleck Manuscript, the text before *Degaré* is a poem on "The Assumption of the Blessed Virgin" (*DIMEV* 6596), which discusses Mary as both "Clene maiden" and "clene virgine" (47, 49); see *The Auchinleck Manuscript*, ed. David Burnley and Alison Wiggins (Edinburgh: National Library of Scotland, 2003), http://auchinleck. nls.uk/mss/assumpt.html.

24   *Emaré* is edited in *The Middle English Breton Lays*, ed. Laskaya and Salisbury, TEAMS: Middle English Texts (Kalamazoo, Mich.: Medieval Institute Publications, 1995); *Eglamour* in *Four Middle English Romances: Sir Isumbras, Octavian, Sir Eglamour of Artois, Sir Tryamour*, ed. Harriet Hudson, TEAMS: Middle English Texts (Kalamazoo, Mich.: Medieval Institute Publications, 2006).

25   Geoffrey Chaucer, *Troilus and Criseyde*, in *The Riverside Chaucer*, gen. ed. Larry D. Benson (Boston: Houghton Mifflin, 1987).

FIELD NOTES IN THE ECOLOGY OF MEDIEVAL ROMANCE 115

For hi wist wel forwhi:
That hi scholde ispoused ben
To a knight that sche never had sen,
And lede here lif with swich a man
That sche ne wot who him wan,   590
No in what londe he was ibore;
Carful was the levedi therefore.
Than seide the King to Degarre,
"Min hende sone, com hider to me:
And thou were al so gentil a man   595
As thou semest with sight upan,
And ase wel couthest wisdomes do
As thou art staleworht man therto,
Me thouwte mi kingdoms wel biset:
Ac be thou werse, be thou bet,   600
Covenaunt ich wille the holde."

Here, the lords' cry that "Child Degarre hath wonne the pris!" (584) is true in two senses: he is the best in the tournament, and he has won the princess as his prize. But at this moment of triumph for Degaré, the poem immediately swaps to the princess's perspective. The next lines focus on her anxiety that that she, as a piece of marriageable property, will be "ispoused … To a knight that sche never had sen" (587–88), and she does not know his family or "in what londe he was ibore" (591). There is a nice irony in the re-use of *winnen* in "sche ne wot who him wan" (590).[26] The truth about Degaré's birth is about to be revealed, but he has also formed his own identity through the accumulated challenges that he has overcome. The text aptly pauses at this moment when Degaré both is and is not his mother's son.

This passage could be ignored as a conventional aside that barely starts to construct the princess's subjectivity, but like the exchange between the princess and her maid earlier, this female-focalized moment provides a point of reflection and speculation. It also has the effect of prolonging the king's embarrassment: shame is not only thought about, but openly proclaimed here ["The King was sor asschamed forthi" (580)], and then held in place during the lines about the princess. When we return to the king, it is as if the narrative pause has allowed him to choose which path to follow. He models a generous response to failure, assuming (and in a sense provoking) Degaré to have the qualities of a good leader, by matching his outward appearance with other attributes (being as "gentil" as he looks, and as wise as he is "staleworht": words that are themselves on a journey from external descriptors to markers of inward qualities). He then makes a promise to him: "Covenaunt ich wille the holde" (601). It is this recuperative response to shame that allows the narrative to move forward, first narrowly avoiding incest between the

---

[26] Here "wan" means "conceived, begat"; *MED*, s.v. "winnen," meaning 4.

116   NICHOLAS PERKINS

princess and her son Degaré, and then enabling Degaré to find, challenge and eventually incorporate his father into the narrative and the family.

Both these passages thicken *Degaré's* narrative texture. They allow the audience to reflect on its story from a different perspective, and to make connections both across this romance (the ecosystem proposed in James's reading) and outside it, to wider systems and networks. While contributing to the poem's narrative progress, they do not wholly fold difficult questions into an overarching, rebalancing story. Instead, the consequences of sexual violence, shame, incest, honor, status, love and marriage, and keeping your word are directly on display. If "interrelations of systems" are fundamental to romance, we can also find evidence for them in places that a broader structural analysis of the poem must in some sense treat as distractions. They are roads not travelled, or desires briefly recognized but then subdued. If the story is performed in sections, scenes of danger or loss might be the last thing the audience hears for some time, until the next episode is read.[27] They incorporate discourses, voices and perspectives that are not those of the dominant generic texture, but they are nevertheless part of an ecosystem of and beyond the text, helping to provide that sense of possibility which characterizes the pleasure of romance reading.[28]

Romance ecology is, then, a productive idea that we can explore at the level of individual stories and more locally, opening these texts to broader intertextual flows. How does this ecology interact with James's stress on romance as a comic genre, driving towards reintegration? There is certainly reintegration at the end of *Degaré*, though its ending leaves lingering questions about the cost of family reunions, and its opening is framed by the dangerous consequences of grief. A harder proposition would be a text whose trajectory is towards death, as with Malory's *Balyn le Sauvage*, or *The Knight with the Two Swords*. James has argued for clarity about what romance is, stressing that unhappy endings such as *Balyn's* do not fit this plan. Likewise for K. S. Whetter "[t]he happy ending is thus not merely a romance commonplace (as is often said), it is one of the genre's *essential* features."[29] In *Reform and Cultural Revolution*, James had navigated some of

---

27 See for example *Sir Tryamour*, in *Four Middle English Romances*, ed. Hudson, note to line 343, where Hudson points to a larger initial in the manuscript that indicates a new section of the text, just after a dramatic and bloody fight; and also Bennett, "'Romanz reding on the bok.'"

28 On pleasure and possibility in romance reading, see Nicola McDonald, "A Polemical Introduction," in *Pulp Fictions of the Middle Ages: Essays in Popular Romance*, ed. Nicola McDonald (Manchester: Manchester University Press, 2004), pp. 1–21; and idem., "The Wonder of Middle English Romance," in *Thinking Medieval Romance*, ed. Little and McDonald, pp. 13–35.

29 K. S. Whetter, *Understanding Genre and Medieval Romance* (Aldershot, UK: Ashgate, 2008), p. 77; and see idem., "On Misunderstanding Malory's Balyn," in *Re-viewing "Le Morte Darthur"*, ed. K. S. Whetter and Raluca L. Radulescu (Cambridge: D. S. Brewer, 2005), pp. 149–62. In the latter, Whetter summarizes previous approaches to *Balyn* and foregrounds Balyn's credentials as an epic or

FIELD NOTES IN THE ECOLOGY OF MEDIEVAL ROMANCE   117

this territory, in particular describing Malory's *Morte Darthur* as having outer "panels" about Arthur's rise and fall, with inner romances "each exploring in its own way how the balance of inward power may be sustained within Arthur's imperial success." But here the affirmation of romance as generically comic comes under renewed pressure. Despite *Gareth* being "as fully achieved as a romance can be," Malory "leaves a small loose end in it, from which, in part, the entire system of Arthur's court unravels." Further, "[t]he very neatness and narrative rigour of 'Gareth' point to the messiness of its adjacent narratives, focused on the royal adulterers Lancelot and Tristram respectively, which seek yet fail to be romances."[30] *Balyn* also shadows Malory's collection: "Romance in Malory is haunted by the fate of Balin, the hero and victim of the second narrative in the very first sequence of stories."[31]

Bringing together the flexibility of romance ecology with the patterning of Malory's own Arthurian compilation, especially in *Balyn*'s foreshadowing of later disasters, I think we can read *Balyn* as a "haunted romance."[32] At least, the problems that it raises cannot easily be resolved by drawing the boundary around the genre of romance a little tighter and turning this story away at the gate: "[a]s soon as the word *genre* is sounded, as soon as it is heard, as soon as one attempts to conceive it, a limit is drawn."[33] Instead, we can look to approaches that highlight romance's hybridity and flexibility: Melissa Furrow, who uses "radial categories" to consider how romances can incorporate material or textures that are contrary to our overall sense of the genre; Simon Gaunt, who talks of a Jaussian "horizon of expectations" for romance – expectations that may be "confirmed, but they may also be toyed with or foiled"; Yin Liu, who describes romance as a "prototype genre," where a text's generic identity is gauged by its proximity to the prime examples of its kind; Ad Putter, who characterizes romance as having "a complex network of relationships and similarities."[34] In this context, we can use James's ecological

---

  tragic protagonist. He describes Malory's *Morte* as "a generic hendiadys best termed epic- or tragic-romance" (p. 162).

[30] James Simpson, *Reform and Cultural Revolution*, pp. 289, 290, 291. Lancelot and Tristan are so embedded in the development of romance that their stories demand to be read at least in relation to romance. See, for example, their inclusion in Middle English lists of exemplary romance figures: Yin Liu, "Middle English Romance as Prototype Genre," *The Chaucer Review* 40 (2006), 335–53, at 348–50.

[31] *Reform and Cultural Revolution*, p. 291.

[32] Several readers have noted *Balyn*'s uncanny quality: for example, Sarah Stanbury, "The Embarrassments of Romance," *Arthuriana* 17 (2007), 114–16, who notes that *Balyn* is "recapitulative, dreamlike, haunted by [its] founding events" (115); Thomas H. Crofts, *Malory's Contemporary Audience: The Social Reading of Romance in Late Medieval England* (Cambridge: D. S. Brewer, 2012), p. 90, who mentions the "doubling or haunting with which Balyn is met at every turn."

[33] Jacques Derrida, "The Law of Genre," tr. Avital Ronell, repr. in *Modern Genre Theory*, ed. David Duff (London: Routledge, 2000), pp. 219–31, at p. 221.

[34] Melissa Furrow, *Expectations of Romance* (Cambridge: D. S. Brewer, 2009), esp. pp. 51–61; Simon Gaunt, "Romance and other Genres," in *The Cambridge Companion to*

approach to explore how *Balyn* enables haunting reflection and commentary on romance at the same time as disabling or disrupting it. Its audience and its protagonists seek to understand the story's action in relation to romance, but *Balyn* shows that "privileged generic knowledge may be wrong."[35] *Balyn*, in its querying of romance motifs, is not just an exception that proves the rule of genre; although it may be read via the epic or tragic, its excesses and reversals are also bound up with the ecology of romance narrative.

Events in *Balyn* are both romance and reflection on romance's discontents. A lady arrives at Arthur's court, girt with a sword. No man may pull the sword from its sheath unless he is "a passing good man of hys hondys and of hys dedis, and withoute velony other trechory and withoute treson."[36] Nobody achieves this, and in a passage that echoes the Green Knight's ostentatious disappointment with the Arthurian court in *Sir Gawain and the Green Knight*, the lady complains "Alas! I wente in this courte had bene the beste knyghtes of the worlde withoute trechory other treson" (I.48). After the lady initially rejects his request to try the challenge, Balyn lectures her on how not to judge a knight by his poor appearance. He in turn receives a prophetic warning, once he has unsheathed the sword but refused to return it:

> "Well," seyde the damesell, "ye ar nat wyse to kepe the swerde fro me, for ye shall sle with that swerde the beste frende that ye have and the man that ye most love in the worlde, and that swerde shall be youre destruccion." (I.50)

These episodes are both narrative and commentary; romance and its undoing. They are ecological, by foregrounding balancing structures and the interplay of different elements in the narrative, but that interplay is here discussed by the protagonists themselves: the story is being glossed and debated intradiegetically. Later, Balyn beheads the Lady of the Lake, who was demanding his head as a gift from Arthur, and the king responds to him angrily: "For what cause soever ye had ... ye sholde have forborne in my presence. Therefore thynke nat the contrary: ye shall repente it, for such anothir despite had I nevir in my courte" (I.51–52). Arthur's "thynke nat the contrary" rhetorically emphasizes his judgement on Balyn's impetuous violence. However, it also draws attention to the acts of contrary thinking that this narrative provokes: the prophesy, speculation, justification, regret, and

---

Romance, ed. Roberta Krueger (Cambridge: Cambridge University Press, 2000), pp. 45–59, at p. 46; Liu, "Prototype Genre"; Ad Putter, "A Historical Introduction," in *The Spirit of Medieval English Popular Romance*, ed. Gilbert and Putter, pp. 1–15, at p. 2.

[35] Cooper, *English Romance in Time*, p. 367. See also idem., "Counter-Romance: Civil Strife and Father-Killing in the Prose Romances," in *The Long Fifteenth Century: Essays for Douglas Gray*, ed. Helen Cooper and Sally Mapstone (Oxford: Clarendon, 1997), pp. 141–62.

[36] Thomas Malory, "Balyn le Sauvage," in *Le Morte Darthur*, ed. P. J. C. Field, 2 vols. (Cambridge: D. S. Brewer, 2013), I.48. Subsequent references will appear in the text.

FIELD NOTES IN THE ECOLOGY OF MEDIEVAL ROMANCE   119

resignation that are folded into the text, sometimes filling the gaps left by the absence of rational or generically stable explanations.[37]

Space does not allow for a fuller discussion of all these episodes, but as with the two passages of *Degaré* that we read, so in *Balyn*, the moments of reversal, reflection or shift in perspective allow for connections with a network of romance and other discourses and genres to rise to the surface. They include the death of Columbe (the lover of Lanceor whom Balyn has just killed) who with a brief lyric lament kills herself while Balyn delays disarming her, for fear of hurting her: "too bodyes thou haste slayne in one herte, and too hertes in one body, and too soules thou hast lost" (I.54). Echoing this is the episode when Balyn helps another knight, Garnysh of the Mownte, find his lover. He succeeds, but finds her in the arms of another man. When Balyn brings Garnysh to them, the latter kills both his lover and her new man, and then blames Balyn, before killing himself: "O Balyn! Moche sorow hast thow brought unto me, for haddest thow not shewed me that syght I shold have passed my sorow" (I.70). Balyn hurries away, but soon comes across a mysterious old man who warns him not to proceed; he then hears a horn, and recognizes that it "is blowen for me, for I am the pryse, and yet am I not dede" (I.70). Alongside these commentaries, new texts and memorials are created, as with the tomb of Lanceor and Columbe, set up by King Mark, to which Merlin adds the names of Lancelot and Tristram who will later fight in that spot. *Balyn*'s excessive, haunted romance narrative is also generative, both of story and commentary.

As the narrative draws to a close, Balyn must fight another knight who by custom challenges all who pass. In *Degaré*, as we have seen, the hero secures his identity through fighting his grandfather and father, but Balyn's final combat transforms this motif. Balyn has obscured his identity by swapping his own shield for an "unknowen" one, and his opponent, his brother Balan, does not recognize him (I.71). The two knights fight to a standstill, their blood mingling and their strength fading. Eventually they reveal their identity to (and with) one another. They realise that they have misread their own romance: "I aspyed wel your two swerdys, but bycause ye had another shild I demed ye had ben another knyght," says Balan (I.72–73).[38] Washed with one another's blood and "naked ... on every syde" (I.72), they ask to be buried together: "We came bothe oute of one wombe, that is to say one moders bely, and so shalle we lye bothe in one pytte" (I.73).

---

[37] For the way that Malory's version removes explanatory material and focuses on Balyn's decisions to "take the adventure" – key moments in the formation of knightly action and romance narrative, see Jill Mann, "'Taking the Adventure': Malory and the *Suite de Merlin*," in *Aspects of Malory*, ed. Toshiyuki Takamiya and Derek Brewer (Cambridge: D. S. Brewer, 1981), pp. 71–91.

[38] Compare the fight between Gareth and Gawain in *Gareth*, which is rescued from a similar outcome by Lynet happening to ride past and recognizing both knights (I.282). This is a generically comic version of the episode, but still foreshadows fraternal conflict later in the *Morte*.

NICHOLAS PERKINS

This is a tragic outcome, but I want to "thynke the contrary" and read it also as romance reintegration. It reveals identities, brings the central protagonist together with his kin, provokes an emotional response (here the burial "pytte" produces "the grettist pité" (I.74) in Arthur, and us too), and gives rise to textual offspring, through the brothers' joint tomb and Merlin's subsequent acts of telling, making and prophesying – for example the prediction that Merlin has inscribed on the new pommel of Balyn's sword, marking it out for either Lancelot or Galahad and predicting that Lancelot will use it to kill Gawayne.[39] In its narrative potential, released later in the *Morte*, in its querying of ethical structures and assumptions, and in its invitation to comment and reflect from inside the narrative, *Balyn*'s networks are not circumscribed by its textual borders, but enmeshed in that larger ecology of romance, at all the levels of discourse and thinking that I have discussed here. *Balyn* helps us to think the contrary about romance structures and expectations, at the moment when they are most pressurized or mingled with others. In other words, it enables us to "suppose for a moment that it were impossible not to mix genres."[40]

James Simpson's discussions of medieval romance have sharpened our appreciation for their narrative organization, their ethical commitments and silences, and their ecological systems. His work has also given new attention to texts that will always be in an uneasy relationship with romance, or working with other powerful conceptions of history or agency. Here I have only been able to address one or two instances of romance genre and (un)thinking to which James provokes us to pay attention. Nevertheless, I suggest that just as a movement towards order in romance narrative "necessitates negotiation with … all that threatens it," we should keep as open as possible the unsettling force of romance ecology as always enmeshed rather than clearly bounded, at the level of discourse, narrative, and the ethical commitments that they produce. Drew Daniel has described genre as "what nobody really believes in but everyone relies on," and this might be a provocative description of romance itself.[41] In reading ecologically, and especially when their language or narrative seems at odds with the generic cues that we initially rely on, if not believe in, we can understand better how romances are always at interplay both with one another, and with the networks of discourses, performances and thinking processes that shape them.

---

[39] I.74. For the way that objects in romance can both carry narrative and provoke reflection, see Nicholas Perkins, "Ekphrasis and Narrative in *Emaré* and *Eglamour of Artois*," in *Medieval Romance, Medieval Contexts*, ed. Rhiannon Purdie and Michael Cichon (Cambridge: D. S. Brewer, 2011), pp. 47–60; idem., *The Gift of Narrative*.

[40] Derrida, "The Law of Genre," p. 222.

[41] Drew Daniel, "Redistributing the Sensible: Genre Theory after Rancière," *Exemplaria* 31 (2019), 129–40, at 129.

7

FILLING IN THE LINES: TEXT, IMAGE, AND LATE MEDIEVAL LITERARY FORMS[1]

Jessica Brantley

James Simpson's scholarship has long been committed to the idea that "literary texts both illuminate and unsettle discursive patterns in disciplines that might seem more powerful."[2] These powerful alternative disciplines are generally based in language – Simpson goes on to name them as "theology, economics, psychology, politics" – but this idea might inspire questions also about the power of literary words to illuminate or unsettle discursive patterns in other media. In this essay, I will borrow the Simpsonian framework to explore how literary words engage visual media, in particular, and how visual media engage them. Do they illuminate each other? Do they unsettle each other? Which is more powerful? And what is the role of *literary* language, specifically, in the relation between visual and verbal representational forms?

These are questions that Simpson has also taken up in his influential work on iconoclasm.[3] If images offer a powerful force countering the dominance

---

[1] I am indebted to the organizers and attendees of the September 2022 Harvard symposium, and especially to Daniel Donoghue, Nicholas Watson, and Sebastian Sobecki, for all the ways in which they enriched this piece. Audiences at New York University, the Fribourg Colloquium, and the New York Comics and Picture Book Symposium made helpful comments on earlier versions of the material. Finally, I am exceedingly grateful to James Simpson for his inspirational example over many years.

[2] See the epigraph to the Introduction, p. 1 above.

[3] See, e.g., *Images, Idolatry, and Iconoclasm in Late Medieval England: Textuality and the Visual Image*, ed. Jeremy Dimmick, James Simpson, and Nicolette Zeeman (Oxford: Oxford University Press, 2002); James Simpson, *Under the Hammer: Iconoclasm in the Anglo-American Tradition* (Oxford: Oxford University Press, 2010); and James Simpson, *The Oxford English Literary History, Vol. 2: 1350–1547.*

of the word, iconoclasm registers the results of a contest between words and images in which words have ostensibly won. But does iconoclasm lead, also, to the development of a language that is precisely literary? Or, put another way: is the relegation of images to the sidelines necessary somehow for the development of literature? I will suggest here that it is not – that understanding late-medieval texts and images as mutually illuminating, mutually unsettling, allows us to ask how literary language emerges from an environment that includes both words and pictures. Iconoclastic discourses claim a separation of text and image that – for all its stridence – is almost always illusory.[4] Simpson himself describes the ways in which an iconoclastic yet idolatrous poet like Milton refuses the opposition, even while the refusal causes "psychic pain."[5] But refusing the opposition between text and image is characteristic of medieval aesthetics, and seems to cause, in general, much less pain. Indeed, late medieval artifacts often reinforce the necessary reliance of one art form upon the other, illuminating and unsettling each other in a dynamic that seems less like a power struggle, perhaps, than a dance. Reading the intermedial engagements of the manuscript page counter-intuitively as an exploration of verbal form, I will suggest that some kinds of literary language in the fourteenth and fifteenth centuries developed in concert with the visual textures of literacy.

To explore this general proposition all too briefly here, I will take up the example of line-fillers, humble manuscript decorations that offer an intriguingly material opportunity to explore the interdependence of medieval words and pictures. Line-fillers are one of the most common – and yet still under-considered – design features of late-medieval books. Visual placeholders that occupy what would otherwise be empty space at the end of a line of text, these bits of ornament are familiar hallmarks of medieval liturgical manuscripts, in particular. They seem entirely unprepossessing – hardly the most elaborate part of what is often a highly decorated page. And because they are arguably neither linguistic nor pictorial, they also would seem to be among those material features of books that are "less readily interpreted," like the ruling lines that Daniel Wakelin has recently studied.[6] Or, like the printers'

    Reform and Cultural Revolution (Oxford: Oxford University Press, 2002), esp. pp. 383–457.

[4] For some of the many critical challenges to any absolute separation between text and image, see, e.g., W. J. T. Mitchell, *Iconology: Image, Text, Ideology* (Chicago: University of Chicago Press, 1986); Mitchell, *Picture Theory: Essays on Verbal and Visual Representation* (Chicago: University of Chicago Press, 1994); and, for early modern England, Brian Cummings, "Iconoclasm and Bibliophobia in the English Reformations, 1521–1558," in *Images, Idolatry, and Iconoclasm*, pp. 185–206.

[5] *Under the Hammer*, p. 110.

[6] Daniel Wakelin, *Immaterial Texts in Late Medieval England: Making English Literary Manuscripts, 1400–1500* (Cambridge: Cambridge University Press, 2022), pp. 69–111, at p. 73.

TEXT, IMAGE, AND LATE MEDIEVAL LITERARY FORMS   123

flowers that Juliet Fleming has analyzed in three fascinating essays, they "first evoke, and then eschew, both semiotic registers."[7] Line-fillers reinforce the linear forms of the text rather than its sense (like ruling lines), and they fill empty space with ornament that challenges interpretation (like printers' flowers). In the relatively luxurious manuscripts in which they usually appear, line-fillers have remained largely resistant to analysis: they register a practice of medieval bookmaking that has decorative but not interpretative force.

But one might, conversely, argue that line-fillers play roles that are both linguistic and pictorial, that they work at once to visualize and to articulate the text. Their appearance within the text-block asserts the rights of the image to that space, and yet they also contribute there to the appearance of the text. Line-fillers serve to elucidate the structure of the texts they accompany, and yet they reveal that one of the text's most fundamental properties is visual: these decorative additions shape the text-block to look complete, to take on an orderly, regular shape. Line-fillers both offer opportunities for visual expression and also use those opportunities to mark textual form – whether for reading out loud, for elucidating grammatical and intellectual structures, or for enabling an experience we might call literary.

As oblong blocks of color, line-fillers function in a variety of ways as part of the decorative apparatus of a medieval book. They suit the visual environment of the manuscript they adorn, ranging from very simple penwork flourishes (figure 1),[8] to geometrically patterned ornament (figure 2),[9] to elaborate – if small and constrained – figural paintings (figure 3).[10] Nigel Morgan has usefully traced the origin and development of these graphical forms in the thirteenth century (from which all of these examples come) and has pointed towards their increasing prominence in the fourteenth and fifteenth centuries.[11] On a formal level, something about these additions solves a visual problem for the designers of the medieval page: they regularize the text-block, justifying the right margin to create the symmetrical and

---

[7] Juliet Fleming, "How to Look at a Printed Flower," *Word & Image* 22 (2006), 165–87; "How Not to Look at a Printed Flower," *JMEMS* 38 (2008), 345–71, quotation at 351; and "Changed Opinion as to Flowers," in *Renaissance Paratexts*, ed. Helen Smith and Louise Wilson (Cambridge: Cambridge University Press, 2011), pp. 48–64.

[8] For a description of the manuscript, see Nigel Morgan, *Early Gothic Manuscripts*, 2 vols., A Survey of Manuscripts Illuminated in the British Isles 4 (London: Harvey Miller, 1988), I: 1190–1250, No. 40.

[9] For a description of the manuscript, see Morgan, *Early Gothic Manuscripts*, II: 1250–1285, No. 112. See also Nigel Morgan, "The Artists of the Rutland Psalter," *British Library Journal* 13 (1987), 159–85.

[10] For a description of the manuscript, see, e.g., Lucy Freeman Sandler, *Gothic Manuscripts 1285–1385*, A Survey of Manuscripts Illuminated in the British Isles 5 (London: Harvey Miller, 1986), No. 15. See also n. 16, below.

[11] Nigel Morgan, "The Decorative Ornament of the Text and Page in Thirteenth-Century England: Initials, Border Extensions and Line Fillers," *English Manuscript Studies, 1100–1700* 10 (2002), 1–33, at 2.

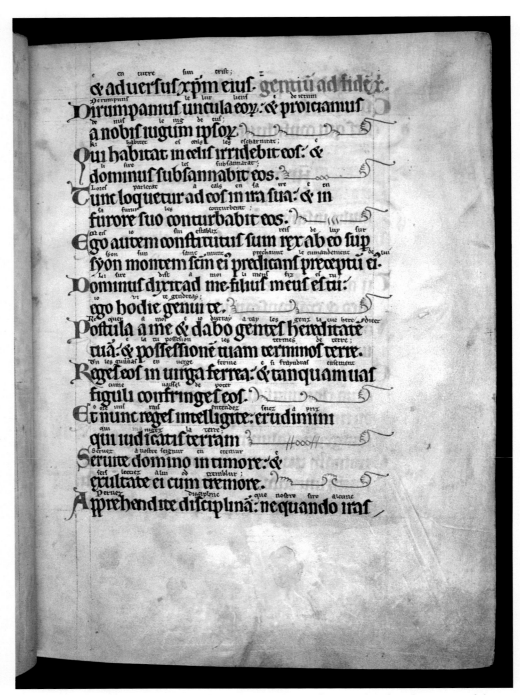

1   Line-fillers: simple penwork flourishes. Psalter with Canticles, fourth quarter of the twelfth century to first quarter of the thirteenth century, England. London, British Library MS Harley 5102, f. 2r. © The British Library Board.

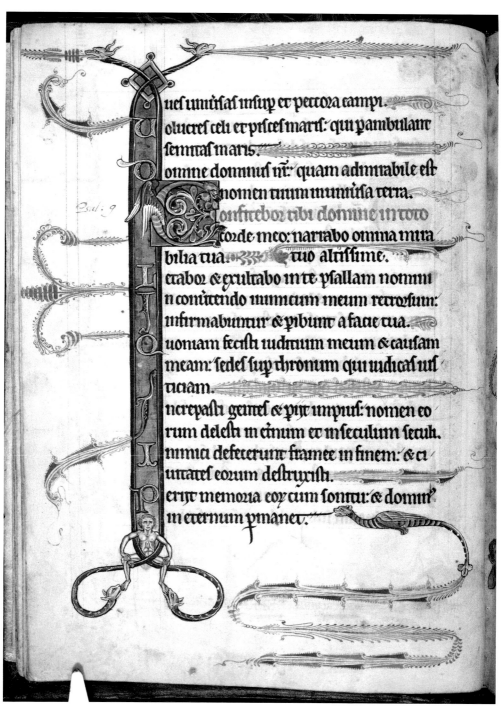

2   Line-fillers: geometrically patterned ornament. Psalter ("Rutland Psalter"), c. 1260, England. London, British Library MS Additional 62925, f. 13v. © The British Library Board.

3   Line-fillers: figural paintings. Book of Hours, c. 1300, England. Baltimore, Walters Art Museum MS W.102, f. 2r.

TEXT, IMAGE, AND LATE MEDIEVAL LITERARY FORMS   127

rectangular shape that Daniel Wakelin has cited as a fundamental feature of medieval book design. In a manuscript whose lines are filled, one can easily "sense the power of the rectangle as an idea about the page."[12] In occupying space that would otherwise be empty, line-fillers also reinforce the density of ornament that is key to a Gothic aesthetic.

But although line-fillers do just what their name suggests – they fill empty space in the lines of the text-block – they also sometimes do more. Revisiting the page from the Rutland Psalter (figure 2), one notices that the geometric forms in the line-fillers are strikingly mirrored in the shapes filling the margins at the left, top, and bottom. On the right, the line-fillers exceed the text-block that they might have been expected to regularize, extending elaborate flourishes towards the edge of the page. And although this manuscript is known for the extensive figural imagery in its margins, at the bottom of this text-block the line filler seems to have usurped that spot: a long narrow dragon sidles up to the text and snaky geometric forms have moved to the *bas de page*. Similar examples of line-fillers exceeding their bounds can be found throughout late medieval liturgical manuscripts, including the famous Hours of Jeanne d'Evreux, where they explode into the margins, transforming themselves into large grisaille figures.[13] Although it might seem that line-fillers should be constrained by the text-block they are employed to regularize, then, in significant examples such as these they reach beyond it, to connect text with image, to associate the look of the textual space with the margins, and with the other images on the page.

In some cases, rather than escaping into the margins, the line-fillers redefine pictorial space within the text block itself. For example, in a small and heavily illustrated book of hours made in Liège c. 1300, Walters Art Museum MS W.37, even the most modest line-fillers make a strong claim for the importance of the visual in the balance of the page.[14] They include geometric and floral designs, as well as birds, or beasts; in the litany, a number of small line-fillers take the shape of dragons. The artist seems to have had only a few dragon templates, which he repeated in different lengths and colors.[15] And perhaps it was the practical considerations surrounding his models that led the artist occasionally to expand the reach of his dragons (figure 4). Instead of remaining securely within a single line, these small line-fillers sometimes occupy two lines, or more, where they

---

[12] Wakelin, *Immaterial Texts*, p. 58.

[13] This manuscript is widely reproduced, and digital images are provided on the website of the Metropolitan Museum of Art: https://www.metmuseum.org/art/collection/search/470309 (accessed 31 January 2023). For line-fillers transformed into grisaille figures in the margins, see, e.g., fols. 20v–21r.

[14] Baltimore, Walters Art Museum MS W.37 is a small book of hours made around 1300–10 for a woman, perhaps a Beguine living in Huy, near Liège. For a full description, see Lilian M. C. Randall, *Medieval and Renaissance Manuscripts in the Walters Art Gallery*, vol. 3, pt. 1. (Baltimore, Md.: Johns Hopkins University Press, 1997), No. 220.

[15] Similar dragons and other elongated beasts appear throughout the *bas de page*; see, e.g., fols. 30r, 45r, 52v, 66v, 84v, 98v, 107v, 111v, 113v, 114r, 119v.

4 Line-fillers: dragons. Book of Hours, c. 1300, Liège. Baltimore, Walters Art Museum MS W.37, f. 128r.

have the space to do so. Here the dragons beside the names Simon and Thaddeus, Matthew and Matthias, needed more space, whereas Mark and Luke are each matched with one of the narrower beasts. The two-line dragons may have come from another exemplar, but their use here shows this artist's willingness to expand the image beyond the constraints imposed by the ruled lines of text. He has taken a small opportunity to treat this space of the line-filler as pictorial, rather than textual.

5   Elephant and castle. Book of Hours, c. 1300, England. Baltimore, Walters Art Museum MS W.102, f. 28r.

130 JESSICA BRANTLEY

The pictorial spaces offered by the litany become an irresistible opportunity in another Walters book of hours made c. 1300 in England, MS W.102.[16] The manuscript is rich and complicated, but it is probably best-known for an arresting mix of text and image: *bas de page* pictures that recreate the false funeral of Renart the Fox and bring into the liturgical hours, as Emma Dillon has noted, an alternative medieval soundscape.[17] The line-fillers in this manuscript also repay attention. Some of them act as line-fillers do: they mimic the shape of text-lines, simply filling in the lines where there are no letters with hybrid creatures sporting human heads (sometimes arms) and elongated bodies (see, e.g., figure 3). On other folios, however, this manuscript's line-fillers take off in a new direction. The artist tasked with this decoration did not always see the space available as a series of discrete horizontal blocks, but (when possible) as an aggregate of those spaces, resulting in a larger and less constricted visual field. When a sequence of short texts leaves a large space to their right on the manuscript page, as in the litany of saints' names, the artist has innovated. In that open visual field, he painted an Elephant and Castle (figure 5). Although there are conventional individual line-fillers on this page, the larger ones (including the two-line grotesque at the bottom) extend beyond the space they necessarily should fill: the elephant's trunk, for example, reaches out into the margins *between* two lines of text. Far from justifying the text-block on the right, this elephant gratuitously breaks the rectangle.

On the verso of this folio, what might have been a long series of single line-fillers has been re-imagined as a striking full-length portrait of Adam: the image gives way to the intrusion of saint Bartholomew's lengthy name, but it also creeps out with Adam's foot over the apostles and evangelists, seeming to rest on the one conventional line-filler below (figure 6). Across the opening, more empty spaces created by the parallel names of saints are filled with an image resembling the Holy Face above and a pair of chess players below (figure 7). Turning the leaf, further unusual images picture Romulus and Remus suckling the she-wolf who raised them, and an ape riding a bear (fol. 29v). In these curious line-fillers (really, space-fillers), image overbalances text, working at literally cross-purposes; we read the pictures vertically, crossing over the horizontal lines created by the succession of words. They also tell a different story, for these are – clearly – not pictures of the saints who are named in succession. Lilian Randall has explored the iconographic significance of these unusual images, arguing that they should be decoded for their ethical or

[16] Baltimore, Walters Art Museum MS W.102 is an English book of hours also made c. 1300, containing unusual texts in Latin and French as well as numerous complicated images and image-sequences. For descriptions of the manuscript, see, e.g., Dorothy Miner, *Illuminated Books of the Middle Ages and Renaissance* (Baltimore, Md.: Trustees of the Walters Art Gallery, 1949), No. 153; and Sandler, *Gothic Manuscripts 1285–1385*, No. 15.

[17] Emma Dillon, *The Sense of Sound: Musical Meaning in France, 1260–1330* (Oxford: Oxford University Press, 2012), pp. 243–86. For the foundational study of the Renart images, see Florence McCulloch, "The Funeral of Renart the Fox in a Walters Book of Hours," *The Journal of the Walters Art Gallery* 25 (1962), 8–27.

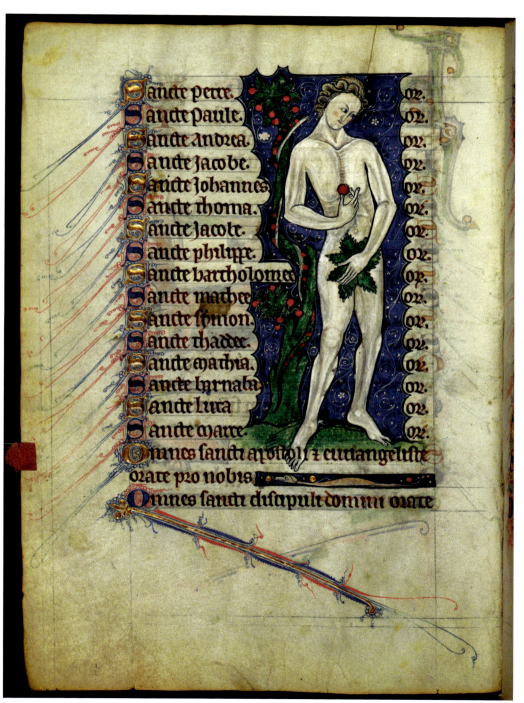

6   Adam. Book of Hours, c. 1300, England. Baltimore, Walters Art Museum MS W.102, f. 28v.

7   Holy Face and game of chess. Book of Hours, c. 1300, England. Baltimore, Walters Art Museum MS W.102, f. 29r.

TEXT, IMAGE, AND LATE MEDIEVAL LITERARY FORMS 133

historical significance.[18] The elephant and castle, for example, might refer to contemporary moralizations of the animal in the bestiary, as well as perhaps commemorating the arrival of an actual elephant in London, presented as a gift to Henry III by Louis IX in 1255.[19] Adam can be easily understood as an emblem of sin and penance.[20] The wound on the forehead of the Holy Face might index the stoning of St. Stephen in what Randall calls the "conflated Christ-Stephen visage" appearing next to St. Stephen's name in the litany.[21] The chess game might allude to games of chance associated with St. Silvester, also named on the page.[22] Although Randall occasionally connects these images with the words on the page, it is their own elaboration of visual motifs that convinces her that their meaning is not far to seek, that their "riddles" should be solved. Having become fully pictorial, line-fillers are capable of bearing meaning.

Whether or not we accept Randall's specific suggestions, these overgrown line-fillers insist by their placement within the text-block that they must be considered a central part of the manuscript's design. Effacing any division of the page into individual lines, the space-fillers in Walters MS W.102 transform a block of text into a visual zone. If these pages present an *agon* between image and text, I would say that these pictures unsettle more than illuminate the words, demanding that a reader's attention be paid, contrariwise, not to a sequential verbal list but to a single visual field. This artist's visual purpose, superseding any original connection with the linear shapes of the verbal text, reminds readers that line-fillers always engage the visual aspects of the text on the page – they turn words into images. Moreover, line-fillers in a manuscript such as this one illustrate the imaginative workings of the manuscript matrix as described by Martha Rust, in which "physical form and linguistic content function in dialectical reciprocity," participating in "one overarching, category-crossing metasystem of systems of signs."[23] For these decorative fragments occupy textual spaces, and while they call attention to the visual elements of the manuscript's words, in other contexts line-fillers also work to illuminate literary forms. By highlighting the periodic absence of text, they articulate textual divisions and showcase textual structures, whether logical, syntactical,

---

[18] Lilian M. C. Randall, "An Elephant in the Litany: Further Thoughts on an English Book of Hours in the Walters Art Gallery (W. 102)," in *Beasts and Birds of the Middle Ages. The Bestiary and Its Legacy*, ed. Willene B. Clark and Meradith T. McMunn (Philadelphia: University of Pennsylvania Press, 1989), pp. 106–33.

[19] Randall, "Elephant in the Litany," pp. 109–10. Randall notes that this event has also been connected to the two-line elephant line-filler at the canticle *Te Deum* in the Windmill Psalter (New York, Morgan Library MS M.102, fol. 162).

[20] Randall, "Elephant in the Litany," pp. 110–11.

[21] Randall, "Elephant in the Litany," p. 111.

[22] Randall, "Elephant in the Litany," pp. 111–14. The game of chess was also elaborately moralized in the period.

[23] Martha Dana Rust, *Imaginary Worlds in Medieval Books: Exploring the Manuscript Matrix* (New York: Palgrave MacMillan, 2007), p. 9.

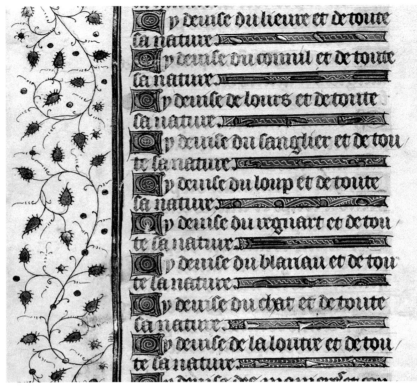

8   Index with line-fillers. Gaston Phoebus, *Livre de la Chasse*, first quarter of the fifteenth century, Paris. New York, The Morgan Library & Museum MS M.1044, f. 2r. Bequest of Clara S. Peck, 1983.

or prosodic.[24] Line-fillers can thereby facilitate reading, enhance understanding, and, at times, secure the integrity of the text. In legal or financial documents, for example, line-fillers serve to reassure readers that any gap is intentional and to prevent anyone from adding to or changing the original. Even around holes in parchment, scribes sometimes drew lines to connect words and direct the reader across the unavoidable empty space.[25] Because line-fillers perform these textual functions, we might consider them a form of punctuation – that is, visual signals intended to help readers navigate the experience of reading words.

[24] Lucy Freeman Sandler notes the way textual divisions sometimes correspond to changing patterns in line-fillers. See, e.g., Sandler, *The Peterborough Psalter in Brussels and Other Fenland Manuscripts* (London: Harvey Miller, 1974), p. 35.

[25] Wakelin, *Immaterial Texts*, p. 52, citing the following examples: New Haven, CT, Beinecke Rare Book and Manuscript Library MS 360, fol. 36v; New Haven, CT, Beinecke Rare Book and Manuscript Library MS 661, fol. 37r; Cambridge, Cambridge University Library MS Add. 3137, fol. 42r–v; New Haven, CT, Beinecke Rare Book and Manuscript Library MS Takamiya 22, fol. 63r.

TEXT, IMAGE, AND LATE MEDIEVAL LITERARY FORMS

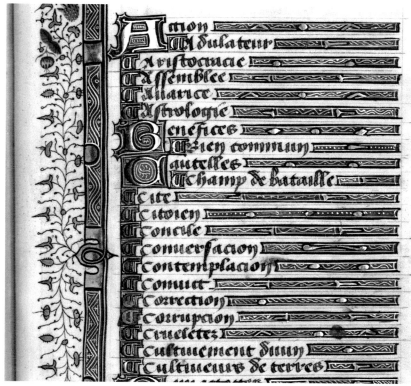

9 Table of contents with line-fillers. Nicole Oresme's translation of Aristotle's *Ethics*, mid-fifteenth century, Rouen. Rouen, Bibliothèque municipale de Rouen MS I 2, f. 410r.

It is no accident that the line-fillers such as the Elephant and Castle in Walters MS W.102, those that take maximal pictorial advantage of the space they are given, accompany the text of the litany.[26] The litany, a series of petitions to specific saints by name, is a list: a textual form whose layout is likely to produce unevenly unfilled spaces. Other kinds of medieval lists also make use of line-fillers. For example, they sometimes appear in medieval calendars, filling out the lines listing saints with shorter names.[27] Another common use of line-fillers in lists occurs in indices and tables of contents, such as a list of chapters by subject in a copy of the *Livre de la chasse* (figure 8), an alphabetical list of topics in a copy of Nicolas Oresme's translation of Aristotle (figure 9),

---

[26] For another solution to the problem of the litany's odd spaces, see the Ruskin Hours (Los Angeles, Getty Museum of Art MS Ludwig IX 3), made c. 1300 in northeastern France. Here, the page is divided into three columns, with the petitions of the litany on the left, illustrations of each saint on the right, and a column of individual horizontal line-fillers in the middle (see, e.g., fol. 105r).

[27] E.g., *Horae ad usum Romanum*, Paris, Bibliothèque nationale de France MS NAL 3111, fol. 8r.

10 Table of
contents with
line-fillers.
Custumal, early
fourteenth century.
Ipswich, Suffolk
Record Office,
Ipswich C/4/1/1, f.
9a. (Image Credit:
Esther L. Cuenca).

TEXT, IMAGE, AND LATE MEDIEVAL LITERARY FORMS 137

or the interesting table of contents in the "black" Domesday book of Ipswich (figure 10). In this final example, the decorative filler in the center of the page plays a mediating role between one part of the list and the other, allowing a reader to follow a line of text without interruption all the way across. This kind of line-filler has a twentieth-century analogue in the dotted lines that often connect chapter titles on the left with page numbers on the right in a table of contents. Such additions do not regularize the right margin of the text-block (which is here, instead, forcefully enclosed by a red and blue frame); instead, they eradicate any white space within it, directing the gothic aesthetic of the filled page towards the purpose of easier reading.

The line-fillers that fill the space after an item in a list call to mind their most familiar use in late-medieval manuscripts: in the layout of the psalms, that most important and influential of biblical books. The psalms took many physical forms in the early Middle Ages: they were sometimes laid out in a continuous script, for example, without any break between lines or even words. The psalms were also laid out *per cola et commata*, following Jerome's plan for the text of his Vulgate; in this system, each clause or phrase begins a new line, marking both a syntactical unit and a new unit of thought. As the psalms were recognized as non-metrical verse, they were laid out to display the parallel stichic verses that have become familiar – these structures were believed to suggest, even in translation, the forms of the Hebrew poetry from which they derived. In the presentation of the psalms in the eighth-century Vespasian Psalter, for example, each verse begins with a new line and a *littera notabilior*, while any overrun from line to line is indented (figure 11).[28] Spaces at the ends of verses are unfilled. But by the later Middle Ages, this layout was frequently modified such that all lines were aligned with the left margin, and any space left at the end of the verse at the right was filled with decoration: that is, line-fillers. Such line-fillers at the end of psalmic verses create the dominant look of psalters and books of hours throughout the fourteenth and fifteenth centuries.[29]

There are several ways of understanding the function of these visible forms with relation to adjacent words. Like all punctuation, they tell readers something about how to interact with the verbal structures they see, both for smoother public performance of texts and also for better understanding of them. The ancient system of *distinctiones* marked units of sense, whereas the medieval *positurae* one finds in liturgical texts developed primarily

---

[28] For an introduction to this well-known manuscript, see the British Library online Catalogue of Digitised Manuscripts, https://www.bl.uk/manuscripts/FullDisplay. aspx?ref=Cotton_MS_Vespasian_A_I (accessed 31 January 2023).

[29] Malcolm Parkes notes that in breviaries and some books of hours this layout was "abandoned to save space" (leaving the psalms instead written as punctuated prose, across the page). See Parkes, *Pause and Effect: An Introduction to the History of Punctuation in the West* (Aldershot, UK: Ashgate, 1992), p. 104.

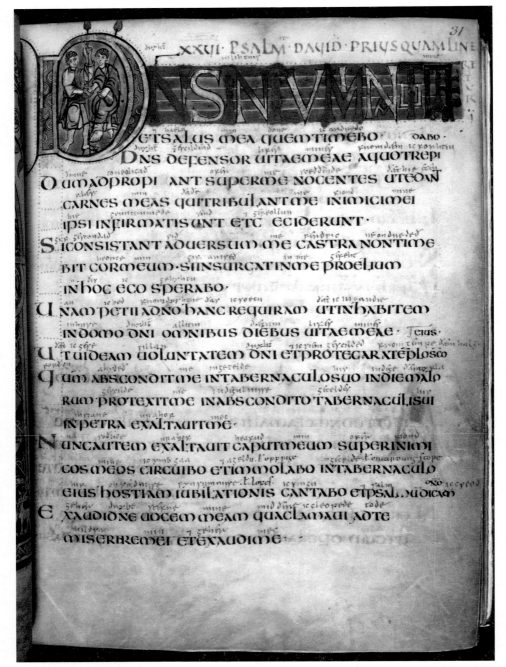

11 Layout of Psalm-verses. Psalter ("Vespasian Psalter"), second quarter of the eighth century to mid-ninth century, England. London, British Library Cotton MS Vespasian A I, f. 31r. © The British Library Board.

TEXT, IMAGE, AND LATE MEDIEVAL LITERARY FORMS 139

to aid in recitation.[30] Because the psalms were characteristically used in performance, their layout and punctuation serves, in part, to help a reader to parse a text quickly for singing or chanting out loud.[31] Moreover, laying out a psalmic text *per cola et commata* (or phrase by phrase) emphasizes its constituent intellectual parts, its *sententiae*, as well as syntactical patterns of repetition, and the logical and rhetorical effects that such patterns can have. Punctuation and layout thereby produce readings of texts, by indicating which words to group with which others – in other words, this is a potentially significant interpretative engagement. The most extreme and funny example of such meaningful groupings is the kind of poem whose sense is completely inverted by different kinds of punctuation – of which there are medieval examples (*Trusty, seldom/to his friends unjust*) and modern ones (*Let's eat, grandma* v. *Let's eat grandma.*)[32]

Both sound and sense were of interest to writers and readers over the medieval centuries, and visual systems of manuscript design could be deployed to help with either one.[33] Moreover, these traces of punctuation as clues to meaningful structure in the psalms open further questions about the visual aspects of verse layout in other contexts. The layout and punctuation of texts can reflect literary structures, as well as grammatical and rhetorical ones, providing revealing insights into medieval readers' understanding of prosody, verse form, and genre.[34] The recognition that lines of verse should be separated

---

[30] For an interesting discussion of the complex and overlapping development of *distinctiones* and *positurae*, see Parkes, *Pause and Effect*, pp. 9–40.

[31] Eyal Poleg, "Memory, Performance, and Change: The Psalms' Layout in Late Medieval and Early Modern Bibles," in *From Scrolls to Scrolling: Sacred Texts, Materiality, and Dynamic Media Cultures in Judaism, Christianity, and Islam*, ed. Brad A. Anderson (Berlin: De Gruyter, 2020), pp. 119–51. Poleg writes, "the Psalms were typically written in lines of poetry. In earlier manuscripts they were written *in lines of meaning*, spaciously representing their poetical structure, and the way they were chanted in churches" (122).

[32] *DIMEV* 6077. For other examples of early punctuation poems, see James R. Kreuzer, "Some Earlier Examples of the Rhetorical Device in *Ralph Roister Doister* (III. iv. 33 ff.)," *The Review of English Studies* 14 (1938), 321–23; R. H. Robbins, "Punctuation Poems: A Further Note," *Review of English Studies* 15 (1939), 206–07; and R. H. Robbins, *Secular Lyrics of the XIVth and XVth Centuries* (Oxford: Clarendon Press, 1952), nos. 110–02. For valuable readings of them, see Christopher Cannon, *Middle English Literature* (Cambridge: Polity Press, 2008), pp. 46–47; and Jenni Nuttall, "One Poem, Two Ways," *Stylisticienne*, 27 March 2014, https://stylisticienne.com/one-poem-two-ways/ (accessed 25 January 2023).

[33] For discussion of these "complementary" modes of punctuation, see Alderik H. Blom, *Glossing the Psalms: The Emergence of the Written Vernaculars in Western Europe from the 7th to the 12th Centuries* (Berlin and Boston: De Gruyter, 2017), pp. 51–53, and references there.

[34] For an example of how layout might engage with literary genre, see Juliet Fleming's gentle suggestion that the nature of the sonnet sequence was shaped by the ornaments printed alongside the poems ("Changed Opinion"). For selected studies of how medieval verse forms were experienced on the page, see, e.g., my "Reading the Forms of *Sir Thopas*," in *Medieval English Manuscripts: Form, Aesthetics, and*

140 JESSICA BRANTLEY

into list-like lines on the page is not universal, of course; verse is laid out in prose lineation in Old English, for example, and often also for various reasons in Middle English. But when a poem is displayed in a way that fully separates its verse lines, it indicates that literary forms have become a visual concern. Layout could gesture both towards logical and semantic organization and also towards literary structures, in what Malcolm Parkes calls "the coincidence of sense with verse form."[35]

How do line-fillers fit into this picture? The empty spaces that are a by-product of verse lineation both signal how the text should be divided and demonstrate the proper rhythm of reading. The designs that occupy those spaces both obscure and emphasize the pauses – they emphasize the pauses in that they offer something different from lines of verbal text, and, as visual forms, they are unpronounceable. Like most other marks of punctuation, but much more visually dramatic, line-fillers are representations of silence. Paradoxically, though, in consolidating the text-block, filling in even where a pause should be, they also efface the emptiness that might be a visual analogue of silence. Mixing the media of image and word, line-fillers make the text-block visually uniform in aspect.

It is worth considering the role of line-fillers as indications of verse-forms, for – although they are most familiar from devotional books such as psalters and books of hours – they play a role in the layout of vernacular poetry, as well. To take just one interesting example from a liturgical book, a French poem in the Entwisle Hours has decorative bars after each line (figure 12).[36] This French hymn to the Virgin, a paraphrase of the *Ave Maria* beginning "Dame je te rent le salut," is written in stanzaic verse, each stanza concluding with a Latin phrase from the prayer: *Ave Maria, gracia plena*, and so on (fols.

---

the Literary Text, ed. Alexandra Gillespie and Arthur Bahr, special issue of *Chaucer Review* 47 (2013), 416–38; Daniel Wakelin, *Designing English: Early Literature on the Page* (Oxford: Bodleian Library, University of Oxford, 2018); and especially Daniel Sawyer, *Reading English Verse in Manuscript, c. 1350–c. 1500* (Oxford: Oxford University Press, 2020).

[35] Parkes, *Pause and Effect*, p. 105.

[36] London, British Library MS Sloane 2321, known as the Entwisle Hours after its probable first owners, Sir Bertin Entwisle (d. 1455) and his wife Lucy, whom he married in 1437. The book was made c. 1440, most likely in northern France, although the liturgical use is Sarum and it seems to have been intended from the start for the English market, perhaps even for the Entwisle family. For other notices of the MS, see Walter de Gray Birch and Henry Jenner, *Early Drawings and Illuminations: An Introduction to the Study of Illustrated Manuscripts* (London: Bagster and Sons, 1879), p. 16; Kathleen Scott, "Caveat Lector: Ownership and Standardization in the Illustration of Fifteenth-Century English Manuscripts," *English Manuscript Studies* 1 (1989), 19–63 (p. 59, n. 54); Janet Backhouse, *Illumination from Books of Hours* (London: British Library, 2004), figure 1; and Kathleen L. Scott, *Later Gothic Manuscripts 1390–1490*, A Survey of Manuscripts Illuminated in the British Isles 6, 2 vols. (London: Harvey Miller, 1996), II, 281, figure 14.

12 Vernacular verse with line-fillers. Book of Hours ("Entwisle Hours"), c. 1440, England. London, British Library MS Sloane 2321, f. 14r. © The British Library Board.

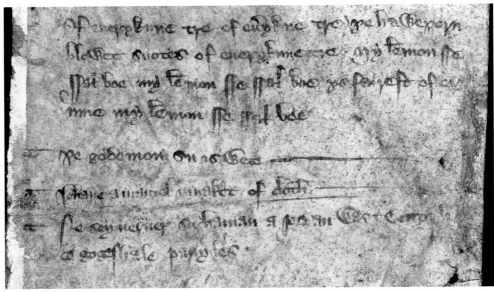

13 Poetic fragments with line-fillers. Collection of fragments, fourteenth–sixteenth century, England. Oxford, Bodleian MS Rawlinson D. 913.

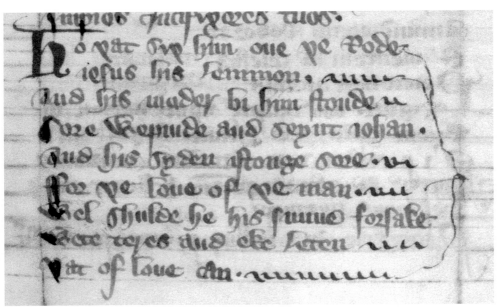

14 "Ho that sith him one the rode." Miscellany, ?fourteenth century, England. London, British Library MS Harley 7322, f. 7. © The British Library Board.

TEXT, IMAGE, AND LATE MEDIEVAL LITERARY FORMS 143

14v–15v). The stanzas begin with decorated initial at the start, as well as a *littera notabilior* at the start of each line.[37] But the line-fillers that flag the rhyming endings of these lines are equally important: they mark the rhymes at the end of each line and extend the text block into a regular rectangle. This poem looks like a psalm, one might say – or, one might conclude that the layout of the psalms has taught the designer of this manuscript how to represent poetry on the page.[38] And because the poetic lines, unlike the psalmic verses, do not carry over from line to line, the line-fillers here are even more visually insistent than they are on a page of a psalter.

Although line-fillers provide opportunities for visual exuberance in litanies and play a role in the decoration of a luxury book like the Entwisle Hours, one can also find more utilitarian and minimally visual instances of them, particularly in English verse – instances that highlight their operations as punctuation and suggest that the impetus behind the form is as much textual as visual. To take one extreme example, on the verso of the surplus strip of vellum bound into Rawlinson D.913, which contains the famous Middle English lyric "Maiden in the mor lay," line-fillers are used to mysterious purpose (figure 13). They appear after single English lines – "þe gode mon on is weie," for instance, in the middle – which are also marked by paraphs at the head. Ardis Butterfield usefully compares these elucidations of text to an index of first lines – that is, to the sort of lists we saw earlier – though, as she emphasizes, it is not at all certain that these are the first lines of longer poems.[39]

A more conclusive example of line-fillers in English vernacular poetry comes in Harley MS 7322. The short lyric "Ho that sith him one the rode," for example, includes both conventional punctuation – the *punctus* visible at the ends of lines 2, 4, 5, 6, and 9 – and also rubricated squiggles definitively functioning as line-fillers (figure 14). In this vernacular setting, the line-filler relates to the visual forms of brackets (also called braces or rhyme-lines) that are so common in Middle English verse, and, indeed, a desultory attempt has been made to bracket these verses.[40] Most often rubricated, brackets work to display the structure of the rhymes: connecting rhyming lines in patterns of *abba*, *abab*, etc. The Harley brackets do

---

[37] Due to the initial at the start of the poem, the first four verses occupy five lines. After that, each verse is laid out on a single line (fol. 14r).

[38] Interestingly, in an even stronger echo of a psalmic layout, the French couplets in the Hours of Christ Crucified in MS Walters W.102 are laid out as two hemistichs separated by punctuation, rather than as two individual verses. They are followed, when necessary, by a line-filler. See, e.g., figure 3, lines 12–13.

[39] Ardis Butterfield, "Poems without Form? *Maiden in the mor lay* Revisited," in *Readings in Medieval Textuality: Essays in Honour of A. C. Spearing*, ed. Cristina Maria Cervone and D. Vance Smith (Cambridge: D. S. Brewer, 2016), pp. 169–94. Butterfield notes possible parallels with the Vernon manuscript, John Grimestone's preaching book, and BL Harley 7322 (p. 175, n. 9).

[40] Sawyer notes that, in some contexts, brackets are "cognate" with decorative line fillers; see *Reading English Verse*, pp. 124, 130, 136–38.

144 JESSICA BRANTLEY

not clearly indicate rhymes, but they create interesting and symmetrical visual patterns on the page, and they recall the sound effects of which the text is built. Intriguingly, they break open the text-block visually, rather than working to preserve solid right justification. In using both line-fillers and brackets, this scribe commits to displaying both the metrical structure of the verses and the idea of rhyme. I would say that the brackets here, which seem almost like an afterthought, merely gesture towards rhyme as a concept.[41] But the confident line-fillers speak to the metrical form of the text; its meter is irregular, its lines are ragged, and the simple rubricated designs signal to readers that it is, in fact, a poem.

A few further examples can suggest the range of uses to which line-fillers were put in marking out the forms of vernacular poetry. Sometimes, they reinforce the rectangle of the text-block when the uneven right edge of verse lines leaves it implicit. In a copy of Hoccleve's *Regement of Princes*, for example, otiose strokes stretching out from the final letter of each line help to demarcate a rectangle, even though the manuscript is unruled.[42] Other times their purpose is less clear: in another manuscript of Hoccleve, in this case *Jereslaus's Wife*, short marks at the end of every verse seem to allude to line-fillers. Though their purpose is obscure – they do not, for example, regularize the right edge of the text-block – Daniel Sawyer guesses that these unachieved line-fillers might echo the fuller apparatus of an exemplar, and he suggests that they might indicate "just the idea of poetry."[43] They certainly emphasize or display the ends of lines, just as large initials and red-tipped capitals emphasize the start, marking end rhyme as an important feature of this poem's form. In a striking example from another manuscript, containing Lydgate's *Troy Book* and *Siege of Thebes*, shorter stanzaic poems by Lydgate, Skelton, and others consistently display formal line-fillers made up of fanciful red curlicues (figure 15).[44] This manuscript, at least, seems to recognize that part of the necessary apparatus of short verse (interestingly, not of the longer narrative poems) is decoration that calls attention to the forms of its lines. This manuscript seems to recognize that images might illuminate as

---

41 For a valuable account of manuscript evidence for the importance of rhyme to late medieval English scribes and readers, see Sawyer, *Reading English Verse*, pp. 110–43. Sawyer observes, however, that occasionally brackets "do not correspond to rhyme scheme, or adorn unrhymed verse: they might merely indicate the idea of poetry" (p. 124).

42 Cambridge, St. John's College I.22, fol. 5v. Cited by Wakelin, *Immaterial Texts*, pp. 108–09.

43 Oxford, Bodleian Library MS Eng. Poet. D.4, fols. 4r–30v. Cited by Sawyer, *Reading Verse*, p. 124, n. 46.

44 London, British Library MS Royal 18 D 2, fols. 1v–5r; fols. 163r–211v. The poems with line-fillers include John Lydgate, *Testament*; William Cornish, "A Treatise between Information and Truth"; John Skelton, "On the Death of the Earl of Northumberland"; "Le assemble de dyeus"; Lydgate, "The reignes of the kyngis of Englande"; "The blsyoure of the arms of kyngis"; William Peeris, "Descent of the Lords Percy"; and proverbial and moral verses transcribed from the walls and ceilings of Percy's houses. Cited in Sawyer, *Reading Verse*, p. 138, n. 94.

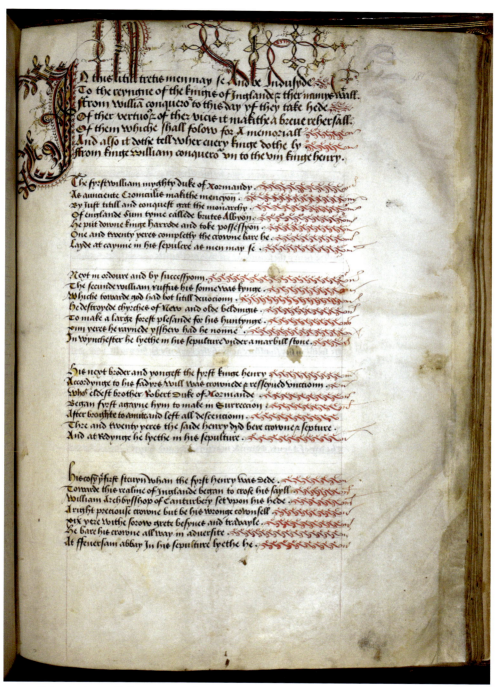

15   John Lydgate, "The reignes of the kyngis of Englande," mid-fifteenth century to the second quarter of the sixteenth century, England. London, British Library MS Royal 18 D 2, f. 181r. © The British Library Board.

146 JESSICA BRANTLEY

well as unsettle texts, and that – iconoclasts aside – medieval literature emerges necessarily from that intermedial context.

I have not attempted here a comprehensive description of line-fillers in late medieval manuscripts, nor even offered a full account of their appearance in vernacular verse. Much remains to be done in studying this subject, but, in the absence of definitive answers, I hope at least to have raised useful questions. Just as scholars have recently begun to develop a better understanding of the rhyme-lines or brackets that are so striking in Middle English poetry, so I suspect that we would benefit from thinking more deeply about line-fillers.[45] Line-fillers are an integral part of the design of the text block, not an afterthought, and in some profound ways they frame or structure readers' encounter with the text. These small decorative additions, operating fascinatingly at the center of the page, can provide insight into how the scribes who designed the look of written poetry understood its forms to work. Line-fillers reinforce the experience of looking at manuscript pages as central to reading medieval verse, and they make the visual experience of poetry an important component of its literary understanding. Through line-fillers, one might even say that images structure readers' encounters with medieval poetry – its sound, its sense, and its verse forms.

A satisfying definition of the literary in any period is tricky to come by, and, in order to get close, one needs to gesture in multiple directions at once. James Simpson, for example, usefully lists "five plausible definitions" of the texts he will treat as literature in *Reform and Cultural Revolution*: formally engaged, entertaining in function, positivistically connected to a sense of tradition, unconcerned with historical truth, and discursive.[46] These definitions are useful to think with. If the category of the literary is plausibly conceived in terms of a text's formal commitments, for example – as much recent work in medieval studies has suggested it might be – then the simple but evocative forms of decorative line fillers deserve further consideration. They are also entertaining, part of a tradition, and products of the imagination rather than reality. I would suggest, also, that they are "discursive," a Simpsonian category defined by the ability to illuminate by unsettling. Line-fillers, in occupying that uncertain ground between text and image, as well as between psalms and vernacular verse, prompt close readers to wonder how these representational systems work together, or at odds with each other, how they mirror each other, and how they differ. For all the familiarity of their forms, line-fillers, upon closer inspection, do not stay in their lane; instead, they unsettle norms of both text and image in a manner that necessitates an interpretative practice allied to the literary. Unsettling scholarly norms, as well, they remind us that the most seemingly inconsequential of forms can productively occupy the center of our attention.

---

[45] For examples of recent work on rhyme-lines, see, e.g., Sawyer, *Reading Verse*, pp. 123–43; and Jane Gilbert, "Form and/as Mode of Existence," *Romantic Review* 111 (2020), 27–47.

[46] Simpson, *Reform and Cultural Revolution*, pp. 4–5.

8

Catching at Words: The Literal, the Metaphorical, and the Obvious

Chris Barrett

CATCH/WORDS

This essay considers obviousness as both an expressive and hermeneutic mode, one long dismissed and yet oddly well-positioned to do humane work in the narrative-receiving and narrative-making work of the twenty-first century. This study of the obvious, though, involves parsing the relationship of obviousness to textual interpretation, a practice that often begins with terms like "literal" and "metaphorical." Disentangling the material sense of a sentence from its symbolic or figurative rendering has long vexed the study of literature, and it has sometimes had history-inflecting effects, given the weaponization of interpretation by institutional interests and authorities. James Simpson's *Burning to Read* offers one such example in the case of Reformation England. Observing that "the literal sense" of a text is always already a "fairly tenuous fiction," one shaped by "interpretive, unwritten assumptions of the interpretive community," Simpson traces how the alluring hope of an absolute meaning, independent of its readers' expectations and hermeneutic labors, can lead to fundamentalist approaches to texts.[1] In Reformation England, the fantasy of a liberating literalism only entrenched the institutional powers entrusted with resolution of interpretive difference, and the result was centuries of sectarian violence among Catholic and Protestant denominations. While that case offers readers today a cautionary tale about the authoritarian creep of invoking the literal as self-evident or stable, plenty of early modern writers in their own moment perceived this danger clearly, developing language for this kind of motivated, sharp-bladed interpretation. By the late sixteenth and early seventeenth

---

[1] James Simpson, *Burning to Read: English Fundamentalism and its Reformation Opponents* (Cambridge, Mass.: Harvard University Press, 2007), p. 107

148   CHRIS BARRETT

centuries, writers invoked a phrase for the implicitly strategic, often cynical, always interested interpretation of words without regard to their contextual valences – that is, a term for a perverse literalism: it was "to catch at words." For example, Richard Bancroft, in a 1588 sermon, cites authority to complain of false, scholarly prophets: "If they catch but a word … they straight insult upon it … They wring and wrest the Scriptures according as they fansie."[2] Likewise, William Burton in 1602 decried those who listen to sermons "only to watch and catch, at a word and a halfe, taking only what will serue their turne (like the diuell himselfe) …."[3] And Robert Holland in 1594 warns that when "a man Gods word doth heare, / And understands thereof no more / Then ere he heard," it is as if "The deuill did catch the word away, / That seed by the way side it lay."[4] To catch at words was, then, to deform the possibilities of interpretation by insisting on an impoverishing and dangerous singularity of meaning; catching words involved presenting a text as though its sense were self-evident, even though that supposedly literal sense was, and always is, the product of convention and elaboration. Another way to put this: literalist catching at words creates a fictive but powerful sense of obviousness, with which to deny the viability of alternative interpretive efforts. And it is that sense of obviousness that this essay seeks to unpack and reimagine.

As an expressive mode, obviousness is curiously positioned in relation to interpretive labor. If the literal purports to require no interpretation beyond a single, readily available clarity, the adjacent category of the obvious takes things further, actively resisting the project of interpretation itself. To class something as obvious is to position it outside the realm of interpretation: it is immediate and irrefutable in ways that foreclose continued exploration. Supposedly, nothing may be gleaned from the monolithic surface of the stony obvious, and this makes the obvious dismissible. One who "states the obvious" usually brackets it off, apologizing for introducing it into otherwise interrogatable speech.

For this reason, the obvious tends to be overlooked, hiding in plain sight, even in literary criticism. There is, for example, no entry for "obvious" in the *Princeton Encyclopedia of Poetics*. Indeed, the entry on "representation" even seems to suggest that poetry and the obvious might be at odds: "Poetry aims to show that relationships exist among the things of the world that are not otherwise obvious," writes T. V. F. Brogan.[5] The obvious, here, appears as that which is not suited to poetic expression. Despite (or perhaps because of) the

---

2   Richard Bancroft, *A sermon preached at Paules Crosse …* (London: Printed by E. B[ollifant] for Gregorie Seton, 1588), p. 39.
3   William Burton, *Ten sermons vpon the first, second, third and fourth verses of the sixt of Matthew …* (London: Printed by Richard Field for Thomas Man, 1602), p. 63.
4   Robert Holland, *The holie historie of our Lord and Sauiour Iesus Christs natiuitie, life, actes …* (London: George Tobie, 1594), p. 93.
5   T. V. F. Brogan, "Representation," in *The Princeton Encyclopedia of Poetry and Poetics*, 4th ed., ed. Roland Greene, Stephen Cushman, Clare Cavanagh et al. (Princeton, N.J.: Princeton University Press, 2012), pp. 1171–74, at p. 1173.

THE LITERAL, THE METAPHORICAL, AND THE OBVIOUS 149

dominance of hermeneutics of suspicion in literary criticism, obviousness has not often appeared as the subject of investigation.[6]

To get to the essence of the obvious, then, it might be necessary to start with the word itself, which according to the *OED* is as much an early modern phenomenon as the Reformation, appearing first in printed English in the sixteenth century.[7] The most common sense of "obvious" for us today might be the word's oldest sense: "Plain and evident to the mind; perfectly clear or manifest; plainly distinguishable; clearly visible." Shortly after its appearance, though, "obvious" acquired another sense – "Lacking in subtlety, sophistication, or originality; banal, predictable" – a sense perhaps reflective of the period's celebration of rhetorical complexity and strategic self-presentation. Within a short period of time, the denotations of "obvious" associated "perfectly clear or manifest" with banality, and the obvious has never really regained any sort of rhetorical stature. The term "obvious" emerged to describe the category of phenomena that, being self-evident, require no interpretive labor – but came to describe, too, the category of phenomena that, lacking the need for interpretive labor, deserved only derogation, as though what were plain must necessarily be without merit.

I linger over this history of the word "obvious" because the term's association with the immediate and abundantly clear has somewhat ironically obfuscated its core paradox, a paradox perceptible in its etymology and essential to revisiting the representational possibilities of the obvious, liberated from the constraints of its historical deprecation. The etymology of "obvious" is itself amusingly obvious: the word comes from the "classical Latin obvius," meaning "presenting itself to the mind or senses, ready to hand … exposed or open (to), in the way." The word "obvious" is itself the combination of the prefix *ob-*, in the way of, and *via-*, a road or way, meaning that the obvious is that which is *in the way of* the way. And therein lies the enabling, generative paradox of obviousness: the ostensible self-evidence of the obvious asserts that nothing stands in the way of its interpretation; at the same time, obviousness appears as some hulking bulk in the hermeneutic road, defying and interrupting interpretive action. The provocative premise of obviousness is, then, that there is an expressive register that defies the application of available interpretive systems. To say something obvious is to say something outside interpretation.

That power of the obvious to frustrate existing hermeneutics and to assert expression outside that which can be elaborated in critique makes it a fascinating discursive category on its own. But the reason I am seeking to understand the workings of the obvious right now is tied to the historical context of this essay's writing. The obvious – a term that came into English in the sixteenth century – demands attention now, in the twenty-first century, because it is the dominant perceptual, conceptual, aesthetic, and ethical category of this moment. The

---

[6] One exception is Stanley E. Fish, "Normal Circumstances, Literal Language, Direct Speech Acts, the Ordinary, the Everyday, the Obvious, What Goes without Saying, and Other Special Cases," *Critical Inquiry* 4 (1978), 625–44, especially at 626–27.

[7] *OED*, "obvious, adj. and n."

150   CHRIS BARRETT

obvious is the register of the Anthropocene, a period that might be said to have begun, too, in the early modern period, when the social, economic, and political conditions for the climate crisis (i.e. the plantation systems that anticipated and enabled fossil fuel-based agro-industrial capitalism) were laid. Every day, the obvious effects of the climate emergency unfold. Definitive and enervating, self-evident and yet even still dismissible in some halls of power, the twenty-first century's carbon nightmare is obvious, even if its palpable immediacy is as unequally distributed around the planet as responsibility for the crisis itself.

And so I find myself wondering about the supposed intractability of obviousness. Is there a way to redefine obviousness such that it does not unleash the violence of literalism but rather functions as an engine of novel, diverse thought? Can we learn from fundamentalist reading practices the danger of treating the obvious as some kind of ontological given, external to the project of critique and creativity, instead of the pliant and potential-filled cultural construct it is? This essay proposes theorizing obviousness as an invitation to productive detour, rather than a boulder blocking the interpretive path. In place of its obstacularity, I suggest restoring to the register of the obvious its power to unsettle and regenerate the practices of communal meaning-making, in a moment when new reading practices are urgently needed.

The instances of literary obviousness are many and diverse – they may be generic, thematic, rhetorical, and more. This chapter considers a bibliographic instance of literary obviousness in order to think the generative workings of its resistance to assimilation into existing forms of interpretive action. Recalling the start of this chapter, I turn not to the catching at words that defined willful literalism, but to the literal catchword of early modern printed books. The catchword has a long and varied history that precedes its appearance in this historical context, but in late fifteenth-century English printing, it refers to the first word of a codex's printed page of type, positioned by early modern compositors at the bottom of the preceding page to ensure that the pages stayed in sequence during imposition and to guarantee the accurate folding of the printed sheets. Those of us who work with early modern printed materials have disciplined ourselves to ignore the catchword, or to bracket its bibliographic significance, but if you have ever had the pleasure of introducing your students to an early modern printed book, or to its digital surrogate, you know that a student will invariably ask about the tiny word at the bottom of each page. Our students' reading reminds us of the hypervisibility of the catchword, and of how obvious a thing the catchword might be to consider when reading an early modern book. The status of the catchword vis-à-vis our available interpretive paradigms might be contingent on the nature of that obviousness.

So while the reading practice I seek to imagine in this chapter would offer a way to assimilate the catchword into the literary labor of its surrounding text, the catchword turns out to be a case study for thinking more broadly about the hermeneutics of the obvious. Indeed, the catchword might be the ideal specimen for doing so. For one thing, catchwords are

THE LITERAL, THE METAPHORICAL, AND THE OBVIOUS 151

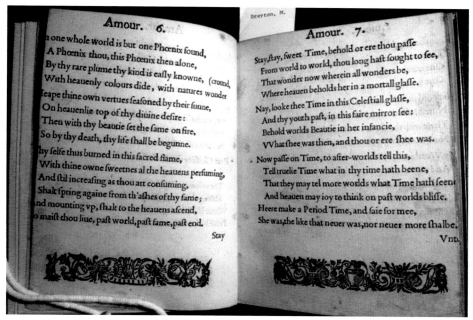

1   Facing pages in Michael Drayton, *Ideas Mirrour* (London, 1594). STC 7203, B3v to B4r. Photograph by Chris Barrett, from the collection of the Folger Shakespeare Library.

definitionally obvious: they are very much in the way of the way, appearing on the eyeline path from the end of one page to the top of the next in a continuous reading practice. And they are self-evident in their presence: the catchword effectively appears twice, a doubly-visible object that, because it presents – in the language of the *OED* definition of the obvious – as "perfectly clear or manifest; plainly distinguishable; clearly visible," ends up being conventionally ignored for (again in *OED* definition of the obvious) "Lacking in subtlety, sophistication, or originality." But catchwords, because of their obviousness, actually invite some creative meaning-making, beyond presently available interpretive frameworks. Considering the possibilities of their workings might reveal how redefining the obviousness might lead to literally meaning-full encounters with obvious things.

STAY

In Michael Drayton's 1594 *Ideas Mirrour*, each of 51 sonnets, or "Amours," appears on its own page. These amours tend to be fairly self-contained, without many overt linkages among preceding and following sonnets. Even so, between Amour 6 ("In one whole world is but one Phoenix found") and Amour 7 ("Stay, stay, sweet Time, behold or ere thou passe") on their facing

152   CHRIS BARRETT

pages, there appears an unlikely but poignant connection between the two poems: the catchword "Stay" (see figure 1).

Before I say more about this catchword "Stay," let me say some things about the early modern printing purposes catchwords served. Appearing at the bottom of a page, the catchword is a preview of the first word of the following page; it helps to ensure that sequential pages follow one another. Because catchwords can save printings from going awry, the catchword is itself almost as old as professional printing in England, having been introduced in the late fifteenth century by Richard Pynson, one of England's earliest printers.[8] After Pynson introduced the catchword, it swiftly became ubiquitous in early modern English printing. Even before Pynson introduced the catchword to English printing, though, the catchword had been used in the production of medieval manuscripts. Possibly introduced to Spain, Italy, and France under Islamic influence around 1000 CE, the catchword appeared on the last page of a quire and anticipated the first word of the subsequent quire, to ensure the gatherings are sequenced accurately during the binding process.[9] In short, while the catchword became quite rare by the twentieth century, it had enjoyed a nearly millennium-long run of being immensely useful to the work of making a book.[10]

Modern readers of early modern printed texts learn to ignore the catchword, to treat it as a non-signifying element of the page. Given the near-total absence of any reference to catchwords in early modern English texts themselves (the *OED*'s earliest attestation of the term comes in 1693, some two hundred years after catchwords' use in printed English books began), it seems that early modern readers, too, naturalized the presence of this bottom-of-the-page item as an unremarkable artifact of the printing process.[11]

In the case of the catchword between Amour 6 and Amour 7 in the 1594 *Ideas Mirrour*, however, the catchword tempts the reader to read the "Stay" as interacting with the literary text. Most immediately, the catchword

---

8   For more on Pynson and his contributions to and competitors in early English printing, see Valerie Hotchkiss and Fred C. Robinson, *English in Print: from Caxton to Shakespeare to Milton* (Urbana, Ill.: University of Illinois Press, 2008), pp. 9, 48–49, 53; and H. S. Bennett, *English Books & Readers 1475–1557*, 2nd ed. (Cambridge: Cambridge University Press, 1969), pp. 182–93.

9   Michelle B. Brown, *Understanding Illuminated Manuscripts: A Guide to Technical Terms* (Los Angeles: The J. Paul Getty Museum in association with the British Library, 1994), p. 36.

10 The term "catchword" now tends to refer either to a word that becomes widely and frequently used, or to the guidewords at the top of alphabetically-organized texts (dictionaries or encyclopedias, for example). Law texts sometimes use "catchwords," tags to flag the central legal matters at stake in a case.

11 *OED*, "catchword, n." The term "catchword" seems to have been at least briefly preceded by the term "direction word." See, for examples, Joseph Moxon, *Mechanick Exercises ...* (London: Printed for Joseph Moxon, 1683), vol. 2, p. 264; and Randle Holme, *The academy of armory ...* (Chester: Printed for the author, 1688), p. 120.

THE LITERAL, THE METAPHORICAL, AND THE OBVIOUS   153

amplifies the injunction with which Amour 7 begins and which undergirds the poem: "Stay, stay, sweet Time," begins the sonnet, urging the personified Time to pause and consider the beloved, who is at once that which Time has been looking forward to, and that which coming years will never see again. Amour 7 carves out a moment for Time to regard this exceptional being in the exceptional moments of her extraordinary presence. The "Stay" which precedes this poem anticipates Amour 7; but at the same time, this same "Stay" continues the sentiment of Amour 6's conclusion. Amour 6 centers on the conceit of the beloved as a phoenix whose virtuous immolation produces a new bird and, by extension, immortality: "So maist thou live, past world, past fame, past end," concludes the poem. The catchword "Stay" thus seems especially expressive in this context: if the beloved is to live on indefinitely, the "Stay" at once speaks to her endless presence in the world (she is staying) and to the desire for her to linger in the lover's present before moving "past world, past fame, past end." The catchword begs the beloved to "Stay," quite literally "past end" of the poem. In inviting the subjects of these two sonnets to wait, if just a moment, the catchword posits an unexpected connection between the two texts, foregrounding the temporal preoccupations of sonnet convention.

At the same time as the catchword attends to the process or interruption of time sought within the situation of the sonnets' subjects, it also attends to the process or interruption of the reader's own practice. Appearing at the bottom of the left facing page as a single word, "Stay," read as an imperative (the sense in which it is used in the first lines of Amour 7), seems to command not Time, but the reader: "Stay" on this page. The catchword elaborates what comes before, in the final lines of Amour 6, while simultaneously reduplicating Amour 7's initial injunction, all the while arresting the reader's gaze with the possibility of an epideictic command. The catchword here thus bridges these two sonnets while marking – perhaps even extending – the moment at which the reader's gaze pauses at the page break. In the phenomenologically minute process of lifting the continuously reading gaze from the bottom of one page to the top of the next, across the material gap of the book, the "Stay" catchword prescribes and indexes readerly experience, in the same way it connects and severs these two poems.

While this catchword strikes me as doing something remarkable in these pages, it can be hard to know exactly how to account for what it is doing. Because it is a word, it appears to have semantic content – something that distinguishes it from other intratextual navigational apparatuses, like the page number. Because the catchword emerges from the text itself, it seems a part of the textual project even while it exists because of the production of the book. Because it appears in a space distinct from the text and invites comparison with the text, it resembles a gloss, but one governed by different expectations of topicality; and because it duplicates a following word in a displaced location, it resembles an internal quotation,

154 CHRIS BARRETT

but without an apparent principle of selection and inclusion. Because the catchword is part of the unaltered book, it differs from marginalia, despite having a similarly emphatic relationship to the material volume. Made from the text but included in the book under conditions that generally exclude it from being read as integral to the text across printings, the catchword sits, quite literally and figuratively, on the margins of analysis, apart from considerations of poetics and hermeneutics. It is hard to know how to read the catchword.

Literary criticism shares this trouble with the early modern printed catchword. Because reading conventions from the early modern period to our own have disregarded the catchword as subject to the same interpretive labor as the set text of each printed page, the catchword appears in literary criticism of the period's works chiefly through book historical accounts. (By contrast, the medieval manuscript catchword occupies a different kind of stature from the usually-ignored early modern printed catchword; because for medievalists the catchword helps to assess the quiring of manuscripts, it is crucial to the work of interpreting the handwritten book.[12]) The catchword typically assists in the reconstruction of printing conditions and processes, and often proves most useful when it constitutes or indexes errors.[13] The catchword makes mis-pagination and mis-assigned signatures readily visible, and thus tends to show up in literary study in close proximity to error, bibliographically defined. Indeed, because the catchword can indicate material hiccups in book printing, it is sometimes invoked as error to explain the elusive. That sense of error can be liberating; Julian Yates encourages attention to the possibility of errors in printed books as a way to recover "the forgotten labors of the print shop ... the strangeness of the medium."[14] Yet the catchword as error often appears more explanatory than recuperative. For example, the notorious ending to Mary Wroth's *Urania* (the word "And" followed by a period) has sometimes been treated as the product of an erroneous catchword printing, though, as Colleen Ruth Rosenfeld notes, such a reading tends to foreclose other accounts of narrative experiment enclosed within this unusual conclusion.[15]

Given current literary critical models, the most likely ways of reading "Stay" on these pages from *Ideas Mirrour* are three in number and not mutually exclusive; in the interests of space, I paint them here in glaringly broad brushstrokes. The first model is to consider the "Stay" entirely as an

[12] My gratitude to Sebastian Sobecki for this observation.
[13] See, for example, Hao Tianhu's account of how catchwords in an eighteenth-century edition of Milton's poetry reveal lineation changes and difficulties with casting off copy: "Lines Per Page, Engravings, and Catchwords in Milton's 1720 *Poetical Works*," *Studies in Bibliography* 59 (2015), 191–95.
[14] Julian Yates, *Error, Misuse, Failure: Object Lessons from the English Renaissance* (Minneapolis: University of Minnesota Press, 2003), p. 115.
[15] Colleen Ruth Rosenfeld, "Wroth's Clause," *ELH* 76 (2009), 1049–71, at 1050–51.

THE LITERAL, THE METAPHORICAL, AND THE OBVIOUS 155

artifact of printing, and useful insofar as it reveals something about the conditions of this book's production. The second model is to consider the "Stay" as the product of some intentionality – on the part of the author, the compositor, or another participant in the collaborative process of creating or preparing this text for print. The third model might be to undertake a close reading of "Stay" as it interacts with these two poems or with the readerly experience – perhaps in a way similar to my reading just above – but to treat those interactions as accidental, a felicitous happenstance otherwise unassimilable into a critical account of this literary work beyond its reception. Each of these modes of analysis would make sense, given our current ways of reading and our contemporary logics of meaning – logics which tend to the etiological to determine the significance of an item for critical analysis. Each of these modes of analysis sets aside the possibility of the catchword participating in the interpretive labor of this text, because each of these modes posits the catchword as somehow distinct from the real subject of study (the book, the agent, the reader). None of these modes, in other words, takes the catchword seriously as a literary element.

Yet the "Stay" on these pages suggests that the catchword does many serious literary things. In my reading, it collapses the reader's phenomenological experience of reading into the signifying work of the text, while it also interjects a genuinely poignant note between two highly stylized, affectively abstract sonnets. Imagining "Stay" as part of the literary project of this work opens up these and other interpretive possibilities. Evelyn B. Tribble's *Margins and Marginality* calls attention to the numerous ways and tonalities with which the margins of early modern printed pages related to their texts, and it seems plausible to imagine the marginal phenomenon of the catchword as inhabiting a variety of postures with regard to its relationship to the set text of its page.[16] In this way, "Stay" is part of this essay's thought experiment in imagining the sort of reading practice that would license incorporating catchwords into the literary critical analysis of the works in which they appear – a practice of reading that embraces the interpretive variety invited by the catchword.

TRANSFORMED

As obvious as catchwords might be to new viewers of the early modern printed page, the catchword appears relatively little in early modernist literary criticism, and the critical vocabulary for catchwords proves limited. For example, no terms describe the relationship between the catchword and its matching word(s) on the subsequent page, though the complexity of those relationships could offer any number of possibilities: shadow, double,

---

[16] Evelyn B. Tribble, *Margins and Marginality: The Printed Page in Early Modern England* (Charlottesville, Va.: University Press of Virginia, 1993), p. 6.

pair, companion, echo, parent/child (or orphan), ghost, second, and so on. Likewise, the nature of these page-crossing linking terms might command any of a variety of terms – complement, completion, repetition, anticipation, and so on – and yet no standard term has emerged. This under-theorization of the early modern printed catchword comes despite the catchword's appearance in most printed early modern books, not discriminating among folios and quartos, poetry and playtexts, imaginative and informational literature. This practical, democratic feature attends almost every genre and format of book printing, and, as such, invites consideration in any of its settings: the catchword's obviousness – including its obviousness qua ubiquity in early modern English printed books – might be, precisely, a reason for its critical examination. Treating the catchword as significant beyond its etiology as a printing artifact only serendipitously relevant to its surrounding text shifts attention to the way the catchword in all its obviousness anticipates and disrupts the interpretive labor of the reader, in ways that may be more or less spectacularly notable, but which are consistently obstructive invitations to reconfigure the protocols of readerly interpretation.

In some moments, the catchword turns its conceptual obviousness into insistence on its own literary significance. Because, unlike the page number or the signature, the catchword emerges from the text itself, it often displaces pieces of the text to form suggestive adjacencies that are spatial, figurative, and temporally mischievous. Consider the 1597 edition of John Gerard's *The Herball or Generall Historie of Plantes*, in which catchwords intermittently engage their preceding and following text in ways that exploit the location of the catchword and its context to achieve affecting results. On pages 53 to 54, for example, the text describes that among the "vertues" or medicinal uses of the "stinking Gladdon" or "Spurgewoort" plant (*Iris foetidissima*) is its ability to assist in treating injury: the plants can "cover with flesh, bones that be bare, being used in plaisters" (see figures 2a and 2b). The page break between "flesh," and "bones" ensures that the catchword "bones" appears immediately below "flesh," creating a stack of words that themselves mimic the action of the spurge-wort plasters, which cover a bone-showing wound. The catchword's placement below the spurge-wort-plastered flesh anticipates the sense of the sentence, revealed only on the next page, and in so doing, performs for the reader the information only available for interpretation later. Presenting (or maybe *pre*-senting) itself in this way, the catchword "bones" appears obvious, inhabiting a state of anterior interpretive labor, such that subsequent elaboration in the text of the sentence becomes redundant. At the same time, by calling attention to its obviousness, the catchword turns its artefactual nature into expression. These "bones," as skeletal element of book production, engage in strikingly signifying labor: they appear below the text's flesh, and, in so doing, demand the reader attend to the significance of the bones' obvious placement. In the case of the

THE LITERAL, THE METAPHORICAL, AND THE OBVIOUS 157

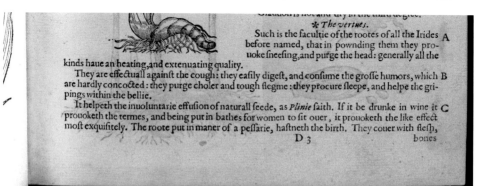

2a   Detail from John Gerard, *The Herball or Generall Historie of Plantes* ... (London: John Norton, 1597); QK41 .G3 1597 OVER, page 53. Special Collections, Louisiana State University Libraries, Baton Rouge, LA.

2b   Detail from Gerard's *Herball*. QK41 .G3 1597 OVER, page 54. Special Collections, Louisiana State University Libraries, Baton Rouge, LA.

Herball's "bones," the catchword unsettles an etiological logic of significance: the catchword's occasion might be as a facilitating technology of accurate bookbinding, but that genesis does not define or control the catchword's expressive power. Indeed, the fact of the catchword's obvious placement on the page and its obvious association with the making of the book, external to the writing of the text, licenses the catchword to behave in unexpectedly communicative ways.

Let me offer another instance from this *Herball* of the catchword linking obviousness with interpretive suggestiveness. On facing pages 112–13, the

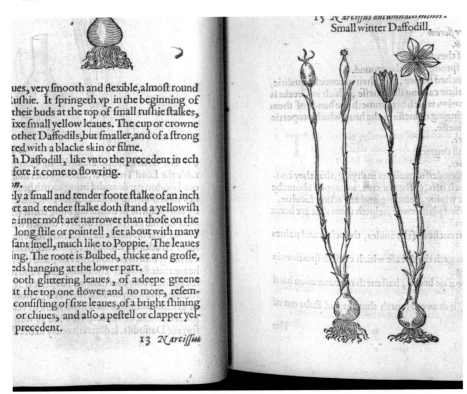

3   Detail from facing pages of Gerard's *Herball*. QK41 .G3 1597 OVER, pages 112–13. Special Collections, Louisiana State University Libraries, Baton Rouge, LA.

Herball continues its account of various daffodils, grouped under their Latin category *Narcissus*, deploying both descriptive text and images of the various kinds of "Daffodill." The *Herball* does not explicitly recount the mythological story of Narcissus or explain why there might be a category of flowers bearing that name until later, on p. 114, but the catchword "13 *Narcissus*" at the bottom of p. 112 nonetheless imports this story into the volume (see figure 3). The catchword anticipates the image of "*Narcissus Persicus*. The Persian Daffodill" at the top left of p. 113, but sits opposite the image of "*Narcissus autumnalis minor*. Small winter Daffodill" at the bottom left of p. 113. The effect is strikingly obvious: across the gutter of the book sit mirrored Narcissuses: the catchword name and the flower image. Even if the *Herball* declines to rehearse the story of the mirror-image-loving youth until later, when in the section on "The names" it makes concise reference to "the transformation of the faire boie Narcissus into a flower of his owne name," the catchword insists on re-presenting the story, transforming Narcissus into flower.

For these pages of the *Herball*, the mythic origins of the bloom belong, ostensibly, outside the margins of these pages. Yet the catchword here performs

THE LITERAL, THE METAPHORICAL, AND THE OBVIOUS 159

that story in the midst of the volume's discussion of the flower, inserting into the middle of the plant's profile its dreamy origins in a metamorphosis imagined (and imaged) as occurring across a page break. The catchword's obvious invocation of this myth makes it impossible not to consider the *Herball's* Ovidian intertexts. By anticipating the next page's Narcissus, the catchword here has turned itself and its mirror into a literary, multitemporal event: into a description of the present state of a flower, the catchword imports a before-and-after story, with a mirrored image of flower over time.

This might seem like a serendipitous anomaly in this volume, but I can't help but think it is significant that this *Herball*, which so assiduously seeks a learned practicality and urgent usefulness, nonetheless encloses imaginative flourishings in its catchwords – imaginative flourishings that offer alternative models of interpretive labor for the reader. In the case of the "bones," the *Herball's* catchword uses its location to anticipate and perform the sense of a subsequent text, effectively urging the reader to consider the obvious catchword as the key to the sentence's sense; in the case of "Narcissus," the catchword demands an allusive reading practice, one demonstrated by the catchword's performance of the flower's mythic origin, and one that demands the reader acknowledge the signifying work of the catchword. The interpretive labor of the catchword foregrounds its textual origins and material conditions to exploit its obviousness: the catchword recuperates and diversifies the expressive register of the obvious, and the result is the expansion of what, in literary critical analysis, might be signifying and significant on the page.

Let me look at another volume – this time the 1590 first edition of the first three Books of Spenser's *The Faerie Queene* – to consider some catchwords that similarly leverage their obviousness as a representational register that allows them to participate in the interpretive work of the text. The catchword at the bottom of p. 370 (Aa2v) comes halfway through stanza 31 in Book 2, Canto 12, amid Guyon's encounter with the mermaids on his epic sea voyage. The catchword "Transform'd" appears midway into the account of the mermaids' anterior transformation, and it anticipates the beginning of line 5, "Transformd to fish" (location hereafter cited in Book.Canto.stanza. line format). There is a notable difference between the catchword and its next-page mate, though. The catchword features an apostrophe in its spelling of "Transform'd" while the first word of line 5 as printed on the following page is spelled without: "Transform'd" becomes "Transformd." There are plausible material explanations for this spelling change (not least among them compositors making spelling and punctuation decisions that met the local exigencies of preparing a page).[17] Yet this word's spelling change does

---

[17] Some critics have sought to use catchwords as a tool for identifying specific compositors (see, for example, Frank B. Evans, "The Printing of Spenser's 'Faerie Queene' in 1596," *Studies in Bibliography* 18 (1965), 49–67), but Jeffrey Masten persuasively critiques this identificatory practice as grounded in anachronistic, and perhaps troublingly symptomatic, assumptions about spelling differences and

160   CHRIS BARRETT

more than provide a signal of early modern orthographic diversity: the word "Transform(')d" transforms as it swims across the facing page break.

In an essay on technologies of early modern printed dis/continuity, Randall McLeod (here pseudonymously Random Clod) notes that minute changes in running headlines or catchwords or other forms of virtuous redundancy suggest that "when a Renaissance text talks about itself, it is often not *quite* what it claims to be. Its structural redundancies are, crucially, both *of* its text and *about* it." For Clod, the advantage of attending to these moments of a text's "non-identity with itself" provides the opportunity to track what he calls its "'transformission' – how it was *transformed* as it was *transmitted*" (original emphasis).[18] In the case of this Spenserian "Transform(')d," the transformation of the word certainly points to this bibliographic transformission: on its surface, the obvious discontinuity of the catchword and its match highlight the vicissitudes of material change text undergoes as it transmits itself in the book.

At the same time, this non-identity of the catchword text with its match on the facing page participates in the interpretive labor of *The Faerie Queene* reader's dutiful allegoresis. The instructional program of the poem makes the history of the mermaids important for the reader, who should appreciate the multivalent significance of the sirens' appeal to the sailing Knight of Temperance. While the mermaids appear to Guyon as dangerously seductive creatures, the poem's account of their anterior transformation asserts their state of excessive allure as a punishment for tangling with the gods. The catchword appearing in the middle of this metamorphic narrative sheds, on its own transformative journey from catchword to first word of the following page, its apostrophe, the punctuational marker of some element's removal or loss. When the catchword becomes the initial word of 2.12.31.5, it erases its previous record of erasure, and the resulting orthography of "Transformd" naturalizes the sense of loss the catchword performs. Metamorphosis – the non-identity with itself of a word, of a siren – would seem like a simple change, were it not for the catchword, insisting that before the mermaids appeared, they underwent processual loss, performed (or perhaps pre-formed) by the catchword "Transform'd." The catchword's reappearance in altered form activates something new in the reading of the stanza, by way of asserting that the interpretation of this transformation has already been undertaken, before the reader has come to examine the line of verse begun by the catchword. Before the mermaids were made half-fish in the text, the catchword had already shown that the transformation involves a process of naturalizing loss, by denaturalizing the fluidity of early modern spelling.

The result of the catchword's interaction with its surrounding text is obvious (the word "Tranformd" transforms) and, in its obviousness, it demands the

---

perceived habits of typesetting (*Queer Philologies: Sex, Language, and Affect in Shakespeare's Time* (Philadelphia: University of Pennsylvania Press, 2016), pp. 39–66).

[18] Random Clod, "Information on Information," *Transactions of the Society for Textual Scholarship* 5 (1991), 241–81, at 246.

THE LITERAL, THE METAPHORICAL, AND THE OBVIOUS   161

reader attend to words in a way that strikingly disrupts the allegorical reading practice that ostensibly governs Spenser's "dark conceit." The literalization of metamorphosis in the word "Transform(')d" upends the interpretive paradigm in which the allegorical tenor of something should take interpretive priority over its vehicle. Here, the transformation of "Transform(')d" causes a riot of unruly concretization where symbolism should dominate. The catchword seems to advance its own representational program, one that resists the interpretive labors the reader brings to the set text of the surrounding pages.

In each of these cases of the catchword – "bones," "Narcissus," "Transform'd" – the obviousness of this printing artifact creates the opportunity for an alternative engagement with the work in which it appears. These catchwords interact with their surrounding text in suggestive ways, upending expectations around chronology, figuration, and interpretation, and insisting on the expansion of the category of signifying elements on a page to include the catchword, the extra-textual occasion for which fails to circumscribe its expressive possibilities. Though seemingly resistant to critical methodologies of making textual meaning, the catchword nonetheless proves a way to diversify the rigorous principles of meaning-making deployed in critical accounts of these works. An object simultaneously in the way of meaning and a way to other meanings, the catchword demands a reading practice willing to absorb the strikingly complex improvisations of the obvious.

DROP

So far I have offered examples of catchwords that seem to be in conversation with their context, in ways that might be vexed or idiosyncratic, but which take the catchword's obviousness as license to deploy multiple interpretive systems in the course of continuous reading. This might seem to require a serendipitous concatenation of felicitous catchword and welcoming context – an etiology of significance that seems, by its unsubtle reliance on chance, to militate against a regular and consistent reading practice. Catchwords in general, though, provoke confrontations with hermeneutic narrowness by virtue of their obviousness, even when that obviousness does not seem on its surface reconcilable with symbolic work. If nothing else, a catchword reduplicates a word in the text, and thus forces, on every catchword-ed page, a reckoning with how a reader processes repetition. A catchword requires on every page a minute re-reading of parts of the text, and if structured re-readings like the excerpt and the passage are the basal elements of literary criticism, attending to the labors of the catchword might prove generative for understanding the very principle by which a whole text is interrogated by way of its parts. It sounds obvious, I know, to say that critical encounter with a text requires re-reading, but the catchword makes this demand of un-critical reading, too, suggesting that the very act of encountering an early modern printed book requires a strategy for acknowledging or suppressing the experience of re-reading. For literary critics, reliant on re-reading, the catchword emerges as the most

Io. What wilt thou doe?

Mar. I will drop in his way fome obfcure Epiftles of love, wherein by the colour of his beard, the fhape of his legge, the manner of his gate, the expreffure of his eye, forehead, and comple£tion, he fhall find himfelfe moft feelingly perfonated. I can write very like my Lady your Neece, on a forgotten matter we can hardly make diftin£tion of our hands.

To. Excellent, I fmell a device.

An. I hav't in my nofe too.

To. He fhall thinke by the Letters that thou wilt d

rop

4   From the Second Folio: *Mr. William Shakespeares comedies, histories, and tragedies: published according to the true originall copies* (London: Thomas Cotes, for Robert Allot, 1632); PR2751 .A2 1632 VAULT, page 261 (Y5r). Special Collections, Louisiana State University Libraries, Baton Rouge, LA.

persistent and ubiquitous agent of literary re-reading, and in so doing, demands consideration of how the basal practices and elements of analysis are entangled with interpretive interactions with literary work.

In that light, let me look at one last catchword. In the Second Folio of Shakespeare's works, *Twelfth Night* boasts a curious catchword at the bottom of page 261 (see figure 4). The catchword appears at the end of a line from Sir Toby, who is conspiring with Maria, Andrew, and Feste in the gulling of Malvolio. Toby's line, "He shall thinke by the Letters that thou wilt drop," ends the page, and the line continues on the verso, "that they come from my Neece ...." The catchword here ought to be "that," the first word on the verso. Instead, the catchword here is "rop," the last three letters of the final word "drop," itself incompletely printed as "d" just above and to the left of the catchword, vertically aligning the right edge of the "d" with the left edge of the "r." This catchword effectively catches the final letters of "drop," which have fallen to the bottom margin of the page, as though themselves having been dropped.

A reader might look at this catchword and assess it to be the evidence of a bored compositor's wit, or simply an amusingly felicitous typographical error, or a failure to create a true catchword with a match on the following page – in any of these three cases, this catchword is received as external to the work of this textual locus. But the catchword resists being excluded from these systems of rationalization: it is obviously a site of play with this line, literalizing the "Letters" in this act of d/ropping, and insisting on the catchword's membership in the line itself. Refusing to participate in its own critical dismissal, the catchword here demands to be taken as part of a line that is incomplete without it. What is more, it refuses to allow the following page's first line to proceed without the catchword's own inclusion in the text. The

THE LITERAL, THE METAPHORICAL, AND THE OBVIOUS   163

conventions of ignoring or dismissing or rationalizing the catchword prove insufficient here. This mischievous catchword, perhaps engaged in its own readerly gulling, could very viably be categorized as a mistake or a joke, a kink excised from regularized texts in the pursuit of regular logics of interpretation. But its obviousness turns it into an agent of interpretive disruption. The catchword here is integral to the play, precisely because the catchword is not willing to hide in plain sight. The obvious catchword becomes part of the line; no matter how these two pages are read, the reader has to reckon with the catchword, in all its obviousness.

I find myself catching catchwords in the process of asserting that their obviousness is significant – specifically, that obviousness is significant because it upsets, precedes, disobeys, modifies, or obstructs our usual interpretive labors. That obstruction creates the opportunity to face what is simultaneously *in* the way of meaning and also *the way* of meaning: by resisting available interpretive frameworks, the obvious invites new techniques, new methodologies, all dependent on a creative approach to thinking anew the possibilities of what seems given.

If the catchword helps advance the development of a hermeneutics of the obvious as representational mode, we can hope that the practice of thinking the obstructive, already-accomplished interpretive labor of the obvious makes us better attuned to similarly obvious and obstructive phenomena that present as already-interpreted, but which nonetheless demand a critical practice to assimilate them into new modes of interpreting the text and world. The catchword, after all, participates in the obvious only insofar as it is subject to a specific and specifically-abled reading technique, of moving the eyes across pages. For those for whom this form of reading is not possible, the catchword exists differently. Additionally, the catchword is available only to those readers with access to early modern printed texts, or to their digital surrogates – access that, while perhaps broader now than ever, is still circumscribed by socio-economic and other factors. It might be obvious that a reader's multidimensional subject positionality affects the reader's interpretive practice, but it might be worth considering how that obviousness can help all readers become more attuned to, and more creative about, the ways we make sense of text and of one another.

In inviting readers to make sense of obvious things, obviousness ruptures the fantasy of expression outside the work of interpretation, and ruptures, too, the sense that interpretive innovation can ever cease. In a world in need of new, less injurious, more sustainable stories, the obvious might be a chance to imagine all sorts of entanglements of author, reader, text, and medium. I say entanglements because I propose that the catchword – as avatar for the obvious more broadly – operates somewhat like the mycorrhizal fungi that network the wood-wide web, connecting diverse species in highly complex systems of communication and exchange.[19] With a logic that transcends the intentional or serendipitous, these fungi, like catchwords, telegraph information among units (pages, text, readers, printers, compositors, et alia) that prove less discrete than one might at first imagine. The fungi and the catchwords link the minute elements of an immense whole, forming something that looks like thought itself – the sort of more-than-human, distributed thought that was, until recently, unimaginable. To modify a common and uncannily apt idiom, we could not see the forest for the trees; but in thinking about that obvious forest, about what it means to reimagine the forest as a dynamic nexus of multispecies intimacies and relationalities forming a kind of mind, we find all sorts of new stories to be told – stories subtle and mysterious, subterranean and astounding.

Catchwords, with all their tiny stories evincing rebellious dreams of what interpretation might look like, point to the possibilities of the obvious to generate the unexpected and the marvelous in understanding the complexities of living in a world that is both self-evidently full of wonders, and wonderfully resistant to assimilation into the narratives we bring to it. And if it does so, it obviously will be because it is built on Simpsonian scholarship that has long done self-evidently marvelous work, highlighting the dangerous legacies of the literal while simultaneously making legible visions of more recuperative knowledge-making and -sharing processes. That work has long illuminated how we have made meaning for and with one another, and how, even in periods of obvious peril, we might make meaning anew.

---

[19] "Wood wide web" introduced with publication of S. W. Simard, D. A. Perry, M. D. Jones, D. D. Myrold, D. M. Durall, and R. Molina, "Net Transfer of Carbon between Tree Species with Shared Ectomycorrhizal Fungi," *Nature* 388 (1997), 579–82.

PART III
CULTURE AND INSTITUTIONS

9 PETITION, JUSTICE, AND PEACE IN *PIERS PLOWMAN*

Yun Ni

This essay expands James Simpson's observation that William Langland's *Piers Plowman* develops its meanings out of the dynamics of different institutional discourses. By examining petitions recorded in the fourteenth-century English Parliament Rolls and William of Pagula's *De Speculo Regis Edwardi III* (*Mirror of King Edward III*, written in the 1330s), in tandem with Peace's bill in *Piers Plowman*, this essay argues that the emergence and development of political theory in the poem observe a particular kind of rhetorical logic with a distinctive dynamic. Langland's allegorical personification adds sophistication and sensitivity to the poem's political analysis and qualifies institutional discourses to comment on the "secular."

For many critics, the two-way traffic between the secular and the spiritual constitutes the heart of Langland's allegory.[1] However, in my reading of allegorical personification in the first vision of *Piers Plowman*, the secular Peace, deprived of the mutual containment and interpenetration of the secular and the spiritual, cannot sustain its own congruity. The suspension of mercy and grace makes justice and peace impossible.

In the first vision, the dreamer-narrator Will witnesses the King's justice in the court. One focus of the first vision in all versions of the poem is the marriage of Lady Mede, whose name has the double meaning of profit and bribery on the one hand, and gift, including the spiritual gift of God, on the other.[2] Mede is to be

---

[1] Jill Mann, for instance, argues: "If on the one hand the material world is interpenetrated by a spiritual reality which transcends material laws, on the other hand the laws of the material world interpenetrate spiritual reality and resolve some of its most fundamental problems." See Jill Mann, "Eating and Drinking in *Piers Plowman*," *Essays and Studies* 32 (1979), 26–43, at 27.

[2] The B-text used in this essay is William Langland, *The Vision of Piers Plowman*, ed. A. V. C. Schmidt (London: J. M. Dent, 1978). All citations of the Middle English text, cited by line number, are from Schmidt's edition. The C-text discussed in this essay is William Langland, *Piers Plowman, A New Annotated Edition of the*

168   YUN NI

wedded to the knight Conscience, whose name seems to suggest he is merely an
ethical and mental abstraction but who proves to be an emphatically public figure,
a diplomat, knight, and lawyer. Conscience rejects Mede and initiates a heated
debate with her in the royal court, prompting the King to summon Reason.

A second, equally important focus is Peace's petition in court against the
bully Wrong. Mede bribes Peace in order to appease the petitioner and acquit
the abuser. Although Peace then agrees to withdraw the petition, Conscience
and Reason persuade the King to execute the law strictly and punish both
Mede and Wrong. In the C-text, the King then appoints Reason as Chancellor
and Conscience as Chief Justice. Two conceptual problems stand out. First, the
poem's allegorical narrative places the personification of private mental faculties,
such as Reason, Conscience, and Kynde Witte (the natural reason), in the public
sphere of national politics, translating figures of individual intellectual prowess
(reason) and ethical judgment (conscience) into figures of public administrative
power. Second, the flat figure of Peace at the center of the court scene has neither
psychological depth nor control over his own identity. The porous boundaries
between the private and the public in *Piers Plowman* create ambiguities in
Langland's poetics of justice, shaping and reshaping how the poem defines it.

Most critics approach the scenes described in the first vision by linking the
allegorical figures and fictional court to various historical referents.[3] Given the
presence of the King and Peace, the obvious allusion is to the court of King's
Bench, the highest criminal court, in which crimes adjudicated were always
defined as crimes against the King's peace.[4] Conrad van Dijk argues that equity
functions as a general principle for the king to execute law with impartiality,
so that "each gets his due."[5] Noting the administrative role accorded Reason,
Matthew Giancarlo argues for a parliamentary instead of chancery setting;
petitions like Peace's bill were often examined in parliament, where reason, law,
and royal prerogative in theory worked together to balance justice and grace.[6]

   C-text, ed. Derek Pearsall (Exeter, UK: University of Exeter Press, 2008). For the
   variations in the A-, B-, and C-texts of Passus 4, see Andrew Galloway, *The Penn
   Commentary on Piers Plowman. Volume 1, C Prologue-Passus 4; B Prologue-Passus
   4; A Prologue-Passus 4* (Philadelphia: University of Pennsylvania Press, 2006), pp.
   375–76. See *MED*, s.v. "mēde, n. (4)." For the ambiguous nature of Mede, see also
   John A. Yunck, *The Lineage of Lady Meed: the Development of Mediaeval Venality
   Satire* (Notre Dame, Ind.: University of Notre Dame Press, 1963), pp. 10–11.

3 In addition to those mentioned below, Lady Mede on trial is frequently identified
   with King Edward III's mistress Alice Perrers, who was impeached by Parliament in
   1376. See Stephanie Trigg, "The Traffic in Medieval Women: Alice Perrers, Feminist
   Criticism and *Piers Plowman*," *The Yearbook of Langland Studies* 12 (1998), 5–29.

4 I thank Sebastian Sobecki for directing me to this legal context. For the disagreements
   about the location of this episode as a reflection of the fluid petitionary system in
   the second half of the fourteenth century, see also Rebecca Davis, *Piers Plowman
   and the Books of Nature* (Oxford: Oxford University Press, 2016), pp. 202–03.

5 Conrad van Dijk, "Giving Each His Due: Langland, Gower, and the Question of
   Equity," *Journal of English and Germanic Philology* 108 (2009), 310–35.

6 Matthew Giancarlo, *Parliament and Literature in Late Medieval England* (Cambridge:
   Cambridge University Press, 2007), pp. 195–96.

PETITION, JUSTICE, AND PEACE IN *PIERS PLOWMAN* 169

But while Giancarlo's argument is persuasive, it also raises a new question. In Passus 3 and Passus 4 of the B-Text, followers of Mede convene in the King's Court, providing a context for Peace's abrupt appearance and petition. To some extent the poem uses Mede, or the general desire for Mede, as a premise for staging this petition. Since material wealth brings these followers together, and if Peace himself is satisfied by monetary compensation, why cannot the petition be resolved by Mede's action?

One obvious answer, as mentioned above, is that the status of Peace as a plaintiff is a conceptual paradox: as Andrew Galloway argues, in Langland's allegory, Peace can be both a hapless individual plaintiff and a personification of the principle of "the king's peace."[7] If the trespass is identified with a breach of the King's peace instead of representing a merely personal grievance, Peace should not be allowed to accept a private reconciliation.[8] Therefore, if Wrong's actions are *contra pacem domini regis* (against the peace of the king), he is not only violating private rights of property but disrupting public order. Thus, when Peace is bribed to withdraw his petition, he is not only giving up his right to self-defense but undermining the whole justice system. Peace's petition exemplifies how one move can trigger a powerful process "that the individual initiator cannot control."[9]

The aftermath is unpredictable. When Peace is forced to be the King's peace, he cannot control the petition process or his allegorical identity. Moreover, not even the King can reverse this profound transformation of Peace. When the King refuses the reconciliation proposed by Peace to defend the peace of the realm, the King commits himself to a principle greater than royal authority. As an executor of the law, the King is below the law when the engine of legal procedure is activated. By the end of the episode, the King himself has turned from a judge for petitions to a petitioner for a mode of justice higher than himself. As Giancarlo notes, "[w]e are left with the king in the position of a petitioner, since he seeks the best way to ensure payment – meed – by inquiring responsibly and deliberatively through 'reason' and law, not through prerogative control."[10] The King does not shy away from succumbing to the rule of Reason because the latter is no longer a personification of the King's rational power but embodies the rigor and consistency of law. Likewise, the King cannot leave Peace alone as the private peace or the government unreformed. When the King identifies justice with law and reason, the petition gains a momentum unforeseen by the initiator and inconceivable to the ruler.

The major problem Giancarlo and others leave unaddressed is why Langland creates an allegorical figure who cannot control his own identity and, more

---

[7] Galloway, *The Penn Commentary*, p. 374.
[8] See Gwilym Dodd, *Justice and Grace: Private Petitioning and the English Parliament in the Late Middle Ages* (Oxford: Oxford University Press, 2007). Historically, the petition "significantly expanded the legal concept of trespass in which a petitioner's grievance was implicitly identified with a breach of the king's peace as well as a personal injury" (p. 36).
[9] Galloway, *The Penn Commentary*, p. 400.
[10] Giancarlo, *Parliament and Literature*, p. 198.

170 YUN NI

importantly, why Langland accommodates Peace's paradoxical allegorical status at the cost of blurring private and public justice. To understand this better we need to turn to petitions recorded in the fourteenth-century English Parliament Rolls and William of Pagula's *De Speculo Regis Edwardi III* (*Mirror of King Edward III*). The purpose of this discussion, however, is not to provide a topical reading, prioritizing history over literature. Poetry and allegory have their own logic. While *Piers Plowman* engages with institutional conditions of its time, Langland does not replicate historical documents or political treatises but adapts them to suit his own literary ends.

PEACE'S BILL: PRIVATE OR COMMON PETITION?

Parliamentary petitions gained increasing prominence in fourteenth-century England. Three features of these petitions are relevant to a parliamentary reading of the petition scene in *Piers Plowman*. First, Parliament for the first time was not only a political but a juridical body. Second, because the petitions brought to Parliament often originated in complaints that local authorities had been unable to resolve, its new receptivity to public demand made it a point of contact between local people and the central government. Third, the king's presence in Parliament to address grievances was a manifestation of royal grace.[11] All these elements are present in the King's dealings with Peace's petition bill. In order to understand how Langland adapts and allegorizes bureaucratic documents in illustrating his idea of justice, it is necessary to compare the structure and diction of Peace's bill and the Parliament Rolls in the 1370s.

Peace's bill lists evils so comprehensively that it seems designed to represent contemporary petitions in general, rather than be taken as an actual example of the genre:

> And thanne com Pees into parlement and put up a bille –
> How Wrong ayeins his wille hadde his wif taken,
> And how he ravysshede Rose, Reignaldes love,
> And Margrete of hir maydenhede maugree hire chekes.
> "Both my gees and my grys his gadelynges feccheth;
> I dar noght for fere of hem fighte ne chide.
> He borwed of me bayard and broughte hym hom nevere
> Ne no ferthying therfore, for nought I koude plede,
> He maynteneth hise men to murthere myne hewen,
> Forstalleth my feires and fighteth in my chepyng,
> And breketh up my berne dores and bereth awey my whete,
> And taketh me but a taille for ten quarters otes.
> And yet he beteth me therto and lyth by my mayde;
> I am noght hardy for hym unnethe to loke!" (IV. 47–60)

---

[11] Dodd, *Justice and Grace*, p. 11.

PETITION, JUSTICE, AND PEACE IN *PIERS PLOWMAN* 171

Peace lists a wide range of possible trespass in the realm, including but not limited to rape, manslaughter, robbery, and forced transactions based on unfair prices. While noting that the petition is procedurally correct, Giancarlo argues that "[t]he bill is so overdone that its allegorical seriousness is somewhat playfully undercut by its hyperbole."[12] True, the reader can hardly imagine one individual committing so many wrongs, even though the culprit is named "Wrong." Yet the impression that Peace's bill is overstated fades if one looks at it in light of actual parliamentary petitions, such as the following, raised in the Good Parliament of 1376:

> 180. CXXI. To their most gracious lord, our lord the king; his lieges of the county of Devon declare: whereas the duke of Brittany, and many others of his retinue, at his last passage to Brittany was residing in the said county for a long time before the passage, many of his retinue, and many of the retinue of others, by night as well as by day took oxen, cows, lambs, corn, hay, oats and all other victuals from various people, and for the most part paid nothing for the same; and some of them set the price of the victuals which they took from the same people at their will at less than one half of the price the victuals were worth, for which nothing is yet paid, to the great destruction and ruin of the said commonalty.
>
> Wherefore the said commons pray that it should be ordered that payment should be made to those to whom such debt is due, after our lord the king has paid them; and no protection should be allowed in writs where the debt is required for this reason; and a general proclamation should be made that if any passage to cross overseas is made in any region in times to come, no man should take any victuals from anyone against the will of him to whom they belong, paying for the same immediately before their passage as they have agreed. And if they take otherwise, they should be treated as the common law of the land requires. (fn. ii-321-941a-1)
>
> [Answer]
>
> For times past the trespassers should answer; and for times to come, the king by the advice of his great council will ordain suitable remedy thereon.[13]

This example illustrates how a range of specific and localized demands as wide as those made in Peace's petition are made "common" and how a complaint that had originated in a particular region due to specific local conditions could be turned into a grievance with a much more general application.

Thematically, Peace's major complaints replicate the social ills named in the Good Parliament petition. For example, Peace complains how Wrong "maynteneth his men" to murder Peace's servants and take away the wheat and oats without payment but leaving "a taille" (a record of transactions as proof

---

[12] Giancarlo, *Parliament and Literature*, p. 194.

[13] The petitions in the Parliament Rolls and their English translations cited in this article are from Chris Given-Wilson, gen. ed., *Parliament Rolls of Medieval England*, 16 vols. (Woodbridge, UK: Boydell, 2005). This petition is in vol. 5, "Edward III: April 1376," No. 180.

for loans) instead (IV. 55–58). The cataloguing of the 1376 petition, which mentions all sorts of livestock and other things that are taken, is mirrored by Peace's petition. Peace's bill also imitates a historical petition by specifying commonly recognizable damages.

However, it is important to note that Peace's bill does not strictly follow the format of a parliamentary petition. The usual structure of a petition was as follows:

1. address
2. identification of the petitioner
3. statement of grievance or difficulty
4. request for redress
5. appeal for remedy.[14]

In Petition 180, the address is "A lour tresgraciouse seignur, nostre seignur le roi" (To their most gracious lord, our lord the king), clauses that ask directly for the king's justice. In Peace's petition, however, there is no address: only a direct statement of grievance. Through these arrangements, Langland does not caricature the petitioner or provide comic relief but implies that someone has already acted as a lobbyist for Peace, making formalities unnecessary.

The petition is *preceded* by the King talking to Reason and Conscience, which is procedurally irregular, particularly in a parliamentary petition:

> And thane Reason rood faste the righte heighe gate,
> As Conscience hym kenned, til thei come to the Kynge,
> Curteisly the Kyng thane com ayeins Reason,
> And bitwene himself and his sone sette hym on benche,
> And worabeden wel wisely a gret while togideres. (IV. 42–46)

Although they are yet to be appointed to administrative roles, Reason and Conscience have already influenced the King, as is obvious from the King's immediate reception of Peace's petition. "The Kyng knew he seide sooth, for Conscience hym tolde / That Wrong was a wikked luft and wroghte muche sorwe" (IV. 61–62). The King does not ask for further evidence or investigate the case but immediately chooses to believe Peace. "Conscience hym tolde" implies that in the previous conversations, Conscience has already complained about Wrong. The reader may infer that Reason's presence also prompts the King to make judgments quickly after Conscience calls the King's attention to Wrong's atrocities. The reader is also invited to suspect that Conscience had previous knowledge of Peace's petition and to question Conscience's commitment to acting as an advocate for Peace. Therefore, Peace's petition and its aftermath violate procedural correctness instead of affirming it.

Moreover, the historical parliamentary petition identifies the petitioner in "ses liges du counte de Devenschire" (his lieges of the county of Devon), but

---

[14] Dodd, *Justice and Grace*, p. 281.

PETITION, JUSTICE, AND PEACE IN *PIERS PLOWMAN* 173

there is no self-identification in Peace's Bill as a liege of one specific area. The absence of Peace's declaration of his identity underlines the paradox of Peace's legal status: the narrator does not clarify whether Peace should be identified as a local victim or the king's Peace of the realm. The impossibility of pinning Peace's identity down makes it hard for the reader to decide at the very beginning of Peace's abrupt appearance whether the following petition is private or common.

Another significant difference is that the documented petition ends with "a grant destruccion et arerissement de la dite commune" (to great destruction and ruin of the said community) but Peace's complaint embraces both private and public violations, oscillating between an individual and the communal in phrases like "my feirs" and "my chepyng." Moreover, Peace often retreats to his timidity and suffering: "I am noght hardy for hym unnethe to loke!" (IV. 60). Peace finishes his petition by murmuring that he does not dare to look at Wrong, as if unable to confront the impact of Wrong's misdeeds on the wider community.

As for the appeal for remedy, the parliamentary petition proposes three specific solutions: first, debts must be paid; second, no such forced loans should be allowed; third, no purveyance should be enacted against the buyers' will. It asks for a general proclamation and reinforces the need for the legislature, suggesting that all violators should be punished according to common law. In contrast, Peace asks for nothing specific in his bill, which leaves the means of settling the dispute unclear and leads to the possibility of monetary compensation, which enables Mede's bribery and is thus cast in an unfavorable light in Langland's narrative. However, in the historical petition, once escalated and made common, some private petitions can no longer prioritize the petitioner's financial interests.

This episode, therefore, can be read as Langland's commentary not only on royal justice but also on the blurred distinctions between private and common petitions in late fourteenth-century England. In this period, private petitions often hijacked the term "common" and used it to advance their ends.[15] Two consequences are noteworthy: first, members of Parliament formed competing lobby groups to represent individual supplications with fierce rivalry; second, the link between common petitions and statuary legislation was weakening.[16] In *Piers Plowman*, the first point is alluded to by Wrong's supporters, Waryn Wisdom and Wit, as well as Peace's supporters, Conscience and Reason, turning into lobbyists to manipulate the law and exercise political influence. The second point partly explains why Peace's private petition is made "common" or "public" but fails to initiate a legislative instead of administrative reform. An administrative reform reshuffles the personnel in the governmental body, such as the appointments of Conscience and Reason in the C-text, without systematically changing the bureaucratic structure. By contrast, a legislative reform changes the rules of the game by implementing substantial changes in the common law, such as decreeing the prohibitions of delayed payment in purveyance mentioned in

---

[15] Dodd, *Justice and Grace*, p. 133.
[16] Dodd, *Justice and Grace*, p. 153.

174 YUN NI

the historical petition cited above. Langland uses this poetic moment of Peace's petition to criticize the opportunistic maneuver of hijacking public discourse and reveals the consequences of privatizing public resources.

ROYAL PURVEYANCE AND *PIERS PLOWMAN* AS *MIRROR OF PRINCES*

Understanding how the petitioners make their voices heard puts the King's prerogative and self-restraint in sharper relief. The most significant complaints of Peace revolve around purveyance, which permitted not only the greater nobility but the king and royal family to pre-empt victuals and military supplies at an arbitrarily determined fixed price below the market value.[17] The 1376 petition bill cited in the above section is a petition against the Duke of Brittany. However, in the fourteenth century, the nobles' abuses of purveyance were far less common than those caused by royal purveyance.[18] It is the king who often used purveyance as arbitrary indirect taxation, which, as a royal prerogative, needed no parliamentary approval.[19] During the 1340s, various exactions in purveyance to feed Edward III's continental army during the Hundred Years' War propelled the parliamentary commons to voice grave discontent on behalf of the general public.[20] Peace's petition bill in Langland's allegory can thus be read as directed against the nobility, or the purveyors, or even the King himself. These options offer two interpretative possibilities: if the complaints were against the nobility, the King's unrelenting justice might seem overreaching and inflexible; if the complaints were against the King's purveyors, or the King himself, however, the King could not disown Peace because he would indeed be *his* Peace.

As early as the 1320s, William of Pagula, the vicar of Winkfield, condemned the evils of purveyance in his *De Speculo Regis Edwardi III* and cautioned Edward III about the consequences of a tyrannical rule.[21] Pagula holds Edward III complicit for using purveyance as outright extortion. "Sed que

---

[17] W. R. Jones, "Purveyance for War and the Community of the Realm in Late Medieval England," *Albion* 7 (1975), 300–16, at 300. Mark W. Ormrod, *The Reign of Edward III: Crown and Political Society in England, 1327–1377* (New Haven, Conn.: Yale University Press, 1990), p. 11.

[18] For a marked decline in the number of common petitions directed against the nobles after 1341, see Ormrod, *The Reign of Edward III*, p. 112.

[19] C. J. GivenWilson, "Purveyance for the Royal Household, 1362–1413," *Historical Research* 56 (1983), 145–63, at 148 and 158.

[20] Ormrod, *The Reign of Edward III*, p. 21.

[21] William of Pagula, *De Speculo Regis Edwardi III*, ed. Joseph Moisant (Paris: Alphonse Picard, 1891), pp. 115–17. For the English translation of the two versions, see *Political Thought in Early Fourteenth-Century England: Treatises by Walter of Milemete, William of Pagula, and William of Ockham*, ed. and tr. Cary J. Nederman (Tempe, Ariz: Arizona Center for Medieval and Renaissance Studies in collaboration with Brepols, 2002), pp. 73–139. See Cary J. Nederman, "The Monarch and the Marketplace: Economic Policy and Royal Finance in William of Pagula's *Speculum Regis Edwardi III*," *History of Political Economy* 33 (2001), 51–69. See also Leonard E. Boyle, "William of Pagula and the *Speculum Regis Edwardi III*," *Mediaeval Studies* 32 (1970), 329–36.

PETITION, JUSTICE, AND PEACE IN *PIERS PLOWMAN* 175

est illa justicia vel equitas his diebus, emere res aliquas pro minori precio quam venditor velit eas dare, cum empcio et vendicio sunt de jure gencium, et contrahuntur consensus?"[22] (But how it is either justice or equity these days to buy something for a lesser price than the seller wishes to sell them for, and contrary to the consent, when buying and selling are fixed by the law of people?).[23] William of Pagula's *Mirror* stands out in the tradition of mirrors for princes because it examines the conditions and consequences of commercial activity in light of moral and spiritual values.[24] For both Pagula and Langland, the king's responsibility for a healthy market affects the health of his soul.

Emphatically, Pagula broaches the topic of regicide. Since Edward III has just started his reign in the 1330s, Pagula reminds the young king of his father's untimely death. Pagula attributes Edward II's troubled reign to unrestrained purveyances.[25] His account of Edward II's death as retribution for abusing the royal prerogative is a blunt reminder of the worst part of kingship. Adding insult to injury, Pagula argues that the unjustly acquired goods were never thoroughly enjoyed by Edward II but were seized by Queen Isabella and her lover Mortimer. Later, Pagula goes so far as reminding Edward III that he should be grateful to be freed by God and his people from the control of his mother and her lover. Edward III, therefore, must be a gracious ruler and show gratitude for the grace God has bestowed on him and for the support of his people. Pagula's admonition often resorts to focusing on the king's personal history instead of public discourse of justice, which nearly justifies regicide.

Pagula's politicization of the fair exchange in the market as the reciprocity between the king and the subjects helps us understand a fraught passage alluding to regicide in the First Vision of *Piers Plowman*. When Conscience, in his debate with Mede, cites the Book of Kings (i.e. 1 Samuel 15) to illustrate how monarchs are destroyed by money (III. 259–79), he is speaking in the voice of an author of a *Mirror for Princes*: "God seide to Samuel that Saul sholde deye, / And al his seed for that synne shenfulliche ende. / Swich a meschief Mede made the kyng to have / That God hated hym for evere and alle his heires after" (III. 276–79). Conscience, like William of Pagula, cites the Biblical history of regicide and in the process puts Mede in a perilous situation. In order to escape this position, Mede then has to circumvent this charge, redirecting the audience's attention to her positive role in diplomacy and warfare, which are beneficial for the King's rule.[26]

Pagula sets the precedent of equating commercial fairness and political equity, but Langland makes Mede distort economic reciprocity into political reciprocity when she bribes Peace into accepting a temporary reconciliation. When Mede

---

[22] The Latin quotation, cited by page number, is from Moisant's edition. William of Pagula, *De Speculo Regis Edwardi III*, p. 84.

[23] The English quotation, cited by page number, is from Nederman's translation. Nederman, *Political Thought in Early Fourteenth-Century England*, p. 74.

[24] Nederman, "The Monarch and the Marketplace," p. 66.

[25] William of Pagula, *De Speculo Regis Edwardi III*, p. 116, and Nederman, *Political Thought in Early Fourteenth-Century England*, p. 98.

[26] Galloway, *Penn Commentary*, p. 316.

176 YUN NI

is bringing the market economy principle to court, what should have been applicable in mercantilism turns out to be a disaster in politics. In Conscience's debate with Mede, both characters work around the idea of money as equal exchange and reciprocity in Aristotle's *Ethics* (5:10–11).[27] As Andrew Galloway notes, "Conscience has already approached the Aristotelian principle of money's equalization as Meed's complete promiscuity … Meed seizes his terms of desire and approaches the Aristotelian principle from another direction, as universal desire for her, rather than for some higher principle of justice (as Aristotle does)."[28] Aristotle's *Ethics* functions as the touchstone for the principle of fair exchange as justice, but in Langland's courtly setting uncontainable desires of all parties – including Wrong, Peace, Wrong's lawyers, and the King – make equal give-and-take impossible. What can be easily stated as clear-cut principles in William of Pagula's political treatise is made impossible in Langland's poetry.

Pagula's *Mirror* helps the reader understand how Langland politicizes and spiritualizes economic reciprocity, but in *Piers Plowman*, when Mede is bringing the market economy principle to court, what should have been applicable in mercantilism turns out to be a disaster in politics. Political reciprocity is based on economic reciprocity in Pagula's admonition to the king, but Langland emphasizes that economic and political reciprocity are equally hard to achieve, in which Peace is the meeting point of many strands of private-public desires. In what follows, Peace's allegorical personification will be more carefully examined.

ALLEGORY BEYOND "SURFACE" AND "DEPTH"

Reading the tension between historical and fictional documents as Langlandian social criticism does not quite do justice to Langland as a poet, because a solely historical reading still leaves Peace's personification unexplained. Delving into the mechanism of allegory aids a better understanding of the inner logic of Langland's poetics. The traditional model of reading allegory as "saying one thing, meaning another," or identifying "surface" and "deeper" meanings of the allegorical narrative, is unproductive in reading *Piers Plowman*. As Nicolette Zeeman points out, the congruence between surface and referent is absent in Langland's narrative.[29] The poet problematizes all allegorical personifications and categories by drawing on the classical rhetoric *paradiastole*, in which vice transforms into its adjacent virtue and virtue transforms into its neighboring vice.[30] For example, in *paradiastole*, insensibility can be masqueraded as temperance, and extravagance can imitate liberality. The same can be true the other way around: courage may turn into recklessness and prudence can be recast as cowardice.[31] Zeeman notes that the consistent application of *paradiastole* throughout *Piers Plowman*

---

[27] For the medieval reception of this Aristotelian principle, see Galloway, *Penn Commentary*, pp. 315–16.

[28] Galloway, *Penn Commentary*, p. 316.

[29] Nicolette Zeeman, *The Arts of Disruption: Allegory and* Piers Plowman (Oxford: Oxford University Press, 2020), p. 56. See also Zeeman's essay in this volume.

[30] Zeeman, *The Arts of Disruption*, pp. 31–74.

[31] Zeeman, *The Arts of Disruption*, pp. 40–42.

PETITION, JUSTICE, AND PEACE IN *PIERS PLOWMAN* 177

is exemplified in Langland's deflation of Conscience and Patience. Working outwards from the historical reading of Peace's status given above, this section further develops Zeeman's observations through an analysis of Peace's allegorical status to enrich our understanding of Langland's disruptive poetics.

The difficulties with understanding Peace's personification in the paradiastolic mode lie in identifying its corresponding vice and virtue in the political scenario. To map out the spectrum of political virtues and translate Zeeman's abstract observation into the political and economic conditions Langland is here taking as his subject, the reader must be aware that at the two ends of the ethical spectrum are not corruption and justice, nor centralized justice and local injustice. As Mark Ormrod states, "[w]hat distinguished the strong rulers of the later Middle Ages was their ability to restrain the more corrupt elements in the aristocracy and to ensure that the crown, rather than the magnates, derived the principal benefit from this system."[32] Ormrod dismantles the myth that the king's centralized justice will always work against local injustice to protect the people of the whole realm. Often, the royal power only remedies, for instance, local corruption when the magnates take a greater share of the benefits deriving from corruption. So long as the local governments do not infringe on royal privileges, the king is complicit in the corrupt system in order to reap benefits for the crown. The king's political virtue is the ability to maintain balance and harmony between the Crown and the magnates, and between the central and local governments.

In considering Peace as a character through the lens of private and public dialectics, it will be useful to unpack thoroughly the meaning of the terms "private peace" and "public peace." In the First Vision of *Piers Plowman*, private peace can mean (1) "psychological peace" or "inner feeling of satisfaction" as against external circumstances; (2) "individual or local" peace as against collective peace or national stability. Correspondingly, public peace can mean (1) fully publicized, universally recognized, collective, or even "national" peace as against "individual," "domestic," or narrowly "local, regional" peace; (2) the King's peace, or royal prerogative to manage peace of the realm according to the ruler's perception; (3) parliamentary, or institutional peace, or the perennial stability of the central government, undisturbed by royal intervention or local misgivings. These categories and subcategories of peace are doomed to clash with each other on different levels.

In what follows, I pair the above categories up one by one, in order to tease out the potential tensions within Peace as an allegorical personification.

(1) COLLECTIVE PEACE

Individual peace is compatible with public, collective, and national peace, although not necessarily easily. In order to achieve individual peace of mind, one must leverage the discourse of collective peace, albeit instrumentalizing it

---

[32] Ormrod, *The Reign of Edward III*, p. 110.

in the process. An individual's peace of mind in Vision One of *Piers Plowman* means no more than the complacency of an ordinary man. In this scenario, one form of peace uses another form of peace as an instrument to reinforce Peace's allegorical status.

However, when "private peace" is understood as local peace, it is hard for the term in this sense to coexist with ideas of national peace. As discussed in the previous section, purveyance, for instance, is one of the many ways to relieve the burdens of centralized taxation. If the armies can be supplied by fixing lower prices to purchase, or even rob, local goods of some affluent regions, there is no need to use the poll tax to deplete the whole nation. From the perspective of the inevitably uneven geographical distribution of purveyance, local peace is often sacrificed for the peace of the whole realm. Collective peace is achieved by inflicting wrongs on specific regions, such as extorting more wealth from more affluent areas.

Despite the politico-economic conditions, there was still a possible balance between the national and the provincial, especially during the reign of Edward III. Local authority and even bastard feudalism were not intolerable to the king. Peace's petition touches on bastard feudalism, or maintenance, according to which a lord can amass his own retainers and pay them for services instead of relying on the stock of vassals bestowed to him by his feudal position.[33] The greater nobility's maintenance depended on Mede or the cash nexus: under what has been traditionally known as the "feudal system," the bond between lord and vassal was symbolized by the grant of a piece of land (a fief), but in the "bastard feudalism" that later replaced it, retainers were kept by a regular payment. Such arrangements started in the thirteenth century, but the reign of Edward III witnessed the development and fruition of their more sinister implications: "The development of contract armies during the 1340s supposedly encouraged magnates to take on larger numbers of permanent retainers, and the king's apparent deference to the nobility allowed lords to use their client networks as a means of infiltrating local government, intimidating rivals, and securing favorable judgments in the courts."[34] Instead of curbing the magnates' expansion of power, the Crown and the central government were willing to involve the nobility in local and central politics. As a result, bastard feudalism did not establish itself as the prime threat, and this balance of power secured both local and central peace.

The two political situations are different, but the similarity is that the conflicting forms of peace justify the existence of the allegorical figure Wrong. Partial injustice and disturbance are necessary to achieve larger peace beyond specific areas. In this scenario, one form of public peace must eliminate a form of private peace.

---

[33] James Simpson, *Piers Plowman: An Introduction*, rev. ed. (Exeter, UK: University of Exeter Press, 2007), p. 46.

[34] Ormrod, *The Reign of Edward III*, p. 152.

(2) ROYAL PEACE

As another form of the public peace, the King's peace is not equivalent to collective peace. If communal peace is achieved through Peace's reconciliation with Wrong, the King remains implacable. Langland's most brilliant stroke in Passus 4 is that the King refuses to sacrifice regional peace to achieve his own peace. "The Kyng swor by Crist and by his crowne bothe / That Wrong for hise werkes sholde wo tholie" (IV. 83–84). Unlike national peace, which is often realized through the sacrifice of local interest, royal peace depends on regional stability. The King does not allow his realm to "rest in peace" if there is one single unjust attempt to "buy" peace, either through purveyance (compulsory purchase of goods) or bribing the plaintiff. The King insists that local peace and royal peace must coexist. From the King's perspective, these two forms of peace are equivalent. In this scenario, both public and private forms of peace are forced to coexist.

However, under this pressure, individual peace cannot coexist with the King's peace. When the King follows Reason's advice, *paradisatole* finds its way into Langland's allegory. The King's peace transforms into absolute, merciless justice while Peace is recast as cowardly and spineless. Reason acts out as the mouthpiece for this form of royal justice: "'I seye it by myself,' quod he, 'and it so were / That I were kyng with coroune to kepen a reaume, / Sholde nevere Wrong in this world that I wite myghte" (IV. 137–38). Here, one form of peace eliminates another and transforms these two forms into their adjacent vices. Worse still, this transformation generates more evils. Peace's individual satisfaction is suppressed to achieve the King's peace. Peace, as a person, desires monetary compensation and fears revenge, but this kind of peace is denied him. At the end of the vision, the reader knows neither whether Peace has been adequately recompensed nor whether Wrong will in practice be imprisoned for as long as he should be. In protecting local peace, both individual and local peace must give way to royal peace, which on this scenario is no less than an arbitrary imposition of order. Yet this kind of justice is unjust, since its consequences, such as revenge and local disturbances, are unpredictable. Peace is doomed to suffer from more unrest because strict justice maintains only momentary peace within the court. Once the King is absent or distant, all levels of peace may be destroyed again.

(3) PARLIAMENTARY PEACE

The only visible positive result of Peace's petition is governmental reform. On the face of it, the episode ends as parliamentary peace is achieved with the introduction of a new system of governance by Reason and Conscience. However, in this optimistic reading, some inner tensions remain unaccounted for.

In the old, unreformed government, Peace's individual peace is achieved purely by political maneuvering. When Reason and Conscience are not in power, lower forms of reason (the men of law) and diminished forms of conscience (Peace's self-complacency) start to work towards a basic form of temporary reconciliation. Individual peace is achieved through a corrupted form of governmental consensus. Here, *paradiastole* also applies. Governmental peace is transformed into veiling faults and wrongs; individual peace is also reduced to the gratification of personal desires. Individual and governmental peace can coexist in this form, but their enabling force is corruption.

In terms of local peace, the unreformed central government is too ready to sacrifice it. "Clerkes that were confessours coupled hem togideres / Al to construe this clause, and for the Kynges profit, / Ac noght for confort of the commune, ne for the Kynges soule" (IV. 149–51). Purveyance allows the King to circumvent the Parliament to get taxation from the lower tiers of society, which provides peace to the central government. The peace of the unreformed central government depends on exploiting local people and disturbing local peace.

After the governmental reform, Conscience and Reason will be able to direct the King to maintain peace in the central and local governments, but local bullies can never be appeased. Even in an uncorrupted central government, petitions must be submitted to disrupt the peace of the Parliament in order to restore local peace. Precisely because the Parliament is a route to achieving local peace, parliamentary peace and local peace are always in competition.

The six possible relationships between the various forms of peace I have traced can be summarized as follows:

1. Individual peace uses collective peace as an instrument.
2. National peace sacrifices local peace or benefits from local magnates' monopoly of power.
3. From the King's perspective, absolute local peace is royal peace.
4. But individual peace cannot coexist with the peace of the King.
5. In a corrupted central government, peace is the concealment of faults, which leaves room for individual peace.
6. Local peace always competes with the peace of central government, even in a reformed government.

Such is Peace's paradoxical status in Langland's allegory. These incompatible and divergent levels of peace create friction and contravene one another.

As a result, at different moments in the narrative, Peace's transformation into adjacent vices can be read differently. Peace becomes cowardice and selfishness when he succumbs to the bribery of Wrong and Mede. He becomes tyranny when the King claims Peace to be his own. He becomes arbitrary centralization of power when parliamentary peace inevitably competes with regional peace. The allegorical existence of Peace must be a paradox, as there is no way to guarantee peace for all parties involved; in other words, there is no way not to sacrifice parts of Peace for the survival of others. Peace is so fragmented and self-contradictory that he is hardly an allegorical figure at all. Instead, Langland's allegorical narrative requires Peace to function as a

PETITION, JUSTICE, AND PEACE IN *PIERS PLOWMAN* 181

plot device that brings coherence to what might otherwise fall apart with the centrifugal but related ideas contained within the allegorical figure.

More importantly, as Peace cannot exist by and for itself, Wrong is inevitable. Thanks to Peace, the most fragmented and self-contradictory character in this episode, different forms of Wrong always coexist with Peace. Reason's ideal kingship, which completely erases Wrong, is not only partial but also impossible. A "well-rounded" Peace simply cannot exist. Through Peace, situational and shifting, Langland's allegory denies intellectual, moral, or political complacencies.

CONCLUSION

In Langland's allegory, Peace is less a character than an embodiment of relations or how different forces should connect. As a set of temporary, shifting relations, Peace engages with both the private and the public. His petition bill is hyperbolic, but only such exaggerations can accommodate the perspectives from all ranks of society. Langland uses allegory to create a web of meaning that brings together multiple literary formulations, including a petition, a *speculum*, and a debate under the theoretical umbrella. When these episodes are read together, the reader becomes aware that the King cannot do without Wrong. Something must be wrong, and someone must be wronged to achieve a delicate balance of power. Peace cannot be blamed for being flat or lacking personality because he is no more than a temporary reconciliation or a meeting point of all forces and genres.

Therefore, what makes Langland's particular political allusions universal is exactly the flatness of Peace. This Utopian character seems the most cowardly, unimportant, and at the mercy of all exercise of power. Still, if it were fully realized, it could have eliminated many characters in *Piers Plowman*. If examined in the light of *paradiastole*, other characters become the opposite of their names. For instance, Patience is not patient with Haukyn; Conscience is not always driven by ethical awareness; Mede is both fair payment and bribery, but these transformations are still all based on relative oppositions. Only the character Peace is based on the impossibility of fulfilling itself. Reciprocity, strict requital, and retribution all seem to maintain Peace but simultaneously eliminate peace. The inherent contradictions of Peace cannot sustain an integral personality of Peace. Peace never lives up to his name.

If Peace is situational, justice is also situational. This observation conforms to Simpson's idea that justice for Langland at this point in the first vision is still partial justice: "The justice that is stressed is the strict, unremitting justice administered by the King; anything short of this on the side of mercy to Wrong is seen as an offence to justice, and to genuine mercy."[35] This version not only is waiting for a fuller justice, but also is preparing the ground for a later understanding of why grace is necessary. In contrast the transcendent,

---

[35] Simpson, *Piers Plowman: An Introduction*, p. 53.

theological Peace in Passus XVIII of the B-text, the purely secular Peace in Passus IV can be read as a commentary on the secular itself, especially considering that the first vision is introduced by none other than Holy Church. In Passus I, the Holy Church weaves the material and spiritual worlds – and their values – together, provisionally, and then separates them. After the unique blending and separation in the first vision, the second vision moves on to define the English polity in a new way, by making everyone in it virtuous. Although the secular figures are mostly doomed, the movements towards and within the purely secular are theoretically interesting and heuristically important.

My reading of the secular Peace as an essentially fragmented figure demonstrates why the poem must move on from the temporary end of the first vision and why it can go only in the direction that it does. Wrong always exists even in the most competent ruler's governance. This is a deeper sort of political wisdom invisible even to the King, who acts as a judge but is merely a participant in this web of meaning. Due to the interdependence between kingship and injustice, justice must be empowered by grace.

In the broader, trans-Reformation comparative parameter established by Simpson, Langland's discussion of justice and mercy calls to mind Portia's "quality of mercy" speech in Shakespeare's *Merchant of Venice* (4.1.179–200), in which mercy is a divine virtue that supplements human justice: "But mercy is above this sceptred sway; / It is enthroned in the hearts of kings, / It is an attribute to God himself, / And earthly power doth then show likest God's / When mercy seasons justice" (4.1.188–92).[36] Portia proposes that human justice has its own existence, but mercy, as an "attribute to God himself," must be added to it, dropping "as the gentle rain from heaven." However rhetorically powerful and socially constructive Portia's speech may be, Simpson argues that it is presented as a dramatic failure.[37] In the post-Reformation era, human access to divinity is denied and the literalism of the law is so rigorous that mercy is external to it; the law can only be sabotaged by playing it at "its own inhumane, inhuman game."[38] Portia's astute rebuttal that the contract allows Shylock to remove only the flesh, not the blood, of Antonio reveals that rigorous justice based on the letter of the law is "wholly unworkable as a way of dealing with the world."[39] By contrast, in Langland's allegory grace is less of an opportunistic expression of a ruler's leniency than an integral part of the proper functioning of human society.

---

[36] Quoted from *The Arden Shakespeare, Third Series Complete Works*, ed. Ann Thompson, David Scott Kastan, H. R. Woudhuysen, and G. R. Proudfoot (London: Bloomsbury, 2021), p. 970.

[37] James Simpson, *Permanent Revolution: The Reformation and the Illiberal Roots of Liberalism* (Cambridge, Mass.: The Belknap Press of Harvard University Press, 2019), p. 305.

[38] Simpson, *Permanent Revolution*, p. 305.

[39] Simpson, *Permanent Revolution*, pp. 305–06.

10 IN PLACE OF THE PAST: *SAINT ERKENWALD*'S VERSIONS OF CONVERSION[1]

Aparna Chaudhuri

Sainthood imprints itself on space. Michel de Certeau remarks that saints' lives feature a "predominance of precise indications of place over those of time," indications that anchor holy communities to the places of the saints' lives and deaths.[2] The seventh-century English saint, Erkenwald, is closely associated with three specific places: Barking and Chertsey, where he founded monasteries, and London, of which he was bishop from 675 to 693. The late eleventh-century *Vita Sancti Erkenwaldi* describes Erkenwald traveling constantly around his diocese, even when ill and needing to be carried on a litter; the mid-twelfth-century *Miracula Sancti Erkenwaldi* details the miraculous signs that appeared after the bishop's death to indicate that his final resting-place should be St. Paul's Cathedral in London, rather than either of the abbeys he had founded.[3] Before and after the Norman Conquest, Erkenwald's body occupied various positions of honor in the evolving structure of St. Paul's, coming to reside in an imposing Gothic-style tomb behind the high altar after the thirteenth-century reconstruction of the cathedral.[4]

---

[1] My deepest thanks to Nicholas Watson, Daniel Donoghue, and Sebastian Sobecki for their helpful comments on this essay, to Leah Whittington, in whose graduate seminar a very early version of it was written, and, of course, to James Simpson, who has influenced all my thought on periodization, historical boundary-crossing, and iconoclasm.

[2] Michel de Certeau, *The Writing of History*, tr. Tom Conley (New York: Columbia University Press, 1988), p. 280.

[3] For texts and translations, see E. Gordon Whatley, ed., *The Saint of London: The Life and Miracles of Saint Erkenwald* (Binghampton, N.Y.: State University of New York Press, 1989).

[4] See Whatley, *The Saint of London*, pp. 57–70.

The monumental presence of Erkenwald's relics in London's civic space registers itself unmistakably in the topographic imagination of the fourteenth-century alliterative poem *Saint Erkenwald*. Yet, instead of the splendidly entombed body of the saint, the poem gives us its uncanny double, telling a story of how the miraculously incorrupt corpse of a judge from remote pre-Christian antiquity is discovered during the laying of the foundations of St. Paul's in seventh-century London, where Erkenwald is bishop. Erkenwald's enshrined relics are thus made out to occupy a space inhabited by other bodies in the past. The poem also represents Britain as the site of successive incursions and conversions – by Saxon invaders, then by Christian missionaries from Rome.

This essay argues that *Saint Erkenwald* defamiliarizes the ambient presence of Christianity in the fourteenth-century English context of the poem's composition in order to raise challenging questions about the grounds of Christianity's occupation of literal ground: in London, Britain, and the world at large. When Christ himself declared that his kingdom is not of this world (John 18:36), what justifies the occupation of space by the earthly Church, especially when such occupation follows the pattern of other territorial conquests such as the Saxon settlement? The question is made sharper by the fact that Christian conversion was often theorized precisely as a "conquest of space": a conversion of pagan religious sites to the purpose of Christian worship.[5] Though at least notionally bloodless, and effected through adaptation rather than outright destruction, such conversion establishes Christianity as a monumental presence on the earth, housing Christ's mystical body, the church, in a constellation of physical churches and shrines, and engendering spatial rituals like pilgrimage.

Saint Erkenwald explores a particular medieval historiographic mode which operates through the study of urban topographies, and envisions pre-Christian architecture as an "allegorical grid" anchoring the Christian city of the present. In her seminal study of "topography as historiography" in representations of medieval Rome, Jennifer Summit argues that this historiographic method "represents historical change as a form of conversion that did not so much destroy or supplant the past as conserve its outward forms

---

5   The phrase "conquest of space" is from Jennifer Summit, "Topography as Historiography: Petrarch, Chaucer, and the Making of Medieval Rome," *Journal of Medieval and Early Modern Studies* 30 (2000), 211–46, especially 221. See, more generally, Robert Bartlett, *Why Can the Dead Do Such Great Things?: Saints and Worshippers from the Martyrs to the Reformation* (Princeton, N.J.: Princeton University Press, 2013), pp. 444–70; John M. Howe, "The Conversion of the Physical World: The Creation of a Christian Landscape," in *Varieties of Religious Conversion in the Middle Ages*, ed. James Muldoon (Gainesville, Fla.: University Press of Florida, 1997), pp. 63–78; and Robert Markus, "How on Earth Could Places Become Holy? Origins of the Christian Idea of Holy Places," *Journal of Early Christian Studies* 2 (1994), 257–71.

while assigning them new meanings."[6] Found in works as seemingly diverse as the twelfth-century pilgrim guide, *Mirabilia Urbis Romae*, Petrarch's letter to Giovanni Colonna about their shared walks through Rome, and Chaucer's Second Nun's Tale, the vision of history as a succession of conversions entails seeing each current architectural form as inhabiting the space or shape of an older one. Summit likens this topographical hermeneutic to the doubled reading of classical texts that Petrarch suggests at the beginning of his letter to Colonna: "Let us thus read philosophical, poetic, or historical writings so that the Gospel of Christ sounds always in our heart. With it alone we are sufficiently happy and learned, without it, no matter how much we learn, we become more ignorant and wretched."[7] Petrarch's formulation, in which the Gospel enriches the inevitable poverty of secular learning, inverts an Augustinian hermeneutic scheme, where it is the treasure of classical wisdom that is to be appropriated by Christianity, its "rightful" possessor.[8] *Saint Erkenwald*, I argue, remains critically cognizant of this appropriative logic that can drive both textual and topographic allegoresis. The Christian "recuperation" of pagan spaces and pagan persons is not only a preoccupation but a problematic in the poem.

As it examines the validity of the Church's territorial manifestation, the poem draws upon texts by and about a principal agent in the establishment of Christianity in England: Gregory I (540–604), the "pope" who sent "Saynt Austyn" to evangelize among the English (12).[9] The plot of *Saint Erkenwald* has long been recognized as based on the story of Gregory's intercession for the soul of the pagan emperor Trajan, after finding out about the latter's deed

---

6   Summit, "Topography as Historiography," p. 227.

7   Francesco Petrarca, *Rerum familiarium libri (I—VIII)*, tr. Aldo S. Bernardo (Albany, N.Y.: SUNY Press, 1975), VI. 6, p. 291. See Summit, "Topography as Historiography," p. 218. On *Saint Erkenwald*'s historical vision in general, see, among others, Laura Varnam, "Sacred Space, Memory and Materiality in *St Erkenwald*," in *Old St Paul's and Culture*, ed. Shanyn Altman and Jonathan Buckner (London: Palgrave Macmillan, 2021), pp. 73–98; Cynthia Turner Camp, "Spatial Memory, Historiographic Fantasy, and the Touch of the Past in *St Erkenwald*," *New Literary History* 44 (2013), 471–91; and Ruth Nisse, "'A Coroun Ful Riche': The Rule of History in 'St Erkenwald,'" *ELH* 65 (1998), 277–95. On the connections between *Saint Erkenwald*'s poetic form and its sense of history, see Christine Chism, "*St Erkenwald*: The Body in Question," in *Alliterative Revivals* (Philadelphia: University of Pennsylvania Press, 2002), pp. 41–65, and Eric Weiskott, "The *Erkenwald*-Poet's Sense of the Past," in *English Alliterative Verse: Poetic Tradition and Literary History* (Cambridge: Cambridge University Press, 2016), pp. 127–47.

8   Augustine, *De Doctrina Christiana*, tr. R. P. H. Green (Oxford: Oxford University Press, 1997), Book 2, chapter 40, p. 64; quoted in Summit, "Topography as Historiography," p. 219.

9   All references to *Saint Erkenwald* are to the text in *The Complete Works of the Pearl-poet*, ed. Malcolm Andrew, Ronald Waldron, Clifford Peterson, tr. Casey Finch (Berkeley, Calif.: University of California Press, 1993), pp. 324–39. Line numbers are given parenthetically in the text.

of justice and compassion towards a poor widow.[10] But the *Erkenwald*-poet was evidently a wide-ranging reader of Gregorian texts, for he frames the story of the virtuous pagan's salvation in Gregory's own influential theorizations of the assimilation of pagan spaces, and their architecture and art, into Christian religious practice. Indeed, as the first part of this essay shows, the Gregory-Trajan legend itself contains a striking example of Christian topographic allegoresis. *Saint Erkenwald* critically examines the grounds and implications of such allegoresis while it translates the Roman legend into an English context and the vernacular that was born of what the poem describes, probably with a measure of irony, as England's "ronke ʒeres" of paganism (11).[11]

GREGORY, TRAJAN, AND TRAJAN'S FORUM

The story of Gregory and Trajan first occurs in Gregory's earliest surviving *vita*, written in the early eighth century by an anonymous monk of Whitby Abbey. Subsequent *vitae*, written in the later eighth and ninth centuries by the deacons Paul and John, reproduce the basic details of the Whitby *Life*'s account, which is as follows:

> One day as he was crossing the Forum [Trajan's Forum], a magnificent piece of work for which Trajan is said to have been responsible, he found on examining it carefully that Trajan, though a pagan, had done a deed so charitable that it seemed more likely to have been the deed of a Christian than of a pagan. For it is related that, as he was leading his army in great haste against the enemy, he was moved to pity by the words of a widow, and the emperor of the whole world came to a halt. She said, "Lord Trajan, here are the men who killed my son and are unwilling to pay me recompense." He answered, "Tell me about it when I return and I will make them recompense you." But she replied, "Lord, if you never return, there will be no one to help me." Then, armed as he was, he made the defendants pay forthwith the compensation they owed her, in his presence. When Gregory discovered this story, he recognized that this was just what we read about in the Bible, "Judge the fatherless, plead for the widow. Come now and let us reason together, saith the Lord." Since Gregory did not know what to do to comfort the soul of this man who brought the words of Christ to his mind, he went to Saint Peter's Church

---

[10] See Gordon Whatley, "Heathens and Saints: *St Erkenwald* in its Legendary Context," *Speculum* 61 (1986), 330–63, as well as "The Uses of Hagiography: The Legend of Pope Gregory and the Emperor Trajan in the Middle Ages," *Viator* 15 (1984), 25–64; and Frank Grady, *Representing Righteous Heathens in Late Medieval England* (New York: Palgrave Macmillan, 2005), pp. 17–44.

[11] Emily Dalton argues that the poem uses the topos of classical recovery/survival to figure its own representation of a "culturally and linguistically remote Anglo-Saxon past," in "'Clansyd hom in Cristes nom': Translation of Spaces and Bodies in *St Erkenwald*," *The Journal of English and Germanic Philology* 117 (2018), 56–83.

SAINT ERKENWALD'S VERSIONS OF CONVERSION 187

and wept floods of tears, as was his custom, until he gained at last by divine revelation the assurance that his prayers were answered, seeing that he had never presumed to ask this for any other pagan.[12]

In the Whitby *Life* and others modeled on it, Gregory's intercession builds on the coexistence of classical and Christian architectures in Rome's topography, and forges a further connection between them. Trajan's Forum is here a third participant in "the drama of intercession."[13] In the hagiographer's phrasing, Trajan's considerable *opera* contributing to Roman art and architecture stands parallel to his ethical *opus*. Architectural space preserves the memory of Trajan's merciful deed – not by accident but by the deliberate investment of imperial power (we are reminded, at the risk of tautology, that Trajan's Forum is Trajan's work). Indeed, the Forum perpetuates Trajan's memory in a distinctive way, a fact of which the Whitby hagiographer appears at least tangentially aware. The last and largest of the imperial fora in Rome, Trajan's Forum foregrounds the emperor's *res gestae*: the narrative of his Dacian campaigns winds its way in elaborate relief engravings up the towering column that stands today in the northern part of the forum complex, guarding the entrance to the temple of deified Trajan and Plotina. Whereas the Forum of Augustus displayed statues of the Roman *summi viri*, and focused on relating the present Augustan age to the Greek past, Trajan's Forum depicts Trajan's own recent deeds in war, in vivid storiated art of unprecedented refinement and extensiveness.[14]

If any aspect of the Forum conveyed the story of Trajan and the widow to Gregory, it was probably among the reliefs on Trajan's Column. Vickers's influential essay develops Gaston Paris's speculation that what Gregory saw, or is believed to have seen, was a bas-relief halfway up Trajan's Column, depicting the emperor on horseback, surrounded by troops, and with a supplicant figure kneeling before him. The scene, as Vickers comments, is a stock one, found on the arch of Trajan at Benevento as well: the kneeling

---

[12] For the Latin original and English translation, see *The Earliest Life of Gregory the Great by an anonymous monk of Whitby*, ed. and tr. Bertram Colgrave (Lawrence, Kans.: University of Kansas Press, 1968), chapter 29, pp. 127–29. For the texts of Paul and John's *Lives* of Gregory, see *Sancti Gregorii Magni Vita: Auctore Paulo Diacono Monachio Cassinensi*, PL 75, cols. 11–60 and *Sancti Gregorii Magni Vita: Auctore Joanne Diacono*, PL 75, cols. 61–212.

[13] Nancy J. Vickers, "Seeing is Believing: Gregory, Trajan, and Dante's Art," *Dante Studies* 101 (1983), 67–85, see especially 80.

[14] This discussion of Trajan's Forum is indebted to Eric M. Thienes, "Remembering Trajan in Fourth-Century Rome: Memory and Identity in Spatial, Artistic, and Textual Narratives" (unpublished Ph.D. dissertation, University of Missouri, 2015), pp. 47–48. See also Alain Gowing, *Empire and Memory: The Representation of the Roman Republic in Imperial Culture* (Cambridge: Cambridge University Press, 2005), pp. 146–51, and Penelope Davies, "The Politics of Perpetuation: Trajan's Column and the Art of Commemoration," *American Journal of Archaeology* 101 (1997), 41–65.

188   APARNA CHAUDHURI

figure represents a conquered nation submitting to its conqueror.[15] Whether
accidentally or intentionally, Gregory "misreads" this convention of imperial
art such that it conveys a story of mercy, which in turn activates Gregory's
own Biblical knowledge and exegetical capabilities. Perhaps the story is one
already in circulation, or perhaps Gregory derives it directly from the relief,
in a form dictated by the hermeneutic anteriority of the Christian scriptures
in his practice of reading.[16] Knowingly or unknowingly, he might identify
the Bible's stock figures of helplessness – the widow and the orphan – in the
conventional symbol of political submission in imperial art.

The early hagiographic accounts of the Gregory-Trajan episode thus
portray Gregory as a reader of history in art and architecture. Gregory himself
issued some of the medieval west's most famous statements on how images
can teach of the deeds of the past. These appear in two letters sent to the
bishop of Marseilles, Serenus, at the end of the sixth century, reproaching
Serenus for having destroyed certain images in his church so that the people
should not commit idolatry by adoring them.[17] Gregory's letters aver that
images must indeed not be adored; yet Serenus should not have had them
broken and ejected from the church. For:

> [I]t is one thing to adore a picture, another through a picture's story to learn
> what must be adored. For what writing offers to those who read it, a picture
> offers to the ignorant who look at it, since in it the ignorant see what they
> ought to follow, in it they read who do not know letters, since especially for
> the gentile nations [*gentibus*] a picture stands in place of reading.[18]

The images to which Gregory refers are "of holy persons" (*sanctorum*), but
clearly not static images of saints. They are pieces of narrative art: *visio
historiae* or *visio rei gestae*.[19] These images, painted or sculpted within
churches, presumably depict events in sacred history: as Celia Chazelle
speculates, they may have included stories from the Old Testament, which are
known to have been depicted in the churches of Gregory's time and earlier.[20]
Nothing suggests that Gregory would have extended the meaning of *res gestae*

---

15 Vickers, "Seeing is Believing," p. 76.
16 On how Christian allegoresis of classical texts operates by assigning anteriority
    to the Bible as a point of reference, see Rita Copeland and Stephen Melville,
    "Allegory and Allegoresis: Rhetoric and Hermeneutics," *Exemplaria* 3 (1991),
    159–87, especially 172.
17 Gregory the Great, *Epistolarum Registrum*, Book 9, Epistle 105 and Book 11, Epistle
    13 (PL vol. 77, cols. 1027–28 and 1128–30).
18 Gregory, *Epistolarum Registrum*, Book 11, Epistle 13 (PL 77, col. 1128). The English
    translations of both Gregory's letters to Serenus are by Celia M. Chazelle, in "Pictures,
    books, and the illiterate: Pope Gregory I's letters to Serenus of Marseilles," *Word and
    Image: A Journal of Verbal/Visual Enquiry* 6 (2012), 138–53, lightly adapted. My
    discussion of Gregory's image-theory is greatly indebted to Chazelle's.
19 Gregory, *Epistolarum Registrum*, Book 11, Epistle 13 (PL 77, col. 1129).
20 Chazelle, "Pictures, books," p. 141.

SAINT ERKENWALD'S VERSIONS OF CONVERSION 189

to secular deeds such as Trajan's conquests. Nevertheless, at the literal level, even events in sacred history are "past deed[s]," capable of being captured in tangible representations which, Gregory argues, are not to be rejected outright, but preserved as external stimuli for the apprehension of a formless God. Moreover, Gregory's words implicitly uphold the continuous history of artistic representation itself. Christian images follow upon a "gentile" history of iconography and visual representation. In reminding Serenus that "especially for the gentiles, a picture stands in place of reading" (*unde praecipua gentibus pro lectione pictura est*) Gregory specifies that the Christian image *should* function as a continuation of pagan artistic tradition, in order that the human subjects of conversion – the "gentiles" turned, or turning, Christian – should not experience a disorienting rupture in their cognitive and interpretive practices, or have to erase (rather than adapt) their older selves to accommodate the new truths of Christianity.

Thus, the earliest story of Gregory and Trajan attributes to Gregory an appreciation of both pagan virtue and pagan art (the vehicle of historical *res gestae*). It places Gregory in a hybrid urban space, the Christian and classical elements of which are connected by his own movements: perhaps a daily walk, as Vickers speculates, from the Lateran Palace, passing through (*transiens*) Trajan's Forum, to St. Peter's (where he finally weeps for Trajan's soul). As it localizes the saint, placing him in his city, the Whitby *Life* simultaneously historicizes the presence of Christianity in Rome, reminding us of the city's pre-Christian past. As Summit argues, this kind of historical vision sees the pagan past as a repository of forms that can be filled with Christian significance, thereby coming to point forward in time, towards the ascendancy of Christianity in the Rome of Gregory's day.[21] Gregory's hermeneutic itinerary, from the Bible (already in his mind), to the classical monument, and back to Christian scripture (which the monument causes him to recall), resembles his physical progress, if the latter is mapped from the papal palace through the Forum to St. Peter's.

In the Whitby *Life*, Gregory learns of a classical instance of justice and/or mercy through classical art and architecture that has survived Rome's conversion to Christianity. A later rendering of the tale produces a sharper sense of the historical distance between the emperor and the Pope by making Trajan's *body* the main remnant of the pagan past in Christian Rome. This version provides a closer analogue to the plot of *Saint Erkenwald*, where too it is a pagan corpse that appears in a recently-converted city. In Jacopo della Lana's commentary (c. 1330) on the *Divine Comedy*, the story of Gregory and Trajan is recounted to provide background for Dante's portrayal of Trajan as an example of humility in the tenth canto of the *Purgatorio* (which describes the penitence of the prideful).[22]

---

[21] See Summit, "Topography as Historiography," especially pp. 214 and 227.
[22] Jacopo della Lana, *Commento*, in *Comedia di Dante Allagheri col commento Jacopo della Lana*, 3 vols. (Bologna: Tipografia Regia, 1866), 2:116–17.

According to della Lana, some Roman workmen were digging a ditch when they came upon a very old coffin containing some bones and a skull with a perfectly preserved tongue. When the hue and cry about the discovery reached the pope's ears, he had the coffin brought before him. Conjured to speak in the name of Christ, the tongue revealed that it belonged to the emperor Trajan, damned for lacking Christian faith. Gregory then turned to books to learn more about Trajan, found the story of his mercy and justice towards the widow, and was moved to pray for his resuscitation, so that he could be baptized and saved.[23]

This version of the Gregory-Trajan story affords a darker view of history as rupture and forgetting, only somewhat mitigated by the memorial and affective capacities of art. Although Trajan's memory is preserved in the books to which Gregory eventually refers, the emperor's sarcophagus is accidentally discovered at a nondescript construction site. It opens to reveal bones and a skull; the miraculously whole tongue appears to exist only to reveal the dichotomy between Trajan's imperial identity and ultimate fate. A humanist fantasy of touching the past glimmers in the detail that Gregory's prayers caused Trajan to revive, live in Gregory's sixth-century world, accept baptism, and finally be saved ("*risuscitò, e visse al mondo, e fu battezzato, e tiensi ch'elli sia mo salvo*"); but the fantasy is framed in an acute consciousness of the loss of the classical past – represented by Trajan's dead, decayed, and forgotten body.[24]

This characteristically humanist consciousness of the past as past causes Gregory to appear like a learned antiquarian, piecing together the scattered fragments of Trajan's history and body. The Whitby *Life* emphasizes a different aporia: what can the Christian of the present day do *as a Christian* for the pagan of the past? Gregory's answer, following initial bewilderment, is to weep over the fate of Trajan's soul. These tears constitute the intercession that Dante terms Gregory's *gran vittoria* (a phrase that recalls the military victories of Trajan depicted in the Forum's reliefs). Once the pagan past is seen as somehow Christian, Trajan's deed as "more likely to have been the deed of a Christian than of a pagan," that past is felt to require present action which will make real its figural Christianity. For Petrarch, writing to Colonna of the need to read classical texts so that "the Gospel of Christ sounds always in one's heart," hermeneutics can forestall the self's potential division between Christian faith and admiration of antiquity. Allegoresis thus solves a problem for Petrarch, whereas it generates a problem for Gregory. For the latter, the coherence between classical and Christian values must be made to manifest itself in the outer world, sometimes through a conversion of spaces, but in this case through a radical departure from the temporal world altogether, as the pope exercises an institutional office with claimed eschatological influence: the power of the keys.

---

[23] On the "resuscitation motif" as a feature of the Gregory-Trajan legend from the twelfth century onwards, see Whatley, "Uses of Hagiography," pp. 36–40.

[24] Jacopo della Lana, *Commento*, p. 117.

SAINT ERKENWALD'S VERSIONS OF CONVERSION   191

Through this selective account of different stages in the development of the Gregory-Trajan legend, and brief foray into Gregory's theories of the artistic image, I have tried to highlight three main elements that *Saint Erkenwald* combines and recombines. The first is the setting of the legend in a spatially and temporally complex urban space, where pagan monuments coexist with the structures of the Christian present. Here, classical art and architecture survive to tell stories of classical virtue: imperial Rome provides a typological framework for the Christian city. The second is a consciousness of the *loss* of the past, which informs della Lana's account of the accidental discovery of Trajan's almost entirely decayed and unidentifiable (except by means of a miracle) body. The third is an aporia between figural and real Christianity that troubles the Christian vision of history, at least as the latter is represented in both Gregory's *vitae* and in *Saint Erkenwald*. If the past is not to be replaced or effaced but incorporated into the present, this incorporation cannot happen only on earth, in material and architectural terms alone: it must involve heaven as well. A poetics of heavenly space develops in response to this historiographic need.

PAGAN PAST AND CHRISTIAN FUTURE IN *SAINT ERKENWALD*

The assimilation of the past to the needs of the present can itself create historical ruptures, to which *Saint Erkenwald* alerts us at its very outset. Indeed, the poem itself appears complicit in their creation, collapsing the period after the Saxon warrior Hengist's arrival in England into a single dark phase – "mony ronke зeres" – of paganism. This "middle age," so to speak, ends with another arrival: that of Augustine of Canterbury, sent to preach Christianity to the English by Pope Gregory. There follows a bloodless conversion of the people to Christianity and the pagan shrines and temples into Christian churches and shrines of saints. If Hengist's incursion was from Saxon hostility ("unsaзt"), what motivated Augustine's? The poem's account of "Austyn's" evangelistic program may provide some answers, especially if we look to their probable source, in instructions sent by the historical Pope Gregory to Augustine for the conversion of England:

> the idol temples of that race should by no means be destroyed, but only the idols in them. Take holy water and sprinkle it in these shrines, build altars and place relics in them. For if the shrines are well built, it is essential that they should be changed from the worship of devils to the service of the true God. When this people sees that their shrines are not destroyed, they will be able to banish error from their hearts and be more ready to come to the places they are familiar with, but now recognizing and worshipping the true God.[25]

[25] Bede, *Historia Ecclesiastica Gentis Anglorum*, in *Bede's Ecclesiastical History of the English People*, ed. and tr. Bertram Colgrave and R. A. B. Mynors (Oxford: Clarendon Press, 1969) Book 1, chapter 30, p. 107.

192 APARNA CHAUDHURI

The readiness with which Gregory feels Christianity should adapt to pagan spatial practices may be interpreted as a function of what Robert Markus termed Christianity's general "indifference to space," born of the conviction that Christ's kingdom is not of this world.[26] The missionary must convert hearts, not spaces, from error. Yet Gregory's words also assign value to the "well-built shrine," and express a desire to possess the latter on behalf of Christianity through the alteration of its inner significance, much as he famously expressed admiration for the external beauty of the English (Angle) slave boys he encountered in a Roman marketplace, and desired to draw them into the Christian fold, making them "fellow-heirs of the angels of heaven."[27] Conquest, in *Saint Erkenwald*, is hate-driven; by contrast, conversion may be libidinal, driven by desire for the tangible outward forms of the persons, places, or structures to be converted.

Meanwhile, the actual power to convert begins to operate in the realm of language before it can express itself in territorial and cultural forms. Gregory puns on the names and toponyms by which the boys identify themselves. Thus, "Angles" should reign with the "*angelorum in caelis*," the "Deiri" (natives of the province from which the boys hail) are "snatched from the wrath of Christ" (*de ira eruti*) and their ruler's name, Aella, is a sign that "alleluia" or "the praise of God the creator must be sung in those parts."[28] Gregory's adeptness at finding Christian significance, expressed in Latin phrases, in the forms of Germanic words makes for learned play on Augustine's assertion in *De Doctrina Christiana* that: "any statements by those who are called philosophers ... which happen to be true and consistent with our faith should not cause alarm, but be claimed for our own use, as it were from owners who have no right to them."[29] As Summit comments, this reading method is akin to the architectural adaptations whereby pagan temples and monuments are converted to Christian uses, and made to prophesy the ultimate ascendancy of Christianity in Rome. Gregory too appropriates a kind of pagan text for Christian use, but whereas Augustine's concern is with proto-Christian truths expressed in the words of pagans, Gregory's wordplay evacuates pagan words of their own meanings (as if throwing idols out of shrines) and replaces them with alien significances.

Saint Erkenwald begins with a similar assimilation, playing out through the conducive form of alliterative verse. Augustine launches a physically and linguistically energetic program of spatial conversion:

> He turnyd temples þat tyme þat temyd to þe deuelle
> And clansyd hom in Cristes nome and kyrkes hom callid

---

[26] Robert Markus, *The End of Ancient Christianity* (Cambridge: Cambridge University Press, 1990), p. 140.

[27] Bede, *Historia Ecclesiastica*, Book 2, chapter 1, p. 133.

[28] Ibid.

[29] Augustine, *De Doctrina*, Book 2, chapter 40, p. 64. See the discussion in Summit, "Topography as Historiography," pp. 219–20.

SAINT ERKENWALD'S VERSIONS OF CONVERSION 193

> He hurlyd owt hor ydols and hade hym in sayntes
> And chaungit chevely hor nomes and chargit hom better.
> Þat ere was of Appolyn is now of Saynt Petre,
> Mahoun to St Margrete oþer to Maudelayne;
> Þe synagogue of the Sonne was sett to oure Lady,
> Jubiter and Jono to Jhesus or to James. (15–22)

There is no mention of the truths of pagan religion, nor even the admission that such truths exist. The gods of different non-Christian faiths are all equated: with each other, and with "Sathanas." While the passage seems to show the influence of medieval pilgrims' guides to Rome, such as the twelfth-century *Mirabilia Urbis Romae*, it omits most of the historical and etymological connections that the *Mirabilia* makes between Christian and pagan structures. Thus, while the detail that the basilica of St. Peter was erected on the site of Apollo's temple occurs both in the *Mirabilia* and *Saint Erkenwald*, the latter otherwise builds mostly on the incidental phonetic similarities of Christian and pagan names, like this passage in the *Mirabilia*:

> Where Saint Peter *ad vincula*, was the temple of Venus. At Saint Mary in Fontana, the temple of Faunus; this was the idol that spake to Julian, and beguiled him.[30]

Locational connections are reinforced by aural assonances (*vincula*-Venus, Fontana-Faunus) – a muted version of the *Erkenwald*-poet's alliterative play on Mahoun/Margrete/Maudelayne or Jupiter/Juno/Jesus/James.[31]

This initial scheme of spatial conversions through alliterative connections lends itself, further on in the poem, to forming a crux between two views of paganism – mere form without meaning, and a substantive faith with its own truths, which are distinctly like those of Christianity, and perhaps better upheld by pagans than by Christians. Mapped on to civic space, this crux takes the form of a change from architectural assimilation to entire destruction and building anew: the largest pagan temple in the city is razed to the ground, and a new "fundament" sought for St. Paul's Cathedral, which is to be established in the temple's place. But deep underground, among the "humic foundations" of both temple and cathedral, a pagan body is discovered, and, through it, a deep resonance between the core values of Christianity and pagan religion.[32] An apparently total iconoclasm thus reveals an uncannily profound identity between paganism and Christianity, which threatens to undermine the logic of Christianity's present ascendancy in Britain, or at least to expose it in an

---

[30] *Mirabilia Urbis Romae: The Marvels of Rome or A Picture of the Golden City*, ed. Francis Morgan Nichols (London: Ellis and Elvey, 1989), p. 108.
[31] On these alliterating conversions, see Jennifer L. Sisk, "The Uneasy Orthodoxy of St. Erkenwald," *ELH* 74 (2007), 89–115; Chism, *Alliterative Revivals*, pp. 50–51.
[32] Robert Pogue Harrison, *The Dominion of the Dead* (Chicago: University of Chicago Press, 2003), p. 27.

194 APARNA CHAUDHURI

appropriative relationship with the pagan past. It is for Bishop Erkenwald to make this unsettling discovery into a pastoral lesson that will consolidate the Christian faith of the recently-converted London citizens who gather in numbers around the body, and speculate on its origins.

Yet, before moving to the pastoral resolution, let us consider the ways in which the appearance of the body problematizes the vision of history as a continuous conversion of old forms to accommodate new meanings. Amidst all of Augustine's assimilation of pagan spaces and structures to Christian uses, the beautiful, immaculately preserved, yet unidentifiable body suggests that a rupture between the past and the present has nevertheless occurred. No one can remember such a man being buried in royal pomp, no document records his existence or death, and the bright golden letters carved on the tomb are unreadably "roynyshe" to all who see them (52). To be sure, when the corpse begins to speak on Erkenwald's command, it reveals that it is immeasurably older than the monuments of the Saxons, having lived in the time of King Belinus, almost five hundred years before the birth of Christ. Even so, the speech of this noble "Trojan" judge – for so he describes himself, with reference to the mythical foundation of London by the Trojan Brutus – invites one to acknowledge possible connections between Saxon and classical paganism, and to wonder what moral values, philosophies, and histories of virtuous individuals might have been effaced from memory in the process of converting pagan forms – considered as no more than forms – to Christian ends.[33]

More fundamentally, the corpse's revelation of its identity raises unsettling questions about the material bases of the "history as conversion" thesis. Though buried with royal honor, the corpse is not that of a king, but a mere judge, albeit one who personifies Trajan's medieval reputation for justice and virtue.[34] Indeed, the *Erkenwald*-author might almost be playing upon an idea expressed by John of Salisbury in his account of ideal kingship in the *Policraticus*: that the quality of being righteous (*rectus*) is *constitutive* of Trajan's identity as king (*rex*):[35] "Amongst all these (Julius Caesar, Augustus Caesar, Trajan), I do not hesitate to prefer Trajan, for he built the majesty of his reign solely upon the practice of virtue. This is akin to the remark of the moralist (Horace), that he who does right may be adjudged king (*Ethicum*

---

[33] For a detailed discussion of how early modern humanists understood Gregory himself as a destroyer of pagan architecture and art, see Tilmann Buddensieg, "Gregory the Great, the Destroyer of Pagan Idols: The History of a Medieval Legend Concerning the Decline of Ancient Art and Literature," *Journal of the Warburg and Courtauld Institutes* 28 (1965), 44–65.

[34] For the argument that the judge represents an ethical ideal of kingship, all the more powerful for standing outside the history of the British monarchy, see Nisse, "'A Coroun Ful Riche.'"

[35] I am grateful to Daniel Donoghue for bringing this pun to my attention.

SAINT ERKENWALD'S VERSIONS OF CONVERSION 195

iuxta qui recte fecerit, regem arbitratur)."[36] The righteous pagan judge of *Saint Erkenwald*, too, is "adjudged king" at his death by a mourning population:

> For þe honour of myn honeste of heghest enprise
> Þey coronede me þe kidde kynge of kene iustises
> Þer euer was tronyd in Troye, oþer trowid euer shulde
> And for I rewarded euer riȝt þey raght me the septre. (253–56)

Yet, replete though he may have been in kingly virtues, and rewarded by royal honors heaped on him by a grateful populace, a judge's existence would not be recorded as a king's would have been – as the lives of the judge's contemporary, King Belinus, and Belinus's warlike brother, Brennin, are rehearsed by Geoffrey of Monmouth, for instance.[37] Nor would a judge be able to direct the perpetuation of his own memory by the creation of a monument or complex of monuments such as Trajan's Forum.[38] In abstracting justice from the figure of the just king, modeled by Trajan, *Saint Erkenwald* subtly reminds us of the wealth and power required to build the monuments that exist through time and furnish the grounds of typological reading. Christianity may infuse new meanings into pagan forms, but, in the process, it acquires those outward shapes of grandeur as its own and must negotiate the potential contradictions they pose to Christ and his apostles' messages of simplicity, poverty, and unworldliness.

Thus complicated, the space that Christianity occupies on the earth requires a new justification, the grounds of which are found in the entirely other spaces of hell and heaven. Where earthly morality is concerned, the judge's account of his virtue suggests that there is no essential difference between pagans and Christians or, indeed, between pagan and Christian religions. (The pagan judge's righteousness is not simply an example of secular virtue, it reflects his faith: "Non gete me fro þe heghe gate to glente out of riȝte, / Als ferforthe as my faithe confourmyd my hert.") This blurring of distinctions is seen in the Gregory-Trajan legend as well; nevertheless, the Whitby *Life* suggests its own reliance on the Augustinian paradigm of appropriative exegesis when it describes Trajan's deed as "more likely to have been the deed of a Christian than a pagan." Such interpretations are withheld in *Saint Erkenwald*, where

---

[36] John of Salisbury, *Policraticus*, in *Ioannis Saresberiensis Policraticus, sive De nugis curialum, et vestigiis philosophorum, libri octo* (Leiden: Johannes Maire, 1639), Book 5, ch. 8, p. 282. The English translation is from John of Salisbury, *Policraticus*, ed. Cary J. Nederman (Cambridge: Cambridge University Press, 2007), pp. 79–80.

[37] Geoffrey of Monmouth, *Historia Regum Britanniae*, in *The History of the Kings of Britain: An Edition and Translation of De Gestis Britonum (Historia Regum Britanniae)*, ed. Michael Reeve, tr. Neil Wright (Woodbridge, UK: Boydell, 2007), pp. 49–59.

[38] For the argument that the judge represents an ethical ideal of kingship, all the more powerful for standing outside the history of the British monarchy, see Nisse, "'A Coroun Ful Riche.'"

196 APARNA CHAUDHURI

God himself has rewarded the pagan, *qua* pagan, for his virtue with the miraculous preservation of his body, and Erkenwald too, building on the promise of Psalm 15 ("Lord, who may abide in thy tabernacle?"), assumes that the pagan's soul is *already* saved:

He þat rewardes uche a renke as he has riȝt served
Myȝt euel forgo þe to gyfe of His grace summe brawnche,
For as He says in His sothe psalmyde writtes:
Þe skilfulle and þe unskathely skelton ay to me.
Forþi say me of þi soule in sele quere ho wonnes. (275–79)

On earth, at least, there is little to distinguish pagan from Christian religion, or the pagan from the Christian righteous. It is left to the pagan soul, speaking from its bitter experience of hell, to point out that the real difference between the two faiths lies in the eschatological realm, whose space cannot be "conquered" by the human being, but lies entirely in God's merciful grant. Here, as another alliterative poem of the period reminds us, human "right" does not translate into the prerogative to possess:

"Anende ryȝtwys men ȝet saytz a gome,
Dauid, in sauter, if ever ȝe seȝ hyt:
Lorde, Þy servaunt draȝ neuer to dome,
For non lyuyande to Þe is justyfyet."
Forþy to corte quen þou schalt com
þer alle oure causez schal be cryed,
Alegge þe ryȝt, þou may be innome.[39]

Pearl capitalizes on two meanings of "corte": the legal court, where humans cannot hope to out-argue or disprove God's judgments, and the royal court, where they may humbly entreat for and receive their lord's mercy. In *Saint Erkenwald*, the judge's baptism by Erkenwald's tears results in heaven – imagined as the feasting-hall of a noble or royal household – being thrown open to the pagan's now Christian soul, when all the pagan's righteousness could not win him this entry. This heavenly "cenacle" has its historical analogue in the "upper room" (Acts 1:13) where the Apostles used to gather with Christ. Like *Pearl*, with its vision of the New Jerusalem, *Saint Erkenwald* too establishes a pattern of translations between earthly and heavenly, historical and eternal spaces, arranging heaven and eternity according to a logic of divine sovereignty that can both uphold and undermine forms of earthly dominion. Thus, in *Pearl*, a human custodian is but a "jeweller" compared to the divine "prince" to whom the "pearl" belongs in the true spiritual sense. In *Saint Erkenwald*, human justice, embodied in the person of a judge, is invested with a figural kingship that finds fulfilment in a heavenly sovereign who

---

[39] *The Poems of the Pearl Manuscript*, ed. Malcolm Andrew and Ronald Waldron (London: Edward Arnold, 1981), pp. 53–110, lines 697–703.

SAINT ERKENWALD'S VERSIONS OF CONVERSION 197

allowed himself to be annihilated in order to redeem his people. The discourse of sovereignty itself is shifted from earth to heaven: there is no historical king, no Trajan, in the poem.

And if the sovereignty – the "kingdom" – of Christ "is not of this world," the church's claim to a place in the world must be founded on its ability to provide a chance of entry to the other world: the court of heaven. Therefore the poem's emphasis on the sacraments, through which the faithful are absorbed into Christ's *corpus mysticum*, and redeemed by his shedding of blood.[40] The poem's sacramentalism has been interpreted as a sign of conservatism in an age of ubiquitous anticlerical satire.[41] Yet, doctrinally orthodox though the poem may be, its orthodoxy is driven on the one hand by a humanist readiness to consider the values of pre-Christian religion as universal moral values, and on the other by a logic that might be called ascetic, for it dictates that death – the point of entry into that other world to which baptism gives access – be preferred over life. It is this logic that is expressed in Erkenwald's desire that the judge's incorrupt corpse return to life just long enough to be baptized, *and no longer*: "then yf thou dropped doun dede, hyt daungered me the lasse." The phrasing of Erkenwald's wish could mean either that the bishop would be less grieved by the judge's death as a Christian than his damnation as a pagan, or that it would be *better* for the baptized Christian to die than to live (we may recall that the resuscitated and baptized Trajan "lives in the world" in della Lana's commentary). By the latter interpretation, Erkenwald facilitates a kind of martyrdom for the judge, enacted in full view of the bishop's seventh-century congregation, who are taught thereby to prefer death as Christians than life as pagans.

They are also taught to see the Christian cathedral as a *memento mori*, albeit one that fills death with the promise of eternal life. In early Christian Rome, the conversion of pagan buildings to Christian uses brought death to the very center of urban life. Previously, since the pagan Romans believed in removing their dead far from the city, Christians' veneration of the bodies of their martyrs had made them congregate in spaces such as the suburban and subterranean catacombs.[42] Christianity's historical rise brought the religion – and its relics – into the central spaces of the city, setting up a deliberate visual conflict between architectural splendor and bodily decay. But there is reason to suspect that, over time, the conflict became less apparent to the

---

[40] John Marenbon contrasts *Saint Erkenwald*'s emphasis on the pagan's baptism with Langland's emphasis on Trajan's virtue in *Piers Plowman*. I have tried to show, however, that paganism is no less an open-ended problem in *Saint Erkenwald* than in *Piers*. John Marenbon, *Pagans and Philosophers: The Problem of Paganism from Augustine to Leibniz* (Princeton, N.J.: Princeton University Press, 2015), pp. 253–62.

[41] For the most detailed such interpretation, see Whatley, "Heathens and Saints."

[42] Peter Brown, *The Cult of the Saints: Its Rise and Function in Latin Christianity* (Chicago: University of Chicago Press, 1981). See, in relation, Bartlett, *How Can the Dead*, pp. 7–13, and Summit's discussion of Chaucer's *Second Nun's Tale*, "Topography as Historiography," pp. 233–39.

198 APARNA CHAUDHURI

later Christians who flocked to Rome as a center of pilgrimage, viewed the grandeur of its churches and shrines, and identified the physical and economic act of visiting sacred relics as a means of absolution from sin.[43] As Christian worship assumes the aspect of a spatial ritual, centered in a few select, sacred, urban topographies, there arises a strong risk, at least, that Christians may come to understand their religion in terms of physical manifestations rather than spiritual verities. In view of this risk, Erkenwald's ascetic wish seeking the death of the body so that the soul may have an immediate chance of salvation is also an implicit statement that, if there is to be a body within the nascent Christian church, it should be a *dead* body, its decay – grotesquely total and immediate in the case of the corpse – a reminder of the brevity and insignificance of earthly life from the perspective of eternity. Of course, this statement gestures towards the saintly body as well. The decayed corpse of the convert might indeed "daunger" Erkenwald less, if the meaning of "daunger" is taken to be the keeping of an aloof distance between oneself and another.[44] By dying in order to attain salvation, the anonymous pagan affords the Christian saint, destined to become a powerful and venerated relic in St. Paul's, a form that he can safely inhabit.[45]

CONCLUSION: EXEGESIS AND ALLEGORY

In conclusion, I would like to consider the relationship briefly mentioned at the beginning of this essay: between Christian exegeses of topography and of texts. As Summit argues, the conversion of pagan architectural space to Christian uses is akin to, and perhaps based on, an Augustinian strategy of mapping classical texts to a scheme of Christian significances.[46] In this hermeneutic process, the Christian exegete acquires responsibility for producing the meaning of the text. Even so, traditional exegesis continues

---

43   On the promotion of Rome as a pilgrimage center, see, in addition to Summit, Debra J. Birch, *Pilgrimage to Rome in the Middle Ages: Continuity and Change* (Woodbridge, UK: Boydell, 1998) and John F. Baldovin, *The Urban Character of Christian Worship: The Origins, Development and Meaning of Stational Liturgy* (Rome: Pontificale Institutum Studiorum Orientalium, 1987). Stational worship, in particular, associated the physical act of visiting the various churches and shrines of the city with years of indulgence, often set at a precise number, as in the Middle English "Incypyt the Stacyons of Rome" (1370), in *Political, Religious, and Love Poems*, ed. F. J. Furnivall, EETS, os 15 (London: K. Paul, Trubner, Trench and co., 1866), pp. 143–73.

44   *MED*, s.v. "daunger" (n.), senses 3: "resistance, opposition, objection," and 4: "resistance offered to a lover by his ladylove; disdain, aloofness, reluctance, reserve."

45   On the symmetries between Erkenwald's tomb and the fictional pagan's, see D. Vance Smith, "Death: Terminable and Interminable: St. Erkenwald," in *Arts of Dying: Literature and Finitude in Medieval England* (Chicago: University of Chicago Press, 2020), pp. 279–305.

46   Summit, "Topography as Historiography."

SAINT ERKENWALD'S VERSIONS OF CONVERSION   199

to define itself as supporting an original, older, work. However, as Rita Copeland has shown, a new kind of exegetical model forms to fit the needs of fourteenth-century vernacular secular literary production. The role of "service or supplementation" to an authoritative, usually classical, original is discarded in this new paradigm. Now the *inventio* of materials from the old text supports the artistic and ethical motives of the new one under production: these motives may include, as they famously do in the case of Chaucer, critical experiments with the very idea of literary authority.[47]

Mapping seventh-century Christian London to the topography of the earlier pagan city as it does, *Saint Erkenwald* appears to understand the past as assimilable to the needs of the present. In a parallel, literary-historical world, the poet's opening claim that the event that he describes is recorded in "crafty chronicles" (44) – a claim so phrased that "chronicles" could as well refer slyly to the poem itself as to other, older, texts – likewise suggests that the poem's vernacular "maker" too might be deploying the idea of antique authority only to appropriate it for himself and his own text. This is especially so since the story he tells appears nowhere in the existing cult and legends of Erkenwald, and is similarly absent from chronicles like Bede's *Ecclesiastical History*. An adaptation of a story told about an early Roman pope and a classical Roman emperor, *Saint Erkenwald* certainly draws upon older Latin sources with confidence in their pliability to its own ends: making a new vernacular poem about a saint of the seventh century who is himself the subject of a species of remaking in the fourteenth, as his cult is promoted with special vigor, and his shrine enhanced by additional work in gold, gems, and iron under the auspices of London's then bishop, Robert Braybrooke.[48]

Yet *Saint Erkenwald*, itself an instance of *translationes studii et imperii*, sifts finely through the implications of such translation, both to point towards the losses of translation and to underline the essential worldliness of translated knowledge and *imperium*. Thus, its own poetics do not facilitate a transfer of authority from past *auctor* to present "maker" so much as they gesture towards a figural relation – one which stops well short of identity – between earth and heaven, the forms of knowledge and expression they respectively afford, and the human and divine authors who respectively inhabit them. Though it does not go as far as *Pearl* in presenting all earthly language (that of the Christian poet is no different, in this regard, from that of the pagan author) as allegory for eschatological reality, *Saint Erkenwald* does suggest that the "conversion" of classical spaces, texts, or values to Christian ones establishes ascendancy for neither the ancient poet nor the modern maker. Rather, conversion's importance proves to be in creating connections of transhistorical sympathy,

---

[47] Rita Copeland, *Rhetoric, Hermeneutics, and Translation in the Middle Ages: Academic Traditions and Vernacular Texts* (Cambridge: Cambridge University Press, 1991), see pp. 179–220. For the phrase "service and supplementation," see p. 7.

[48] Whatley, *Saint of London*, pp. 66–67.

which might *figure* the compassion of Christ for humankind, but, at the earthly level on which both pagan and Christian writer operate, actually translate into a shared disavowal of conclusive authority. In contrast to *Pearl*, *Saint Erkenwald* also does not develop a symbolic system of earthly objects that can figure heavenly verities (the "pearl" itself, for instance), and therefore acquire a transcendence of their own. Rather, the poem presents language as locked within history and subject to its vicissitudes: the bright golden letters on the judge's tomb remain indecipherable to the end of the poem, their "roynyshe" code a secret that the present cannot wrest from the past. At a metapoetic level, *Saint Erkenwald* seems to accept historical contingency with an absoluteness that can make our access to the poem in the twenty-first century appear at least a minor miracle.

11

PROVERB AND SATIRICAL TIME: THE DIGBY POEMS AND THEIR FIFTEENTH CENTURY[1]

Spencer Strub

The serious reflection is composed
Neither of comic nor tragic but of commonplace.
– Wallace Stevens[2]

In a 1990 essay that helped set the terms for a reemergent historicism in Middle English literary studies, James Simpson offers a new understanding of late-medieval satire. Speech in early fifteenth-century England was genuinely constrained by newly punitive secular and ecclesiastical legislation, he argues, but to understand the satires of the period – his case examples are *Piers Plowman* and *Mum and the Sothsegger* – critics must also "account for their formal properties as a way of negotiating the constraints which both surround and inhabit them."[3] Simpson's reading reveals the feints and dodges that alliterative poets incorporated into their *modus dicendi*: they place incontrovertible wisdom in the mouths of suspect speakers; they defer to the pronouncements of authoritative institutions, only to reveal their inadequacies.

---

[1] I am grateful to Sebastian Sobecki and Nicholas Watson for their careful reading and editorial advice, as well as Taylor Cowdery and Esther Liberman Cuenca for their insights.

[2] Wallace Stevens, "An Ordinary Evening in New Haven," in *Collected Poetry and Prose*, ed. Frank Kermode and Joan Richardson (New York: Library of America, 1997), p. 408.

[3] James Simpson, "The Constraints of Satire in *Mum and the Sothsegger* and *Piers Plowman*," in *Langland, the Mystics and the Medieval English Religious Tradition*, ed. Helen Phillips (Cambridge: D. S. Brewer, 1990), pp. 11–30 (at p. 21).

202   SPENCER STRUB

Such tactics authorize a satirical poetic voice but also leave space for that voice
to reflect on its own limits.

This essay proceeds from Simpson's insights on the relation between
context and form in fifteenth-century satire. Its subject, however, poses
a special problem in understanding that relation. The twenty-four lyrics
uniquely attested in Oxford, Bodleian Library MS Digby 102 – sandwiched
in thirty folia that fall between copies of the comparatively ubiquitous *Piers
Plowman* C and Richard Maidstone's *Penitential Psalms*, all written as prose
in a single hand – seem to address specific historical events, but they almost
exclusively speak in commonplaces unlocatable in any specific time, place,
or institution. As Helen Barr has observed, the poems are characterized by
their "sparseness of specific temporality," operating in the timeless realm of
ethical guidance rather than the time-bound realm of political commentary.[4]
Unlike Simpson's case examples, which veil and displace their critiques but
nevertheless make unambiguous and sometimes obviously partisan reference
to historical events, the Digby poems speak almost entirely in truisms – some
creatively extended, some deftly reworked, all lacking the kind of particularity
that would allow us to place the poet in a specific place or party.

This essay will argue that such proverbial obliquity might be understood as
another formal strategy available to the late-medieval English satirist, albeit
one aimed as much against the risk of obsolescence as the constraints of
censorship. It will do so in part by extending our account of the provenance of
Digby 102. In what follows, I identify one likely early owner of the manuscript:
the London alderman Robert Horne (d. 1468?), whose career in politics began
in the late 1430s.[5] Both manuscript and poems have been dated to the first
quarter of the fifteenth century – that is, twenty years before Horne would
have read them. Satire defined by contemporaneity alone would lose its edge
after two decades. But the Digby poems' *sense* of topicality, their proverbial
style, and a homiletic deferral to a reader's actions permit them to speak
to new historical conjunctures with the same urgency. Between their likely
composition and their remaking at midcentury, they disclose what Simpson
has called, describing the minor genres of late-medieval satire, the "irreducible
continuities of political involvement" in fifteenth-century London.[6] They also
point to the particular affordances of the late-medieval proverb: an authority
unfixed from an author or a moment, open to reapplication in new contexts.

---

4   Helen Barr, "'This Holy Tyme': Present Sense in the *Digby Lyrics*," in *After Arundel:
    Religious Writing in Fifteenth-Century England*, ed. Vincent Gillespie and Kantik
    Ghosh (Turnhout, Belgium: Brepols, 2011), pp. 307–24, at p. 307.
5   On Horne's death date, see *Calendar of Letter-Books of the City of London: L,
    Edw. IV – Henry VII*, ed. Reginald R. Sharpe (London: Corporation of the City of
    London, 1912), pp. 78–79.
6   James Simpson, *The Oxford English Literary History, Vol. 2: 1350–1547. Reform and
    Cultural Revolution* (Oxford: Oxford University Press, 2002), p. 254.

THE DIGBY POEMS AND THEIR FIFTEENTH CENTURY   203

SATIRE AND THE COMMONPLACE

The Digby poems present an especially keen instance of a challenge general to the study of medieval political verse: how do we reconcile such poetry's timeless moralizing with the specific historicity of its satire?[7] Critics are comparatively well-equipped to decode heraldic allegories or retrospective prophecies, modes that, in their very obfuscations, promise to reveal a pointed meaning behind their fictive apparatus. (*Piers Plowman* and *Mum and the Sothsegger* dabble in both modes.) But the broad truisms of the Digby poems are harder to decode. Most of the poems adopt an admonitory-instructional mode of direct address, eschewing narrative or description in favor of aphoristic rumination on ethics and politics. All but two are written in eight-line rhyming stanzas that sometimes read as a single thought and sometimes as a drumbeat of apothegms. Their subjects generally sit at intersections of public and private life conventional to a broad swathe of fifteenth-century English writing: truth-telling, dying well, knowing oneself and keeping the sacraments, serving the common profit and eschewing division.

The poems' first editor, Josef Kail, remarked upon this broad moralizing tendency in his summary account of Digby 102. He held that their promotion of virtue was a response to the turbulence of Henry IV's reign and Henry V's return to the war in France, arguing that "nearly all the pieces are occasional poems" written by a cleric who "occupied a seat in parliament, and voted with the Commons."[8] Proceeding from these convictions, Kail looked for allusions to parliamentary procedure in the poems, finding enough to date sixteen of them to specific years between 1401 and 1421. These dates were generally accepted for a century, until Helen Barr's 2009 edition definitively dismantled nearly all of Kail's purported allusions.[9] For Barr, the time of the poems is "present time," a "timeless world of common sense and ethical behavior."[10] But like Kail (albeit with considerably better evidence and more circumspection), Barr takes this timelessness as evidence of the historical particularity of the poems: she argues that they were likely written by a Benedictine monk in 1413–14, during the early years of Henry V's reign, when a sense of moral

---

[7]   On this challenge, see Elizabeth Salter, "The Timeliness of *Wynnere and Wastoure*," *Medium Ævum* 47 (1978), 40–65; George Kane, "Some Fourteenth-Century 'Political' Poems," in *Medieval English Religious and Ethical Literature: Essays in Honour of G. H. Russell*, ed. Gregory Kratzmann and James Simpson (Cambridge: D. S. Brewer, 1986), pp. 82–91; Derek Pearsall, "The Timelessness of *The Simonie*," in *Individuality and Achievement in Middle English Poetry*, ed. O. S. Pickering (Cambridge: D. S. Brewer, 1997), pp. 59–72.

[8]   *Twenty-Six Political and Other Poems*, ed. J. Kail, EETS, os 124 (London: Trübner, 1904), p. ix.

[9]   *The Digby Poems: A New Edition of the Lyrics*, ed. Helen Barr (Exeter, UK: University of Exeter Press, 2009). Unless otherwise noted, all quotations from the Digby poems are drawn from this edition.

[10] Barr, "This Holy Tyme," p. 311.

204   SPENCER STRUB

permanence shorn of specific reference would have affirmed a new era of political stability and unity of purpose.[11]

Not all critics concur with this revised dating: R. H. Nicholson relocates the poems to Henry VI's minority, while Louis Verheij's edition affirms Kail's dates.[12] (All agree that the collection is the work of a single poet, as do I.)[13] Though the essay below will quibble with some of Barr's suggestions about the provenance of the poems, a date late in Henry IV or early in Henry V's reign seems likely. As I see it, the poems are not bound by historical reference but intend to speak beyond the moment of their composition.

The poetry might speak to an era of stability, or it might speak to an era of tumult. As Barr puts it, the very texture of the poetry is "sedimented with recycled old lore," legible as affirmation or admonition.[14] Take this stanza in the third lyric, "Treuth, Reste, and Pes":

> Defaute of wit makeþ long counsayle:
> For witteles wordes in ydel spoken,
> Þe more cost, þe lesse auayle;
> For fawte of wyt, purpos broken.
> In euyl soule, no grace is stoken,
> For wikked soule is graceless:
> In good lyuere, Goddis wille is loken,
> Þat mannys counsell makeþ pes.[15]

The poem belongs to a tradition of truth-telling poetry encapsulated in an oft-repeated axiom: "whoso sayth soth, he shalbe shent."[16] It begins with one stanza in the first person, declaring that dread often keeps the speaker's lips closed, before slipping back into a more distanced sententious voice to deliver an encomium to truth and good counsel, essential to maintaining a kingdom in "pes" [peace], the word around which the poem's refrain is built.

This stanza is representative of the poem's densely aphoristic style. The syntax of the first quatrain could be parsed a number of ways – Barr's punctuation makes two-line units of assertion and explanation; Kail treats the first and

---

[11] Barr, "This Holy Tyme," p. 314; for a fuller argument on dating, see *Digby Poems*, pp. 6–41.

[12] R. H. Nicholson, "Poetry and Politics: 'A Remembraunce of LII Folyes' in Context," *Viator* 41 (2010), 375–410; and L. J. P. Verheij, "'Where of is mad al mankynde': An Edition of and Introduction to the Twenty-Four Poems in Oxford, Bodleian Library MS Digby 102" (unpublished Ph.D. dissertation, Leiden University, 2009).

[13] For a suggestion of multiple authorship, see Wendy Scase, Review of *The Digby Poems: A New Edition of the Lyrics, Journal of English and Germanic Philology* 110 (2011), 136–38.

[14] Barr, *Digby Poems*, p. 59.

[15] Barr, *Digby Poems*, 3.89–96. Subsequent citations will be made in-text, noting poem number and lines.

[16] On this tradition, see Andrew Wawn, "Truth-Telling and the Tradition of *Mum and the Sothsegger,*" *The Yearbook of English Studies* 13 (1983), 270–87.

THE DIGBY POEMS AND THEIR FIFTEENTH CENTURY 205

fourth lines as standalone gnomic statements, the second and third as a single thought; I have rendered each quatrain as a passage of thesis and extrapolation – but almost every line of the quatrain could function as a standalone expression. (B. J. Whiting's *Proverbs, Sentences, and Proverbial Phrases* includes only "the more cost, the less avail" from this stanza, but one could imagine choosing any of the other lines instead.)[17] Each contains at least two elements in a description, the minimal condition of a proverbial phrase, arranged in a little sententious equation expressed in characteristically compressed fashion, its linking verbs and some conjunctions suppressed.[18] The second quatrain proceeds in much the same fashion, albeit offering more complex constructions. Read as a whole, the stanza simply presents complementary truths: the sinful offer worthless counsel; the virtuous give good counsel. The scribe has added a *nota* in the margins, recognizing that these *sententiae* would appeal to readers. Unlike the proverb collections that circulated widely in the late Middle Ages, these lines are not presented as dialogue or citation, nor do they mark the intrusion of some other voice that underlines or ironizes the poetic voice itself as they might in narrative poetry (on which, more below). Rather, the commonplace *is* the poetic voice.

"Treuth, Reste, and Pes" addresses its moment with evergreen wisdom. Its nostrums are delivered in Barr's "present sense," its advice sufficiently abstract as to apply universally. The stanza that follows might therefore seem like a surprising turn in the poem:

> To wete ȝif parlement be wys
> Þe comoun profit wel it preues:
> A kyngdom in comouns lys,
> Alle profytes and alle myscheues.
> Lordis wet neuere what comouns greues
> Til her rentis bigynne to ses;
> Þere lordis ere, pore comons releues,
> And maytene hem in were and pes. (3.96–104)

The preceding stanza's fuzzy discourse on counsel becomes more institutionally specific here: this is a statement about Parliament, and more specifically about the disjunction between the pressures on the Commons and the willful ignorance of the Lords. Abstractions arranged in proverbial oppositions – good and evil, wit and will, grace and gracelessness – are replaced by explicit references to "rentis" and governing institutions. These lines still proceed in

---

[17] Bartlett Jere Whiting with Helen Wescott Whiting, *Proverbs, Sentences, and Proverbial Phrases from English Writings Mainly Before 1500* (Cambridge, Mass.: Belknap Press, 1968), C446.

[18] On these elements, see, e.g., Alan Dundes, "On the Structure of the Proverb," in *The Wisdom of Many: Essays on the Proverb*, ed. Wolfgang Mieder and Alan Dundes (New York and London: Garland, 1981), pp. 43–64, at pp. 51–52; on compression, Nancy Mason Bradbury, "The Proverb as Embedded Microgenre in Chaucer and *The Dialogue of Solomon and Marcolf*," *Exemplaria* 27 (2015), 55–72, at 57.

an unbound present sense. But they increasingly hint at a motivating occasion to ground their vague universals. The opening lines here promise as much. To "prove" something in late medieval England, one tests it by experience: virtue through tribulation, gold in the fire, an illness through examination, an argument through examples.[19] To prove the wisdom of Parliament, one must assess the concrete conditions of the realm.

Kail thus placed this poem between January and March 1401 on account of "the allusions which it contains to the parliamentary transactions" in those months: allusions to tale-tellers, inconstant governance, and noble discord.[20] As Barr points out, however, any dating grounded in such evergreen complaints is tenuous at best.[21] Rather than the one-to-one referentiality upon which topical commentary depends, the poem depends on the potential multiplicity of the proverb: Matthew Giancarlo observes, for instance, that the stanza quoted above collocates multiple senses of the late-medieval keyword "commons," including not just the parliamentary Commons but also "the imagined social totality of the *communitas regni* in the *comouns* of the kingdom; the abstract *bonum commune* of the *comoun profit*; and, at the end, the grievances of the clearly lower-class *pore comons* subject to lordly abuse and neglect."[22] So the stanza might be construed thus: to know if Parliament is wise, look to the collective wellbeing for evidence; a kingdom consists in its community, all its goods and all its ills; lords do not know what afflicts the lower classes until their rents begin to cease; where lords are merciful and maintain the lower classes through war and peace, the lower classes are revived.

Such displacements are not unusual in late medieval English political discourse. As John Watts has shown, from the late fourteenth to the early sixteenth century, the "commons" rather broadly signified the third estate as class and political community.[23] "Treuth, Reste, and Pes," like most of its companions in Digby 102, expresses a politics that (in its broad conceptual strokes) remained consistent from the tumult of the 1380s through the minority of Henry VI. As the poet observes in the twelfth poem, entitled in manuscript "God kepe our kynge and saue the croune," the king's crown signifies "lordis, comouns, and clergye / [that] ben all at on assent" (12.11–12): the ideal of governance is the mutual coordination and interdependence of the three estates, operating for the benefit of the community, their will condensed and channeled through the person of the king, who serves simultaneously as symbolic representation of the

---

[19] *MED*, s.v. "preven," 1, 2, 5, 6.

[20] Kail, *Twenty-Six Political and Other Poems*, p. xi.

[21] Barr, *Digby Poems*, p. 106.

[22] Matthew Giancarlo, "Troubling the New Constitutionalism: Politics, Penitence, and the Dilemma of Dread in the Digby Poems," *JEGP* 110 (2011), 78–104, at 87.

[23] On the contradictions in the term "commons," see John Watts, "Public or Plebs: The Changing Meaning of 'The Commons,' 1381–1549," in *Power and Identity in the Middle Ages: Essays in Memory of Rees Davies*, ed. Huw Pryce and John Watts (Oxford: Oxford University Press, 2007), pp. 242–60.

THE DIGBY POEMS AND THEIR FIFTEENTH CENTURY   207

realm as a whole and as the independent agent whose actions guide and protect it.[24] As Simpson has shown, such a schema becomes in practice a politics of mutual constraint, where the common good is served by contending parties' willing and reciprocal deference to counsel and compromise.[25] The greatest vice in this discourse is division, marked in various forms by the self-promotion of a counselor's flattery, an aristocrat's "singulere," the urban disorder of craft factionalism, unconstrained non-cooperation between estates, and the catastrophe of civil war (3.113–20; 12.129–30; 15.119–44; 16.57–60).

While such a message would have had particular purchase at specific moments – as in the factional struggles of the 1380s and 1390s; or in the years after the Lancastrian usurpation, when the king was repeatedly threatened by magnate rebellions and popular disillusionment; or immediately after Henry V's death, when Lydgate warned against "þe contagious damages & þe importable harmes of devision" – its basic points slide easily from regnal politics into personal ethics.[26] Lydgate himself, implicitly but obviously addressing the king's council, ends *The Serpent of Division* by advising his noble readers "teschewe stryf and dissencion / within yowreself beth not contrarious" as they jockey for power in a suddenly acephalous realm.[27] The Digby poet in turn sometimes seems to speak to the king, sometimes to the commons, but regardless always operates on a blurry boundary between the person and the realm. Even the most concrete political commentary, like the poet's endorsement of war in France in "Dede is worchyng," is bracketed by statements of political principle that read as ethical universals: the highest point of charity is to stand with the commons (13.33–34); the most profit and highest honor comes from listening to your tenants' complaints (13.41–43); "syngulerte" will lead to ruin, as the commons can observe (13.81); make peace within before you go to battle (13.105). In other words, even the positions that might be associated with a specific party are framed and hedged in axioms that emphasize consensus and common purpose.

Returning to "Treuth, Reste, and Pes" helps show how such oscillations disclose a satirical strategy concerned as much with shaping a reader as with articulating political critique. Its appearance of targeted contemporaneity

---

[24] See further John Watts, *Henry VI and the Politics of Kingship* (Cambridge: Cambridge University Press, 1996), pp. 21–31. Barr suggests (*Digby Poems*, p. 193, n. 12) that "on assent" echoes 1410 parliamentary procedure, but the formula is widely found in fourteenth- and late fifteenth-century rolls as well. Gower's *Confessio amantis* prefigures fifteenth-century discourse on the singular and the common; see the discussion in Sebastian Sobecki, *Unwritten Verities: The Making of England's Vernacular Legal Culture* (Notre Dame, Ind.: University of Notre Dame Press, 2015), pp. 84–88.

[25] Simpson, *Reform and Cultural Revolution*, p. 214.

[26] John Lydgate, *The Serpent of Division*, ed. Henry Noble MacCracken (New Haven, Conn.: Yale University Press, 1911), p. 65. On the complex historicity of this text in 1422, see Maura Nolan, "The Art of History Writing: Lydgate's *Serpent of Division*," *Speculum* 78 (2003), 99–127.

[27] Lydgate, *Serpent of Division*, p. 67.

SPENCER STRUB

repeatedly unfolds into broader, less time-bound ideas.[28] Two stanzas in a row in fact begin with paradigmatic markers of proverbial wisdom. "Old speche is spoken 3ore," one begins, before enumerating the goods in "a kyngdom tresory": livestock, grain, a rich commons, wise clergy, knights ready to charge and a king gifted at leading in war and governing in peace (3.65–66). The next gestures to the books made "among philosofres wyse" (3.73). A few stanzas earlier, immediately following the discussion of governance from afar that helped Kail anchor the poem in early 1401, the poet disclaims *any* specific satirical point:

> I speke not in specyale
> Of oo kyngdom the lawe to telle;
> I speke hool in generale
> In eche kyngdom the lawe to telle. (3.49–52)

"Specyale" and "generale" distinguish between a comment on a specific place and a universal comment; the distinction, inherited from scholarly Latin, is common in Middle English expository writing.[29] In an essay on the poet's approach to Wycliffism, Barr takes the refusal to explicitly name "lollards" or Wycliffites as an act of *damnatio memoriae* that condemns by silencing.[30] Tactical nonspecificity is indeed common in medieval satire, reflecting by varying degrees a concern for accuracy, genuine fears of reprisal, and a conventional rhetorical toolkit that prized strategies of effective misdirection. When Gower invokes a parallel general/special distinction in his criticism of the clergy in the preface to the *Confessio amantis*, refusing to speak "in general" – that is, universally – "for ther ben somme in special / in whom that alle vertu duelleth," he preserves a model for emulation while criticizing all who fall short.[31] In *Mum and the Sothsegger*, a critique of the friars is venomous and unambiguous in its topical reference, but after calling the mendicant orders the descendants of Cain, the poet hedges his attack with a vague excuse: "I seye of hem suche been and cesse agaynes other."[32] It seems unlikely that any friars who happened to read *Mum* would be convinced that

---

[28] On the interpretative openness of "misty" proverbs, see Alastair Bennett, "*Brevis oratio penetrat celum*: Proverbs, Prayers, and Lay Understanding in Late Medieval England," *New Medieval Literatures* 14 (2012), 127–63.

[29] E.g., M. C. Seymour et al., eds., *On the Properties of Things: John Trevisa's Translation of Bartholomæus Anglicus "De Proprietatibus Rerum"*, 2 vols. (Oxford: Clarendon Press, 1975), 21.2.5, 1.5.8–9, 1.6.4–5, 1.12.13, etc.

[30] Helen Barr, "The Deafening Silence of Lollardy in the *Digby Lyrics*," in *Wycliffite Controversies*, ed. Mishtooni Bose and J. Patrick Hornbeck II (Turnhout, Belgium: Brepols, 2011), pp. 243–60.

[31] John Gower, *Confessio amantis*, vol. 1, ed. Russell Peck, tr. Andrew Galloway, TEAMS: Middle English Texts (Kalamazoo, Mich.: Medieval Institute Publications, 2006), prologue, lines 431–33.

[32] *Mum and the Sothsegger*, from *The Piers Plowman Tradition*, ed. Helen Barr (London: J. M. Dent, 1993), l. 505. A corrector has added a marginal note extending the disclaimer, cautioning, "sum and of certayn, I say not of alle"; London, British

THE DIGBY POEMS AND THEIR FIFTEENTH CENTURY   209

the poet's vitriol was not directed at them. The poet's dodge proceeds from his satirical method. In his pathbreaking essay on *Mum*, Simpson suggests that the poet adopts a number of textual strategies "designed to convey the impression that the narrator adopts the role of satirist despite himself."[33]

But the Digby poet does not perform the same satirical maneuver. Rather than the winking preterition that denies an attack as it is being made, these poems depend more on a homiletic mode of address that recruits a reader's participation. The distinction between special and general address seems to serve an exculpatory function in "Treuth, Reste, and Pes." The next poem in the collection, "Lerne say wele, say litel, or say no3t," returns to the special/general distinction from another perspective:

> To synge or preche generale,
> Werkys of vices for to blame,
> Summe tak to hem speciale,
> And say, "Felow þu dost vs blame"
> Þere he accuseþ his owen name.
> All þat hym se, knowe it may;
> He can not hele his owen shame,
> And so all folk wole say. (4.41–48)

That is to say, when one sings or preaches in general terms and someone takes it as a particular criticism, the offended party "accuseþ his owen name." As the American proverb puts it, a hit dog will holler.

Of course, such expressions might serve as an exculpatory statement: after yet another broadside against the mendicants, for instance, the *Mum*-corrector adds, "Hit shal not greue a good frere though gilty be amendid."[34] But the Digby poet's gesture toward a reader's painful, shameful, public confrontation with their own sin – or, alternatively, their sense of their virtue affirmed, seeing another person's defensiveness – is not simply defensive. It provides a kind of capsule *ars poetica* for the lyrics, an account of how the ethical force of a broad commonplace might be activated by a guilty conscience. The poet repeatedly invokes, in direct address to the reader, their God-given moral capacities. A binary choice between right and wrong follows from this descriptive statement. So "Treuth, Reste, and Pes" ends: "3e haue fre wille: chese 3oure chaunce / to haue wiþ God or pes" (3.167–68). The fifth poem, "Wyt and Wille," ends by telling the addressee, "God haþ lent 3ow discrecioun, / boþe of wele and of woo … Siþ 3e can part hem wel o two, / let vyces on 3ow brynge no bille" (5.65–70). "God & Man Ben Made Atte On" – a poem in Christ's voice – declares, "In oure fre wille, þe choys it lys, / Heuene or helle, to haue that on" (11.61–62).

Library Additional MS 41666, 6v. Here and elsewhere, the corrector tends to moderate the poem's anticlericalism.

[33] Simpson, "Constraints of Satire," p. 21.

[34] London, British Library Additional MS 41666, fol. 6r.

210   SPENCER STRUB

These formulae depend on a reader's application. In a few rare instances, the poet actually models a communal response to these individual prompts. In "God kepe oure kyng and saue the croune," a poem Barr and Kail both place soon after Henry V's coronation, England's victories in France are compared to a father's chastisement of a child:

> The fadir þe wanton child wole kenne:
> Chastyse wiþ ȝerde, and bete hit sore,
> So after þe fadyr þe ȝerde wole brenne
> When child is wys, and takeþ to lore.
> We han ben Goddis ȝerde ȝore:
> Chastysed kyngdom, castell and towne:
> Twyggis of oure ȝerde we haue forlore.
> God saue þe kyng and kepe þe crowne! (12.113–20)

When the father finishes beating the child and he has learned his lesson, the father burns the "yerde," the stick. England, once God's "yerde," is now losing twigs – in other words, losing territory it once held. The analogy comes from Augustine's exposition of Psalm 73, though the Digby poet may have encountered it in *Ancrene Wisse* instead.[35] The similitude shows that divine discipline can come through wicked instruments, which are ephemeral. But in the poet's hands, it underlines collective guilt: after all, the similitude would seem to make England the stick to be burned. Individual penance is refashioned for collective commentary.

This movement across political, ethical, and devotional registers has long been understood as evidence of clerical or monastic authorship. Kail suggested they were written by "a priest, most probably an abbot or a prior."[36] Barr points to the macaronic sermons in Oxford, Bodleian Library MS Bodley 649 as a potential comparand.[37] The sermons, addressed to a mixed lay-clerical audience, are a product of Henry V's reign; their author seems to have been affiliated with Oxford, and perhaps with the abbey of St. Peter's in Gloucester as well.[38] The Digby poet may well have been a preacher, given that the poems consistently present singing and preaching as a parallel acts of moral instruction, and Barr identifies ample parallels in theme and content between the lyrics and the sermons.[39] As Barr speculates on the basis of these parallels,

---

[35] Augustine, *Enarrationes in Psalmos* (CPL 0283, SL 39), ps. 73, para. 8; *Ancrene Wisse: A Corrected Edition of the Text in Cambridge, Corpus Christi College, MS 402, with Variants from Other Manuscripts*, ed. Bella Millett, with E. J. Dobson and Richard Dance, 2 vols., EETS, os 325–26 (Oxford: Oxford University Press, 2005), IV.97–104.

[36] Kail, *Twenty-Six Political and Other Poems*, p. ix.

[37] Barr, *Digby Poems*, pp. 73–75.

[38] See *A Macaronic Sermon Collection from Late Medieval England: Oxford, MS Bodley 649*, ed. and tr. Patrick J. Horner (Toronto: Pontifical Institute of Mediaeval Studies, 2006), pp. 4–7. What follows refers exclusively to the twenty-five sermons in this edition, which Horner refers to as "set 1."

[39] Parallels are exhaustively catalogued in Barr, *Digby Poems*, pp. 76–78.

THE DIGBY POEMS AND THEIR FIFTEENTH CENTURY   211

"if we must seek an author for these poems ... then a Benedictine monk who was part of the cultural milieu of the pro-Henrician writing of the order is as likely a candidate as any."[40] The Digby poems might thus be read alongside Lydgate as Lancastrian-Benedictine political commentary.[41]

These connections are suggestive but not dispositive. The devotional tropes the poems and sermons share are omnipresent in medieval English writing, their shared religious views consistent with fifteenth-century orthodox reform, their political commentary largely in line with a wide swathe of regiminal and satirical writing.[42] Barr identifies eight proverbial expressions shared by the poems and the sermons (though they are all worded differently), but, as she acknowledges, they are attested elsewhere too.[43] Even close parallels reveal divergent purposes: when the Bodley preacher advises his listeners to "fle not to hye for fallinge," he intends to warn them not to meddle in theology and "sta ad tuum credo" [stand on your Creed] instead; when the Digby poet warns "to fliӡe to hyӡe treste not þy wyng" (14.47), he cautions against overweening ambition and overconfidence at the top of Fortune's wheel – there are no ecclesiological or theological questions at play.[44] There are few formal conjunctions between the works. The twenty-nine short verses in the macaronic sermons show no particular similarity to the Digby poems.[45] All but three are couplets; none are in the Digby poet's characteristic eight- and fourteen-line stanzas, nor do they show the same metrical expertise. Unsurprisingly, many are macaronic. The Digby poems are by contrast remarkable for their relative *lack* of Latin, a monolingualism particularly marked given their placement between *Piers Plowman* and Maidstone's *Penitential Psalms*, both densely studded with Latin.

That is to say, though the Digby poems may well emerge from the same milieu as the Bodley macaronic sermons, they probably do not come from the same hand. The comparison is still instructive because it suggests that the Digby poems might best be understood according to other generic protocols in addition to those of poetic satire. In their anonymity, admonitory style, and interwoven concern with proper piety and good governance, the Digby lyrics could also be compared to the London householders' devotional books that their manuscript resembles.[46] As in catechetical and conduct writing, their

---

40 Barr, *Digby Poems*, p. 75.
41 Barr, "Present Sense," pp. 308–10. Derek Pearsall suggests the poet may have been abbot of Bury St. Edmunds; see Derek Pearsall, *John Lydgate* (London: Routledge & Kegan Paul, 1970), p. 205.
42 See Barr, *Digby Poems*, p. 78.
43 See, e.g, Whiting, *Proverbs*, V3–V6 (weathervane); G488 (hooded guile); and *MED*, s.v. "favel" and "Fauvel," 2.
44 *Bodley 649*, 6.297 (tr. p. 169).
45 See *Bodley 649*, pp. 27, 45, 55, 61, 151, 155, 159, 245, 263, 282, 321, 369, 373, 383, 385, 387, 397, 401, 429, 449, 451, 461, 467, 485, 487, 505, and 519.
46 On these books, see Amy Appleford, *Learning to Die in London, 1380–1540* (Philadelphia: University of Pennsylvania Press, 2014).

212   SPENCER STRUB

general truths are meant to be read specially. The drama of free-speaking
and concealment that animates so much of the satire in the tradition of *Mum
and the Sothsegger* is dispelled by their homiletic deferrals: rather than the
bedraggled truth-teller cast out of court, these poems generally speak in a
voice of moral counsel already half-internalized by their audience.

THE FUNCTION OF THE PROVERB
IN THE FIFTEENTH CENTURY

"Treuthe, Reste, and Pes" exemplifies the particular proverbial style of the
Digby poems, in which commonplace and satirical commentary are so
blurred as to be inextricable. Indeed, the poems reflect a broader traffic
between the forms of proverb and lyric: both medieval and modern lyric are
defined by their complex temporality, "lyric" denoting both the suspended
time of the poem itself and its resistance to historicity as a self-unfolding
aesthetic object.[47] The qualities that differentiate the Middle English lyric
from its post-Romantic counterpart – its absent or comparatively impersonal
lyric I, its tendency toward amplification rather than compression, its lack of
aesthetic autonomy and literary originality – mark an even greater similarity
between forms (and are apt shorthand for describing the Digby poems).[48]
As Wendy Scase points out, the poems in Digby 102 are comparable to the
Vernon and Simeon manuscripts' lyrics, likewise built around end-stopped
and amplified articulations of orthodox piety and conventional wisdom.[49]
Middle English writers often seem to have understood the sententious lyric
as a kind of collection of proverbs. So Chaucer ends "Lenvoy a Bukton,"
a finely-crafted little library of misogamist saws, by declaring "this lytel
writ, proverbes, or figure / I sende yow" – three names for the same thing,
emphasizing the materiality of the poem, the nature of its contents, and the
rhetorical invention that crafted it respectively.[50]

---

[47] For the most influential account of the lyric as a category of abstraction away
from history, see Virginia Jackson, *Dickinson's Misery: A Theory of Lyric Reading*
(Princeton, N.J.: Princeton University Press, 2005).

[48] See Ardis Butterfield, "The Construction of Textual Form: Crosslingual Citation in
Some Medieval Lyrics," in *Citation, Intertextuality and Memory in the Middle Ages and
Renaissance*, ed. Yolanda Plumley, Giuliano Di Bacco, and Stefano Jossa (Exeter, UK:
University of Exeter Press, 2011), pp. 41–57, and "Why Medieval Lyric?," *ELH* 82 (2015),
319–43; and Andrew Galloway, "Theory of the Fourteenth-Century English Lyric," in
What Kind of Things is a Middle English Lyric?, ed. Cristina Maria Cervone and Nicholas
Watson (Philadelphia: University of Pennsylvania Press, 2022), pp. 303–41.

[49] Scase, Review of *The Digby Poems*, p. 137.

[50] *The Riverside Chaucer*, gen. ed. Larry D. Benson, 3rd ed. (Boston: Houghton
Mifflin, 1987), p. 656, ll. 25–26. On these lines, see also Galloway, "Theory," p. 306,
and John Scattergood, "*Chaucer a Bukton* and Proverbs," *Nottingham Medieval
Studies* 31 (1987), 98–107.

THE DIGBY POEMS AND THEIR FIFTEENTH CENTURY 213

Fifteenth-century English writing is notoriously dense with proverbial expressions. Manuscript collections and early printed books made Chaucer a repository of *sententiae*; traditions of wisdom writing like the *Distichs of Cato* or the *Secreta secretorum*, always popular in the Middle Ages, saw new translations and adaptations achieve a wide dissemination.[51] For readers, they promise a particular kind of pleasure, produced by what Christopher Cannon calls "the acts of recognition that are produced by the repetition of well-worn truths."[52] Drawing on Kenneth Burke's account of the proverb as "equipment for living," Cannon argues that the proverbial mode speaks to a literary aesthetic that allows readers "not to encounter something new, but to re-encounter the wholly familiar."[53] The authority of the proverb rests in a confirmation of gut intuition guaranteed by an appeal to the common voice or to antiquity. But what seems to be the emanation of the common voice can, upon closer inspection, express the tendentious interests of a particular party, and the wisdom of antiquity might belong to a more recent past.

In *Mum and the Sothsegger*, for instance, a nasty bit of antifraternal invective is capped by a brief proverb:

> The secund is a pryvy poynt, I pray hit be helid;
> Thay cunne not reede redelles a-right, as me thenketh;
> For furst folowid freres Lollardz manieres,
> And sith hath be shewed the same on thaym-self,
> That thaire lesingz have lad thaym to lolle by the necke;
> At Tibourne for traison y-twyght up thay were;
> For as hit is yseide by eldryn dawes,
> *That the churle gafe a dome whiche came by hym aftre.*[54]

A Latin line from the *Monostichs* of Cato appears, misattributed to Seneca, in the margins of this passage in the manuscript: "*Patere legem quam ipse tuleris*" [You must suffer the law that you yourself imposed].[55] These lines are notoriously jumbled in the manuscript, but the broad strokes are clear. *Mum* is telling a story of just deserts and ironic comeuppances. The friars "folowid," that is, attacked or prosecuted, Lollards: the line may invoke the 1382 Blackfriars Council (attended by Franciscans and Dominicans among others), or the burning of William Sawtre in 1401, or perhaps it refences anti-Wycliffite

---

51 Julia Boffey, "Proverbial Chaucer and the Chaucer Canon," *Huntington Library Quarterly* 58 (1995), 37–47.

52 Christopher Cannon, "Proverbs and the Wisdom of Literature: *The Proverbs of Alfred* and Chaucer's *Tale of Melibee*," *Textual Practice* 43 (2010), 407–34, at 408.

53 Cannon, "Wisdom of Literature," p. 426; and see Kenneth Burke, "Literature as Equipment for Living," in *The Philosophy of Literary Form: Studies in Symbolic Action* (Baton Rouge, La.: Louisiana State University Press, 1941), pp. 293–304.

54 *Mum and the Sothsegger*, from *The Piers Plowman Tradition*, ed. Helen Barr (London: J. M. Dent, 1993), lines 415–22; emphasis added.

55 London, British Library Additional MS 41666, fol. 5v, printed as l. 422*a* in Barr's edition.

214   SPENCER STRUB

polemicists like the Franciscan William Woodford or the Dominican Roger
Dymmok.[56] Regardless, the friars found themselves prosecuted in turn, and
here the reference is unmistakable. Rumors of Richard II's return began
to circulate in spring 1402; Henry IV and his subordinates responded to
this potentially seditious rumor-mongering by making an example of the
offenders. Dozens of people were prosecuted for conspiracy.[57] The largest of
these supposed conspiracies emanated from a set of Franciscan houses in the
Midlands; fourteen plotters, among them eight Franciscans, were tried and
executed.[58] The poetry is charged with the logic of reversal even at the level of
lexis: Andrew Cole observes that the poet "takes the punitive energy stored
up in 'lollard' and directs it back at the friars"; as Barr points out, the hanged
friars' lolling echoes the "lollardz" invoked two lines earlier.[59] The point, as the
proverb underlines, is that they got what they had coming.

The poem, probably written between 1406 and 1409, discusses this event
in its characteristic satirical idiom: an ostentatious, transparent fiction of
secrets shared (the narrator whispers to readers "a pryvy poynt, I pray hit be
helid" [i.e. kept secret]) coupled with what James Simpson has identified as its
pointed "apparent deference" to authoritative discourses, marked in this case
by the polemical repurposing of legal terms like "folwen."[60] This form of satire
draws on proverbs to punctuate and summarize its critiques. As Nancy Mason
Bradbury explains, in moments like this, the proverb is bounded and distinct,
commenting on the narrative situation from a standpoint outside the poetic
voice; it "functions as a miniature theory, a formulation that testifies to its
self-sufficient completeness and also captures its generative quality."[61] Siegfried
Wenzel found *Mum*'s English and Latin churl-judgment proverbs first attested
in the Dominican John Bromyard's *Summa praedicantium*.[62] Bromyard cites
them to the effect that to do evil is to both open yourself to retribution and invite
God's punishment. In *Mum*'s hands, they say: you get as good as you give. Anne
Middleton has described the fundamental form of the proverb as "expressing a

---

56 On the allusion to Blackfriars, see Helen Barr, *Signes and Sothe: Language in the
    Piers Plowman Tradition* (Cambridge: D. S. Brewer, 1994), p. 114.
57 "Clergy and common law in the reign of Henry IV," ed. R. L. Storey, in *Medieval
    Legal Records Edited in Memory of C. A. F. Meekings*, ed. R. F. Hunnisett and J. B.
    Post (London: Her Majesty's Stationery Office, 1978), pp. 341–408 (at p. 355).
58 Storey, "Clergy and Common Law," p. 357.
59 Andrew Cole, *Literature and Heresy in the Age of Chaucer* (Cambridge: Cambridge
    University Press, 2008), p. 34; Barr, *Signes and Sothe*, p. 114. On the links between
    Sawtre's burning and the execution of the friars, see also Paul Strohm, *England's
    Empty Throne: Usurpation and the Language of Legitimation, 1399–1422* (New
    Haven, C.T.: Yale University Press, 1998), pp. 139–42.
60 James Simpson, "The Constraints of Satire in *Mum and the Sothsegger* and *Piers
    Plowman*," in *Langland, the Mystics and the Medieval English Religious Tradition*,
    ed. Helen Phillips (Cambridge: D. S. Brewer, 1990), pp. 11–30, at p. 23.
61 Bradbury, "Proverb as Embedded Microgenre," p. 64.
62 Siegfried Wenzel, "*Mum and the Sothsegger*, Lines 421–22," *ELN* 14 (1976), 87–90.
    Cf. also Whiting D342.

THE DIGBY POEMS AND THEIR FIFTEENTH CENTURY 215

relationship of cause to consequence."[63] In this case, that mechanistic relationship is crucial: the proverb applies conventional wisdom retrospectively to the friars' plot while translating its specific circumstances into a universal law. The turn to the proverbial thus mediates between truism and historical event. The proverb serves as a kind of auto-allegoresis, a pendant to narrative that restates events at a level of abstraction and compression sufficient to be portable. Its authorlessness and non-specificity – the fact that it comes from the common wisdom of "eldryn dawes" and simply offers an account of how the world works – buttresses invariably subjective polemic with an impersonal sense of truth.

But proverbs are, by their nature, ripe for reappropriation. When Margery Kempe arrives in London near the end of her *Book*, exhausted, disheveled, and broke after a difficult sojourn on the continent, she finds herself haunted by a sentence that travels ahead of her: "A, thu fals flesch, thu schalt no good mete etyn."[64] Margery never said these words, the narrator explains, and no one could prove she did; they were made up by the devil and sustained by envious people, powerless to hinder Margery except through slander. Only after this furious denial are we made to understand why this gnomic expression dogs Margery so. One or more people had contrived a tale about Margery: on a fish day, at a good man's table, she made a show of refusing cheap red herring in favor of fancier pike. "A, thu fals flesch," she supposedly proclaimed, "thu woldist now etyn reed heryng, but thu schalt not han thi wille."[65] The juxtaposition of luxury and an ostentatious claim to ascetic refusal makes her laughable:

> Thus it sprong into a maner of proverbe agen hir that summe seydyn, "Fals flesch, thu schalt ete non heryng." And sum seydyn the wordys the whech arn beforn wretyn, and al was fals, but yet wer thei not forgetyn; thei wer rehersyd in many a place wher sche was nevyr kyd ne knowyn.[66]

Where recollection, repetition, and mockery meet, "a maner of proverbe" is born. This sense of "proverbe" reflects a late-medieval usage more capacious than its modern definition.[67] Medieval rhetoricians and exegetes did not

---

[63] Anne Middleton, "Dowel, the Proverbial, and the Vernacular: Some Versions of Pastoralia," in *Medieval Poetics and Social Practice: Responding to the Work of Penn R. Szittya*, ed. Seeta Chaganti (New York: Fordham University Press, 2012), pp. 143–69 (at p. 145).

[64] *Book of Margery Kempe*, ed. Lynn Staley, TEAMS: Middle English Texts (Kalamazoo, Mich.: Medieval Institute Publications, 1996), II.9.554.

[65] *Book of Margery Kempe*, II.9.567–68.

[66] *Book of Margery Kempe*, II.9.569–73.

[67] Though *MED*, s.v. "proverbe," cites this passage under sense 1a ("A proverb, maxim; a saying"), it seems equally likely to apply to sense 1e ("an object of general reproach or derision, a byword"). The Latin construction that lies behind "into a maner of proverbe," i.e., *in proverbium*, is most familiar from the Vulgate 3 [1] Kings 9:7: "erit ... Israel in proverbium, et in fabulam cunctis populis" [Israel will be made into a proverb and a byword among all peoples]. When the Digby poems invoke "oo prouerbe," they reference Ecclesiasticus (4.33).

216 SPENCER STRUB

always agree on what *proverbium* meant, but most treated it as a subcategory of figures of thought and *parabolae*, comparable to other tools of the preacher's art like the similitude or the exemplum.[68]

Kempe's fish story shows by contrast how the proverb was understood and used as vernacular shorthand. Two qualities seem particularly important. First, though this "maner of proverbe" changes in circulation, it retains its basic shape: its four iterations in this short chapter are all slightly different, but all are recognizable variations on the same address to the "fals flesch." They loosely resemble other Middle English expressions – like beans or straw, red herring is proverbially worthless – but are clearly distinct from them.[69] Paremiologists argue that the structure of a proverb is essential to its recognition *as* proverb.[70] But its particulars, what folklorist G. L. Permyakov called the *realia*, provide "emotiveness," "local color," and "artistic value."[71] *Realia* are also subject to variation in a way that underlying structures are not. Take the four instances of Kempe's proverb:

> "A, thu fals flesch, thu schalt no good mete etyn."
> "A, thu fals flesch, thu woldist now etyn reed heryng, but thu schalt not han thi wille."
> "Fals flesch, thu schalt ete non heryng."
> "Thu fals flesch, thu schalt non etyn of this good mete."[72]

Only two include herring, the *reale* most bound to the foodways of late-medieval England. But "fals flesch" is always present, as is some kind of reference to food. The structure that matters is bipartite: the first opposition obtains between chastised flesh and the food that the chastising refuses; the second, implicit but central to the proverb's ironic sting, between the food that is passed over and the finer fare that is chosen instead. This structure of comparison is one foundation of the Digby poems' omnipresent moral binaries: "the more cost, the less avail" and its ilk depend on similar binaries.

Second, the proverb emanates from a specific person and situation, but in its retelling becomes authorless. Margery notionally uttered the original phrase, and she first encounters it because her antagonists lob it at her with

---

68 See Barry Taylor, "Medieval Proverb Collections: The West European Tradition," *Journal of the Warburg and Courtauld Institutes* 55 (1992), 19–35 and Cameron Louis, "The Concept of the Proverb in Middle English," *Proverbium* 14 (1997), 173–86.

69 See Whiting F235 and H367.

70 Alan Dundes, "On the Structure of the Proverb," in *The Wisdom of Many: Essays on the Proverb*, ed. Wolfgang Mieder and Alan Dundes (New York and London: Garland, 1981), pp. 43–64. See also the "perception of proverbiality" in Nancy Mason Bradbury, "The Proverb as Embedded Microgenre in Chaucer and *The Dialogue of Solomon and Marcolf*," *Exemplaria* 27 (2015), 55–72 (at 59).

71 G. L. Permyakov, *From Proverb to Folk-tale: Notes on the General Theory of Cliché*, tr. Y. N. Filippov (Moscow: Nauka, 1979), pp. 28–29; see also Karla Taylor, *Chaucer Reads 'The Divine Comedy'* (Stanford, Calif.: Stanford University Press, 1989), p. 156.

72 *Book of Margery Kempe*, ll. 554, 567–68, 570–71, 582.

THE DIGBY POEMS AND THEIR FIFTEENTH CENTURY   217

the express intent of turning her words against her; a dozen lines later, she simply overhears it at a meal, repeated by people cracking jokes over their food. But it still carries her story as by synecdoche. When Margery asks her table companions if "yf thei had any knowlach of the persone whech schulde a seyd thes wordys," they respond:

> Nay forsothe, but we have herd telde that ther is swech a fals feynyd ypocrite in Lynne whech seyth sweche wordys, and, leevyng of gret metys, sche etith the most delicyows and delectabyl metys that comyn on the tabyl.[73]

When Margery tells them that she herself is that woman from Lynn and had never said any such thing, her interlocutors become embarrassed, humbling themselves in the face of her honest bearing. Margery's interlocutors do not know her and they do not seek to mock her – it seems they only want to poke fun at each other. They are still able to name the place and personage behind the proverb. And yet it is already mobile, an axiom defined by its authorlessness: when slanderers repeat it, "evyr thei madyn other lyars her autorys, seying in excusyng of hem self that other men telde hem so."[74] From the perspective of penitential theology, such self-excusing is delusional. The single act of backbiting slays three: the backbiter who sins in speaking, the listener who sins in consenting to hear, and the victim, whose reputation is destroyed.[75]

But such deferral offers a useful account of the emergence of a proverb. As B. J. Whiting held in a formative study on the proverb form, "Nothing is more likely than that certain sayings can be traced to the utterances of specific individuals, but this has nothing to do with the origin of the proverb as a type or with the origin of most proverbs."[76] As I noted above, whether a proverb is understood to crystallize common knowledge or transmit the wisdom of antiquity, its status as something "that other men telde" vouchsafes its authority. Margery's experience, however, suggests that the proverb is also an uncontrolled utterance: it is invented to suit one circumstance, but once spoken, might be deployed to fit new situations to the same structure of thought. This unsettled dynamic is crucial to the operation of the Digby poems, explaining how many seem to remark upon a specific historical juncture without definitively belonging to it. These poems are built for new occasions.

---

[73] *Book of Margery Kempe*, II.9.585–88.

[74] *Book of Margery Kempe*, II.9.560–62.

[75] See Edwin Craun, *Lies, Slander, and Obscenity in Medieval English Literature: Pastoral Rhetoric and the Deviant Speaker* (Cambridge: Cambridge University Press, 1997), pp. 47–52.

[76] Bartlett Jere Whiting, "The Origin of the Proverb (1931)," in *When Evensong and Morrowsong Accord: Three Essays on the Proverb*, ed. Joseph Harris (Cambridge, Mass.: Department of English and American Literature and Language, Harvard University, 1994), pp. 25–26.

DIGBY 102 IN MID-FIFTEENTH-CENTURY LONDON

Digby 102 itself points to one such occasion. Wherever the poems originated, the manuscript that transmits them is almost certainly a London production. It was likely commissioned and used by members of the urban craft-guild elite – that is, by people proximate to (but not part of) the royal and parliamentary debates that modern critics generally see as the poetry's implied context. In his study of the codex, Simon Horobin finds the Digby-scribe's hand working in the Memorandum Book of the London Brewers' Guild between 1418 and 1441. Horobin tentatively identifies the scribe as Robert Lynford, a junior clerk for the guild, and dates the manuscript to late in the first quarter of the fifteenth century or slightly thereafter.[77]

No colophon identifies the scribe, nor are there any medieval ownership marks. But the manuscript has two rebuses, which probably encode the name "Horne."[78] If Lynford was the scribe, the rebus likely identifies the book's owner. Though Horne is an august London surname, the fifteenth-century city furnishes a single likely candidate: the Bridge Ward alderman and one-time sheriff Robert Horne.[79] (Horobin proposes that a large R written in the upper margin of fol. 128r may mark Lynford's given name; it may instead mark Horne's.)[80] Horne was a fishmonger, not a brewer, but as craftsman and local politician, he would have had extensive contact with guild clerks like Lynford.[81]

Horne was a public figure, entangled in the mounting crises of his era, and thus left a robust documentary record. He served in various civic capacities from at least 1437 onward, served as alderman from 1444–56, was elected sheriff by the mayor in 1446, and was dead by 1468.[82] In 1450, he was charged with defending London Bridge against Jack Cade's rebels, whom he vociferously opposed. When

---

[77] Simon Horobin, "The Scribe of Bodleian Library, MS Digby 102 and the Circulation of the C Text of *Piers Plowman*," *YLS* 24 (2010), 89–112.

[78] Digby 102, fols. 97v (following explicit to *Piers* C) and 139v (following explicit to *Disputatio inter corpus et animam*). *Will's Visions of Piers Plowman and Do-Well*, in *Piers Plowman: The C Version*, ed. George Russell and George Kane, rev. ed. (London: Athlone, 1997), p. 16, notes that the rebus "seems to contain the letters H E R O N." Nicholson, "Poetry and Politics," p. 408, also offers "Horne" as solution to the rebus.

[79] Sylvia L. Thrupp, *The Merchant Class of Medieval London, 1300–1500* (Ann Arbor, Mich.: University of Michigan Press, 1989), p. 350. The London Robert Horne should not be confused with the Kentish Robert Horne, a member of Parliament and Yorkist knight who died at Towton.

[80] Horobin, "Digby 102," p. 97.

[81] Alfred P. Beaven, *The Aldermen of the City of London Temp. Henry III – 1912* (London: Corporation of the City of London, 1908), p. 329, identifies Horne as a brewer, but corrects the identification in the *corrigenda*, p. 444. Horne approved a 1453 *ordinacio de berebuers*, governing London brewers; see *Calendar of Letter-Books of the City of London: K, Henry VI*, ed. Reginald R. Sharpe (London: Corporation of the City of London, 1911), p. 354.

[82] *Letter-Book K*, p. 218 (first appearance), pp. 295–96 (alderman election), p. 315 (election as sheriff); *Letter-Book L*, pp. 78–79 (posthumous execution of will).

THE DIGBY POEMS AND THEIR FIFTEENTH CENTURY   219

the gates opened anyway, the rebels imprisoned him in Newgate, where he might have been executed had his wife and associates not intervened and ransomed him.[83] He seems to have earned rebel odium at least in part by being associated with the much-loathed party of William de la Pole, Duke of Suffolk. After Suffolk was kidnapped and executed in 1450, one of the events that precipitated Cade's rising, a mock *dirige* circulated celebrating his death and wishing ill on his allies. Horne earned two contemptuous lines in this unambiguously topical macaronic satire: "*Pelle me consumptus carnibus* to the nynne, / Robart Horne, alderman, that shall be thy vers."[84] (The final Digby poem, "The Lessouns of the Dirige," likewise takes the *dirige* as its inspiration, though it offers instead an earnest vernacular adaptation of the Office of the Dead.) Aside from this unfortunate cameo appearance, Horne's role in fifteenth-century English literary culture is decidedly peripheral, though he was tied to bigger players: his first appearance in the documentary record registers a debt to John Shirley incurred in 1432 – early in Horne's career, but well after Shirley began his prodigious project of literary bookmaking. Four years earlier, Shirley had joined the confraternity of the Benedictine St. Albans Abbey.[85] If the Digby poems indeed have a Benedictine origin, perhaps Shirley was the vector of their transmission to Horne or to the London guildhall at large.

Horne's career suggests a new context in which to read the Digby poems. Middleton, working from Kail's dates, argues that Digby 102 as a whole addresses "the broadly ethical and devotional concerns of men of affairs, lay and ecclesiastical, at the coming of the Lancastrians."[86] How might the same book speak to a lay "man of affairs" during the midcentury Lancastrian crack-up, when the optimism central to both Kail and Barr's readings of the Digby poems had curdled into factionalism and fear?

Poem 16, "A Remembraunce of LIJ Folyes," immediately announces its subject with a characteristically direct address: "Loke how Flaundres doþ fare wiþ his folyhede!" (16.1). Flanders's follies include civil strife and the fall of a prince. As Barr points out, the poem belongs to a longstanding English "discourse of Flanders"; she suggests its "remembraunce" was prompted

---

[83] "William Gregory's Chronicle of London," in *The Historical Collections of a Citizen of London in the Fifteenth Century*, ed. James Gairdner (Westminster, UK: Camden Society, 1876), p. 192; and Ralph A. Griffiths, *The Reign of King Henry VI: The Exercise of Royal Authority, 1422–61* (London: Ernest Benn, 1981), pp. 625–26.

[84] *Three Fifteenth-Century Chronicles*, ed. James Gairdner (Westminster, UK: Camden Society, 1880), p. 103, NIMEV 1555 (2). The Latin is drawn from Job 19:20. On the circumstances that occasioned this poem, see I. M. W. Harvey, *Jack Cade's Rebellion of 1450* (Oxford: Clarendon Press, 1991), pp. 75–77.

[85] Kew, The National Archives, C 241/225/52. On Shirley's dates, see Margaret Connolly, *John Shirley: Book Production and the Noble Household in Fifteenth-Century England* (Aldershot, UK: Ashgate, 1998), pp. 27, 52.

[86] Anne Middleton, "The Audience and Public of *Piers Plowman*," in *Middle English Alliterative Poetry and Its Literary Background: Seven Essays*, ed. David Lawton (Cambridge: D. S. Brewer, 1982), pp. 101–23, at p. 108.

220 SPENCER STRUB

by the civil war in France in 1410–11.[87] R. H. Nicholson proposes that the poem instead reflects on the failure of Philip the Good's 1436 siege of Calais, suggesting it is propaganda on behalf of Humphrey, Duke of Gloucester – Suffolk's rival – thus resituating the entire sequence in Henry VI's minority.[88] Kail read the poem as commentary on the assassination of John the Fearless, duke of Burgundy, who "was indeed guilty of some of the follies which, as our poet pretends, caused his fall."[89] Given the manuscript's date and the poem's allusions to the fall of a prince, Kail may be closest to the mark: a reader in the early 1420s, reading these gnomic references, would naturally think of John's death.[90] Within a few years, however, such clarifying context would likely already be forgotten.

So what would Robert Horne see in this poem, had he read it during his career in office, which began nearly twenty years after John's death? Flanders was a major importer of English wool and thus crucial to London merchants. It remained a concern in English politics throughout Horne's life – it was a point of contention between Gloucester's war party and Suffolk's peace party, for instance. But the poem is more a *memento mori* for a commonwealth than an articulation of any opinion about trade or the war: "Flaundres was þe richest land and meriest to mynne," the poet writes, "now it is wrapped in wo and moche welþe raft" (16.57–58). Such a turn of Fortune's wheel becomes more grist for the poet's commonplace-making mill. The final stanza, flagged by a scribal *nota* in the manuscript (fol. 116r), declares that the speaker has only found four true people on earth: sickness, sorrow, death, and dread, who claim us by custom, sparing neither prince nor pauper, old nor young (16.113–20).

These universals are nevertheless prefaced by specifics that might particularly tweak a London alderman. Flanders suffers "for defaute of iustice and singulere to wynne, / Þey were rebelle to ryse craft aȝen craft" (16.59–60). The antagonisms between the governing guilds of the Three Cities of Ghent, Bruges, and Ypres and both the dukes of Burgundy and the workers of other cities spawned a number of revolts and internal conflicts. For a London alderman elected in 1444, however, the threat of risings of "craft aȝen craft" would strike closer to home. Midcentury London politics was defined by years of strife between the ruling merchant Drapers and the comparatively disempowered artisan Tailors. Radical organizing and conservative resistance led to a series of contested mayoral elections, juridical suppression of urban sedition, and (in late 1443) a foiled uprising.[91] Insofar as magnates were

---

[87] Barr, *Digby Poems*, pp. 11–13, referencing David Wallace, "In Flaundres," *Studies in the Age of Chaucer* 19 (1997), 63–91.
[88] Nicholson, "Poetry and Politics."
[89] Kail, *Twenty-Six Political and Other Poems*, p. xxi.
[90] I am grateful to Sebastian Sobecki for this suggestion.
[91] Caroline M. Barron, "Ralph Holland and the London Radicals, 1438–1444," in *Medieval London: Collected Papers of Caroline M. Barron*, ed. Martha Carlin and Joel T. Rosenthal (Kalamazoo, Mich.: Medieval Institute, 2017), pp. 335–60.

THE DIGBY POEMS AND THEIR FIFTEENTH CENTURY   221

involved, Suffolk supported the merchants, Gloucester the artisans. The Fishmongers were part of the oligarchic merchant ascendancy. So Horne might have read these lines as an endorsement of the status quo, warning against the disasters that follow dissension from below – a factional position articulated in a shared language, like the later Yorkist poems that Paul Strohm argues turn descriptive political theory into polemic "available to the leader, and his followers, who can claim it."[92]

But a commonplace can cut two ways, and admonition lurks here too. In her reading of the Digby poems, Natalie Calder argues that they articulate a Benedictine critique that constrains even as it endorses the policies of Lancastrian kings.[93] Read by a merchant alderman, the sequence channels a Gowerian vein of double-edged advice that warns the ruling class as it castigates disobedient commoners. "Defaute of iustice" and "singulere" interest – sins of rulers and rebels alike – give rise to craft conflict. "Treuth, Reste and Pes" also laments the mess that follows "whan craft riseþ aȝen craft," insisting that the law rule rather than the mob (3.33). But the same poem includes these lines, quoted above:

> A kyngdom in comouns lys,
> Alle profytes and alle myscheues.
> Lordis wet neuere what comouns greues
> Til her rentis bigynne to ses. (3.98–101)

These truisms might have struck a midcentury London alderman as particularly timely. In January 1450, the Tailors rose and were suppressed again.[94] As Cade's rebels gathered in Kent five months later, they drafted bills of complaint: "They seye the Kynge schuld lyve upon his Comyns, and that her bodyes and goodes ern his; the contrarie is trew."[95] Horne and his colleagues were neither lords nor King, but seeing Cade on their doorstep, might still have taken the Digby poem's broad statement and read it "to hem speciale," just as the poet intended.

CONCLUSION

The Digby poems only use the word "proverb" once. "Oo prouerbe loke ȝe preue," the poet writes: "Look what neyȝebore most may greue, / By al way make hym þi frende" (4.33–36). In other words, befriend the neighbor who

---

[92] Paul Strohm, *Politique: Languages of Statecraft between Chaucer and Shakespeare* (Notre Dame, Ind.: University of Notre Dame Press, 2005), p. 192.

[93] Natalie Calder, "'The Puple is Godes, and Not ȝoures': Lancastrian Orthodoxy in the Digby Lyrics," *Review of English Studies* 65 (2013), 403–20.

[94] Eliza Hartrich, *Politics and the Urban Sector in Fifteenth-Century England, 1413–1471* (Oxford: Oxford University Press, 2019), p. 131.

[95] Harvey, *Jack Cade's Rebellion*, p. 189.

can harm you most – a more pointed variation on the Biblical injunction to love thy neighbor that was rearticulated in a variety of pithy ways in late medieval England.[96] In the lines that follow, the poet explains why: your enemies will turn from you, afflicted by "here owen þouȝt" instead (4.38); and from this point unfolds the second of the Digby poems' two sustained ruminations on general critique and special guilt. The directive to look that you *prove* the proverb, in part just a bit of poetic flab filling out a line, nevertheless underlines a central conviction of these poems: just as the common profit proves the wisdom of Parliament, so too does the conduct of the addressee prove the proverb relayed by the poem. The meaning of the poetry is fulfilled in the domain of the reader's experience.

That particular relation to the world – an affordance of the proverbial form, elevated into a poetic method – explains why these poems seem at once topical and timeless. They offer guidance that emerges from a specific situation but is intended to speak to another. As Vincent Gillespie observes of the Digby poems, "if moral poetry is not susceptible of application to contemporary events, it has effectively lost its purpose."[97] But that susceptibility is framed by the poet's invocations of a reader's will. Any topical relevance depends on the reader's application of its truisms, rather than the poet's articulation of them.

Ingrid Nelson observes that the medieval lyric is especially vulnerable to degradation over time: words might lose their music, flyleaf jottings their integrity as a poetic unit. But Nelson encourages critics to understand such losses as "tactics of transformation, positive signs of a network of practice and protean agglomeration rather than entropic decay."[98] The unresolved critical debate over the referentiality of the Digby poems – the fact that they seem to comment on topical issues while remaining "largely illocatable, at times it seems studiously so," as Giancarlo puts it – might likewise be taken as evidence not only of the satirist's plausible deniability, but also the capacity for recontextualization afforded by the commonplace style itself.[99] James Simpson has described literary reading as "the recovery of the somehow already known": meaning emerges from the encounter with the old, made new in the act of recognition.[100] The Digby poet's proverbial style is primed for those acts of recovery and recognition, reviving its truisms, giving new force to its satire in the face of new crises.

---

[96] The Digby version is Whiting N82; but cf. N74, N83, N84, N86.

[97] Vincent Gillespie, "Moral and Penitential Lyrics," in *A Companion to the Middle English Lyric*, ed. Thomas G. Duncan (Cambridge: D. S. Brewer, 2005), pp. 68–95, at pp. 91–92.

[98] Ingrid Nelson, *Lyric Tactics: Poetry, Genre, and Practice in Later Medieval England* (Philadelphia: University of Pennsylvania Press, 2017), p. 152.

[99] Giancarlo, "Troubling the New Constitutionalism," p. 78.

[100] James Simpson, "Cognition is Recognition: Literary Knowledge and Textual 'Face,'" *New Literary History* 44 (2013), 25–44 (at 40).

12 COMMON STYLE AND THE BOURGEOIS ETHOS IN JOHN LYDGATE'S *DIETARY*

Taylor Cowdery

Over twenty years ago, James Simpson observed that John Lydgate was a "thoroughly public" poet, one whose "corpus was riven by distinct, often exclusive, generic and discursive commitments."[1] This essay grows out of Simpson's insights about Lydgate's adaptable style and public orientation, although it considers a poem that is a far cry from the maximalist work for which Lydgate is best known today. This is the so-called *Dietary*, a ten-stanza lyric about the many benefits of honest dealing, personal hygiene, a healthy diet, and clean living.[2] A poem that survives in at least fifty-six manuscripts, the notional topic of the *Dietary* is "the gouernans of man," as rubrics to the text often put it, and many of its lines are indeed given over to the proper habits that a person ought to keep up if they wish to remain in sound physical health.[3] For instance, we are told to wear a hat when it is cold (1), to keep away from the "eyre of pestelens" (42), to go to bed early (7), and to take it easy on the salt (69–70). At the same time, however, the *Dietary* also devotes about

---

[1] James Simpson, *The Oxford English Literary History, Vol. 2: 1350–1547: Reform and Cultural Revolution* (Oxford: Oxford University Press, 2002), pp. 38 and 52.

[2] See item no. 1356 in *DIMEV*. All citations of the *Dietary* will be given parenthetically in the text, with reference to John Lydgate, "Dietary," item no. 78 in *Secular Lyrics of the XIVth and XVth Centuries*, ed. Rossell Hope Robbins, 2nd ed. (Oxford: Clarendon Press, 1955). For further discussion of the poem in the manuscript record, see Jake Walsh Morrissey, "'Termes of Phisik': Reading Between Literary and Medical Discourses in Geoffrey Chaucer's *Canterbury Tales* and John Lydgate's *Dietary*" (unpublished Ph.D. dissertation, McGill University, 2011), pp. 261–301, and compare my account below.

[3] For an example of one such rubric, see item no. 31 in *Codex Ashmole 61: A Compilation of Popular Middle English Verse*, ed. George Shuffleton, TEAMS Middle English Texts (Kalamazoo, Mich.: Medieval Institute Publications, 2008).

half of its space to the voicing of conventional moral sentiments – by making comments, for instance, about such things as the need to remain "content with suffisaunce" (14) or to shun "mowthes þat ben doubill" (25) – and this mixture of proverbial wisdom with wellness advice has prompted some debate about what Julie Orlemanski terms the "generic flexibility" of the poem.[4] Some scholars have suggested that it is a courtesy text, or even a text designed to appeal to a new type of consumer, while others have contended that it is a work of medicine at heart.[5] What both positions tend to have in common, however, is a tacit assumption that, as Derek Pearsall once put it, this is a poem for which "literary criticism" has "no part."[6] In each case, that is, the operating premise is that the *Dietary* must have been popular because it was useful for some instrumental end, and not because it appealed to the aesthetic or literary sensibilities of its readers.

In what follows, I would like to make two claims about the *Dietary* in support of a different theory about its popularity. My first claim has to do with the manuscript record of the poem. Surviving copies of the *Dietary* are mostly to be found in literary miscellanies or in wide-ranging compilations of material associated with the London middle classes.[7] While it is true that the poem did appear in certain dedicated medical compilations, it is very unlikely that fifteenth-century readers would have taken the *Dietary* for a guide to practical medicine, for as I explain below, there are key formal and generic differences between the *Dietary* and the Middle English recipes, or "receipts," that often traveled alongside it.[8] Indeed, Lydgate himself twice distinguishes the *Dietary* from such texts. It is, he tells us, not the sort of "resceyte" that is "bought" at a "poticarye" (78), but a text to which we might turn if "physike lakke" (16) and "leches" fail us (9).[9]

---

4   Julie Orlemanski, *Symptomatic Subjects: Bodies, Medicine, and Causation in the Literature of Late Medieval England* (Philadelphia: University of Pennsylvania Press, 2019), p. 75.
5   For two strong positions on the genre of the poem, see respectively Jake Walsh Morrissey, "'To Al Indifferent': The Virtues of Lydgate's 'Dietary,'" *Medium Ævum* 84 (2015), 258–78, who argues that it was received as a "bona fide medical text" (p. 270), and Claire Sponsler, "Eating Lessons: Lydgate's 'Dietary' and Consumer Conduct," in *Medieval Conduct*, ed. Kathleen Ashley and Robert L. A. Clark (Minneapolis, Minn.: University of Minnesota Press, 2001), pp. 1–22, who suggests that "the poem teaches the reader how to be a good consumer" (p. 7).
6   Derek Pearsall, *John Lydgate* (London: Routledge & Kegan Paul, 1970), p. 220.
7   See Julie Orlemanski, "Thornton's Remedies and the Practices of Medical Reading," in *Robert Thornton and his Books: Essays on the Lincoln and London Thornton Manuscripts*, ed. Susanna Fein and Michael Johnston (York: York Medieval Press, 2014), pp. 235–55, at pp. 251–55, and compare the discussion below.
8   For discussion of Middle English recipes, see especially Hannah Bower, *Middle English Recipes and Literary Play, 1375–1500* (Oxford: Oxford University Press, 2022).
9   Compare again Orlemanski, "Thornton's Remedies," p. 254.

COMMON STYLE AND BOURGEOIS ETHOS IN LYDGATE'S *DIETARY*   225

This distinction leads me to my second claim, which is that the popular appeal of the *Dietary* has as much to do with the style and voice of the lyric as it does with its notional utility for any practical end. By speaking in warm tones about the virtues of "welfare, prosperite, and fusoun" (31), as the poem puts it, the *Dietary* authorizes and even helps to create a set of social values that came to be seen as normative and desirable by the merchants and artisans who were its primary audience. These are basically what Anne Middleton has identified as the values of "public poetry," a set of civic-minded commitments to a pious, urban, and decidedly bourgeois way of life. "The voice of public poetry," she explains,

> is neither courtly, nor spiritual, nor popular. It is pious, but its central pieties are worldly felicity and peaceful, harmonious communal existence. It speaks for bourgeois moderation, a course between the rigorous absolutes of religious rule on the one hand, and, on the other, the rhetorical hyperboles and emotional vanities of the courtly style, whether that style is conceived in its narrower sense of a distinctive manner of speech or as the mode of living and personal values associated with the noble estate. This poetic voice is vernacular, practical, worldly, plain, public-spirited, and peace-loving – in a word, "common," rather than courtly or clerical, in its professed values and social allegiances.[10]

As I will demonstrate, the *Dietary* celebrates these "common" values in two ways. First, it plays upon many of the keywords and key phrases associated with the civic and legal cultures of fifteenth-century London, a fact that is gauged easily enough if we compare its lexis with that of the London custumals and the surviving ordinances of the London guilds. Like the custumals and the guild-texts, the *Dietary* also speaks of living "worschypfuly" (40), or of having "compassion" upon the "nedy" (46), or of maintaining "rest and pes" with one's "neyghbors" (32), and at the very least, these echoes suggest that the poem aimed to catch the attention of readers for whom such phrases had the force of a social imperative – the merchants and craftspeople for whom Lydgate composed many other works of poetry and drama alike.[11] Second, and still more important, the *Dietary* employs a distinctive idiom to speak of these values, one that I will call the "common style." While the common style may

---

[10] Anne Middleton, "The Idea of Public Poetry in the Reign of Richard II," *Speculum* 53 (1978), 94–114, at 95–96.

[11] For Lydgate and the merchant and artisan classes, see especially C. David Benson, "Civic Lydgate: The Poet and London," in *John Lydgate: Poetry, Culture, and Lancastrian England*, ed. Larry Scanlon and James Simpson (Notre Dame, Ind.: University of Notre Dame Press, 2006), pp. 147–68; Lisa H. Cooper, "The Poetics of Practicality," in *Oxford Twenty-First Century Approaches to Literature: Middle English*, ed. Paul Strohm (Oxford: Oxford University Press, 2007), pp. 491–505; and Maura Nolan, *John Lydgate and the Making of Public Culture* (Cambridge: Cambridge University Press, 2005), pp. 71–119.

TAYLOR COWDERY

226

be understood as a collection of concrete features – consistent end-stopping, or the imperative mood, or the use of couplet rhymes, or a frequent recourse to the half-line clause – its most notable characteristic is a certain mode of address, or even a certain voice, that is either reassuring or stifling, depending upon one's point of view. Like Middleton's "voice of public poetry," this voice is indeed pious and moderate, but it is also avuncular, or even fatherly. It tells us that we are right to feel how we feel, and right to believe what we believe in. It assures us that our "governans" (10) of ourselves and our households has been well-considered, temperate, and correct. It offers us advice, not merely for the sake of the advice, but because listening to advice allows us to feel a certain way.

It would seem, then, that while the *Dietary* is obviously designed to sell us something, the product on offer is not what it has often been taken to be. This is not a poem, in my view, whose commercial appeal hinges upon its translation of Latin knowledge into the vernacular, or upon its conveyance of professional secrets to a wider and non-specialist audience.[12] Rather, what the *Dietary* sells is a kind of affective validation. It allows each reader to feel that his "housholde" is a castle, even if he only has small "Rente" for its maintenance (60). It assures its audience that the "common values" of the London merchant and artisan classes are a path to "all þe welth / of soule and of body" (73–74), never mind what gentlemen or clerks might say. Most of all, it offers these classes a new way of speaking and feeling about their emerging way of life – a local habitation, and perhaps even a name, for a social formation coming into its own during the early fifteenth century.

THE *DIETARY* AND ITS MANUSCRIPTS

Perhaps the first thing that one should say about the *Dietary* is that its textual form was misrepresented by its first critical editor, Henry Noble MacCracken. He chose for his base text London, British Library MS Lansdowne 699, which offers up a composite version of the *Dietary*, one that interpolates eight additional stanzas – which are "perhaps genuine," as MacCracken remarks – into the body of the lyric.[13] As Jake Walsh Morrissey has observed, this recension of the *Dietary* appears only in the Lansdowne book and one other manuscript, and the additional stanzas, which are primarily concerned "with the healthful consumption of food and drink," differ sharply in tone and character from the

---

[12] For readings of the *Dietary* in this vein, compare, e.g., Morrissey, "To Al Indifferent," p. 258, and Pearsall, *John Lydgate*, pp. 218–19. Many fifteenth-century texts did, however, make claims just like this. For discussion, see especially Sebastian Sobecki, *Unwritten Verities: The Making of England's Vernacular Legal Culture, 1463–1549* (Notre Dame, Ind.: University of Notre Dame Press, 2015), pp. 137–39.

[13] For the interpolated material, see item no. 48, "The Dietary," in *The Minor Poems of John Lydgate*, ed. Henry Noble MacCracken, vol. 2, EETS, os 192 (Oxford: Oxford University Press, 1934), lines 33–96; for the remark, see p. 702, n. 1.

COMMON STYLE AND BOURGEOIS ETHOS IN LYDGATE'S *DIETARY*   227

standard, ten-stanza version of the lyric, which "contains proportionally less information on dietary habits."[14]

I have begun with MacCracken's choice of base text because it has led scholars to focus their attention on a variant recension of the *Dietary* instead of the version of the lyric that was most widely known to Lydgate's contemporaries.[15] This matters for anyone concerned with questions of reception and audience, of course, but it is an especially pressing issue with respect to the *Dietary* because the interpolated stanzas found in MacCracken's variant edition have predisposed modern readers to view it as a text concerned primarily with medicine and "practical content," to use Hannah Bower's term.[16] To a certain extent, this position is warranted by the poem, which certainly takes pains to advertise itself as a work concerned with the "governance" of the body, and which does offer up a modicum of relatively sound medical advice.[17] But what does the manuscript record have to say about the genre of the poem? In my own survey, I concluded that fifteen of the fifty-six manuscripts reproduce material that is exclusively, or almost exclusively, concerned with medicine.[18] The remaining forty-one codices may be divided into two groups. Eleven might be classed as anthologies of poems by Lydgate and other Middle English poets that are self-consciously "literary," and that were likely commissioned to serve either as exemplars for other anthologies or as miscellanies of items that could be written out for bookshop customers on spec.[19] The remaining thirty

14 Morrissey, "To Al Indifferent," p. 260.
15 Compare again Morrissey, "To Al Indifferent," pp. 259–61.
16 Bower, *Middle English Recipes*, p. 86.
17 On "governance" and the genre of the poem, see Morrissey, "To Al Indifferent," p. 270.
18 These manuscripts are as follows: Bethesda, Md., National Library of Medicine MS E 4; Cambridge, Fitzwilliam Museum MS 261; Cambridge, Trinity College Library MS O.2.13; London, British Library MSS Egerton 1995, Harley 941, Harley 5401, Sloane 775, Sloane 989, and Sloane 3534; London, Lambeth Palace Library MS 444; London, Wellcome Historical Medical Library MSS 406, 411, and 8004; Oxford, Bodleian Library MSS Add. B. 60 and e Musaeo 52; and a privately held and untraced MS, *olim* Schwerdt (for a discussion of the contents see Morrissey, "Termes of Phisik," pp. 300–01). For a similar but slightly more selective list of medical manuscripts containing the *Dietary*, compare Orlemanski, "Thornton's Remedies," p. 253, n. 65.
19 The literary anthologies are as follows: Cambridge, Jesus College MS Q. G. 8; Oxford, Bodleian Library MSS Ashmole 61, Bodley 686, and Laud. Misc. 683; Edinburgh, National Library of Scotland MS Advocates 1.1.6 (the Bannatyne MS); Leiden University Library MS Vossius Germ. Gall. Q. 9; London, British Library MSS Arundel 168, Harley 116, Harley 2251, and Lansdowne 699; and Rome, English College, AVCAU MS 1405. For the possibility of work done on spec and the claim that fascicular copies of minor Lydgatian works, such as the *Dietary*, were a staple of London bookshops, see Julia Boffey and John J. Thompson, "Anthologies and Miscellanies: Production and Choice of Texts," in *Book Production and Publishing in Britain, 1375–1475*, ed. Jeremy Griffiths and Derek Pearsall (Cambridge: Cambridge University Press, 1989), pp. 279–315, at pp. 287–91 and 309, n. 71, and compare Pearsall, *John Lydgate*, pp. 75–76.

manuscripts are more eclectic in character, and situate the text of the *Dietary* alongside everything from anticlerical satire to *The Book of the Craft of Dying*. Of these thirty, roughly eleven adhere to the genre of the "commonplace book" or "citizens' custumal," and most of these are reliably associated with the merchant and artisan classes of medieval London.[20] Such books are of special importance to my argument, and I will return to them below.

From this survey of the manuscripts, I would draw two conclusions. The first is that scholarship has overrepresented the extent to which the *Dietary* was read, and received, as a text of practical medicine. Indeed, most of its manuscripts are not primarily medical, and while it is true that miscellanies often feature the *Dietary* alongside recipes and other texts concerned with healthy living, it is unlikely, as Bower suggests, that such texts were "thought of as possessing the same modal and formal flexibility as Lydgate's works."[21] In one respect, this is because literature is the exception rather than the rule in these miscellanies, for as Malcolm Richardson has observed, most urban compilations are dominated by the "rhetorical genres" of writing that readers found most useful "to conduct their daily lives."[22] But the same point can be made more directly if we simply compare the *Dietary* with medical texts that were more obviously instrumental. Consider, for example, the following text, which may be found on the page immediately preceding the *Dietary* in Oxford, Bodleian Library MS Rawlinson C. 86.

> A good medecyne for the paynes of a horsse
> Take oyle de baye a quantyte halffe a alpurth of sope a alpurth of mustard
> a halpurth of verdegrece a alpurth of brymstone and make it into powder
> and boyle al þeyse togedir and Anoynte þe horsse hote and it wyll make
> hym hole.[23]

---

[20] See London, British Library MSS Royal 17 B.XLVII, Harley 2252, Harley 541, Harley 4011, Additional 34360, Additional 10099, Egerton 1995, and Cotton Caligula A. II; Oxford, Bodleian Library MSS Rawlinson C. 48 and Rawlinson C. 86; and London, Lambeth Palace Library MS 853. On the difference in the nomenclature, see Boffey and Thompson, "Anthologies and Miscellanies," pp. 292–93; Julia Boffey, "London Books and London Readers," in *Cultural Reformations: Medieval and Renaissance in Literary History*, ed. Brian Cummings and James Simpson (Oxford: Oxford University Press, 2010), pp. 420–37, at pp. 423–25; and Malcolm Richardson, *Middle-Class Writing in Late Medieval London* (London: Pickering and Chatto, 2011), pp. 154–69.

[21] Bower, *Middle English Recipes*, p. 92.

[22] Richardson, *Middle-Class Writing*, p. 8.

[23] Oxford, Bodleian Library MS Rawlinson C. 86, fol. 60v; all abbreviations have been silently expanded. Compare S. J. Ogilvie-Thomson, ed., *The Index of Middle English Prose: Handlist XXIII: The Rawlinson Collection, Bodleian Library, Oxford* (Cambridge: D. S. Brewer, 2017), p. 94. "Alpurth" seems to be a contraction of "halpeni-worth."

COMMON STYLE AND BOURGEOIS ETHOS IN LYDGATE'S *DIETARY*   229

Now, contrast this recipe with what I take to be the most topical and prescriptive stanza in the *Dietary*, at least with respect to the matters of physical health.

> Dyne not at morow Afore þyn appetyte–
> Clere ayre & walkyng maketh good digestioun;
> Betwene mealys drynke not for no froward delyte,
> But thurste or traveyle geve þe occasioun;
> Ouer-salte metys do gret oppressioun
> To febill stomakys whanne þey cannot refrayn,
> ffro þynges contrarie to her complexioun;
> Of gredy handis þe stomake hath grete payn. (65–72)

One of these texts is obviously unlike the other, and not just because the recipe is intended for a horse. While both offer the reader instructions on how to maintain or restore good health, each one approaches this question at a different scale, and in a different mode. The recipe is specific and topical: it lists the ingredients needed for the ointment, and then offers the reader a step-by-step guide to its mixing ("make it into powder and boyle al þeyse togedir") and application ("anoynte the horsse hote"). The *Dietary* also provides the reader with good wellness advice, such as taking a walk after a meal to aid the digestion, but it does so in a gnomic and universalizing way, and on a greater range of topics. In one moment, we are told to "preserve aye from colde" our "hede, fote, and stomake" (58), while in the next, we are warned to "swere no othyes no man to begyle" (62). What is more, these differences cannot be attributed merely to the use of rhyme or meter, for Middle English verse recipes often managed to be quite literary without sacrificing the topical and concrete aspects of the recipe-form. Consider, for example, the following recipe against the headache from San Marino, Huntington Library MS HM 64:

> A medycyn here I have in mynde. Ffor hedde-werke to telle as I fynde. To take ayeselle and puliolle ryalle. And camamylle and seethe hit withe alle. And that Iouce anoynte thy nasse threllis welle. And make a plaster of that othere deele. And doo hit in a goode grete clowte. And wynd the hedde therewithe abowte. So sone as hit is Layde thereon. Alle the hedde werke awaye schalle gon.[24]

This may not be great poetry, but it is certainly informative poetry. If one had chamomile, vinegar, and pennyroyal on hand, one could distill this recipe without too much difficulty.

It is likely, then, that the *Dietary* would have seemed rather weak tea to a fifteenth-century audience accustomed to a richer diet of medical texts in

---

[24] San Marino, Huntington Library MS HM 64, fol. 113v. All abbreviations have been silently expanded. For discussion of this recipe, see Bower, *Middle English Recipes*, pp. 82–83.

Middle English. But if this is the case, was the appeal of the *Dietary* more strictly literary instead? Once again – and this is my second conclusion – the manuscript record argues against such a view. Partly, this is because the *Dietary* is obviously ill at ease when it is found alongside many of the items in the literary compilations of Lydgate's works, and it often appears to have been included in such compilations because of its association with Lydgate's name and not because of its generic resemblance to whatever else might be found in the book.[25] What is more, the poem is durably associated, in certain manuscripts, with conduct and courtesy literature, and this suggests that fifteenth-century readers did indeed believe that it had an instrumental social function, even if such a function had little to do with specific regimens of health.[26] Here, we might recall Simpson's observation that Lydgate's work was "riven by distinct, often exclusive, generic and discursive commitments."[27] The key terms here are "exclusive" and "commitments." Lydgate wrote for many audiences, and so he quickly learned to adapt his style and mode of address as needed. Rather like Gower, he sought to speak to each of his implied audiences in the terms, and even with the voice, that was best aligned with their orientation towards each other and towards the world in which they lived.[28] He understood, in other words, that the appeal of a work of art often has less to do with what it says than with the affinities it creates. Readers consume poetry not merely for the sounds and sense, but because it tells them who they are and where they belong.

THE *DIETARY* AND THE "BOURGEOIS ETHOS"

Evidence from the manuscript record would suggest, then, that the *Dietary* appealed to its readers neither because it was seen as a useful authority on *materia medica* nor because it made available to a middle-class audience an otherwise inaccessible sort of cultural or intellectual capital. But what then accounts for its wild popularity? Perhaps one answer to this question may be found if we examine more closely the London manuscripts in which the *Dietary* often appeared – and in particular, those manuscripts that

---

[25] See, for example, Oxford, Bodleian Library MS Laud 683, which features the *Dietary* (fols. 60r–61v) and whose fifteenth-century pages are entirely comprised of Lydgate's poems (see fols. 1r–107v). For the power of Lydgate's name as a fifteenth-century brand, see especially Robert J. Meyer-Lee, *Poets and Power from Chaucer to Wyatt* (Cambridge: Cambridge University Press, 2007), pp. 50–54.

[26] In London, British Library MS Stowe 982, for example, the *Dietary* (fols. 11r–12r) appears exclusively alongside conduct material, including the *Boke of Kervynge*, Lydgate's *Stans Puer ad Mensam*, and a treatise on the keeping of horses. For discussion of texts such as these, see again Cooper, "Poetics of Practicality."

[27] Simpson, *Reform and Cultural Revolution*, p. 52.

[28] See Meyer-Lee, *Poets and Power*, pp. 36–38, and R. D. Perry, "Lydgate's Virtual Coteries: Chaucer's Family and Gower's Pacifism in the Fifteenth Century," *Speculum* 93 (2018), 669–98, at 688–94.

COMMON STYLE AND BOURGEOIS ETHOS IN LYDGATE'S *DIETARY* 231

have been called "commonplace books" or "citizens' custumals." As I noted above, these books were associated with the merchants and craftspeople of fifteenth-century London, and they typically featured an eclectic mixture of local history, pious poetry, medical recipes, romances, and lists of useful information. London, British Library MS Egerton 1995, for example, features the *Dietary* alongside a chronicle of London; lists of London churches, monasteries, and hospitals; accounts of laws and customs specific to the city; and matrices of definitions and terms in Latin, English, and French, including the "properteys that longythe to a yonge gentylleman," the "condyscyons of a grehounde," terms of hunting, and "the namys of hawkys and to what maner of personys that they longe vnto."[29] As Julia Boffey has observed, such books "suggest the interpenetrating worlds of business, politics, ceremony, and diversion which fuelled metropolitan textual production."[30] They are at once practical-minded and frivolous, concerned with the proper management of the household and the spirit alike, and so perhaps it would be best to say, with Felicity Riddy, that such books testify to the "bourgeois ethos" of a certain class of fifteenth-century readers.[31] This ethos, as Riddy explains, is a certain social orientation towards civic life and the place of the reader within it, one that is broadly associated with "the citizens or freemen of urban society" and is typically masculine, or even patriarchal, in its self-identifications.[32]

How might we understand this "bourgeois ethos" in more specific terms? To answer this question, we could study the texts that often traveled with the *Dietary* in manuscript and that bear a strong resemblance to it – texts such as the "Book of Courtesy" or the "ABC of Aristotle," for instance.[33] But perhaps a still more illuminating answer may be found if we examine the civic and legal sources that lie behind the "citizens' custumals," and especially, the sources that are most directly concerned with the rights and privileges of the London citizenry. Consider, for instance, the *Liber albus*, an official custumal produced in 1417 and 1418 for the Guildhall by John Carpenter, an

---

29 On Egerton 1995, see especially Lisa H. Cooper, "Nothing Was Funny in the Late Middle Ages: The 'Tale of Ryght Nought' and British Library MS Egerton 1995," *Journal of Medieval and Early Modern Studies* 47 (2017), 221–53, and compare Sheila Lindenbaum, "London Texts and Literate Practice," in *The Cambridge History of Medieval English Literature*, ed. David Wallace (Cambridge: Cambridge University Press, 1999), pp. 284–309, at pp. 307–08, and Richardson, *Middle-Class Writing*, p. 162.

30 Boffey, "London Books and London Readers," p. 425.

31 See Felicity Riddy, "Mother Knows Best: Reading Social Change in a Courtesy Text," *Speculum* 71 (1996), 66–86, at 67. Compare Morrissey, "To Al Indifferent," p. 259, who notes that the sense of "diete" in Middle English often referred to a certain "way of living or thinking."

32 Riddy, "Mother Knows Best," pp. 67 and 77; on the masculinity of the "bourgeois ethos," compare too Sponsler, "Eating Lessons," pp. 8–9.

33 See, e.g., London, British Library MS Harley 541, which features the *Dietary* (fols. 211r–v) alongside the "ABC of Aristotle" (fols. 213r–v) and the "Book of Courtesy" (210r–v).

232   TAYLOR COWDERY

important civic figure whose name is often associated with Lydgate during
the 1420s and 1430s.[34] Here, we may find a lexis that is consonant with that of
the *Dietary*, one that is keyed, as it were, to certain terms. In the discussions
of city ordinances, the assize, and the articles of the wardmotes, for instance,
one finds frequent references to preventing any "nuisance" or "annoyance" to
others and to upholding a standard of "neighborliness."[35] Such social norms,
we are often told, will allow not just for individual benefit, but for the "profit"
of the "people" or the "city."[36] If we turn back to the *Dietary*, we will find
that Lydgate's poem likewise stresses living "in reste and pease" with one's
"neyghbours" (32) alongside the importance of reasonable and "prudent"
judgment (22) and the maintenance of good reputation, or "a good name"
(40). These are values that are also prized, again, by the *Liber albus*.[37] Indeed,
so insistent is the *Liber* about the virtues of technocratic and "reasonable"
good governance that some of its passages may sound a bit like parody. In
one statute commenting on the regulation of day-laborer wages, for example,
the text remarks that, in addition to what they "receive throughout the year,"
laborers should also benefit from "all the good usages and good and reasonable

[34] For the generic differences between the official custumal and the citizens' custumal,
see n. 20 above. For the association of Carpenter and Lydgate, see especially Maura
Nolan, *John Lydgate*, pp. 233–41, and Amy Appleford, "The Dance of Death in
London: John Carpenter, John Lydgate, and the Daunce of Poulys," *Journal of
Medieval and Early Modern Studies* 38 (2008), 285–314.

[35] On avoiding "annoyance" or "nuisance," see Henry Thomas Riley, ed., *Munimenta
Gildhallae Londoniensis: Liber Albus, Liber Custumarum, et Liber Horn*, vol.
1 (London: Longman, Brown, Green, Longmans, and Roberts, 1859), p. 260
("desturbance" and "nusaunce"), p. 271 ("en desturbance ne anusaunce des gentz"),
and p. 288 ("saunz … destourbances"). On being respectful to one's "neighbors,"
see again Riley, ed., *Munimenta Gildhallae*, p. 271 ("a la leggance des veisyns"),
p. 319 (avoiding disputes "inter vicinos in civitate"), p. 322 (regulations "de muro
vicinorum communi custu constructo"), p. 331 ("sine damno vicini sui"), and p.
288 (large houses must be ready with two ladders "pur socurere lour veisins en case
qe mal aventure").

[36] On the "profit" of the city or the people, see Riley, ed., *Munimenta Gildhallae*, p.
266 ("al profit du poeple"), p. 285 ("al profit de la citee"), and p. 288 ("le profit de la
citee").

[37] On the importance of a citizen's reputation, often signaled by the phrase "a good
and lawful man," see Riley, ed., *Munimenta Gildhallae*, p. 268 ("afferme par le Maire
et les Audermans comme boun et leal homme"), p. 282 ("afferme par le Gardeyn
et Meire et Aldermanns come boun et leal homme"), p. 294 ("bouns et leaux
hommes"). On the standard of "reasonable" judgment, especially as it is levied
by the twelve aldermen, see again Riley, ed., *Munimenta Gildhallae*, p. 289 (the
"bounes custumes et resonables" of the city administration), p. 320 (aldermen must
be present at Hustings "nisi causa rationabili … impediti"), p. 324 (concerning
whether privies have been "rationabiliter factae sint an non" according to the
judgment of the twelve aldermen).

COMMON STYLE AND BOURGEOIS ETHOS IN LYDGATE'S *DIETARY*   233

[*resonables*] customs made and ratified by the Mayors and Aldermen in the past, for the profit [*profit*] and improvement of the City."[38]

Still more evocative, perhaps, are the echoes of the *Dietary* that we may find in another important source for the citizens' custumals: the surviving ordinances of the London guilds. Here again, we find many of the same values pointed up by the *Liber albus* – most notably, an emphasis on "common profit," maintaining a "good name," and practicing "neighborliness" – alongside a few new ideas as well.[39] The open performance of piety emerges as a central concern. For example, the first item in a set of ordinances is often an injunction that the whole company attend mass together in a certain church at a certain time.[40] Equally important is the care that guild members are expected to extend towards the poor; the role that "common assent" must play in the ratification of guild rules; and the close regulation of standards of dress and livery.[41] Sometimes, these concerns intersect, as they do in this passage from the Grocers' Company ordinances, which describes the proper procedure for the funeral of one of the Company in this way.

> And whan eny of the Brothyrhode dyen in london the Maystres that ben for the ӡer shul don her Bedel to Warn hem in what clotyng they schull comyn to the dirige, and the morwe to the messe, And tho that fayle paye xij d. And ӡyf any of the same Brethyrhode die, and is nouӡt of power to paye for the costes of the berying, Than the same Brothyrhod grauntyth that it be don of the comyn good, And they to be ther in her clotyng, as they schuld for the richest man of the same bretherhode, Apon the payn fornseyde.[42]

---

[38] Riley, ed., *Munimenta Gildhallae*, p. 289: "touz les bonz usages et bounes custumes et resonables par les Meirs et Audermans avaunt ses hours fetes et ordenez, pur le profit et amendment de la citee."

[39] I draw upon the returns of the Carpenters Guild (in 1389) and the ordinances of the Grocers' Company (dated 1418) and the Physician's Company (recorded in Letter-Book K in 1423), all reproduced in R. W. Chambers and Marjorie Daunt, eds., *A Book of London English, 1384–1425* (Oxford: Clarendon Press, 1931). For "common profit," see pp. 109 and 110; for the "good name" or alternately "evil name" of the guilds and their members, see pp. 43, 109, 111, and 197; and for "neighborliness," see p. 198. On the many senses of "common profit" in fifteenth-century London, see Kellie Robertson, "Common Language and Common Profit," in *The Postcolonial Middle Ages*, ed. Jeffrey Jerome Cohen (London: Palgrave, 2000), pp. 209–28.

[40] See Chambers and Daunt, eds., *A Book of London English*, pp. 41–42 (the Carpenters) and pp. 113–15 (the Physicians). For discussion of bourgeois piety in fifteenth-century London, see especially Amy Appleford and Nicholas Watson, "Merchant Religion in Fifteenth-Century London: The Writings of William Litchfield," *Chaucer Review* 46 (2011), 203–22.

[41] Compare again Chambers and Daunt, eds., *A Book of London English*. On caring for the poor, see pp. 42, 112, and 199; on "common assent," see pp. 195, 196, and 199; and on livery and clothing, see pp. 197 and 199.

[42] Chambers and Daunt, eds., *A Book of London English*, p. 199.

234   TAYLOR COWDERY

This characteristic blend of piety, corporate identity, and a concern for the "common good" can likewise be found, once more, in the *Dietary*, which also insists upon the imperative to "visite þe pore" and "haue compassioun" upon the "nedy" (45); instructs us to "be clenly clad aftyr" our "estate" (33); and urges us to attend "masse" punctually and "do to god reuerence" (43–44) each morning upon rising from bed. What is more, such imperatives are presented, as in the guild ordinances, not merely as a social good, but as a good that will redound upon the individual. Through the exercise of charity and piety, the reader will accrue a distinctly material benefit: "god shall send grace and influence / the to encrese and þy possessioun" (47–48).

Sentiments such as these were ubiquitous, of course, in fifteenth-century urban culture, and it is unlikely that they would have been unknown to the readers of the *Dietary*, especially if those readers were members of the artisan and merchant classes, as I believe they typically were.[43] But it seems to me that the *Dietary* would have appealed to these readers less because of what it said and more because of how it said it. Indeed, what this poem really seems to do is to provide a style that was useful as a vessel of self-definition for the members of these relatively new classes – a certain way of speaking, or even a certain voice, that was felt to be fitting to their ethos and situation. Critics have often remarked upon the way that fifteenth-century conduct literature seems centrally concerned with "processes of differentiating subjects, displaying status, and allotting power," as Claire Sponsler puts it.[44] Conduct texts, in other words, are often centrally concerned with the class striations and subtle hierarchies that are to be found within mercantile culture and the orders of the guilds alike. But this literature could serve just as easily to project an identity or ethos that grouped together a disparate set of classes under a single banner – that of the "middle class" or the "bourgeois" or the "common." It could define for its readers a certain "place in the world," as Sheila Lindenbaum puts it, a place that was "desirable" precisely because it had an assured position within the greater "symbolic order" of bourgeois London life.[45]

Consider in this regard how the *Dietary* speaks to its reader about his worldly station. To some extent, the poem casts the value of remaining content with one's situation as a form of vaguely Boethian Stoicism. Be "ryche with litell," it advises, and "glad in pouerte," and then, provided you are "temperat" in "dyet" and "traveyle" (11), you will find yourself "mery lyke þy degre" (13–15). Here, the half-line rhythms and frequent use of imperatives project a lyric speaker whose voice is sententious and perhaps a little pedantic. But it is also a reassuring voice, for it has all the answers the reader would ever need.

---

[43] Compare Sponsler, "Eating Lessons," pp. 10–13, who proposes that the "implied reader" of the *Dietary* was a member of precisely this class, a "prosperous, leisured householder" (p. 11).

[44] Sponsler, "Eating Lessons," p. 3, and for this view of the citizens' custumals, see Richardson, *Middle-Class Writing*, p. 169.

[45] Lindenbaum, "London Texts and Literate Practice," p. 305.

COMMON STYLE AND BOURGEOIS ETHOS IN LYDGATE'S *DIETARY* 235

It tells us how to look; it tells us how to respect ourselves and our fellows; and it lays out for us the very course of our lives, from the moment of our birth up until the time of our death. As it instructs us,

> Be clenly clad aftyr thyne estate;
> Passe not þy bondys, kepe þy promise blyve;
> With thre folks be not at debate –
> ffirst with thy bettir beware for to strive,
> A-geyne þy felawe no quarell do cont[r]ive[46],
> With þy soget to striue it were shame;
> Wherfor I counsell pursue all þy lyve
> To lyve in pease and gete þe A good name. (33–40)

Everything about this passage, from its use of small-scale allegory (e.g. "thre folks") to its exceedingly reasonable rhyming pairs (e.g. "shame … name") and the perfectly regular iambic pentameter of the last two lines, seems designed to assure us that the world is an orderly and predictable place – so much so that we need merely follow the rules if we wish to "lyve in pease" and obtain "a good name." No need, here, to "strive" or "contrive." Much better to keep our "estate" happily, by avoiding "debate."

This voice is most comfortable in the mode of command; it is at once reassuring and monitory; and it sounds brusque or even a little reproachful at times. It is, in other words, a masculine voice – the voice of a father, perhaps, or maybe an uncle or older brother – and this is no coincidence. After all, a masculine voice would have been synonymous with authority in many fifteenth-century London households, and a certain style of patriarchy was endemic to the social and civic order of the city. If we turn again to the *Liber albus*, we will find that the homosocial bonds between men were often at center stage during guild and city ceremonies for the transmission of power from year to year.[47] In its discussion of the transfer of the office from one mayor to the next, for example, the *Liber* observes that the current mayor must take his successor "by the hand [*per manum*]" and "lead him down into the hall below."[48] Later, the old mayor must again "lead the future mayor by the hand" through the city streets "until they arrive at the home [*domum*] of the future mayor."[49] As Barbara Hanawalt observes, these ceremonies certainly aim to demonstrate "the continuity of the

---

[46] I have corrected Robbins's edition in this instance against the manuscript, which clearly reads "contrive" and not (as Robbins has it) "contive." See Oxford, Bodleian Library MS Rawlinson C. 86, fol. 61v.

[47] For discussion of these ceremonies and the *Liber albus*, see Barbara Hanawalt, *Ceremony and Civility: Civic Culture in Late Medieval London* (Oxford: Oxford University Press, 2017), pp. 52–80.

[48] Riley, ed., *Munimenta Gildhallae*, p. 22: "… Major, descendendo in aulum, consuevit procedure ducens secum per manum Majorem futurum pro anno sequente."

[49] Riley, ed., *Munimenta Gildhallae*, p. 24: "Gladius vero deferebatur ante conducentem secum per manum Majorem futurum … et abinde praecedebat gladius Majorem praeteritum usque in domum suam."

office and the power of the mayor," but their fatherly resonances could hardly have been lost on members of a culture that, both in the household and in the workshop, understood the transmission of power in patriarchal terms – as the passing of authority from fathers to sons, or masters to apprentices.[50] The same might be said, perhaps, of another passage in the *Liber*, one that stipulates that each alderman should "personally supervise and correct" the behavior of those serving under him if they are negligent, up to the point of acting to "reasonably [*rationabiliter*] punish and chastise them" himself.[51] Such advice would be right at home in the *Dietary*, which likewise advises the patriarchs of London to observe the members of their households with a loving but watchful eye.

> Suffir at þy tabill neuer detraccioun,
> Haue despite of folke þat ben trouble;
> Of fals rowners and adulacioun;
> Within þy court suffir no devisoun,
> Whych in þyn houshold shulde cause gret excesse. (26–30)

While the term "court" may seem to shift the poem into an aristocratic context, this "court" is surely a city or guild court instead.[52] Here, as in the "housholde" or at the "tabill," authority is said to derive not from the rights of nobility or blood, but from the civic privilege afforded to a male London citizen.[53] To "suffir no devisoun" in such a space, particularly in the face of "folke þat ben trouble," will require patience, moderation, and sound judgment, precisely the civic values that the *Dietary* celebrates.

To be sure, these privileges were not for everyone – and the same could likely be said for the avuncular tone and proverbial rhythms of the common style. But for the reader who felt an affinity to that voice, and who hoped to find a place within the bourgeois world for which it spoke, it may be that reading the *Dietary* brought forth comforting associations – say, the feeling of a warm but firm handshake. Indeed, Riddy has noted that certain fifteenth-century conduct poems notionally directed to daughters were likely intended to be read by mothers, and the equivalent is probably true of the *Dietary* as well.[54] No doubt, this poem has sometimes been cast as a lyric for young men, perhaps because it once addresses the reader as "sonn" (17).[55] But in offering the reader an occasion

---

[50] Hanawalt, *Ceremony and Civility*, p. 62.

[51] Riley, ed., *Munimenta Gildhallae*, pp. 38–39: "Et debet Aldermannus in propria persona sua supervidere et corrigere omnes defectus et nocumenta in Wardemoto … remissos vel negligentes … ipsos rationabiliter puniet et castigabit."

[52] For confusion about the meaning of "court," see Sponsler, "Eating Lessons," p. 9. For the city and guild courts, see Richardson, *Middle-Class Writing*, pp. 83–87.

[53] This "tabill" could well have been a public table, and not just a board within the household; for the role that banquets played in the construction of civic authority, see again Hanawalt, *Ceremony and Civility*, pp. 75–77.

[54] Riddy, "Mother Knows Best," p. 83.

[55] See, e.g., Pearsall, *John Lydgate*, p. 220, who is amusingly skeptical of the claim.

COMMON STYLE AND BOURGEOIS ETHOS IN LYDGATE'S *DIETARY*   237

to pronounce in his mind, or even aloud, the gospel of "suffisaunce" (14) and "gouernaunce" (16), it is more likely that the poem appealed primarily to men who sat at the head of the table in fifteenth-century London.

CONCLUSIONS

We might say, then, that the *Dietary* is a poem more concerned with the projection of a certain class sensibility than it is with the purveyance of any specific medical advice – that it may indeed be called a "dietarie," but only in the capacious sense ("way of living") that the term possessed in Middle English.[56] We might also say that the *Dietary* appealed to the merchants and artisans of fifteenth-century London not merely because it rehearsed the values that those groups prized – values such as piety, or neighborliness, or "common profit" – but because it spoke of them with a particular voice, one designed to evoke certain feelings in its audience or even to provide that audience with a new way of feeling about themselves and their place in the world.

As I have noted above, the provenance of this voice is easy enough to track. It belongs to the father, or to the head of the household, or even to the alderman – to a man, that is, who presides over his "table" or "court" as a benevolent patriarch. But the feelings that the voice plays upon are perhaps more complex. Pride, and especially pride in one's profession and one's household, is obviously one of them. But so too is a certain suspicion towards the claims of expert knowledge. Consider, for example, the final stanza of the poem, which, as I noted in my introduction, distinguishes the *Dietary* from the kinds of "resceytes" one might purchase from an accredited "poticarye."

> Thus in two þinges standith all þe welth
> Of soule and of body, whoso hem sue,
> Moderat fode gevyth to man his helth,
> And all surfetys doth from him remewe;
> And charite to þe soule is due,
> This resceyte bought is at no poticarye,
> Of master Antony nor of master hewe,
> To all indifferent þe rycheste dietarye. (73–80)

As Morrissey has noted, "Antony" and "hewe" are likely "the celebrity physicians Antonio Cermisone and Hugh of Siena," whose technical expertise is positioned as a foil to the more holistic advice offered by Lydgate's poem, here described as "þe rycheste dietarye" one could buy.[57] More important than this claim to authority, however, is the affective force behind the claim, for the *Dietary* doesn't just say that we must exercise "charite to þe soule" (77),

---

[56] For this sense of "dietarie," see Morrissey, "To Al Indifferent," p. 259 and 259, n. 14.
[57] Morrissey, "To Al Indifferent," p. 258.

be "mery" with our "degre" (15), and commit ourselves to living in "reste and pease" with our "neyghbours" (32). Rather, it declares that these notions are correct – that they are right, and that we are right to believe them, no matter what "master Antony" or "master hewe" or any other "master" might say.

What the *Dietary* really offers its readers, then, is a feeling of security and comfort. Here, the citizen is assured that the certainties of bourgeois thought still hold true; that he occupies a place in the world that is exactly right for him; and that his role in the household and his professional status are warranted, not just by his merits or social privileges, but right thinking and reasonable judgment, if not even by the will of God himself. This is high ideological fantasy, and we may wonder if some of Lydgate's readers regarded it with a skeptical eye. As Simpson would remind us, however, fifteenth-century London was a place of multiple, competing social jurisdictions, each one producing its own, "differently figured" vision of history.[58] Lydgate wrote for many of these jurisdictions. Perhaps his bourgeois public felt it was only fair that they receive a history figured on their terms as well.

[58] Simpson, *Reform and Cultural Revolution*, p. 55.

PART IV
REFORMATIONS

13

Rewriting *Robert the Devil*: Thomas Lodge and Medieval Romance

Cathy Shrank

"Romance survives the Tudor revolution," notes James Simpson: "While the events of the 1530s and 1550s provoked the radical limitation or the official repudiation of many varieties of Middle English writing, romance continued to be produced."[1] The essay that follows uses Thomas Lodge's *Famous, True and Historicall Life of Robert, Second Duke of Normandy* (1591) to examine how one such romance – in Simpson's words – "adapt[ed] to new discursive, commercial, and political environments."[2] In particular, this essay traces how Lodge's text reflects the impact of humanism and religious reformation in later Elizabethan England. It explores how Lodge's recourse to seemingly "papist" material is inflected by his confessional position, but also how it challenges reformist polemic which painted romances as morally-corrupting works, made for pleasure and time-wasting, by using romance to make moral and political arguments, and – as Edmund Spenser does from a Calvinist perspective in *The Faerie Queene* (1590) – to try to cultivate an active, ethically engaged readership.

The legend of Robert the Devil comes into English from France where it has a long literary tradition, in verse, prose, and drama; in Latin and the vernacular, going back until at least the thirteenth century.[3] Prior to Lodge's *Life*, there were at least four English versions: two lost plays (performed in Lincoln in 1453 and Chester in 1529); a prose account, *The Lyf of the Moste Myschevoust Robert the*

---

[1] James Simpson, *The Oxford English Literary History, Vol. 2: 1350–1547. Reform and Cultural Revolution* (Oxford: Oxford University Press, 2002), p. 292.

[2] Ibid., p. 293.

[3] See Élisabeth Gaucher, *Robert le Diable: histoire d'une légende* (Paris: Honoré Champion, 2003).

242 CATHY SHRANK

Devyll, published by Wynkyn de Worde, around 1500 (second edition 1517?), which is translated fairly faithfully from *La Vie de terrible Robert le Diable* (first printed in Lyon in 1496); and a version in metrical verse, derived from de Worde's *Lyf*, printed, probably by Richard Pynson, around 1510. Aside from a small fragment in the Bodleian Library, Oxford (MS Douce, Fragmn. f. 4), this version only survives in a mid-sixteenth-century manuscript transcription (London, British Library MS Egerton 3132A), which seems to have belonged to a recusant named Edward Banyster.[4]

These multiple versions share the same basic plot. The Duke and Duchess of Normandy, long-married, lack an heir, until – in despair – the Duchess abandons praying to God for a child and instead pledges any baby that she conceives to the devil. From the outset, the resulting child (Robert) is trouble. He is born in a prodigious storm, after a protracted labor (as much as a month long in some versions). His infancy and boyhood are a litany of crimes: he bites the teats off his wet-nurses; he kills his tutor; and, once of age, he becomes the leader of a band of outlaws, wreaking havoc on the surrounding countryside, raping, pillaging, and sacking religious houses. Then, at the height of his crimes, comes a moment of realization: that he is cursed, and that everyone fears him and runs from him. The second half of the narrative recounts Robert's repentance. He travels to Rome where he undergoes a penance, akin to that endured by the protagonist of the fourteenth-century *Robert of Sicily*: he must not talk; he must assume the role of a fool; and he must sleep and eat with the dogs, consuming only the food that is thrown to them. Robert consequently lives, in silence, as a fool at the Emperor's court, in most versions for a suitably mythical seven years. In the early fourteenth-century *Croniques de Normandie*, Robert – having served his penance – then departs for Jerusalem, where he dies.[5] All other versions transform him into a military hero, saving Rome from the Saracens, when the emperor's own seneschal either leads these invaders or refuses to come to the Emperor's aid. In either case, the seneschal betrays his overlord because he wants to compel the emperor to give him in marriage his beautiful – but mute – daughter. Things look bleak for the defending forces, until an angel gives Robert a white horse and armor, an incident witnessed only by the emperor's daughter. Three times (another mythic number), Robert rides out in disguise and repels the attackers. By the third occasion, the Emperor is anxious to know the identity of his savior and arranges that some of his men waylay him. Robert is wounded in the thigh in the scuffle, and the emperor sends out a proclamation that he will wed his

---

4   M. C. Seymour, "MSS Douce 261 and Egerton 3132A and Edward Banyster," *Bodleian Library Record* 10 (1980), 162–65. Banyster's recusancy is suggestive in light of Lodge's confessional position (explored below). However, as James Wade argues, penitential romances were not the sole preserve of Catholic writers and readers. See Wade, "Penitential Romance after the Reformation," in *Medieval into Renaissance: Essays for Helen Cooper*, ed. Andrew King and Matthew Woodcock (Cambridge: D. S. Brewer, 2016), pp. 91–106.

5   *Les Vraies Croniques de Normandie* (1301–25), Paris, Bibliothèque Nationale de France (BNF) MS fr. 5388, fol. 11v.

THOMAS LODGE AND MEDIEVAL ROMANCE

243

daughter to the stranger in white armor with an injured thigh. The seneschal sees his chance: he wounds himself, acquires a suitably colored horse and armor, and rides into Rome to claim his bride. The emperor's daughter, who knows the truth, tries to protest, without success, until – on the brink of marriage – she is miraculously given the power of speech and tells all; the emperor then offers her to Robert. At this point, the various endings diverge. In the thirteenth-century verse *récit*, Robert refuses the princess and ends his days as a hermit in the forest near Rome (a similar conclusion to the *Croniques*, albeit in a different geographical location).[6] Later versions impose a romantic ending, where Robert marries the princess and returns with her to Normandy where – his father dead – he rescues his mother from the persecutions of a treacherous nobleman.[7]

The precise version of the story that Lodge follows has either been lost, or he draws on more than one source, since the combination of events found in his narrative does not map onto a single, known text.[8] Lodge also transforms this conversion narrative, or penitential romance, for the marketplace of late Elizabethan print. Lodge certainly needed a nose for what would sell. The son of a bankrupt Lord Mayor of London, Lodge attended Merchant Taylors' School, and then Trinity College, Oxford, as a poor scholar.[9] After graduating, he enrolled at Lincoln's Inn, but rather than pursuing the law, made his living as a professional writer, a dereliction of duty that saw him disinherited from his mother's will. His output covers every fashionable Elizabethan genre. His prodigal fiction, *An Alarum against Usurers*, was printed in 1584 in a patently modish miscellany alongside his pastoral romance, *Forbonius and Prisceria*, and verse satire "The lamentable complaint of truth over England." *Scillaes Metamorphosis* (1589) pre-empts the 1590s vogue for Ovidian epyllia, and – following the success of Samuel Daniel's *Delia ... with the Complaint of Rosamond* (1592) – Lodge strategically coupled his sonnet sequence (*Phillis*, 1593) with female-voiced complaint ("The tragicall complaint of Elstred"), throwing in for good measure a handful of eclogues, a long-established genre given new impetus by Spenser's *Shepheardes Calender* (1579).

Lodge consequently refashions Robert's story for contemporary literary tastes. The woods in which Robert is conceived are not, as in the *Croniques*,

---

[6] Samuel N. Rosenberg, tr., *Robert the Devil: The First Modern English Translation of* Robert le Diable*, An Anonymous French Romance of the Thirteenth Century* (Pennsylvania: University Park: Pennsylvania State University Press, 2018).

[7] In order to condense the material sufficiently for dramatic representation, *Le Miracle de Robert le Diable* (c. 1339–50) omits the staging of Robert's birth and childhood, and his return to Normandy. See Gaucher, *Robert le Diable*, pp. 112–15.

[8] Lodge, for instance, follows the *Croniques* in the immediate build-up to Robert's repentance (by having him wounded by a vengeful father) but includes material that the *Croniques* omits, including the assault on Rome, marriage to the emperor's daughter, and Robert's return to Normandy.

[9] Biographical details in this paragraph from Alexandra Halasz, "Lodge, Thomas (1558–1625)," *Oxford Dictionary of National Biography* (Oxford: Oxford University Press, 2004), https://www.oxforddnb.com (accessed 26 January 2023).

244 CATHY SHRANK

a forbidding place, beyond the civil bounds, in which the duke forces himself upon his wife.[10] Rather, they are transformed into a bower of bliss and erotic delight, from which the couple will "return ... homewards with privie smiles":

> Heere saw [the duke] a faire delicious brooke, recording musick in his course, being christall in cleerenes, environed with faire Ceders so orderly arranged, as Arte could not in more excellence exemplifie the effects of perfection. On that side a closed Arbor beawtifyed with Roses, paved with Violets, on the top whereof, the byrds with melodious musick animated the flowres, and the flowres assisted by the Westerne coole wyndes, seemed to daunce for delight, and to florish.[11]

The landscape here described by Lodge is not wild and threatening, but is firmly located within a then voguish mode of pastoral romance, as exemplified by Philip Sidney's *Arcadia* or Lodge's own *Rosalynde* (both printed in 1590).[12] The countryside in this tradition is decorous, tamed by the obvious artifice of the description, with its tendency to frame nature in terms of human activities (such as gardening, architecture, or other arts).

This self-conscious updating of his source material is also evident in Lodge's style, as can be seen by comparing his opening sentence with that in de Worde's version. De Worde's reads:

> It befel in tyme past there was a duke in normandye whiche was called ouberte the whiche duke was passinge ryche of goodes & also vertuous of lyvynge and loved and dred god above al thinge and dede greate almosse dedes and exceded all other in ryghtwysnesse and justice / and mooste chevalrouse in dedes of armes and notable actes doinge.[13]

This paratactic style characterizes much late medieval English prose. In contrast, Lodge deploys subordinate clauses to the point of digressiveness:

> In the populous and plentifull Dukedome of *Normandie*, (in times past called *Neustria*) at such time as *Pepin* the Father of the great King *Charlemaigne* governed the flourishing Kingdome of *Fraunce*, *Aubert* the first Duke of that Countrey, by some supposed to be *Ron* of *Denmarke*, began to signorize in the same about the yeare of our Lord 750[,] a Prince by nature affable, in nurture fortunate, as glorious for his Conquests, as

---

10   BNF MS fr. 5388, fol. 10r.
11   Thomas Lodge, *The Famous, True and Historicall Life of Robert, Second Duke of Normandy* (London: Thomas Orwin, 1591), sigs. B3v, B2r–v.
12   Compare the descriptions of landscapes in Philip Sidney, *The Countess of Pembrokes Arcadia* (London: John Windet for William Ponsonby, 1590), fol. 7r, and Thomas Lodge, *Rosalynde* (London: Thomas Orwin for T. G[ubbin] and John Busbie, 1590), sig. E4r.
13   Anon., *The Lyf of the Moste Myschevoust Robert the Devyll* (London: Wynkyn de Word, 1500?), sig. A2r.

THOMAS LODGE AND MEDIEVAL ROMANCE

245

gratious in his curtesies, enterprising his attempts with *Metellus* constancie, and finishing the same with *Alexanders* fortune.[14]

Lodge's meandering opening sentence (nearly twice as long as de Worde's) is highly mannered, the parallel constructions (*isocola*) further highlighted by sonic repetition (such as alliteration or prose rhyme), a feature of Euphuism, the literary style that became fashionable in the wake of John Lyly's *Euphues* (1578).

The difference in style between de Worde's and Lodge's version owes much (if not everything) to the spread, over the course of the sixteenth century, of humanist educational practices, not least of which was the promotion of a written style which abhorred, and actively avoided, monotony of vocabulary and syntax. Desiderius Erasmus's *De copia* – a staple school text-book from its publication in 1512 – famously celebrates and promotes a varied and copious style (for instance, teaching its users to say "your letter pleased me greatly" in 150 different ways). As Erasmus declares (in Betty I. Knott's translation), "Exercise in expressing oneself in different ways will be of considerable importance in general for the acquisition of style .... Variety is so powerful in every sphere that there is absolutely nothing, however brilliant, which is not dimmed if not commended by variety."[15] The use of double translation, meanwhile, was intended to test, and improve, pupils' Latin style.[16] However, the process also invited scrutiny of English style, as can be seen from William Cecil's memories of his own tutelage under the influential Cambridge academic John Cheke:

> One manner of his, amongst dyvers excellent, was this; – to appoint those that weare under hym, and that he desired shoulde moste profytt, to take a peece of Tullie [Cicero], and to translate it into Englishe, and after, (laying their bookes asyde,) to translate the same againe into Latine, and then to compare them with the booke, and to consider whiche weare don aptelie, or unproperlie; and howe neare Tullie's phrase was followed in the Latine, *and the most sweete and sensyble wrytinge in Englishe*; contynewinge with this kinde of exercise once or twice in a weeke, for two or three yeres, *you shall come to write (as he dyd) singularlie in both tongues.*[17]

Imitating Latin – particularly Ciceronian Latin, with its propensity for complex, periodic sentences (the benchmark for a mature Latin style) – and the promotion of a copious style shaped assumptions about what constituted "good" English prose.

---

[14] Lodge, *Life*, sig. B1r.

[15] Desiderius Erasmus, *Copia: Foundations of the Abundant Style: De duplici copia verborum ac rerum Comentarii duo*, in *Collected Works of Erasmus*, vol. 24, ed. and tr. Betty I. Knott (Toronto: Toronto University Press, 1978), p. 302.

[16] William E. Miller, "Double Translation in English Humanistic Education," *Studies in the Renaissance* 10 (1963), 163–74.

[17] William Cecil to John Harington (1578), in John Harington, *Nugae Antiquae*, ed. Henry Harington (London: J. Wright, 1804), vol. I, 133–34 (emphases added).

246 CATHY SHRANK

Lodge's refashioning of Robert's story is thus a measure of how perceptions of, and discourses about, the linguistic resources of English had changed since the opening decades of the sixteenth century when – at the beginning of a self-consciously neologizing phase – the poet Thomas Wyatt lamented the "lacke of such diversyte in our tong" which left it wanting "a great dele of the grace" available to writers in Latin.[18] In contrast, if the authors of Lodge's generation apologize, it is (usually with notable insincerity) for their own lack of proficiency, not for the inadequacies of their native language.[19] They revel in linguistic display, rarely using one word where ten will do, as seen in Lodge's lists of Euphuistic similes: the attempt of Robert's schoolmaster to discipline his pupil is as "frustrate [as those] who seeke to bring *Caucasus* into a plaine, to bereave *India* of gems, *Candia* of oyles, *Cochim* of pepper, or *Hibla* of honey"; Robert himself is "more obstinate than the Northern wind, more indurate than the hard Marble, more cruell than the *Libian* Lyonesse, more perverse than the *Lidian* tyrryant."[20] Such use of amplification – saying the same thing more than once – is recommended by the rhetorician Thomas Wilson as the "chief" help "if either wee purpose to make our tale appere vehemente, to seme pleasaunt, or to be well stored with muche copie."[21] That this linguistic exuberance is designed to speak to contemporary tastes is evident from the way it is used to sell Lodge's book, with the "manie conceits" (i.e. "ingenious, witty expressions") that it contains advertised on the title page.[22]

As Lodge infuses the *Robert* narrative with classical allusions and recasts it in a style that is indebted to the humanist education that he and the previous generation of English authors had received, he epitomizes the way in which, as Helen Cooper notes, "humanism was a development added on to strong and deeply embedded native cultural and literary traditions," with "romance ... one of the most strongly rooted of all those traditions."[23] Whilst Cooper proceeds to observe that "any classical air about [romance] was rarely more than a surface gloss, for a humanist author to show off his fashionability," in the section that follows, I want to argue that Lodge's *Life* is one of the rarities this comment allows for: its classicism is not simply a veneer; it is used to interrogate – and stress-test – the ideological foundations of his humanist education.

---

[18] Thomas Wyatt, *The Quyete of Mynde* (London: Richard Pynson, 1528), sig. A1v.

[19] This humility is not unique to later sixteenth-century writers. See David Lawton, "Dullness in the Fifteenth Century," *English Literary History* 54 (1987), 761–99. For the later sixteenth-century confidence in the vernacular, see Richard Mulcaster (Lodge's former head teacher): "such a period in the Greke tung was that time, when *Demosthenes* lived ...: such a period in the Latin tung, was that time, when *Tullie* lived, and those of that age: Such a period in the English tung I take this to be in our daies, for both the pen and the speche," *The First Parte of the Elementarie* (London: Thomas Vautrollier, 1582), sig. K2r.

[20] Lodge, *Life*, sigs. C1r, C2v.

[21] Thomas Wilson, *The Arte of Rhetorique* (London: Richard Grafton, 1553), sig. Q4r.

[22] *OED*, "conceit, n.," sense 10b.

[23] Helen Cooper, *The English Romance in Time: Transforming Motifs from Geoffrey of Monmouth to the Death of Shakespeare* (Oxford: Oxford University Press, 2004), pp. 5, 6.

THOMAS LODGE AND MEDIEVAL ROMANCE

In the words of Lodge's former headmaster, Richard Mulcaster, the whole purpose of that education was to train its pupils to "serve abrode in publik functions of the common weal."[24] The public utility of education permeates Mulcaster's writings, from his discussion about which social background was most likely "to bring forth that student, which must serve his country best" to his call to limit the numbers receiving a university education, lest too many be "left gaping for preferment," threatening the peace of the realm. "To[o] many learned be to[o] burdenous," Mulcaster warns: "wittes well sorted be most civill, that the same misplaced be most unquiet and seditious."[25] Mulcaster's qualms were realized, and Lodge was part of that "unquiet" generation graduating from university in the 1570s and 1580s: men who had been trained to serve in offices of state, but for whom few such employment opportunities were on offer. As Richard Helgerson recounts (drawing on Laurence Stone's research), by the middle years of the sixteenth century,

> gentry made up about half the population of Oxford and over 80 percent of that of the inns of court. The extraordinary recourse of gentlemen's sons to the seats of learning … had, however, an unforeseen result. It quickly saturated the offices of the state with men trained in good letters, leaving few openings for those who came behind.[26]

As a consequence, according to Helgerson, many – like Lyly, Lodge, or their contemporary Robert Greene – turned to their pen. The works they wrote "express rebellion, defensiveness, and guilt – an acute consciousness that they were not doing what they had been brought up to do."[27]

Lodge's position in the *Life* is more complex and equivocal than Helgerson's words suggest: as we will see, he does not entirely abandon a fittingly civic humanist interest in the proper workings of government, nor lose faith in the ethical potential of literature. Nonetheless, there is, undoubtedly, a strong vein of defiance. At least at the outset, the very choice and treatment of his subject matter appear to be in opposition to humanist beliefs about the proper – that is, morally instructive – purpose of literature. Lodge produces exactly the tale of "open mans slaughter, and bold bawdrye" denounced by that arch-humanist Roger Ascham (one of Cheke's acolytes) in both *Toxophilus* (1545) and *The Scholemaster* (1570).[28] In the process, Lodge systematically increases both the amount of violence in his narrative and the detail with which those events are

---

[24] Mulcaster, *First Part*, sig. ¶2v.

[25] Richard Mulcaster, *Positions wherin those Primitive Circumstances be Examined, which are Necessarie for the Training up of Children* (London: Thomas Vautrollier for Thomas Chard, 1581), sigs. S2v, R3v.

[26] Richard Helgerson, *The Elizabethan Prodigals* (Berkeley, Calif.: University of California Press, 1976), p. 23. The oversupply of graduates was not unique to this period. See Kathryn Kerby-Fulton, *The Clerical Proletariat and the Resurgence of Medieval English Poetry* (Philadelphia: University of Pennsylvania Press, 2021).

[27] Helgerson, *Elizabethan Prodigals*, p. 23.

[28] Roger Ascham, *The Scholemaster* (London: John Day, 1570), sig. I2r; cf. Ascham, *Toxophilus* (London: Edward Whitchurch, 1545), sig. A1r.

248 CATHY SHRANK

recounted. Take the various outrages that Robert commits on the religious houses of Normandy. In the versions most readily available to Lodge (*La Vie*, de Worde's *Lyf*, Pynson's metrical version), the accounts of Robert's viciousness lack specificity. De Worde's summative headings characteristically supply as much detail as the chapters they introduce: "How Robert the devyll rode aboute the countree of normandy robbynge stelinge morderynge & brennynge chyrches abbayes & other holy places of religion & forsynge of women & ravysshynge of maydens."[29] They rarely focus on individual victims, or do so only fleetingly. Lodge, in contrast, lingers over episodes. The account of the rape and murder of a nun on the eve of Robert's inauguration as knight, covered in the *Croniques* within a few lines, is expanded to fill almost a page, for instance, as Lodge catalogues the parade of nuns, from which Robert "made choyce of the fairest," her entreaties, his violation of her, and his final act of aggression, in which he kills her by "cut[ting] off both her papps."[30]

However, it is not simply that Lodge increases cruelty and violence: he also aestheticizes it. The episode with the nun epitomizes this narrative mode, chillingly juxtaposing horror and beauty. As the moon "beautifie[s] with her sparkling brightnesse the diffused darkenesse," we are reminded that Robert is "more vigilant in vilanie, than valiant in vertue." The linguistic patterning threatens to gloss over, or lend verbal logic to, the depravity of the scene, which ends with "the bloodsucking wretch" (Robert), having "satisfied his lewd lust," riding back to the city, "embrued in the purple drops of the murthered Lady." At this point the narrative shifts startlingly in tone (but not in colour palate), describing how "the mornings roseate coatch beawtifie[d] the East with vermelion rednesse, and the faire breathing Steeds of the Sunne mount[ed] above the bosome of *Oceanus*." This type of periphrastic description of the dawn recurs throughout Lodge's *Rosalynde*, but has a rather different tenor embedded in a pastoral romance, rousing lovers from their beds, than here, following a sadistic murder.

The aestheticization, or even eroticization, of violence sets Lodge's treatment of brutality apart from the analogous material, which frequently treats bloodshed and cruelty with grim humor: a "diabolic, cynical laughter," Élisabeth Gaucher writes of the fourteenth-century *Dit de Robert Le Diable*.[31] So, for example, when the *Dit*'s Robert kills his schoolmaster, he does so with a pun: "Mestre, moustrez vo maistrise de la" ("Master, demonstrate your mastery of that"). Or we have the importation into the *Vie* of elements belonging to the jest book tradition (sections subsequently adopted in both de Worde's prose and the English metrical version): whilst enduring his penance as a mute fool at the Emperor's court in Rome, Robert "made a Jewe to kysse his dogges arse at the

---

[29] Anon., *Lyf*, sig. A7v; cf. "Comment Robert sen alia par le pays de normandie roubant & pillant tout le pays forcant et destruisant femmes & violant poures filles pucelles," Anon., *La vie de terrible Robert le diable* (Lyon: Pierre Mareschal et Barnabé Chaussard, 1496), sig. A6v.

[30] BNF MS fr. 5388, fol. 10v; Lodge, *Life*, sigs. C3r–v.

[31] "l'auditeur entend résonner un rire diabolique, cynique," Gaucher, *Robert le Diable*, p. 109.

THOMAS LODGE AND MEDIEVAL ROMANCE   249

Emperours table."[32] He also leads a bride "through a passyng foule dong hyll," before catching "a lyvynge catte," which he casts into a "sethynge potte [of] podred befe" being prepared for the wedding feast.[33] These events, we are told, constitute "madde or mery conceyte[s] to cause the Emperour to laugh."[34] Brutal humor is certainly present in Lodge's narrative: his Robert bites off, not merely his wet-nurse's nipples, but also the nose of the Lady of Sancerre when she stoops to kiss him in his cradle.[35] For the most part, though, the violence tends not towards what readers (or auditors) are invited to understand as "comic," but to the sensational: incidents which dwell upon Robert's sadistic acts, such as the piecemeal dismemberment of a bridegroom, whilst Robert attempts to coerce the bride to have sex with him (an episode – again expanded from a few lines in the *Croniques* – which occupies three pages of narrative).[36]

Lodge's amplification and aestheticization of violence is not a purely commercially-minded, crowd-pleasing gesture, however: it serves to probe assumptions underpinning his humanist education. He does not only update the legend by lending it a voguish Euphuism, or elements of pastoral romance. He also imbues the text with an anxiety which resonates throughout much later Elizabethan writing: namely, a compulsion to test the efficacy, or not, of humanist belief in the improving powers of education and of persuasion, which (following authors such as Cicero) is given a key role in the founding, and maintenance, of civil society. As Thomas Elyot writes:

> noble autours do affirme that, in the first infancie of the worlde, men, wandring like beastes in woddes and on mountaines, regardinge neither the religion due unto god, nor the office pertaining unto man, ordred all thing by bodily strength: untill Mercurius (as Plato supposeth) or some other man holpen by sapience and eloquence, by some apt or propre oration, assembled them togeder and perswaded them what commodite was in mutual conversation and honest maners.[37]

Tudor educationalists, such as Elyot, further assert that reading the right books will make you a good person. Sidney's *Defence of Poesy*, for example, written in the early 1580s, deems poetry "prince" over all other skills because it is the

---

[32] Anon., *Lyf*, sig. C7r; "Comment Robert sit baiser le cul de son chien a ung juif qui disnoit avec lempereur," *Vie*, sig. C2r.

[33] Anon., *Lyf*, sigs. C7v–C8r; "lamena en la plus grande fange que fust en toute la rue & la fit tomber tellement quelle en fut toute soillee"; "il print ung chat & le getta tout vif en une chaudiere en laquelle cuysoient les viands du disner," *Vie*, sig. C2v.

[34] Anon., *Lyf*, sig. C7v; "quelque esbatement pour rire & passer son temps," *Vie*, sig. C2r.

[35] Lodge, *Life*, sig. B4v.

[36] BNF MS fr. 5388, fol. 11r; Lodge, *Life*, sigs. D1r–D2v.

[37] Thomas Elyot, *The Governour* (London: Thomas Berthelet, 1531), fol. 47r. For Cicero's version, see *De Inventione*, ed. and tr. H. M. Hubbell (Cambridge, Mass.: Harvard University Press, 1949), 1.2–3. Versions of this passage recur throughout sixteenth-century works of a humanist bent; see, for example, the preface of Wilson's *Rhetorique*.

250 CATHY SHRANK

one best able to "bring forth" "virtuous action."[38] It is this same notion that late Elizabethan authors recurrently subvert: in Shakespeare's *Titus Andronicus* (first performed c. 1588–93; printed in 1594), the lesson that Tamora's sons take from their boyhood study of Ovid's *Metamorphoses* is that, if you want to rape someone and escape detection, you need to cut off your victim's hands as well as her tongue, so that – unlike Philomel – she cannot weave her narrative into a tapestry. Or think of Sidney's own *Astrophil and Stella* (printed in 1591), where we see the humanistically educated protagonist disappointing the "great expectation" of his birth and education, uninterested in great matters of state, unmoved by ancient authors (like Plato), and instead deploying all his learning and rhetorical skills to seduce a married woman.[39] It is this failure of education, or literature, to guarantee its moral efficaciousness that Lodge exposes in his retelling of Robert's story. Robert murders his schoolmaster, not with any old knife, but with a pen-knife: a necessary piece of schoolroom equipment.[40] Like Robert in the *Dit*, he takes pleasure in this (as in his other crimes); he does it "smiling," but he does not seal his act with a pun (as in the French version), but with a quotation from Ovid's *Metamorphoses*, from the killing of Pentheus in Book 3: "Ille mihi feriandus aper" ("That boar is mine for the striking").[41] The protagonist of traditional *Robert* narratives is generally portrayed as unwilling to learn, hurling his books "ageynst the walles" or at his master's head ("ala testa").[42] In contrast, Lodge's Robert displays an appetite and ability for study, although the lessons he draws from his schoolbooks are disturbing, as illustrated by an incident added by Lodge, when

> Hearing his Tutor one day discoursing upon the nature of *Cicuta* [hemlock], he gave diligent attention to his doctrine, and finding out the simple, he prepared the same according as hee was instructed, and presented it to his masters sonne[,] a child of rare towardnesse, who no sooner tasted thereof, but with vehement and bitter agonies gave up the ghost.[43]

This callous murder becomes a vehicle by which Lodge can emphasize not only his protagonist's depravity but also the fiction that education necessarily makes you a better person. Responding to the schoolmaster's understandably "pitiful bemonings," Robert cruelly flaunts the fact that he has undertaken this murder as an educational experiment: "Master (sayd he) I have but put in practise that which you have taught me in precept, and since I find you a man of such credite, I will boldly write under your lesson *probatum est* [it is proven]."[44] Elsewhere we

---

[38] Philip Sidney, *The Defence of Poesy*, in *Sir Philip Sidney: The Major Works*, ed. Katherine Duncan-Jones (Oxford: Oxford University Press, 2002), p. 220.

[39] Philip Sidney, *Astrophil and Stella*, in *Major Works*, ed. Duncan-Jones, Sonnet 21, lines 7, 5.

[40] Lodge, *Life*, sig. C1v.

[41] Ovid, *Metamorphoses*, ed. Frank Justus Miller, rev. G. P. Goold (Cambridge, Mass.: Harvard University Press, 1916), 3.715. Translation mine.

[42] Anon., *Lyf*, sig. A5r; *Vie*, sig. A4r.

[43] Lodge, *Life*, sigs. B4v–C1r.

[44] Ibid., sig. C1r.

THOMAS LODGE AND MEDIEVAL ROMANCE

find Robert Latinising *ex-tempore*, as with the ominous quip, "*Quae superflua sunt, abscidenda sunt*" ("what is superfluous must be removed"), when he cuts off the beards of old men who dare to offer him counsel (the threat being that they risk being as redundant, and as easy to prune, as their facial hair).[45] "Studie" for Robert is not scholarship, but "how to invent new lamentable stratagems"; eloquent he might be, but he is "eloquent, but in impietie."[46]

Books, then, do not inevitably make their readers virtuous, and nor do books always seek to do so. In one of his many Euphuistic parallelisms, for example, Lodges notes how "in reading the Poets [Robert] despised the precepts of worth, and delighted in the poems of wantonnes."[47] Readers have the opportunity to experience some such lascivious poetry in a sequence which Lodge adds to the source material. En route to Rome, the now penitent Robert has to pass through a "thicke Wood," a symbolic landscape which owes much to the Arthurian tradition, and which he later discovers from a handy hermit is called "le bois du temptation."[48] Here he slays a lion (which he and we are later told is emblematic of overcoming fear) and demonstrates his resistance to lust when he staves off the advances of a "faire delicious Damosell" who tries to seduce him with a *carpe diem* song: "Plucke the fruite and tast the pleasure", "After death when you are gone, / Joy and pleasure is there none."[49] Poetry thus occupies a rather ambivalent position within Lodge's *Life*, and the unease about the morality of the literary arts threatens to extend to the fiction that Lodge himself is writing.

In one of the few extended critical discussions of Lodge's writings, Helgerson contrasts Lodge's fictions with those of his "prodigal" generation: "Unlike [George] Gascoigne, Lyly, Greene, or Sidney, Lodge rarely invites his reader to make the leap from literature to life," he argues; "Prodigal and critic may be the roles most often dramatized in his fiction, but Lodge does not ask us to think him the one playing those roles."[50] Lodge certainly does not, like those other authors, insert playful *alter egos* into his works: there is no equivalent to Sidney's Astrophil to lure us into autobiographical readings, or Greene's frame authors, repenting their waywardness. However, in the *Life*, Lodge does align narrator and protagonist, and – in doing so – invites us to reflect on the ethics of authorship, just as those other writers do, with their use of morally flawed personae. As Lodge's narrator slips into citing Latin commonplaces and lines of poetry, his voice starts to sound uncomfortably like that of his protagonist, particularly as this is a practice that he, like Robert, only displays in the opening, pre-conversion part of the story. Like Robert, the narrator reaches for Ovid's *Metamorphoses* in the face of brutality. "Great were the clamours of the poore," he writes:

---

[45] Ibid., sig. C2r.
[46] Ibid., sigs. C3v, B4v.
[47] Ibid., sig. B4v.
[48] Ibid., sig. F4r.
[49] Ibid., sig. F3r.
[50] Helgerson, *Elizabethan Prodigals*, p. 107.

252 CATHY SHRANK

the cryes of the oppressed, the complaints of the fatherlesse, the weepings of the widdowes, the father for his child, the child for his father, the mother for her sonne, the sonne for his mother.

> *Nec quicquam nis vulnus erat, cruor undique manat.*[51]

The *mise-en-page* – with the quotation on a separate line, off-set from the margin, in italic type – is that also used for Robert's Latin quotations. Voice of narrator and protagonist sound, and look, the same. The source of the quotation – Ovid's description of Apollo flaying Marsyas, in *Metamorphoses* 6 – is also telling: this is an episode which displays profound anxiety about the relationship between art and violence. As Bruce Holsinger shows, this problematic dynamic is often revealed most clearly through visual representations, which recurrently portray Marsyas with his arms twisted back above his head, mirroring the shape of Apollo's discarded lyre, whilst the knife that Apollo uses to skin him resembles the plectrum that the god would use to pluck its strings.[52] Lodge's choice of this quotation is thus loaded with resonance: it is a profoundly self-scrutinizing moment, in which the writer/artist is forced to recognise their own complicity, as they make art out of violence. This moment of reflection is further enabled by the switch into Latin, which halts the narrative drive: a cue to readers that they too should step back from the narrative and think about what is occurring.

Lodge's romance is not a manifesto against poetry and eloquence, in other words. Rather, the work probes the double-edged nature of verbal proficiency. Despite the humanist maxim that "the good will not speake evill, and the wicked can not speake well," Lodge's *Life* is all too aware that this is not the case, as is made apparent through some of the changes that Lodge makes to the events leading up to the attack on Rome.[53] In Lodge's account, the Emperor's mute daughter has a name, Emine.[54] Her would-be lover is now the Sultan of Babylon, a substitution for the seneschal in the other versions that may owe something to the story of Sir Gowther (a fifteenth-century English romance which has almost exactly the same plot as *Robert the Devil*). This alternative allows for a shift in the examination of power. When the frustrated lover was the seneschal, the attack on Rome was an act of treachery, a violation of feudal loyalties. Making the lover a ruler in his own right changes the dynamic and provides Lodge with the opportunity to depict the potent – but problematic – role of counsel. When we first meet the Sultan, he is fairly harmless: love-sick, he has retreated into a

---

51 Lodge, *Life*, sig. D1r. The quotation is Ovid, *Metamorphoses*, 6.388: "he is all one wound; blood flows down on every side."

52 Bruce Holsinger, *Music, Body, and Desire in Medieval Culture* (Stanford, Calif.: Stanford University Press, 2002), esp. pp. 55–57.

53 Wilson, *Arte of Rhetorique*, sig. 2G3r; cf. Quintilian, *The Orator's Education*, ed. and tr. Donald A. Russell (Cambridge, Mass.: Harvard University Press, 2002), 2.15.28.

54 That this is the same name as the Lady of Beaumont, whom Robert attempts to rape and then murders, is possibly an error on Lodge's part, but it also underscores the similarities between the two women, both of whom excite desire and both of whom are seen as objects there for the taking.

THOMAS LODGE AND MEDIEVAL ROMANCE

253

pleasure palace, and has taken to composing sonnets, the archetypal sign of a lover in the literature of this period, as can be seen from Shakespeare's parody of such behaviour in *Love's Labours Lost*, where the "affected Spanish braggart" Armado renounces his military profession: "Adieu, valour! rust rapier! be still, drum! for your manager is in love; yea, he loveth. Assist me, some extemporal god of rhyme, for I am sure I shall turn sonnet. Devise, wit; write, pen; for I am for whole volumes in folio."[55] With the Sultan similarly turned lover, his formerly warlike nation is now left idly – and dangerously – kicking its heels. He is only persuaded out of this pacific torpor by his nobleman, Behenzar.

The role Lodge gives to counsel in fomenting war connects the way in which he uses the *Robert* legend to explore the ambivalence of the art of eloquence with another facet that he brings to the *Robert* tradition: namely, a greater focus on governance. Lodge consistently increases the attention paid to the impact of Robert's predations on his father's dukedom. All versions mention Robert's victims, but only in Lodge's account are those victims also explicitly positioned as members of a political ecosystem. Lodge highlights the economic consequences of Robert's crimes: "leaving no meanes unattempted whereby he might glorie in his ungodlines, there was no free passage to any citie, the Merchants were beaten and their goods taken from them, the Market wives spoyled, and their victualls bereft them, so that this flourishing Dukedome seemed almost decayed," he records.[56] Robert's conversion is not simply a religious one in which he recognises his sinfulness; he also becomes aware of the effect on the polity of his criminality. When his followers will not repent, Robert "put them all to death, as being vipers in his fathers common weale," the first time that the narrative deploys the word "common weale," a term which depicts the workings of state as symbiotic.[57] Robert's coming to consciousness is thus mirrored by the narrative, which now recognizes a model of governance that is not simply a hierarchical one of ruler and ruled, but one where everyone's fates are intertwined.

Aside from spawning a sociopathic son, Robert's father (Aubert) is presented in Lodge's narrative as a responsible ruler, concerned for the succession, using appropriate mechanisms of government, and viewing his dukedom – in his own words – as a "common weale" to which he has responsibilities.[58] We are repeatedly told, for instance, that he consults his council, as was expected in a properly functioning polity.[59] Yet even so, Lodge uses one of his additions to the *Robert* tradition to highlight the dangers of autocratic systems of government, however benign. When Lodge's first, French hermit comes to the palace to inform Robert's parents that their son is alive and penitent, he begins

---

[55] William Shakespeare, *Love's Labours Lost*, in *The Oxford Shakespeare*, ed. John Jowettt et al., 2nd ed. (Oxford: Oxford University Press, 2005), *dramatis personae* (p. 308), 1.2.172–75.

[56] Lodge, *Life*, sig. D3r.

[57] Ibid., sig. C4r.

[58] Ibid., sig. D4v.

[59] Ibid., sigs. D2v, D4v.

254   CATHY SHRANK

his speech – not with his news – but with a digression on the sycophantic malleability of a ruler's subjects:

> At the entraunce of thy Pallace[,] *Aubert*[,] I see men weeping, because the report runneth thou are wretched; thus are all affections ruled by the affaires of the mightie, and honour is so a savourie a thing in those mens mindes, who would be great, that it sootheth, and is soothed by all sorts of them. In *Trajans* time, all men loved justice, because he was just: in *Octavians* before him, all hunted after peace, in that he was peaceable: in *Heliogabulus* dayes all were wanton, in that he was wanton: and now, since thy minde is vexed with doubtfull griefe, thy subjects likewise are attaynted.[60]

There is, in other words, a greater attention in Lodge's version to the complexities – and complications – of the ties that bind leader and led.

Despite its often sensational violence and its subversion of the notion that eloquence and education are necessarily tools of social improvement, Lodge's retelling of the *Robert* narrative is consequently not an outright rejection of humanist precepts. At its core remains a key tenet of humanist thinking, namely a concern to analyze the workings of state and to interrogate the best form of government. In taking on Robert's story, Lodge fashions this long-established narrative to suit later Elizabethan tastes and expectations: his version displays a penchant for *copia*; it frets about the ethics and efficacy of eloquence; and it makes space for moments in which we see, not just the actions of a ruling elite, but also the consequences for the people they govern. This latter point is not unconnected to the text's intended audience. Peppered with untranslated snippets of Latin, the text assumes a primary readership of educated men (boys being much more likely in this period to receive a classical education). The maleness of this intended audience is made apparent in the prefatory and valedictory addresses, both of which begin "Gentlemen": a status which Lodge also claims for himself, using the initials "TLG" ("Thomas Lodge, Gent") no less than four times in the opening four pages.[61] Lodge, in other words, is writing for his male peers, exactly the sort of readers who might be expected both to know Latin and concern themselves with matters of state.

Writing post-Reformation, Lodge also has to modify the theological elements of his base tale. Traces of the Reformation can certainly be seen in the British Library copy of de Worde's 1517 edition, where a zealous reader has attempted either to score or scratch out every mention of the word *pope*.[62] Lodge allows the word *pope* to remain (he does not demote him to the Bishop of Rome, in line with reformist terminology), but, tellingly, a propensity for "greate almosse dedes" is not used as a sign of Aubert's good character, as it is in de Worde; nor is such a Catholic practice deemed a suitable response to his wife's danger

---

[60] Ibid., sig. F1r. Lodge's narrative has three hermits, more than other versions: the first heals Robert and witnesses his initial conversion; Robert meets the second en route to Rome; the third, near Rome, sets his penance.

[61] Ibid., A2v, M3v; A1r, A2r (twice), A2v.

[62] British Library C.21.c.11.

THOMAS LODGE AND MEDIEVAL ROMANCE

in childbirth, whereas – in de Worde's version – she is saved by "good prayers … & almesse dedes / good works & grete penaunce done for her."[63] As Wade notes, "Gone, too, is any … correlation between penance and absolution …. The major spiritual battle in this 1591 version has nothing to do with the austerity of Robert's pilgrimage to Rome, nor with any adversary he may face there."[64] Instead, like Spenser's Red Crosse Knight in Book 1 of *The Faerie Queene*, "the principal adversary is 'despair', or as Lodge also put it, 'cursed melancholie.'"[65]

Lodge also diminishes the supernatural elements. Robert is armed by Emine, not – as in other versions – by an angel. Similarly, the forces which lead characters to sin or repentance are internalized. The duke in the *Vie* and de Worde's version is "tempted" by the devil whilst out hunting, who "troublede his mynde," prompting him to return to the castle, the bedchamber, and Robert's ill-fated conception; in the accompanying woodcut in the 1517 de Worde edition we can see the devils surrounding the marital bed.[66] In contrast, Lodge's Aubert is driven into the woods by the excessive heat of the day, where he overhears, and is moved by, his wife's despair, as – over the course of an entire page – she laments her barrenness in another favourite Elizabethan rhetorical set-piece: *prosopopoeia* (speaking in the voice of another), a staple classroom exercise, the legacy of which we see playing out in Elizabethan vernacular literature, not least the vogue for female-voiced complaint, such as Lodge's own *Elstred*.[67] The conception of Lodge's Robert is occasioned by both material factors and Aubert's compassion for his wife's sorrow, as comforting her soon leads to more intimate embraces.

Robert's conversion is similarly given a logical context. Gravely wounded by the Duke of Coutances, the vengeful father of one of his hapless victims, Robert is ripe for conversion: weakened by "the great expence of blood, the long and wearie course of travell …[,] a hidden affliction of the minde began with such horror to attaine him."[68] That Robert's repentance comes at a moment when the protagonist is at a low physical ebb lends his otherwise sudden conversion some degree of realism. Moreover, the actual catalyst for contrition is due, not to a miracle, but to the lessons of Robert's schoolmaster, which finally, belatedly take effect: Robert remains unable to articulate his penitence, "neither knowing how to amend [his faults] they were so infinite, nor reconcile himselfe he had been so dissolute," until

> lifting up his eyes to heaven, he beheld the Moone performing her course, the Starres ministring their dueties, and by their celestiall beautie began with himselfe to imagine the beautie of their maker, then called he to

---

[63] Anon., *Lyf*, sigs. A2r, A5r.

[64] Wade, "Penitential Romance," pp. 104–05.

[65] Ibid., p. 105, citing Lodge, *Life*, sig. E2v.

[66] Anon., *Robert the Devyll* (London: Wynkyn de Worde, 1517?), sig. A4v; "le dyable & qui tousjours est prest a decepuoit le genre humain si tempta le duc & luy troubla lentendement," *Vie*, sig. A4r.

[67] Lynn Enterline, *Shakespeare's Schoolroom: Rhetoric, Discipline, Emotion* (Philadelphia: University of Pennsylvania Press, 2012), esp. pp. 9–32.

[68] Lodge, *Life*, sig. E1r. The 1591 text has "*Constances*." Since the name is spelled like this throughout, the misreading must lie with Lodge rather than the compositor.

256 CATHY SHRANK

remembrance the olde rudiments of his master, as touching the essence and power of God.[69]

Nonetheless, the narrative cannot be entirely denuded of wonder. Emine's sudden acquisition of the power of speech, ascribed to "the wonderous works of almightie GOD," is too integral to the plot to be avoidable; and the totality of Robert's transformation is miraculous, even without the presence of angels.[70]

Despite the stripping out or downplaying of miracle and religious ritual, Lodge's choice of a story, tracking the conversion of its protagonist from a state of error to a state of grace, is striking, and must have been personal, not least because – as we have seen – the narrative voice mirrors the hero's own literary-linguistic propensities. Lodge was certainly Catholic in later life. After 1611, he "was protected from prosecution for recusancy by order of the privy council," and there are indications that he held this faith earlier: in 1581, he was denied his MA; that same year, "a Thomas Lodge was imprisoned at the king's bench" on evidence supplied by an anti-Catholic informer, and a man surnamed "Lodge" appears on a list of recusants in Paris in 1580, whilst the institutions he attended – Trinity College, Oxford and Lincoln's Inn – were "hospitable to recusants."[71] In the "Epilogus" Lodge affixes a moral to his *Robert* narrative: "Here may the dispayring father finde hope in his sonnes untowardnesse, and the untoward sonne take example to please his dispayring father."[72] Since Aubert dies before the end of the story and before he has proof of his son's reformation, this maxim does not adequately encapsulate the work that we have read unless we understand "father" and "son" – as Arthur Kinney suggests – as denoting God and humankind.[73] In telling the tale of an errant but ultimately redeemed child, Lodge thus takes on the narrative of the prodigal son that was so germane to the work of contemporaries such as Greene and Gascoigne.[74] Yet, in doing so, he makes it not their secular, semi-autobiographical mode of writing, but restores it to its original usage in the Bible, where it is a parable (told in Luke 15:11–32) expressive of the proper relationship between God and humankind.

As the secular genre of Elizabethan prodigal fiction is reinfused with spirituality, Lodge again draws close to his protagonist. This time, he does not share the younger Robert's perversion of literature and scholarship, but the repentant Robert's repurifying of it. After his conversion, Robert turns to poetry, carving his poems into the barks of trees, like the lovelorn hero of Lodge's *Rosalynde*.[75] However, Robert is not doing this as an expression of love, at least not love of anything earthly. Rather, he transforms secular gestures and genres into worship

69 Ibid., sigs. E1r–E1v.
70 Ibid., sig., K4v.
71 Halasz, "Lodge."
72 Lodge, *Life*, sig. M3v.
73 Arthur F. Kinney, *Humanist Poetics: Thought, Rhetoric and Fiction in Sixteenth-Century England* (Amherst, Mass.: University of Massachusetts Press, 1986), p. 409.
74 See Helgerson, *Elizabethan Prodigals*, passim.
75 Lodge, *Life*, sigs. F2r–F3r.

THOMAS LODGE AND MEDIEVAL ROMANCE

of the divine. "Roberts Meditation" takes as its starting point the opening lines of Troilus's song in Book 3 of Chaucer's *Troilus and Criseyde*, which comes after the consummation of his affair with Criseyde, and is itself indebted to Boethius's *Consolation of Philosophy*. "Love, that of erthe and se hath governance, / Love that his hestes hath in hevene hye," opens Chaucer's version.[76] "O Heavenly God that governst every thing, / Whose power in heaven and in the earth we know," begins Robert's.[77] Lodge's rewriting of Chaucer is thus an act of reconstitution and return, as Boethius's poem, appropriated by the pagan Troilus for an outpouring of post-coital bliss, is reinstituted as an expression of Christian devotion.

Analyzing Lodge's *Life* against earlier treatments of the *Robert* legend allows us to tease out ways in which ideas and practices associated with the Renaissance and Reformation played out in late sixteenth-century English culture. Lodge's version is testament to the hybrid roots which the early moderns revisited when they embarked on their journeys of rediscovery. It was not simply a pagan, classical past to which they returned and which they revivified: a vernacular, pre-Reformation heritage also offered rich territory for reclamation (and the consequent negotiation of doctrinal change). The consolidation of humanist education both enriched the English vernacular and endorsed virtues of public service: of using one's learning, including one's writings, to serve the state. Even as Lodge's narrative questions the assumptions on which humanist education rested, it never backs away from a civic humanist interest in proper governance. There is also something profoundly ethical and urgent in probing the limits of a belief in the improving powers of literature and eloquence and – further to that – in encouraging one's readers to reflect actively on these very same issues. In doing both these things, Lodge contests the simplistic correlation between morality and reading "good" or "bad" books made by Ascham a generation before, when he attacked "bokes of fayned chevalrie, wherein a man by redinge, shuld be led to none other ende, but onely to manslaughter and baudrye."[78] Lodge's blood-thirsty, ethically-testing tale demonstrates that it is not necessarily what you read that matters, but how you read it. "Bad" books might paradoxically be capable of doing "good."

---

[76] Geoffrey Chaucer, *Troilus and Criseyde*, in *The Riverside Chaucer*, 3rd ed., gen. ed. Larry Benson (Boston: Houghton Mifflin, 1987), 3.174–75.

[77] Lodge, *Life*, sig. F2r.

[78] Ascham, *Toxophilus*, sig. A1r.

1 Binham Priory screen, detail of surviving bay fragment (photo by A. Massouras).

14   ICONOCLASM AND THE EPIGRAPHIC IMAGE

Jessica Berenbeim

The chancel screen of Binham Priory has figured in twentieth- and twenty-first-century academic literature as a perfect embodiment of the Reformation's iconoclastic effacement of Image with Word. Where the image of the Risen Christ now emerges from beneath the inscribed words (figure 1), the screen has inspired a more implicit historiographic reading, the pentimento a kind of perfect allegory for its own scholarship, for the intellectual resurrection of that enduring pre-Reformation past. However what makes the screen's expression of sixteenth-century epigraphic culture so suggestive is not so much the superimposition of image with word, but the replacement of one kind of image with another: the epigraphic image. Understanding the screen's inscription as an iconoclastic image, an image that attacks but can't escape its own visuality, prompts a reading of the text as itself a kind of historiography: iconoclasm as an historiographical battle of "cultural rupture" that is ultimately unwinnable.[1]

The distinctive materiality of the Binham screen has made it the subject of frequent references by historians of literature, art, religion, and of both medieval and early modern history.[2] The screen therefore has come to represent "Reformation

---

[1] In the formulation of James Simpson, "The Rule of Medieval Imagination," in *Images, Idolatry, and Iconoclasm in Late-Medieval England: Textuality and the Visual Image*, ed. Jeremy Dimmick, James Simpson, and Nicolette Zeeman (Oxford: Oxford University Press, 2002), pp. 4–24, especially pp. 23–24.

[2] Probably the most-cited notice is by Eamon Duffy in *The Stripping of the Altars*, for which the Risen Christ panel also serves as the second edition's cover image: Eamon Duffy, *The Stripping of the Altars: Traditional Religion in England, c. 1400–c. 1580*, 2nd ed. (New Haven, Conn.: Yale University Press, 2005). The wide dissemination of this book has probably contributed to the familiarity of the image in subsequent decades of research and teaching; for the book's influence in the field, see Peter Marshall, "(Re) defining the English Reformation," *Journal of British Studies* 48 (2009), 571–72, 581–83. Details of the Binham screen also serve as cover images for at least two other academic books about English culture in this period: Christopher Marsh, *Popular Religion in Sixteenth-Century England: Holding Their Peace* (Basingstoke, UK: Macmillan, 1998),

260   JESSICA BERENBEIM

iconoclasm" in general terms, but a detailed study of precisely what makes it so distinctive raises a specific and significant question: how do such inscriptions – as iconoclastic images – respond to what they replace? In the following discussion, I will argue that this particular object can serve, first, as the basis for a theory of the iconoclastic inscription; and second, as a model for its interpretive practice.[3]

---

and Shannon Gayk, *Image, Text, and Religious Reform in Fifteenth-Century England* (Cambridge: Cambridge University Press, 2010). Among a great many brief references, the most detailed discussions of the Binham screen are: M. R. James, *Suffolk and Norfolk: A Perambulation of the Two Counties with Notices of their History and their Ancient Buildings* (London: J. M. Dent, 1930), p. 171; John Mitchell, catalogue entry for the Risen Christ panel in *Gothic: Art for England, 1400–1547*, ed. Richard Marks and Paul Williamson (London: V&A, 2003), no. 357; Duffy, *Stripping of the Altars*, pp. xxxv–xxxvii; Margaret Aston, *Broken Idols of the English Reformation* (Cambridge: Cambridge University Press, 2016), pp. 920–21; David Griffith, "Texts and Detexting on Late Medieval English Church Screens," in *The Art and Science of the Church Screen in Medieval Europe: Making, Meaning, Preserving*, ed. Spike Bucklow, Richard Marks, and Lucy Wrapson (Woodbridge, UK: Boydell, 2017), pp. 71–99, at pp. 74–75.

[3] Discussions of idolatry and iconoclasm that particularly inform the analysis that follows include: Margaret Aston, *England's Iconoclasts*, vol. 1 (Oxford: Clarendon Press, 1988); Michael Camille, *The Gothic Idol: Ideology and Image-Making in Medieval Art* (Cambridge: Cambridge University Press, 1989); David Freedberg, *The Power of Images: Studies in the History and Theory of Response* (Chicago: University of Chicago Press, 1989); *Iconoclash*, ed. Bruno Latour and Peter Weibel (Cambridge, Mass.: MIT Press, 2002); Joseph Koerner, *The Reformation of the Image* (Chicago: University of Chicago Press, 2004), see especially pp. 11–13; Dimmick, Simpson, and Zeeman, "Introduction," in *Images, Idolatry, and Iconoclasm*, pp. 1–3; James Simpson, *Under the Hammer: Iconoclasm in the Anglo-American Tradition* (Oxford: Oxford University Press, 2010); *Art Under Attack: Histories of British Iconoclasm*, ed. Tabitha Barber and Stacy Boldrick (London: Tate Publishing, 2013), as well as the exhibition this catalogue accompanied. In an extensive epigraphic literature, relatively few studies concern post-Conquest Britain; some of the historical, art-historical, and literary, as well as more strictly epigraphic studies most relevant to this discussion are: John Higgit, "Epigraphic Lettering and Book Script in the British Isles," in *Inschrift und Material, Inschrift und Buchschrift*, ed. Walter Koch and Christine Steiniger (Munich: Bayerische Akademie der Wissenschaften, 1997), pp. 137–49; A. S. G. Edwards, "Middle English Inscriptional Verse Texts," in *Texts and their Contexts*, ed. J. Scattergood and Julia Boffey (Dublin: Four Courts Press, 1997), pp. 26–43; Jerome Bertram, "Inscriptions on Late-Medieval Brasses and Monuments," and Sally Badham, "The Contribution of Epigraphy to the Typological Classification of Medieval English Brasses and Slabs," in *Roman, Runes, and Ogham: Medieval Inscriptions in the Insular World and on the Continent*, ed. John Higgitt, Katherine Forsyth, and David N. Parsons (Donington, UK: Shaun Tyas, 2001), pp. 190–97 and pp. 202–10; Richard Marks, "Picturing Word and Text in the Late-Medieval Parish Church," in *Image, Text, and Church, 1380–1600*, ed. Linda Clark, Maureen Jurkowski, and Colin Richmond (Toronto: Pontifical Institute of Mediaeval Studies, 2009), pp. 162–88; Jerome Bertram, *Mediaeval Inscriptions: The Epigraphy of the City of Oxford* (Oxford: Boydell Press for the Oxfordshire Record Society, 2020). For studies of the visual culture of premodern writing, see especially *Viewing Inscriptions in the Late Antique and Medieval World*, ed. Anthony Eastmond (Cambridge: Cambridge University Press, 2015); *Sign and Design: Script as Image in Cross-Cultural Perspective (300–1600 CE)*, ed. Brigitte Bedos-Rezak and Jeffrey Hamburger (Washington, D.C.: Dumbarton Oaks, 2016).

ICONOCLASM AND THE EPIGRAPHIC IMAGE 261

In this object, the Binham screen, the rejected image remains underneath. In other instances of iconoclastic epigraphy, the superseded image may not literally be present but is nevertheless in some sense still there.[4] The artists of the later, epigraphic paintings on the Binham screen could not at that point see the earlier ones: they were painting words against a white ground. It is simply an accident of history and chemistry that the painted letters have often protected the under-layer of white from flaking, such that in places the words appear directly against the superseded figures. So what appears to us now is, in fact, a modern image: an anachronism. But conceptually, perhaps it is the opposite of an anachronism: a rare modern visual manifestation of early modern visuality. For this arbitrary survival gives to present-day vision a kind of training ground for the "period eye," including the ways in which the "public mind ... was an active institution of interior visualization with which every painter had to get along."[5] Exceptionally, one can in some respects see the Binham screen as it looked to people of the mid-sixteenth century, seeing simultaneously both what appeared to their eyes and what appeared before their minds' eyes. That is, the earlier past that we half-see, and that they half-remembered.

The Binham screen was first painted with figures c. 1500 and overpainted with inscriptions c. 1540–53. The earlier, figurative campaign can be dated on the basis of style and imagery, and the later, epigraphic one on the basis of source text. The original figures include Henry VI, and the later inscriptions most closely follow the Great Bible; the date of 1539 for the Great Bible's first version therefore serves as the *terminus post quem* of the overpaint's conventional dating, with the death of Edward VI in 1553 taken as the *terminus ante quem*.[6] The political context of Edward's reign offers reasonable grounds to date the iconoclastic inscriptions most likely between 1547 and 1553: these are the years when such reforming activities are best documented to have taken place elsewhere, as well as the years that saw the promulgation of consonant liturgical changes.

Although Binham Priory was a Benedictine monastery, as was the case with a number of other foundations its nave was in parochial use both before and after the monastic community's suppression in May 1539.[7] Of the larger site, it is this nave that survives best. The screen is no longer in its original position, but from the location of the surviving rood stairs it is clear where it would have been

---

4   For some examples, see Aston, *Broken Idols*, Chapter 9; there are similar inscriptions at St. Albans Abbey, later Cathedral, once the mother church of Binham Priory. These are all very clear instances, and I would suggest that the category could be defined more broadly.

5   Michael Baxandall, *Painting and Experience in Fifteenth-Century Italy*, 2nd ed. (Oxford: Oxford University Press, 1988), pp. 29–108, especially pp. 34–48 (quoted text from p. 45); Michael Baxandall, *The Limewood Sculptors of Renaissance Germany* (New Haven, Conn.: Yale University Press, 1980), pp. 143–63.

6   James, *Perambulation*, p. 171; *Gothic*, no. 357.

7   *The Cartulary of Binham Priory*, ed. Johanna Margerum (Exeter, UK: Norfolk Record Society, 2016), p. xl.

2 Binham Priory site, view from south-east (photo by author).

3   Binham Priory screen, full surviving bay (photo by author).

located, surmounted by a rood loft. An important aspect of the screen's initial context, both physical and institutional, is the distinct character of the parochial space within the site, even more so within the wider monastic precinct. It had a separate access route, and standing remains of the monks' choir indicate how far it extended beyond the parochial nave (figure 2). Beyond what is now the nave's blocked-up east end is in effect a whole second, larger monastic church in ruins. In the immediate aftermath of the priory's suppression, the monks did not remain in the community or nearby; rather, they appear to have been relocated to another part of Binham's county of Norfolk.[8] The iconic and iconoclastic images are not those of two different communities, monastic and lay – but of one community, at two different points in time.

It is equally critical to understand, inasmuch as it can be known, what the archaeology of the screen itself can reveal. Four bays of the screen survive, along with the "Risen Christ" fragment of another (figures 3–6 and 1). The

[8] James G. Clark, *The Dissolution of the Monasteries: A New History* (New Haven, Conn.: Yale University Press, 2021), p. 436.

4 Binham Priory screen, full surviving bay (photo by author).

only publication to venture a guess as to the screen's original dimensions and configuration is the entry for the Risen Christ panel in the catalogue that accompanied its display in the V&A's 2003 *Gothic* exhibition. The entry suggests that there were eight original bays: four complete ones from the south side, and the Risen Christ fragment from the north side (on the viewer's left when facing the altar). On the face of it, however, this seems implausible, as the width of the nave is approximately 7.47m, measured from the screen's original position, and each of the bays is about 1m wide. By contrast, an unattributed explanatory wall-text at the site alludes to six original bays, without suggesting an original order, and reproduces an early nineteenth-century watercolor by John Sell Cotman of the church interior.[9] Cotman's drawing, as well as another roughly contemporary watercolor by John Thirtle, both show the screen *in situ*, and both clearly show three bays on each side.[10]

[9] Anon., "The Binham Rood Screen," wall-text on the south side of the nave.
[10] John Sell Cotman, *Church Interior of Binham Abbey* (undated), NWHCM 1951.235.247; John Thirtle, *Interior of Binham Priory* (undated), NWHCM 1951.235.1352.B65. Norfolk Museums Collections, https://www.museums.norfolk.gov.uk/collections.

ICONOCLASM AND THE EPIGRAPHIC IMAGE 265

5   Binham Priory screen, full surviving bay (photo by author).

It does not seem possible to determine which bays were on the north side and which were on the south. But the configuration of surviving panels into two north-or-south groups, and the order within each group, can be deduced from the inscriptions. The superimposed text of the fragment is continuous with that of one other inscribed biblical extract, so it is overwhelmingly likely that they were already adjoining bays on one side (figures 3 and 1).

The remaining three bays (figures 4, 5, and 6) belonged together on the other side. Their order can be determined from an earlier inscription, which is equally – and more significantly – revealing about the screen's social history. Before the biblical extracts were overpainted at the Reformation, there were already inscriptions on the screen: in particular, on the dado rail (most visible in figure 4). Two layers of paint are visible here as well, black and red; the black lettering belongs to the initial campaign of c. 1500. This original inscription has previously been read as *Orate pro bono fratu*, and interpreted as a commemorative inscription for two monk benefactors.[11] However it actually must read *Orate pro bono statu*; that is, it is an injunction to "pray for the

---

[11]   *Gothic*, no. 357.

6   Binham Priory screen, full surviving bay (photo by author).

good estate" of the donors. The same formula is not infrequently attested in contemporary inscriptions elsewhere; for example, a 1462 text once inscribed across the bottom of the east window at St. Mary's church in Oxford: *Orate pro bono statu Walteri Lyhert Norwiciensis Ep(iscop)i qui hoc cancellum suis sumptibus edificavit. A(nn)o D(omi)ni M.CCCC.LXII.º*.[12] The next legible word on the Binham screen's dado rail is *et*. The inscription continues on one of the two remaining bays, although none of the words is legible. Then, the dado rail of the third remaining bay concludes with the word *eius*, followed by a decorative line-filler. This original intercessory inscription therefore links these three surviving bays together, with *Orate* at the beginning and *eius*, followed by the line-filler, at the end. In addition to clarifying aspects of the screen's original configuration, the intercessory inscription also confirms its lay patronage: not only because *fratu* is to be read as *statu*, but also because the final word *eius* strongly suggests the common collocation *uxor eius*, a reading that is consistent with legible letter-elements of the inscription's penultimate word.

[12] Bertram, *City of Oxford*, no. 138; see also nos. 57, 92, 97, 124, and 154.

7 Binham Priory screen, detail of full surviving bay in figure 4 (photo by author).

268   JESSICA BERENBEIM

Along with this intercessory inscription, the artists working around 1500 painted four holy figures in each bay. Many of these can plausibly be identified: St. Alban, St. Helena, St. Christopher, Henry VI (visible in figure 5), Mary of Egypt (?), St. Catherine, St. Michael (visible in figure 4), and of course the Risen Christ (figure 1). Others remain mysterious, such as the unidentified female saint with the unsettling gaze, who now seems to stare out from between the prison bars of Reformation lettering (figure 7).

The epigraphic image then covered these figurative images. During most of the years 1540–53, and certainly during the most probable range of Edward's reign from 1547, the living of Binham would have fallen within the control of the Paston estate, with the logistics of Reformation renovations falling within the remit of churchwardens. Peter and Albreda de Valognes had founded the priory as a cell of St. Alban's in the late eleventh or early twelfth century, and their son confirmed the grant of the church and everything belonging to it to the monks of Binham at some point in the first half of the twelfth century.[13] In 1541, a little over two years after the Priory's suppression, the king granted Binham Priory and all its properties to Thomas Paston, a member of his privy chamber, who then controlled the estate for the rest of the 1540s. Thomas Paston died in 1550, at which point it all passed to his son, Edward, who was only baptized in that same year.[14] In the early 1550s, the estate's executor was Edward's mother, Agnes Paston, who is mentioned in a document dated to before 1553 as Thomas's "executrix."[15] The narrative of Edward's life has an evocative echo of the screen itself: though the godson and namesake of Edward VI, as an adult he became a devoted recusant; according to an (apocryphal?) story, after he demolished parts of Binham's monastic site to build his manor house, he called off the project on account of his conscience.

Many records survive of analogous destructive creations during the years 1547–53, where the iconoclastic inscriptions themselves have now vanished. Often, these acts of iconoclasm belonged to reforming campaigns that also included the purchase of liturgical books in English, and came within recent memory of the destroyed objects' creation or repair. The extant churchwardens' accounts for Binham only cover part of the seventeenth century,[16] but records of precisely this kind of campaign survive in churchwardens' accounts from many other institutions during the same period, even if in most cases these inscriptions themselves do not. For example, at St. Mary-at-Hill in London, in the account year 1547–48 the wardens paid 5s. "for taking downe of the Rode lofte," 13s. 4d. "for taking down of the tabernacle ouer the vestry doore, being all stone, and other stone workes in the churche," 8s. "for vi new sawters

---

[13] *Binham Cartulary*, nos. 1 and 2 (datable to 1109x1142); commentary on pp. xiii–xv of Introduction.

[14] See Michael Riordan, "Henry VIII, privy chamber of," *Oxford Dictionary of National Biography* (Oxford: Oxford University Press, 2004), https://www.oxforddnb.com (accessed 31 January 2023); Philip Brett, "Paston, Edward," ibid.; *Binham Cartulary*, p. lix.

[15] London, The National Archives, STAC 3/7/74.

[16] Norfolk Record Office, NRO BL/GT 3/1-20.

ICONOCLASM AND THE EPIGRAPHIC IMAGE 269

in englisshe for the quyer," 14d. "for cariage of tymbre for scaffoldes for the
Rode loft when yt was paynted," 16d. "for Ropes to bynde the scafoldes," and
4l. "for paynting of the Rode lofte with scriptures."[17] At Ashburton in Devon,
the accounts of that same year record a payment of 3s. 4d. for taking down
"le rode" and other images, and then another payment of 3s. 8d. for removing
more images and "tabernaclez," as well as "burnyng the same" – when these
had only been mended or made about a decade or so earlier.[18]

The artist or artists of Binham's biblical inscriptions covered the screen's
saints with broad strokes of white paint, and then ruled the bays for nine lines
of text each; on these lines, they painted inscriptions in black. All five surviving
inscriptions derive from the epistles: two from the first Epistle of Peter; two from
Paul's first Epistle to Timothy; and one from Paul's Epistle to the Colossians. It
does therefore seem highly plausible that the missing inscription also derives
from Colossians, but there is no way to know. However, one can reasonably
speculate that it was an epistle extract: the words of, say, Deuteronomy, Kings,
or the Creed would have been extremely rhetorically and tonally discordant
here, which seems unlikely given the otherwise carefully curated nature of
the project. The lineation, spacing, and lettering are uniform, such that each
extract needed to be of similar length, and the whole project thus had to be
methodically constructed. The Reformation inscriptions also refashion the text,
in that they do not follow any one version of the Great Bible more closely than
any other, and to some degree they depart from all versions in the particularities
of their textual detail. And of course, their form and composition are entirely
different: out of textually and materially modified fragments of the Great Bible,
they collectively create a new text (itself now fragmentary).

The overpainted inscriptions on the partially surviving side read:[19]

---

[17] *The Medieval Records of A London City Church: St Mary At Hill, 1420–1559*, ed.
Henry Littlehales (London: Trübner, 1905), pp. 385–88.

[18] *Churchwardens' Accounts of Ashburton, 1479–1580*, ed. Alison Hanham (Torquay:
Devon & Cornwall Record Society, 1970), pp. 121, 124; cf. "5d. to Peter Cerver for
mendyng of the roodelofte" in 1535–36 and 9s. to a Peter Rowallying, which was
a down payment on an unspecified total, for an image of St. Christopher, pp. 97,
104. For other records along these lines, see: *The Early Churchwardens' Accounts
of Bishop's Stortford, 1431–1558*, ed. Stephen G. Doree ([Hitchin]: Hertfordshire
Record Society, 1994), pp. 110, 123, 178, 289, 290, 291–94, 295, 301, 302; *The
Churchwardens' Accounts of St Michael, Spurriergate, York, 1518–1548*, ed. C. C.
Webb ([York]: Borthwick Institute of Historical Research, 1997), p. 331; *Records of the
Churchwardens of Mildenhall: Collections (1446–1454) and Accounts (1503–1553)*, ed.
Judith Middleton-Stewart (Woodbridge, UK: Suffolk Records Society, 2011), pp. xxv,
44, 109, 110, 118; *Wing Churchwardens' Accounts, 1527–1662*, ed. Maureen Brown
and Paul Brown (Aylesbury, UK: Buckinghamshire Record Society, 2019), pp. 49, 52.

[19] There is no national corpus with established transcription conventions; of those
that exist, the most relevant are: R. G. Collingwood and R. P. Wright, *The Roman
Inscriptions of Britain* (Oxford: Clarendon, 1965), most recently updated and
very substantially expanded as Scott Vanderbilt, *Roman Inscriptions of Britain*
(2017–), https://romaninscriptionsofbritain.org, see "Reference: Critical Signs";
Elisabeth Okasha, *Hand-list of Anglo-Saxon Non-runic Inscriptions* (Cambridge:

270 JESSICA BERENBEIM

Godlynes is greate ryches If a man be ~ | content with that he hath for we broughe not<yng> | Into the worlde nether maye we cary any | thyng out But when we haue fode and | rayment we must ther with be content | They that wylbe ryche fall into temptac|yon and snares {of} the deuyll & into many | folysshe & no{yso}me lustes which droune | men into per{dicion and} destruccyon ~[20]

{For couetousnes of money is the} rote of all | {euel: which whyle some lusted afte}r they ~| {erred from the fayth and tangled t}he(m) selues | {wyth many sorowes. But thou man} of god | {flye suche thynges. Folowe ryghteousnes, godlynes, fayth, loue, pacyence, me}akenes ~| {Fyght the good fyght of fayth. L}aye hande | {on eternal lyfe, wher vnto thou} art also | {called, & hast professed a good p}rofession | {before many wytnesses}[21]

The three bays from the other side read:

Be sober and trust perfectly on the grace that | is brought vnto you by th(e) declaryng of Jesus | chryst as obedient chyldren that ye geue not ~ | your selues ouer unto your o{l}de lustes by ~ | whyche ye were led whan as yet ye were ~ | ignoraunt of christ but as he whiche called you | is holy euen so be ye holy also {i}n all maner ~ | of conuersacion because it is written Be ye | holy for I am holy saithe the lor{d} ~[22]

Holy and beloued put on tender mercy, ~ | kyndnes{,} humblenes of mynde, mekenes, ~ | longe suffrynge, forbearynge one another, and |forgeu{y}nge one another, yf any man have a | quarel agaynst another : as christ forgaue you | euen so do ye aboue all t{h}ese thynges put on | loue which is the bonde o{f} per{f}ectnes and th{e} | peace of god rule in your h{eart}es to the ~ | which peace ye are call{e}d {in o}ne bodye and | ~ {see that} ye be t{hankful}[23]

Be readye alwayes to geue an answere to | euery man that asketh you a reason of the | hope th(at) is in you & that with meaknes | and feare hauynge a good conscience that | where as they backbyte you as euyll doar<s> | they maye be ashamed th(at) falsely accuse your | good conuersacion in Christ for it is better | yf the wyll of god be so {that} ye suffre for | well doinge than for e{uyll doinge}[24]

Cambridge University Press, 1971), p. 45; Robert Favreau et al., *Corpus des inscriptions de la France médiévale* (Paris: CNRS, 1974–), 16 (2016), p. 14. None is entirely appropriate to this context, but I have adopted the CFM's conventions as the closest, with the addition of the following conventions borrowed from palaeographical transcription: colored or otherwise decorated letters are transcribed in bold type-face; line breaks are noted by the | sign.

[20] I Tim. 6:6–9.

[21] I Tim. 6:10–12; suggested missing words supplied from STC (2nd ed.), 2075.

[22] I Pet. 1:13–16.

[23] Col. 3:12–15.

[24] I Pet. 3:15–17.

ICONOCLASM AND THE EPIGRAPHIC IMAGE

Like the screen's holy figures, the earlier intercessory inscription on its dado rail was overpainted in the Reformation. The later inscription is visible on top of the earlier one, in red letters painted over the earlier black ones (figures 4, 5, and 6). Where it is legible at this point, the overpainted inscription in the first bay of the surviving group of three reads:

The fyrst epistle of S peter the

In the next bay:

Colossians the thyrd

In other words: they are rubrics. That designation fits both their verbal and visual features, that is to say their textual function (identification) and form (contrasting color, specifically red). Furthermore, they are rubrics that – in at least one case – identify the chapter. The nature of the overpainted rubrics, then, is potentially significant in light of Cranmer's 1549 directive that priests should now announce biblical chapters before each lesson in liturgical performance.[25] The rubric inscriptions can be considered in that context, as indeed the screen's full repainting can be seen in the context of the wholesale printing and dissemination of his *Book of Common Prayer* that same year (and this is another good reason to place Binham's Reformation inscriptions in the early 1550s). These superimposed inscriptions are also a *damnatio memoriae*, in which the names of individuals – whom the viewer was once called upon to make the object of individual intercession – have been obliterated by the names of apostles and the objects of their collective evangelization. These epigraphic images are therefore expressions of a concept of image-worship as part of an inextricably linked constellation of condemned practices.

Indeed, the words themselves – as opposed to the location and circumstances of their painting – are not, in fact, explicitly iconoclastic *stricto sensu*. Rather, an ideological matrix emerges from the fusion of these texts, their associations, and their early viewers' "interior visualizations" of what is now actually visible. Of course, the inscription on the missing bay may have directly addressed images, image-worship, or idolatry. That said, if it is impossible to say definitively that direct references were absent, oblique references are certainly present. Far more ostensibly direct engagements appear in epistle passages virtually adjacent to the sources of the inscriptions; for example, in I Peter 1:

> the tryall of your faythe beynge muche more precyous then golde that perisheth (thoughe it be tryed wyth fyre) myghte be founde unto laude, glory, and honoure at the appearyng of Jesus Christ, whom ye haue not

---

[25] In a recent groundbreaking material-text study of the Bible, Eyal Poleg has described this directive as "a key moment in the parallel evolution of Bible and liturgy," because "[f]or the first time in English history priests were instructed to utter the chapter divisions in the performance of the liturgy." Eyal Poleg, *A Material History of the Bible: England 1200–1553* (Oxford: Oxford University Press/British Academy, 2020), p. 74.

272   JESSICA BERENBEIM

> sene, and yet loue hym, in whom euen nowe, though ye se him not, yet
> do you beleue

and

> For all fleshe is grasse, and all the glorye of man is as the floure of grasse.
> The grasse wydereth, & the floure falleth awaye, but þe worde of the
> Lorde endureth euer.

The passage from I Timothy, extending over two bays, also perhaps calls attention to idolatry by implication. Its warning that "couetousnes of money is the rote of all euel" clearly offers a general repudiation of materialism – and therefore not only of the predecessor holy images themselves, but also of the donations that enabled both their creation and the consequent intercessory prayers for their donors. Indeed, when compared with the same text in the Great Bible, it's striking that the inscription starts in the middle of a sentence, refashioning it as a beginning and re-casting the text in more immediately imperative form:

> [GB:] Wherefore gyrde vp the loynes of youre mynde, be sober, & trust
> perfectly …

> [Screen:] **Be** sober and trust perfectly …

With the early viewers' "interior visualizations" in mind, remember that this line of writing – "Be sober and trust perfectly" – is precisely adjacent to where the same people would, a decade earlier, have read *Orate*. One plural imperative, to perform a particular action of intercessory prayer, has been reinscribed with another kind of command – to *be*, to trust. Such a strong emphasis on "couetousnes of money" further suggests a direct reference to the newly-consolidated Tenth Commandment (against covetousness), which in the Reformation reformulation was locked in an inverse and intimate textual relationship with the Second (against idolatry).[26] It is in that fusion of oblique reference and context that the epigraphic paintings are able to construct the rejection of "idolatry" as a kind of synecdoche for the ideological matrix as a whole. The object doesn't need to express a rejection of idolatry in words, because it embodies that rejection in paint.

The epistle inscriptions also depart from the Great Bible in their orthography and visuality. In addition to specific variations like the one quoted above, more generally they are less abbreviated and – especially – less punctuated. They look far more like liturgical manuscripts contemporary with, or even earlier than, their predecessor images on the screen than they do like the printed pages of the Great Bible on which they are based. The painted writing

---

[26] See the detailed discussion of "The Structure of the Decalogue," in Aston, *England's Iconoclasts*, pp. 371–400.

8 Thornham church screen, north bays (photo by author).

274 JESSICA BERENBEIM

on the screen is closer to formal textualis scripts than to the Great Bible's textura type-face, in its general aspect – lateral compression, contrasted with pronounced word- and line-separation – in the individual letter-forms, and in the inscription artist's representation of formal features (e.g. figures 6 and 7). For example: the emphatically but somewhat idiosyncratically squared (quadratus) treatment of feet and heads of minims; variable forked ascenders; and, most ingeniously, a stylized imitation, with the tip of a brush, of the elaborated hairline pen-strokes that are themselves stylized graphic features. These letter-forms, along with the rubrics, the colored initials, and the ruling (almost certainly functional, but nevertheless with a visual effect) combine to evoke a manuscript rather than a printed page.

The rhetorical structure of the extracts also seems to be conditioned by underlying patterns of its past formal character. The first two bays of the full surviving side have structurally complementary extracts, in which the passages mirror each other: "*as* he whiche called you is holy, *even so* be ye holy"/"*as* christ forgave you, *even so* do ye above all these things put on love" (see figures 4 and 5, transcribed above; emphasis added). The relation of these passages is therefore one of pairing, evoking the patterns of paired figures that were so common a feature of East Anglian screen painting in the fifteenth and early sixteenth centuries; compare, for example, the screen from Thornham, nearby to Binham (figure 8). The surviving pair of bays from the other side are sequential extracts: one continues the other to complete the passage from I Timothy (figures 3 and 1, transcribed above). These in turn evoke the continuous, multi-figure narratives that are particularly common where such screens depict christocentric imagery, rather than figures of saints; and indeed this is the passage that covered the "Risen Christ," and from which he now seems to emerge.

Even before the white paint began to flake away, this epigraphic image was haunted by its past. Although the ghosting figures from that past were not what the inscriptions' initial viewers physically saw, it is in some way what they perceived. The message of these curated extracts is specifically oppositional, predicated on the persistence of spiritual and ideological challenge: "Be readye alwayes to geue an answere ...." And the visible language of this inscription, its evangelical medium on a persisting orthodox surface, expresses iconoclasm's insistent but unstable articulation of a periodic break. It has been significant to emphasize that the initial audiences of the superseded and superimposed images were members of the same community at different points in time. These two different points in time were chronologically close, but nevertheless what the iconoclastic ideology conceived – and constructed – as epochally divided. Epigraphic writing more generally can be characterized by its endeavor to speak across time. But in its more classic mode, it speaks to the future: *orate pro animabus* ...; all you who may pass by ...; "I am Ozymandias ...." The epigraphic image of iconoclasm reverses that mode: it also speaks across time, but to the past.

15 THE LETTER KILLS BUT THE SPIRIT GIVES LIFE (2 CORINTHIANS 3:6): OR, WHAT HAPPENED TO ENEMY LOVE?

David Aers

> … onely add
> Deeds to thy knowledge answerable, add Faith,
> Add Vertue, Patience, Temperance, add Love,
> By name to come calld Charitie, the soul
> Of all the rest …[1]
>
> (Milton, *Paradise Lost*, XII.581–85)

This brief essay explores some central puzzles in Christian doctrine and practice. As its title indicates, it addresses hermeneutics and violence, writing and killing. It does so by attending to Jesus Christ's challenging but luminous teaching on enemy-love. And despite its brevity, it also seeks to suggest why diachronic study is as important as James Simpson has been showing for many years and across many substantial books.[2] Purely synchronic history, encouraged by institutionalized period divisions in

---

[1] I quote from *The Poetical Works of John Milton*, ed. Helen Darbishire, 2 vols. (Oxford: Oxford University Press, 1962).

[2] I refer to these works by James Simpson: *The Oxford English Literary History, Vol. 2: 1350–1547. Reform and Cultural Revolution* (Oxford: Oxford University Press, 2002); *Burning to Read: English Fundamentalism and Its Reformation Opponents* (Cambridge, Mass.: Harvard University Press, 2007); *Under the Hammer: Iconoclasm in the Anglo-American Tradition* (Oxford: Oxford University Press, 2010); *Permanent Revolution: The Reformation and the Illiberal Roots of Liberalism* (Cambridge, Mass.: Harvard University Press, 2019).

276   DAVID AERS

university departments of history and literature, diminishes our ability to understand the historical moment or writer that the synchronic specialist studies. One common consequence is the abundance of false claims about origins, innovations, and novelty. It begets an inability to discern, let alone study, the complex ways in which traditions develop, transform, and encounter rivals, either assimilating them or being defeated by them and, in the process, becoming unintelligible.[3] Of course, diachronic work is as risky as it is demanding. The demands are obvious, but what are the risks? The risks are those of working against the specialized compartmentalizations of period and coterie boundaries. We can only be grateful that James Simpson has so exuberantly and so eruditely taken these risks.

I should also note that this essay is in dialogue with a central preoccupation of James Simpson's work from *Burning to Read* to *Permanent Revolution*: namely, the relation between the distinctive hermeneutics of the Reformation, and the practices of persecutory violence (and vehement legitimizations of such violence) germane to the period.[4] In *Permanent Revolution* Simpson shows, often in dismaying detail, how the Reformation continued to produce an "unending, uncompromising, physical, cultural, and psychic violence grounded on an entirely new and revolutionary understanding of divine textuality" (p. 260). He demonstrates, as in his discussion of Bunyan's *Grace Abounding* (pp. 292–98), "[t]he violence unleashed by Lutheran and Calvinist reading programs," first against Catholic Christianity but then becoming "a practice of permanent revolution, dividing Protestantism from itself much more vigorously than it divided Protestantism from Catholicism" (p. 263). Simpson's account coheres perfectly with the very different form of analysis offered by historian Karl Gunther in *Reformation Unbound*.[5] Particularly relevant is Gunther's account of evangelical Christians urging their governors to massacre Catholics and all who were judged to be impeding the Reformation. He shows in detail that English Protestants in the sixteenth century took Jesus's observations on the divisiveness of his own teaching with unequivocal literalism: "Think not that I am come to send peace on earth: I come not to send peace but a sword" (Matthew 10:34). The letter apparently urged early modern Christians to take up the carnal sword to exterminate their Catholic neighbors.[6]

---

3   Like James Simpson, the issues have concerned me for many years: explicitly in "A Whisper in the Ear of Early Modernists, or, Reflections on Literary Critics Writing the History of the Subject," in *Culture and History, 1350–1600*, ed. David Aers (London: Harvester, 1992), pp. 177–202; most recently in *Versions of Election: From Langland and Aquinas to Calvin and Milton* (Notre Dame, Ind.: University of Notre Dame Press, 2020).
4   This theme runs through *Burning to Read* and *Permanent Revolution*.
5   Karl Gunther, *Reformation Unbound: Protestant Visions of the Reformation in England, 1525–1590* (Cambridge: Cambridge University Press, 2014).
6   See Gunther, *Reformation Unbound*, chapter 2, centered on this saying of Jesus in Protestant ideology; Simpson quotes this version in *Permanent Revolution*, pp.

THE LETTER KILLS BUT THE SPIRIT GIVES LIFE 277

Like Simpson, I think we can only understand what happened to Christian hermeneutics in the Reformation by paying attention to what it saw as its adversary: medieval traditions of exegesis and their relation to the Catholic Church. So, for example, with Matthew 10:34 (quoted above), medieval exegesis characteristically includes an allegorical dimension, interpreting the sword as the word of God poured into human hearts rather than an evangelical command to slaughter one's neighbors.[7] I envisage this essay as a footnote to Simpson's work in this area. A footnote, however, which seeks to introduce a tradition that quite understandably is absent from his accounts of the Reformation. This tradition has no adequate name since it comprises multiple strands of Christian teaching and experience in complex, often obscure relations. But its makers have been known, or abused, as Anabaptists, Spiritualists, Libertines, Antinomians, Familists, Behmenists, Quakers.[8] These groups and individuals were habitually scorned and violently persecuted by the magisterial Reformation. This is perhaps not surprising, for they called into question many of its core doctrinal and ecclesiological tenets, including hermeneutics and, especially, the relations between the letter which kills and the Spirit which gives life.

As I observed at the beginning of this essay, Jesus Christ's teaching on enemy-love is luminous. For example: "Ye have heard it hath been said, An eye for an eye and a tooth for a tooth: But I say unto you, That ye resist not evil: but whosoever shall smite thee on thy right cheek, turn to him the other also" (Matthew 5:38–39). Or:

> Ye have heard that it hath been said, Thou shalt love thy neighbour, and hate thine enemy. But I say unto you, Love your enemies, bless them that curse you, do good to them that hate you, and pray for them which despitefully use you, and persecute you; That ye may be the children of your Father which is in heaven: for he maketh his sun to rise on the evil and on the good and sendeth rain on the just and on the unjust. (Matthew 5:43–45)

The conclusion: "Be ye therefore perfect, even as your Father which is in heaven is perfect" (Matthew 5:48). Another lucid example comes from a narrative in Luke's gospel. Jesus is going to Jerusalem and he wants to stay

---

271–72. For Simpson's exemplification of the similar violence in early Reformation exegesis see *Burning to Read*, pp. 148, 191–94.

[7] For example: Thomas Aquinas, *Catena Aurea*, tr. John Henry Cardinal Newman, 4 vols. (London: Saint Austin Press, 1999), I.396.

[8] There is a vast literature here. One place to begin is George Williams, *The Radical Reformation*, 3rd ed. (Kirksville, Mo.: Truman State University Press, 1995); with Nigel Smith, *Perfection Proclaimed: Language and Literature in English Radical Religion, 1640–1660* (Oxford: Clarendon, 1989); David Como, *Blown by the Spirit: Puritanism and the Emergence of an Antinomian Underground in Pre-Civil-War England* (Stanford: Stanford University Press, 2004).

278   DAVID AERS

in a village of the Samaritans. They refuse to receive him because he is
going to Jerusalem. His disciples James and John want to exterminate the
villagers with fire from heaven and seek Jesus's agreement. Their model
of holiness and God comes from Elijah; in the second book of Kings it is
recorded that the prophet killed over two hundred men with fire sent from
heaven (2 Kings 1:5–15). Perhaps they also recalled how his successor Elisha
cursed little children who mocked his baldness so that forty-two of them
were mauled by bears (2 Kings 2:23–25). But Jesus sees no precedent in
Elijah's mass killings or violence against those children who mocked him.
He rebukes his disciples and tells them he has come to save people's lives,
not to destroy them (Luke 9:51–56). On the Cross itself, Jesus lives out his
teaching on enemy-love as he prays for those who tortured him and killed
him: "Father forgive them; for they know not what they do" (Luke 23:34).
The apostle Paul rehearses this teaching: "Bless them which persecute you:
bless, and curse not. ... Recompense to no man evil for evil" (Romans 12:14,
17; see too 12:20–21).

In these passages from Matthew 5 and Luke 9, as elsewhere (Luke
6:27–38), Jesus initiates a new form of holy community centered on mutual
acts of forgiveness, reconciliation, and enemy-love. In fact, the command
to love one's enemy only becomes intelligible within the new, revolutionary
community he was making with its peculiar form of virtues. As his disciple
Paul wrote, if anyone is in Christ there is a new creation: "old things are
passed away; behold all things are become new." And so disciples are
given "the ministry of reconciliation." God himself had initiated this
by reconciling us to God through his Son "when we were enemies" to
God. Indeed, "God was in Christ reconciling the world unto himself not
imputing their trespasses unto them" (2 Corinthians 5:17–18; Romans
5:10; 2 Corinthians 5:9). All luminous. All perfectly clearly showing that
neither Elijah's violence, nor Moses's (to which we will come when we
turn to Calvin), nor the holy wars of the Old Testament remain models
for disciples of Jesus in the new community. This teaching was perfectly
well understood in the early Church. Origen, for example, affirmed it. He
reminded Christians that the wars apparently given divine blessing in the
Old Testament must be read allegorically by disciples of Jesus; they could
not be literal models for Christian practice. As Frederick Russell observes:

> Origen considered the Old Testament as an allegory of the New,
> consequently Christians should study the historical books of the Old
> Testament with the understanding that these wars should be understood
> as spiritual wars against the devil. They function as *exempla* for moral
> edification rather than as guides for making decisions.[9]

---

[9] Frederick H. Russell, *The Just War in the Middle Ages* (Cambridge: Cambridge
University Press, 1975), pp. 11–12.

THE LETTER KILLS BUT THE SPIRIT GIVES LIFE   279

The wars sacralized in the Old Testament belonged to a distinct historical process of nation formation in the making of Israel. But God had allowed the Jewish kingdoms "to disintegrate" and Christians had no calling to repeat this history.[10] It was by listening to Ambrose that Augustine was to encounter this tradition of allegorical hermeneutics around the Old Testament, an encounter decisive in changing his contempt for the Christian Church and the Old Testament.[11] He gradually discovered that the Church did not teach the wicked things he had thought it did. By drawing him to hear Ambrose preach and practice Christian hermeneutics, God was turning Augustine around ("convertebar"), showing him that his Church – the body of his only son ("ecclesia unica, corpus unici tui") – did not have a taste for infantile trifles ("non saperet infantiles nugas"). Now what had seemed absurd turned out to be quite other: Augustine now delighted to hear Ambrose declaring that "the letter kills, but the spirit gives life (littera occidit, spiritus autem vivificat [2 Corinthians 3:6])." With this hermeneutic, Ambrose removed the mystical veil ("remoto mystico velamento") and opened out the spiritual meaning of texts that had seemed to teach wickedness. These exegetical experiences, central to his conversion to Christianity, shape all Augustine's homilies on the Psalms and pervade his preaching.

Medieval exegesis, as Henri de Lubac demonstrated in massive and loving detail, followed Origen and Augustine.[12] In this hermeneutic tradition allegorical exegesis springs from the incarnation of Christ with his crucifixion and resurrection. Allegorical interpretation of the Old Testament emerges from the seeds of providential history, a history which made the Hebrew Bible into the Old Testament which yearns for its fulfilment in Christ and his Church. As Henri de Lubac wrote in his great study of Origen's understanding of Scripture, Christ's act of incarnation initiates a "supernatural metamorphosis."[13] Like St. Paul, says de Lubac, "Origen made 'spiritual' equivalent to 'new.'" For the spirit is "a creation, a radiation from the Christian event" (pp. 309–10). The water becomes wine in "the redemptive drama and the Paschal Mystery" (p. 310). Indeed, after Christ,

---

[10] Russell, *Just War*, p. 11. On the early Church and its views on Christian discipleship in relation to war, see Roland H. Bainton, *Christian Attitudes toward Peace and War* (Nashville, Tenn.: Abingdon, 1960), chapter 5.

[11] I follow Augustine's account in the *Confessions*, VI.1.1–VI.5.7. The quotation here is from VI.4.5–6. I use *Confessions*, ed. James J. O'Donnell, 3 vols. (Oxford: Clarendon Press, 1992). Of the many fine translations of the *Confessions*, I tend to use Henry Chadwick's *Confessions* (Oxford: Oxford University Press, 1991).

[12] Henri de Lubac, *Exégèse médiévale*, 4 vols. (Paris: Aubier, 1959–64); see too Gilbert Dahan, *L'Exégèse chrétienne de a Bible en Occident médiéval: XII–XIV siècle* (Paris: Cerf, 1999).

[13] Henri de Lubac, *History and Spirit: The Understanding of Scripture according to Origen*, tr. Anne Englund Nash (San Francisco: Ignatius Press, 2007 [French ed. 1950]): page references given in text.

280   DAVID AERS

"the old Scripture in a way lost its literal meaning" (p. 311). It must now be read not only in a historical perspective but also through the divine and eternal view disclosed in Christ (p. 312): "Let us say, therefore, that Jesus Christ does not so much explain the Old Testament as transform it" (p. 316). From Augustine to William Langland and Denis the Carthusian this hermeneutic guided those who read Scripture in the Catholic Church.[14]

What happened in the Calvinist Reformation?[15] Calvin insisted on the identity of the Old Testament and the New Testament. In the second book of his *Institutes of the Christian Religion* Calvin stresses that the Old and New Covenants are one and the same: their doctrine and ethics are identical (II.8.7; II.10.1–23).[16] Calvin insists that it is "very important" to recognize that the two covenants consist of "the same law" and "the same doctrine" (II.10.1). Those who deny this are heretical like that "rascal Servetus," whom Calvin burnt to death outside the gates of Geneva, and those "madmen" known as Anabaptists (II.10.1). Indeed, the covenant made with the patriarchs in the Old Testament is "one and the same" as that disclosed by Jesus Christ (II.10.2). Furthermore, Calvin asserts that the Israelites share the same sacraments and the same understanding of eternal life as Christians (II.10.5 and 8). In fact, Calvin assures us, we can be certain that Jesus Christ never taught anything that Moses did not teach. To deny this is "a most pernicious opinion" (II.8.7). And Moses, of course, was a champion of holy war in the formation of Israel on its way to the promised land.

---

[14] This statement does not entail subjecting Langland's *Piers Plowman* to Robertsonian hermeneutics: consult my exemplification of Langland's ways within the tradition in *Salvation and Sin* (Notre Dame, Ind.: University of Notre Dame Press, 2009), chapter 4; and before that, David Aers, *Piers Plowman and Christian Allegory* (London: Arnold, 1975). For a brilliant description of Langland's allegorical modes, see Nicolette Zeeman, *The Arts of Disruption: Allegory and* Piers Plowman (Oxford: Oxford University Press, 2020).

[15] There have recently been some attempts to claim continuity between medieval allegorical exegesis and the magisterial Reformation: for example, see Thomas Fulton, *The Book of Books: Biblical Interpretation, Literary Culture, and the Political Imagination from Erasmus to Milton* (Philadelphia: University of Pennsylvania Press, 2021), pp. 10–17. Such claims seem to be the product of early modernists who have not much direct acquaintance with medieval hermeneutics and practices. However, there is a very fine synchronic study by an early modernist which overlaps in illuminating ways with some arguments and examples of the present essay: Achsah Guibbory, *Christian Identity, Jews, and Israel in Seventeenth-Century England* (Oxford: Oxford University Press, 2010), pp. 14–17; on Calvin, see pp. 86–120, 283–90.

[16] *Institutes of the Christian Religion*, ed. John T. McNeill, tr. Ford L. Battles, 2 vols. (Philadelphia: Westminster Press, 1960). Michael Walzer noticed this in a book that has been oddly ignored by historians: *The Revolution of the Saints: A Study in the Origins of Radical Politics* (Cambridge, Mass.: Harvard University Press, 1965), p. 56: "Calvin always insisted that the two testaments were essentially similar"; see too the examples from England, pp. 278–85.

THE LETTER KILLS BUT THE SPIRIT GIVES LIFE   281

It is thus not surprising that against Anabaptists like Menno Simons and Spiritualists like Hans Denck Calvin takes Moses as the ideal model of Christian magistracy. As an example of such distinctively Christian practice, Calvin relates how Moses slaughtered three thousand of his erring sisters and brothers in one day. Admiringly Calvin recalls how, "sprinkled and dripping with the blood of his brethren, he [Moses] dashes through the camp to new carnage" (IV.20.10). Not for Calvin and the magisterial Reformation the deployment of allegorical hermeneutics to guide Christians in reading the celebrations of mass slaughter in the Old Testament.[17] Not even when commenting on the end of Psalm 137, the famous exultation at the imminent destruction of those who have captured Israel: "Happy shall he be, that taketh and dasheth thy little ones against the stones [Vulgate, 'ad petram,' the rock]." Calvin's commentary on the Psalms was translated into English by Arthur Golding in 1571 and here is the response to Psalm 137:

> And although it seeme a cruell thing, when hee wysheth theyr tender babes, whiche as yet coulde do no harme, too be dashed and brayned agaynst the stones: yet nothwithstanding forasmuche as he speaketh not as his own head, but fetcheth his words at God's mouth, it is nothing else but a proclayming of God's juste judgement.[18]

To grasp what has gone on here, to understand the revolution in Christian hermeneutics and its consequences evident in Calvin's teaching, the kind of diachronic study pursued in James Simpson's *Burning to Read* is indispensable. We must set Calvin and his followers in Europe and across the Atlantic against Augustine and medieval commentaries. Augustine observes that the newborn Babylonian child is "potentially a citizen of Jerusalem." We are all Babylonian

---

[17] For Calvin's frequent attacks on allegorical exegesis in the *Institutes*, see G. Sujin Pak, *The Judaizing Calvin: Sixteenth Century Debates over the Messianic Psalms* (Oxford: Oxford University Press, 2010), p. 192, n. 42, and passim; her later study is relevant to this topic: *The Reformation of Prophecy: Early Modern Interpretations of the Prophet and Old Testament Prophecy* (Oxford: Oxford University Press, 2018), pp. 73–79, 84–88, 299–307. For James Simpson's detailed and nuanced analysis of Tyndale's attacks on allegorical exegesis combined with extensive uses of allegorical modes of reading, see *Burning to Read*, pp. 192–217. In her study of early modern hermeneutics, Alison Knight offers a strangely simplified and distorted account of Simpson's arguments and exemplification of early Protestant relations to allegory, one which might well encourage her readers to assume that Simpson's work is not an important contribution to the rich field she explores and so not one they need to study: *The Dark Bible: Cultures of Interpretation in Early Modern England* (Oxford: Oxford University Press, 2022), p. 239.

[18] I quote from the discussion in Hannibal Hamlin, *Psalm Culture and Early Modern English Literature* (Cambridge: Cambridge University Press, 2004), p. 271. See too the commentary in Claudia Richter, *The Calvinesque: An Aesthetics of Violence in English Literature after the Reformation* (New York: Lang, 2014), pp. 77–78 and the whole section on "The Maledictory Psalms," pp. 69–78.

282   DAVID AERS

children until we are converted by divine grace. So how are we to read the violent, murderous letter of the Psalm's final verse? "Who are these little ones in Babylon?" Augustine replies: "Evil desires newly come to birth." He notes that some of us have to fight against inveterate habits, doubtless recalling his intimate experience of this in his *Confessions* (VIII.5.10–11). But he tells his congregation that they can do better than this. How? Here is his answer:

> When evil desire is born, before your bad habits reinforce it, while it is still in its infancy and has not yet fortified itself by alliance with depraved custom, dash it to pieces. It is only a baby still. But make sure it does not survive your violent treatment: dash it on the rock. *And the rock is Christ* (I Cor 10:4).[19]

Because Protestants liked to appropriate Wyclif and Wycliffites as glorious forerunners to their own glorious Reformation, it is salutary to compare here the Wycliffite English Psalter commentary (following Augustine and the conventions of medieval exegesis) as it addresses Psalm 136 [137]:9: "Thes infants [smale] ben yvel stirynges in mannes þouʒte: of pride, coveitise and lechery." The reader is told to knock these infant vices on the rock which is Christ.[20]

I will now turn to the seventeenth-century English revolution and the British civil wars. From late 1641 a drive for war was articulated and publicized by preachers reared and immersed in Calvinist ideology and culture. As some historians have so richly illustrated, these preachers' sermons to Parliament were almost exclusively drawn from the Old Testament, from the narratives of Israel's holy wars and their massacres.[21] Just as, according to Milton and others, God was now an Englishman, so England was the new Israel called to crush the Protestant enemy in England.[22] Just as Moses had slaughtered

---

[19] I use the translation by Sister Maria Boulding: *Exposition of the Psalms*, 6 vols., III.15–20 in *The Works of Saint Augustine, A Translation for the 21st Century* (Hyde Park, N.Y.: New City Press, 2004), here Exposition of Psalm 136.21, III/20, 240.

[20] *Two Revisions of Rolle's English Psalter Commentary and the Related Canticles*, ed. Anne Hudson, 3 vols., EETS, os 343 (Oxford: Oxford University Press, 2014): on Psalm 136 (137), vol. 3, pp. 1061–64, here I quote from p. 1064.

[21] See especially Hugh Trevor-Roper, "The Fast Sermons of the Long Parliament," in *Religion, the Reformation and Social Change and Other Essays* (London: Macmillan, 1967), pp. 294–344; Walzer, *Revolution of the Saints*, pp. 212, 214–29; James Spalding, "Sermons Before Parliament (1640–1649) as a Public Puritan Diary," *Church History* 36 (1967): 24–35; John F. Wilson, *Pulpit in Parliament: Puritanism During the English Civil Wars, 1640–1648* (Princeton: Princeton University Press, 1969), pp. 197–235. Also illuminating here: P. D. L. Avis, "Moses and the Magistrate: A Study in the Rise of Protestant Legalism," *Journal of Ecclesiastical History* 26 (1975): 149–72; and John W. McKenna, "How God Became an Englishman," in *Tudor Rule and Revolution*, ed. DeLloyd Guth and John McKenna (Cambridge: Cambridge University Press, 1982), pp. 25–43.

[22] On God, the English, and the nation state see Elizabeth Sauer, *Milton, Toleration and Nationhood* (Cambridge: Cambridge University Press, 2014), chapter 2; John

THE LETTER KILLS BUT THE SPIRIT GIVES LIFE 283

his idolatrous fellow Israelites on the way to the promised land, so the new Moses (first Parliament, then Cromwell) should slaughter their fellow Protestants who defended the pre-war Church of England and its supreme governor, Charles I.

I only have the stomach to illustrate the conventional war-preaching of Calvinist divines from one sermon, a very famous one preached over sixty times by its author, Stephen Marshall. The sermon is entitled *Meroz Cursed*. Preached to the House of Commons in February 1642, it was published in 1642 "by order of that House" and later reprinted.[23] In it Marshall deploys one of the holy war stories in the Book of Judges to stir up support for Parliament, and especially for the group around Pym pressing towards war against the King. In Judges 5 the people of Meroz (like most English people in 1641–43) seek to keep out of war. For this they are cursed with God's "wrath." Today, says Marshall, those fellow members of the Church of England whom he calls "neuters" will be cursed by God's clergyman and by God for refusing "the helpe of the Lord and his cause." God's cause in the spring of 1642 was of course that of Parliament, or at least of Pym's supporters there. Marshall does acknowledge that Christ ordered his disciples to bless and *not* curse their enemies (for example, Luke 6:28). But whatever Christ says, Marshall proclaims that now is "the most seasonable time" to curse and kill in support of God's cause: "Cursed is everyone that withholds his hands from the shedding of blood." Here Marshall trumps Christ with an Old Testament text (Jeremiah 48:10), one invoked a few years later by Marshall's onetime supporter John Milton when writing about war in *De Doctrina Christiana*.[24] Like Marshall, Milton teaches that there is no reason to think making war is any less licit for Christians than it was for Israel in the Old Testament. He argues that this activity is not prohibited in the New Testament. In this domain at least still a thoroughly orthodox Calvinist, Milton's first proof text comes from the Old Testament: "[The sons of Zion] *having a two-edged sword in their hand*" (II.17, 1243). In neither Milton nor Marshall is there any Christological allegory nor any hint that Christ's teaching might, as Origen argued, undermine uses of the Old Testament as models of slaughter for Christians.

Not surprisingly, Marshall moves easily from cursing "neuters" and those who are holding back from willingness to shed blood in the looming

---

K. Hale, "England as Israel in Milton's Writings," *Early Modern Literary Studies* 2 (1996): 31–54.

[23] The order is on the title page of the 1641 edition: I modernize February 1641 to 1642. See Trevor-Roper, "The Fast Sermons," pp. 297–99, 304–08, 331–32; and Hamlin, *Psalm Culture*, pp. 250–51. On the historical contexts of such uses of Meroz see Jordan S. Downs, "The Curse of Meroz and the English Civil War," *Historical Journal* 57 (2014): 343–68.

[24] Milton's *De Doctrina Christiana*, ed. and tr. John K. Hale and J. Donald Cullington, 2 parts being volume 8 of *The Complete Works of John Milton* (Oxford: Oxford University Press, 2012), II.17, p. 1240.

284 DAVID AERS

civil war to Psalm 137: "blessed is the man that takes their little ones and dashes them against the stones."[25] As with Calvin, Marshall of course offers no Augustinian and medieval Christological allegory. We are given only a deadly literalism. This is precisely the literalism that guided the new Joshua, Oliver Cromwell, during his massacres in Ireland during 1649, at Drogheda and Wexford. These massacres and the campaigns of ethnic cleansing were unequivocally supported by Milton.[26]

Be that as it may, Marshall reflects on Psalm 137:9 in these words:

> What *Souldiers heart* would not start at this, not only when he is in *hot blood* to cut downe *armed* enemies in the *field*, but afterwards *deliberately* to come into a subdued *City*, and take the *little ones* upon the *speares point*, to take them by the heeles and *beat* out their *braines against the walles*, what inhumanitie and barbarousnesse would this be thought? Yet if this work be to revenge Gods Church against *Babylon*, he is a *blessed man that takes and dashes the little one against the stones* (10; italics in Marshall's text).

So excited is the Calvinist preacher by this verse in Psalm 137 that he sets aside Protestant commitment to the strict letter of Scripture to add images: the infants on soldiers' "*speares point*" together with images of infants being taken "by the heeles" so that the soldiers could "beat out their brains against the walles."[27] The preacher's imagination is being activated and shaped by Calvinist hermeneutics around the Old Testament. As so many medieval exegetes observed, *the letter kills.*

The next year (1643) Marshall's Smectymnuan friend Edmund Calamy published a work for parliamentary forces: *The souldiers pocket Bible: containing the most (if not all) those places contained in holy Scripture, which doe show the qualifications of his inner man, that is a fit souldier to fight the Lords battels, both before he fight, in the fight, and after the fight.*[28] Calamy's Bible is a collection of scriptural texts assembled to encourage

---

25 Hamlin discusses *Meroz Cursed* in relation to Psalm 137 in *Psalm Culture*, pp. 250–51.

26 For Cromwell's massacres and his deployment of the language of holy war in the Old Testament, see Ian Gentles, *The New Model Army in England, Ireland, and Scotland: 1645–1653* (Oxford: Blackwell, 1994), pp. 357–68; also consult J. C. Davis, *Oliver Cromwell* (New York: Oxford University Press, 2001), pp. 107–11 with chapter 6.

27 On Marshall's additions, see Hamlin, *Psalm Culture* and Richter, *The Calvinesque.*

28 References are given in the text. There was another edition in 1644. This little book was discussed by Roland Bainton, *Christian Attitudes*, p. 150. On Calamy's popular sermon to Parliament in December 1641 (published as *England's Looking Glass*, 1642) see Simpson, *Permanent Revolution*, pp. 43–47. In *Burning to Read*, James Simpson refers to an earlier example of Protestant identification of England with Israel and encouragement to "English soldiers to read the Scriptures for Israelite victories" (pp. 148–49): Thomas Becon, *The new pollecye of war* (1542).

THE LETTER KILLS BUT THE SPIRIT GIVES LIFE   285

and sacralize Parliament's war against Charles I. The vast majority of the chosen texts are extracted from the Old Testament. What happens to Jesus Christ's commands concerning enemy-love? Here is Calamy's unironic answer: "A Souldier must love his enemies, and hate them as they are gods enemies" (6). He cites Jesus from Matthew 5:44: "But I say unto you love your enemies." Without comment, he immediately follows this with two texts from the Old Testament: first, "Wouldest thou help the wicked and love these that hate the Lord?"; second, "Doe not I hate them O Lord that hate thee and do not I earnestly contend with them that rise up against thee? I hate them with an unfained hatred, as they were mine utter enemies" (6, citing 2 Chronicles 19:2 and Psalm 139:21–22). Love your enemy and thus obey Jesus, but simultaneously kill him as God's enemy. Calamy assures Parliament's soldiers that God will fight for them (5, citing Deuteronomy 20:4) and that God now speaks to them in the words of Deuteronomy 3:32: "fear them not for I have given them into thine hand" (6). The minister also provides examples of mass killing from the Old Testament, exclaiming that "[t]he Lord is a man of warre" (15).

In 1644 Robert Ram wrote a longer work for Calamy's audience: *The Souldiers Catechisme: composed for The Parliaments Army ... Written for the Incouragement and Instruction of all that have taken up Armes in the Cause of God and his People; especially the common Souldiers.*[29] Here too we are assured that the God Christians worship "Calls himself a man of war" and "himself taught *David* to fight" (1–2). But what could Jesus mean by teaching us not to resist evil with carnal actions, he asks, citing Matthew 5:39? The answer is twofold. First, "Christ there onely forbids private revenge and resistance." Second, because Protestants know that Scripture is self-interpreting, "we know that other places of Scripture do warrant taking up of Arms in some cases" (2). Typical of the CalvoReformation hermeneutics I have been following, it is not at all incongruent for Ram that Christ's utterances be set alongside the plethora of texts from Israel's wars and subordinated to Moses. We recall Calvin insisting that the New Testament adds nothing new to the doctrine of the Old Testament, that Christ could not innovate in relation to Moses. And Robert Ram is confident that Parliament's armies "fight to recover the King out of the hands of a Popish Malignant Company" (2). His soldier declares: "I fight for the defence and maintenance of the true Protestant Religion" (3). So we are not killing followers of Reformed Christianity but members of "the Popish Religion." In doing so, "Wee take up Armes against the enemies of Jesus Christ" (3). But are we not fighting fellow Protestants, some of whom do not wish to fight us? Ram responds to this query by insisting that both the armed enemy and "Newters" are actually "secret enemies of God and his Cause." Both active enemy and "such Newters" are cursed as Meroz (Judges 5:23), and will be "spued out of

---

[29] *The Souldiers Catechisme* (London, 1644): references given in text.

286 DAVID AERS

Christ's mouth" (Revelation 3:16). Our opponents are "Papists," "enemies of God" maintaining "the cause of Antichrist" (7). If they are not "Papists" they are "Atheists." If they claim to be Protestants, they really "feare Reformation" and have joined the enemies of Christ (8). What is our aim? To pull down Babylon: here Ram cites the Psalm Marshall invoked in cursing Meroz: Psalm 137:8 (9). Again he stresses that the armed struggle is against "Papists and Atheists," blasphemers, "enemies to God" (12, 15). And without any doubt, "God now calls upon us to avenge the blood of his Saints that hath been shed in the Land" (14). So let the civil war continue, the killing be intensified. Remember you are killing God's enemies who include idolaters who propose "stinking ceremonies," "abominable Monuments of Idolatrie" (16). Let the Reformation begin at last (17–18, 21–25). Such a reformation has all the marks of what James Simpson so powerfully analyzed as "permanent revolution."[30]

His analysis in some haunting ways is foreshadowed during a sermon preached in Oxford, "Shortly after the Surrender of that Garrison" to parliamentary forces in June 1646. The preacher, Jasper Maine, a doctor of divinity, characterized the victorious forces as led by false prophets who have "made it their businesse to put *Holy colours* on their *Slaughters*."[31] Alongside *"Holy colours"* he notes the language of "publique *Utility & necessity*" to smooth over *"Murthers* also and *Bloud-sheds*, together with the *Cries of Widdowes*, and *Tears* of *Orphans*" (8). He sees the victorious forces as driven by a mixture of secular ambitions and religious claims, but here it is the latter that interest me. He tells his congregation that for "almost five years" parliamentary ministers have "preacht up … a *Holy* war," proclaiming a zealous war "for the *Reformation* of a corrupted, degenerate *Church*." Or, in their language, "for the *Restitution* of the *Protestant Religion* growne *Popish*" (11). He also notes that *"Liberty* of *Conscience*" has been a proclaimed cause (11). But Maine argues that even were it true that the Reformation needed further reforming, even were it true that "the *Protestant Religion*" needed restitution, the organized violence of a holy war is utterly alien to the teachings of Christ (11–12). He notes a text discussed by both James Simpson and Karl Gunther, one referred to earlier in the present essay: Christ *"came not to send peace but a Sword into the World"* (Matthew 10:34). Maine argues its use by parliamentary preachers subordinates the Christian gospel to an alien religion of violent conversion and makes Christ "the Author of all those *Massacres*, which from his time to ours, have worne that *Holy Impression*." The problem here includes the ministers' hermeneutic practices, reading "over-litterally" (12). The same applies to their use

---

[30] See *Permanent Revolution*, chapter 2.
[31] *A Sermon Against False Prophets. Preached in St. Maries Church in Oxford, shortly after the Surrender of that Garrison.* The title page names Jasper Maine as author, "D. D. and one of the Students of *Christ. Church* OXON." It was printed in 1647. Here I quote from p. 4 and give all future references in the text.

THE LETTER KILLS BUT THE SPIRIT GIVES LIFE   287

of Christ's statement that the kingdom of heaven is taken "by *violence*" (Matthew 11:12). Where, asks Maine, does Jesus urge his disciples "to come into the field with an *armed Gospel*" to make "Proselites" (13)? Once again, the letter kills while the spirit gives life. Maine then unfolds a Simpsonian account of "permanent revolution." The current false prophets claim that the reformation needs reforming, but this claim is actually a demand for "farther endlesse *changes* as unreasonably still pursued by the *Prophets* of our times" (17).[32] He sees this insatiable desire for continuing "*reformation*" as one in which we see "so much *novelty* mistaken for *reformation*" but driven by a self-interested "*zeale*" (17). Central to this has been the utterly fluid charge of "*Idolatrie*." For example, parliamentary preachers have "taught people to conclude that all *pictures* in *Church-windowes* are *Idols*," that the Book of Common Prayer includes the Catholic "*Masse*," that all images must be banished out of our churches "because *some* (if yet there have been any so stupid) have made them *Idols*" (18–19). He works away at the putative logic legitimizing permanent iconoclasm and revolution, exploring the "*Language of Saints*" (21).

~

Here I must leave this fascinating sermon to turn to an example of the anti-magisterial Reformation mentioned near the beginning of this essay. This example needs to be set alongside the revolutionary regime's understanding of the place of the Old Testament in Christian ethics and legislation. In May 1648, a Presbyterian-led Parliament passed the Blasphemy Ordinance prescribing the death penalty for what Austin Woolrych describes as "numerous deviations from 'orthodox' doctrine."[33] In May 1650 the purged Parliament passed an Act prescribing the death penalty for adultery and in August a Blasphemy Act against "divers men and woman ... most monstrous in their opinions, and loose in all wicked and abominable practices ... even to the dissolution of all humane society."[34] This act did not stipulate the death penalty, though the Blasphemy Ordinance which did so was not repealed. In 1655 the prolific Calvinist John Owen (Cromwell's chaplain and vice-chancellor of Oxford University) defended Calvin for burning Servetus to death for what Owen called "blasphemy": that is, rejecting the scriptural warrants for Nicene Trinitarianism.[35] Martin Bucer, whom John Milton praised as "this faithfull Evangelist" on the path "to a perfectest reforming,"

---

[32] I follow the pagination which moves from 14 to 17.

[33] Austin Woolrych, *Britain in Revolution: 1625–1660* (Oxford: Oxford University Press, 2002), p. 407.

[34] Quoting Blair Worden, *The Rump Parliament* (Oxford: Oxford University Press, 1977), p. 233.

[35] See John Coffey, "The Toleration Controversy in the English Revolution," in *Religion in Revolutionary England*, ed. Christopher Durston and Judith Maltby (Manchester: Manchester University Press, 2006), pp. 50, 64, n. 43.

288   DAVID AERS

would have been delighted.[36] Writing for the Edwardian Reformation, Bucer had demanded the introduction of the death penalty for adultery and blasphemy, citing clusters of texts from the Old Testament. He also advocated that those who broke laws concerning the Sabbath should also be killed. This was in *De Regno Christi*, presented to the young king in 1550. Bucer's hermeneutics assume the identity of New and Old Testaments, of Christ and Moses.[37] And it is in this tradition of the Reformation that the revolutionary legislators of 1648 and 1650 worked.

In 1656 the Quaker James Nayler was charged with blasphemy. Many Presbyterians in Parliament demanded the death penalty for Nayler. Typical of this demand was Richard Shapcote's invocation of the Old Testament: "by the old law this very blasphemy is punishable by death." Here we see the logical outcome of Bucer, Calvin, and their Reformation. As Blair Worden observes, the debate about Nayler in Parliament was in "Old Testament language."[38] Nevertheless, by a vote of 96 to 82, it was decided that instead of the death penalty Nayler was to be tortured and maimed. This was the judgment:

> he was to be placed in the pillory at Westminster for two hours, and then whipped through the streets from there to the Old Exchange where he would again be placed in a pillory for another two hours. Then his tongue would be bored through with a hot iron, he would have the letter B (for blasphemer) branded upon his forehead, and he would finally be sent to Bridewell where he would be kept to hard labour.[39]

As for Nayler's crime, he had ridden into Bristol in October 1656 with some followers shouting hosannas and strewing garments in his path. He was thus enacting Christ's entry into Jerusalem (Luke 19:35–48; Matthew 21:6–16).

---

36 John Milton, *The Judgement of Martin Bucer Concerning Divorce* (1644): I quote from the edition in the *Complete Prose Works of John Milton* (New Haven, Conn.: Yale University Press, 1959), II.438.

37 For Bucer's *De Regno Christi* I refer to the English translation in *Melanchthon and Bucer*, ed. William Pauck (Philadelphia: Westminster Press, 1969): here see II.60 (pp. 378–84) with I.2 (p. 182). On Bucer and his appeals to the Old Testament, see Fulton, *Book of Books*, pp. 99–104.

38 Blair Worden, *God's Instruments: Political Conduct in the England of Oliver Cromwell* (Oxford: Oxford University Press, 2014), pp. 79–81. For Shapcote see the account of the trial in Patrick Little and David Smith, *Parliaments and Politics during the Cromwellian Protectorate* (Cambridge: Cambridge University Press, 2007), p. 212.

39 I quote from Little and Smith, *Parliaments*, p. 185: see pp. 183–88, 211–15. See too Leo Damrosch, *The Sorrow of the Quaker Jesus: James Nayler and the Protestant Crackdown on Free Speech* (Cambridge, Mass.: Harvard University Press, 1996); and David Loewenstein, *Treacherous Faith: The Specter of Heresy in Early Modern Literature and Culture* (Oxford: Oxford University Press, 2013), pp. 224–35 (on Nayler).

THE LETTER KILLS BUT THE SPIRIT GIVES LIFE   289

He was offering a complex sign. One of the speakers in the parliamentary debate glimpsed this. William Sydenham, a soldier, observed "the nearness of [Nayler's] opinion to that which is a most glorious truth, that the spirit is personally in us." Sydenham saw that Nayler's hermeneutic and Christology was quite distinct from Calvinist ones assumed by his persecutors. This, he argued, could not be blasphemy. Besides, killing Nayler "scarcely agrees with the rule of the Gospel."[40] Nayler too had served in the revolutionary army and General Lambert gave him an unequivocally supportive character reference. In the army many forms of anti-Calvinist Christianity flourished, but the forms of theology and spirituality embodied in Nayler were anathema to the revolutionary Parliament's version of the Reformation and the new Israel in England's green and pleasant land.

In 1658 the imprisoned Quaker wrote *The Lamb's War Against the Man of Sin*.[41] Nayler urges "returning love for hatred ... evil with good" (107). He declares that such are the demands of the Spirit disclosed by Christ. Participation in the Lamb's form of holy war means using "weapons [that] are not carnal nor hurtful to the creation: for the Lamb comes not to destroy man's life nor the work of God" (106). Nayler thus echoes Jesus's teaching to his disciples seeking to exterminate an unwelcoming Samaritan village, related in Luke 9:51–56, and summarized at the beginning of this essay. Nayler writes that Jesus Christ puts "spiritual weapons" into the hands and hearts of his followers. The Lamb's war is "not as the prince of this world in his subjects, with whips and prisons, tortures and torments on the bodies of creatures, to kill and destroy men's lives, who are deceived and so become his enemies" (107). Discipleship of Christ, says Nayler, is discipleship of one "who laid down his life for his enemies" (110). He tells his fellow heirs of the Reformation: "Search the Scriptures and read the life of them, and your own lives, with the light of Christ Jesus" (112). No wonder the Quaker merchant Robert Rich, in his *Love Without Dissimulation* (1667), refers to "Innocent and Patient James Nayler."[42]

Gerrard Winstanley himself seems to have completed his life as a Quaker, but I will look briefly at a pamphlet he wrote in 1650, *A New-Yeers Gift Sent to the Parliament and Armie*.[43] Winstanley's works offer a profound account of the shared material interests of landowner, church, and law – interests

---

[40] Little and Smith, *Parliaments*, p. 212.

[41] I quote from the *Lamb's War* in *Early Quaker Writings, 1650–1700*, ed. Hugh Barbour and Arthur Roberts (Grand Rapids, Mich.: Eerdmans, 1973), pp. 102–16. For Quaker Christology see T. L. Underwood, *Primitivism, Radicalism, and the Lamb's Wars: The Baptist-Quaker Conflict in Seventeenth-Century England* (Oxford: Oxford University Press, 1997), chapters 3–4.

[42] Robert Rich, *Love Without Dissimulation* (1667?), 3: contrast the distinguished historian Blair Worden (admirer of Marchamont Nedham and John Milton) dismissing Nayler as "A sorry lunatic" in *The Rump Parliament*, p. 129.

[43] I use the edition in *The Works of Gerrard Winstanley*, ed. George Sabine (New York: Russell and Russell, 1965), pp. 353–96.

in expropriating, exploiting, and controlling those whose labors sustain dominating elites. The serpent of the Fall in Genesis lured humanity to invent private property, a fall from the common treasury of the creation. Fascinating as this is, here I only want to highlight his teaching on enemy-love and the spirit. In 1650 he observes that the demonic kingly power which Parliament and Army claim to have overthrown still flourishes in them and their sword. This kingly power enslaves people, causes wars, and denies the "freedom in the earth" to all (355). Yet Parliament and Army claim to own Scripture: so they have privatized that too! But God will not be mocked by those who use the sword to dominate and to create private property from common land (355–56). The clergy, of course, are beneficiaries of the system which yields them coerced tithes and they support it. What becomes of enemy-love in this context? Winstanley observes that the Diggers had acted without violence in cultivating common land but had nonetheless been violently treated. Yet enemy-love is the end of all preaching and prayer (354–65). Indeed, Love is the creator, the creation, the Word: in the beginning is "the Spirit of Universal Love," "*Love* is the *Word*." When this Spirit of Love rules within us we are at peace; once we are dominated by "Self or Particular love" we create "Bondage" and misery (375). He tells the victors of the civil wars, "Victory that is gotten by the Sword, is a Victory that slaves get one over another" (379). False Christs and false prophets defend the current order, deploying the Calvinist doctrine of double predestination to cement its subjugations of the "reprobated" (381). The true Christ, however, teaches "*Love your enemies, do as you would be done by*" (385). He practices a "true Levelling": "for Jesus Christ the Saviour of all men, is the greatest, first, and truest Leveller that ever was spoke of in the world" (386). In his light the current revolution is one where claims to "set Christ upon his throne in *England*" and to make England "a FREE Commonwealth" are "abominable dissembling Hypocrisie" (386). He discusses the wages paid to laborers forced to work for minimal subsistence by those who have used the sword and the law to enslave them (388). He, always on the parliamentary side as he emphasizes, criticizes the treatment of those defeated in the civil wars: "I was alwayes against the Cavaleers cause; yet their persons are part of the Creation" (389). Those who now oppress them "act contrary to the Scripture which bids you, *Love your enemies, and do as you would be done by*." Why do those who claim to live by Scripture not "practice it" (389)? Enemy-love has uncomfortable entailments for Milton or Cromwell: "Come, make peace with the Cavaliers your enemies, and let the oppressed go free, and let them have a livelihood … let them go in peace, and let love wear the Crown" (389). Like Nayler or Fox, Winstanley invokes the "inward power of love," the inner light. But in 1650, as at any time, this light demands thoroughly specific practices embodying enemy-love taught by Jesus Christ, "the head *Leveller*" (390). Not Calamy's version of enemy-love as slaughter but a Christologically shaped non-violence.

THE LETTER KILLS BUT THE SPIRIT GIVES LIFE   291

Near the end of *Permanent Revolution* James Simpson has a celebratory chapter entitled "Escaping Literalism's Trap" (chapter 17). It concludes with a happy account of how "Milton's hermeneutics recovered, without him ever saying so (perhaps without him knowing so), pre-Reformation traditions of interpretation" (313). Simpson follows Milton's "anti-literalism" from "the disaster of Milton's actual marriage" to *Paradise Lost* (310–14). This happy demonstration concurs with work by Dayton Haskin, Stanley Fish, and Thomas Fulton.[44] And yet the development had a thoroughly bizarre consequence in relation to the subject of the present essay: it enabled Milton to set aside Jesus Christ's teaching on enemy-love. To demonstrate this, I turn now to the strikingly explicit statement in his *De Doctrina Christiana* alluded to earlier. There Milton maintains that all sane Christians will interpret Christ's teachings on the mount *not* literally but according to the kind of hermeneutics Milton had worked out in *Tetrachordon* and the other writings on divorce, a hermeneutics of what he called "charity." So not only can we dissolve the literal sense of Christ's teaching on divorce, by Milton's logic we can do the same to his literal teaching on enemy-love and on the practice of non-violence. Without any intentional irony, Milton teaches that "through a supreme regard for charity" we will sometimes "deviate from the letter even of the gospel commands." We can treat Christ's commands as he treated the literal "sabbath observances" (II.1 and II.27).[45] Are we in Joachim of Fiore's third age of the Holy Spirit superseding the New Testament? While some of Milton's contemporaries imagined something like this, he himself was convinced that he sustained a distinctively Protestant conviction that all Christian doctrine emerges from Scripture without human mediation (see *DDC*, "Epistle to all the churches of Christ" and I.30). Yet to me this hermeneutic practice seems thoroughly congruent with Chaucer's Summoner's Friar describing his own preaching:

> Glosing is a glorious thing, certein,
> For lettre sleeth, so as we clerkes seyn.
> Ther have I taught hem to be charitable.
> (*Canterbury Tales*, III.1793–95)[46]

I doubt that Milton would have appreciated this genealogy, but to me it seems peculiarly fitting. The plainer and more luminous Jesus's commands on love and non-violence, the more harrowing his own pursuit of his teaching, the more we need a glorious gloss. Jesus says, "If ye love me, keep my commandments" (John 14:15), and Milton declares that Jesus is

---

[44] Dayton Haskin, *Milton's Burden of Interpretation* (Philadelphia: University of Pennsylvania Press, 1994); Stanley Fish, *How Milton Works* (Cambridge, Mass.: Harvard University Press, 2001); Fulton, *Book of Books*, chapter 8.

[45] In the edition by Hale and Cullington, part 2, pp. 708–10 and p. 908 (see n. 24 for full bibliographical reference).

[46] I quote from Chaucer, *The Canterbury Tales*, ed. Jill Mann (London: Penguin, 2005).

indeed Theanthrōpos, Deus Homo, God Man (*DDC*, I.14). But Milton has forged a hermeneutics in which his own "charity" can confidently set aside Jesus's own teaching when the spirit moves him (*DDC*, I.30). So, ironically, "anti-literalism" can yield the same results as a literalism in which the letter kills. In *De Doctrina Christiana* Milton writes about the slaughters of holy wars in the Old Testament without any allegorical exegesis (*DDC*, I.11). The understanding of the relations between letter and spirit in this eclectic theologian of the Reformation is far removed from the Catholic and Christological hermeneutics of the medieval Church which Protestants so loved to hate.

16 JAMES SIMPSON'S FREEDOMS: AN APPRECIATION

Jason Crawford

The first time I met James Simpson, I found him in the form of a single printed sentence: *If literary history and criticism is, as I believe it should be, ancillary to the complex history of freedoms, then this is a narrative of diminishing liberties.*[1]

It happened, I think, sometime in the fall of 2003. I was a young doctoral student in the English Department at Harvard. James had just been hired as the department's new medievalist and was soon to arrive on campus. His *Reform and Cultural Revolution* had been published a few months before, and everyone said it was supposed to be bodacious stuff: a field-changing, boundary-crossing, nose-tweaking book, a whisper in the ear of early modernists and many others. I liked the sound of that, and I wanted to know what I was in for at the hands of this new teacher. So I bought the book, hauled it over to Widener Library, opened to paragraph one, and found that sentence: *If literary history and criticism is, as I believe it should be, ancillary to the complex history of freedoms, then this is a narrative of diminishing liberties.*

The thing that startled me, reading that sentence for the first time, was its sheer confidence. *I believe*, it said. This was a *credo*, a declaration. This writer had convictions about what literary history and criticism should be. He could name his enterprise in five words: "the complex history of freedoms." I didn't know exactly what that phrase meant, "the complex history of freedoms." But I could tell it named something strong enough to give this writer his bearings. Already he had my attention.

---

[1] *The Oxford English Literary History, Vol. 2: 1350–1547. Reform and Cultural Revolution* (Oxford: Oxford University Press, 2002), p. 1.

294 JASON CRAWFORD

He had my attention in part because belief, at that moment, seemed to me especially elusive. I was a working-class Protestant with an ingrained mistrust of established institutions, and I found myself now reading medieval literature at an institution that was very well established indeed. I was skeptical about the whole enterprise, resistant to the possibility that history, or historical scholarship, could make any claims on the business of living in the present. I doubted whether I could honestly say what purpose, truth, or community my own scholarship served. So it landed with a jolt, this declaration from a fellow medievalist about exactly what purposes literary history and criticism should serve. I began to expect that what I'd discover in this book, more than anything else, was the bold and bracing assertiveness that I couldn't quite muster up myself.

I was partly right about that, and mainly wrong. In any case, I kept reading, and it turned out that the claims of *Reform and Cultural Revolution* landed with a jolt again and again. If you want to understand the difference of medieval cultural forms, the emergence of modern cultural forms, and even the very notions of *medieval* and *modern* as we understand them, James Simpson said, you have to understand the logic of revolution. Really? This was supposed to be the "late medieval" volume in the Oxford English Literary History: revolution was not what I expected. James went on then to describe the cultural forms of fourteenth- and fifteenth-century England as characterized by heterogeneity and plurality. He described institutions that overlap, intersect, collide, cooperate, and haggle their way toward consensus. He described texts in which languages, genres, and interpretive possibilities multiply and intermingle. And he described, framing it all, an economy of salvation that includes the manifold forms of human agency within itself, a divine grace that disperses itself into many practices and local habitations. In the proliferating texts and institutions of this cultural order, James found freedoms – not *Freedom*, singular and absolute, but *freedoms*, a whole rabble of them, fragile and contingent, jostling together like the motley weirdos of a Langlandian dream. He tracked the forms and practices of these freedoms in all sorts of texts, from *Piers Plowman*, where satire is "reformative rather than damnatory" because it "circles back on itself, recuperating that which it had seemed to reject," to *Sir Gawain and the Green Knight*, where the games of inversion and paradox are so pervasive that "even the pentangle's uncompromising ethical system contains its opposite."[2] These texts, in James's readings, enact a complex history of freedoms in their attempts to contain multitudes, to hold seemingly incommensurable literary, ethical, and temporal registers in juxtaposition.

This already was something to think about, a full-spectrum experiment in redefining the medieval. But then came the book's account of the English sixteenth century. What to call the cultural ruptures of that century's first

---

[2] *Reform and Cultural Revolution*, pp. 374, 281.

JAMES SIMPSON'S FREEDOMS: AN APPRECIATION   295

few decades? Renaissance? Reformation? Secularization? James had another suggestion: *diminishing liberties*. He read the ruptures of the early Tudor period as a cultural revolution, a sudden concentration of power in a regime that demolishes old institutions, repudiates old ideologies, and asserts itself as a transcendent source of authority. In this revolutionary culture, he found a rejection of historical accretion in favor of radical novelty, a suppression of heterogeneity in favor of rigorously policed coherence, a new machinery of judicial torture and state violence. And he found that the subjects of this revolutionary regime were busy having their own crises of belief, mistrustful of established institutions and skeptical about the claims of history on the present. Their emergence, in James's telling, belonged to a story of centralization, expurgation, and a "newly conceived transcendence of power" – a narrative of diminishing liberties.[3]

For James, that story of revolutionary violence played out in early Tudor texts such as Thomas Wyatt's *Paraphrase of the Penitential Psalms*, in which the agency of an absolutist God negates the agency and history of the human sinner, and the interludes of John Bale, in which dramatic action tends to be confined to an errant middle movement and then purged, in the end, by the world-negating pronouncements of a single authoritative voice.[4] Like *Piers Plowman* and *Gawain*, these texts circle back on themselves, fixing their attention on their own histories and rejected possibilities. But James found them circling back to the past in the service not of recuperation but of demolition.

This, too, was something to think about. As I read and digested James's account of these sixteenth-century ruptures, it happened that I was discovering my own affinities with later post-Reformation writers, from Donne and Herbert to Bunyan and Behn. *Reform and Cultural Revolution* goaded me to read these writers with a particular sort of alertness, and with a heightened attunement to the stakes of my reading. Its bold assertions about early modern revolution helped me to start asking questions both about the cultural predicaments of these writers – their mingling of radical and conservative energies, their crises of belief and allegiance, their peculiar forms of historical repudiation and spiritual violence – and about my own embeddedness in those predicaments, my own involvement in a complex history of freedoms. I began, slowly, to see the stories I wanted to tell in my own work.

What I didn't yet understand was that the live-wire argumentation of this book was powered not so much by the imperative of bold assertion as by something else: the imperatives of plurality, the demands of writing multiple complex histories of multiple freedoms. In his 2019 book *Permanent Revolution*, James confesses that when he drafted that defining first-page sentence in *Reform and Cultural Revolution*, he at first wrote the following: "If literary history and criticism is, as I believe it should be, ancillary to the

---

[3]   *Reform and Cultural Revolution*, p. 559.
[4]   See *Reform and Cultural Revolution*, pp. 322–27, 529–33.

complex history of freedom, then this is a narrative of diminishing liberty."[5] Immediately, though, he says, he saw that this sentence missed something decisive, that the story he had to tell was a story of multiplicity: *freedoms*, *liberties*. In asserting the plurality of these freedoms, James wanted to unsettle the notion of absolutist Freedom that the revolutionary culture of early modern England itself produced as a corollary of absolutist Power. His was a story not of Freedom but of freedoms, of liberties that open up in many locations and take many forms. The more I've read James and the longer I've known him, the more I've come to think that this plurality is crucial, not just to his accounts of cultural history, but also to the way he *practices* cultural history. That's my claim here, such as it is: that James Simpson's freedoms, in the plural, inform the way he conceives of his own longue durée narratives, the way he reads and teaches and writes, the way he fosters intellectual community.

But it would take me some years to discover all that. In the meantime, I had to meet the man. At last, in the fall of 2004, he arrived: James Simpson, in all his James Simpsonness. I'm pretty sure the first thing that struck me about him was his sheer personal voltage. He was fully charged, live with intellectual and collegial energy. He emanated a kind of vitality – even, I would say, a kind of radiance. In office hours, over our weekly medievalist lunches at Dolphin Seafood, at the English Department's Thursday-afternoon Medieval Colloquium, he practiced conversation as an exercise in passionate inquiry and artful exchange. His mind ranged all over; his curiosity seemed boundless. When he had something particularly emphatic to posit or to ask, he would fix you in his gaze, peering just over his spectacles, his face animated with conviction and alacrity and mischief. It was electric. For James, clearly, it was fun. His very presence was a running tutorial in the practice of conversing with all channels open.

Then again, there were plenty of conversations I was eager not to have. I was still busy having my crisis of belief. Whenever James invited me to come by his office, or talked about the future, or asked about things like dissertation topics, I deployed intricate tactics of resistance and evasion. To my dismay, he didn't let up. He kept finding me, kept asking questions I didn't want to answer. And before long I began to discover some things about the author of the boldly assertive *Reform and Cultural Revolution*. I discovered, first, that James Simpson was unfailing in his warmth. Even in our most pointed exchanges, he was always engaged, utterly free of arrogance or reserve. Every time I took a step forward, he practically glowed with gladness. He seemed intent on coaxing me out, alert to every sign of conviction or insight in my work. And he cheered most of all when I tacked in unexpected directions, when I departed from his own notions of what my work was about. I began to see early on that there was a remarkable selflessness in James's practice of

---

5   *Permanent Revolution: The Reformation and the Illiberal Roots of Liberalism* (Cambridge, Mass.: Harvard University Press, 2019), p. 320.

teaching. He *wanted* me to take my departures, because he wanted to see a young scholar who would be unlike himself emerge out of our exchanges. His pointed questions and bold assertions served what I'm inclined to call a *pedagogy of freedoms*, rooted in his commitment to the agency and difference of others.

Over the four years that followed, I came to see how very free James is in that commitment. In our department's weekly Medieval Colloquium, he (along with two other uncommonly generous teachers, Daniel Donoghue and Nicholas Watson) worked to invite students to the center of things, treating us as the owners of the conversation, endeavoring to fill this space not with himself but with many others. As I slogged through my own dissertation project, and again as I moved on into the world of the post-recession academy, he kept pace alongside, sharing the yields of his own thinking and writing, making sure there was wind in the sails, and – more and more – making himself my colleague, a friend and fellow-pilgrim in this enterprise. At every stage, James has offered to me the gift of his delight in my work, with all its peculiarities and all its differences from his own. Quite a few times he has said to me, in response to something I've written or attempted or applied for, "*you* are the person to do this!" Those words of celebration distill, for me, James's pedagogy of freedoms, his affirmation of the plural selves and stories that emerge in the work of intellectual exchange.

At the end of *Reform and Cultural Revolution*, James offers another *credo*, a final pair of sentences that attempts to distill his ethos of plurality: "Even books that make a strong case are," he says, "properly transitional. Cultural history necessarily provokes the exhilarating yet always unfinished business of unwriting and rewriting ourselves."[6] You can, of course, spot a James Simpson book by its provocative claims, its vigorous assertion of bold narratives, the intensity of its critiques and confrontations. But here, in the last words of this book, James declares his work unfinished, part of an ongoing process of unwriting and rewriting. In his "Envoi" to the book, he reports that he changed his mind in the course of writing it, that he set out to dissolve the boundaries between medieval and early modern only to find that he was rewriting these boundaries in unanticipated ways; the process of writing, he says, "persuaded me that the dissolution of the boundary line would be a misrepresentation of history."[7] Which is to say that the boldly asserted narratives of this book are subject to revision, up for grabs. The powerful voltage of James's argumentation has been calculated not to foreclose debate but to open it wide, and his provocations have been calls not for silence but for company, for many voices joining in generous discussion. The long penultimate paragraph of *Reform and Cultural Revolution* explicitly appeals to scholars practicing other forms of history to step in and tell their own

6   *Reform and Cultural Revolution*, p. 561.
7   *Reform and Cultural Revolution*, p. 558.

298　　　　　　　　　　　　JASON CRAWFORD

versions of the story.[8] In the book's final pair of sentences, I imagine that James is directing that appeal even to himself: it's time, he says, to get busy unwriting and rewriting this unfinished narrative.

In the years since, James has done just that, following his complex history of freedoms in many directions and across many boundaries. He published *Burning to Read* in 2007, *Under the Hammer* in 2010, and essays along the way on everything from Elizabethan torture and Dutch still life painting to linguistic pragmatism and Rita Felski's *The Limits of Critique*. In *Permanent Revolution*, published in 2019, he returned to his large narrative of early modern revolution and carried it forward, to 1688 and the long history of liberalism. And he announced unambiguously that this new book would take up the invitation he issued to himself back in 2002. James opens the conclusion of *Permanent Revolution* by summing up the project of the book as follows: "If literary history and criticism is, as I believe it should be, ancillary to the complex history of freedoms, then this is a narrative of both newly forged and partially recovered liberties."[9]

Any reader who remembers the opening paragraph of *Reform and Cultural Revolution* will, of course, recognize that sentence: here is James Simpson, seventeen years later, unwriting and rewriting the words of his earlier self. And the change here, from *diminishing liberties* to *newly forged and partially recovered liberties*, indicates not just an extension of his earlier narrative into the later history of post-Reformation liberalism, but also a circling back on himself, a project of returning to his previous narrative and recovering the things he has missed, rejected, or left behind. In some cases that return is very direct. As I've mentioned already, the chapter on "The Dramatic" in *Reform and Cultural Revolution* takes John Bale's religious interludes of the 1530s as exemplars of a revolutionary drama. If, James argues, earlier religious plays such as the York and Wakefield cycles concern themselves with human action in a historically particular world, and with a form of "materialist spirituality" or "light sacramentalism" according to which "Christ is born out of the relentless imperatives of that material world," Bale privileges assent over action, making summaries of scriptural texts so central to his plays that "that pre-dramatic text effectively pre-empts the dramatic itself."[10] In the course of making these arguments, James casts a glance at a passage in Bale's *Three Laws* in which Infidelity gets up to no good alongside her subordinates Idolatry and Sodomy. He notes briefly, in half a paragraph, that Idolatry is associated with magic and that her appearance heralds a period of English history in which folk magic, midwifery, and witchcraft would come under new forms of suppression and control. And

---

8　*Reform and Cultural Revolution*, pp. 560–61.
9　*Permanent Revolution*, p. 344.
10　*Reform and Cultural Revolution*, pp. 527, 557, 532.

JAMES SIMPSON'S FREEDOMS: AN APPRECIATION 299

then he moves on, leaving this thought aside and faring forward with his main discussion of how Bale's drama represents historical action.[11]

But then, in *Permanent Revolution*, he circles back, again to the history of early Tudor drama and again to this passage in the *Three Laws*. This time James notices that Infidelity is not just the associate or supervisor but in fact the *conjuror* of Idolatry, a magician whose enchantments make dramatic characters spring to life onstage.[12] Through the portal of that insight, he enters into a sustained investigation of theater and black magic, considering polemical texts from the fourteenth-century *Treatise on Miracles Playing* to William Prynne's 1633 *Histriomastix* and dramatic texts from the Corpus Christi cycles to the plays of Marlowe, Shakespeare, and Milton. It's as if he has journeyed into the wormhole of his earlier passing comment and found there a new set of narratives about trans-Reformation drama, entangled with but different from the narratives he pursued in his earlier work. As he writes these new narratives, he returns to various points in his old narratives: not just Bale but also, for instance, the York cycle, where he now notices that it is not Infidelity but Christ who is accused of producing theatrical effects by witchcraft. In Christ's recalcitrant silence before his inquisitor Herod, James sees a refusal of theatrical action that is itself "powerfully theatrical and performative" and that therefore "illuminates the sacramental sense of the whole cycle, here by having his exposed body totally transform the world around it."[13] His reading of the York *Christ Before Herod* play thinks again about the materialist spiritualities and sacramentalisms of the pre-Reformation dramatic cycles, reconsidering their theatricality and opening doors onto possibilities that *Reform and Cultural Revolution* never brought fully into view.

Across the two decades of work that have followed on from his earlier narrative, James has engaged in this sort of unwriting and rewriting in many ways, entering into the long history of the Reformation by various approaches and each time discovering paradoxes, ethical problems, and possible futures that weren't visible before. And in *Permanent Revolution*, he parlays his discoveries into a rewriting not just of himself, but also of the whole liberal tradition within which he locates himself. He begins the book by announcing his intention to engage in just this sort of circling back: "Every book," he says in the first sentence of his Preface, "derives from the always unfinished business of unwriting and rewriting the self as one engages with history."[14] If we remember the final sentence of *Reform and Cultural Revolution* – with its "unfinished business of unwriting and rewriting ourselves" – we know that James here is revising his earlier text yet again. There's an intricate symmetry

---

[11] See *Reform and Cultural Revolution*, p. 532.
[12] See *Permanent Revolution*, pp. 209–15.
[13] *Permanent Revolution*, pp. 216–19 (quoted at p. 219).
[14] *Permanent Revolution*, p. ix.

in these passages: the later book begins where the earlier ended and ends where the earlier began. It's like something from the *Pearl* poet, a forging forward that moves ever back, into an unfinished history. In that recursive movement, voices and selves multiply; a later Simpson enters into exchange with an earlier. His grand narratives become visible as themselves sites of plurality, teeming with juxtapositions and accretions, the products of histories and inquiries not yet finished.

Near the end of *Permanent Revolution*, James reflects on the moment in *Paradise Lost* when, after Adam and Eve have fallen, they turn to each other in mutual dependence, in what Eve calls "faithful love unequalled" and what Adam describes as a kind of shared identity, "my own in thee, for what thou art is mine."[15] These professions, in James's account, are freedoms, what he calls "speeches of mutually generous solidarity in the face of overpowering and threatening historical conditions."[16] They belong to the moment when Milton's primal human speakers take up the demands and burdens of a newborn history, grant prerogatives to each other, open themselves to the risk of genuine exchange. Inasmuch as these speeches promise a human community grounded in plurality, they might have something to say about James's own work of inquiring, conversing, and teaching. He has spent a career cultivating his own practice of mutually generous solidarity, discovering in the process that this sort of solidarity is ever unfinished and ever in need of recovery, the ground and the reward of a still-unfinished history of freedoms. And "the discussion" – as he himself reminded himself in the aftermath of *Reform and Cultural Revolution* – "has hardly begun."[17] It's just getting started, alive with possibility, even as the conditions of history seem threatening and overpowering as ever.

---

[15] *Permanent Revolution*, pp. 341, 342; John Milton, *Paradise Lost*, IX.958, 982.
[16] *Permanent Revolution*, p. 342.
[17] "Not the Last Word," *Journal of Medieval and Early Modern Studies* 35 (2005), 111–19 (at 119).

James Simpson's Publications from 1984 to 2024

BOOKS

The Index of Middle English Prose, Handlist VII: Manuscripts Containing Middle English Prose in Parisian Libraries. Cambridge: D. S. Brewer, *1989.*

Piers Plowman: An Introduction to the B-Text. Longman Medieval and Renaissance Library 1. Harlow, UK: Longman, 1990. (Selection r*epr. in Piers* Plowman. Edited by Elizabeth Robertson and Stephen Shepherd. New York: Norton, 2006. 584–91.)

Sciences and the Self in Medieval Poetry: Alan of Lille's "Anticlaudianus" and John Gower's "Confessio amantis". Cambridge: Cambridge University Press, *1995.*

The Oxford English Literary History, Vol. 2: 1350–1547. Reform and Cultural Revolution. Oxford: Oxford University Press, *2002.*

*Piers Plowman: An Int*roduction. Rev. ed. Exeter Medieval Texts and Studies. Exeter, UK: Exeter University Press, *2007.*

Burning to Read: English Fundamentalism and its Reformation Opponents. Cambridge, Mass.: The Belknap Press of Harvard University Press, *2007.*

Under the Hammer: Iconoclasm in the Anglo-American Tradition. The Clarendon Lectures. Oxford: Oxford University Press, *2010.*

*Reynard the Fox: A New Tra*nslation. New York: Liveright/Norton, *2015.*

*John Hardyng, Chronicle: Edited from British Library MS Lansd*owne 204. Co-edited with Sarah Peverley. Vol. 1. TEAMS Middle English Texts. Kalamazoo, Mich.: Medieval Institute Publications, *2015.*

*Permanent Revolution: The Reformation and the Illiberal Roots of Li*beralism. Cambridge, Mass: The Belknap Press of Harvard University Press, *2019.*

The Oxford Chaucer. Edited by Christopher Cannon and James Simpson. Oxford: Oxford University Press, 2024.

302 JAMES SIMPSON'S PUBLICATIONS FROM 1984 TO 2024

COLLECTIONS AND ANTHOLOGIES

Medieval English Religious and Ethical Literature: Essays in Honour of G. H. Russell. Edited by Gregory Kratzmann and James Simpson. Cambridge: D. S. Brewer, 1986.

Images, Idolatry and Iconoclasm in Late Medieval England. Edited by Jeremy Dimmick, James Simpson, and Nicolette Zeeman. Oxford: Oxford University Press, 2002.

John Lydgate: Poetry, Culture, and Lancastrian England. Edited by Larry Scanlon and James Simpson. Notre Dame, Ind.: University of Notre Dame Press, 2006.

"The Middle Ages." Edited by Alfred David and James Simpson. Volu*me A of The Norton Anthology of English Li*terature. Edited by Stephen Greenblatt and M. H. Abrams. 8*th ed. New York: W. W. Norton, 2006.*

The Morton Bloomfield Lectures, 1989–2005. Edited by Daniel Donoghue, James Simpson and Nicholas Watson. Kalamazoo, Mich.: Medieval Institute Publications, 2010.

*Premodern Sha*kespeare. Edited by Sarah Beckwith and James Simpson. Special *issue of The Journal of Medieval and Early Modern* Studies 40 (2010).

"The Middle Ages." Edited by Alfred David and James Simpson. Volu*me A of The Norton Anthology of English Li*terature. Edited by Stephen Greenblatt. 9th ed. New York: W. W. Norto*n, 2012.*

Cultural Reformations: Medieval and Renaissance in Literary History. Edited by Brian Cummings and James Simpson. Oxford Twenty-First Century Approaches to Literature 2. Oxford: Oxford University Press, 2010.

"The Middle Ages." *Edited by James Simpson. Volume A of The* Norton Anthology of English Literature. Edited by Stephen Greenblatt. 10*th ed. New York: W. W. Norton,* 2017.

The Oxford Handbook to Chaucer. Edited by Suzanne Akbari and James Simpson. Ox*ford: Oxford University Press, 2020.*

*Enlistment: Lists i*n Medieval and Early Modern Literature. Edited by Eva von Contzen and James Simpson. Interventions: New Studies in Medieval Culture. Columbus, Ohio*: Ohio State University Press, 2022.*

*The Prac*tice and Politics of Reading, 650–1500. Edited by Daniel Donoghue, James Simpson, Nicholas Watson and Anna Wi*lson. Cambridge: D. S. Brewer,* 2022.

*Inten*tion and Interpretation, Now and Then. Edit*ed by James Simpson. Special issue of The Journa*l of Medieval and Early Modern Studies 53 (2023).

"The Middle Ages." Edited b*y Julie Orlemanski and James Simpson. The* Norton Anthology of English Literature. Edited by Stephen Greenblatt. 11th ed. New York: W. W. Norton, 2023.

ARTICLES AND ESSAYS

"Spiritual and *Earthly Nobility in 'Piers P*lowman.'" Neuphilologisc*he Mitteilungen* 86 *(1985). 467–*81.

"Et Vidit Deus Cogitationes Eorum: a Parallel Instance and Possible Source for L*angland's Use* of a Biblical *Formula at Piers* Plowman B.XV.200a." Notes and Queries n.s. 33 (1986). 9–13.

"Dante's 'Astripetam Aquilam' and *the Theme of* Poetic Discretion i*n* the House of Fame." Essays and Studies n.s. 39 (1986). 1–18.

JAMES SIMPSON'S PUBLICATIONS FROM 1984 TO 2024

"The Transformation of Meaning: a Figure of Thought in Piers Plowman." Review of English Studies n.s. 37 (1986). 161–83.

"From Reason to Affective Knowledge: Modes of Thought and Poetic Form in Piers Plowman." Medium Ævum 55 (1986). 1–23.

"The Role of Scientia in Piers Plowman." In Medieval English Religious and Ethical Literature: Essays in Honour of G. H. Russell. Edited by Gregory Kratzmann and James Simpson. Cambridge: D. S. Brewer, 1986. 49–65.

"Spirituality and Economics in Passus I–VII of the B-Text of Piers Plowman." The Yearbook of Langland Studies 1 (1987). 83–103.

"Ironic Incongruence in the Prologue and Book I of Gower's Confessio Amantis." Neophilologus 72 (1988). 617–32.

"Poetry as Knowledge: Dante's Paradiso XIII." Forum for Modern Language Studies 25 (1989). 329–43.

"The Constraints of Satire in Mum and the Sothsegger and Piers Plowman." In Langland, the Mystics and the Medieval English Religious Tradition. Edited by Helen Phillips. Cambridge: D. S. Brewer, 1990. 11–30.

"Madness and Texts: Hoccleve's Series." In Chaucer and Fifteenth Century Poetry. Edited by Janet Cowen and Julia Boffey. London: King's College, 1991. 15–29.

"The Information of Alan of Lille's Anticlaudianus: a Preposterous Interpretation." Traditio 47 (1992). 113–60.

"'After Craftes Conseil clotheth yow and fede': Langland and the City of London." In England in the Fourteenth Century (the 1991 Symposium). Harlaxton Medieval Studies 3. Edited by Nicholas Rogers. Stamford, UK: Paul Watkins, 1993. 109–27.

"The Information of Genius in Book III of the Confessio Amantis." Mediaevalia 16 (1993, for 1990). 159–95.

"The Death of the Author?: Skelton's Bowge of Court." In The Timeless and the Temporal, Writings in Honour of John Chalker. Edited by Elizabeth Maslen. London: Queen Mary and Westfield College, 1993. 58–79.

"'Ut Pictura Poesis': A Critique of Robert Jordan's Chaucer and the Shape of Creation." In Interpretation Medieval and Modern: J. A. W. Bennett Memorial Lectures, Eighth Series. Edited by Piero Boitani and Anna Torti. Cambridge: D. S. Brewer, 1993. 167–87.

"Nobody's Man: Thomas Hoccleve's Regement of Princes." In London and Europe. Edited by Julia Boffey and Pamela King. London: Westfield Publications in Medieval Studies, 1995. 150–80.

"Desire and the Scriptural Text: Will as Reader in Piers Plowman." In Criticism and Dissent in the Middle Ages. Edited by Rita Copeland. Cambridge: Cambridge University Press, 1996. 215–43.

"'Dysemol daies and Fatal houres': Lydgate's Destruction of Thebes and Chaucer's Knight's Tale." In The Long Fifteenth Century: Essays in Honour of Douglas Gray. Edited by Helen Cooper and Sally Mapstone. Oxford: Oxford University Press, 1997. 15–33.

"Ageism: Leland, Bale and the Laborious Start of English Literary History, 1350–1550." New Medieval Literatures 1 (1997). 213–35.

"The Other Book of Troy: Guido delle Colonne's Historia destructionis Troiae in Fourteenth and Fifteenth-Century England." Speculum 73 (1998). 397–423. Repr. in Classical and Medieval Literature Criticism. Vol. 90. Detroit, Mich.: Gale Research Co., 2007.

"Hoccleve," "Usk," and "Beast Fable." In Medieval England: An Encyclopaedia. Edited by Paul E. Szarmach. New York: Garland, 1998. 111–12.

"Ethics and Interpretation: Reading Wills in Chaucer's Legend of Good Women." Studies in the Age of Chaucer 20 (1998). 73–100.

"Breaking the Vacuum: Ricardian and Henrician Ovidianism." Journal of Medieval and Early Modern Studies 29 (1999). 325–55.

"Violence, Narrative and Proper Name: Sir Degaré, 'The Tale of Sir Gareth of Orkney', and the Anglo-Norman Folie Tristan d'Oxford." In The Spirit of Medieval English Popular Romance. Edited by Jane Gilbert and Ad Putter. London: Routledge, 2000. 122–41.

"The Sacrifice of Lady Rochford: Henry Parker's Translation of De claris mulieribus." In "Triumphs of English": Henry Parker, Lord Morley, Translator to the Tudor Court. New Essays in Interpretation. Edited by Marie Axton and James P. Carley. London: British Library Publications, 2000. 153–69.

"Contemporary English Writers." In A Companion to Chaucer. Edited by Peter Brown. Oxford: Blackwell, 2000. 114–32.

"Medieval Literature, Class 1." In The Virtual Classroom. https://www.english. cam.ac.uk/classroom/class2/index.htm (accessed 16 July 2023).

"Bulldozing the Middle Ages: The Case of 'John Lydgate.'" New Medieval Literatures 4 (2000). 213–42.

"Grace Abounding: Evangelical Centralisation and the End of Piers Plowman." Yearbook of Langland Studies 14 (2000). 1–25.

"The Power of Impropriety: Authorial Naming in Piers Plowman." In William Langland's Piers Plowman: A Book of Essays. Edited by Kathleen M. Hewett-Smith. New York: Routledge, 2001. 145–65.

"The Rule of Medieval Imagination." In Images, Idolatry and Iconoclasm in Late Medieval England. Edited by Jeremy Dimmick, James Simpson and Nicolette Zeeman. Oxford: Oxford University Press, 2002. 4–24.

"Faith and Hermeneutics: Pragmatism versus Pragmatism." Journal of Medieval and Early Modern Studies 33 (2003). 215–39.

"Chaucer's Presence and Absence, 1400–1550." In A Chaucer Companion. Edited by Jill Mann and Piero Boitani. 2nd ed. Cambridge: Cambridge University Press, 2003. 251–69.

"Humanism." In Dictionary of the Middle Ages. Supplement 1. Edited by William Chester Jordan. New York: Charles Scribner's Sons, 2004. 279–82.

"Martyrdom in the Literal Sense: Surrey's Psalm Paraphrases." Medieval and Early Modern English Studies (South Korea) 12 (2004). 133–65.

"Reginald Pecock and John Fortescue." In A Companion to Middle English Prose. Edited by A. S. G. Edwards. Cambridge: D. S. Brewer, 2004. 271–88.

"Not the Last Word." Journal of Medieval and Early Modern Studies 1 (2005). 111–20.

"Saving Satire after Arundel: John Audelay's Marcol and Solomon." In Text and Controversy from Wyclif to Bale: Essays in Honour of Anne Hudson. Edited by Ann Hutchison and Helen Barr. Medieval Church Studies 4. Turnhout, Belgium: Brepols, 2005. 387–404.

"Subjects of Triumph and Literary History: Dido and Petrarch in Petrarch's Trionfi and Africa." Journal of Medieval and Early Modern Studies 35 (2005). 489–508. Translated and republished as "Soggetti di trionfo e storia letteraria: Didone e Petrarca nell'Africa e nei Trionfi di Petrarca." In Petrarca: canoni, esemplarità. Edited by Valeria Finucci. Rome: Bulzoni, 2006. 73–92.

JAMES SIMPSON'S PUBLICATIONS FROM 1984 TO 2024   305

"Consuming Ethics: Caxton's History of Reynard the Fox." In Studies in Late Medieval and Early Renaissance Texts in Honour of John Scattergood. Edited by Alan Fletcher and Anne-Marie D'Arcy. Dublin: Four Courts Press, 2005. 321–36.

"Literary Terminology." In Norton Anthology of English Literature. Edited by Stephen Greenblatt. 8th ed. New York: W. W. Norton, 2006. A56–A77.

"Chaucer as a European Writer." In The Yale Companion to Chaucer. Edited by Seth Lerer. New Haven, Conn.: Yale University Press, 2005. 55–86.

"'For al my body … weieth nat an unce': Empty Poets and Rhetorical Weight in Lydgate's Churl and the Bird." In John Lydgate: Poetry, Culture, and Lancastrian England. Edited by Larry Scanlon and James Simpson. Notre Dame, Ind.: University of Notre Dame Press, 2006. 129–46.

With Larry Scanlon. "Introduction." In John Lydgate: Poetry, Culture, and Lancastrian England. Edited by Larry Scanlon and James Simpson. Notre Dame, Ind.: University of Notre Dame Press, 2006. 1–11.

"Confessing Literature." English Language Notes 44 (2006). 121–26.

"Making History Whole: Diachronic History and the Shortcomings of Medieval Studies." e-Colloquia 3 (2005). http://www.ecolloquia.com/issues/200501/index.html.

"Diachronic History and the Shortcomings of Medieval Studies." In Reading the Medieval in Early Modern England. Edited by David Matthews and Gordon McMullan. Cambridge: Cambridge University Press, 2007. 17–30.

"Bonjour Paresse: Literary Waste and Recycling in Book 4 of Gower's Confessio amantis." The Sir Israel Gollancz Memorial Lecture. Publications of the British Academy 151 (2007). 257–84.

"Tyndale as Promoter of Figural Allegory and Figurative Language: A Brief Declaration of the Sacraments." Archiv für das Studium der Neueren Sprachen und Literaturen 245 (2008). 37–55.

With Kevin Brownlee, Tony Hunt, Ian Johnson, Alastair Minnis, and Nigel F. Palmer. "Vernacular Literary Consciousness, c. 1100–c. 1500: French, German and English Evidence." In The Cambridge History of Literary Criticism, Vol. 2: The Middle Ages. Edited by Alastair Minnis and Ian Johnson. Cambridge: Cambridge University Press, 2009. 422–27.

"The Economy of Involucrum: Idleness in Reason and Sensuality." In Through a Classical Eye: Transcultural and Transhistorical Visions in Medieval English, Italian, and Latin Literature in Honor of Winthrop Wetherbee. Edited by Andrew Galloway and R. F. Yeager. Toronto: University of Toronto Press, 2009. 390–414.

"John Lydgate." In The Cambridge Companion to Medieval Literature. Edited by Larry Scanlon. Cambridge: Cambridge University Press, 2009. 205–16.

"Sixteenth-Century Fundamentalism and the Specter of Ambiguity, or The Literal Sense is Always a Fiction." In Writing Fundamentalism. Edited by Klaus Stierstorfer and Axel Stähler. Newcastle Upon Tyne: Cambridge Scholars Publishing, 2009. 133–54.

"Rhetoric, Conscience and the Playful Positions of Sir Thomas More." In The Oxford Handbook to Tudor Literature, 1485–1603. Edited by Mike Pincombe and Cathy Shrank. Oxford: Oxford University Press, 2009. 121–36.

With Sarah Beckwith. "Premodern Shakespeare." In Premodern Shakespeare. Edited by Sarah Beckwith and James Simpson. Special issue of The Journal of Medieval and Early Modern Studies 40 (2010). 2–5.

306   JAMES SIMPSON'S PUBLICATIONS FROM 1984 TO 2024

"*Place.*" In *Cultural Reformations: Mediev*al and Renaissance in Literary History. Edited by Brian Cummings and James Simpson. Oxford Twenty-First Century Approaches to Literature 2. Oxford: Oxford University Press, 2010. 95–112.

With *Brian Cummings.* "*Introduction.*" In *Cultural Reformations: Mediev*al and Renaissance in Literary History. Edited by Brian Cummings and James Simpson. Oxford Twenty-First Century Approaches to Literature 2. Oxford: Oxford University Press, 2010. 1–9.

"'And that was litel nede': *Poetry's Need in Robert Henry*son's *Fables and Testament of Cresseid.*" In *Mediev*al Latin and Middle English Literature. Edited by Christopher Cannon and Maura Nolan. Cambridge: D. S. Brewer, 2011. 193–210.

"'*Not Just a Museum*'? Not so Fast." Religion and Literature 42 (2010). 141–61.

"Visiona*ry Writing in England, 1534–1550s.*" In *The Cam*bridge Companion to Medieval Mysticism. Edited by Vincent Gillespie and Samuel Fanous. Cambridge: Cambridge University Press, 2011. 249–64.

"*Killing Auth*ors: *Skelton's Dreadful Bouge of Court.*" In *Form and* Reform: Reading the Fifteenth Century. Edited by Kathleen Tonry and Shannon Gayk. Columbus, Ohio: Ohio State University Press, 2011. 180–96.

"Orthodoxy's Image T*rouble: Image*s in a*nd After Arundel's Constitutions.*" In *After Arundel: Religiou*s Writing in Fifteenth-Century England. Edited by Vincent Gillespie and Kantik Ghosh. Medieval Church Studies 21. Turnhout, Belgium: Brepols, 2011. 91–113.

"No Brainer: *The Early Modern Traged*y of Torture." Religion and Literature 43 (2011). 1–23.

"The Reformation of S*cholarship: A Reply to Debora Shuger.*" *The Journal* of Medieval and Early Modern Stu*dies 42 (*2012). *249–68.*

"*John Bale's Three Laws.*" In The Oxford Handbook to Tudor Drama. Edited by Greg Walker and Tom Betteridge. Oxford: Oxford University Press, 2012. 109–22.

"Cognition is Recognition: L*iterary Knowledge and* Textual 'Face,'" New Literary History 44 (2013). 25–44.

Harvard University Arts and Humanities Division. "The Teaching of the Arts and Humanities at Harvard College: Mapping the Future." 2013. http://artsandhumanities.fas.harvard.edu/ (accessed 16 July *2023).*

"*Derek Brewer's Romance.*" In *A Modern Medievalist: Traditions and Innovation*s in the Study of Medieval Literature. Edited by Charlotte Brewer and Barry Windeatt. Cambridge: D. S. Brewer, 2013. 154–72.

"*Religious F*orms a*nd Institutions in Piers Pl*owman." In The Cambridge Companion to Piers Plowman. Edited by Andrew Cole and Andy Galloway. Cambridge: Cambridge University Press, 2013. 97–116.

"Iconoc*lasm and the Enlightenment Museum.*" In *Strikin*g Images: Iconoclasms Past and Present. Edited by Stacy Boldrick, Leslie Brubaker, and Richard Clay. Farnham, UK: Ashgate, 2013. 113–27.

"Iconoclasm: *Early Modern Britain and America.*" In Oxford Encyclopaedia of Aesthetics. Edited by Michael Kelly. 2nd ed. 6 vols. Oxford: Oxford University Press, 2014. 3: 400–03.

"Glassy Temporalities: The Chapel Win*dows of King's College Cambridge.*" In *King's College Chapel 1515–2015*: Art, Music and Religion in Cambridge. Edited by Nicolette Zeeman and Jean Michel Massing. Studies in Medieval and Early Renaissance Art History 75. Turnhout, Belgium: Brepols, 2014. 79–95.

JAMES SIMPSON'S PUBLICATIONS FROM 1984 TO 2024   307

"Human Prudence versus the Emotion of the Cosmos: War, Deliberation and Destruction in the *Late Medieval Statian Tradition.*" *In Emotions an*d War: Medieval to Romantic Literature. Edited by Andrew Lynch, Stephanie Downes, and Katrina O'Loughlin. Palgrave Studies in the History of Emotions. London: Palgrave McMillan, 2015. 98–116.

"*Not Yet: Chaucer and An*agogy." Studies in the Age of Cha*ucer 37 (2015). 31–54. Republished in Asynchronien: Formen der* verschränkter Zeit in der Vormoderne. Edited by Jutta Eming and Johannes Traulsen. Vandenhoeck & Ruprecht: Göttingen, 2022. 63–84.

"The Psalms and Threat in Six*teenth-Century Englis*h Court Culture." Renaissance Studies 29 (2015). 576–94.

"'The Form*less Ruin of Oblivion*': Shakespeare's Troilus and *Cressida and Literary Defacement.*" *In Love, History an*d Emotion in Chaucer *and* Shakespeare: Troilus and Criseyde and Troilus and Cressida. Edited by Andrew Johnston, Russell West Pavlov, and Elizabeth Kempf. Manchester: Manchester U*niversit*y Press, 2016. 189–206.

"The Aeneid Translations of Henry Howard, Earl of Surr*ey: The Exiled Reader's Presence.*" *In The Oxford History of Classical Reception in Englis*h Literature, Vol. 1: The Middle Ages. Edited by Rita Copeland. Oxford: Oxford University Press, 2016. 601–23.

"Br*ad Gregory's Unintended Revelations.*" *Journa*l of Medieval and Early Modern Studies 46 (2016). 545–54.

"2016. Interrogation *Over. A Review Essay of Rita* Felski, The Limits of Critique." PMLA 132 (20*17). 377–83.*

"Subver*sive Laughter in R*eynard the Fox." In Animals: A History. Edited by Peter Adamson and G. Fay Edwards. Oxford Philosophical Concepts. Oxford: Oxford University Press, 2017. 157–62.

"Textua*l Face: Cognition as Recognition.*" *In Contemporary Chaucer across the Centur*ies: A Festschrift for Stephanie Trigg. Edited by Helen M. Hickey, Anne McHendry, and Melissa Raine. Manchester: Manchester University Press*, 2018. 218–*33.

"*Unthinking Romance: Sir* Degaré." In Thinking Medieval Romance. Edited by Katherine C. Little and Nicola McDonald. Oxford: Oxford University Press, 2018. 36–54.

"Anti-Virgilianism *in Late Medieval Troy Narrative*s." In Troie en Europe au Moyen Âge. Edited by Catherine Croizy-Naquet, Anne Roch*ebouet, and Florenc*e Tanniou. Vol. 2, Troianalexandrina *19 (2019). 293–312.*

"*Rich*ard II." In A New Companion to Chaucer. Edited by Peter Brown. Oxford: Wiley, 2019. 359–78.

"Working, across the *Very Long* Reformation: Four Models." Reformation 24 (2019). 181–94.

"Trans-Refo*rmation English Literary History.*" *In Early Modern Histories of Time: The Periodizations of Sixt*eenth- and Seventeenth-Century England. Edited by Kristen Poole and Owen Williams. Philadelphia: University of Pennsylvania Press, 2019. 88–101.

"Stilled Lives, Still *Lives: Reformation Memorial* Focus." In Remembering the Reformation. Edited by Brian Cummings, Ceri Law, Bronwyn Wallace, and Alexandra Walsham. London: Routledge, 2020. 23–40.

JAMES SIMPSON'S PUBLICATIONS FROM 1984 TO 2024

"'Gaufred, deere maister *soverain*': *Chaucer and Rhetoric*." In The Oxford Handbook to Chaucer. Edited by Suzanne Akbari and James Simpson. Oxford: Oxford University Press, 2020. 126–46.

"Giving and Gaining Voice *in Civil War: the* Alain Chartier's Quadrilogue Inve*ctif in Fifteenth-Century England*." *In* Literature, Emotions and Pre-Modern War. Edited by Claire McIroy and Anne M. Scott. Leeds: ARC Humanities Press, 2021. 151–66.

"*The Not Yet Wife of Bath*." *In Gender, Poetry, and the Form of Thought in Later Medieval Literature: Ess*ays in Honor of Elizabeth A. Robertson. Edited by Ingrid Nelson and Jennifer Jahner. Bethlehem, Penn.: Lehigh University Press, 2022. 201–22.

"Capaneus' Atheis*m and Criseyde's Reading in Chaucer's Troilus and Criseyde*." In *"Of latine and of othire lare"*: Essays in Honour of David R. Carlson. Edited by Richard Firth Green and R. F. Yeager. Papers in Mediaeval Studies 35. Toronto: Pontifical Institute of Mediaeval Studies, 2022. 67–*81*.

"*Prisonniers de la* 'Liberté!'" Le Journal des Libertés 17 (2022). 123–37.

"Reformation Lists: Syntax, the S*acred, and the Production of Junk*." *In Enlistment: Lists i*n Medieval and Early Modern Literature. Edited by Eva von Contzen and James Simpson. Interventions: New Studies in Medieval Culture. Columbus, Ohio: Ohio State University Press, 2022. 195–212.

"Unwritten Virtues, Selves a*nd Texts: Early Modern Self-Erasure*." *Journal* of Medieval and Early Modern Studies 52 (2022). 415–44.

With Daniel Donoghue, Nicholas Watson*, and Anna Wilson*. "Introduction." *In The Prac*tice and Politics of Reading, 650–1500. Edited by Daniel Donoghue, James Simpson, Nicholas Watson and Anna Wilson. Cambridge: D. S. Brewer, 2022. 1–17.

With Eva von Contzen. "Enlistme*nt as Poetic as Poetic Stratagem*." *In Enlistment: Lists i*n Medieval and Early Modern Literature. Edited by Eva von Contzen and James Simpson. Interventions: New Studies in Medieval Culture. Columbus, Ohio: Ohio State University Press, 2022. 1–14.

"The Elle*smere Manuscript: T*he *Once and Future Canterbury* Tales." Huntington Library Quarterly 85 (2023). 197–218.

"Literary T*raditions: Continuity and Change*." *In T*he *Oxford History of Poetry in English*. Volume 3: Poetry in English: 1400–1500. Edited by Julia Boffey and A. S. G. Edwards. Oxford: Oxford University Press, 2023. 28–45.

"Intention *and Interpretation, Now and Then*." *In Int*erpreting Interpretation, Now and Then. Edit*ed by James Simpson. Special issue of The Journa*l of Medieval and Early Modern Studies 53 (*2023). 451–65.*

REVIEWS

J. A. Burrow. Medieval W*riters and their Work. Boris* Ford, ed. Medieval Li*terature, Part I. Stephe*n *Medcalf, e*d. The Later Middle Ages. Medium Æ*vum 53 (1984).* 307–11.

Janet *Coleman. Piers* Plowman and the Moderni. Medium Ævum *53 (1984).* 125–27.

William Whallon. Inconsi*stenci*es: Stud*ies in t*he N*ew* Testame*nt, the Inferno,* Othello and Beowulf. Notes and Queries n.*s. 31 (1984).* 413–15.

Piero Boitani. Chaucer and the Italian Trecento. Medium Ævum 54 (1985). *306–08.*

JAMES SIMPSON'S PUBLICATIONS FROM 1984 TO 2024 309

Guy Bourquin. Piers Plowman: Etudes sur la genèse littéraire des trois versions. Medium Ævum 54 (1985). 302–04.

M. L. Colish. The Mirror of Language: A Study in the Medieval Theory of Knowledge. Medium Ævum 55 (1986). 123–25.

Howard H. Schless. Chaucer and Dante: a Revaluation. Medium Ævum 56 (1987). 120–23.

David Wallace. Chaucer and the Early Writings of Boccaccio. Medium Ævum 56 (1987). 323–24.

Lavinia Griffiths. *Personification* in Piers Plowman. Notes and Queries n.s. 34 (1987). 63–64.

Julia Bolton Holloway. The Pilgrim and the Book: a Study of Dante, Langland and Chaucer. Medium Ævum 59 (1990). 144–46.

A. J. Minnis and A. B. Scott, eds. Medieval Literary Theory and Criticism, c. 1100–c. 1375: the Commentary Tradition. Medium Ævum 59 (1990). 140–42.

Wendy Scase. Piers Plowman and the New Anticlericalism. Notes and Queries n.s. 37 (1990). 455–56.

Cindy L. Vitto. The Virtuous Pagan in Middle English Literature. Cahiers de Civilisation Médiévale (1991). 281.

Derek Pearsall. An Annotated Bibliography of Langland. Notes and Queries n.s. 38 (1991). 358–59.

Anna Torti. The Glass of Form: Mirroring Structures from Chaucer to Skelton. Medium Ævum 61 (1992). 323–24.

Pamela Raabe. Imitating God: the Allegory of Faith in Piers Plowman. Medium Ævum 61 (1992). 121–23.

Kathryn Kerby-Fulton. Reformist Apocalypticism and Piers Plowman. Journal of Ecclesiastical History 42 (1991). 664.

Piero Boitani and Anna Torti, eds. Religion in the Poetry and Drama of the Late Middle Ages in England. Notes and Queries n.s. 40 (1993). 361–62.

A. J. Minnis, ed. Chaucer's Boece and the Medieval Tradition of Boethius. Notes and Queries n.s. 41 (1994). 544–45.

Helen Barr, ed. The Piers Plowman Tradition. Studies in the Age of Chaucer 16 (1994). 150–52.

J. A. Burrow. Langland's Fictions. Medium Ævum 63 (1994). 328–29.

J. A. Burrow. Thomas Hoccleve. Medium Ævum 65 (1996). 179.

Richard G. Newhauser and John Alford, eds. Literature and Religion in the Later Middle Ages: Philological Studies in Honor of Siegfried Wenzel. Yearbook of Langland Studies 11 (1997). 230–32.

Richard J. Utz, ed. Literary Nominalism and the Theory of Rereading Late Medieval Texts. Anglia 116 (1998). 537–39.

Seth Lerer. Courtly Letters in the Age of Henry VIII: Literary Culture and the Arts of Deceit. Medium Ævum 68 (1999). 135–36.

Theresa M. Krier, ed. Refiguring Chaucer in the Renaissance. Mediaevalia et Humanistica n.s. 26 (1999). 197–99.

David Wallace, ed. The Cambridge History of Medieval English Literature. Medium Ævum 69 (2000). 127–30.

John Scattergood. The Lost Tradition: Essays on Middle English Alliterative Poetry. Review of English Studies 53 (2002). 109–11.

Kathryn L. Lynch. Chaucer's Philosophical Visions. Modern Language Review 98 (2003). 426–27.

Russell A. Peck, ed. John Gower, Confessio Amantis. Speculum 76 (2001). 943–44.

310 JAMES SIMPSON'S PUBLICATIONS FROM 1984 TO 2024

Ethan Knapp. *The Bureaucratic Muse: Thomas Hoccleve and the Literature of Late Medieval* England. Studies in the Age of Chaucer 25 (2003). 394–97.

Ian Gadd and Alexandra Gillespie, eds. *John Stow (1525–1605) and the Making of the English Past: Studies in Early Modern Culture* and the History of the Book. Speculum 81 (2006). 849–50.

Ralph Hanna. *London Literature, 1300–1380.* Studies in the Age of Chaucer 28 (2006). 290–93.

Bruce Holsinger. *The Premodern Condition: Medievalism and the Making of Theory.* Speculum 82 (2006). 198–200.

John Bowers. *Chaucer and Langland: The Antagonistic Tradition.* Studies in the Age of Chaucer 30 (2008). 343–46.

J. A. Burrow. *The Poetry of Praise.* Notes and Queries n.s. 56 (2009). 278–80.

Bruce Gordon. *Calvin.* Times Literary Supplement, 18 and 25 December (2009). 34.

Alastair Minnis. *Translations of Authority in Medieval English Literature: Valuing the Vernacular.* Notes and Queries n.s. 57 (2010). 578–80.

David Aers. *Sanctifying Signs: Making Christian Tradition in Late Medieval England. David Aers. Salvation and Sin: Augustine, Langland, and Fourteenth-Century Theology.* Yearbook of Langland Studies 24 (2011). 205–09.

James Kearney. *The Incarnate Text: Imagining the Book in Reformation England.* Modern Philology 110 (2012). E228–30.

Lee Patterson. *Acts of Recognition: Essays on Medieval Culture.* Speculum 87 (2012). 268–70.

Rosemarie McGerr. *A Lancastrian Mirror for Princes: The Yale Law School New Statutes of England.* American Historical Review 118 (2013). 569–70.

William Kuskin. *Recursive Origins: Writing at the Transition to Modernity.* Modern Philology 112 (2014). 35–37.

Ruth Morse, *Helen Cooper, and Peter Holland, eds. Medieval Shakespeare: Pasts and Presents.* Medieval and Renaissance Drama in England 28 (2015). 196–99.

Margaret Aston, *Broken Idols of the English Reformation.* Material Religion 14 (2018). 263–64.

Andrew Hiscock and Helen Wilcox, eds. *Early Modern English Literature and Religion.* Renaissance Quarterly 71 (2018). 1585–86.

Jill Mann, ed. Geoffrey Chaucer: *The Canterbury Tales. David Lawton, with Jennifer Arch and Kathryn Lynch, eds. The Norton Chaucer.* Speculum 96 (2021). 791–94.

Robert Meyer-Lee, *Literary Value and Social Identity in the Canterbury Tales.* JEGP 120 (2021). 426–27.

BIBLIOGRAPHY

MANUSCRIPTS

Baltimore

Walters Art Museum, W.37
Walters Art Museum, W.102

Bethesda, Md.

National Library of Medicine, E 4

Cambridge

Fitzwilliam Museum, 261
Jesus College, Q. G. 8
St. John's College, I.22
Trinity College Library, O.2.13
University Library, Additional 3137
University Library, Ff.2.38

Edinburgh

National Library of Scotland, Advocates' 1.1.6
National Library of Scotland, Advocates' 18.7.21
National Library of Scotland, Advocates' 19.2.1
National Library of Scotland, Advocates' 19.2.2 (ii)

Exeter

Cathedral Library, 3501

Ipswich

Suffolk Record Office, Ipswich C/4/1/1

Leiden

University Library, Vossius Germ. Gall. Q. 9

BIBLIOGRAPHY

London

British Library, Additional 10099
British Library, Additional 27879
British Library, Additional 34360
British Library, Additional 41666
British Library, Additional 62925
British Library, Arundel 168
British Library, Cotton Caligula A I
British Library, Cotton Vespasian A I
British Library, Cotton Vitellius A XV
British Library, Egerton 1995
British Library, Egerton 2862
British Library, Egerton 3132A
British Library, Harley 116
British Library, Harley 541
British Library, Harley 941
British Library, Harley 2251
British Library, Harley 2252
British Library, Harley 4011
British Library, Harley 5102
British Library, Harley 5401
British Library, Harley 7322
British Library, Lansdowne 699
British Library, Royal 18 D 2
British Library, Royal 17 B.XLVII
British Library, Sloane 775
British Library, Sloane 989
British Library, Sloane 2321
British Library, Sloane 3534
Kew, The National Archives, C 241/225/52
Kew, The National Archives, STAC 3/7/74
Lambeth Palace Library, 444
Lambeth Palace Library, 853
Wellcome Historical Medical Library, 406
Wellcome Historical Medical Library, 411
Wellcome Historical Medical Library, 8004

Los Angeles

Getty Museum of Art, Ludwig IX 3

New Haven, Conn.

Beinecke Rare Book and Manuscript Library, 360
Beinecke Rare Book and Manuscript Library, 661
Beinecke Rare Book and Manuscript Library, Takamiya 22

New York

Metropolitan Museum of Art, Cloisters Collection, 54.1.2
Morgan Library, M.102
Morgan Library, M.1044

BIBLIOGRAPHY

Norwich

Norfolk Record Office, NRO BL/GT 3/1-20

Oxford

Bodleian Library, Add. B. 60
Bodleian Library, Ashmole 61
Bodleian Library, Bodley 649
Bodleian Library, Bodley 686
Bodleian Library, Digby 102
Bodleian Library, Douce 261
Bodleian Library, Eng. Poet. A.1
Bodleian Library, Eng. Poet. D.4
Bodleian Library, e Musaeo 52
Bodleian Library, Laud. Misc. 683
Bodleian Library Rawlinson C. 48
Bodleian Library, Rawlinson C. 86
Bodleian Library, Rawlinson F.34

Paris

Bibliothèque nationale de France, fr. 5388
Bibliothèque nationale de France, NAL 3111

Rome

English College, AVCAU 1405

Rouen

Bibliothèque municipale de Rouen, I 2s

ONLINE RESOURCES

Anglo-Norman Dictionary. https://www.anglo-norman.net.
British Library. *Catalogue of Digitised Manuscripts*. https://www.bl.uk/manuscripts/ Default.aspx.
Database of Middle English Romance. York: University of York, 2012. https://www. middleenglishromance.org.uk.
Dictionary of Old English Web Corpus, compiled by Antonette diPaolo Healey with John Price Wilkin and Xin Xiang. Toronto: Dictionary of Old English Project, 2009. https://tapor.library.utoronto.ca/doecorpus.
Dictionnaire de moyen français (1330–1500). http://zeus.atilf.fr/dmf/.
DIMEV. Digital Index of Middle English Verse. Compiled, edited, and supplemented by Linne R. Mooney, Daniel W. Mosser, and Elizabeth Solopova, with Deborah Thorpe, David Hill Radcliffe, and Len Hatfield. http://www.dimev.net.
MED. Middle English Dictionary. Edited by Hans Kurath, Sherman Kuhn, and Robert E. Lewis. 115 fascicules. Ann Arbor, Mich.: University of Michigan Press, 1952–2001. https://quod.lib.umich.edu/m/middle-english-dictionary/ dictionary.
Oxford Dictionary of National Biography. https://www.oxforddnb.com.
OED. Oxford English Dictionary. https://www.oed.com.

BIBLIOGRAPHY

PRIMARY SOURCES

A Macaronic Sermon Collection from Late Medieval England: Oxford, MS Bodley 649. Edited and translated by Patrick J. Horner. Studies and Texts 153. Toronto: Pontifical Institute of Mediaeval Studies, 2006.

Ælfric of Eynsham. "Dominica VIII Post Pentecosten." In *Ælfric's Catholic Homilies, Second Series, Text*. Edited by Malcolm Godden. EETS, ss 5. Oxford: Oxford University Press, 1979. 230–34.

Alan of Lille. *Anticlaudianus*. In *Alan of Lille: Literary Works*. Edited and translated by Winthrop Wetherbee. DOML 22. Cambridge, Mass.: Harvard University Press, 2013. 219–517.

Aldhelm. *Enigmata*. In *Aldhelmi Opera*. Edited by Rudolf Ehwald. Monumenta Germaniae Historica Auct. Antiq. 15. Berlin: Weidmann, 1919.

Ancrene Wisse: A Corrected Edition of the Text in Cambridge, Corpus Christi College, MS 402, with Variants from Other Manuscripts. Edited by Bella Millett, with E. J. Dobson and Richard Dance. 2 vols. EETS, os 325, 326. Oxford: Oxford University Press, 2005.

Andrew, Malcolm, and Ronald Waldron, eds. *The Poems of the Pearl Manuscript*. London: Edward Arnold, 1981.

——, and Clifford Peterson, eds. *The Complete Works of the Pearl-poet*. Berkeley, Calif: University of California Press, 1993.

Aquinas, Thomas. *Catena Aurea*. Translated by John Henry Cardinal Newman. 4 vols. London: Saint Austin Press, 1999.

——. *Commentary on the Nicomachean Ethics*. Edited and translated by C. I. Litzinger. O.P. 2 vols. Chicago: Henry Regnery Company, 1964.

——. *Summa Theologica*. Edited and translated by the Fathers of the English Dominican Province. 3 vols. New York: Benziger Brothers, 1947–48.

Aristotle. *Metaphysics*. In *The Complete Works of Aristotle*. Edited and translated by Jonathan Barnes. 2 vols. Princeton, N.J.: Princeton University Press, 1984. 2.1552–728.

——. *Poetics*. In *Aristotle, Poetics. Longinus, On the Sublime. Demetrius, On Style*. Edited by Stephen Halliwell. Translated by W. Hamilton Fyfe. Cambridge, Mass.: Harvard University Press, 1995.

Ascham, Roger. *The Scholemaster*. London: John Day, 1570.

——. *Toxophilus*. London: Edward Whitchurch, 1545.

"The Assumption of the Blessed Virgin." In *The Auchinleck Manuscript*. Edited by David Burnley and Alison Wiggins. Edinburgh: National Library of Scotland, 2003. http://auchinleck.nls.uk/mss/assumpt.html. Fols. 73r–78r.

Augustine of Hippo. *Confessions*. Translated by Carolyn J. B. Hammond. 2 vols. Cambridge, Mass.: Harvard University Press, 2014.

——. *Confessions*. Edited by James J. O'Donnell. 3 vols. Oxford: Clarendon Press, 1992.

——. *Confessions*. Translated by Henry Chadwick. Oxford: Oxford University Press, 1991.

——. *On Christian Doctrine*. Translated by D. W. Robertson. New York: Liberal Arts Press, 1958.

——. *De Doctrina Christiana*. Translated by R. P. H. Green. Oxford: Oxford University Press, 1997.

——. *Enarrationes in Psalmos*. Edited by E. Dekkers and J. Fraipont. CCSL 38–40. Turnhout, Belgium: Brepols, 1956.

BIBLIOGRAPHY

315

——. *Exposition of the Psalms*. In *The Works of Saint Augustine, A Translation for the 21st Century*. Translated by Maria Boulding. 6 vols. Hyde Park, N.Y.: New City Press, 2004.

——. *The Trinity*. Translated by Stephen McKenna. Washington: Catholic University of America Press, 1963.

Bancroft, Richard. *A sermon preached at Paules Crosse the 9. Of Februarie* …. London: Printed by E. B[ollifant] for Gregorie Seton, 1588.

Barr, Helen, ed. *The Piers Plowman Tradition*. London: J. M. Dent, 1993.

Beckett, Samuel. *The Complete Dramatic Works*. London: Faber and Faber, 1986.

Bede. *Historia Ecclesiastica Gentis Anglorum*. In *Ecclesiastical History of the English People*. Edited and translated by Bertram Colgrave and R. A. B. Mynors. Oxford: Clarendon Press, 1969.

——. *Venerabilis Baedae Opera Historica*. 2 vols. Edited by Charles Plummer. Oxford: Oxford University Press, 1896.

Benedict of Nursia. *Regula*. In *Benedicti Regula*. Edited by Rudolph Hanslik. CSEL. Vienna: Hoelder-Pichler-Tempsky, 1960.

Boccaccio, Giovanni. *Boccaccio on Poetry: Being the Preface and the Fourteenth and Fifteenth Books of Boccaccio's* Genealogia Deorum Gentilium. Translated by Charles G. Osgood. Repr. Indianapolis, Ind.: Bobbs-Merrill, 1956.

——. *Die Proemia, Lib. XIV, Und Lib. XV, sowie die Conclusio der Genealogia deorum im Wortlaut des Originals des Laurenziana*. In *Boccaccio-Funde*. Edited by Oskar Hecker. Braunschweig: George Westermann, 1902. 159–299.

——. *Esposizioni sopra la Comedia di Dante*. In *Tutte le opere di Giovanni Boccaccio*. Gen. ed. Vittore Branca. Vol. 6. Florence: Arnoldo Mondadori, 1965.

——. *Il Filostrato: The Filostrato of Giovanni Boccaccio*. Edited and translated by Nathaniel Edward Griffin and Arthur Beckwith Myrick. Philadelphia: University of Pennsylvania Press, 1929.

——. *Trattatello in laude di Dante*. In *Tutte le opere di Giovanni Boccaccio*. Edited by Pier Giorgio Padoan. Gen. ed. Vittore Branca. Vol. 3. Florence: Arnoldo Mondadori, 1974. 423–911.

Boethius. *Consolatio Philosophiae*. Translated by S. J. Tester. Loeb Classical Library. Cambridge, Mass.: Harvard University Press, 2014.

Bonde, William. *Pilgrimage of Perfection*. ESTC S108952. London: Wynkyn de Worde, 1531.

Brown, Maureen, and Paul Brown, eds. *Wing Churchwardens' Accounts, 1527–1662*. Aylesbury, UK: Buckinghamshire Record Society, 2019. 49, 52.

Bucer, Martin. *De Regno Christi*. In *Melanchthon and Bucer*. Edited by William Pauck. Philadelphia: Westminster Press, 1969.

Burton, William. *Ten sermons vpon the first, second, third and fourth verses of the sixt of Matthew* …. London: Printed by Richard Field for Thomas Man, 1602.

Calamy, Edmund. *The souldiers pocket Bible: containing the most (if not all) those places contained in holy Scripture, which doe show the qualifications of his inner man, that is a fit souldier to fight the Lords battels, both before he fight, in the fight, and after the fight*. London: G.B. and R.W. for G.C., 1643.

Calendar of Letter-Books of the City of London: K, Henry VI. Edited by Reginald R. Sharpe. London: Corporation of the City of London, 1911.

Calendar of Letter-Books of the City of London: L, Edw. IV–Henry VII. Edited by Reginald R. Sharpe. London: Corporation of the City of London, 1912.

Calvin, John. *Institutes of the Christian Religion*. Edited by John T. McNeill. Translated by Ford L. Battles. 2 vols. Philadelphia: Westminster Press, 1960.

BIBLIOGRAPHY

Carle, Eric. *The Very Hungry Caterpillar*. New York: World Publishing Company, 1969.

Chambers, R. W., and Marjorie Daunt, eds. *A Book of London English, 1384–1425*. Oxford: Clarendon Press, 1931.

Chaucer, Geoffrey. *The Canterbury Tales*. Edited by Jill Mann. London: Penguin, 2005.

——. *The Riverside Chaucer*. 3rd ed. Gen. ed. Larry Benson. Boston: Houghton Mifflin, 1987.

——. *Troilus and Criseyde*. Edited by Stephen A. Barney. In *The Riverside Chaucer*. Gen ed. Larry Benson. Boston: Houghton Mifflin, 1987.

Cicero. *De Inventione*. Edited and translated by H. M. Hubbell. Loeb Classical Library. Cambridge, Mass.: Harvard University Press, 1949.

——. *De oratore*. In *De oratore Book III, De Fato, Paradoxa Stoicorum, De partitione oratoria*. Edited and translated by H. Rackham. Loeb Classical Library. Cambridge, Mass.: Harvard University Press, 1942. 3–185.

——. *Orator*. In *Brutus. Orator*. Edited and translated by H. M. Hubbell. Loeb Classical Library. Cambridge, Mass.: Harvard University Press, 1962. 295–509.

"Clergy and common law in the reign of Henry IV." Edited by R. L. Storey. In *Medieval Legal Records Edited in Memory of C. A. F. Meekings*. Edited by R. F. Hunnisett and J. B. Post. London: Her Majesty's Stationery Office, 1978. 341–408.

Codex Ashmole 61: A Compilation of Popular Middle English Verse. Edited by George Shuffleton. TEAMS Middle English Texts. Kalamazoo, Mich.: Medieval Institute Publications, 2008.

Colgrave, Bertram, ed. and tr. *The Earliest Life of Gregory the Great, by an anonymous monk of Whitby*. Lawrence, Kans.: University of Kansas Press, 1968.

Copeland, Rita, and Ineke Sluiter, eds. *Medieval Grammar and Rhetoric: Language Arts and Literary Theory, AD 300–1475*. Oxford: Oxford University Press, 2009.

Dante Alighieri. *Convivio: A Dual-Language Edition*. Edited and translated by Andrew Frisardi. Cambridge: Cambridge University Press, 2018.

——. *Epistle to Can Grande*. In *Dantis Alagherii Epistolae. The Letters of Dante*. Edited by Paget Toynbee. 2nd ed. Oxford: Clarendon Press, 1966. Epistola 10.

——. *La Divina Commedia*. Edited by Natalino Sapegno. 2nd ed. 3 vols. Florence: Nuova Italia, 1971.

Demetrius, On Style. Edited by Doreen C. Innes. Based on the translation of W. Rhys Roberts. In *Aristotle, Poetics. Longinus, On the Sublime. Demetrius, On Style*. Loeb Classical Library. Cambridge, Mass.: Harvard University Press, 1995. 309–525.

De Montaigne, Michel. *Les Essais de Michel de Montaigne*. Edited by Pierre Villey and Verdun L. Saulnier. 3rd ed. Paris : Presses universitaires de France, 1978.

De spirituali amicitia. In *Aelredi Rievallensis Opera omnia: I. Opera ascetica*. Edited by A. Hoste and C. H. Talbot. CCCM I. Turnhout, Belgium: Brepols, 1971.

Degaré. In *The Middle English Breton Lays*. Edited by Anne Laskaya and Eve Salisbury. TEAMS Middle English Texts. Kalamazoo, Mich.: Medieval Institute Publications, 1995.

Della Lana, Jacopo. *Commento*. In *Comedia di Dante Allagheri col commento Jacopo della Lana*. 3 vols. Bologna: Tipografia Regia, 1866.

The Digby Poems: A New Edition of the Lyrics. Edited by Helen Barr. Exeter Medieval Texts and Studies. Exeter, UK: University of Exeter Press, 2009.

BIBLIOGRAPHY 317

Donati ars grammatica. In *Grammatici latini.* Edited by Heinrich Keil. 7 vols. Leipzig: Teubner, 1857–80. 4.353–402.

Doree, Stephen G., ed. *The Early Churchwardens' Accounts of Bishop's Stortford, 1431–1558.* [Hitchin]: Hertfordshire Record Society, 1994.

Drayton, Michael. *Ideas Mirrour.* London: James Roberts, for Nicholas Linge, 1594.

Eglamour. In *Four Middle English Romances: Sir Isumbras, Octavian, Sir Eglamour of Artois, Sir Tryamour.* Edited by Harriet Hudson. TEAMS Middle English Texts. Kalamazoo, Mich.: Medieval Institute Publications, 2006.

Eliot, T. S. *Collected Poems 1909–1962.* London: Faber and Faber, 1963.

Elyot, Thomas. *The Governour.* London: Thomas Berthelet, 1531.

Emaré. In *The Middle English Breton Lays.* Edited by Anne Laskaya and Eve Salisbury. TEAMS Middle English Texts. Kalamazoo, Mich.: Medieval Institute Publications, 1995.

Ephron, Nora. *Sleepless in Seattle.* TriStar Pictures, 1993. Film.

Erasmus, Desiderius. *Copia: Foundations of the Abundant Style: De duplici copia verborum ac rerum Comentarii duo.* In *Collected Works of Erasmus.* Edited and translated by Betty I. Knott. Vol. 24. Toronto: Toronto University Press, 1978.

Exeter Riddles. In *The Old English and Anglo-Latin Riddle Tradition.* Edited by Andy Orchard. DOML 69. Cambridge, Mass.: Harvard University Press, 2021.

Favreau, Robert, et al. *Corpus des inscriptions de la France médiévale.* Paris: CNRS, 1974–.

The First Commentary on the First Six Books of the Aeneid *of Vergil commonly attributed to Bernardus Silvestris.* Edited by Julian Ward Jones and Elizabeth Frances Jones. Lincoln, Nebr.: University of Nebraska Press, 1977.

Furnivall, F. J., ed. "Incypyt the Stacyons of Rome." In *Political, Religious, and Love Poems.* EETS, os 15. London: K. Paul, Trubner, Trench and co., 1866.

Geoffrey of Monmouth. *Historia Regum Britanniae: The History of the Kings of Britain: An Edition and Translation of De Gestis Britonum (Historia Regum Britanniae).* Edited by Michael Reeve. Translated by Neil Wright. Woodbridge, UK: Boydell, 2007.

Geoffrey of Vinsauf. *Poetria nova.* In *Les Arts poétiques du XIIe et XIIIe siècle.* Edited by E. Faral. Paris: Champion, 1924. 194–262.

——. *Poetria nova.* Translated by M. F. Nims. Rev. ed. Toronto: Pontifical Institute of Mediaeval Studies, 2010. 49–50.

Gerard, John. *The Herball or Generall Historie of Plantes ….* London: John Norton, 1597.

Given-Wilson, Chris, gen. ed. *Parliament Rolls of Medieval England.* 16 vols. Woodbridge, UK: Boydell, 2005.

Gower, John. *Confessio amantis.* Edited by Russell Peck with Latin translations by Andrew Galloway. 3 vols. TEAMS Middle English Texts. Kalamazoo, Mich.: Medieval Institute Publications, 2006.

Gregory the Great. *Epistolarum Registrum.* PL 77, cols. 441–1328.

Guido da Pisa. *Expositiones et glose super Comediam Dantis, or Commentary on Dante's Inferno.* Edited by Vincenzo Cioffari. Albany, N.Y.: State University of New York Press, 1974.

Guillaume de Lorris, and Jean de Meun. *Le Roman de la Rose.* 3 vols. Edited by Félix Lecoy. Paris: Librairie Honoré Champion, 1965–70.

——. *The Romance of the Rose.* Translated by Charles Dahlberg. 3rd ed. Princeton, N.J. : Princeton University Press, 1995.

BIBLIOGRAPHY

Guillaume de Machaut. *Le Jugement dou roy de Behaingne*. In *Guillaume de Machaut: The Complete Poetry and Music, Volume 1: The Debate Series*. Edited by R. Barton Palmer and Yolanda Plumley, with Dominic Leo and Uri Smilansky. Kalamazoo, Mich.: Medieval Institute Publications, 2016.

——. *Remede de Fortune*. In *Guillaume de Machaut: The Complete Poetry and Music, Volume 2: The Boethian Poems*. Edited by R. Barton Palmer, with Dominic Leo and Uri Smilansky. Kalamazoo, Mich.: Medieval Institute Publications, 2019.

Hanham, Alison, ed. *Churchwardens' Accounts of Ashburton, 1479–1580*. Torquay: Devon & Cornwall Record Society, 1970. 121, 124.

Harington, John. *Nugae Antiquae*. Vol. I. Edited by Henry Harington. London: J. Wright, 1804.

Hawes, Stephen. *The Pastime of Pleasure*. Edited by William Edward Mead. EETS, os 173. London: Oxford University Press, 1928.

Henry the Minstrel. *The Actis and Deidis of The Illustere and Vailðeand Campioun Schir William Wallace, Knicht of Ellerslie*. Edited by James Moir. Edinburgh: William Blackwood and Sons, 1889.

Heraclitus. *Homeric Problems*. Edited and translated by Donald A. Russell and David Konstan. Leiden: Brill, 2005.

Holland, Robert. *The holie historie of our Lord and Sauiour Iesus Christs natiuitie, life, actes, miracles …*. London: George Tobie, 1594.

Holme, Randall. *The academy of armory …*. Chester: Printed for the author, 1688.

Homer. *The Odyssey*. Translated by A. T. Murray. Revised by George E. Dimock. 2 vols. Cambridge, Mass.: Harvard University Press, 1995.

Isidore of Seville. *Etymologiarum sive originum libri XX*. Edited by W. M. Lindsay. Oxford: Clarendon Press, 1957.

John of Salisbury. *Policraticus*. In *Ioannis Saresberiensis Policraticus, sive De nugis curialum, et vestigiis philosophorum, libri octo*. Leiden: Johannes Maire, 1639.

——. *Policraticus*. Translated by Cary J. Nederman. Cambridge: Cambridge University Press, 2007.

John the Deacon. *Sancti Gregorii Magni Vita: Auctore Joanne Diacono*. PL 75, cols. 61–212.

Johnson, Samuel. "No. 71." 20 November 1750. In *The Rambler*. Vol. II. London: P. Dodsley, R. Owen, and Other Booksellers, 1794.

"Joseph's Troubles about Mary." In *The York Corpus Christi Plays*. Edited by Clifford Davidson. TEAMS Middle English Texts. Kalamazoo, Mich.: Medieval Institute Publications, 2011.

Kempe, Margery. *The Book of Margery Kempe*. Edited by Lynn Staley. TEAMS Middle English Texts. Kalamazoo, Mich.: Medieval Institute Publications, 1996.

Klaeber's Beowulf. Edited by R. D. Fulk, Robert E. Bjork, and John D. Niles. 4th ed. Toronto: University of Toronto Press, 2008.

Krapp, George Philip, and Elliot van Kirk Dobbie, eds. *The Exeter Book*. New York: Columbia University Press, 1936.

La vie de terrible Robert le diable. Lyon: Pierre Mareschal et Barnabé Chaussard, 1496.

Langland, William. *Piers Plowman, A New Annotated Edition of the C-text*. Edited by Derek Pearsall. Exeter Medieval Texts and Studies. Exeter, UK: University of Exeter Press, 2008.

——. *The Vision of Piers Plowman*. Edited by A.V.C. Schmidt. London: J. M. Dent, 1978.

BIBLIOGRAPHY

319

——. *Will's Visions of Piers Plowman and Do-Well*. In *Piers Plowman: The C Version*. Rev. ed. Edited by George Russell and George Kane. London: Athlone, 1997.

Les Vraies Croniques de Normandie. Paris, Bibliothèque Nationale de France, MS fr. 5388.

Littlehales, Henry, ed. *The Medieval Records of A London City Church: St Mary At Hill, 1420–1559*. London: Trübner, 1905.

Locke, John. *An Essay Concerning Human Understanding*. Edited by Alexander Campbell Fraser. Oxford: Clarendon Press, 1894.

Lodge, Thomas. *Rosalynde*. London: Thomas Orwin for T. G[ubbin] and John Busbie, 1590.

——. *The Famous, True and Historicall Life of Robert, Second Duke of Normandy*. London: Thomas Orwin, 1591.

Lydgate, John. *The Minor Poems of John Lydgate*. Edited by Henry Noble MacCracken. Vol. 2. EETS, os 192. Oxford: Oxford University Press, 1934.

——. *The Serpent of Division*. Edited by Henry Noble MacCracken. New Haven, C.T.: Yale University Press, 1911.

The Lyf of the Moste Myschevoust Robert the Devyll. London: Wynkyn de Worde, 1500?

Maine, Jasper. *A Sermon Against False Prophets. Preached in St. Maries Church in Oxford, shortly after the Surrender of that Garrison*. Oxford?: Publisher not known. 1647.

Malory, Thomas. *Le Morte Darthur*. Edited by P. J. C. Field. 2 vols. Cambridge: D. S. Brewer, 2013.

Margerum, Johanna, ed. *The Cartulary of Binham Priory*. Norfolk Record Society 80. Exeter, UK: Norfolk Record Society, 2016.

Marie de France. *Guigemar*. In *Lais*. Edited by A. Ewert. Oxford: Blackwell, 1965.

Matthew of Vendôme. *The Art of Versification*. Translated by Aubrey E. Galyon. Ames, Iowa: Iowa State University Press, 1980.

McCarey, Leo. *An Affair to Remember*. 20th Century Fox, 1957. Film.

Metropolitan Museum of Art. New York. https://www.metmuseum.org/art/collection/search/470309. The Cloisters Collection, 1954.

Middleton-Stewart, Judith, ed. *Records of the Churchwardens of Mildenhall: Collections (1446–1454) and Accounts (1503–1553)*. Woodbridge, UK: Suffolk Records Society, 2011.

Milton, John. *De Doctrina Christiana*. In *The Complete Works of John Milton*. Edited and translated by John K. Hale and J. Donald Cullington. Vol. 8. Oxford: Oxford University Press, 2012.

——. *Paradise Lost*. In *The Poetical Works of John Milton*. Edited by Helen Darbishire. Vol. 1. Oxford: Oxford University Press, 1962.

——. *The Judgement of Martin Bucer Concerning Divorce*. In *The Complete Prose Works of John Milton*. Edited by Ernest Sirluck. New Haven, Conn.: Yale University Press, 1959.

Moxon, Joseph. *Mechanick Exercises* …. London: Printed for Joseph Moxon, 1683.

Mulcaster, Richard. *Positions wherin those Primitive Circumstances be Examined, which are Necessarie for the Training up of Children*. London: Thomas Vautrollier for Thomas Chard, 1581.

——. *The First Part of the Elementarie*. London: Thomas Vautrollier, 1582.

320 BIBLIOGRAPHY

Nayler, James. *The Lamb's War Against the Man of Sin*. In *Early Quaker Writings, 1650–1700*. Edited by Hugh Barbour and Arthur Roberts. Grand Rapids: Eerdmans, 1973. 102–16.

Nederman, Cary J., ed. and tr. *Political Thought in Early Fourteenth-Century England: Treatises by Walter of Milemete, William of Pagula, and William of Ockham*. Tempe, Ariz: Arizona Center for Medieval and Renaissance Studies in collaboration with Brepols, 2002.

Nichols, Francis Morgan, ed. *The Marvels of Rome or A Picture of the Golden City: Mirabilia Urbis Romae*. London: Ellis and Elvey, 1989.

Okasha, Elisabeth. *Hand-list of Anglo-Saxon Non-runic Inscriptions*. Cambridge: Cambridge University Press, 1971.

Ovid. *Metamorphoses*. Edited and translated by Frank Justus Miller. Revised by G. P. Goold. Cambridge, Mass.: Harvard University Press, 1916.

Paul the Deacon. *Sancti Gregorii Magni Vita : Auctore Paulo Diacono Monachio Cassinensi*. PL 75, cols. 11–60.

Petrarca, Francesco. *Le Familiari*. Edited by Vittorio Rossi. 4 vols. Florence: G. C. Sansoni, 1933–41.

——. *Rerum familiarium libri (I–VIII)*. Translated by Aldo S. Bernardo. Albany, N.Y.: State University of New York Press, 1975.

Pietro Alighieri. *Comentum super poema Comedie Dantis: A Critical Edition of the Third and Final Draft of Pietro Alighieri's "Commentary" on Dante's "The Divine Comedy"*. Edited by Massimiliano Chiamenti. Tempe, Ariz.: Arizona Center for Medieval and Renaissance Studies, 2002.

Plato. *Meno*. Edited and translated by W. Lamb. Cambridge, Mass.: Harvard University Press, 1924.

——. *"Timaeus", a Calcidio translatus commentarioque instructus*. Edited by Jan H. Waszink. Leiden and London: Brill and Warburg Institute, 1975.

Pseudo-Cicero. *Rhetorica ad Herennium*. Edited and translated by Harry Caplan. Loeb Classical Library. Cambridge, Mass.: Harvard University Press, 1954.

Puttenham, George. *The Art of English Poesy: A Critical Edition*. Edited by Frank Whigham and Wayne A. Rebhorne. Ithaca, N.Y.: Cornell University Press, 2007.

Quintilian. *The Orator's Education*. Edited and translated by Donald A. Russell. Loeb Classical Library. 5 vols. Cambridge, Mass.: Harvard University Press, 2002.

Ram, Robert. *The Souldiers Catechisme: composed for The Parliaments Army … Written for the Incouragement and Instruction of all that have taken up Armes in the Cause of God and his People; especially the common Souldiers*. London: 1644.

Rich, Robert. *Love Without Dissimulation*. London: 1667?

Riley, Henry Thomas, ed. *Munimenta Gildhallae Londoniensis: Liber Albus, Liber Custumarum, et Liber Horn*. Vol. 1. London: Longman, Brown, Green, Longmans, and Roberts, 1859.

Robbins, Rossell Hope, ed. *Secular Lyrics of the XIVth and XVth Centuries*. 2nd ed. Oxford: Clarendon Press, 1955.

Robert the Devyll. London: Wynkyn de Worde, 1517?

Rosenberg, Samuel N., tr. *Robert the Devil: The First Modern English Translation of* Robert le Diable, *An Anonymous French Romance of the Thirteenth Century*. University Park: Pennsylvania State University Press, 2018.

BIBLIOGRAPHY

Shakespeare, William. *Love's Labours Lost*. In *The Oxford Shakespeare*. Edited by John Jowettt et al. 2nd ed. Oxford: Oxford University Press, 2005. 773–844.
——. *Mr. William Shakespeares comedies, histories, and tragedies: published according to the true originall copies*. London: Thomas Cotes, for Robert Allot, 1632.
——. *The Arden Shakespeare Third Series Complete Works*. Edited by Ann Thompson, David Scott Kastan, H. R. Woudhuysen, and G. R. Proudfoot. London: Bloomsbury, 2021.
——. *Titus Andronicus*. In *The Oxford Shakespeare*. Edited by John Jowettt et al. 2nd ed. Oxford: Oxford University Press, 2005. 183–250.
Sidney, Philip. *Astrophil and Stella*. In *Sir Philip Sidney: The Major Works*. Edited by Katherine Duncan-Jones. Oxford: Oxford University Press, 2002. 153–211.
——. *The Countess of Pembrokes Arcadia*. London: John Windet for William Ponsonby, 1590.
——. *The Defence of Poesy*. In *Sir Philip Sidney: The Major Works*. Edited by Katherine Duncan-Jones. Oxford: Oxford University Press, 2002. 220.
Solomon and Saturn I. In *The Old English Dialogues of Solomon and Saturn*. Edited by Daniel Anlezark. Cambridge: D. S. Brewer, 2009.
Sophocles. *Oedipus Tyrannos*. Edited and translated by Hugh Lloyd-Jones. Cambridge, Mass.: Harvard University Press, 1994.
Spenser, Edmund. "A Letter of the Authors." In *The Faerie Queene*. Edited by A. C. Hamilton. Assisted by R. J. Manning. London: Longman, 1977. 737.
Stevens, Wallace. *Collected Poetry and Prose*. Edited by Frank Kermode and Joan Richardson. New York: Library of America, 1997.
Symphosius. *Enigma 16*. In *Variae collectiones aenignmatvm Merovingicae aetatis (pars altera)*. Edited by Fr. Glorie. CCSL 133a. Turnhout, Belgium: Brepols, 1968. 637.
Three Fifteenth-Century Chronicles. Edited by James Gairdner. Westminster, UK: Camden Society, 1880.
Trevisa, John. *On the Properties of Things: John Trevisa's Translation of Bartholomæus Anglicus "De Proprietatibus Rerum"*. Edited by M. C. Seymour et al. 3 vols. Oxford: Clarendon Press, 1975.
Tryamour. In *Four Middle English Romances*. Edited by Harriet Hudson. 2nd ed. TEAMS Middle English Texts. Kalamazoo: Medieval Institute Publications, 2006.
Twenty-Six Political and Other Poems. Edited by J. Kail. EETS, os 124. London: Trübner, 1904.
Two Revisions of Rolle's English Psalter Commentary and the Related Canticles. Edited by Anne Hudson. EETS, os 343. 3 vols. Oxford: Oxford University Press, 2014.
Vercelli VII. In *The Vercelli Homilies and Related Texts*. Edited by D. G. Scragg. EETS, os 300. Oxford: Oxford University Press, 1992. 133–38.
Verheij, L. J. P. "'Where of is mad al mankynde': An Edition of and Introduction to the Twenty-Four Poems in Oxford, Bodleian Library, MS Digby 102." Unpublished Ph.D. dissertation, Leiden University, 2009.
Webb, C. C., ed. *The Churchwardens' Accounts of St Michael, Spurriergate, York, 1518–1548*. [York]: Borthwick Institute of Historical Research, 1997. 331.
Whatley, Gordon E., ed. *The Saint of London: The Life and Miracles of Saint Erkenwald*. Binghampton, N.Y.: State University of New York Press, 1989.

322 BIBLIOGRAPHY

Whiting, Bartlett Jere, with Helen Wescott Whiting. *Proverbs, Sentences, and Proverbial Phrases from English Writings Mainly Before 1500*. Cambridge, Mass.: Belknap Press, 1968.

"William Gregory's Chronicle of London." In *The Historical Collections of a Citizen of London in the Fifteenth Century*. Edited by James Gairdner. Westminster, UK: Camden Society, 1876.

William of Ockham. *Ordinatio*. In *Opera Theologica: Vol. I: Scriptum in Librum Primum Sententiarum Ordinatio (Prol. Et Dist. I)*. Edited by Gedeon Gál et al. St. Bonaventure, N.Y.: The Franciscan Institute, 1967.

William of Pagula. *De Speculo Regis Edwardi III*. Edited by Joseph Moisant. Paris: Alphonse Picard, 1891.

Wilson, Thomas. *Arte of Rhetorique*. Edited by Thomas J. Derrick. New York: Garland, 1982.

———. *The Arte of Rhetorique*. London: Richard Grafton, 1553.

Winstanley, Gerrard. *A New-Yeers Gift Sent to the Parliament and Armie*. In *The Works of Gerrard Winstanley*. Edited by George Sabine. New York: Russell and Russell, 1965. 353–96.

The Wonders of the East. In *The Beowulf Manuscript*. Edited and translated by R. D. Fulk. DOML 3. Cambridge, Mass.: Harvard University Press, 2010.

Wyatt, Thomas. *The Quyete of Mynde*. London: Richard Pynson, 1528.

SECONDARY SOURCES

Aers, David. "A Whisper in the Ear of Early Modernists, or, Reflections on Literary Critics Writing the History of the Subject." In *Culture and History, 1350–1600*. Edited by David Aers. London: Harvester, 1992. 177–202.

———. *Piers Plowman and Christian Allegory*. London: St. Martin's Press, 1975.

———. *Salvation and Sin*. Notre Dame, Ind.: Notre Dame University Press, 2009.

———. *Versions of Election: From Langland and Aquinas to Calvin and Milton*. Notre Dame, Ind.: University of Notre Dame Press, 2020.

Afros, Elena. "*Sindrum begrunden* in Exeter Book Riddle 26: the Enigmatic Dative Case." *Notes and Queries* n.s. 51 (2004). 7–9.

Akbari, Suzanne Conklin. *Seeing through the Veil: Optical Theory and Medieval Allegory*. Toronto: University of Toronto Press, 2004.

Allen, Elizabeth. *False Fables and Exemplary Truth: Poetics and Reception of Medieval Mode*. New York: Palgrave Macmillan, 2005.

Allen, Peter L. *The Art of Love: Amatory Fiction from Ovid to the Romance of the Rose*. Philadelphia: University of Pennsylvania Press, 1992.

Appleford, Amy, and Nicholas Watson. "Merchant Religion in Fifteenth-Century London: The Writings of William Litchfield." *Chaucer Review* 46 (2011). 203–22.

Appleford, Amy. *Learning to Die in London, 1380–1540*. Philadelphia: University of Pennsylvania Press, 2014.

———. "The Dance of Death in London: John Carpenter, John Lydgate, and the Daunce of Poulys." *Journal of Medieval and Early Modern Studies* 38 (2008). 285–314.

Ascoli, Albert R. "Dante and Allegory." In *The Cambridge Companion to Allegory*. Edited by Rita Copeland and Peter T. Struck. Cambridge: Cambridge University Press, 2010. 128–35.

BIBLIOGRAPHY

Ashe, Laura. *The Oxford English Literary History, Vol. 1: 1000–1350. Conquest and Transformation*. Oxford: Oxford University Press, 2017.

Aston, Margaret. *Broken Idols of the English Reformation*. Cambridge: Cambridge University Press, 2016. 920–21.

——. *England's Iconoclasts*. Vol. 1. Oxford: Clarendon Press, 1988.

Avis, P. D. L. "Moses and the Magistrate: A Study in the Rise of Protestant Legalism." *Journal of Ecclesiastical History* 26 (1975). 149–72.

Backhouse, Janet. *Illumination from Books of Hours*. London: British Library, 2004.

Badham, Sally. "The Contribution of Epigraphy to the Typological Classification of Medieval English Brasses and Slabs." In *Roman, Runes, and Ogham: Medieval Inscriptions in the Insular World and on the Continent*. Edited by John Higgitt, Katherine Forsyth, and David N. Parsons. Donington, UK: Shaun Tyas, 2001. 202–10.

Bahr, Arthur. *Fragments and Assemblages: Forming Compilations of Medieval London*. Chicago: University of Chicago Press, 2013.

Bainton, Roland H. *Christian Attitudes toward Peace and War*. Nashville, Tenn.: Abingdon, 1960.

Baldovin, John F. *The Urban Character of Christian Worship: The Origins, Development and Meaning of Stational Liturgy*. Rome: Pontificale Institutum Studiorum Orientalium, 1987.

Barber, Tabitha, and Stacy Boldrick, eds. *Art Under Attack: Histories of British Iconoclasm*. London: Tate Publishing, 2013.

Barr, Helen. *Signes and Sothe: Language in the Piers Plowman Tradition*. Cambridge: D. S. Brewer, 1994.

——. "The Deafening Silence of Lollardy in the *Digby Lyrics*." In *Wycliffite Controversies*. Edited by Mishtooni Bose and J. Patrick Hornbeck II. Turnhout, Belgium: Brepols, 2011.

——. "'This Holy Tyme': Present Sense in the *Digby Lyrics*." In *After Arundel: Religious Writing in Fifteenth-Century England*. Edited by Vincent Gillespie and Kantik Ghosh. Turnhout, Belgium: Brepols, 2011.

Barron, Caroline M. "Ralph Holland and the London Radicals, 1438–1444." In *Medieval London: Collected Papers of Caroline M. Barron*. Edited by Martha Carlin and Joel T. Rosenthal. Kalamazoo, Mich.: Medieval Institute, 2017.

Bartlett, Robert. *Why Can the Dead Do Such Great Things?: Saints and Worshippers from the Martyrs to the Reformation*. Princeton, N.J.: Princeton University Press, 2013.

Baumgartner, Emmanuèle. "Le livre et le roman (XII–XIIIe siècles)." In *Livre et littérature: dynamisme d'un archétype*. Nanterre: Université de Paris X-Nanterre, 1986. 7–19.

Baxandall, Michael. *Painting and Experience in Fifteenth-Century Italy*. 2nd ed. Oxford: Oxford University Press, 1988. 29–108.

——. *The Limewood Sculptors of Renaissance Germany*. New Haven, Conn.: Yale University Press, 1980. 143–63.

Beaven, Alfred P. *The Aldermen of the City of London Temp. Henry III - 1912*. London: Corporation of the City of London, 1908.

Bedos-Rezak, Brigette, and Jeffrey Hamburger, eds. *Sign and Design: Script as Image in Cross-Cultural Perspective (300–1600 CE)*. Washington, D.C.: Dumbarton Oaks, 2016.

BIBLIOGRAPHY

Bennett, Alana. "'Romanz reding on the bok': 'Reauralising' Romances from Later Medieval English Household Manuscripts." Unpublished Ph.D. dissertation, University of York, 2022.

Bennett, Alastair. "*Brevis oratio penetrat celum*: Proverbs, Prayers, and Lay Understanding in Late Medieval England." *New Medieval Literatures* 14 (2012). 127–63.

Bennett, H. S. *English Books & Readers 1475–1557*. 2nd ed. Cambridge: Cambridge University Press, 1969.

Benson, C. David. *Chaucer's Drama of Style: Poetic Variety and Contrast in the Canterbury Tales*. Chapel Hill, N.C.: University of North Carolina Press, 1986.

——. "Civic Lydgate: The Poet and London." In *John Lydgate: Poetry, Culture, and Lancastrian England*. Edited by Larry Scanlon and James Simpson. Notre Dame, Ind.: University of Notre Dame Press, 2006. 147–68.

Benton, John F. "Consciousness of Self and Perceptions of Individuality." In *Renaissance and Renewal in the Twelfth Century*. Edited by Robert L. Benson and Giles Constable, with Carol D. Lanham. Cambridge, Mass.: Harvard University Press, 1982.

Benveniste, Émile. "The Nature of Pronouns." In *Problems in General Linguistics*. Translated by Mary Elizabeth Meek. Coral Gables, Fla.: University of Miami Press, 1971. 217–22.

Berenbeim, Jessica. "The Past of the Past: Historical Distance and the Medieval Image." *New Medieval Literatures* 21 (2021). 191–220.

Bertram, Jerome. "Inscriptions on Late-medieval Brasses and Monuments." In *Roman, Runes, and Ogham: Medieval Inscriptions in the Insular World and on the Continent*. Edited by John Higgitt, Katherine Forsyth, and David N. Parsons. Donington, UK: Shaun Tyas, 2001. 190–97.

——. *Mediaeval Inscriptions: The Epigraphy of the City of Oxford*. Oxford: Boydell, 2020.

Birch, Debra J. *Pilgrimage to Rome in the Middle Ages: Continuity and Change*. Woodbridge, UK: Boydell, 1998.

Birch, Walter de Gray, and Henry Jenner. *Early Drawings and Illuminations: An Introduction to the Study of Illustrated Manuscripts*. London: Bagster and Sons, 1879.

Bitterli, Dieter. *Say What I Am Called: The Old English Riddles of the Exeter Book & the Anglo-Latin Riddle Tradition*. Toronto: University of Toronto Press, 2009.

Bloch, R. Howard. *Medieval Misogyny and the Invention of Western Romantic Love*. Chicago: University of Chicago Press, 1991.

Blom, Alderik H. *Glossing the Psalms: The Emergence of the Written Vernaculars in Western Europe from the 7th to the 12th Centuries*. Berlin and Boston: De Gruyter, 2017.

Boboc, Andreea. "Theorizing Legal Personhood in Late Medieval England." In *Theorizing Legal Personhood in Late Medieval England*. Edited by Andreea Boboc. Leiden: Brill, 2015. 1–28.

Boffey, Julia, and John J. Thompson. "Anthologies and Miscellanies: Production and Choice of Texts." In *Book Production and Publishing in Britain, 1375–1475*. Edited by Jeremy Griffiths and Derek Pearsall. Cambridge: Cambridge University Press, 1989. 279–315.

Boffey, Julia. "London Books and London Readers." In *Cultural Reformations: Medieval and Renaissance in Literary History*. Edited by Brian Cummings and James Simpson. Oxford: Oxford University Press, 2010. 420–37.

BIBLIOGRAPHY 325

——. "Proverbial Chaucer and the Chaucer Canon." *Huntington Library Quarterly* 58 (1995). 37–47.

Boitani, Piero. *Riconoscere è un dio: scene e temi del riconoscimento nella letteratura*. Milan: Einaudi, 2014.

Bowers, Hannah. *Middle English Recipes and Literary Play, 1375–1500*. Oxford: Oxford University Press, 2022.

Boyde, Patrick. *Dante Philomythes and Philosopher*. Cambridge: Cambridge University Press, 1981.

Boyle, Leonard E. "William of Pagula and the *Speculum Regis Edwardi III*." *Mediaeval Studies* 32 (1970). 329–36.

Bradbury, Nancy Mason. "The Proverb as Embedded Microgenre in Chaucer and *The Dialogue of Solomon and Marcolf*." *Exemplaria* 27 (2015). 55–72.

Brantley, Jessica. "Reading the Forms of *Sir Thopas*." In *Medieval English Manuscripts: Form, Aesthetics, and the Literary Text*. Edited by Alexandra Gillespie and Arthur Bahr. Special issue of *Chaucer Review* 47 (2013). 416–38.

Breen, Katharine. *Machines of the Mind. Personification in Medieval Literature*. Chicago: University of Chicago Press, 2021.

Brett, Philip. "Paston, Edward." *Oxford Dictionary of National Biography*. Oxford: Oxford University Press, 2004. https://www.oxforddnb.com.

Brewer, Derek. *Symbolic Stories: Traditional Narratives of the Family Drama in English Literature*. London: Longman, 1980.

Brljak, Vladimir, ed. *Allegory Studies: Contemporary Perspectives*. New York: Routledge, 2021.

——. "The Age of Allegory." *Studies in Philology* 114 (2017). 697–719.

——. "Introduction: Allegory Past and Present." In *Allegory Studies: Contemporary Perspectives*. New York: Routledge, 2021. 1–40.

Brogan, T. V. F. "Representation." In *The Princeton Encyclopedia of Poetry and Poetics*. 4th ed. Edited by Roland Greene, Stephen Cushman, Clare Cavanagh et al. Princeton University Press, 2012. 1171–74.

Brown, Michelle B. *Understanding Illuminated Manuscripts: A Guide to Technical Terms*. Los Angeles: The J. Paul Getty Museum in association with the British Library, 1994.

Brown, Peter. *The Cult of the Saints: Its Rise and Function in Latin Christianity*. Chicago: University of Chicago Press, 1981.

Brümmer, Vincent. *The Model of Love: A Study in Philosophical Theology*. Cambridge: Cambridge University Press, 1993.

Buchanan, Peter. "Reading Bodies, Books, and beyond: Experience and Contingency in *Troilus and Criseyde*." *Textual Practice* 36 (2022). 1892–912.

Buddensieg, Tilmann. "Gregory the Great, the Destroyer of Pagan Idols: The History of a Medieval Legend Concerning the Decline of Ancient Art and Literature." *Journal of the Warburg and Courtauld Institutes* 28 (1965). 44–65.

Burke, Kenneth. "Literature as Equipment for Living." In *The Philosophy of Literary Form: Studies in Symbolic Action*. Baton Rouge, La.: Louisiana State University Press, 1941.

Burrow, John. "Autobiographical Poetry in the Middle Ages: The Case of Thomas Hoccleve." *Proceedings of the British Academy* 68 (1982). 389–412.

Butler, Judith. *Giving an Account of Oneself*. New York: Fordham University Press, 2005.

Butterfield, Ardis. "Poems without Form? *Maiden in the mor lay* Revisited." In *Readings in Medieval Textuality: Essays in Honour of A. C. Spearing*. Edited by

BIBLIOGRAPHY

Cristina Maria Cervone and D. Vance Smith. Cambridge: D. S. Brewer, 2016. 169–94.

——. "The Construction of Textual Form: Crosslingual Citation in Some Medieval Lyrics." In *Citation, Intertextuality and Memory in the Middle Ages and Renaissance*. Edited by Yolanda Plumley, Giuliano Di Bacco, and Stefano Jossa. Exeter, UK: University of Exeter Press, 2011.

——. "Why Medieval Lyric?" *ELH* 82 (2015). 319–43.

Bynum, Caroline Walker. "Did the Twelfth Century Discover the Individual?" In *Jesus as Mother: Studies in the Spirituality of the High Middle Ages*. Berkeley, Calif.: University of California Press, 1982. 82–109. (Revised from *Journal of Ecclesiastical History* 31 (1980), 1–17.)

Calder, Natalie. "'The Puple is Godes, and Not ʒoures': Lancastrian Orthodoxy in the Digby Lyrics." *Review of English Studies* 65 (2013). 403–20.

Camp, Cynthia Turner. "Spatial Memory, Historiographic Fantasy, and the Touch of the Past in *St Erkenwald*." *New Literary History* 44 (2013). 471–91.

Cannon, Christopher. "Lyric Romance." In *What Kind of a Thing is a Middle English Lyric?* Edited by Christina Maria Cervone and Nicholas Watson. Philadelphia: University of Pennsylvania Press, 2022. 88–105.

——. *Middle English Literature*. Cambridge: Polity Press, 2008.

——. "Proverbs and the Wisdom of Literature: *The Proverbs of Alfred* and Chaucer's *Tale of Melibee*." *Textual Practice* 43 (2010). 407–34.

Cartlidge, Neil. "'Alas, I go with chylde': Representations of Extra-Marital Pregnancy in the Middle English Lyric." *English Studies* 79 (1998). 395–414.

Cave, Terence. *Recognitions: A Study in Poetics*. Oxford: Oxford University Press, 1988.

Camille, Michael. *The Gothic Idol: Ideology and Image-Making in Medieval Art*. Cambridge: Cambridge University Press, 1989.

Certeau, Michel de. *The Writing of History*. Translated by Tom Conley. New York: Columbia University Press, 1988.

Cervone, Cristina Maria, and Nicholas Watson, eds. *What Kind of Thing is a Middle English Lyric?* Philadelphia: University of Pennsylvania Press, 2022.

Chazelle, Celia M. "Pictures, books, and the illiterate: Pope Gregory I's letters to Serenus of Marseilles." *Word and Image: A Journal of Verbal/Visual Enquiry* 6 (2012). 138–53.

Cheyette, Fredric L., and Howell Chickering. "Love, Anger, and Peace: Social Practice and Poetic Play in the Ending of Yvain." *Speculum* 80 (2005). 75–117.

Chism, Christine. *Alliterative Revivals*. Philadelphia: University of Pennsylvania Press, 2002.

Clark, James G. *The Dissolution of the Monasteries: A New History*. New Haven, Conn.: Yale University Press, 2021. 436.

Clod, Random. "Information on Information." *Transactions of the Society for Textual Scholarship* 5 (1991). 241–81.

Coffey, John. "The Toleration Controversy in the English Revolution." In *Religion in Revolutionary England*. Edited by Christopher Durston and Judith Maltby. Manchester: Manchester University Press, 2006. 42–68.

Cohen, Jeffrey Jerome. *Of Giants: Sex, Monsters, and the Middle Ages*. Minneapolis, Minn.: University of Minnesota Press, 1999.

Cole, Andrew. *Literature and Heresy in the Age of Chaucer*. Cambridge: Cambridge University Press, 2008.

BIBLIOGRAPHY

Colish, Marcia L. *The Mirror of Language: A Study in the Medieval Theory of Knowledge*. Rev. ed. Lincoln, Nebr.: University of Nebraska Press, 1983.

Collingwood, R. G., and R. P. Wright. *The Roman Inscriptions of Britain*. Oxford: Clarendon, 1965.

Como, David. *Blown by the Spirit: Puritanism and the Emergence of an Antinomian Underground in Pre-Civil-War England*. Stanford: Stanford University Press, 2004.

Conner, Patrick W. *Anglo-Saxon Exeter: A Tenth-Century Cultural History*. Woodbridge, UK: Boydell, 1993.

Connolly, Margaret. *John Shirley: Book Production and the Noble Household in Fifteenth-Century England*. Aldershot, UK: Ashgate, 1998.

Cooper, Helen. "Counter-Romance: Civil Strife and Father-Killing in the Prose Romances." In *The Long Fifteenth Century: Essays for Douglas Gray*. Edited by Helen Cooper and Sally Mapstone. Oxford: Clarendon, 1997. 141–62.

——. *Oxford Guides to Chaucer: The Canterbury Tales*. 2nd ed. Oxford: Oxford University Press, 1996.

——. *The English Romance in Time: Transforming Motifs from Geoffrey of Monmouth to the Death of Shakespeare*. Oxford: Oxford University Press, 2004.

Cooper, Lisa H. "Nothing Was Funny in the Late Middle Ages: The 'Tale of Ryght Nought' and British Library, MS Egerton 1995." *Journal of Medieval and Early Modern Studies* 47 (2017). 221–53.

——. "The Poetics of Practicality." In *Oxford Twenty-First Century Approaches to Literature: Middle English*. Edited by Paul Strohm. Oxford: Oxford University Press, 2007. 491–505.

Copeland, Rita, and Peter T. Struck. "Introduction." In *The Cambridge Companion to Allegory*. Edited by Rita Copeland and Peter T. Struck. Cambridge: Cambridge University Press, 2010. 1–11.

Copeland, Rita, and Stephen Melville. "Allegory and Allegoresis: Rhetoric and Hermeneutics." *Exemplaria* 3 (1991). 159–87.

Copeland, Rita. *Rhetoric, Hermeneutics, and Translation in the Middle Ages: Academic Traditions and Vernacular Texts*. Cambridge: Cambridge University Press, 1991.

——. "Allegory and Rhetoric." In *The Oxford Handbook to Allegory*. Edited by David Parry. Oxford: Oxford University Press, forthcoming.

Courcelle, Pierre. *Connais toi-même de Socrate à saint Bernard*. 2 vols. Paris: Etudes Augustiniennes, 1974.

Craun, Edwin. *Lies, Slander, and Obscenity in Medieval English Literature: Pastoral Rhetoric and the Deviant Speaker*. Cambridge: Cambridge University Press, 1997.

Crawford, Jason. *Allegory and Enchantment: An Early Modern Poetics*. Oxford: Oxford University Press, 2017.

Crocker, Holly A. *Chaucer's Visions of Manhood*. New York: Palgrave Macmillan, 2007.

Crofts, Thomas H. *Malory's Contemporary Audience: The Social Reading of Romance in Late Medieval England*. Cambridge: D. S. Brewer, 2012.

Cummings, Brian. "Iconoclasm and Bibliophobia in the English Reformations, 1521–1558." In *Images, Idolatry, and Iconoclasm in Late Medieval England: Textuality and the Visual Image*. Edited by Jeremy Dimmick, James Simpson, and Nicolette Zeeman. Oxford: Oxford University Press, 2002. 185–206.

BIBLIOGRAPHY

Dahan, Gilbert. *L'Exégèse chrétienne de la Bible en Occident médiéval: XIIe–XIVe siècle*. Paris: du Cerf, 1999.

Dailey, Patricia. "Riddles, Wonder and Responsiveness, in Anglo-Saxon Literature." In *The Cambridge History of Early Medieval English Literature*. Edited by Claire A. Lees. Cambridge: Cambridge University Press, 2013. 451–72.

Dalton, Emily. "'Clansyd hom in Cristes nom': Translation of Spaces and Bodies in *St Erkenwald*." *The Journal of English and Germanic Philology* 117 (2018). 56–83.

Damrosch, Leo. *The Sorrow of the Quaker Jesus: James Nayler and the Protestant Crackdown on Free Speech*. Cambridge, Mass.: Harvard University Press, 1996.

Daniel, Drew. "Redistributing the Sensible: Genre Theory after Rancière." *Exemplaria* 31 (2019). 129–40.

Davidson, Clare. "Reading in Bed with *Troilus and Criseyde*." *Chaucer Review* 55 (2020). 147–70.

Davies, Penelope. "The Politics of Perpetuation: Trajan's Column and the Art of Commemoration." *American Journal of Archaeology* 101 (1997). 41–65.

Davis, J. C. *Oliver Cromwell*. New York: Oxford University Press, 2001.

Davis, Rebecca. Piers Plowman *and the Books of Nature*. Oxford: Oxford University Press, 2016.

de Lubac, Henri. *Exégèse médiévale*. 4 vols. Paris: Aubier, 1959–64.

——. *History and Spirit: The Understanding of Scripture according to Origen*. Translated by Anne Englund Nash. San Francisco: Ignatius Press, 2007.

de Man, Paul. "Autobiography as De-facement." *MLN* 94 (1979). 919–30.

Delhaye, Philippe. *Le Microcosmos de Godefroy de St.-Victor: étude théologique*. Lille: Facultés catholiques, 1951.

Derrida, Jacques. "The Law of Genre." Translated by Avital Ronell. Repr. in *Modern Genre Theory*. Edited by David Duff. London: Routledge, 2000. 219–31.

Dijk, Conrad van. "Giving Each His Due: Langland, Gower, and the Question of Equity." *Journal of English and Germanic Philology* 108 (2009). 310–35.

Dillon, Emma. *The Sense of Sound: Musical Meaning in France, 1260–1330*. Oxford: Oxford University Press, 2012.

Dimmick, Jeremy, James Simpson, and Nicolette Zeeman, eds. *Images, Idolatry, and Iconoclasm in Late Medieval England: Textuality and the Visual Image*. Oxford: Oxford University Press, 2002.

Dodd, Gwilym. *Justice and Grace: Private Petitioning and the English Parliament in the Late Middle Ages*. Oxford: Oxford University Press, 2007.

Downs, Jordan S. "The Curse of Meroz and the English Civil War." *Historical Journal* 57 (2014). 343–68.

Dronke, Peter. *Poetic Individuality in the Middle Ages: New Departures in Poetry, 1000–1150*. Oxford: Clarendon Press, 1970.

——. *Fabula: Explorations into the Uses of Myth in Medieval Platonism*. Leiden: Brill, 1974.

Duffy, Eamon. *The Stripping of the Altars: Traditional Religion in England, c. 1400–c. 1580*. 2nd ed. New Haven, Conn.: Yale University Press, 2005.

Dundes, Alan. "On the Structure of the Proverb." In *The Wisdom of Many: Essays on the Proverb*. Edited by Wolfgang Mieder and Alan Dundes. New York and London: Garland, 1981.

Eastmond, Anthony, ed. *Viewing Inscriptions in the Late Antique and Medieval World*. Cambridge: Cambridge University Press, 2015.

BIBLIOGRAPHY

Edwards, A. S. G. "Middle English Inscriptional Verse Texts." In *Texts and their Contexts*. Edited by J. Scattergood and Julia Boffey. Dublin: Four Courts Press, 1997. 26–43.

Enterline, Lynn. *Shakespeare's Schoolroom: Rhetoric, Discipline, Emotion*. Philadelphia: University of Pennsylvania Press, 2012.

Evans, Frank B. "The Printing of Spenser's 'Faerie Queene' in 1596." *Studies in Bibliography* 18 (1965). 49–67.

Farber, Lianna. "The Creation of Consent in the *Physician's Tale*." *The Chaucer Review* 39 (2004). 151–64.

Felski, Rita. *The Limits of Critique*. Chicago: University of Chicago Press, 2015.

Festugière, André Jean. *La revelation de Hermes Trismegiste*. 4 vols. Paris: Les Belles Lettres, 1944–54.

Fish, Stanley E. "Normal Circumstances, Literal Language, Direct Speech Acts, the Ordinary, the Everyday, the Obvious, What Goes without Saying, and Other Special Cases." *Critical Inquiry* 4 (1978). 625–44.

——. *How Milton Works*. Cambridge, Mass.: Harvard University Press, 2001.

Fleming, Juliet. "Changed Opinion as to Flowers." In *Renaissance Paratexts*. Edited by Helen Smith and Louise Wilson. Cambridge: Cambridge University Press, 2011. 48–64.

——. "How Not to Look at a Printed Flower." *JMEMS* 38 (2008). 345–71.

——. "How to Look at a Printed Flower." *Word & Image* 22 (2006). 165–87.

Fletcher, Angus. *Allegory: The Theory of a Symbolic Mode*. Repr. Princeton: Princeton University Press, 2012.

——. "The Sentencing of Virginia in the Physician's Tale." *The Chaucer Review* 34 (2000). 300–08.

Fowler, Roger. Review of Morton W. Bloomfield, *Essays and Explorations: Studies in Ideas, Language, and Literature* (Cambridge, Mass.: Harvard University Press, 1970). *Journal of European Studies* 1 (1971). 95.

Foys, Martin. "The Undoing of Exeter Book Riddle 47: 'Bookmoth.'" In *Transitional States: Cultural Change, Tradition and Memory in Medieval England*. Edited by Graham D. Caie and Michael D. C. Drout. Tempe, Ariz.: Arizona Center for Medieval and Renaissance Studies, 2018. 101–30.

Freedberg, David. *The Power of Images: Studies in the History and Theory of Response*. Chicago: University of Chicago Press, 1989.

Frye, Northrop. *Anatomy of Criticism: Four Essays*. Princeton, N.J.: Princeton University Press, 1957.

Fulton, Thomas. *The Book of Books: Biblical Interpretation, Literary Culture, and the Political Imagination from Erasmus to Milton*. Philadelphia: University of Pennsylvania Press, 2021.

Furrow, Melissa. *Expectations of Romance*. Cambridge: D. S. Brewer, 2009.

Galloway, Andrew. *The Penn Commentary on Piers Plowman. Volume 1, C Prologue-Passus 4; B Prologue-Passus 4; A Prologue-Passus 4*. Philadelphia: University of Pennsylvania Press, 2006.

——. "Theory of the Fourteenth-Century English Lyric." In *What Kind of Things is a Middle English Lyric?* Edited by Cristina Maria Cervone and Nicholas Watson. Philadelphia: University of Pennsylvania Press, 2022.

Gaston, Kara. *Reading Chaucer in Time: Literary Formation in England and Italy*. Oxford: Oxford University Press, 2020.

Gaucher, Élisabeth. *Robert le Diable: histoire d'une légende*. Paris: Honoré Champion, 2003.

BIBLIOGRAPHY

Gaunt, Simon. *Gender and Genre in Medieval French Literature*. Cambridge: Cambridge University Press, 2009.

——. "Romance and other Genres." In *The Cambridge Companion to Romance*. Edited by Roberta Krueger. Cambridge: Cambridge University Press, 2000. 45–59.

Gentles, Ian. *The New Model Army in England, Ireland, and Scotland: 1645–1653*. Oxford: Blackwell, 1994.

Giancarlo, Matthew. *Parliament and Literature in Late Medieval England*. Cambridge: Cambridge University Press, 2007.

——. "Troubling the New Constitutionalism: Politics, Penitence, and the Dilemma of Dread in the Digby Poems." *Journal of English and Germanic Philology* 110 (2011). 78–104.

Gilbert, Jane. "Form and/as Mode of Existence." *Romanic Review* 111 (2020). 27–47.

Gillespie, Vincent. "Moral and Penitential Lyrics." In *A Companion to the Middle English Lyric*. Edited by Thomas G. Duncan. Cambridge: D. S. Brewer, 2005. 68–95.

Given-Wilson, C. J. "Purveyance for the Royal Household, 1362–1413." *Historical Research* 56 (1983). 145–63.

Goodman, Jennifer R. "'That Wommen Holde in Ful Greet Reverence': Mothers and Daughters Reading Chivalric Romances." In *Women, the Book, and the Worldly*. Edited by Lesley Smith and Jane H. M. Taylor. Cambridge: D. S. Brewer, 1995. 25–30.

Goulet, Richard, and Gilbert Dahan. "Présentation." In *Allégorie des poètes, allégorie des philosophes: Etudes sur la poétique et l'hermeneutique de l'allégorie de l'Antiquité à la Réforme*. Edited by Richard Goulet and Gilbert Dahan. Paris: Vrin, 2005. 5–8.

Gowing, Alain. *Empire and Memory: The Representation of the Roman Republic in Imperial Culture*. Cambridge: Cambridge University Press, 2005.

Greene, Roland, Stephen Cushman, Clare Cavanagh, Jahan Ramazani, and Paul Rouzer, eds. *The Princeton Encyclopedia of Poetry and Poetics*. 2 vols. Princeton, N.J.: Princeton University Press, 2012.

Griffith, David. "Texts and Detexting on Late Medieval English Church Screens." In *The Art and Science of the Church Screen in Medieval Europe: Making, Meaning, Preserving*. Edited by Spike Bucklow, Richard Marks, and Lucy Wrapson. Woodbridge, UK: Boydell, 2017. 71–99.

Griffiths, Ralph A. *The Reign of King Henry VI: The Exercise of Royal Authority, 1422–61*. London: Ernest Benn, 1981.

Grove, Kevin G. *Augustine on Memory*. Oxford: Oxford University Press, 2021.

Guibbory, Achsah. *Christian Identity, Jews, and Israel in Seventeenth-Century England*. Oxford: Oxford University Press, 2010.

Gunther, Karl. *Reformation Unbound: Protestant Visions of the Reformation in England, 1525–1590*. Cambridge: Cambridge University Press, 2014.

Halasz, Alexandra. "Lodge, Thomas (1558–1625)." *Oxford Dictionary of National Biography*. Oxford: Oxford University Press, 2004. https://www.oxforddnb.com.

Hale, John K. "England as Israel in Milton's Writings." *Early Modern Literary Studies* 2 (1996). 31–54.

Hamlin, Hannibal. *Psalm Culture and Early Modern English Literature*. Cambridge, Mass.: Cambridge University Press, 2004.

BIBLIOGRAPHY

Hanawalt, Barbara. *Ceremony and Civility: Civic Culture in Late Medieval London*. Oxford: Oxford University Press, 2017.

Hanning, Robert W. *The Individual in Twelfth-Century Romance*. New Haven, Conn.: Yale University Press, 1977.

Harbus, Antonina. *The Life of the Mind in Old English Poetry*. Amsterdam: Rodopi, 2002.

Harf-Lancner, Laurence. "Chrétien's Literary Background." *A Companion to Chrétien de Troyes*. Edited by Norris J. Lacy and Joan Tasker Grimbert. Cambridge: D. S. Brewer, 2005. 26–42.

Harrison, Robert Pogue. *The Dominion of the Dead*. Chicago: University of Chicago Press, 2003.

Hartrich, Eliza. *Politics and the Urban Sector in Fifteenth-Century England, 1413–1471*. Oxford: Oxford University Press, 2019.

Harvey, I. M. W. *Jack Cade's Rebellion of 1450*. Oxford: Clarendon Press, 1991.

Haskin, Dayton. *Milton's Burden of Interpretation*. Philadelphia: University of Pennsylvania Press, 1994.

Hayes, Mary. "The Talking Dead: Resounding Voices in Old English Riddles." *Exemplaria* 20 (2008). 123–42.

Helgerson, Richard. *The Elizabethan Prodigals*. Berkeley, Calif.: University of California Press, 1976.

Hermanson, Lars. *Friendship, Love, and Brotherhood in Medieval Northern Europe, c. 1000–1200*. Translated by Alan Crozier. Leiden: Brill, 2019.

Hiatt, Alfred. "Genre without System." In *Oxford Twenty-first Century Approaches to Literature. Middle English*. Edited by Paul Strohm. Oxford: Oxford University Press, 2007. 277–94.

Higgit, John. "Epigraphic Lettering and Book Script in the British Isles." In *Inschrift und Material, Inschrift und Buchschrift*. Edited by Walter Koch and Christine Steiniger. Munich: Bayerische Akademie der Wissenschaften, 1997. 137–49.

Hirsh, John C. "Modern Times: The Discourse of the *Physician's Tale*." *Chaucer Review* 27 (1993). 387–95.

Hoffman, Richard L. "Jephthah's Daughter and Chaucer's Virginia." *Chaucer Review* 2 (1967). 20–31.

Holsinger, Bruce. *Music, Body, and Desire in Medieval Culture*. Stanford, Calif.: Stanford University Press, 2002.

——. "Of Pigs and Parchment: Medieval Studies and the Coming of the Animal." *PMLA* 124 (2009). 616–23.

Horobin, Simon. "The Scribe of Bodleian Library, MS Digby 102 and the Circulation of the C Text of *Piers Plowman*." *Yearbook of Langland Studies* 24 (2010). 89–112.

Hotchkiss, Valerie, and Fred C. Robinson. *English in Print: from Caxton to Shakespeare to Milton*. Urbana, Ill.: University of Illinois Press, 2008.

Howe, John M. "The Conversion of the Physical World: The Creation of a Christian Landscape." In *Varieties of Religious Conversion in the Middle Ages*. Edited by James Muldoon. Gainesville, Fla.: University Press of Florida, 1997. 63–78.

Howe, Nicholas. *Writing the Map of Anglo-Saxon England: Essays in Cultural Geography*. New Haven, Conn.: Yale University Press, 2008.

BIBLIOGRAPHY

——. "The Cultural Construction of Reading in Anglo-Saxon England." In *The Ethnography of Reading*. Edited by Jonathan Boyarin. Berkeley, Calif.: University of California Press, 1993. 58–79.

Hunt, Tony. *Chrétien de Troyes:* Yvain. London: Grant and Cutler, 1986.

Irvine, Martin. "Heloise and the gendering of the literate subject." In *Criticism and Dissent in the Middle Ages*. Edited by Rita Copeland. Cambridge: Cambridge University Press, 1996. 87–114.

Jackson, Virginia. *Dickinson's Misery: A Theory of Lyric Reading*. Princeton, N.J.: Princeton University Press, 2005.

Jacobs, Nicolas. *The Later Versions of Sir Degarre: A Study in Textual Degeneration*. Oxford: Society for the Study of Medieval Languages and Literature, 1995.

Jaeger, C. Stephen. *Ennobling Love: In Search of a Lost Sensibility*. Philadelphia: University of Pennsylvania Press, 1999.

James, M. R. *Suffolk and Norfolk: A Perambulation of the Two Counties with Notices of their History and their Ancient Buildings*. London: J. M. Dent, 1930. 171.

Johnston, Michael. *Romance and the Gentry in Late Medieval England*. Oxford: Oxford University Press, 2014.

Jones, W. R. "Purveyance for War and the Community of the Realm in Late Medieval England." *Albion* 7 (1975). 300–16.

Kay, Sarah. "Desire and Subjectivity." In *The Troubadours: An Introduction*. Edited by Simon Gaunt and Sarah Kay. Cambridge: Cambridge University Press, 1999. 212–27.

——. *Parrots and Nightingales: Troubadour Poetry and the Development of European Poetry*. Philadelphia: University of Pennsylvania Press, 2013.

——. "Touching Singularity: Consolation, Philosophy, and Poetry in the *Dit*." In *The Erotics of Consolation: Desire and Distance in the Late Middle Ages*. Edited by Catherine E. Léglu and Stephen J. Milner. New York: Palgrave Macmillan, 2008. 21–38.

Kane, George. "Some Fourteenth-Century 'Political' Poems." In *Medieval English Religious and Ethical Literature: Essays in Honour of G. H. Russell*. Edited by Gregory Kratzmann and James Simpson. Cambridge: D. S. Brewer, 1986.

Kelly, Douglas. *The Art of Medieval French Romance*. Madison, Wis.: University of Wisconsin Press, 1992.

Kerby-Fulton, Kathryn. *The Clerical Proletariat and the Resurgence of Medieval English Poetry*. Philadelphia: University of Pennsylvania Press, 2021.

Kinney, Arthur F. *Humanist Poetics: Thought, Rhetoric and Fiction in Sixteenth-Century England*. Amherst, Mass.: University of Massachusetts Press, 1986.

Kirk, Elizabeth D. "'Paradis Stood Formed in Hire Yën': Courtly Love and Chaucer's Re-Vision of Dante." In *Acts of Interpretation: The Text in its Contexts, 700–1600: Essays on Medieval and Renaissance Literature in honor of E. Talbot Donaldson*. Edited by Mary J. Carruthers and Elizabeth D. Kirk. Norman, Okla.: Pilgrim Books, 1982. 257–77.

Kline, Daniel T. "Jephthah's Daughter and Chaucer's Virginia: The Critique of Sacrifice in the Physician's Tale." *Journal of English and Germanic Philology* 107 (2008). 77–103.

Knight, Alison. *The Dark Bible: Cultures of Interpretation in Early Modern England*. Oxford: Oxford University Press, 2022.

Knox, Philip. *The Romance of the Rose and the Making of Fourteenth-Century English Literature*. Oxford: Oxford University Press, 2021.

BIBLIOGRAPHY

Koerner, Joseph. *The Reformation of the Image*. Chicago: University of Chicago Press, 2004. 11–13.

Kooper, Erik. "Loving the Unequal Equal: Medieval Theologians and Marital Affection." In *The Olde Daunce: Love, Friendship, Sex, and Marriage in the Medieval World*. Edited by Robert R. Edwards and Stephen Spector. Albany, N.Y.: State University of New York Press, 1991. 44–56.

Kreuzer, James R. "Some Earlier Examples of the Rhetorical Device in Ralph Roister Doister (III. iv. 33 ff.)." *The Review of English Studies* 14 (1938). 321–23.

Lapidge, Michael. *The Anglo-Saxon Library*. Oxford: Oxford University Press, 2005.

Latour, Bruno, and Peter Weibel, eds. *Iconoclash*. Cambridge, Mass.: MIT Press, 2002.

Lawton, David. *Chaucer's Narrators*. Cambridge: D. S. Brewer, 1985.

——. "Dullness in the Fifteenth Century." *ELH* 54 (1987). 761–99.

LeClercq, Jean. *The Love of Learning and the Desire for God: A Study of Monastic Culture*. New York: Fordham University Press, 1982.

Leneghan, Francis. "Making the Psalter Sing: The Old English Metrical Psalms, Rhythm, and *Ruminatio*." In *The Psalms and Medieval English Literature: From Conversion to the Reformation*. Edited by Tamara Atkin and Francis Leneghan. Cambridge: D. S. Brewer, 2017. 173–97.

Lester, G. A. "The Caedmon Story and its Analogues." *Neophilologus* 58 (1974). 225–37.

Lewis, C. S. *The Allegory of Love: A Study in Medieval Tradition*. Oxford: Clarendon Press, 1936.

Liddell, H. G., R. Scott, and J. M. Whiton, eds. *A Lexicon Abridged from Liddell and Scott's Greek-English Lexicon*. New York: American Book Company, 1906.

Lindenbaum, Sheila. "London Texts and Literate Practice." In *The Cambridge History of Medieval English Literature*. Edited by David Wallace. Cambridge: Cambridge University Press, 1999. 284–309.

Liu, Yin. "Middle English Romance as Prototype Genre." *The Chaucer Review* 40 (2006). 335–53.

Loewenstein, David. *Treacherous Faith: The Specter of Heresy in Early Modern Literature and Culture*. Oxford: Oxford University Press, 2013.

Lombardi, Elena. *The Wings of the Doves: Love and Desire in Dante and Medieval Culture*. Montreal: McGill-Queen's University Press, 2012.

Louis, Cameron. "The Concept of the Proverb in Middle English." *Proverbium* 14 (1997). 173–86.

Lynch, Kathryn L. *The High Medieval Dream Vision*. Stanford: Stanford University Press, 1988.

Mann, Jill. "Chaucer and the 'Woman Question.'" In *This Noble Craft: Proceedings of the Xth Research Symposium of the Dutch and Belgian University Teachers of Old and Middle English and Historical Linguistics*. Edited by Erik Kooper. Amsterdam: Rodopi, 1991. 173–88.

——. "Eating and Drinking in *Piers Plowman*." *Essays and Studies* 32 (1979). 26–43.

——. "Langland and Allegory." Morton W. Bloomfield Lectures on Medieval Literature 2. Kalamazoo, Mich.: Medieval Institute Publications, 1992.

——. "Parents and Children in the Canterbury Tales." In *Literature in Fourteenth-Century England*. Edited by Piero Boitani and Anna Torti. Tübingen: Narr, 1983. 165–83.

334 BIBLIOGRAPHY

——. "'Taking the Adventure': Malory and the Suite de Merlin." In *Aspects of Malory*. Edited by Toshiyuki Takamiya and Derek Brewer. Cambridge: D. S. Brewer, 1981. 71–91.

Marenbon, John. *Pagans and Philosophers: The Problem of Paganism from Augustine to Leibniz*. Princeton, N.J.: Princeton University Press, 2015.

Marks, Richard. "Picturing Word and Text in the Late-Medieval Parish Church." In *Image, Text, and Church, 1380–1600*. Edited by Linda Clark, Maureen Jurkowski, and Colin Richmond. Toronto: Pontifical Institute of Mediaeval Studies, 2009. 162–88.

Markus, Robert. "How on earth could places become holy? Origins of the Christian idea of holy places." *Journal of Early Christian Studies* 2 (1994). 257–71.

——. *The End of Ancient Christianity*. Cambridge: Cambridge University Press, 1990.

Marshall, Peter. "(Re)defining the English Reformation." *Journal of British Studies* 48 (2009). 71–72, 581–83.

Masten, Jeffrey. *Queer Philologies: Sex, Language, and Affect in Shakespeare's Time*. Philadelphia: University of Pennsylvania Press, 2016.

Mazzaro, Jerome. "From *Fin Amour* to Friendship: Dante's Transformation." In *The Olde Daunce: Love, Friendship, Sex, and Marriage in the Medieval World*. Edited by Robert R. Edwards and Stephen Spector. Albany, N.Y.: State University of New York Press, 1991. 121–37.

McCulloch, Florence. "The Funeral of Renart the Fox in a Walters Book of Hours." *The Journal of the Walters Art Gallery* 25 (1962). 8–27.

McDonald, Nicola. "A Polemical Introduction." In *Pulp Fictions of the Middle Ages: Essays in Popular Romance*. Edited by Nicola McDonald. Manchester: Manchester University Press, 2004. 1–21.

——. "Chaucer's *Legend of Good Women*, Ladies at Court, and the Female Reader." *The Chaucer Review* 35 (2000). 22–42.

——. "The Wonder of Middle English Romance." In *Thinking Medieval Romance*. Edited by Nicola McDonald and Katherine C. Little. Oxford: Oxford University Press, 2018. 13–35.

McEvoy, James. "*Philia* and *amicitia*: the philosophy of friendship from Plato to Aquinas." *Sewanee Mediaeval Colloquium Occasional Papers* 2 (1985). 1–23.

McKenna, John W. "How God Became an Englishman." In *Tudor Rule and Revolution*. Edited by DeLloyd Guth and John McKenna. Cambridge: Cambridge University Press, 1982. 25–43.

Meale, Carol M., ed. *Women and Literature in Britain, 1150–1500*. 2nd ed. Cambridge: Cambridge University Press, 1996.

Meyer-Lee, Robert J. *Poets and Power from Chaucer to Wyatt*. Cambridge: Cambridge University Press, 2007.

——. *Literary Value and Social Identity in the "Canterbury Tales"*. Cambridge: Cambridge University Press, 2019.

Middleton, Anne. "Dowel, the Proverbial, and the Vernacular: Some Versions of Pastoralia." In *Medieval Poetics and Social Practice: Responding to the Work of Penn R. Szittya*. Edited by Seeta Chaganti. New York: Fordham University Press, 2012.

——. "The Audience and Public of *Piers Plowman*." In *Middle English Alliterative Poetry and Its Literary Background: Seven Essays*. Edited by David Lawton. Cambridge: D. S. Brewer, 1982.

BIBLIOGRAPHY   335

——. "The Idea of Public Poetry in the Reign of Richard II." *Speculum* 53 (1978). 94–114.

——. "The *Physician's Tale* and Love's Martyrs: Ensamples Mo than Ten as a Method in the *Canterbury Tales*." *The Chaucer Review* 8 (1973). 9–32.

——. "Thornton's Remedies and the Practices of Medical Reading." In *Robert Thornton and his Books: Essays on the Lincoln and London Thornton Manuscripts*. Edited by Susanna Fein and Michael Johnston. York: York Medieval Press, 2014. 235–55.

Miller, William E. "Double Translation in English Humanistic Education." *Studies in the Renaissance* 10 (1963). 163–74.

Miner, Dorothy. *Illuminated Books of the Middle Ages and Renaissance*. Baltimore, Md.: Trustees of the Walters Art Gallery, 1949.

Minnis, A. J., A. B. Scott, with the assistance of David Wallace, eds. *Medieval Literary Theory and Criticism c. 1100–c. 1375: The Commentary Tradition*. Oxford: Clarendon Press, 1988.

Mitchell, J. Allan. "Romancing Ethics in Boethius, Chaucer, and Levinas: Fortune, Moral Luck, and Erotic Adventure." *Comparative Literature* 57 (2005). 101–16.

Mitchell, John. *Gothic: Art for England, 1400–1547*. Edited by Richard Marks and Paul Williamson. London: V&A, 2003.

Mitchell, W. J. T. *Iconology: Image, Text, Ideology*. Chicago: University of Chicago Press, 1986.

——. *Picture Theory: Essays on Verbal and Visual Representation*. Chicago: University of Chicago Press, 1994.

Morgan, Nigel. *Early Gothic Manuscripts*. A Survey of Manuscripts Illuminated in the British Isles 4. 2 vols. London: Harvey Miller, 1988.

——. "The Artists of the Rutland Psalter." *British Library Journal* 13 (1987). 159–85.

——. "The Decorative Ornament of the Text and Page in Thirteenth-Century England: Initials, Border Extensions and Line Fillers." *English Manuscript Studies, 1100–1700* 10 (2002). 1–33.

Morris, Colin. *The Discovery of the Individual: 1050–1200*. London: S.P.C.K., 1972.

Morrissey, Jake Walsh. "'Termes of Phisik': Reading Between Literary and Medical Discourses in Geoffrey Chaucer's *Canterbury Tales* and John Lydgate's *Dietary*." Unpublished Ph.D. dissertation, McGill University, 2011.

——. "'To Al Indifferent': The Virtues of Lydgate's 'Dietary.'" *Medium Ævum* 84.2 (2015). 258–78.

Morton, Jonathan. *The* Roman de la Rose *in its Philosophical Context: Art, Nature, and Ethics*. Oxford: Oxford University Press, 2018.

Most, Glen W. "Hellenistic Allegory and Early Imperial Rhetoric." In *The Cambridge Companion to Allegory*. Edited by Rita Copeland and Peter T. Struck. Cambridge: Cambridge University Press, 2010. 26–38.

Murphy, James J. *Rhetoric in the Middle Ages: A History of Rhetorical Theory from St. Augustine to the Renaissance*. Berkeley, Cal.: University of California Press, 1974.

Murrin, Michael. *The Veil of Allegory: Some Notes towards a Theory of Allegorical Rhetoric in the English Renaissance*. Chicago: University of Chicago Press, 1969.

——. "Renaissance Allegory from Petrarch to Spenser." In *The Cambridge Companion to Allegory*. Edited by Rita Copeland and Peter T. Struck. Cambridge: Cambridge University Press, 2010. 162–76.

BIBLIOGRAPHY

Nederman, Cary J. "The Monarch and the Marketplace: Economic Policy and Royal Finance in William of Pagula's *Speculum Regis Edwardi III.*" *History of Political Economy* 33 (2001). 51–69.

Nelson, Ingrid. *Lyric Tactics: Poetry, Genre, and Practice in Later Medieval England.* Philadelphia: University of Pennsylvania Press, 2017.

Neville, Jennifer. "The Unexpected Treasure of the 'Implement Trope': Hierarchical Relationships in the Old English Riddles." *RES* 62 (2011). 505–19.

Newman, Barbara. *God and the Goddesses: Vision, Poetry, and Belief in the Middle Ages.* Philadelphia: University of Pennsylvania Press, 2003.

Nicholas, David. *Medieval Flanders.* New York: Routledge, 1992.

Nicholson, R. H. "Poetry and Politics: 'A Remembraunce of LII Folyes' in Context." *Viator* 41 (2010). 375–410.

Nievergelt, Marco. "Allegory." In *The Encyclopedia of Medieval Literature in Britain.* Edited by Siân Echard and Robert Rouse. Chichester, UK: Wiley Blackwell, 2017. 50–59.

Niles, John D. *Old English Enigmatic Poems and the Play of the Texts.* Turnhout, Belgium: Brepols, 2006.

Nisse, Ruth. "'A Coroun Ful Riche': The Rule of History in 'St Erkenwald.'" *ELH* 65 (1998). 277–95.

Nolan, Maura. *John Lydgate and the Making of Public Culture.* Cambridge: Cambridge University Press, 2005.

——. "The Art of History Writing: Lydgate's *Serpent of Division.*" *Speculum* 78 (2003). 99–127.

Nuttall, Jenni. "One Poem, Two Ways." *Stylisticienne,* 27 March 2014. https://stylisticienne.com/one-poem-two-ways/.

Ogilvie-Thomson, S. J. *The Index of Middle English Prose: Handlist XXIII: The Rawlinson Collection, Bodleian Library, Oxford.* Cambridge: D. S. Brewer, 2017.

Orchard, Andy. *A Commentary on the Old English and Anglo-Latin Riddle Tradition.* Washington: Dumbarton Oaks, 2021.

——. "Enigma Variations: The Anglo-Saxon Riddle Tradition." In *Latin Learning and English Lore: Studies in Anglo-Saxon Literature for Michael Lapidge.* Edited by Katherine O'Brien O'Keeffe and Andy Orchard. 2 vols. Toronto: University of Toronto Press, 2005. 1: 284–304.

Orlemanski, Julie. "Genre." *A Handbook of Middle English Studies.* Edited by Marion Turner. Chichester, UK: Wiley-Blackwell, 2013. 207–21.

——. *Symptomatic Subjects: Bodies, Medicine, and Causation in the Literature of Late Medieval England.* Philadelphia: University of Pennsylvania Press, 2019.

Ormrod, Mark W. *The Reign of Edward III: Crown and Political Society in England, 1327–1377.* New Haven, Conn.: Yale University Press, 1990.

Pak, G. Sujin. *The Judaizing Calvin: Sixteenth Century Debates over the Messianic Psalms.* Oxford: Oxford University Press, 2010.

——. *The Reformation of Prophecy: Early Modern Interpretations of the Prophet and Old Testament Prophecy.* Oxford: Oxford University Press, 2018.

Parkes, Malcolm. *Pause and Effect: An Introduction to the History of Punctuation in the West.* Aldershot, UK: Ashgate, 1992.

Patterson, Lee. *Chaucer and the Subject of History.* Madison, Wis.: University of Wisconsin Press, 1991.

Paxson, James J. *The Poetics of Personification.* Cambridge: Cambridge University Press, 1994.

BIBLIOGRAPHY

Paz, James. "Æschere's Head, Grendel's Mother, and the Sword That Isn't a Sword: Unreadable Things in *Beowulf*." *Exemplaria* 25 (2013). 231–51.

Pearsall, Derek. *John Lydgate*. London: Routledge & Kegan Paul, 1970.

——. *The Life of Geoffrey Chaucer: A Critical Biography*. Oxford: Blackwell, 1992.

——. "The Timelessness of *The Simonie*." In *Individuality and Achievement in Middle English Poetry*. Edited by O. S. Pickering. Cambridge: D. S. Brewer, 1997.

——. "Medieval Literature and Historical Enquiry." *Modern Language Review* 99 (2004). xxxi–xlii.

——. "The Apotheosis of John Lydgate." *Journal of Medieval and Early Modern Studies* 35 (2005). 25–38.

Perkins, Nicholas. "Ekphrasis and Narrative in *Emaré* and *Eglamour of Artois*." In *Medieval Romance, Medieval Contexts*. Edited by Rhiannon Purdie and Michael Cichon. Cambridge: D. S. Brewer, 2011. 47–60.

——. *The Gift of Narrative in Medieval England*. Manchester: Manchester University Press, 2021.

Permyakov, G. L. *From Proverb to Folk-tale: Notes on the General Theory of Cliché*. Translated by Y. N. Filippov. Moscow: Nauka, 1979.

Perry, R. D. "Lydgate's Virtual Coteries: Chaucer's Family and Gower's Pacifism in the Fifteenth Century." *Speculum* 93 (2018). 669–98.

Pizarro, J. M. "Poetry as Rumination: the Model for Bede's Caedmon." *Neophilologus* 89 (2005). 469–72.

Poleg, Eyal. *A Material History of the Bible: England 1200–1553*. Oxford: Oxford University Press for the British Academy, 2020. 74.

——. "Memory, Performance, and Change: The Psalms' Layout in Late Medieval and Early Modern Bibles." In *From Scrolls to Scrolling: Sacred Texts, Materiality, and Dynamic Media Cultures in Judaism, Christianity, and Islam*. Edited by Brad A. Anderson. Berlin: De Gruyter, 2020. 119–51.

Putter, Ad. "A Historical Introduction." In *The Spirit of Medieval English Popular Romance*. Edited by Jane Gilbert and Ad Putter. London: Routledge, 2000. 1–15.

Pépin, Jean. "Allegoria." *Enciclopedia Dantesca*. Edited by Umberto Bosco. Rome: Istituto della Enciclopedia Italiana, 1970. 151–65.

Randall, Lilian M. C. "An Elephant in the Litany: Further Thoughts on an English Book of Hours in the Walters Art Gallery (W. 102)." In *Beasts and Birds of the Middle Ages. The Bestiary and Its Legacy*. Edited by Willene B. Clark and Meradith T. McMunn. Philadelphia: University of Pennsylvania Press, 1989. 106–33.

——. *Medieval and Renaissance Manuscripts in the Walters Art Gallery*. Vol. 3, pt. 1. Baltimore, Md.: Johns Hopkins University Press, 1997. No. 220.

Raskolnikov, Masha. *Body against Soul: Gender and Sowlehele in Middle English Allegory*. Columbus, Ohio: Ohio State University Press, 2009.

Raw, Alice. "Gender, Sexual Discourse, and Women's Pleasure in Later Medieval England, c. 1300–c. 1550." Unpublished D.Phil. dissertation, Oxford University, 2023.

Richardson, Malcolm. *Middle-Class Writing in Late Medieval London*. London: Pickering and Chatto, 2011.

Richter, Claudia. *The Calvinesque: An Aesthetics of Violence in English Literature after the Reformation*. New York: Lang, 2014.

BIBLIOGRAPHY

Riddy, Felicity. "Mother Knows Best: Reading Social Change in a Courtesy Text." *Speculum* 71 (1996). 66–86.

Riordan, Michael. "Henry VIII, privy chamber of." *Oxford Dictionary of National Biography*. Oxford: Oxford University Press, 2004. https://www.oxforddnb.com.

Rippl, Gabriele. "Ekphrasis." In *The Oxford Research Encyclopedia of Literature*, 25 June 2019. https://oxfordre.com/literature (accessed 1 February 2023).

Robbins, R. H. *Secular Lyrics of the XIVth and XVth Centuries*. Oxford: Clarendon Press, 1952. Nos. 110–12.

——. "Punctuation Poems: A Further Note." *Review of English Studies* 15 (1939). 206–07.

Robertson, Kellie. "Common Language and Common Profit." In *The Postcolonial Middle Ages*. Edited by Jeffrey Jerome Cohen. London: Palgrave, 2000. 209–28.

——. *Nature Speaks: Medieval Literature and Aristotelian Philosophy*. Philadelphia: University of Pennsylvania Press, 2017.

Robinson, Fred C. "Artful Ambiguities in the Old English 'Book-Moth' Riddle." In *Anglo-Saxon Poetry: Essays in Appreciation, for John. C. McGalliard*. Edited by Lewis E. Nicholson and Dolores Warwick Frese. Notre Dame, Ind.: University of Notre Dame Press, 1975. 355–62.

Rosenfeld, Colleen Ruth. "Wroth's Clause." *ELH* 76 (2009). 1049–71.

Rosenfeld, Jessica. *Ethics and Enjoyment in Late Medieval Poetry: Love after Aristotle*. Cambridge: Cambridge University Press, 2010.

Russell, Frederick H. *The Just War in the Middle Ages*. Cambridge: Cambridge University Press, 1975.

Russo, Teresa G., ed. *Recognition and Modes of Knowledge: Anagnorisis from Antiquity to Contemporary Theory*. Edmonton: University of Alberta Press, 2013.

Russom, Geoffrey. "Exeter Riddle 47: A Moth Laid Waste to Fame." *Philological Quarterly* 56 (1977). 129–36.

Rust, Martha Dana. *Imaginary Worlds in Medieval Books: Exploring the Manuscript Matrix*. New York: Palgrave MacMillan, 2007.

Salter, Elizabeth. "The Timeliness of *Wynnere and Wastoure*." *Medium Ævum* 47 (1978). 40–65.

Salvador-Bello, Mercedes. *Isidorean Perceptions of Order: The Exeter Book Riddles and Medieval Latin Enigmata*. Morgantown, W. Va.: West Virginia University Press, 2015.

Sandler, Lucy Freeman. *Gothic Manuscripts, 1285–1385*. A Survey of Manuscripts Illuminated in the British Isles 5. 2 vols. London: Harvey Miller, 1986.

——. *The Peterborough Psalter in Brussels and Other Fenland Manuscripts*. London: Harvey Miller, 1974.

Sanok, Catherine. "The Geography of Genre in the *Physician's Tale* and *Pearl*." *New Medieval Literatures* 5 (2002). 177–201.

Sarot, Marcel. "The Value of Infused Love: Nygren, Brümmer and Aquinas on *Agape and Caritas*." *Jaarboek Thomas Instituut te Utrecht* 33 (2013). 111–23.

Sauer, Elizabeth. *Milton, Toleration and Nationhood*. Cambridge: Cambridge University Press, 2014.

Saunders, Corinne. "Affective Reading: Chaucer, Women, and Romance." *The Chaucer Review* 51 (2016). 11–30.

——. "Introduction." In *A Companion to Romance: From Classical to Contemporary*. Edited by Corinne Saunders. Oxford: Blackwell, 2004. 1–9.

BIBLIOGRAPHY

——. *Rape and Ravishment in the Literature of Medieval England*. Cambridge: D. S. Brewer, 2001.

Sawyer, Daniel. *Reading English Verse in Manuscript, c. 1350–c. 1500*. Oxford: Oxford University Press, 2020.

Scala, Elizabeth. *Desire in the* Canterbury Tales. Columbus, Ohio: The Ohio State University Press, 2015.

Scarry, Elaine. "The Well-Rounded Sphere: Cognition and Metaphysical Structure in Boethius's *Consolation of Philosophy*." In *Resisting Representation*. Oxford: Oxford University Press, 1994. 143–80.

Scase, Wendy. Review of *The Digby Poems: A New Edition of the Lyrics*. *Journal of English and Germanic Philology* 110 (2011). 136–38.

Scattergood, John. "*Chaucer a Bukton* and Proverbs." *Nottingham Medieval Studies* 31 (1987). 98–107.

——. "Eating the Book: *Riddle 47* and Memory." In *Text and Gloss: Studies in Insular Learning and Literature Presented to Joseph Donovan Pheifer*. Edited by Helen Conrad O'Brian, Anne Marie D'Arcy, and John Scattergood. Dublin: Four Courts Press, 1999. 119–27.

Schieberle, Misty. "Proverbial Fools and Rival Wisdom: Lydgate's *Order of Fools* and Marcolf." *Chaucer Review* 49 (2014). 204–27.

Scott, Kathleen L. "Caveat Lector: Ownership and Standardization in the Illustration of Fifteenth-Century English Manuscripts." In *English Manuscript Studies* 1 (1989). 19–63.

——. *Later Gothic Manuscripts 1390–1490*. A Survey of Manuscripts Illuminated in the British Isles 6. 2 vols. London: Harvey Miller, 1996.

Seal, Samantha Katz. "Reading Like a Jew: Chaucer's *Physician's Tale* and the Letter of the Law." *Chaucer Review* 52 (2017). 298–317.

Seymour, M. C. "MSS Douce 261 and Egerton 3132A and Edward Banyster." *Bodleian Library Record* 10 (1980). 162–65.

Sheehan, Michael M. "*Maritalis Affectio* Revisited." In *The Olde Daunce: Love, Friendship, Sex, and Marriage in the Medieval World*. Edited by Robert R. Edwards and Stephen Spector. Albany, N.Y.: State University of New York Press, 1991. 32–43.

Silk, Michael. "Invoking the Other: Allegory in Theory, from Demetrius to de Man." In *Allegory Studies: Contemporary Perspectives*. Edited by Vladimir Brljak. New York: Routledge, 2021. 41–65.

Simard, S. W., D. A. Perry, M. D. Jones, D. D. Myrold, D. M. Durall, and R. Molina. "Net Transfer of Carbon between Tree Species with Shared Ectomycorrhizal Fungi." *Nature* 388 (1997). 579–82.

Simpson, James. *Burning to Read: English Fundamentalism and its Reformation Opponents*. Cambridge, Mass.: Harvard University Press, 2007.

——. "Chaucer as a European Writer." In *The Yale Companion to Chaucer*. Edited by Seth Lerer. New Haven, Conn.: Yale University Press, 2006. 55–86.

——. "Cognition is Recognition: Literary Knowledge and Textual 'Face.'" *New Literary History* 44 (2013). 25–44.

——. "The Constraints of Satire in *Mum and the Sothsegger* and *Piers Plowman*." In *Langland, the Mystics and the Medieval English Religious Tradition*. Edited by Helen Phillips. Cambridge: D. S. Brewer, 1990.

——. "Derek Brewer's Romance." In *Traditions and Innovations in the Study of Medieval English Literature: The Influence of Derek Brewer*. Edited by Charlotte Brewer and Barry Windeatt. Cambridge: D. S. Brewer, 2013. 154–72.

BIBLIOGRAPHY

——. "Desire and the Scriptural Text: Will as reader in *Piers Plowman.*" In *Criticism and Dissent in the Middle Ages.* Edited by Rita Copeland. Cambridge: Cambridge University Press, 1996. 215–43.

——. "'Dysemol daies and fatal houres': Lydgate's *Destruction of Thebes* and Chaucer's *Knight's Tale.*" In *The Long Fifteenth Century: Essays for Douglas Gray.* Edited by Helen Cooper and Sally Mapstone. Oxford: Oxford University Press, 1997. 15–33.

——. "Humanism." In *Dictionary of the Middle Ages.* Supplement 1. Edited by William Chester Jordan. New York: Charles Scribner's Sons, 2004. 279–82.

——. "Interrogation Over. A Review Essay of Rita Felski, *The Limits of Critique.*" *PMLA* 132 (2017). 377–83.

——. "John Lydgate." In *The Cambridge Companion to Medieval Literature.* Edited by Larry Scanlon. Cambridge: Cambridge University Press, 2009. 205–16.

——. "Madness and Texts: Hoccleve's *Series.*" In *Chaucer and Fifteenth-Century Poetry.* Edited by Julia Boffey and Janet Cowan. London: King's College, 1991. 15–29.

——. "Nobody's Man: Thomas Hoccleve's *Regement of Princes.*" In *London and Europe in the Later Middle Ages.* Edited by Julia Boffey and Pamela King. London: Centre for Medieval and Renaissance Studies, Queen Mary and Westfield College, 1995. 149–80.

——. "Not the Last Word." *Journal of Medieval and Early Modern Studies* 35 (2005). 111–19.

——. *The Oxford English Literary History, Vol. 2: 1350–1547. Reform and Cultural Revolution.* Oxford: Oxford University Press, 2002.

——. *Permanent Revolution: The Reformation and the Illiberal Roots of Liberalism.* Cambridge, Mass.: Harvard University Press, 2019.

——. *Piers Plowman: An Introduction.* Rev. ed. Exeter Medieval Texts and Studies. Exeter, UK: University of Exeter Press, 2007.

——. "The Rule of Medieval Imagination." In *Images, Idolatry and Iconoclasm in Late Medieval England.* Edited by Jeremy Dimmick, James Simpson and Nicolette Zeeman. Oxford: Oxford University Press, 2002.

——. *Sciences and the Self in Medieval Poetry: Alan of Lille's* Anticlaudianus *and John Gower's* Confessio amantis. Cambridge: Cambridge University Press, 1995.

——. "Spirituality and Economics in Passus 1–7 of the B Text." *Yearbook of Langland Studies* 1 (1987). 83–103.

——. "Textual Face: Cognition as Recognition." In *Contemporary Chaucer across the Centuries, a Festschrift for Stephanie Trigg.* Edited by Helen M. Hickey, Anne McHendry and Melissa Raine. Manchester: Manchester University Press, 2018. 218–33.

——. *Under the Hammer: Iconoclasm in the Anglo-American Tradition.* Oxford: Oxford University Press, 2010.

——. "Unthinking Thought: Romance's Wisdom." In *Thinking Medieval Romance.* Edited by Nicola McDonald and Katherine C. Little. Oxford: Oxford University Press, 2018. 36–52.

——. "Violence, Narrative and Proper Name: *Sir Degaré,* 'The Tale of Sir Gareth of Orkney', and the *Folie Tristan d'Oxford.*" In *The Spirit of Medieval English Popular Romance.* Edited by Jane Gilbert and Ad Putter. London: Routledge, 2000. 122–41.

Sisk, Jennifer L. "The Uneasy Orthodoxy of 'St. Erkenwald.'" *ELH* 74 (2007). 89–115.

Smith, D. Vance. *Arts of Possession: The Middle English Household Imaginary.* Minneapolis, Minn.: University of Minnesota Press, 2003.

BIBLIOGRAPHY 341

——. "Death: Terminable and Interminable." *Arts of Dying: Literature and Finitude in Medieval England*. Chicago: University of Chicago Press, 2020.

Smith, David. *Parliaments and Politics during the Cromwellian Protectorate*. Cambridge: Cambridge University Press, 2007.

Smith, Nigel. *Perfection Proclaimed: Language and Literature in English Radical Religion, 1640–1660*. Oxford: Clarendon, 1989.

Sobecki, Sebastian. *Unwritten Verities: The Making of England's Vernacular Legal Culture, 1463–1549*. Notre Dame, Ind.: University of Notre Dame Press, 2015.

Spalding, James. "Sermons Before Parliament (1640–1649) as a Public Puritan Diary." *Church History* 36 (1967). 24–35.

Spearing, A. C. *Medieval Autographies: The "I" of the Text*. Notre Dame, Ind.: University of Notre Dame Press, 2012.

——. "Narration in Two Versions of 'Virginius and Virginia.'" *The Chaucer Review* 54 (2019). 1–34.

——. *Textual Subjectivity: The Encoding of Subjectivity in Medieval Narratives and Lyrics*. Oxford: Oxford University Press, 2005.

——. "What is a Narrator? Narrator Theory and Medieval Narratives." *Digital Philology* 4 (2015). 59–105.

Speed, Diane. "Language and Perspective in the *Physician's Tale*." In *Words and Wordsmiths: A Volume for H. L. Rogers*. Edited by Geraldine Barnes et al. Sydney: University of Sydney, 1989. 119–36.

Sponsler, Claire. "Eating Lessons: Lydgate's 'Dietary' and Consumer Conduct." In *Medieval Conduct*. Edited by Kathleen Ashley and Robert L. A. Clark. Minneapolis, Minn.: University of Minnesota Press, 2001. 1–22.

Stanbury, Sarah. "The Embarrassments of Romance." *Arthuriana* 17 (2007). 114–16.

Strohm, Paul. *England's Empty Throne: Usurpation and the Language of Legitimation, 1399–1422*. New Haven, Conn.: Yale University Press, 1998.

——. *Politique: Languages of Statecraft between Chaucer and Shakespeare*. Notre Dame, Ind.: University of Notre Dame Press, 2005.

Struck, Peter T. "Allegory and Ascent in Neoplatonism." In *The Cambridge Companion to Allegory*. Edited by Rita Copeland and Peter T. Struck. Cambridge: Cambridge University Press, 2010. 57–70.

Summit, Jennifer. "Topography as Historiography: Petrarch, Chaucer, and the Making of Medieval Rome." *Journal of Medieval and Early Modern Studies* 30 (2000). 211–46.

Sutton, Mark Q., and E. N. Anderson. *Introduction to Cultural Ecology*. 3rd ed. Lanham, Md.: Altamira Press, 2014.

Taylor, Barry. "Medieval Proverb Collections: The West European Tradition." *Journal of the Warburg and Courtauld Institutes* 55 (1992). 19–35.

Taylor, Karla. *Chaucer Reads "The Divine Comedy"*. Stanford, Calif.: Stanford University Press, 1989.

Teskey, Gordon. *Allegory and Violence*. Ithaca, N.Y.: Cornell University Press, 1996.

——. "Langland's Golden Bough." *Yearbook of Langland Studies* 25 (2011). 189–96.

Thienes, Eric M. "Remembering Trajan in Fourth-Century Rome: Memory and Identity in Spatial, Artistic, and Textual Narratives." Unpublished Ph.D. dissertation, University of Missouri, 2015.

Thrupp, Sylvia L. *The Merchant Class of Medieval London, 1300–1500*. Ann Arbor, Mich.: University of Michigan Press, 1989.

BIBLIOGRAPHY

Tianhu, Hao. "Lines Per Page, Engravings, and Catchwords in Milton's 1720 *Poetical Works*." *Studies in Bibliography* 59 (2015). 191–95.

Timperley, Grace A. "The Idea of Disinheritance in Middle English Romances." Unpublished Ph.D. dissertation, Manchester University, 2020.

Trevor-Roper, Hugh. "The Fast Sermons of the Long Parliament." In *Religion, the Reformation and Social Change and Other Essays*. London: Macmillan, 1967. 294–344.

Tribble, Evelyn B. *Margins and Marginality: The Printed Page in Early Modern England*. Charlottesville, V.A.: University Press of Virginia, 1993.

Trigg, Stephanie. "The Traffic in Medieval Women: Alice Perrers, Feminist Criticism and *Piers Plowman*." *The Yearbook of Langland Studies* 12 (1998). 5–29.

Tuve, Rosemond. *Allegorical Imagery: Some Mediaeval Books and their Posterity*. Princeton, N.J.: Princeton University Press, 1966.

Underwood, T. L. *Primitivism, Radicalism, and the Lamb's Wars: The Baptist-Quaker Conflict in Seventeenth-Century England*. Oxford: Oxford University Press, 1997.

Varnam, Laura. "Sacred Space, Memory and Materiality in *St Erkenwald*." In *Old St Paul's and Culture*. Edited by Shanyn Altman and Jonathan Buckner. London: Palgrave Macmillan, 2021. 73–98.

Vickers, Nancy J. "Seeing is Believing: Gregory, Trajan, and Dante's Art." *Dante Studies* 101 (1983). 67–85.

Vines, Amy N. "Invisible Women: Rape as a Chivalric Necessity in Medieval Romance." In *Sexual Culture in the Literature of Medieval Britain*. Edited by Amanda Hopkins et al. Cambridge: Cambridge University Press, 2014. 161–80.

Wade, James. "Penitential Romance after the Reformation." In *Medieval into Renaissance: Essays for Helen Cooper*. Edited by Andrew King and Matthew Woodcock. Cambridge: D. S. Brewer, 2016. 91–106.

Wadiak, Walter. *Savage Economy: The Returns of Middle English Romance*. Notre Dame, Ind.: University of Notre Dame Press, 2016.

Wakelin, Daniel. *Designing English: Early Literature on the Page*. Oxford: Bodleian Library, University of Oxford, 2018.

——. *Immaterial Texts in Late Medieval England: Making English Literary Manuscripts, 1400–1500*. Cambridge: Cambridge University Press, 2022.

Wallace, David, ed. *The Cambridge History of Medieval English Literature*. Cambridge: Cambridge University Press, 1999.

——. "In Flaundres." *Studies in the Age of Chaucer* 19 (1997). 63–91.

——. "'She Lives!': Jephthah's Daughter and Chaucer's Virginia, Jews and Gentiles, Bad Narrative and Ending Happily." *The Chaucer Review* 58 (2023). 403–15.

Walzer, Michael. *The Revolution of the Saints: A Study in the Origins of Radical Politics*. Cambridge, Mass.: Harvard University Press, 1965.

Watts, John. *Henry VI and the Politics of Kingship*. Cambridge: Cambridge University Press, 1996.

——. "Public or Plebs: The Changing Meaning of 'The Commons,' 1381–1549." In *Power and Identity in the Middle Ages: Essays in Memory of Rees Davies*. Edited by Huw Pryce and John Watts. Oxford: Oxford University Press, 2007.

Wawn, Andrew. "Truth-Telling and the Tradition of *Mum and the Sothsegger*." *The Yearbook of English Studies* 13 (1983). 270–87.

Weaver, Erica. "Premodern and Postcritical: Medieval Enigmata and the Hermeneutic Style." *New Literary History* 50 (2019). 43–64.

Wehlau, Ruth. "Rumination and Re-Creation: Poetic Instruction in *The Order of the World*." *Florilegium* 13 (1994). 65–77.

BIBLIOGRAPHY

343

Weiskott, Eric. *English Alliterative Verse: Poetic Tradition and Literary History*. Cambridge: Cambridge University Press, 2016.

Wenzel, Siegfried. "*Mum and the Sothsegger*, Lines 421–22." *ELN* 14 (1976). 87–90.

West, Philip J. "Rumination in Bede's Account of Cædmon." *Monastic Studies* 12 (1976). 217–26.

Wetherbee, Winthrop. *Platonism and Poetry in the Twelfth Century*. Princeton, N.J.: Princeton University Press, 1972.

Whately, Gordon E. "Heathens and Saints: *St Erkenwald* in its Legendary Context." *Speculum* 61 (1986). 330–63.

——. "The Uses of Hagiography: The Legend of Pope Gregory and the Emperor Trajan in the Middle Ages." *Viator* 15 (1984). 25–64.

Whetter, K. S. "On Misunderstanding Malory's Balyn." In *Re-viewing "Le Morte Darthur"*. Edited by K. S. Whetter and Raluca L. Radulescu. Cambridge: D. S. Brewer, 2005. 149–62.

——. *Understanding Genre and Medieval Romance*. Aldershot, UK: Ashgate, 2008.

Whiting, Bartlett Jere. "The Origin of the Proverb (1931)." In *When Evensong and Morrowsong Accord: Three Essays on the Proverb*. Edited by Joseph Harris. Cambridge, Mass.: Department of English and American Literature and Language, Harvard University, 1994.

Whitman, Jon. *Allegory. The Dynamics of an Ancient and Medieval Technique*. Cambridge, Mass.: Harvard University Press, 1987.

Wilcox, Jonathan. "Eating Books: The Consumption of Learning in the Old English Poetic *Solomon and Saturn*." *ANQ* 4 (1991). 115–18.

Williams, George. *The Radical Reformation*. 3rd ed. Kirksville, Mo.: Truman State University Press, 1995.

Williamson, Craig. *The Old English Riddles of the "Exeter Book"*. Chapel Hill, N.C.: The University of North Carolina Press, 1977.

Wilson, John F. *Pulpit in Parliament: Puritanism During the English Civil Wars, 1640–1648*. Princeton: Princeton University Press, 1969.

Wimsatt, James I. "Reason, Machaut, and the Franklin." In *The Olde Daunce: Love, Friendship, Sex, and Marriage in the Medieval World*. Edited by Robert R. Edwards and Stephen Spector. Albany, N.Y.: State University of New York Press, 1991. 201–10.

Woolrych, Austin. *Britain in Revolution: 1625–1660*. Oxford: Oxford University Press, 2002.

Worden, Blair. *God's Instruments: Political Conduct in the England of Oliver Cromwell*. Oxford: Oxford University Press, 2014.

——. *The Rump Parliament*. Oxford: Oxford University Press, 1977.

Yates, Julian. *Error, Misuse, Failure: Object Lessons from the English Renaissance*. Minneapolis: University of Minnesota Press, 2003.

Yunck, John A. *The Lineage of Lady Meed: the Development of Mediaeval Venality Satire*. Notre Dame, Ind.: University of Notre Dame Press, 1963.

Zeeman, Nicolette. *The Arts of Disruption: Allegory and* Piers Plowman. Oxford: Oxford University Press, 2020.

Zink, Michel. *Medieval French Literature: An Introduction*. Translated by Jeff Rider. Binghamton, N.Y.: Medieval and Renaissance Texts and Studies, 1995.

Zurcher, Andrew. *Edmund Spenser's* The Faerie Queene: *A Reading Guide*. Edinburgh: Edinburgh University Press, 2011.

Zweck, Jordan. "Silence in the Exeter Book Riddles." *Exemplaria* 28 (2016). 319–36.

A Note on the Bloomfield Conferences

The Bloomfield lectures and more recently conferences were established in 1987 to honor Morton W. Bloomfield, Arthur Kingsley Porter Professor of English at Harvard from 1971 until 1983. Bloomfield's work in the fields of medieval linguistics, allegory, ethics, hermeneutics, and apocalypticism, as well as his literary and public criticism, made him one of the most wide-ranging medieval scholars of the post-World War II generation. Arguably, his was "a conservative mind," as the critical linguist Roger Fowler suggested in 1971, referring, not to Bloomfield's politics but to his lifelong tendency to seek the point of balance between critical extremes; it was also, in Fowler's accurate judgement, "an overwhelmingly generous, synthesizing and penetrating one."[1] The conferences named in his memory aspire to embody these same last three qualities.

The 2022 Morton W. Bloomfield Lecture, given by one of Bloomfield's successors at Harvard, James Simpson, is Chapter 1 of this book.

---

[1] Roger Fowler, review of Morton W. Bloomfield, *Essays and Explorations: Studies in Ideas, Language, and Literature* (Cambridge, Mass.: Harvard University Press, 1970), *Journal of European Studies* 1 (1971), 95.

GENERAL INDEX

Ælfric of Eynsham   37
Aelred of Rievaulx   68
  On Spiritual Friendship   68
Aenigma   26–27, 29, 30, 93
  see also riddle
Alain of Lille   54, 97
  Anticlaudianus   97
  De planctu naturae   88, 92, 97, 105
Aldhelm   36, 40, 42–43
  Enigmata   36, 40–41, 43
Alighieri, Dante   16, 98, 190
  Divine Comedy   76–77, 88, 92, 101, 190
    commentary of Jacopo della
      Lana   189
    commentary of Guido da Pisa   100
  Convivio   98
  Epistle to Can Grande   99
Alighieri, Pietro   101
allegoresis   94, 95, 160, 185, 186, 190, 215
allegory   54, 90, 102, 105, 199
  allegoria   91, 96–101, 103
    hermeneutic   94–95
    rhetorical   92–94, 96–97
  biblical   30, 277, 278–79, 283
  genre   87–89, 95–96, 98, 104–05
  narrative   87–90, 92, 104–06, 168, 176
  in *Piers Plowman*   167, 169–70, 176,
      177, 180–81
  trope   92–93, 99, 100, 102
  see also Fortune, Nature, William
      Langland, Peace, personification,
      Reason
Allen, Elizabeth   56
Ambrose   279
Anabaptists   277, 280, 281
anagnorisis   15, 71, 78, 80, 84
  see also recognition
Ancrene Wisse   210
animation   50–51, 53, 56, 62
Appius   51, 54, 58, 59, 62
Aquinas, Thomas   68, 80–81
Aristotle   15, 17, 31, 68, 80, 96, 135, 176
  Ethics   135, 176
  Poetics   17, 96

Ascham, Roger   247, 257
Ascoli, Albert   99
Augustine of Canterbury   185, 191, 194
Augustine of Hippo   18–19, 20, 21–22,
      279, 280, 281–82
  Confessions   18, 20, 22, 282
  conversion   279
  De doctrina christiana   192
  Ennarationes in Psalmos   210, 279

Bale, John   295, 298–99
  Three Laws   298–99
Balyn le Sauvage see under Thomas
  Malory
Bancroft, Richard   148
Banyster, Edward   242
Barr, Helen   202, 203–05, 208, 210
Beckett, Samuel   20
Bede   36, 37, 199
  *Ecclesiastical History of the English
      People*   199
Benveniste, Émile   61
Beowulf   36, 46, 47, 48
  Æschere   36, 45–46, 47
  Grendel's mother   45, 46, 47, 48
  Hrothgar   45–46, 47, 48
  manuscript   45, 46
Bible   30
  Deuteronomy
    3:32   285
    20:4   285
  Judges
    5:23   283, 285
    11   64
  1 Samuel
    15   175
  2 Kings
    1:5–15, 2:23–25   278
  2 Chronicles
    19:2   285
  Psalm
    15:1   196
    137:9   281–82, 284
    139:21–22   285

348 GENERAL INDEX

Jeremiah
  48:10   283
Matthew
  5:38–39, 5:43–45, 5:48   277, 285
  10:34   276, 186
  11:12   287
  21:6–16   288
Luke
  6:27–38   278, 283
  9:51–56   278, 289
  15:11–32   256
  19:35–48   288
  23:34   278
John
  18:36   184
Acts
  1:13   196
Romans
  5:10   278
  12:14, 17   278
1 Corinthians
  3:2   37
2 Corinthians
  3:6   279
  5:9, 5:17–18   278
Colossians
  3:12–15   270, 271
1 Timothy
  6:6–12   270, 272
1 Peter
  1:13–16   270, 271–72
  3:15–17   270
Binham Priory   259, 261, 268
  chancel screen   261
    dimensions and order of   263–65
    inscriptions on   265–66, 269–71, 274
    "Risen Christ" image   263
    use of the Great Bible   261, 272
Bitterli, Dieter   41
Boccaccio, Giovanni   98, 99–100
  *Esposizioni sopra la Comedia di
    Dante*   100–01
  Il Filostrato   72, 75, 77, 78, 79, 81
    Criseida   75, 77, 78, 79
    Troilo   77–79
Boethius   73, 83
  Boethian philosophy   76, 79, 83, 234
  Consolation of Philosophy   23, 257
Boffey, Julia   231
Boniface   42
Book of Common Prayer   271, 287
bookchest   36, 40, 41, 46
bookworm   37, 38, 39, 41, 43, 44, 47
Bowers, Hannah   227–28
Bradbury, Nancy Mason   214

Brecht, Bertolt   25
Breen, Katherine   49
Brewer, Derek   108–09
Brljak, Vladimir   96, 103, 105
Brogan, T. V. F.   148
Bromyard, John   214
  Summa praedicantium   214
Bucer, Martin   287–88
  De regno Christi   288
Bunyan, John   295
  Grace Abounding   276
Burckhardt, Jacob   89
Burton, William   148
Butler, Judith   72

Cade, Jack   218, 219, 221
Cædmon   37
Calamy, Edmund   284, 290
  The souldiers pocket Bible   284–85
Calcidius   23
Calder, Natalie   221
Calvinism   282, 283, 289
  doctrine   290
  reading practices   276, 284
Calvin, John   280, 281, 285, 287, 288
  Institutes of the Christian Religion   280
Cannon, Christopher   213
The Canterbury Tales see under Geoffrey
  Chaucer
caritas   68
Carpenter, John   231–32
catchwords   150, 152, 154
  as error   154, 159–60, 162
  need for critical examination   155–56
  obviousness   150–51, 156, 160–61,
    163–64
  as repetition   153
Cecil, William   245
de Certeau, Michel   183
Ceyx   65, 66
Charles I of England   283, 285
Chaucer, Geoffrey   49, 50, 52, 55, 64, 67,
  199
  Book of the Duchess   65
  The Canterbury Tales   55, 57, 62, 105
    "The Physician's Tale"   49, 51–53, 56,
      59, 62, 63, 65–66
      Virginia   49, 52, 53–54, 58–59, 61, 66
        creation   55, 57
        voice   60, 62, 63–64, 65
      Virginius   51, 53, 54–55, 58,
        59–62, 65
    "The Second Nun's Tale"   185
    "The Summoner's Tale"   291
  House of Fame   52, 88

GENERAL INDEX

"Lenvoy a Bukton"   212
literary sources   51, 54, 56, 58, 59, 72, 74, 77, 82–83
Parliament of Fowls   104
Troilus and Criseyde   63, 72, 76, 77, 84, 257
Criseyde   67, 73–74, 75, 77, 114
as moral agent   78, 80, 82
Troilus   67, 74, 75, 77–80, 82, 84, 257
Chazelle, Celia   188
choice   75, 79, 81, 84
Christ, Jesus
comparison to Moses   280, 285
conception   113
disciples   278, 283, 289
image of   259, 263–64, 268, 277
incarnation   279
resurrection   16
teachings of charity   291
teachings on love   275, 277–78, 285, 289, 290, 291
teachings on violence   287, 289
voice   209
Christology   21–22, 283–84, 290
Church of England   283
Cicero   92, 93, 245, 249
Orator   92
climate change   150
cognition   14, 33, 81
see also recognition
Cohen, Jeffrey Jerome   47
Cole, Andrew   214
Compendium rhetorice   98
conduct writings   211, 228, 230, 234, 236
Confessions see under Augustine
Consolation of Philosophy   23, 257
consumption   36–37, 39, 41–42, 47, 230
see also digestion, rumination
Cooper, Helen   52, 246
Copeland, Rita   93, 99, 199
Cotman, John Sell   264
creation   21–22, 53, 65, 268, 278, 290
Crocker, Holly A.   57
Cromwell, Oliver   283, 284, 290
Croniques de Normandie   242, 243, 248, 249
custumals   225, 228, 231, 233
see also Liber albus

Dahan, Gilbert   102
Dante *see under* Alighieri, Dante
Degaré   111–16, 119
Demetrius   96
De nuptiis Philologiae et Mercurii   104
diegesis   61, 87, 88, 89, 91, 95, 96, 104

Dietary see under John Lydgate
Digby poems   202–03, 211, 212, 216, 219, 221–22
"God & Man Ben Made Atte On"   211
"God kepe oure kyng and saue the croune"   206, 210
"Lerne say wele, say litel, or say noȝt"   209
"The Lessouns of the Dirige"   219
MS Digby 102   202, 218
question of authorship   210–11, 218–19
"A Remembraunce of LIJ Folyes"   219–20
"Treuth, Reste, and Pes"   204–05, 206, 209, 212, 221
"Wyt and Wille"   209
see also lyric
digestion   35–36, 38, 39, 41, 44, 45, 48, 229
see also consumption, rumination
van Dijk, Conrad   168
Dillon, Emma   130
discovery   14, 20, 190, 191, 194
dispersonification *see under* personification
Distichs of Cato   213
Dit de Robert le Diable   248, 250
see also Lodge, Thomas, Robert the Devil
Divine Comedy see under Dante Alighieri
Donatus   92, 93
Donestre   36, 45, 46, 47
drama   15, 225, 298–99
Drayton, Michael   151
Ideas Mirrour   151–53, 154

ecology   108, 110–11, 114, 116, 118, 120, 163–64
Edward II   175
Edward III   167, 174, 175, 178
Edward VI   261, 268
ekphrasis   55, 91
elephant and castle imagery   129–30, 133, 135
Elyot, Thomas   249
emotion   15, 17, 20, 25, 27, 112
Enigmata see under Aldhelm
Entwisle Hours   140–41, 143
Erasmus, Desiderius   245
De copia   245
Erkenwald, Saint   183, 194, 196, 199
Miracula sancti Erkenwaldi   183
relics   183–84
Saint Erkenwald   183, 195–97, 198, 200

GENERAL INDEX

plot 185–86, 189
setting 191, 193
sources 199
Vita sancti Erkenwaldi 183
Euphuism 245, 246, 249, 251
Eurycleia 16, 17, 19, 25
Eurydice 42
Eusebius 37, 46
exegesis 64, 195, 198, 215
allegorical 279
Calvinist rejection 280–81, 292
medieval tradition 277, 279, 282, 284
topographical 188, 198–99
Exeter Book riddles 26, 37, 41, 43, 45, 47
Riddle 24 27–30, 43, 44
Riddle 45 36–39, 41, 43–45, 47–48
Riddle 47 40
Riddle 86 43
Exeter, Cathedral Library MS 3501 *see*
Exeter Book riddles

The Faerie Queene see under Edmund
Spenser
*Famous, True and Historicall Life of
Robert... see under* Lodge, Thomas
Farber, Lianna 57
feudalism 178
Il Filostrato see under Giovanni Boccaccio
Flanders 219, 220
Fleming, Juliet 123
Fortune (allegorical figure) 73–73, 76, 83,
211, 220
see also allegory
freedom 76, 80, 81, 298
histories of 293, 294, 295, 300
limited 67
pedagogy of 297
plurality of 294, 295–96
free will 68, 72, 73, 76, 80, 84
see also will
friendship 13–14, 17, 68–69, 70
Foys, Martin 39, 42, 44
Furrow, Melissa 117

Galloway, Andrew 169
Gaucher, Élisabeth 248
Gaunt, Simon 117
genre 14, 52, 109, 117, 120, 139
Elizabethan 243, 256
secular 256
of textuality 93, 96, 98
see also allegory, hagiography, history,
riddle, romance, satire
Geoffrey of Vinsauf 93
Poetria nova 93–94

Gerard, John 156
*The Herball or General Historie of
Plantes* 156–59
Giancarlo, Matthew 168–69, 171
Gillespie, Vincent 222
glossing 88, 90–91, 95, 103, 106, 153
Golding, Arthur 281
Goulet, Richard 102
Gower, John 208, 221, 230
Confessio amantis 104, 208
The Great Bible 261, 269, 272, 274
Greene, Robert 247, 251, 256
Gregory I 185, 187, 188, 191–92
in the *Divine Comedy* 189–90
letters to Serenus 188–89
the Whitby *Life* 186–87, 189, 190, 195
Gunther, Karl 276

hagiography 63, 65, 187, 188
Hanawalt, Barbara 235
Harbus, Antonina 37
Hegel, Georg 71
Helgerson, Richard 247, 251
Henry IV of England 203, 214
Henry V of England 203, 204, 207, 210
Henry VI of England 204, 206, 220, 261,
268
Heraclitus 96–97
hermeneutics 71–72, 88, 147, 149, 161,
277
Christian 95, 185, 188, 189–90, 198,
279–81
Reformation 276, 277, 281, 284, 285,
291–92
see also allegory, exegesis
Hirsch, John 60
history
cultural 296–97
genre 54, 59
literary 293–94
study of 275–76
visions of 185, 190, 191, 194, 238
Hoccleve, Thomas 144
Jereslaus's Wife 144
Regement of Princes 144
Holland, Robert 148
Holsinger, Bruce 48, 252
Horne, Robert 202, 218–19, 220, 221
Horobin, Simon 218
Hours of Jeanne d'Evreaux 127
Howe, Nicholas 47
Huizinga, Johan 89
humanism 24, 252
critique of recognition 26, 30, 31, 33
education 14, 245, 246, 249, 250, 257

GENERAL INDEX

351

government   247, 254, 257
view of the past   190, 197
see also Lodge, Thomas
Hundred Years' War   174

iconoclasm   122, 259, 193, 287
ideology of   271, 274
images   260, 263, 268
inscriptions   260, 261
during the Reformation   122, 268–69, 271
individuality   70, 71, 81, 84
see also subjectivity

Jephthah's daughter   64
see also Bible
Jesus *see* Christ
John of Salisbury   194
Policraticus   194–95

Kail, Josef   203, 206, 210
Kempe, Margery   215, 216–17
King's Bench   168, 256
Kinney, Arthur   256

Langland, William   280
Piers Plowman   105, 175
B-text   169, 182
C-text   168, 173, 202
commentary on justice   172, 177, 181–82
First Vision   167–68
obscurity   90
petition scene   170–71, 172–73, 174
regicide   175
satire   201, 294
poetics   168, 176, 177
see also allegory, peace
Liber albus   231, 232, 233, 235
see also custumal
liberation   14, 147
liberalism   176, 298, 299
library *see* bookchest
line-fillers   122–23, 127, 130, 133, 266
as decorative   137
in lists   135
as punctuation   134
representing silence   140
in vernacular poetry   143–44
unsettling norms   146
literalism   147, 148, 150, 161, 164
in exegesis   97–98, 276, 278, 284, 291, 292
in law   182
Liu, Yin   117

Livy   54, 55, 56, 57, 63
Locke, John   20, 24
An Essay Concerning Human Understanding   24
Lodge, Thomas   241, 243, 256
An Alarum against Usurers   243
Elstred   243, 255
Famous, True and Historicall Life of Robert, Second Duke of Normandy   241, 254–55
classical allusions   246, 250, 251–52, 254
conversion narrative   255–56
critique of humanism   246, 250, 252, 254
humor   249
use of poetry   251, 252
as pastoral romance   244
plot   242–43
sources   242, 243, 257
violence   247–49, 253
Forbonius and Prisceria   243
Philis   243
Rosalynde   244
Scillaes Metamorphosis   243
see also humanism, Robert the Devil
Lollards   208, 213, 214
see also Wycliffites
London   184, 194, 199
fifteenth-century politics   202, 218, 235, 237, 238
love   116, 256
choice of   79, 80
of enemies   277–78, 285, 290–91
loss of   76, 77, 82, 84
theory of   68–70, 77, 80, 81, 84
see also Jesus Christ
love-sickness   252–53
de Lubac, Henri   279
Lydgate, John   144, 211, 223, 224, 225, 230, 238
Dietary
audience   232, 234, 236–37
idiom   229, 232, 235
genre   227–28
manuscript history   224, 226–28, 231
social values   225, 233–36
The Serpent of Division   207
Lyf of the Moste Myschevoust Robert the Devyll see under de Worde, Wynkyn
Lyly, John   245, 247
Euphues   245
see also Euphuism
Lynford, Robert   218
lyric   69, 113, 212, 222, 234

352 GENERAL INDEX

Middle English 105, 143, 202
see also Digby poems, John Lydgate,
voice

MacCracken, Henry Noble 226–27
de Machaut, Guillaume 82–83
Le jugement dou roy de Behaingne 82
Remede de Fortune 83
Maidstone, Richard 202
Penitential Psalms 202, 211
Maine, Jasper 286
"Shortly after the Surrender of that
Garrison" 286–87
Malory, Thomas 116–17
Balyn le Sauvage 117–20
Morte Darthur 117
Mann, Jill 62
manuscripts 29, 43, 48, 122, 137, 139,
152, 272, 274
Baltimore, Walters Art Museum,
W.37 127–28
Baltimore, Walters Art Museum,
W.102 126, 129–33
London, British Library, Additional
62925 125
London, British Library, Cotton
Vespasian A I 138
London, British Library, Egerton
3132A 242
London, British Library, Egerton
1995 231
London, British Library, Harley
5102 124
London, British Library, Harley
7322 142, 143–44
London, British Library, Lansdowne
699 226
London, British Library, Royal 18 D
2 145–46
New York, Morgan Library,
M.1044 134
Oxford, Bodleian Library, Bodley
649 210
Oxford, Bodleian Library, Digby
102 202, 218
Oxford, Bodleian Library, Douce,
Fragmn. f. 4 242
Oxford, Bodleian Library, Rawlinson C.
86 228
Oxford, Bodleian Library, Rawlinson D.
913 142
Rouen, Bibliothèque municipal de
Rouen I 2 135
San Marino, Huntington Library HM
64 229

Marie de France 70
Guigemar 70
Markus, Robert 192
Marshall, Stephen 283
Meroz Cursed 283–84, 286
Mary Magdalene 16
masks 49, 51, 53, 56, 66
McLeod, Randall 160
medical recipes 224, 228–29, 231
memento mori 197, 220
memory 18–19, 22, 187, 190, 195
merchant guilds 218–19, 220–21, 225,
233
metamorphosis 159, 160–61
Metamorphoses see under Ovid
de Man, Paul 51
de Meun, Jean 52, 54, 58
Romance of the Rose 51, 54, 55–56,
88, 90, 92, 105
see also allegory
Middleton, Anne 61, 214, 225–26
Milton, John 122, 282, 284, 287, 290, 299
De Doctrina Christiana 283, 291–92
Paradise Lost 275
Tetrachordon 291
mimesis 73, 81–82
Mirabilia Urbis Romae 185, 193
Miracula sancti Erkenwaldi see under
Erkenwald, Saint
Mirouer des simples ames 88
Mirror of King Edward III see under
William of Pagula
de Montaigne, Michel 70
Morgan, Nigel 123
Morrissey, Jake Walsh 226, 237
Moses 278, 280–83, 285, 288
Most, Glen 96
Mulcaster, Richard 247
Mum and the Sothsegger 201, 203,
208–09, 212, 213, 214
Murrin, Michael 90

Narcissus 158–59, 161
Nature (allegorical figure) 53–57, 59, 62
see also allegory
Nayler, James 288–89, 290
*The Lamb's War Against the Man of
Sin* 289
Nelson, Ingrid 222
neoplatonism *see under* Platonism
Nicholson, R. H. 204
Nievegelt, Martin 103
Niles, John D. 39
nostalgia 15, 18, 25–26

GENERAL INDEX

353

observation 14, 17, 41, 44
obscurity 87–88, 94, 104, 106
  figural 90, 95, 96, 102
  opacity 94
  temporary 44
  trope of 93
obviousness 147, 150–51, 156, 161, 163
  core paradox 148–49
  as disruption 163–64
  history 149
Odysseus 16, 17, 19, 25, 42
Old English 26–28, 36, 48, 140
  see also Exeter Book riddles, riddles
optimism 49, 51
Origen 278, 279, 283
Ormrod, Mark 177
Orpheus 42, 46
Ovid 52, 55, 66
  epic 243
  Heroides 59
  lyric 60, 69
  Metamorphoses 57, 159, 250, 251–52
Owen, John 287

paganism 63, 64, 186, 189, 191–94
  compared to Christianity 195–96,
    197, 198
Pandarus 73, 74
paradiastole 176, 177, 180, 181
Paradise Lost see under John Milton
Parliament 170, 173, 174, 180, 203,
    205–06, 287–89
  army of 284, 285, 286, 290
  the Good Parliament 171
  petitions to 170–73
  support for 282–83
Parliament Rolls 167, 170
Paston family 268
Paz, James 46
Peace (allegorical character) 168, 169,
    174, 181–82
  paradoxical status 173, 180
  personification 176–77, 180–81
  as petitioner 170–73, 178
  secular figure 167, 182
  see also allegory
peace
  collective 178, 180
  individual 177–78, 179, 180
  local 180
  parliamentary 179–80
  private 169, 177
  public 177
  royal 168, 169, 173, 177, 179–80
Pearl 196, 199, 200, 299

Pearsall, Derek 224
pedagogy 14–15, 34, 40, 297
Pèlerinage de vie humaine 88, 104
Pépin, Jean 99
Perlesvaus 88
Permyakov, G. L. 216
personification 49, 56, 89, 91, 106
  dispersonification 58, 65
  see also prosopopoeia
Petrarch, Francesco 98
  Familiar Matters 99, 100
  letter to Giovanni Colonna 185, 190
"The Physician's Tale" see under Geoffrey
  Chaucer
pictorial space 127, 128, 130
Piers Plowman see under William Langland
da Piso, Guido 100
Pizarro, J. M. 37
Plato 20, 21, 250
  Meno 21
  Timaeus 23
Platonism 21, 22, 23, 33
  Christian Neoplatonism 21–22
Plummer, Charles 37
poetics 154, 191, 199
  see also William Langland
Poetics 17, 96
  see also Aristotle
privacy 65, 168, 169, 173, 176, 181
prosopopoeia 49–51, 52, 53, 65, 66, 91,
    255
  literary invention 53, 59, 62, 65
  see also personification
proverbs 102, 206, 209, 212–15, 222
  form 205, 211, 214, 217
  re-use 215
  structure 216, 222
  style 202, 212
  wisdom 208, 215, 224
psalms 39
  layout and structure 137–39, 143
  see also Bible
public poetry 223, 225–26
punctuation 134, 137, 140, 143, 159
  brackets 143–44
  punctus 143
  for recitation 138–39
  for understanding 139, 204
purveyance 173, 174, 175, 178, 179, 180
Puttenham, George 102
  Art of English Poesy 102
Putter, Ad 117
Pygmalion 55, 57
Pynson, Richard 152, 242, 248

354 GENERAL INDEX

Quakerism 277, 288
Queste del sanc graal 104
Quintilian 50, 93, 102
  Institutio Oratoria 50, 92

Ram, Robert 285
Randall, Lilian 130, 133
Raskolnikov, Masha 90
Reason (allegorical figure) 77–78, 168,
  169, 172, 179
  see also allegory
reason 17, 69, 168, 169, 179
recognition 222
  activation 17–18
  delayed 43
  drama of 15–17, 25, 62
  impossibility of 47–48, 84
  literary 33, 45, 51, 52, 65, 73, 76
    limits of 81
  mistaken 51, 62, 65
  moral 70, 84
  pedagogy 34, 40
  Platonic view of 21
  pleasure of 24–25, 213
  renewing force 222
  self-recognition 19
  signs of 13
  timing 15–16
  see also cognition
recovery 14, 20, 30, 33, 53, 65, 222
reform 173, 179, 211
Reformation 149, 182, 254, 272, 292, 295,
  299
  Calvinist 280, 281, 285
  in England 147, 241, 257, 286–89
  magisterial 277, 281, 287
  violence 276
  see also iconoclasm
regicide 175
revolution 276, 282, 286–87, 290,
  294–95, 298
Rhetorica ad Herennium 50
Rich, Robert 289
  Love Without Dissimulation 289
Richardson, Malcolm 228
riddles 26–27, 29–32, 36, 42–43
  see also Aenigma, Aldhelm, Exeter
    Book riddles
Riddy, Felicity 236
Robert the Devil 241–43, 253, 254,
  257
  see also Dit de Robert le Diable, Lodge,
    Thomas, Wynkyn de Worde
Robinson, Fred C. 39

Romance of the Rose see under de Meun,
  Jean
romance 114, 116, 120, 241
  Arthurian 105
  comic 116–17
  courtly 69
  genre definition 108–11, 116, 117–18
  haunted 117, 119
  pastoral 243, 244, 248, 249
  penitential 243
  prose 105
Rome 63, 184–85, 187, 242–43, 252
  Christian 189, 192, 197–98
  pagan 191, 192
  pilgrimage site 193, 198, 255
  Trajan's Forum 186–88, 189, 190, 195
Romulus and Remus 130
Rosenfeld, Colleen Ruth 154
Rufinus of Aquileia 37
The Rule of Benedict 45
rumination 36–37, 38, 41, 47, 48, 203
  see also consumption, digestion
runes 45, 46
Russell, Frederick 278
Rust, Martha 133
Rutland Psalter 127

Saint Erkenwald see under Erkenwald, Saint
St. Paul's Cathedral 183, 184, 193, 198
St. Peter's Basilica 189
Salvador-Bello, Mercedes 39
Sanok, Catherine 63
satire 201–02, 203, 208–09, 211–12, 214,
  222
Seal, Samantha Katz 64
"The Second Nun's Tale" *see under*
  Geoffrey Chaucer
Secreta secretorum 213
Ser Brunetto 16
  see also Dante Alighieri
Serenus, bishop of Marseilles 188–89
The Serpent of Division see under John
  Lydgate
Shakespeare, William 299
  Love's Labours Lost 253
  The Merchant of Venice 182
  The Second Folio 162
  Titus Andronicus 250
  Twelfth Night 162
shame 112–13, 115, 116, 209
Shirley, John 219
Sidney, Philip 251
  Arcadia 244
  Astrophil and Stella 249, 251
  Defence of Poesy 250

GENERAL INDEX

355

Silvestris, Bernardus 97
  Cosmographia 97
Simpson, James
  Burning to Read 5, 147, 276, 281
  as colleague 87, 107
  Permanent Revolution 6, 276, 286, 287, 291, 295, 299–300
  Reform and Cultural Revolution 4–5, 67, 116, 146, 293–95, 297, 298–300
  as teacher 1, 6–7, 296–97
Sir Gawain and the Green Knight 118, 294, 295
Shapcote, Richard 288
Socrates 21
Solomon and Saturn I 36, 39
soul 21, 23, 68–69, 71, 196, 198
soul food 37
Spearing, A. C. 58, 59, 63
Spenser, Edmund 241
  The Faerie Queene 102–03, 159–61, 169, 241, 255
  Shepheardes Calender 243
Sponsler, Claire 234
Stoicism 234
subjectivity 63, 73, 77, 81, 115
  see also individuality
Summit, Jennifer 184, 198
"The Summoner's Tale" *see under* Geoffrey Chaucer
surprise 17, 30
  see also wonder
Sydenham, William 289
Symphosisus 38, 43
  Tinea 38–39, 47

the Ten Commandments 272, 291
Teskey, Gordon 90
Tetrachordon see under John Milton
timelessness 202, 203, 222
theft 41, 45
Thirtle, John 264
Thornham screen 274
tragedy 67–68, 83–84, 118
Trajan, emperor 185, 186, 189–90, 191, 194, 197
Trajan's forum *see under* Rome
Tribble, Evelyn B. 155
Troilus and Criseyde see under Geoffrey Chaucer

The Very Hungry Caterpillar 41–42
Vespasian Psalter 137
Vickers, Nancy J. 187
violence 30, 61, 118, 247–49, 252, 295
  non-violence 291

religious 147, 276, 286, 290
  sexual 112, 116
Vita sancti Erkenwaldi see under Erkenwald, Saint
voice 50, 53, 63, 88, 213, 252
  feminine 55, 59, 113, 243, 255
  in lyric 69, 113, 234
  masculine 235, 236, 237
  poetic 69, 113, 202, 203, 205, 214, 225–26
  satirical 202
  narrative 28, 57–58, 66, 73, 251, 252, 256

Wakelin, Daniel 122, 127
war 203, 206, 207, 220, 253, 282–83
  in the Old Testament 278–79, 285, 292
  see also Hundred Years' War
Watts, John 206
Wenzel, Siegfried 214
Whetter, K. S. 116
Whiting, B. J. 205, 217
Whitman, Jon 93
Winstanley, Gerrard 289
  A New-Yeers Gift Sent to the Parliament and Armie 289–90
will 68, 80–81
  see also free will
William of Ockham 81
William of Pagula 167, 170, 174
  Mirror of King Edward III 167, 170, 174–75, 176
Wilson, Thomas 102, 246
  Arte of Rhetorique 102
wonder 18, 27, 30, 31, 39, 44, 48, 256
The Wonders of the East 46, 48
Woolrych, Austin 287
de Worde, Wynkyn 242
  Lyf of the Moste Myschevoust Robert the Devyll 242, 244, 245, 248, 254–55
Worden, Blair 288
Wright, Thomas 96
Wroth, Mary 154
  Urania 154
Wyatt, Thomas 246, 295
  Paraphrase of the Penitential Psalms 295
Wycliffites 208, 213, 282
  see also Lollards

Yates, Julian 154
York play cycle 113, 299

Zweck, Jordan 43

TABULA GRATULATORIA

David Aers
Amy Appleford
DeVan Ard
Laura Ashe
Anthony Bale
Chris Barrett
Christopher Baswell
Michael Bennett
Jessica Berenbeim
Johan Bergström-Allen
Anke Bernau and David Matthews
Louise M. Bishop
Kenneth Bleeth
Julia Boffey
Jessica Brantley
Peter Brown
Ardis Butterfield
Christopher Cannon
Cristina Maria Cervone
Aparna Chaudhuri
Eva von Contzen
Rita Copeland and David Wallace
Eduardo Correia
Taylor Cowdery
Jason Crawford
Richard Dance
Orietta Da Rold
Jeremy Dimmick
Daniel Donoghue
Siân Echard
Robert R. Edwards
James Engell
Ruth Evans
Susanna Fein and David Raybin
R. D. Fulk
Helen Fulton
Jamie Fumo and Vincent DiMarco
John M. Fyler
Andrew Galloway

Shannon Gayk
Alexandra Gillespie
Luis Manuel Girón Negrón
Richard Firth Green
Stephen Greenblatt
Karen Elizabeth Gross
John C. Hirsh
Rhema Hokama
Jonathan Hsy
M. E. J. Hughes
Ann M. Hutchison and James P. Carley
Ian Johnson
Andrew James Johnston
Hope Johnston
Elizabeth Papp Kamali
Wolfram Keller
Henry Ansgar Kelly
Kathryn Kerby-Fulton
Philip Knox
Katie Little
Andrew Lynch
Deidre Lynch
Kathryn L. Lynch
Jill Mann
Catherine McKenna
Sarah McNamer
Jenna Mead
Robert J. Meyer-Lee
Alastair Minnis
Alex Mueller
Susan Nakley
Yun Ni
Julie Orlemanski
Caroline Palmer
Nicholas Perkins
R. D. Perry
Alessandra Petrina
Ad Putter
Jim Rhodes

TABULA GRATULATORIA

Nicole R. Rice
Elizabeth Robertson
Daniel Rubey
Martha Rust
Sarah Salih
Daniel Sawyer
Larry Scanlon and Aline Fairweather
Misty Schieberle
Catherine Shrank
George Shuffelton
Jeremy J. Smith
Sebastian Sobecki
Sarah Spence
Lynn Staley
John Stauffer
Spencer Strub
Gordon Teskey

Kathleen Tonry
Stephanie Trigg
Yoko Wada
Daniel Wakelin
Laura Wang
Stella Wang
Lawrence Warner
Claire M. Waters
Nicholas Watson
Erica Weaver
Jill Whitelock
Tara Williams
Leah Whittington
R. F. Yeager
Nicolette Zeeman
Lian Zhang
Yating Zhang

Printed in the United States
by Baker & Taylor Publisher Services